CLYMER®

SKI-DOO

SNOWMOBILE SHOP MANUAL
1990-1995

The world's finest publisher of mechanical how-to manuals

PRIMEDIA
Information Data Products

P.O. Box 12901, Overland Park, KS 66282-2901

Copyright © 1996 PRIMEDIA Business Magazines & Media Inc.

FIRST EDITION
First Printing August, 1996
Second Printing November, 1997
Third Printing November, 2000
Fourth Printing November, 2002
Fifth Printing January, 2005

Printed in U.S.A.

CLYMER and colophon are registered trademarks of PRIMEDIA Business Magazines & Media Inc.

ISBN: 0-89287-663-8

Library of Congress: 95-80285

TECHNICAL PHOTOGRAPHY: Ron Wright and Mark Jacobs.

TECHNICAL ILLUSTRATIONS: Steve Amos.

WIRING DIAGRAMS: Robert Caldwell.

TECHNICAL ASSISTANCE:
  Don Anderson, Instructor/Technical Supervisor and Coordinator, Trade and Industrial Development
  Northwest Technical College
  Outdoor Power Equipment & Snowmobile Technology Department
  Detroit Lakes, Minnesota 56501

  Dale Fett, Technical Advisor
  Fett Brothers Performance, Inc.
  Route 4, Box 383C
  Frazee, Minnesota 56544

  Jaye Cheney, Owner/Technical Advisor
  Cheney Motors
  101 8th Avenue Northwest
  West Fargo, ND 58078

Snowmobile Code of Ethics provided by the International Snowmobile Industry Association, Fairfax, Virginia.

CLYMER®

Publisher Shawn Etheridge

EDITORIAL

Managing Editor
James Grooms

Associate Editor
Lee Buell

Technical Writers
Jay Bogart
Michael Morlan
George Parise
Mark Rolling
Ed Scott
Ron Wright

Editorial Production Manager
Dylan Goodwin

Senior Production Editor
Greg Araujo

Production Editors
Holly Messinger
Darin Watson

Associate Production Editors
Susan Hartington
Julie Jantzer-Ward
Justin Marciniak

Technical Illustrators
Steve Amos
Errol McCarthy
Mitzi McCarthy
Bob Meyer

MARKETING/SALES AND ADMINISTRATION

Associate Publisher
Vickie Martin

Advertising & Promotions Manager
Elda Starke

Advertising & Promotions Coordinators
Melissa Abbott

Art Director
Chris Paxton

Associate Art Director
Jennifer Knight

Sales Managers
Ted Metzger, Manuals
Dutch Sadler, Marine
Matt Tusken, Motorcycles

Business Manager
Ron Rogers

Customer Service Manager
Terri Cannon

Customer Service Representatives
Shawna Davis
Courtney Hollars
Susan Kohlmeyer
April LeBlond
Jennifer Lassiter

Warehouse & Inventory Manager
Leah Hicks

PRIMEDIA
Business Magazines & Media
P.O. Box 12901, Overland Park, KS 66282-2901 • 800-262-1954 • 913-967-1719

The following books and guides are published by PRIMEDIA Business Directories & Books.

More information available at *primediabooks.com*

Contents

Quick Reference Data

SKI-DOO MODEL NUMBER

Year	Model	Model number
1990	Formula MX	3742
	Formula MX LT	3743
	Formula MX LT (2)	3749
	Formula Plus	3744
	Formula Plus LT	3745
	Formula Plus LT (2)	3750
	Formula MACH 1	3746
	Formula MACH 1 XTC	3751
1991	Formula MX	3755
	Formula MX E	3756
	Formula MX X	3766
	Formula MX XTC	3757
	Formula MX XTC E	3758
	Formula MX XTC SS/SR	3769
	Formula MX XTC E SS/SR	3770
	Formula Plus	3759
	Formula Plus E	3760
	Formula Plus X	3767
	Formula Plus XTC	3761
	Formula Plus XTC E	3762
	Formula Plus XTC SS/SR	3771
	Formula Plus XTC E SS/SR	3772
	Formula MACH 1	3763
	Formula MACH 1 X	3768
	Formula MACH 1 XTC	3764
	Formula MACH 1 XTC SS/SR	3773
1992	Formula MX	3775
	Formula MX XTC R	3788
	Formula Plus	3777
	Formula Plus E	3778
	Formula Plus XTC	3779
	Formula Plus XTC E	3780
	Formula Plus X	3790
	Formula MACH 1	3781
	Formula MACH 1 X	3789
	Formula MACH 1 XTC	3782
	Formula MACH 1 XTC II	3783
1993	Formula MX	3791
	Formula MX (2)	3846
	Formula MX XTC R	3792
	Formula MX Z	3844
	Formula MX Z A	3847
	Formula Plus	3793
	Formula Plus (2)	3750
	Formula Plus E	3894
	Formula Plus XTC	3795
	Formula Plus EFI	3799

(continued)

Year	Model	Model number
1993 (continued)	Formula Plus X	3849
	Formula MACH 1	3797
	Formula MACH 1 (2)	3852
	Formula MACH 1 XTC	3798
	Formula Grand Touring	3796
1994		
	Formula MX	3868, 3883, 3885
	Formula MX Z	3870, 3886
	Formula MX Z X	3870X, 3886X
	Summit 470 HAC	3871, 3888
	Formula ST	3872, 3889
	Formula STX	3873, 3893, 3892
	Formula STX II	3874, 3894
	Formula Z	3875, 3897, 3896
	Summit 583	3876, 3891
	Summit 583 (2)	3881, 3882, 3890
	MACH 1	3863, 3880
	Grand Touring	3867, 3879
	Grand Touring XTC	3864, 3878
	Grand Touring SE	3866
1995		
	MX	1000, 1001
	MX Z	1036, 1037
	Formula SS	1033, 1034, 1047
	Formula STX	1003, 1004
	Formula STX (LT)	1007, 1008
	Formula Z	1030, 1031, 1032
	Summit 583	1013, 1014, 1015
	Summit 670	1016, 1017, 1018
	MACH 1	1043, 1044, 1045
	Grand Touring SE	1027, 1028, 1029
	Grand Touring 580	1024, 1025, 1026
	Grand Touring 470	1022, 10231-2

ENGINE NUMBER IDENTIFICATION

Year model	Engine number
1990	
Formula MX & MX LT	467
Formula Plus & Plus LT	536
Formula MACH 1 & MACH 1 XTC	583
1991	
Formula MX, MX E, MX X, MX XTC & MX XTC E	467
Formula Plus, Plus E, Plus X, Plus XTC & Plus XTC E	536
Formula MACH 1, MACH 1 X & MACH 1 XTC	643

(continued)

Year model	Engine number
1992	
Formula MX & MX XTC R	467
Formula Plus, Plus E, Plus XTC & Plus XTC E	582
Formula Plus X	583
Formula MACH 1, MACH 1 XTC & MACH 1 XTC II	643
Formula MACH 1 X	670
1993	
Formula MX, MX (2) & MX XTC R	467
Formula MX Z	467 (Z)
Formula Plus, Plus (2), Plus E, Plus XTC & Plus EFI	582
Formula Plus X	643
Formula MACH 1, MACH 1 (2) & MACH 1 XTC	670
Formula Grand Touring	582
1994	
Formula MX, MX Z, MX Z X & ST	467
Summit 470 HAC	467HAC
Formula STX, STX II & Z	583
Summit 583 HAC	583HAC
MACH 1	670
Grand Touring & Grand Touring XTC	582
Grand Touring SE	670
1995	
MX & Grand Touring 470	467
MX Z	454
Formula SS	670
Formula STX, STX (LT) & Z	583
Summit 583	583HAC
Summit 670	670HAC
MACH 1 & Grand Touring SE	670
Grand Touring 580	582

GENERAL ENGINE SPECIFICATIONS

Bore		
454	67.5 mm	(2.658 in.)
467	69.5 mm	(2.736 in.)
536	72.0 mm	(2.835 in.)
582, 583 & 583HAC	76.0 mm	(2.992 in.)
643	76.0 mm	(2.992 in.)
670	78.0 mm	(2.736 in.)
Stroke		
454	61.0 mm	(2.402 in.)
467	61.0 mm	(2.402 in.)
536	64.0 mm	(2.520 in.)
582, 583 & 583HAC	64.0 mm	(2.520 in.)
643	68.0 mm	(2.677 in.)
670	70.0 mm	(2.756 in.)

(continued)

GENERAL ENGINE SPECIFICATIONS (continued)

Displacement

454	436.6 cc	(26.6 cu. in.)
467	462.7 cc	(28.2 cu. in.)
536	521.2 cc	(31.8 cu. in.)
582, 583 & 583HAC	580.7 cc	(35.4 cu. in.)
643	616.9 cc	(37.6 cu. in.)
670	668.7 cc	(40.8 cu. in.)

Compression ratio

454	6.6:1
467	6.8-7.3:1
536	6.1:1
582	6.70-7.5:1
583 & 583HAC	5.2-7.1:1
643	6.3:1
670	6.0-6.4:15-3

SPARK PLUGS

Model	Plug type	Gap mm (in.)
All models	NGK BR9ES	0.45 (0.018)

APPROXIMATE REFILL CAPACITY

Chaincase

1990-1992	200 cc	7 oz.
1993-1995	350 cc	12 oz.

Oil injection reservoir

1990-1993	2.9 L	98 oz.
1994		
Formula STX, GT, MACH 1	2.9 L	98 oz.
Other models	4.1 L	138.7 oz.
1995		
MX Z	2.55 L	86 oz.
Other models	4.1 L	138.7 oz.

Cooling system

1990-1991	4.2 L	142 oz.
1993		
MX Z	4.7 L	159 oz.
Other models	4.2 L	142 oz.
1994		
Formula MX, MX Z, ST, Z	4.7 L	159 oz.
Summit 470 HAC, 583 HAC	4.7 L	159 oz.
Other models	4.2 L	142 oz.
1995		
Formula STX LT	5.0 L	169 oz.
Summit 583, 670	5.0 L	169 oz.
Grand Touring models	5.0 L	169 oz.
Other models	4.7 L	159 oz.

Fuel tank

1990	40.9 L	10.8 gal.
1991 without electric start	40.9 L	10.8 gal.
1991 electric start models	33 L	8.7 gal.

(continued)

APPROXIMATE REFILL CAPACITY (continued)

Fuel tank (continued)		
1992	35.3 L	9.3 gal.
1993		
MX Z	42.1 L	11.1 gal.
Formula Plus EFI	45.3 L	12 gal.
Other models	35.3 L	9.3 gal.
1994		
Formula MX Z	39.0 L	10.3 gal.
MACH 1, GT models	35.3 L	12 gal.
Other models	42.1 L	11.1 gal.
1995		
MX Z	37.0 L	9.8 gal.
Other models	42.1 L	11.1 gal.

RECOMMENDED LUBRICANTS

Item	Lubricant type
Countershaft bearing, hub bearings, bogie wheels, ski legs, idler bearings, leaf spring cushion pads, etc.	A
Oil seal interior lips	A
Engine injection oil	B
Chaincase	C

Lubricant legend:

  A. Bombardier bearing grease or equivalent multipurpose lithium base grease for use through a temperature range of –40° to 95° C (–40° to 200° F). This grease will be referred to as a "low temperature grease" throughout this manual.

  B. Bombardier injection oil or equivalent. Injection oil must flow at –40° C (–40° F).

  C. Bombardier chaincase oil or equivalent. Make sure equivalent oil provides lubrication at low temperatures.

  * WD-40 can be used as a general lubricant.

MAINTENANCE TIGHTENING TORQUES

	N·m	ft.-lb.
Crankcase nuts or screws		
1990		
M6	10	7.5
M8	22	16
1991-on		
M6	10	7.5
M8	24	17
M10	38	28
Cylinder base screws or nuts		
1990-1991	22	16
1992-on	30	22
Cylinder head		
1990-1991		
All models	22	16

(continued)

MAINTENANCE TIGHTENING TORQUES (continued)

	N·m	ft.-lb.
Cylinder head (continued)		
1992		
467 & 582 engines		
Cylinder head	30	22
Head cover	10	7.5
583, 643 & 670 engines	22	16
1993		
467 & 582 Engines		
Cylinder head	30	22
Head cover	10	7.5
583 & 670 engines	22	16
1994-on		
467 & 582 Engines		
Cylinder head	30	22
Head cover	10	7.5
454, 583 & 670 engines	22	16
Engine mounts		
1990-on		
M10 screws	48	35
M10 nuts	38	28
M8 Allen screws	25	18
M8 nuts	25	18
Exhaust valve screws		
454, 583, 643 & 670 engines	10	7.5
Exhaust manifold screws or nuts		
1990-1992		
467 engine model	21	15
536 engine model	25	18
583 engine model	10	7.5
1993		
467 engine model	25	18
582 & 583 engines	25	18
583 engine model	25	18
1994-on		
467 & 582 engines	25	18
454, 583 & 670 engines	10	7.5
Flywheel nut		
1990-1994		
643 & 670 engines	125	92
Other engine models	105	77
1995		
467, 582 & 583	105	77
454, 583HAC, 670	125	92
Rear idler wheel bolts	48	35
Rotary valve cover	22	16

Chapter One

General Information

This Clymer shop manual covers the 1990-1995 Ski-Doo Formula MX, Formula Plus, Formula Mach and Grand Touring models.

Troubleshooting, tune-up, maintenance and repair are not difficult, if you know what tools and equipment to use and what to do. Step-by-step instructions guide you through jobs ranging from simple maintenance to complete engine and suspension overhaul.

This manual can be used by anyone from a first time do-it-yourselfer to a professional mechanic. Detailed drawings and clear photographs give you all the information you need to do the work right.

Some of the procedures in this manual require the use of special tools. The resourceful mechanic can, in many cases, think of acceptable substitutes for special tools—there is always another way. This can be as simple as using a few pieces of threaded rod, washers and nuts to remove or install a bearing or fabricating a tool from scrap material. However, using a substitute for a special tool is not recommended as it can be dangerous and may damage the part. If you find that a tool can be designed and safely made, but will require some type of machine work, you may want to search out a local community college or high school that has a machine shop curriculum. Shop teachers sometimes welcome outside work that can be used as practical shop applications for advanced students.

Table 1 lists model number coverage.

General specifications are listed in **Table 2**. **Table 3** lists vehicle weight.

Metric and U.S. standards are used throughout this manual. U.S. to metric conversion is given in **Table 4**.

Critical torque specifications are found in table form at the end of each chapter (as required). The general torque specifications listed in **Table 5** can be used when a torque specification is not listed for a specific component or assembly.

A list of general technical abbreviations is given in **Table 6**.

Metric tap drill sizes can be found in **Table 7**.

Table 8 lists windchill factors.

Tables 1-8 are found at the end of the chapter.

MANUAL ORGANIZATION

This chapter provides general information useful to snowmobile owners and mechanics. In addition, information in this chapter discusses the tools and techniques for preventive maintenance, troubleshooting and repair.

Chapter Two provides methods and suggestions for quick and accurate diagnosis and repair of problems. Troubleshooting procedures discuss typical symptoms and logical methods to pinpoint the cause of the trouble.

Chapter Three explains all periodic lubrication and routine maintenance necessary to keep your snowmobile operating well.

Chapter Three also includes recommended tune-up procedures, eliminating the need to constantly consult other chapters on the various assemblies.

Subsequent chapters describe specific systems, providing disassembly, repair, assembly and adjustment procedures in simple step-by-step form. If a repair is impractical for a home mechanic, it is so indicated. It is usually faster and less expensive to take such repairs to a dealer or competent repair shop. Specifications concerning a specific system are included at the end of the appropriate chapter.

NOTES, CAUTIONS AND WARNINGS

The terms NOTE, CAUTION and WARNING have specific meanings in this manual. A NOTE provides additional information to make a step or procedure easier or clearer. Disregarding a NOTE could cause inconvenience, but would not cause damage or personal injury.

A CAUTION emphasizes an area where equipment damage could occur. Disregarding a CAUTION could cause permanent mechanical damage; however, personal injury is unlikely.

A WARNING emphasizes an area where personal injury or even death could result from negligence. Mechanical damage may also occur. WARNINGS are to be taken *seriously*. In some cases, serious injury and death have resulted from disregarding similar warnings.

SAFETY FIRST

Professional mechanics can work for years and never sustain a serious injury. If you observe a few rules of common sense and safety, you can enjoy many safe hours servicing your machine. If you ignore these rules you can hurt yourself or damage the equipment.

1. Never use gasoline as a cleaning solvent.

2. Never smoke or use a torch in the vicinity of flammable liquids, such as cleaning solvent, in an open container.

3. If welding or brazing is required on the machine, remove the fuel tank to a safe distance, at least 50 ft. (15 m) away.

4. Use the proper sized wrenches to avoid damage to fasteners and injury to yourself.

5. When loosening a tight or stuck nut, be guided by what will happen if the wrench slips. Be careful and protect yourself accordingly.

6. When replacing a fastener, always use one with the same measurements and strength as the old one. Incorrect or mismatched fasteners can

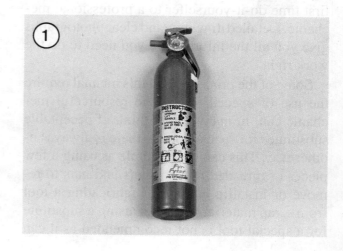

result in damage to the snowmobile and possible personal injury. Beware of fastener kits that are filled with cheap and poorly made nuts, bolts, washers and cotter pins. Refer to *Fasteners* in this chapter for additional information.

7. Keep all hand and power tools in good condition. Wipe greasy and oily tools after using them. They are difficult to hold and can cause injury. Replace or repair worn or damaged tools.

8. Keep your work area clean and uncluttered.

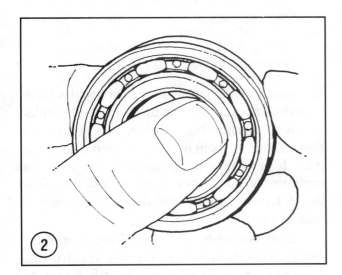

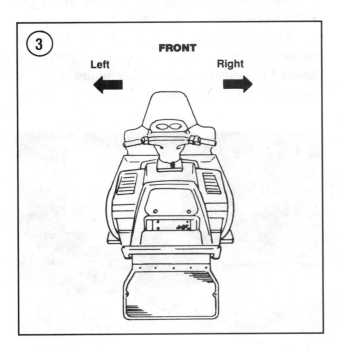

9. Wear safety goggles during all operations involving drilling, grinding, the use of a cold chisel or *anytime* you feel unsure about the safety of your eyes. Safety goggles should also be worn anytime solvent and compressed air are used to clean parts.

10. Keep an approved fire extinguisher (**Figure 1**) nearby. Be sure it is rated for gasoline (Class B) and electrical (Class C) fires.

11. When drying bearings or other rotating parts with compressed air, never allow the air jet to rotate the bearing or part. The air jet is capable of rotating them at speeds far in excess of those for which they were designed. The bearing or rotating part is very likely to disintegrate and cause serious injury and damage. To prevent bearing damage when using compressed air, hold the inner bearing race (**Figure 2**) by hand.

SERVICE HINTS

Most of the service procedures covered are straightforward and can be performed by anyone reasonably handy with tools. However, consider your own capabilities carefully before attempting any operation involving major disassembly.

1. "Front," as used in this manual, refers to the front of the snowmobile; the front of any component is the end closest to the front of the snowmobile. The "left-" and "right-hand" sides refer to the position of the parts as viewed by a rider sitting on the snowmobile facing forward. See **Figure 3**. For example, the throttle control is on the right-hand side. These rules are simple, but confusion can cause a major inconvenience during service.

2. When disassembling any engine or drive component, mark the parts for location and mark all parts which mate together. Small parts, such as bolts, can be identified by placing them in plastic sandwich bags (**Figure 4**). Seal the bags and label them with masking tape and a marking pen. When reassembly will take place immediately, an accepted practice is to place nuts and

bolts in a cupcake tin or egg carton in the order of disassembly.

3. Protect finished surfaces from physical damage or corrosion. Keep gasoline off painted surfaces.

4. Use penetrating oil on frozen or tight bolts, then strike the bolt head a few times with a hammer and punch (use a screwdriver on screws). Avoid the use of heat where possible, as it can warp, melt or affect the temper of parts. Heat also ruins finishes, especially paint and plastics.

5. No parts removed or installed (other than bushings and bearings) in the procedures given in this manual should require unusual force during disassembly or assembly. If a part is difficult to remove or install, find out why before proceeding.

6. Cover all openings after removing parts or components to prevent dirt or small tools from falling in.

7. Read each procedure *completely* while looking at the actual parts before starting a job. Make sure you *thoroughly* understand what is to be done and then carefully follow the procedure, step by step.

8. Recommendations are occasionally made to refer service or maintenance to a snowmobile dealer or a specialist in a particular field. In these cases, the work will be done more quickly and economically than if you performed the job yourself.

9. In procedural steps, the term "replace" means to discard a defective part and replace it with a new or exchange unit. "Overhaul" means to remove, disassemble, inspect, measure, repair or replace defective parts, reassemble and install major systems or parts.

10. Some operations require the use of a hydraulic press. It would be wiser to have these operations performed by a shop equipped for such work, rather than to try to do the job yourself with makeshift equipment that may damage your machine.

11. Repairs go much faster and easier if your machine is clean before you begin work. There are many special cleaners on the market, like Bel-Ray Degreaser, for washing the engine and related parts. Follow the manufacturer's directions on the container for the best results. Clean all oily or greasy parts with cleaning solvent as you remove them.

WARNING
Never use gasoline as a cleaning agent. It presents an extreme fire hazard. Be sure to work in a well-ventilated area when using cleaning solvent. Keep a fire extinguisher, rated for gasoline fires, handy in any case.

12. Much of the labor charge for repairs made by a dealer is for the time involved during in the removal, disassembly, assembly, and reinstallation of other parts in order to reach the defective part. It is frequently possible to perform the preliminary operations yourself and then take the defective unit to the dealer for repair at considerable savings.

13. If special tools are required, make arrangements to get them before you start. It is frustrating and time consuming to get partly into a job and then be unable to complete it.

14. Make diagrams (take a video or Polaroid picture) wherever similar-appearing parts are found. For instance, crankcase bolts are often not the same length. You may think you can remem-

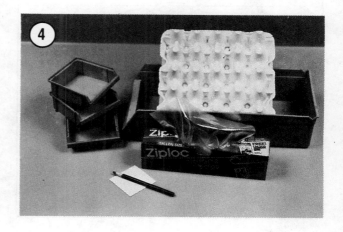

ber where everything came from—but mistakes are costly. There is also the possibility that you may be sidetracked and not return to work for days or even weeks—in which time the carefully laid out parts may have become disturbed.

15. When assembling parts, be sure all shims and washers are replaced exactly as they came out.

16. Whenever a rotating part butts against a stationary part, look for a shim or washer. Use new gaskets if there is any doubt about the condition of the old ones. A thin coat of silicone sealant on non-pressure type gaskets may help them seal more effectively.

17. If necessary to make a cover gasket and you do not have a suitable old gasket to use as a guide, you can use the outline of the cover and gasket material to make a new gasket. Apply engine oil to the cover gasket surface. Then place the cover on the new gasket material and apply pressure

with your hands. The oil will leave a very accurate outline on the gasket material that can be cut around.

> *CAUTION*
> *When purchasing gasket material to make a gasket, measure the thickness of the old gasket (at an uncompressed point) and purchase gasket material with the same approximate thickness.*

18. Heavy grease can be used to hold small parts in place if they tend to fall out during assembly. Be sure to keep grease and oil away from electrical components.

19. A carburetor is best cleaned by disassembling it and cleaning the parts in hot soap and water. Never soak gaskets and rubber parts in commercial carburetor cleaner. Never use wire to clean out jets and air passages, because they are easily damaged. Use compressed air to blow out the carburetor only if the float has been removed first.

20. Take your time and do the job right. Do not forget that a newly rebuilt engine must be broken-in just like a new one.

ENGINE AND CHASSIS SERIAL NUMBERS

Ski-Doo snowmobiles are identified by frame and engine identification numbers. The frame or Vehicle Identification Number (VIN) is stamped on the right-hand side of the tunnel just below the front of the seat (**Figure 5**). The engine number is stamped on the left-hand side of the crankcase as shown in **Figure 6**. **Figure 7** shows the breakdown of the vehicle serial number found on Ski-Doo snowmobiles covered in this manual. The first 4 digits represent the vehicle's model number. The model numbers are listed in **Table 1**. The last 5 digits are the specific vehicle's number.

Factory installed tracks have a serial number stamped on the outside of the track.

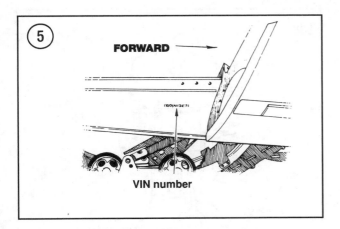

FORWARD

VIN number

Write down all serial and model numbers applicable to your machine and carry the numbers with you when you order parts from a dealer. Always order by year and engine and machine numbers. If possible, compare the old parts with the new ones before purchasing them. If the parts are not alike, have the parts manager explain the reason for the difference and insist on assurance that the new parts will fit and are correct.

ENGINE OPERATION

Ski-Doo snowmobiles are equipped with Rotax 2-stroke rotary-valve engines. Rotary valve engines differ from piston port intake systems in that a disc attached to the crankshaft opens and closes the intake port. On a piston port intake system, the piston skirt acts as a valve to close and open the intake port.

The intake system is mounted on the side of the engine. Two intake ports are machined into the upper crankcase half (**Figure 8**). The rotary

valve (**Figure 9**) is mounted on the crankshaft and is positioned between the intake valve cover and the crankcase. As the crankshaft turns, the rotary valve opens and closes the intake ports.

During this discussion, assume the crankshaft is rotating clockwise in **Figure 10**, starting at the beginning of the intake and cylinder compression phase. As the piston moves up in the cylin-

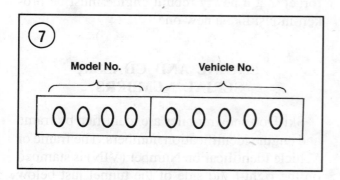

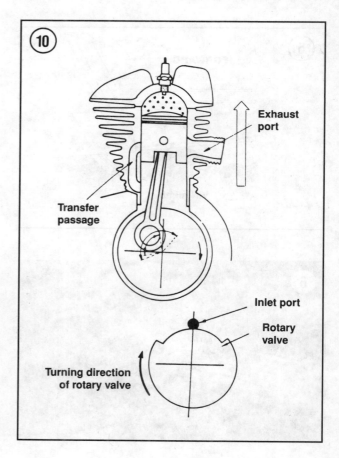

der, it closes the exhaust and transfer ports (**Figure 10**). As the piston continues upward, the air/fuel mixture in the cylinder is compressed. Note also that the space in the crankcase approaches its maximum, and a partial vacuum is created in the crankcase. Further crankshaft movement allows the leading edge of the rotary valve to start to uncover the intake port. A fresh fuel/air charge is then drawn into the crankcase through the intake port because of the vacuum created by the upward piston movement.

Figure 11 illustrates the next phase of the cycle. As the piston approaches top dead center (TDC), the spark plug fires, igniting the compressed fuel/air mixture. The piston is then driven downward by the expanding gases. Because the intake port is closed, the mixture in the crankcase is compressed by the piston as it moves downward.

When the top of the piston uncovers the exhaust port, the third phase begins, as shown in **Figure 12**. The exhaust gases begin to leave the cylinder through the exhaust port. At this point, the rotary valve is blocking the intake port, compressing the mixture in the crankcase.

As the piston continues to move downward, the intake port is still closed, but the main and auxiliary transfer ports are uncovered by the top of the piston (**Figure 13**). The exhaust gases continue to leave the cylinder through the exhaust port. A fresh air/fuel charge moves from the crnakcase to the cylinder through the transfer ports as the port opens. Since the incoming charge is under pressure, it rushes into the cylinder quickly and helps to scavenge the exhaust gases remaining from the previous combustion event. It can be seen by this discussion that every downward stroke of the piston is a power stroke.

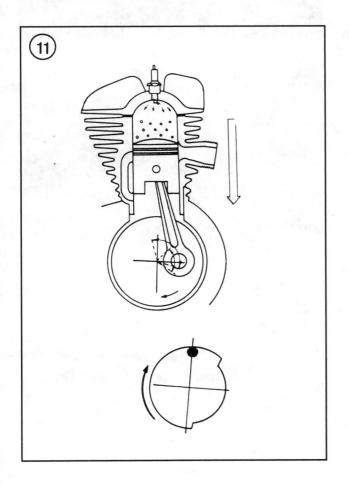

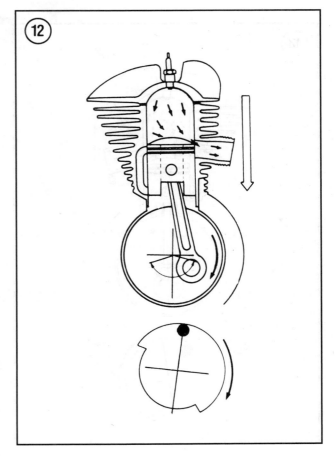

TORQUE SPECIFICATIONS

Torque specifications throughout this manual are given in Newton-meters (N•m) and foot-pounds (ft.-lb.).

Table 5 lists general torque specifications for nuts and bolts that are not listed in the respective chapters. To use the table, first determine the size of the nut or bolt by measuring it with a vernier caliper. **Figure 14** and **Figure 15** show how to do this.

FASTENERS

The materials and designs of the various fasteners used on your snowmobile are not arrived at by chance or accident. Fastener design determines the type of tool required to turn the fastener. Fastener material, size, and thread type is carefully selected to decrease the possibility of physical failure (**Figure 16**).

Nuts, bolts and screws are manufactured in a wide range of thread patterns. To join a nut and bolt, the diameter of the bolt and the diameter of the hole in the nut must be the same and the threads on both parts must be the same.

The best way to tell if the threads on 2 fasteners are matched is to turn the nut on the bolt (or

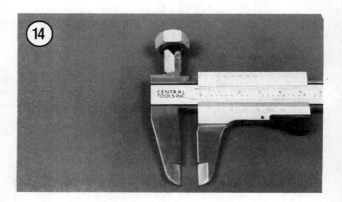

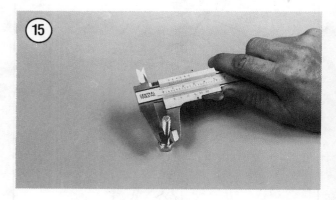

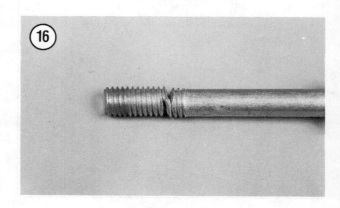

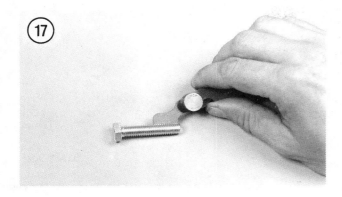

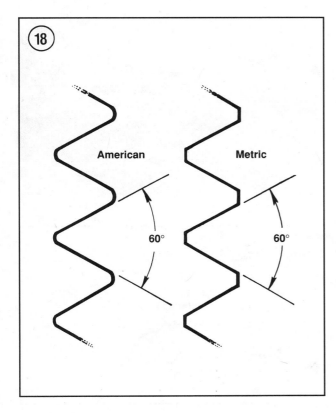

American   Metric

60°   60°

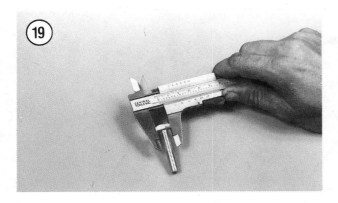

the bolt into the threaded hole in a piece of equipment) with fingers only. Be sure both pieces are clean. If much force is required, check the thread condition on each fastener. If the condition of threads on both parts is good but the fasteners jam, the threads are not compatible. A thread pitch gauge (**Figure 17**) can also be used to determine pitch. Ski-Doo snowmobiles are manufactured with ISO (International Organization for Standardization) metric fasteners. ISO metric threads are cut differently than those of standard American fasteners (**Figure 18**).

Most threads are cut so that the fastener must be turned clockwise to tighten it. These are called right-hand threads. Some fasteners have left-hand threads and must be turned counterclockwise to be tightened. Left-hand threads are used in locations where normal rotation of the equipment would tend to loosen a right-hand threaded fastener.

ISO Metric Screw Threads

ISO (International Organization for Standardization) metric threads come in coarse, fine and constant pitch threads. The ISO coarse pitch is used for most common fastener applications. The fine pitch thread is used on certain precision tools and instruments. The constant pitch thread is used mainly on machine parts and not for fasteners. The constant pitch thread, however, is used on all metric thread spark plugs.

ISO metric threads are specified by the capital letter M followed by the diameter in millimeters and the pitch (or the distance between each thread) in millimeters. For example a M8—1.25 bolt is one that has a diameter of 8 millimeters with a distance of 1.25 millimeters between each thread. The measurement across 2 flats on the head of the bolt (**Figure 19**) indicates the proper wrench size to be used, but is not an indication of thread size. **Figure 20** shows how to determine bolt diameter.

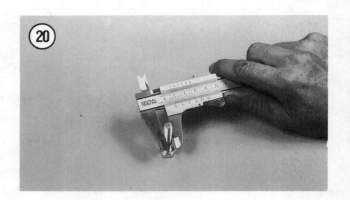

NOTE
*When purchasing a bolt from a dealer or parts store, it is important to also know how to specify bolt length. The correct way to measure bolt length is by measuring the length starting from underneath the bolt head to the end of the bolt (**Figure 21**). Always measure bolt length in this manner to avoid purchasing bolts that are the wrong length.*

Machine Screws

There are many different types of machine screws. **Figure 22** shows a number of screw heads requiring different types of turning tools. Heads are also designed to protrude above the metal (round) or to be slightly recessed in the metal (flat). See **Figure 23**.

Bolts

Commonly called bolts, the technical name for these fasteners is cap screw. Metric bolts are

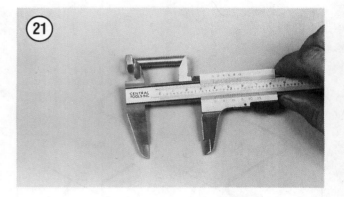

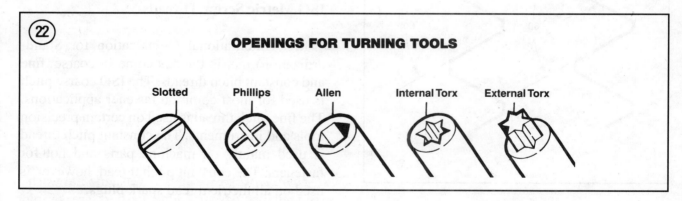

OPENINGS FOR TURNING TOOLS

Slotted   Phillips   Allen   Internal Torx   External Torx

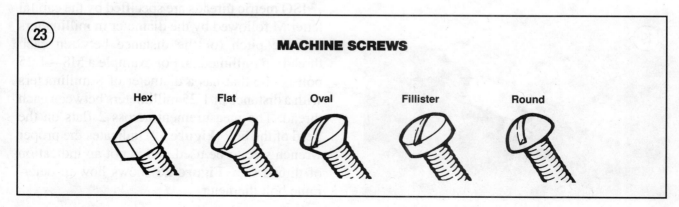

MACHINE SCREWS

Hex   Flat   Oval   Fillister   Round

described by the diameter and pitch (or the distance between each thread).

Nuts

Nuts are manufactured in a variety of types and sizes. Most are hexagonal (6-sided) and fit on bolts, screws and studs with the same diameter and pitch.

Figure 24 shows several types of nuts. The common nut is generally used with a lockwasher. A self-locking nut usually has a nylon insert that prevents the nut from loosening and no lockwasher is required. Wing nuts are designed for fast removal by hand and are used for convenience in non-critical locations.

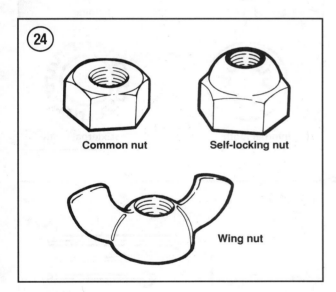

Common nut   Self-locking nut

Wing nut

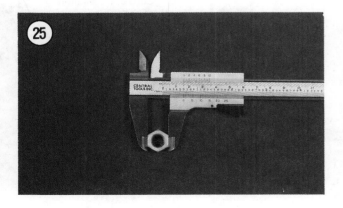

To indicate the size of a metric nut, manufacturers specify the diameter of the opening and the thread pitch. This is similar to bolt specifications, but without the length dimension. The measurement across 2 flats on the nut (**Figure 25**) indicates the proper wrench size to be used.

Self-Locking Fasteners

Several types of bolts, screws and nuts incorporate a system that develops an interference between the bolt, screw, nut or tapped hole threads. Interference is achieved in various ways: by distorting threads, coating threads with dry adhesive or nylon, distorting the top of an all-metal nut, using a nylon insert in the center or at the top of a nut, etc.

Self-locking fasteners offer greater holding strength and better vibration resistance. Some self-locking fasteners can be reused if in good condition. Others, like the nylon insert nut, form an initial locking condition when the nut is first installed; the nylon forms closely to the bolt thread pattern, thus reducing any tendency for the nut to loosen. When the nut is removed, the locking efficiency is greatly reduced. For greatest safety, replace self-locking fasteners whenever components are removed or disassembled.

Washers

There are 2 basic types of washers: flat washers and lockwashers. Flat washers are simple discs with a hole to fit a screw or bolt. Lockwashers are designed to prevent a fastener from working loose due to vibration, expansion and contraction. **Figure 26** shows several types of washers. Washers are also used in the following functions:

 a. As spacers.
 b. To prevent galling or damage of the equipment by the fastener.
 c. To help distribute fastener load during torquing.

d. As seals.

Note that flat washers are often used between a lockwasher and a fastener to provide a smooth bearing surface. This allows the fastener to be turned easily with a tool.

Cotter Pins

Cotter pins (**Figure 27**) are used to secure special kinds of fasteners. The stud or bolt must have a hole in it; the nut or nut lock piece must have castellations around which the cotter pin ends wrap. Cotter pins should *not* be reused after removal.

Snap Rings (Circlips)

Snap rings (sometimes called circlips) can be internal or external design. They are used to retain items on shafts (external type) or within tubes or bores of housings (internal type). In some applications, snap rings of varying thicknesses are used to control the end play of shafts or assemblies. These are often called selective snap rings. Always install new snap rings during reassembly, because removal weakens and deforms them.

Snap rings may be manufactured by either machining or stamping. Machined snap rings (**Figure 28**) can be installed in either direction (on the shaft or in the housing) because both faces are machined, thus creating two sharp edges. Stamped snap rings (**Figure 29**) are manufactured with one sharp edge and one rounded edge. When installing a stamped snap ring in a thrust situation, the sharp edge must face away from the part producing the thrust unless the text directs otherwise. When installing snap rings, observe the following:

a. Remove and install snap rings with snap ring pliers. See *Snap Ring Pliers* in this chapter.

b. Compress or expand snap rings only enough to install them.

c. After the snap ring is installed, make sure it is completely seated in its groove.

LUBRICANTS

Periodic lubrication ensures long life for any type of equipment. The *type* of lubricant used is just as important as the lubrication service itself. The following paragraphs describe the types of

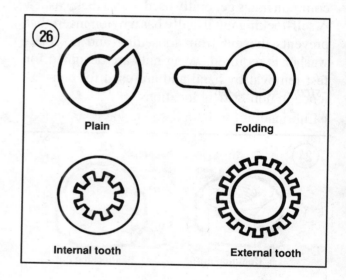

Plain   Folding

Internal tooth   External tooth

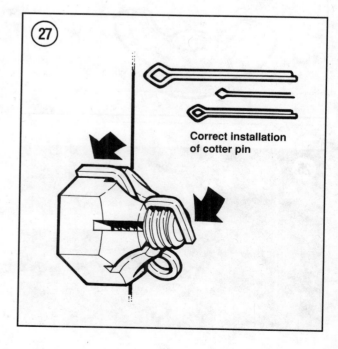

Correct installation of cotter pin

lubricants most often used on snowmobiles. Be sure to follow the manufacturer's recommendations for lubricant types.

Generally, all liquid lubricants are called "oil." They may be mineral-based (including petroleum bases), natural-based (vegetable and animal bases), synthetic-based or emulsions (mixtures). "Grease" is an oil to which a thickening base has been added so the end product is semi-solid. Grease is often classified by the type of thickener added; lithium soap is commonly used.

Engine Oil

2-stroke engine oil

Lubrication for a 2-stroke engine is provided either by oil mixed with the incoming fuel/air mixture or by oil injected into the fuel/air mix-

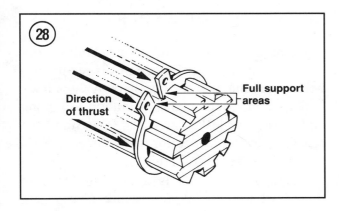

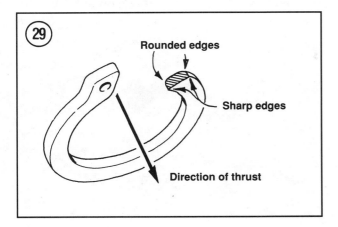

ture. The models included in this manual are equipped with an oil injection system. Some of the oil settles out in the crankcase, lubricating the crankshaft and lower end of the connecting rods. The rest of the oil enters the combustion chamber to lubricate the piston rings and cylinder walls. This oil is burned during the combustion process, then expelled with the engine's exhaust.

Engine oil must have several special qualities to work well in a 2-stroke snowmobile engine. The oil must flow freely in cold temperatures, lubricate the engine sufficiently and burn easily during combustion. It can't leave behind excessive deposits, and it must be appropriate for the high operating temperatures associated with 2-stroke engines. Refer to *Engine Lubrication* in Chapter Three.

> *NOTE*
> *The injection oil used in Ski-Doo snowmobile engines must also be able to flow at temperatures of -40° C (-40° F). See Chapter Three under **Lubrication** for additional information.*

4-stroke engine oil

> *CAUTION*
> *Four-stroke oil is only discussed to provide a comparison. The engines used in these models of Ski-Doo snowmobiles are 2-stroke engines and only 2-stroke oil should be used.*

Four-stroke (cycle) oil for ATV, motorcycle and automotive engines is classified by the American Petroleum Institute (API) and the Society of Automotive Engineers (SAE) in several categories. Oil containers display classifications on the top or label.

API oil classification is indicated by letters; oils for gasoline engines are identified by an "S," such as "SE, SF, SG" or "SH." Using the type recommended by the manufacturer is important, but some earlier classifications of oil may be difficult to find.

Viscosity is an indication of the oil's thickness or ability to flow at a specific temperature. The SAE uses numbers to indicate viscosity; thin oils have low numbers while thick oils have high numbers. A "W" after the number indicates that the viscosity testing was done at low temperature to simulate cold-weather operation. Engine oils fall into the 5 to 50 range.

Multi grade oil (for example 5W-20) has been changed by additives that modify the oil to be less viscous (thinner) at low temperatures and more viscous (thicker) at high temperatures. This allows the oil to perform efficiently across a wide range of engine operating conditions. The lower the number, the easier the engine will start in cold climates. Higher numbers are usually recommended for engine running in hot weather conditions.

Grease

Grease is graded by the National Lubricating Grease Institute (NLGI). Grease is graded by number according to the consistency of the grease; these range from No. 000 to No. 6, with No. 6 being the most solid. A typical multipurpose grease is NLGI No. 2. For specific applications, equipment manufacturers may require grease with an additive such as molybdenum disulfide (MOS2).

NOTE
Use a low-temperature grease wherever grease is required on the snowmobile. Chapter Three lists the low-temperature grease recommended by Ski-Doo.

RTV GASKET SEALANT

Room temperature vulcanizing (RTV) sealant is used on some pre-formed gaskets and to seal some components. RTV is a silicone gel supplied in tubes and can be purchased in a number of different colors.

Moisture in the air causes RTV to cure. Always place the cap on the tube as soon as possible after using RTV. RTV has a shelf life of one year and will not cure properly once the shelf life has expired. Check the expiration date on RTV tubes before using and keep partially used tubes tightly sealed.

Applying RTV Sealant

Clean all gasket residue from mating surfaces. Surfaces must be clean and free of oil and dirt. Remove all RTV gasket material from blind attaching holes, as it can cause a "hydraulic" effect and affect bolt torque.

Apply RTV sealant in a continuous bead 2-3 mm (0.08-0.12 in.) thick. Circle all mounting holes unless otherwise specified. Torque mating parts within 10 minutes after application.

THREADLOCK

Because of the snowmobile's operating conditions, a threadlock (**Figure 30**) is required to help secure many of the fasteners. A threadlock will lock fasteners against vibration loosening and seal against leaks. Loctite 242 (blue) and 271 (red) are recommended for many threadlock requirements described in this manual.

Loctite 242 (blue) is a medium-strength threadlock for general purpose use. Component disassembly can be performed with normal hand

tools. Loctite 271 (red) is a high-strength thread-lock that is normally used on studs or critical fasteners. Heat or special tools, such as a press or puller, may be required for component disassembly.

Applying Threadlock

Surfaces must be clean and free of oil and dirt. If a threadlock was previously applied to the component, this residue should also be removed.

Shake the Loctite container thoroughly and apply to both parts. Assemble parts and/or tighten fasteners.

GASKET REMOVER

Stubborn gaskets can present a problem during engine service as they can take a long time to remove. Consequently, there is the added problem of secondary damage occurring to the gasket mating surfaces from the incorrect use of a gasket scraping tool. To quickly and safely remove stubborn gaskets, use a spray gasket remover. Spray gasket remover can be purchased through Ski-Doo dealers and automotive parts houses. Follow the manufacturer's directions for use.

EXPENDABLE SUPPLIES

Certain expendable supplies are required during maintenance and repair work. These include grease, oil, gasket cement, wiping rags and cleaning solvents. Ask your dealer for the special locking compounds, silicone lubricants and lube products which make vehicle maintenance simpler and easier. Cleaning solvent is available at some service stations.

WARNING
Have a stack of clean shop rags on hand when performing engine and suspension service. Clean shop rags should be
stored safely, but present less danger than solvent and lubricant soaked rags. Most local fire codes require that used rags be stored in a sealed, metal container with a self-closing lid until they can be washed or discarded.

WARNING
Even mild solvents and other chemicals can be absorbed into your skin while cleaning parts. Health hazards ranging from mild discomfort to major infections can often be avoided by using a pair of petroleum-resistant gloves. These can be purchased from industrial supply houses or many hardware stores.

PARTS REPLACEMENT

Always be ready to provide the frame and engine numbers when purchasing or ordering replacement parts. Frequently design changes are made during manufacture and some are relatively major. The vehicle identification number is located on the plate (**Figure 5**) located on the right side of the tunnel. The engine serial number is (**Figure 6**) is located on the plate attached to the left-hand side of the engine crankcase.

NOTE
Use caution when servicing an engine or vehicle if either serial number plate is missing, because it will be much more difficult to identify the specific parts to install. It may also indicate that the vehicle or engine has been stolen.

BASIC HAND TOOLS

Many of the procedures in this manual can be carried out with simple hand tools and test equipment familiar to the home mechanic. Keep your tools clean and in a tool box. Keep them organized with related tools stored together. After using a tool, wipe off dirt and grease with a clean cloth and return the tool to its correct place.

Top quality tools are essential; they are also more economical in the long run. If you are now starting to build your tool collection, avoid "advertised specials" featured at some parts houses, discount stores and chain drug stores. These are usually a poor grade tool that can be sold cheaply and that is exactly what they are—*cheap*. They are usually made of inferior material, and are thick, heavy and clumsy. Their rough finish makes them difficult to clean and they usually don't last very long. If it is ever your misfortune to use such tools, you will probably find out that the wrenches do not fit the heads of bolts and nuts correctly and will often damage the fastener.

Quality tools are made of alloy steel and are heat treated for greater strength. They are lighter and better balanced than cheap ones. Their surface is smooth, making them a pleasure to work with and easy to clean. The initial cost of good quality tools may be more but they are cheaper in the long run. Don't try to buy everything in all sizes in the beginning; do it a little at a time until you have the necessary tools.

The following tools are required to perform virtually any repair job. Each tool is described and the recommended size given for starting a tool collection. Additional tools and some duplicates may be added as you become familiar with the vehicle. Ski-Doo snowmobiles are built with metric standard fasteners—so if you are starting your collection now, buy metric sizes.

Screwdrivers

The screwdriver is a very basic tool, but if used improperly it will do more damage than good. The slot on a screw has a definite dimension and shape. A screwdriver must be selected to conform with that shape. Use a small screwdriver for small screws and a large one for large screws or the screw head will be damaged.

Two basic types of screwdrivers are required: common (flat-blade) screwdrivers (**Figure 31**) and Phillips screwdrivers (**Figure 32**).

Screwdrivers are available in sets which often include an assortment of common and Phillips blades. If you buy them individually, buy at least the following:

a. Common screwdriver—5/16 × 6 in. blade.

b. Common screwdriver—3/8 × 12 in. blade.

c. Phillips screwdriver—size 2 tip, 6 in. blade.

Use screwdrivers only for driving screws. Never use a screwdriver for prying or chiseling metal. Do not try to remove a Phillips or Allen head screw with a common screwdriver (unless the screw has a combination head that will accept either type); you can damage the head so that the proper tool will be unable to remove it.

Keep screwdrivers in the proper condition and they will last longer and perform better. Always keep the tip of a common screwdriver in good condition. **Figure 33** shows how to grind the tip to the proper shape if it becomes damaged. Note the symmetrical sides of the tip.

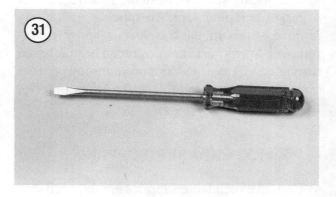

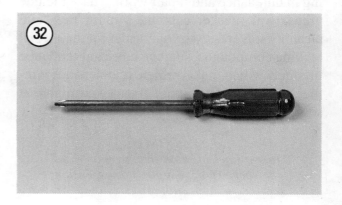

Pliers

Pliers come in a wide range of types and sizes. Pliers are useful for holding, cutting, bending and crimping. They should never be used to cut hardened objects or to turn bolts or nuts. **Figure 34** shows several pliers useful in snowmobile repair.

Each type of pliers has a specialized function. Slip-joint pliers are used mainly for holding things and for bending. Needlenose pliers are used to hold or bend small objects. Groove-joint pliers (commonly referred to as channel locks) can be adjusted to hold various sizes of objects such as pipe or tubing. There are many more types of pliers, but the ones described are the most suitable for snowmobile repair.

> *CAUTION*
> *Pliers should not be used for loosening or tightening nuts or bolts. The plier's sharp teeth will damage the nut or bolt corners.*

> *CAUTION*
> *If it is necessary to use slip-joint pliers to hold an object with a finished surface that can be easily damaged, wrap the object with tape or cardboard for protection.*

Locking (Vise-Grip) Pliers

Locking pliers (**Figure 35**) hold objects very tightly like a vise. Because locking pliers exert more force than regular pliers, their sharp jaws can permanently scar any object that is held. In addition, when locking pliers are locked in position, they can crush or deform thin walled material. Locking pliers are available in many types for specific tasks.

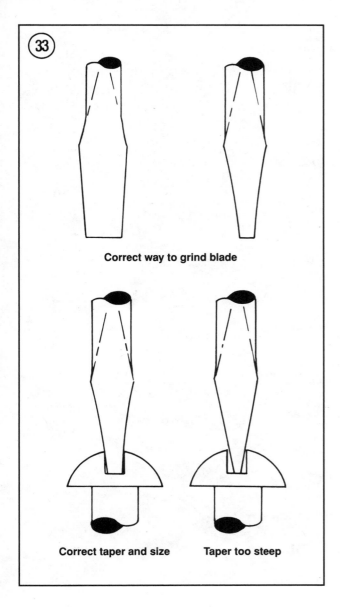

(33)

Correct way to grind blade

Correct taper and size   **Taper too steep**

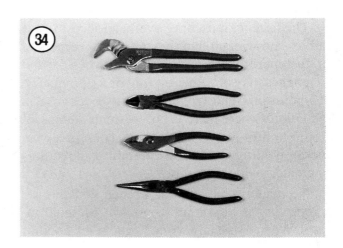

(34)

Snap Ring (Circlip) Pliers

Snap ring pliers (**Figure 36**) are made for removing and installing snap rings and should not be used for any other purpose. External pliers (spreading or expanding) are used to remove snap rings from the outside of a shaft or other similar part. Internal snap rings are located inside a tube, gear or housing and require pliers that squeeze the ends of the snap ring together so the snap ring can be removed.

Box-end, Open-end and Combination Wrenches

Box-end and open-end wrenches (**Figure 37**) are available in sets or separately in a variety of sizes. The number stamped on open- and box-end wrenches refers to the distance between 2 parallel flats of a nut or bolt head. Combination wrenches have a box-end wrench on one end and an open-end wrench of the same size on the other end. The wrench size is stamped near the center of combination wrenches.

Open-end wrenches are speedy and work best in areas with limited overhead access. Their wide jaws make them unsuitable for situations where the bolt or nut is sunken in a well or close to the edge of a casting. These wrenches only grip on two flats of a fastener, so if either the fastener head or wrench jaws are worn, the wrench may slip off.

The fastener must have overhead access to use a box-end wrench, but they grip all 6 corners of a fastener for a very secure grip. Box-end wrenches may be either 6-point or 12-point. The 12-point box-end wrench permits operation in situations where there is only a small amount of room to turn the wrench. The 6-point gives superior holding power and durability but requires a greater swinging radius.

No matter what style of wrench you choose, proper use is important to prevent personal injury. When using any wrench, get in the habit of

pulling the wrench toward you. This reduces the risk of injuring your hand if the wrench should slip. If you have to push the wrench away from you to loosen or tighten a fastener, open and push with the palm of your hand. This technique gets your fingers and knuckles out of the way should

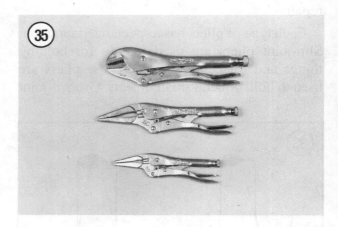

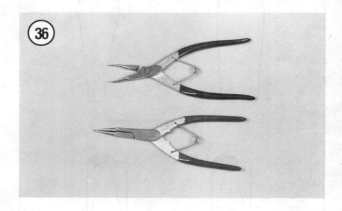

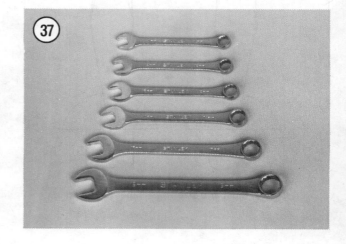

the wrench slip. Before using a wrench, always consider what could happen if the wrench should slip, if the bolt were to slip or if the bolt were to break.

Adjustable Wrenches

An adjustable wrench (sometimes called a Crescent wrench) can be adjusted to fit nearly

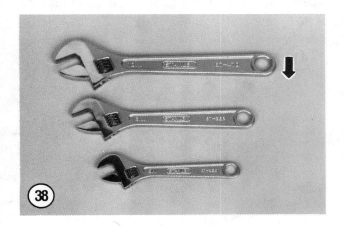

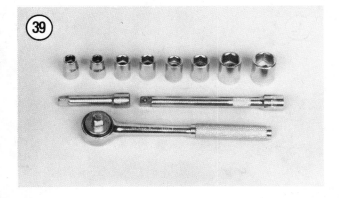

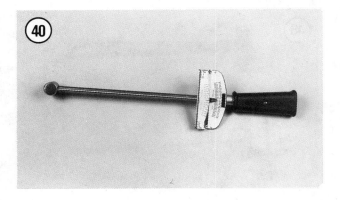

any nut or bolt head which has clear access around its entire perimeter. Adjustable wrenches **Figure 38** are best used as a backup wrench to keep a large nut or bolt from turning while the other end is being loosened or tightened with a proper wrench.

Adjustable wrenches have only two gripping surfaces and one is designed to be moveable. The usually large physical size and the adjustable feature make this type of wrench more apt to slip off the fastener, damaging the part and possibly injuring your hand.

These wrenches are directional; the solid jaw must be the one transmitting the force. Apply force in the direction indicated by arrow in **Figure 38**. If you use the adjustable jaw to transmit the force, it may loosen, allowing the wrench to slip off.

Adjustable wrenches come in several sizes but a 6 or 8 in. size is recommended as an all-purpose wrench.

Socket Wrenches

This type is undoubtedly the fastest, safest and most convenient to use. Sockets which attach to a ratchet handle are available with 6-point or 12-point openings and 1/4, 3/8 and 1/2 in. drives (**Figure 39**). The drive size indicates the size of the square hole which mates with the ratchet handle.

Torque Wrench

A torque wrench (**Figure 40**) is used with a socket to measure how tightly a nut or bolt is installed. They come in a wide price range and with a 1/4, 3/8, or 1/2 in. square drive. The drive size indicates the size of the square drive which mates with the socket.

Impact Driver

This tool makes removal of tight fasteners easy and reduces the chance for damage to bolts and screw slots. Impact drivers and interchangeable bits (**Figure 41**) are available at most large hardware, snowmobile and motorcycle dealers. Sockets can also be used with a hand impact driver; however, make sure the socket is designed for impact use. Regular hand type sockets may shatter (**Figure 42**) if used with an impact driver.

Hammers

The correct hammer (**Figure 43**) is necessary for certain repairs. A hammer with a face (or head) of rubber or plastic or the soft-faced hammer that is filled with lead shot is sometimes necessary during engine teardown. *Never* use a metal-faced hammer on engine or suspension parts, as severe damage will result in most cases. You can produce the same amount of force in most cases using a soft-faced hammer. A metal-faced hammer, however, is required when using a hand impact driver or cold chisel.

PRECISION MEASURING TOOLS

Measurement is an important part of snowmobile service. When performing many of the service procedures in this manual, you are required to make a number of measurements. These include basic checks such as engine compression and spark plug gap. As you get deeper into engine disassembly and service, measurements are required to determine the condition of the piston and cylinder bore, crankshaft and so on. When making these measurements, the degree of accuracy will dictate which tool is required. Precision measuring tools are expensive. If this is your first experience at engine service, it may be worthwhile to have the measurements made at a dealer. However, as your skills and enthusi-

asm increase for doing your own service work, you may want to purchase some of these specialized tools. The following is a description of the measuring tools required in order to perform service described in this manual.

Feeler Gauge

Feeler gauges are available in sets of various sizes (**Figure 44**). The gauge is made of either a

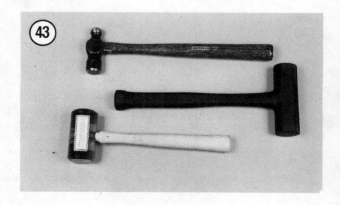

piece of a flat or round hardened steel of a specific thickness. Wire gauges are used to measure spark plug gap. Flat gauges are used for most other measurements.

Vernier Caliper

This tool (**Figure 45**) is invaluable when reading inside, outside and depth measurements with close precision. Common uses of a vernier caliper are measuring the length of springs, the thickness of shims, thrust washers and rotary valve, or the depth of the rotary valve bore. Although a vernier caliper is not as accurate as a micrometer, it allows reasonably precise measurements, typically to within 0.025 mm (0.001 in.).

Outside Micrometers

An outside micrometer is one of the most reliable instruments for precision measurement. Outside micrometers are required to precisely measure piston diameter, piston pin diameter, crankshaft journal and crankpin diameter. Used with a telescopic gauge, an outside micrometer can be used to measure cylinder bore size and to determine cylinder taper and out-of-round. Outside micrometers are delicate instruments; if dropped on the floor, they most certainly will be knocked out of calibration. Always handle and use micrometers carefully to ensure accuracy. Store micrometers in their padded case when not in use to prevent damage. Micrometers can be purchased individually or as a set (**Figure 46**).

Dial Indicator

A dial indicator (**Figure 47**) is a precision tool used to check differences in machined surfaces, such as the runout of a crankshaft or brake disc.

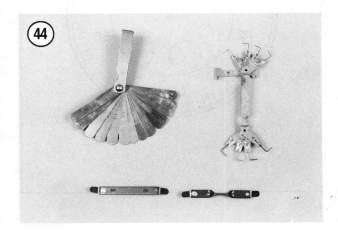

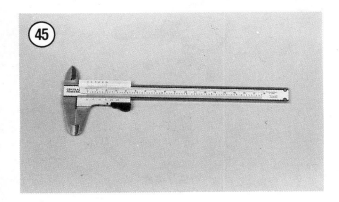

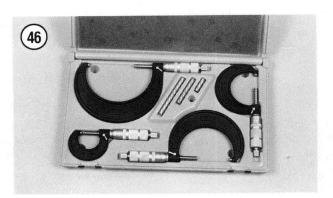

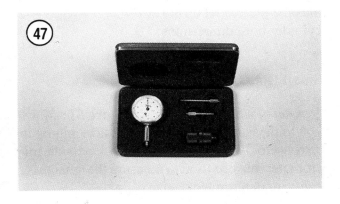

A dial indicator may also be used to locate the piston at a specific position for checking ignition timing. For snowmobile repair, select a dial indicator with a continuous dial (**Figure 48**). Several different mounting types are available, including a magnetic stand that attaches to iron surfaces, a clamp that can be attached to various components, and a spark plug adapter that locates the probe of the dial indicator through the spark plug hole. See *Magnetic Stand* in this chapter. The various mounts are required for specific measuring requirements. The text will indicate the type of mounting necessary.

Degree Wheel

A degree wheel (**Figure 49**) is a specific tool used to measure parts of a circle and angles. For Ski-Doo snowmobiles, a degree wheel is required to mark the rotary valve timing position. A degree wheel can be ordered through Ski-Doo dealers (part No. 414 3529 00).

Cylinder Bore Gauge

The cylinder bore gauge is a very specialized precision tool.

The gauge set shown in **Figure 50** is comprised of a dial indicator, handle and a number of length adapters to adapt the gauge to different bore sizes. The bore gauge can be used to make cylinder bore measurements such as bore size, taper and out-of-round. An outside micrometer must be used to set up the bore gauge to measure cylinder bore dimensions.

Small Hole Gauges

A set of small hole gauges (**Figure 51**) allows you to measure a hole, groove or slot ranging in size up to 13 mm (0.500 in.). An outside micrometer must be used to measure the small hole gauge to determine the size.

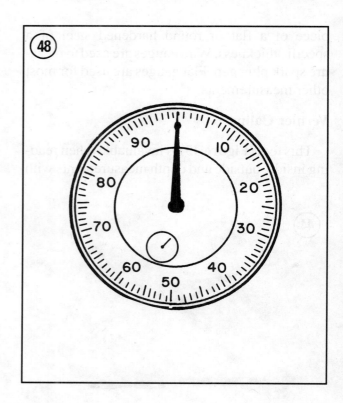

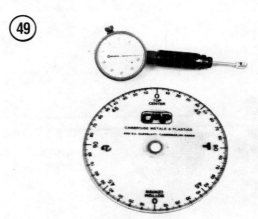

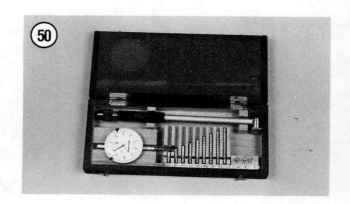

Telescoping Gauges

Telescoping gauges (**Figure 52**) can be used to measure hole diameters from approximately 8 mm (5/16 in.) to 150 mm (6 in.). Like the small hole gauge, the telescoping gauge does not have a scale gauge for direct readings. An outside micrometer must be used to measure the telescoping gauge to determine the size.

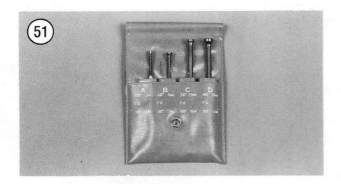

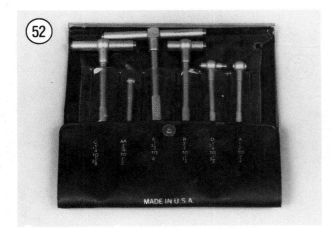

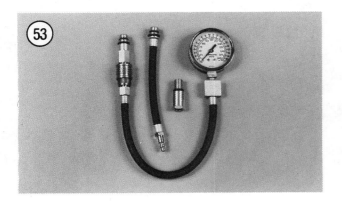

Compression Gauge

An engine with low compression cannot be properly tuned and will not develop full power. A compression gauge (**Figure 53**) measures engine compression. The one shown has a flexible stem with an extension that allows you to hold it while cranking the engine. Open the throttle all the way when checking engine compression. See Chapter Three.

Two-Stroke Pressure Tester

Refer to *Two-Stroke Pressure Testing* in Chapter Two.

Strobe Timing Light

This instrument is used to check ignition timing. By flashing a light at the precise instant the spark plug fires, the position of the timing mark can be seen. The flashing light makes the moving mark appear to stand still so it can be viewed in relation to the stationary mark.

Suitable lights range from inexpensive neon bulb types (**Figure 54**) to powerful xenon strobe lights. A light with an inductive pickup is recommended to eliminate any possible damage to ignition wiring. The timing light should be attached and used according to the instructions provided by its manufacturer.

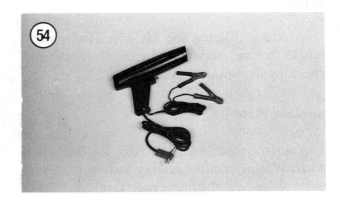

Multimeter

A multimeter (**Figure 55**) is invauable for electrical system troubleshooting and service. It combines a voltmeter, an ohmmeter and an ammeter into one unit, so it is often called VOM.

Two types of multimeters are commonly available, analog and digital. Analog meters have a moving needle with marked bands indicating the volt, ohm and amperage scales. The digital meter (DVOM) is ideally suited for troubleshooting because it is easy to read, more accurate than analog, contains internal overload protection, is auto-ranging (analog meters must be calibrated each time the scale is changed) and has automatic polarity compensation.

Screw Pitch Gauge

A screw pitch gauge (**Figure 56**) determines the thread pitch of bolts, screws, studs, etc. The gauge is made up of a number of thin plates. Each plate has a thread shape cut on one edge to match one thread pitch. When using a screw pitch gauge to determine a thread pitch size, try to fit different blade sizes onto the bolt thread until both threads match exactly.

Magnetic Stand

A magnetic stand (**Figure 57**) is used to securely hold a dial indicator when checking the runout of a round object or when checking the end play of a shaft.

V-Blocks

V-blocks (**Figure 58**) are precision ground blocks that are used to hold a round object when checking its runout or condition.

Surface Plate

A surface plate is used to check the flatness of parts. While industrial quality surface plates are quite expensive, the home mechanic can impro-

vise. A piece of thick, flat metal or plate glass can sometimes be used as a surface plate. The quality of the surface plate will affect the accuracy of the measurement. The metal surface plate shown in **Figure 59** has a piece of fine grit paper on its surface to assist in cleaning and smoothing a flat surface. The machined surfaces of the cylinder head, crankcase, and other close fitting parts may

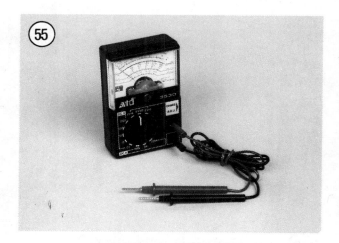

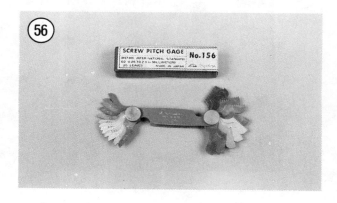

require a very good quality surface plate to smooth nicked or damaged surfaces.

> *NOTE*
> *Check with a local machine shop, fabricating shop or school offering a machine shop course for the availability of a metal plate that can be resurfaced and used as a surface plate.*

SPECIAL TOOLS

This section describes special tools that may be unique to Ski-Doo snowmobile service and repair. These tools are often a valuable asset even if used infrequently and most can be ordered through your Ski-Doo dealer. It is often necessary to know the specific snowmobile or engine model to select the correct special tools.

Flywheel Puller

A flywheel puller (**Figure 60**) is required to remove the flywheel and service the stator plate assembly or when adjusting the ignition timing. In addition, when disassembling the engine, the flywheel must be removed before the crankcase can be split. There is no satisfactory substitute for this tool. Because the flywheel is a taper fit on the crankshaft, makeshift removal often results in crankshaft and flywheel damage. Don't think about removing the flywheel without this tool. A puller can be ordered through Ski-Doo dealers.

Cylinder Aligning Plates

The two cylinders must be attached to the crankcase with both exhaust ports and all of cylinder head studs precisely aligned. Special plates (**Figure 61**) are available to align the two cylinders so the cylinder head, exhaust, and the other parts attached to the cylinders will fit properly. The alignment plates can be ordered through Ski-Doo dealers.

Bearing Pullers

A bearing puller set with long arms is necessary to remove bearings from suspension, wheels and other locations.

Track Clip Remover

This tool is used to remove track cleats (**Figure 62**).

Track Clip Installer

A track clip installer is required to install track clips. See **Figure 63** and **Figure 64**.

Spring Scale

A spring scale (**Figure 65**) is required to check track tension.

Clutch Tools

A number of special tools are required for clutch service. These are described in Chapter Thirteen.

MECHANIC'S TIPS

Removing Frozen Nuts and Screws

If a fastener rusts and cannot be removed, several methods may be used to loosen it. First, apply penetrating oil such as Liquid Wrench or WD-40 (available at hardware or auto supply stores). Apply it liberally and let it penetrate for 10-15 minutes, then tap the fastener several times with a small hammer. Do not hit it hard enough to cause damage. Reapply the penetrating oil if necessary. Using an *Impact Driver* as described in this chapter will often loosen a stuck bolt or screw.

> *CAUTION*
> *Do not pound on screwdrivers unless the steel shank of the tool extends all the way through the handle. Pounding on a plastic handled screwdriver is a sure way to destroy the tool.*

For frozen screws, apply additional penetrating oil as described, insert a screwdriver in the slot and tap the top of the screwdriver with a hammer. This loosens the rust so the screw can be removed. If the screw head is too damaged to use this method, grip the head with locking pliers and twist the screw out.

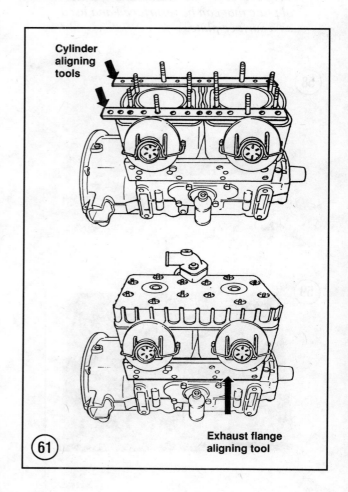

Cylinder aligning tools

Exhaust flange aligning tool

61

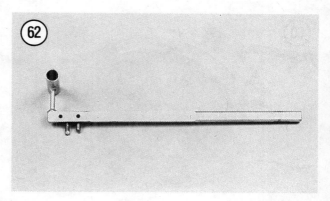

62

Avoid applying heat unless specifically instructed, as it may melt, warp or remove the temper from parts.

Removing Broken Screws or Bolts

If the head breaks off a screw or bolt, several methods are available to remove the remaining portion.

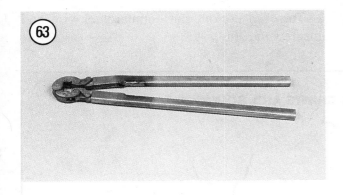

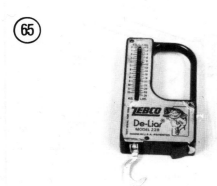

If a large portion of the fastener projects out, try gripping it with locking pliers. If the projecting portion is too small, file it to fit a wrench or cut a slot in it to fit a screwdriver. See **Figure 66**.

If the head breaks off flush, use a screw extractor. To do this, centerpunch as close as possible to the exact center of the remaining part of the screw or bolt. Drill a small hole in the screw and tap the extractor into the hole. Back the screw out with a wrench on the extractor. See **Figure 67**.

Remedying Stripped Threads

Occasionally, threads are damaged during service. Sometimes the threads can be cleaned up by running a tap (for internal threads) or die (for external threads) through the threads. See **Figure 68**. To clean or repair spark plug threads, a spark plug tap can be used.

NOTE
*Tap and dies can be purchased individually or in a set as shown in **Figure 69**.*

If an internal thread is damaged, it may be necessary to install a Helicoil (**Figure 70**) or some other type of thread insert. Follow the manufacturer's instructions when installing their insert.

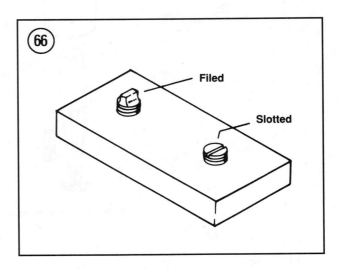

If it is necessary to drill and tap a hole, refer to **Table 7** for metric tap drill sizes.

Removing Broken or Damaged Studs

If the threads on a stud are damaged (**Figure 71**), but some threads remain, the old stud can be removed as follows. A tube of Loctite 271 (red), 2 nuts, 2 wrenches and a new stud are required during this procedure (**Figure 72**).

1. Thread 2 nuts onto the damaged stud. Then tighten the 2 nuts against each other so they are locked.

NOTE
If the threads on the damaged stud do not allow installation of the 2 nuts, remove the stud with a pair of locking pliers.

2. Turn the bottom nut counterclockwise and unscrew the stud.

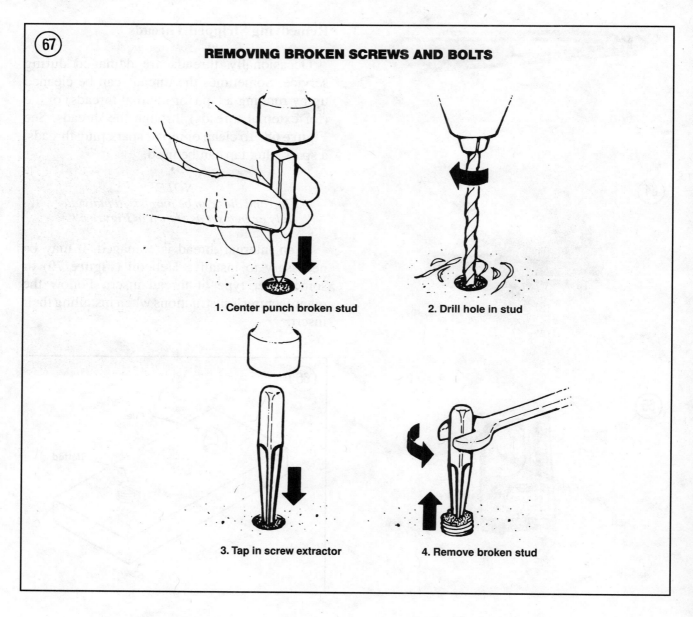

⑥⑦

REMOVING BROKEN SCREWS AND BOLTS

1. Center punch broken stud

2. Drill hole in stud

3. Tap in screw extractor

4. Remove broken stud

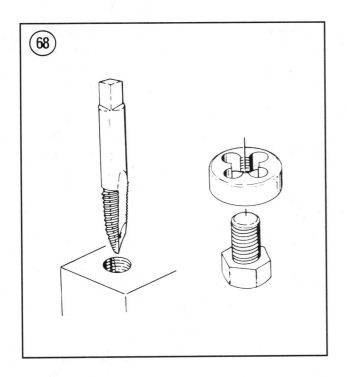

3. Clean the threads with solvent or electrical contact cleaner and allow to dry thoroughly.

4. Install 2 nuts on the top half of the new stud as in Step 1. Make sure they are locked securely.

5. Coat the bottom half of the new stud with Loctite 271 (red).

6. Turn the top nut clockwise and thread in the new stud completely.

7. Remove the nuts and repeat for each stud as required.

8. Follow Loctite's directions on cure time before assembling the component.

BALL BEARING REPLACEMENT

Ball bearings (**Figure 73**) are used throughout the snowmobile engine and chassis to reduce

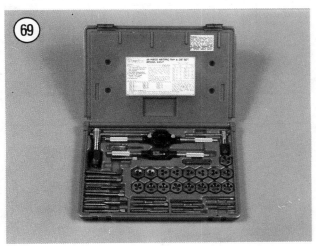

power loss, heat and excessive noise resulting from friction. Because ball bearings are precision made parts, they must be maintained by proper lubrication and maintenance. If a bearing is damaged, it must be replaced immediately. However, when installing a new bearing, use caution to prevent damage to the new bearing. While bearing replacement is described in the individual chapters where applicable, use the following as a guideline.

NOTE
Unless otherwise specified, install bearings with the manufacturer's mark or number facing outward.

Bearing Removal

While bearings are normally removed only when damaged, there may be times when it is necessary to remove a bearing that is in good condition. However, improper bearing removal will damage the bearing and maybe the shaft or case half. Note the following when removing bearings.

1. When using a puller to remove a bearing from a shaft, care must be taken so shaft damage does not occur. Always place a piece of metal between the end of the shaft and the puller screw. In addition, place the puller arms next to the inner bearing race. See **Figure 74**.

2. When using a hammer to remove a bearing from a shaft, do not strike the hammer directly

against the shaft. Instead, use a brass or aluminum rod between the hammer and shaft (**Figure 75**). In addition, support both bearing races with wooden blocks as shown in **Figure 75**.

3. The most ideal method of bearing removal is with a hydraulic press. However, certain procedures must be followed or damage may occur to

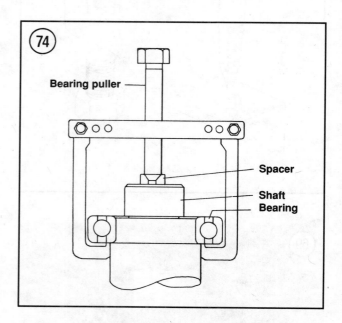

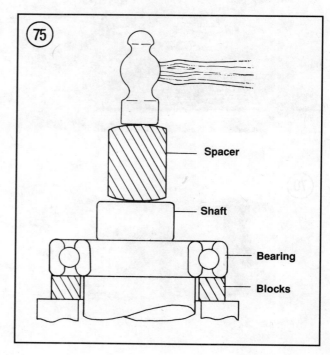

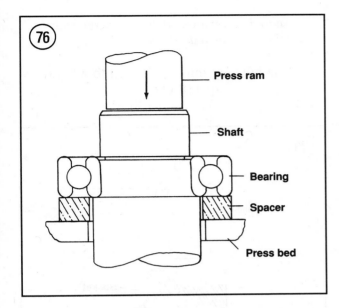

the bearing, shaft or case half. Note the following when using a press:

   a. Always support the inner and outer bearing races with a suitable size wooden or aluminum ring (**Figure 76**). If only the outer race is supported, the balls and/or the inner race will be damaged.

   b. Always make sure the press ram (**Figure 76**) aligns with the center of the shaft. If the ram is not centered, it may damage the bearing and/or shaft.

   c. The moment the shaft is free of the bearing, it will drop to the floor. Secure or hold the shaft to prevent it from falling.

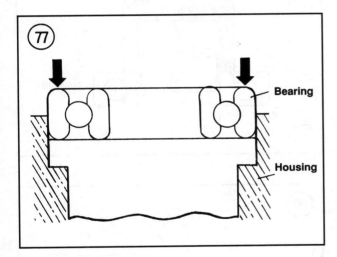

Bearing Installation

1. When installing a bearing in a housing, pressure must be applied to the *outer* bearing race (**Figure 77**). When installing a bearing on a shaft, pressure must be applied to the *inner* bearing race (**Figure 78**).

2. When installing a bearing as described in Step 1, some type of driver is required. Never strike the bearing directly with a hammer or the bearing will be damaged. When installing a bearing, a piece of pipe or a socket with an outer diameter that matches the bearing race is required. **Figure 79** shows the correct way to use a socket and hammer when installing a bearing.

3. Step 1 describes how to install a bearing in a case half and over a shaft. However, when installing over a shaft and into a housing at the same time, a snug fit is required for both outer and inner bearing races. In this situation, a spacer must be installed underneath the driver tool so that pressure is applied evenly across *both* races. See **Figure 80**. If the outer race is not supported as shown in **Figure 80**, the balls will push against the outer bearing track and damage it.

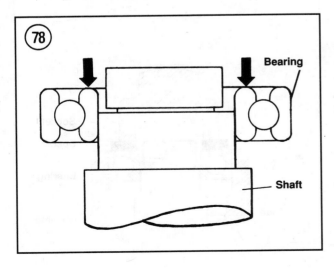

Shrink Fit

1. *Installing a bearing over a shaft:* If a tight fit is required, the bearing inside diameter is smaller than the shaft. In this case, driving the bearing on the shaft using normal methods may cause bearing damage. Instead, heat the bearing before installation. Note the following:

   a. Secure the shaft so it can be ready for bearing installation.

   b. Clean the bearing surface on the shaft of all residue. Remove burrs with a file or sandpaper.

   c. Fill a suitable pot or beaker with clean mineral oil. Place a thermometer (rated higher than 120° C [248° F]) in the oil. Support the thermometer so it does not rest on the bottom or side of the pot.

   d. Secure the bearing with a piece of heavy wire bent to hold it in the pot. Hang the bearing in the pot so that it does not touch the bottom or sides of the pot.

   e. Turn the heat on and monitor the thermometer. When the oil temperature rises to approximately 120° C (248° F), remove the bearing from the pot and quickly install it. If necessary, place a socket on the inner bearing race and tap the bearing into place. As the bearing chills, it will tighten on the shaft so you must work quickly when installing it. Make sure the bearing is installed all the way.

2. *Installing a bearing in a housing*: Bearings are generally installed in a housing with a slight interference fit. Driving the bearing into the housing using normal methods may damage the housing or cause bearing damage. Instead, heat the housing before the bearing is installed. Note the following:

> *CAUTION*
> *Before heating the crankcase in this procedure to remove the bearings, wash the cases thoroughly with detergent and water. Rinse and rewash the case as re-*

quired to remove all traces of oil and other chemical deposits.

   a. The housing must be heated to a temperature of about 100° C (212° F) in an oven or

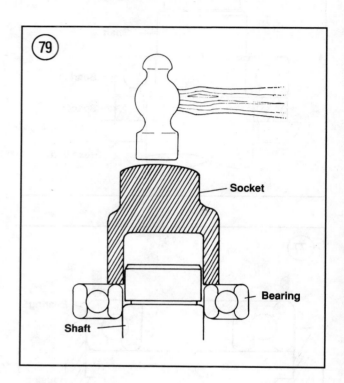

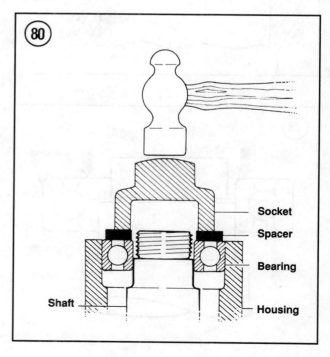

on a hot plate. An easy way to determine if it is at the proper temperature is to drop tiny drops of water on the case; if they sizzle and evaporate immediately, the temperature is correct. Heat only one housing at a time.

CAUTION
Do not heat the housing with a torch (propane or acetylene)—never bring a flame into contact with the bearing or housing. The direct heat will destroy the case hardening of the bearing and will likely warp the housing.

b. Remove the housing from the oven or hot plate. Hold the housing with a kitchen pot holder, heavy gloves or heavy shop cloths—*it is hot.*

NOTE
A suitable size socket and extension works well to remove and install bearings.

c. Hold the housing with the bearing side down and tap the bearing out. Repeat for all bearings in the housing.

d. While heating the housing halves, place the new bearings in a freezer if possible. Chilling them will slightly reduce their overall diameter while the hot housing assembly is slightly larger due to heat expansion. This will make installation much easier.

NOTE
Always install bearings with their manufacturer's mark or number facing outward unless the text directs otherwise.

e. While the housing is still hot, install the new bearing(s) into the housing. Install the bearings by hand, if possible. If necessary, lightly tap the bearing(s) into the housing with a socket placed on the outer bearing race. *Do not* install new bearings by driving on the inner bearing race. Install the bearing(s) until it seats completely.

OIL SEALS

Oil seals (**Figure 81**) are used to contain oil, grease or combustion inside a housing. Improper seal removal can damage the housing or the shaft. Improper installation can damage the seal. Note the following:

a. Prying is generally the easiest and most effective method to remove a seal from a housing. However, always place a rag underneath the pry tool to prevent damage to the housing.

b. A low-temperature grease should be packed in the seal lips before the seal is installed.

c. Oil seals should always be installed so that their manufacturer's numbers or marks face out.

NOTE
A socket of the correct size can often be used as a seal driver. Select a socket that fits the seal's outer diameter properly and clears any protruding shafts.

d. Install oil seals using a seal driver placed on the outside of the seal as shown in **Figure 82**. Make sure the seal is driven squarely into the housing. Never install a seal by

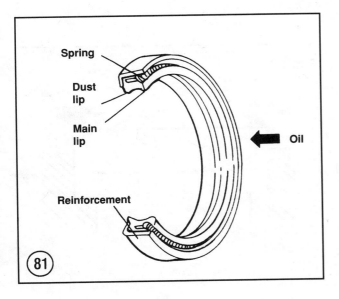

Spring

Dust lip

Main lip

Oil

Reinforcement

81

hitting against the top of the seal with a hammer.

SNOWMOBILE OPERATION

Snowmobiles are ideal machines for getting around otherwise inaccessible areas during winter months. However because snowmobiles are often operated in extreme weather conditions, over rough terrain, and in remote areas, they should be checked before each ride and maintained on a periodic basics.

> *WARNING*
> ***Never*** *lean into a snowmobile's engine compartment while wearing a scarf or other loose clothing when the engine is running or when the driver is attempting to start the engine. If the scarf or clothing should catch in the drive belt or clutch, severe injury or death could result.*

Pre-start Inspection

Always perform a pre-start inspection before heading out on your snowmobile. While the following list may look exhaustive, it can be performed rather quickly after a few times.

1. Familiarize yourself with your snowmobile.

2. Clean the windshield with a clean, damp cloth. Do not use gasoline, solvents or abrasive cleaners.

3. Check track tension (Chapter Three) and adjust if necessary.

4. Check the tether switch and the emergency cutout switch for proper operation. If your machine is new or if you are using a friend's machine, practice using the tether or stop switch a few times. Be certain that its use will be automatic during an emergency.

5. Check the brake operation. Be certain the brake system is correctly adjusted and operates properly.

6. Check the fuel level and top it up if necessary.

7. Check the injection oil tank. Make sure it is full.

8. Check the coolant level.

9. Operate the throttle lever. It must open and close smoothly.

10. Open the belt guard and visually inspect the drive belt. If the belt seems worn or damaged, replace it. Chapter Fourteen lists drive belt wear limit specifications. Close the belt guard after inspecting the belt. Make sure the belt guard mounts are not loose or damaged.

11. While the engine shroud is open, visually inspect all hoses, fittings and parts for looseness or damage. Check the tightness of all bolts and nuts. Tighten as required.

12. Check the handlebar and steering components for looseness or damage. Do not ride the vehicle if any steering component is damaged. Tighten loose fasteners as required.

13. After closing the shroud, make sure the shroud latches are fastened securely.

14. Check the skis for proper alignment (Chapter Three). Check the ski pivot bolt for tightness or damage.

> *WARNING*
> *When starting the engine, be sure that no bystanders are in front of or behind the snowmobile. A sudden lurch of the machine could cause serious injury.*

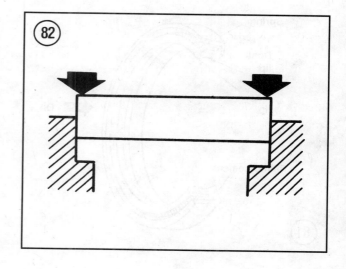

15. Make sure that all lights are working.

NOTE
If abnormal noises are detected after starting the engine, locate and repair the problem before starting out.

NOTE
Refer to the appropriate chapter for tightening torques and service procedures.

Tools and Spare Parts

Before leaving on a trip, make sure that you carry tools and spare parts in case of emergency. A tool kit should include the following:

a. Flashlight
b. Rope
c. Tools
d. Tape

A spare parts kit should include the following:

a. Drive belt
b. Emergency starter rope
c. Light bulbs
d. Spark plugs
e. Main jets
f. Throttle cable
g. Brake cable
h. This book...just in case

If you are going on a long trip, extra oil and fuel should also be carried.

Emergency Starting

If your recoil starter rope breaks (and the electric starter does not work), the engine can be started with an emergency rope that is wrapped around the primary sheave cap.

WARNING
*The drive belt guard must be removed when starting the engine with the emergency starter rope. **Never** lean into a snowmobile's engine compartment while wearing a scarf or other loose clothing while the engine is running or*

when attempting to start the engine. If the scarf or clothing should catch in the drive belt or clutch, severe injury or death could result.

1. Open the shroud.
2. Remove the drive belt guard.
3. Remove the spare starter rope from your tool kit.
4. Wind the rope around the primary sheave cap and start the engine.
5. Reinstall the drive belt guard after starting the engine.
6. Close and secure the shroud.
7. Store the spare starter rope in your tool kit.

Clearing the Track

If the snowmobile has been operated in deep or slushy snow, it is necessary to clear the track after stopping to prevent the track from freezing. This condition would make starting and running difficult.

WARNING
Make sure no one is behind the machine when clearing the track. Ice and rocks thrown from the track can cause injury.

Tip the snowmobile on its side until the track clears the ground *completely*. Run the track at a moderate speed until all the ice and snow is thrown clear.

CAUTION
If the track does freeze, it must be broken loosen manually with the engine turned OFF. Attempting to force a frozen track with the engine will burn and damage the drive belt.

SNOWMOBILE SAFETY

Proper Clothing

Warm and comfortable clothing is a must to provide protection from frostbite. Even mild temperatures can be very uncomfortable and dangerous when combined with a strong wind or when traveling at high speeds. See **Table 8** for windchill factors. Always dress according to what the windchill factor is, not the temperature. Check with an authorized dealer for suggested types of snowmobile clothing.

WARNING
To provide additional warmth as well as protection against head injury, always wear an approved helmet when snowmobiling.

Emergency Survival Techniques

1. Do not panic in the event of an emergency. Relax, think the situation over, then decide on a course of action. You may be within a short distance of help. If possible, repair your snowmobile so you can drive to safety. Conserve your energy and stay warm.

2. Keep hands and feet active to promote circulation and avoid frostbite while servicing your machine.

3. Mentally retrace your route. Where was the last point where help could be located? Do not attempt to walk long distances in deep snow. Make yourself comfortable until help arrives.

4. If you are properly equipped for your trip you can turn any undesirable area into a suitable campsite.

5. If necessary, build a small shelter with tree branches or evergreen boughs. Look for a sheltered area against a hill or cliff. Even burrowing in the snow offers protection from the cold and wind.

6. Prepare a signal fire using evergreen boughs and snowmobile oil. If you cannot build a fire, make an S-O-S in the snow.

7. Use a policeman's whistle or beat cooking utensils to attract attention.

8. When your camp is established, climb the nearest hill and determine your whereabouts. Observe landmarks on the way, so you can find your way back to your campsite. Do not rely on your footprints. They may be covered by blowing snow.

SNOWMOBILE CODE OF ETHICS

1. I will be a good sportsman and conservationist. I recognize that people judge all snowmobilers by my actions. I will use my influence with other snowmobile owners and operators to promote sportsmanlike conduct.

2. I will not litter any trails or areas, nor will I pollute streams or lakes. I will carry out what I carry in.

3. I will not damage living trees, shrubs or other natural features.

4. I will respect other people's properties and rights.

5. I will lend a helping hand when I see someone in need.

6. I will make myself and my vehicle available to assist in search and rescue operations.

7. I will not interfere with the activities of other winter sportsmen. I will respect their right to enjoy their recreational activity.

8. I will know and obey all federal, state or provincial and local rules regulating the operation of snowmobiles in areas where I use my vehicle.

9. I will not harass wildlife.

10. I will not snowmobile where prohibited.

Table 1 SKI-DOO MODEL NUMBER

Year	Model	Model number
1990	Formula MX	3742
	Formula MX LT	3743
	Formula MX LT (2)	3749
	Formula Plus	3744
	Formula Plus LT	3745
	Formula Plus LT (2)	3750
	Formula MACH 1	3746
	Formula MACH 1 XTC	3751
1991	Formula MX	3755
	Formula MX E	3756
	Formula MX X	3766
	Formula MX XTC	3757
	Formula MX XTC E	3758
	Formula MX XTC SS/SR	3769
	Formula MX XTC E SS/SR	3770
	Formula Plus	3759
	Formula Plus E	3760
	Formula Plus X	3767
	Formula Plus XTC	3761
	Formula Plus XTC E	3762
	Formula Plus XTC SS/SR	3771
	Formula Plus XTC E SS/SR	3772
	Formula MACH 1	3763
	Formula MACH 1 X	3768
	Formula MACH 1 XTC	3764
	Formula MACH 1 XTC SS/SR	3773
1992	Formula MX	3775
	Formula MX XTC R	3788
	Formula Plus	3777
	Formula Plus E	3778
	Formula Plus XTC	3779
	Formula Plus XTC E	3780
	Formula Plus X	3790
	Formula MACH 1	3781
	Formula MACH 1 X	3789
	Formula MACH 1 XTC	3782
	Formula MACH 1 XTC II	3783
1993	Formula MX	3791
	Formula MX (2)	3846
	Formula MX XTC R	3792
	Formula MX Z	3844
	Formula MX Z A	3847
	Formula Plus	3793
	Formula Plus (2)	3750
	Formula Plus E	3894
	Formula Plus XTC	3795
	Formula Plus EFI	3799
	Formula Plus X	3849
	Formula MACH 1	3797
	Formula MACH 1 (2)	3852
	Formula MACH 1 XTC	3798
	Formula Grand Touring	3796

(continued)

Table 1 SKI-DOO MODEL NUMBER (continued)

Year	Model	Model number
1994		
	Formula MX	3868, 3883, 3885
	Formula MX Z	3870, 3886
	Formula MX Z X	3870X, 3886X
	Summit 470 HAC	3871, 3888
	Formula ST	3872, 3889
	Formula STX	3873, 3893, 3892
	Formula STX II	3874, 3894
	Formula Z	3875, 3897, 3896
	Summit 583	3876, 3891
	Summit 583 (2)	3881, 3882, 3890
	MACH 1	3863, 3880
	Grand Touring	3867, 3879
	Grand Touring XTC	3864, 3878
	Grand Touring SE	3866
1995		
	MX	1000, 1001
	MX Z	1036, 1037
	Formula SS	1033, 1034, 1047
	Formula STX	1003, 1004
	Formula STX (LT)	1007, 1008
	Formula Z	1030, 1031, 1032
	Summit 583	1013, 1014, 1015
	Summit 670	1016, 1017, 1018
	MACH 1	1043, 1044, 1045
	Grand Touring SE	1027, 1028, 1029
	Grand Touring 580	1024, 1025, 1026
	Grand Touring 470	1022, 10231-2

Table 2 GENERAL DIMENSIONS

	cm	in.
Overall length		
1990		
Formula MX	277	109
Formula MX LT	296.5	117
Formula Plus, Plus LT,		
MACH 1 & MACH 1 XTC	277	109
1991		
Formula MX, MX E,		
Plus, Plus E &		
Formula MACH 1	277	109
Formula MX XTC,		
MX XTC E, Plus XTC,		
Plus XTC E & MACH 1 XTC	296.5	117
1992		
Formula MX	274.3	108
Formula MX XTC R	296.4	116.7
Formula Plus & MACH 1	277	109
Formula Plus XTC &		
MACH 1 XTC	296.4	116.7

(continued)

Table 2 GENERAL DIMENSIONS (continued)

	cm	in.
1993		
Formula MX, Plus, Plus E, Plus EFI, Plus X & MACH 1	277	109
Formula MX XTC R, Plus XTC & MACH 1 XTC	296.5	117
Formula MX Z	280	110.2
Formula Grand Touring	290.8	114.5
1994		
Formula MX, MX Z, ST, STX & STX II	280	110.2
Formula Z	299.4	117.87
MACH 1	277	109
Summit 470 HAC	277	109
Summit 583 HAC	299.4	117.87
Grand Touring	277	109
Grand Touring XTC	290.8	112.49
Grand Touring SE	286.4	112.75
1995		
MX, MX Z, Formula SS, STX, Z, STX LT & MACH 1	272	107.1
Summit 583, Summit 670 & Grand Touring 470	291	114.6
Grand Touring SE & Grand Touring 580	302	119
Overall width		
1990-1991	104.1	41
1992	111.76	44
1993		
Formula MX XTC R, Plus XTC & MACH 1 XTC	106	41.7
Formula MX Z	116.8	46
Formula MX, Plus, Plus E, Formula Plus EFI, Plus X & MACH 1	112.7	44.4
Formula Grand Touring	115.6	45.5
1994		
Formula MX, ST, STX & STX II	115.5	45.5
Formula MX Z	116.8	46
Summit 470 HAC	112.7	44.4
Formula MX Z X	–	–
Formula Z & Summit 583 HAC	105.4	41.5
MACH 1, Grand Touring, Grand Touring XTC & Grand Touring SE	112.7	44.4
1995		
MX	115.6	45.5
MX Z	113.1	44.5
Formula SS, STX, STX LT & Z	115.6	45.5
Summit 583 & Summit 670	108.0	42.5
MACH 1, Grand Touring SE, Grand Touring 580 & Grand Touring 470	115.6	45.5
Overall height		
1990		
Formula MX, MX LT, Plus & Plus LT	117	46
Formula MACH 1 & MACH 1 XTC	99	39

(continued)

Table 2 GENERAL DIMENSIONS (continued)

	cm	in.
Overall height (continued)		
1991		
All Models Except Formula MX X, Plus X & MACH 1 X	121	47.6
Formula MX X, Plus X & MACH 1 X	–	–
1992		
Formula MX, MX XTC R, Formula Plus, Plus E, Plus XTC, Plus XTC E & Plus X	114.3	45
Formula MACH 1, MACH 1 X, MACH 1 XTC & MACH 1 XTC II	96.5	38
1993		
Formula MX, Plus, Plus E & Plus EFI	113.5	44.7
Formula MX XTC R, Plus XTC, MACH 1 XTC & Grand Touring	120	47.2
Formula MX Z	108	42.5
Formula Plus X	91.5	36
Formula MACH 1	96.4	38
1994		
Formula MX & MX Z	108	42.5
Summit 470 HAC	113.5	44.7
Formula MX Z X	–	–
Formula ST, STX, STX II, Z & Summit 583 HAC	128.3	50.52
MACH 1	96.4	38
Grand Touring, Grand Touring XTC & Grand Touring SE	120	47.2
1995		
MX, MX Z, Formula SS, Z & MACH 1	108	42.5
Formula STX & STX LT, Summit 583, Summit 670, Grand Touring SE, Grand Touring 580 & Grand Touring 470	128.3	50.52

Table 3 VEHICLE WEIGHT

	kg	lbs.
1990		
Formula MX	222.2	490
Formula MX LT, Plus LT & MACH 1 XTC	240	529
Formula Plus	227	500
Formula MACH 1	230.4	508
1991		
Formula MX	230	507
Formula MX E	243.5	537
Formula MX XTC	239	527
Formula MX XTC E	252	556
Formula Plus	234	516
Formula Plus E	247	545
Formula Plus XTC	250	550
Formula Plus XTC E	263	580
Formula MACH 1	238	525
Formula MACH 1 XTC	249	549

(continued)

Table 3 VEHICLE WEIGHT (continued)

	kg	lbs.
1992		
Formula MX	225	496
Formula MX XTC R	247	545
Formula Plus	228	504
Formula Plus E	240	530
Formula Plus XTC	250	550
Formula Plus XTC E	263	580
Formula Plus X & MACH 1	233	514
Formula MACH 1 XTC	254	560
1993		
Formula MX	225	496
Formula MX XTC R	247	545
Formula MX Z	213	470
Formula Plus	228	504
Formula Plus E	240	530
Formula Plus XTC	250	550
Formula Plus EFI	232	510
Formula Plus X & MACH 1	233	514
Formula MACH 1 XTC	254	560
Formula Grand Touring	250	550
1994		
Formula MX	214	472
Formula MX Z	213	470
Formula MX Z X	–	–
Summit 470 HAC	225	496
Formula ST	217	478
Formula STX & STX II	220	484
Summit 583 HAC & Formula Z	222	489
MACH 1	233	514
Grand Touring	250	550
Grand Touring XTC	255	562
Grand Touring SE	253	558
1995		
MX	220	484
MX Z	217	477
Formula SS	233	513
Formula STX, STX (LT) & Z	227	500
Summit 583	234	515
Summit 670	237	521
MACH 1	235	517
Grand Touring 470	240	528
Grand Touring 580	250	549
Grand Touring SE	259	570

Table 4 DECIMAL AND METRIC EQUIVALENTS

Fractions	Decimal in.	Metric mm	Fractions	Decimal in.	Metric mm
1/64	0.015625	0.39688	33/64	0.515625	13.09687
1/32	0.03125	0.79375	17/32	0.53125	13.49375
3/64	0.046875	1.19062	35/64	0.546875	13.89062
1/16	0.0625	1.58750	9/16	0.5625	14.28750
5/64	0.078125	1.98437	37/64	0.578125	14.68437
3/32	0.09375	2.38125	19/32	0.59375	15.08125
7/64	0.109375	2.77812	39/64	0.609375	15.47812
1/8	0.125	3.1750	5/8	0.625	15.87500
9/64	0.140625	3.57187	41/64	0.640625	16.27187
5/32	0.15625	3.57187	21/32	0.65625	16.66875
11/64	0.171875	4.36562	43/64	0.671875	17.06562
3/16	0.1875	4.76250	11/16	0.6875	17.46250
13/64	0.203125	5.15937	45/64	0.703125	17.85937
7/32	0.21875	5.55625	23/32	0.71875	18.25625
15/64	0.234375	5.95312	47/64	0.734375	18.65312
1/4	0.250	6.35000	3/4	0.750	19.05000
17/64	2.265625	6.74687	49/64	0.765625	19.44687
9/32	0.28125	7.14375	25/32	0.78125	19.84375
19/64	0.296875	7.54062	51/64	0.796875	20.24062
5/16	0.3125	7.93750	13/16	0.8125	20.63750
21/64	0.328125	8.33437	53/64	0.828125	21.03437
11/32	0.34375	8.73125	27/32	0.84375	21.43125
23/64	0.359375	9.121812	55/64	0.859375	21.82812
3/8	0.375	9.52500	7/8	0.875	22.22500
25/64	0.390625	9.92187	57/64	0.890625	22.62187
13/32	0.40625	10.31875	29/32	0.90625	23.01875
27/64	0.421875	10.71562	59/64	0.921875	23.41562
7/16	0.4375	11.11250	15/16	0.9375	23.81250
29/64	0.453125	11.50937	61/64	0.953125	24.20937
15/32	0.46875	11.90625	31/32	0.96875	24.60625
31/64	0.484375	12.30312	63/64	0.984375	25.00312
1/2	0.500	12.7000	1	1.00	25.40000

Table 5 GENERAL TORQUE SPECIFICATIONS

Item	N·m	ft.-lb.
Bolt		
6 mm	6	4.3
8 mm	15	11
10 mm	30	22
12 mm	55	40
14 mm	85	63
16 mm	130	95
Nut		
6 mm	6	4.3
8 mm	15	11
10 mm	30	22
12 mm	55	40
14 mm	85	63
16 mm	130	95

Table 6 TECHNICAL ABBREVIATIONS

ABDC	After bottom dead center
ATDC	After top dead center
BBDC	Before bottom dead center
BDC	Bottom dead center
BTDC	Before top dead center
C	Celsius (Centigrade)
cc	Cubic centimeters
CDI	Capacitor discharge ignition
cu. in.	Cubic inches
F	Fahrenheit
ft.-lb.	Foot-pounds
gal.	Gallons
H/A	High altitude
hp	Horsepower
in.	Inches
kg	Kilogram
kg/cm2	Kilograms per square centimeter
kgm	Kilogram meters
km	Kilometer
l	Liter
m	Meter
MAG	Magneto
ml	Milliliter
mm	Millimeter
N·m	Newton-meters
oz.	Ounce
psi	Pounds per square inch
PTO	Power take off
pt.	Pint
qt.	Quart
rpm	Revolutions per minute

Table 7 METRIC TAP DRILL SIZES

Metric (mm)	Drill size	Decimal equivalent	Nearest fraction
3 × 0.50	No. 39	0.0995	3/32
3 × 0.60	3/32	0.0937	3/32
4 × 0.70	No. 30	0.1285	1/8
4 × 0.75	1/8	0.125	1/8
5 × 0.80	No. 19	0.166	11/64
5 × 0.90	No. 20	0.161	5/32
6 × 1.00	No. 9	0.196	13/64
7 × 1.00	16/64	0.234	15/64
8 × 1.00	J	0.277	9/32
8 × 1.25	17/64	0.265	17/64
9 × 1.00	5/16	0.3125	5/16
9 × 1.25	5/16	0.3125	5/16
10 × 1.25	11/32	0.3437	11/32
10 × 1.50	R	0.339	11/32
11 × 1.50	3/8	0.375	3/8
12 × 1.50	13/32	0.406	13/32
12 × 1.75	13/32	0.406	13/32

Table 8 WINDCHILL FACTORS

Estimated Wind Speed in MPH	Actual Thermometer Reading (°F)											
	50	40	30	20	10	0	−10	−20	−30	−40	−50	−60
	Equivalent Temperature (°F)											
Calm	50	40	30	20	10	0	−10	−20	−30	−40	−50	−60
5	48	37	27	16	6	−5	−15	−26	−36	−47	−57	−68
10	40	28	16	4	−9	−21	−33	−46	−58	−70	−83	−95
15	36	22	9	−5	−18	−36	−45	−58	−72	−85	−99	−112
20	32	18	4	−10	−25	−39	−53	−67	−82	−96	−110	−124
25	30	16	0	−15	−29	−44	−59	−74	−88	−104	−118	−133
30	28	13	−2	−18	−33	−48	−63	−79	−94	−109	−125	−140
35	27	11	−4	−20	−35	−49	−67	−82	−98	−113	−129	−145
40	26	10	−6	−21	−37	−53	−69	−85	−100	−116	−132	−148
*	Little Danger (for properly clothed person)				Increasing Danger				Great Danger			
					Danger from freezing of exposed flesh.							

*Wind speeds greater than 40 mph have little additional effect.

Chapter Two

Troubleshooting

Diagnosing electrical and mechanical problems is relatively simple if you use orderly procedures and keep a few basic principles in mind. The first step in any troubleshooting procedure is to define the symptoms as closely as possible and then localize the problem. Subsequent steps involve testing and analyzing those areas which could cause the symptoms. A haphazard approach may eventually solve the problem, but it can be very costly in terms of wasted time and unnecessary parts replacement.

Proper lubrication, maintenance and periodic tune-ups as described in Chapter Three will reduce the necessity for troubleshooting. Even with the best of care, however, all snowmobiles are prone to problems which will require troubleshooting.

Never assume anything. Do not overlook the obvious. If the engine will not start, check the position of the emergency cutout switch and the tether switch. Is the engine flooded with fuel from excessive use of the primer?

If the engine suddenly quits, check the easiest, most accessible problem first. Is there gasoline in the tank? Has a spark plug wire broken or fallen off?

If nothing obvious turns up in a quick check, look a little further. Learning to recognize and describe symptoms will make repairs easier for you or a mechanic at the shop. Describe problems accurately and fully.

Gather as many symptoms as possible to aid in diagnosis. Note whether the engine lost power gradually or all at once, what color smoke came from the exhaust and so on. Remember that the more complicated a machine is, the easier it is to troubleshoot because symptoms point to specific problems.

After the symptoms are defined, areas which could cause problems can be tested and analyzed. Guessing at the cause of a problem may provide the solution, but it usually leads to frustration, wasted time and a series of expensive, unnecessary parts replacements.

You do not need fancy equipment or complicated test gear to determine whether you should attempt repairs at home. A few simple checks could save a large repair bill and lost time while your snowmobile sits in a dealer's service department. On the other hand, be realistic and *do not attempt repairs that are beyond your abilities*. Service departments tend to charge heavily for putting together an engine that someone else has disassembled. Some shops won't even take such a job, so use common sense and don't get in over your head.

Electrical specifications are listed in **Tables 1-4** at the end of this chapter.

OPERATING REQUIREMENTS

An engine needs 3 basics to run properly: correct fuel/air mixture, sufficient compression and a spark at the right time (**Figure 1**). If one basic requirement is missing, the engine will not run. Two-stroke engine operating principles are described in Chapter One under *Engine Principles*. Ignition problems are a frequent cause of breakdowns and the ignition system can be quickly and easily checked. Keep that in mind before you begin tampering with carburetor adjustments.

If the snowmobile has been sitting for any length of time and refuses to start, check and clean the spark plugs. Then check the condition of the battery (if so equipped) to make sure it is fully charged. If these are okay, then look to the gasoline delivery system. This includes the tank, fuel shutoff valve, fuel pump and fuel line to the carburetor. Gasoline deposits may have gummed up the carburetor's fuel inlet needle, jets, and small air passages. Gasoline tends to lose its potency after standing for long periods and condensation may contaminate it with water. Drain the old gas and try starting with a fresh tankful.

TESTING ELECTRICAL COMPONENTS

Most dealers and parts houses will not accept returns of any electrical parts. When testing electrical components, make sure that you perform

the test procedures as described in this chapter and that your test equipment is working properly. If a test result shows that the component is defective it is still a good idea to have the component retested by a Ski-Doo dealer to verify the test result before purchasing a new component.

ENGINE ELECTRICAL SYSTEM TROUBLESHOOTING

All models are equipped with a capacitor discharge ignition (CDI) system. This section de-

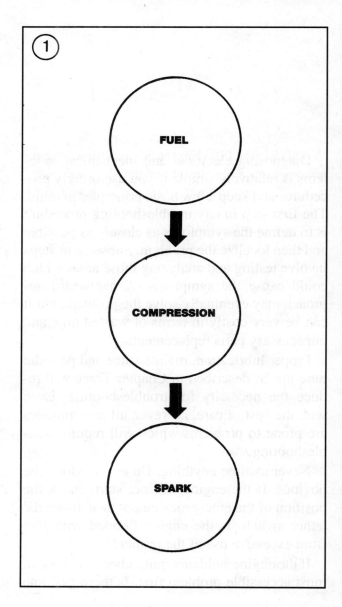

scribes complete ignition and charging system troubleshooting.

This solid state system uses no contact breaker points or other moving parts. Because of the solid state design, problems with the capacitor discharge system are relatively few. Problems are usually limited to no spark, but that lack of spark may only occur when the engine is subjected to certain temperatures, loads or vibrations. It is often easier to find the cause of no spark than those with intermittent problems. If the ignition has no spark, first check for broken or damaged wires.

General troubleshooting procedures are provided in **Figure 2**.

Test Equipment

Complete testing of the engine electrical system requires a Bombardier ignition tester (part No. 419 0033 00) (**Figure 3**) or similar Nippondenso tester. *Basic* testing of the electrical system can be performed with an accurate ohmmeter.

If you do not have access to the special tester shown in **Figure 3**, you can use visual inspection and an ohmmeter to pinpoint electrical problems caused by dirty or damaged connectors, faulty or damaged wiring or electrical components that may have cracked or broken. If basic checks fail to locate the problem, take your snowmobile to a Ski-Doo dealer and have them troubleshoot the electrical system.

Precautions

Certain measures must be taken to protect the capacitor discharge system. Damage to semiconductors in the system may occur if the following is not observed.
1. Do not crank the engine if the CDI unit is not grounded to the engine.
2. Do not disconnect any ignition component when the engine is running or while the battery cables are connected.

3. Keep all connections between the various units clean and tight. Be sure that the wiring connectors are pushed together firmly.

Troubleshooting Preparation

NOTE
To test the wiring harness for poor connections in Step 1, bend the molded rubber connector while checking each wire for continuity.

Refer to the wiring diagram for your model at the end of this book when performing the following.
1. Check the wiring harness for visible signs of damage.
2. Make sure all of the connectors (**Figure 4**) are properly connected as follows:

NOTE
*Never pull on the electrical wires when separating an electrical connector. Pull only on the plastic housing of the connector. See **Figure 5**.*

a. Disconnect each electrical connector in the ignition circuit. Check for bent or damaged male connector pins (**Figure 6**). A bent pin will not connect properly and will cause an open circuit.
b. Check each female connector end. Make sure the metal connector at the end of each wire (**Figure 7**) is pushed all the way into the plastic connector. If not, use a small, narrow-blade screwdriver to carefully push them in. Make sure you do not pinch or cut the wire. Also, make sure that you do not spread the connector.
c. Check the wires to make sure that each is properly attached to a metal connector inside the plastic connector.
d. Make sure all electrical connectors are clean and free of corrosion. If necessary, clean the connectors with an electrical contact cleaner.

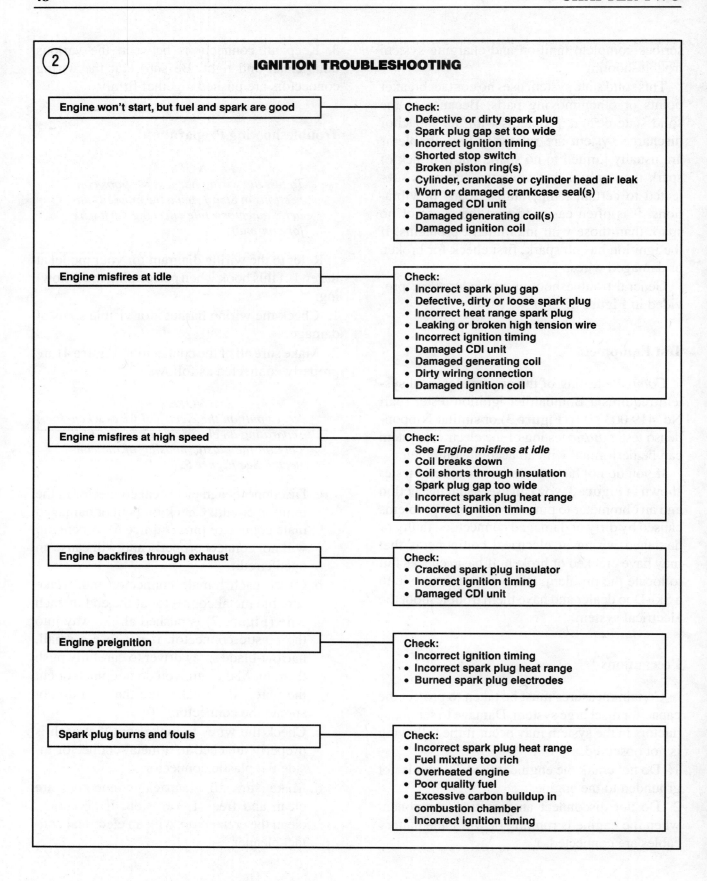

② IGNITION TROUBLESHOOTING

Engine won't start, but fuel and spark are good

Check:
- Defective or dirty spark plug
- Spark plug gap set too wide
- Incorrect ignition timing
- Shorted stop switch
- Broken piston ring(s)
- Cylinder, crankcase or cylinder head air leak
- Worn or damaged crankcase seal(s)
- Damaged CDI unit
- Damaged generating coil(s)
- Damaged ignition coil

Engine misfires at idle

Check:
- Incorrect spark plug gap
- Defective, dirty or loose spark plug
- Incorrect heat range spark plug
- Leaking or broken high tension wire
- Incorrect ignition timing
- Damaged CDI unit
- Damaged generating coil
- Dirty wiring connection
- Damaged ignition coil

Engine misfires at high speed

Check:
- See *Engine misfires at idle*
- Coil breaks down
- Coil shorts through insulation
- Spark plug gap too wide
- Incorrect spark plug heat range
- Incorrect ignition timing

Engine backfires through exhaust

Check:
- Cracked spark plug insulator
- Incorrect ignition timing
- Damaged CDI unit

Engine preignition

Check:
- Incorrect ignition timing
- Incorrect spark plug heat range
- Burned spark plug electrodes

Spark plug burns and fouls

Check:
- Incorrect spark plug heat range
- Fuel mixture too rich
- Overheated engine
- Poor quality fuel
- Excessive carbon buildup in combustion chamber
- Incorrect ignition timing

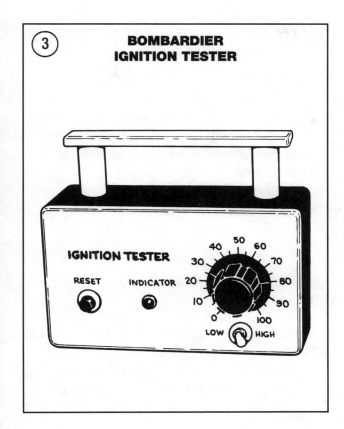

③ **BOMBARDIER IGNITION TESTER**

④

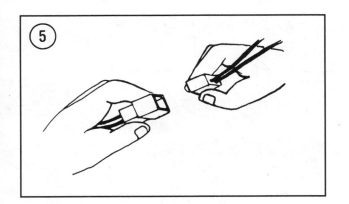

⑤

e. After making sure that all of the individual connectors are alright, push the connectors together until they "click." Make sure they are fully engaged and locked together (**Figure 8**).

3. Check all electrical components for a good ground to the engine.

4. Check all wiring for short circuits or open circuits.

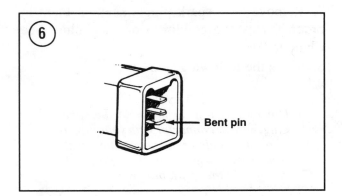

⑥ Bent pin

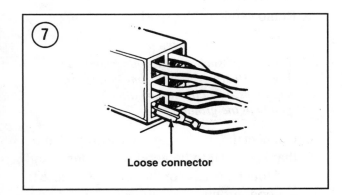

⑦ Loose connector

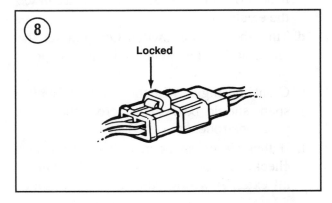

⑧ Locked

2

5. Make sure the fuel tank has an adequate supply of fresh fuel and that the oil tank is properly filled.

6. Check spark plug cable routing (**Figure 9**) and be sure the cables are properly connected to spark plugs.

CAUTION
To prevent expensive engine damage, refer to Caution under Spark Plug Removal in Chapter Three.

7. Remove both spark plugs, keeping them in order. Check the condition of each plug. See Chapter Three.

8. Make the following spark test:

WARNING
During this test do not hold the spark plug, wire or connector with your fingers or a serious electrical shock may result. If necessary, use a pair of insulated pliers to hold the spark plug wire.

a. Open the hood.
b. Remove one of the spark plugs.

NOTE
Test plugs such as the one shown in Figure 10 are available from many parts suppliers. The clip can be attached to a good engine ground.

c. Connect the spark plug cable to a spark plug that is known to be good (or the test plug) and touch the base of the spark plug base to a good ground like the engine cylinder head. Position the spark plug so you can see the electrode.

d. Turn the ignition switch ON and set the tether and cutout switches to the ON position.

e. Crank the engine with the starter. A fat blue spark should be evident across the spark plug electrode.

f. If there is no spark or only a weak one, check for loose connections at the coil. If all external wiring connections are good,

check the remaining components of the ignition system.

g. Turn the ignition switch OFF.

Switch Tests

Test the following switches as described in Chapter Nine.

a. Ignition switch.
b. Tether cutout switch.
c. Emergency cutout switch.

Ignition Testing with the Bombardier Ignition Tester

Prior to testing the ignition system, note the following:

a. The Bombardier Ignition Tester (part No. 419 0033 00) (**Figure 3**) is required for the following tests. The tester can purchased

through Ski-Doo dealers. The Bombardier Ignition Tester includes information and instructions. The procedures given should be followed only after acquainting yourself with the test equipment. If you do not have access to this test instrument, have the tests performed by a Ski-Doo dealer.

b. Perform the *Troubleshooting Preparation* procedures in this section.

c. Tests are similar for all models, but it is important to follow the instructions for the particular model that is being tested.

d. The following tests must be made at cranking speed. This means that while it is not necessary to have the engine running when checking the ignition with the Bombardier

Ignition Tester, it is important to pull vigorously on the starter rope while checking the ignition.

e. Perform each test 3 times to ensure consistent results.

f. The ignition tester should be reset after each test by depressing the reset button on the front of the tester.

g. Have the dealer recheck components to verify that unit is faulty before buying a replacement.

h. Make sure that replacement part is correct. Units are very simil*ar, but similar parts may not be interchangeable.*

WARNING
Do not touch any ignition component when cranking the engine during the following tests. A powerful electric shock may occur if you do so.

1990 Engine Model 583 (Serial No. 3 827 466 and earlier) and 1991 MACH 1 X (643 Engine with 2-speed Generator Coil)

The ignition system used on these models uses a dual generator coil. The coil is easily identified visually by the 2 sets of coil laminations (plates), two windings and three ignition generator wires (black, black/white and black/red). This system uses components that are different from similar units and only parts designed for this system should be installed.

Test 1 —Ignition high tension coil output test

1. Connect the P test lead (**Figure 11**) to the engine ground and the N test lead (**Figure 11**) to an adapter clipped to the high tension cable for the magneto side cylinder near the spark plug adapter.

2. Set the tester dial (**Figure 11**) to 25 and the switch (**Figure 11**) to LOW.

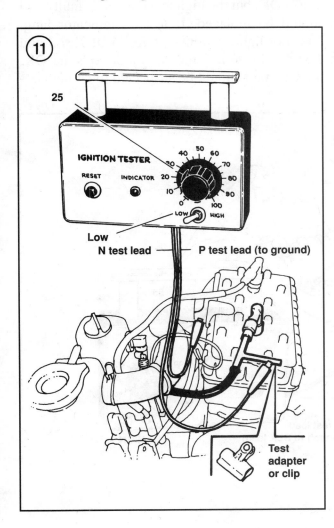

3. Turn ignition switch ON, set the cutout and tether switches to ON and crank engine by pulling the rewind starter handle.

4. If the engine starts, allow it to idle, check the tester's indicator light, then shut engine OFF.

5. Push the tester's reset button and repeat Steps 3 and 4 2 more times.

6. If the tester's indicator lamp lights, the ignition system is OK. If tester's indicator lamp does not light, continue to *Test 2*.

Test 2 —CDI control unit test

1. Disconnect the 2 wire connector located between the CDI unit and the ignition high tension coil.

2. *Install an ignition high tension coil that is known to be good.* Install short jumper wires between the good ignition coil and the CDI unit,

so the tester's wires can be connected to these two wires.

3. Connect the P test lead (**Figure 12**) to the CDI unit's black wire and the N test lead (**Figure 12**) to the CDI unit's white/blue wire.

4. Set the dial (**Figure 12**) to 55 and the switch (**Figure 12**) to HIGH.

5. Turn ignition switch ON, set the cutout and tether switches to ON and crank the engine by pulling the rewind starter handle.

6. If the engine starts, allow it to idle, check the tester's indicator light, then shut the engine OFF.

7. Push the tester's reset button and repeat Steps 5 and 6 2 more times.

8. If the tester's indicator lamp lights, the CDI unit is OK, but the high tension coil is faulty and should be replaced. If tester's indicator lamp does not light, continue at *Test 3*. If *Test 3* and *Test 4* indicate that the generator coils are OK, the CDI unit should be suspected to be faulty.

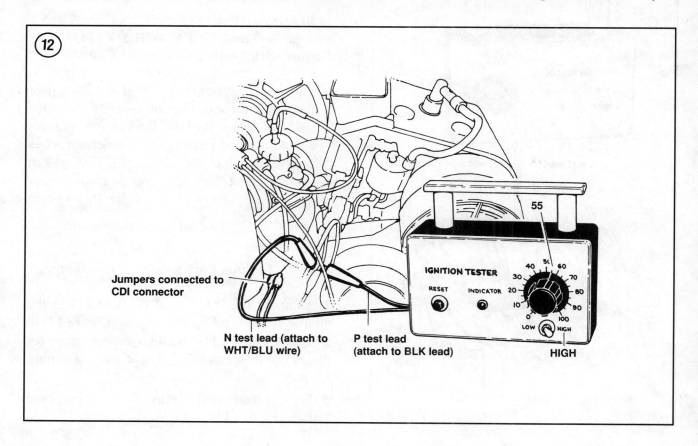

Jumpers connected to CDI connector

N test lead (attach to WHT/BLU wire)

P test lead (attach to BLK lead)

IGNITION TESTER

RESET   INDICATOR

55

HIGH

Test 3 —High speed generator coil test

1. Disconnect the wiring connector from the ignition module harness at the engine.

2. Connect the P test lead (**Figure 13**) from tester to the ignition module wiring harness black/white wire and N test lead (**Figure 13**) to the black/red wire.

3. Set dial (**Figure 13**) to 70 and switch (**Figure 13**) to LOW.

4. Turn ignition switch ON, set the cutout and tether switches to OFF and crank engine by pulling the rewind starter handle.

5. Repeat Step 4 at least 3 more times to verify test.

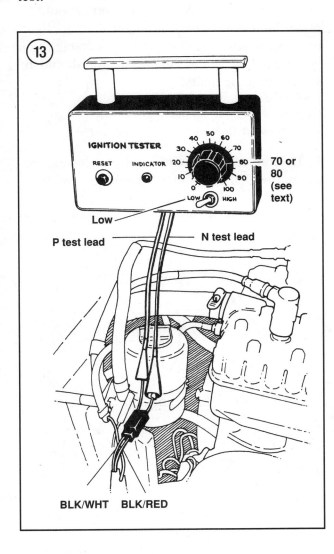

Test 4 —Low speed generator coil test

1. Disconnect the wiring connector from ignition module harness at the engine.

2. Connect the P test lead to the ignition module wiring harness black wire and the N test lead to the black/red wire.

3. Set the dial to 80 and switch to LOW.

4. Turn ignition switch ON, set the cutout and tether switches to OFF and crank engine by pulling the rewind starter handle.

5. Repeat Step 4 at least 3 more times to verify test. Tests should be consistent.

6. If the tester's indicator lamp lights, the low speed generating coil is OK. If tester's indicator lamp does not light, the low speed generator coil is faulty and should be replaced.

Test 5 —Lighting coil test

1. Disconnect the wiring harness junction block at engine.

2. Connect the P test lead to the yellow/black wire and the N test lead to the yellow wire.

3. Set the tester dial to 70 and switch to LOW.

4. Crank the engine by pulling the rewind starter handle and observe the tester's indicator lamp.

5. Repeat Step 4 at least 3 more times to verify test. Tests should be consistent.

6. If the tester's indicator lamp lights, the lighting coil is OK. If tester's indicator lamp does not light, the lighting coil is faulty and should be replaced.

6. If the tester's indicator lamp lights, the high speed generating coil is OK. If tester's indicator lamp does not light, the high speed generator coil is faulty and should be replaced.

1990-1991 Engine Models 467 & 536; 1990 Engine Model 583 (Serial No. 3 827 467 And Higher); 1991 Mach 1, Mach 1 XTC (643 Engine With Single Generator Coil)

The ignition system on these models uses a single generator coil. The coil is easily identified by only one set of coil laminations (plates), one winding and two ignition generator wires (black and white/blue). This system uses components that are different from similar units and only parts designed for this system should be installed.

Test 1 —Ignition high tension coil output test

1. Connect the P test lead (**Figure 11**) to the engine ground and the N test lead (**Figure 11**) to an adapter clipped to the high tension cable for the magneto side cylinder.
2. Set the dial (**Figure 11**) to 45 and the switch (**Figure 11**) to LOW.
3. Turn the ignition switch ON, set the cutout and tether switches to ON and crank the engine by pulling the rewind starter handle.
4. If the engine starts, allow it to idle, check the tester's indicator light, then shut the engine OFF.
5. Push the tester's reset button and repeat Steps 3 and 4 2 more times.
6. If the tester's indicator lamp lights, the ignition system is OK. If tester's indicator lamp does not light, continue to *Test 2*.

Test 2 —CDI control unit test

1. Disconnect the 2 wire connector located between the CDI unit and the ignition high tension coil.
2. *Install an ignition high tension coil that is known to be good.* Install short jumper wires between the good ignition coil and the CDI unit, so the tester's wires can be connected to these 2 wires.

3. Connect the P test lead (**Figure 12**) to the CDI unit's black wire (– terminal of ignition coil) and the tester's N lead (**Figure 12**) to the CDI unit's white/blue wire (+ terminal of the ignition coil). Refer to **Figure 14**.
4. Set the dial (**Figure 12**) to 55 and the switch (**Figure 12**) to HIGH.
5. Turn the ignition switch ON, set the cutout and tether switches to ON and crank the engine by pulling the rewind starter handle.
6. If the engine starts, allow it to idle, check the tester's indicator light, then shut engine OFF.
7. Push the tester's reset button and repeat Steps 5 and 6 2 more times.
8. If the tester's indicator lamp lights, the CDI unit is OK, but the coil is faulty and should be replaced. If tester's indicator lamp does not light, continue to *Test 3*. If *Test 3* indicates that ignition generator coil is OK, the CDI unit should be suspected to be faulty.

Test 3 —Ignition generator coil test

1. Disconnect the 2-wire connector located between the CDI unit and the magneto harness.

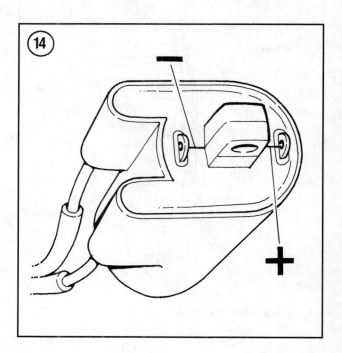

2. Connect the N test lead (**Figure 13**) to the black/red wire of the magneto harness and the P test lead to the black wire of the magneto harness.

3. Set the tester dial to 85 and switch to LOW.

4. Crank the engine by pulling the rewind starter handle and observe the tester's indicator lamp.

5. Repeat Step 4 at least twice to verify test.

6. If the tester's indicator lamp lights, the ignition generating coil is OK. If tester's indicator lamp does not light, the ignition generator coil is faulty and should be replaced.

Test 4 —Lighting coil test

1. Disconnect the wiring harness junction block at the engine.

2. Connect the P test lead to the yellow/black wire and N test lead to the yellow wire.

3. Set the tester dial to 70 and switch to LOW.

4. Crank the engine by pulling the rewind starter handle and observe the tester's indicator lamp.

5. Repeat Step 4 at least 3 more times to verify test. Tests should be consistent.

6. If the tester's indicator lamp lights, the lighting coil is OK. If tester's indicator lamp does not light, the lighting coil is faulty and should be replaced.

1992 Engine Models 467 & 582

The ignition system on these models uses a single generator coil. The coil is easily identified by only one set of coil laminations (plates), one winding and two ignition generator wires (black and white/blue). This system uses components that are different from similar units and only parts designed for this system should be installed.

Test 1 —Ignition high tension coil output test

1. Connect the P test lead (**Figure 11**) to the engine ground and the N test lead (**Figure 11**) to

an adapter clipped to the high tension cable for the magneto side cylinder.

2. Set the tester dial (**Figure 11**) to 45 and the switch (**Figure 11**) to LOW.

3. Turn the ignition switch ON, set the cutout and tether switches to ON and crank the engine by pulling the rewind starter handle.

4. If the engine starts, allow it to idle, check the tester's indicator light, then shut engine OFF.

5. Push the tester's reset button and repeat Steps 3 and 4 2 more times.

6. If the tester's indicator lamp lights, the ignition system is OK. If tester's indicator lamp does not light, continue to *Test 2*.

Test 2 —CDI control unit test

1. Disconnect the 2-wire connector located between the CDI unit and the ignition high tension coil.

2. Install an ignition high tension coil that is known to be good. Install short jumper wires between the good ignition coil and the CDI unit, so the tester's wires can be connected to these two wires.

3. Connect the P test lead (**Figure 12**) to the CDI unit's black wire (– terminal of ignition coil) and the tester's N test lead (**Figure 12**) to the CDI unit's white/blue wire (+ terminal of the ignition coil). Refer to **Figure 14**.

4. Set the tester dial (**Figure 12**) to 55 and the switch (**Figure 12**) to HIGH.

5. Turn the ignition switch ON, set the cutout and tether switches to ON and crank the engine by pulling the rewind starter handle.

6. If the engine starts, allow it to idle, check the tester's indicator light, then shut engine OFF.

7. Push the tester's reset button and repeat Steps 5 and 6 2 more times.

8. If the tester's indicator lamp lights, the CDI unit is OK, but the coil is faulty and should be replaced. If tester's indicator lamp does not light, continue to *Test 3*. If *Test 3* indicates that the

ignition generator coil is OK, the CDI unit should be suspected to be faulty.

Test 3 —Ignition generator coil test

1. Disconnect the 2 wire connector located between the CDI unit and the magneto harness.
2. Connect the N test lead (**Figure 13**) to the black/red wire of the magneto harness and the P test lead to the black wire of the magneto harness.
3. Set the tester dial to 85 and switch to LOW.
4. Crank the engine by pulling the rewind starter handle and observe the tester's indicator lamp.
5. Repeat Step 4 at least twice to verify the test.
6. If the tester's indicator lamp lights, the ignition generating coil is OK. If tester's indicator lamp does not light, the ignition generator coil is faulty and should be replaced.

Test 4 —Lighting coil test

1. Disconnect the wiring harness junction block at engine.
2. Connect the P test lead to the yellow/black wire and N test lead to the yellow wire.
3. Set the tester dial to 70 and switch to LOW.
4. Crank the engine by pulling the rewind starter handle and observe the tester's indicator lamp.
5. Repeat Step 4 at least 3 more times to verify test. Tests should be consistent.
6. If the tester's indicator lamp lights, the lighting coil is OK. If tester's indicator lamp does not light, the lighting coil is faulty and should be replaced.

1992 Engine Models 583 & 670 and 1993 Formula Plus X (583 Engine With Two Speed Generator Coil)

The ignition system on these models uses a dual generator coil. The coil is easily identified by the 2 sets of coil laminations (plates), 2 windings and 3 ignition generator wires (black,

black/white and black/red). This system uses components that are different from similar units and only parts designed for this system should be installed.

Test 1 —Ignition high tension coil output test

1. Connect the P test lead (**Figure 11**) to the engine ground and the N test lead (**Figure 11**) to an adapter clipped to the high tension cable for the magneto side cylinder.
2. Set the tester dial (**Figure 11**) to 25 and the switch (**Figure 11**) to LOW.
3. Turn the ignition switch ON, set the cutout and tether switches to ON and crank the engine by pulling the rewind starter handle.
4. Check to see if the tester's indicator lamp lights when the engine is cranked.
5. If the engine starts, allow it to idle, check the tester's indicator light, then shut the engine OFF.
6. Push the tester's reset button and repeat Steps 3-5 2 more times.
7. If the tester's indicator lamp lights, the ignition system is OK. If tester's indicator lamp does not light, continue to *Test 2*.

Test 2 —CDI control unit test

1. Disconnect the 2-wire connector located between the CDI unit and the ignition high tension coil.
2. Install an ignition high tension coil that is known to be good. Install short jumper wires between the good ignition coil and the CDI unit, so the tester's wires can be connected to these two wires.
3. Connect the P test lead (**Figure 12**) to the CDI unit's black wire (– terminal of ignition coil) and the N test lead to the CDI unit's white/blue wire (+ terminal of the ignition coil). Refer to **Figure 14**.
4. Set the tester dial to 55 and the switch to HIGH.

5. Turn the ignition switch ON, set the cutout and tether switches to ON and crank engine by pulling the rewind starter handle.

6. If the engine starts, allow it to idle, check the tester's indicator light, then shut engine OFF.

7. Push the tester's reset button and repeat the test 2 more times.

8. If the tester's indicator lamp lights, the CDI unit is OK, but the coil is faulty and should be replaced. If tester's indicator lamp does not light, continue to *Test 3* and *Test 4*. If *Test 3* and *Test 4* indicate that generator coils are OK, the CDI unit should be suspected to be faulty.

Test 3 —High speed ignition generator coil test

1. Disconnect the 3-wire connector located between the CDI unit and the magneto harness.

2. Connect the P test lead (**Figure 13**) to the black/white wire of the magneto harness and the N test lead to the black/red wire of the magneto harness.

3. Set the tester dial to 70 and the switch to LOW.

4. Turn the ignition switch ON, set the cutout and tether switches to OFF and crank the engine by pulling the rewind starter handle.

5. Observe the tester's indicator lamp and repeat this test 3 more times to verify test.

6. If the tester's indicator lamp lights, the ignition high speed generating coil is OK. If tester's indicator lamp does not light, the ignition high speed generator coil is faulty and should be replaced.

Test 4 —Low speed ignition generator coil test

1. Disconnect the 3-wire connector located between the CDI unit and the magneto harness.

2. Connect the P test lead (**Figure 13**) to the black wire of the magneto harness and the N test lead to the black/red wire of the magneto harness.

3. Set the tester dial to 80 and the switch to LOW.

4. Turn the ignition switch ON, set the cutout and tether switches to OFF and crank the engine by pulling the rewind starter handle.

5. Observe the tester's indicator lamp and repeat this test 3 more times to verify test. Tests should be consistent.

6. If the tester's indicator lamp lights, the ignition low speed generating coil is OK. If tester's indicator lamp does not light, the ignition low speed generator coil is faulty and should be replaced.

Test 5 —Lighting coil test

1. Disconnect the wiring harness junction block at engine.

2. Connect the P test lead to the yellow/black wire and N test lead to the yellow wire.

3. Set the tester dial to 70 and the switch to LOW.

4. Crank the engine by pulling the rewind starter handle and observe the tester's indicator lamp.

5. Repeat this test 3 more times to verify test. Tests should be consistent.

6. If the tester's indicator lamp lights, the lighting coil is OK. If tester's indicator lamp does not light, the lighting coil is faulty and should be replaced.

1993 Engine Models 467, 582 and 670; 1994 Engine Models 467, 582, 583 and 670

The ignition system on these models uses a separate trigger coil just outside the flywheel (to the rear). A 2-wire plug with one white/yellow wire and one blue/yellow wire attaches the trigger coil to the CDI control unit. A 3-wire plug attaches the generator coil to the CDI control unit. This system uses components that are different from similar units and only parts designed for this system should be installed.

Test 1 —Ignition trigger coil test

1. Disconnect the 2-wire trigger coil connector from the CDI control unit.

2. Connect the P test lead (1, **Figure 15**) to the white/yellow trigger coil wire and N test lead (2, **Figure 15**) to the blue/yellow wire.

3. Set the tester dial to 35 and switch to LOW.

4. Crank the engine by pulling the rewind starter handle and observe the tester's indicator lamp.

5. Repeat Step 4 at least 2 more times to verify test.

6. If the tester's indicator lamp lights, the ignition trigger coil is OK. If tester's indicator lamp does not light, the ignition trigger coil is improperly grounded or faulty.

Test 2 —High tension ignition coil output test

NOTE
A squeeze clamp type paper clip about 20 mm (3/4 in.) long can be used as a test adapter to clamp over the high tension cable if the standard adapter is not available.

1. Connect the N test lead (**Figure 11**) to the engine ground and the P test lead (**Figure 11**) to an adapter clipped to the high tension cable for the magneto side cylinder.

NOTE
Test indications may be different if the test adapter is attached to the spark plug cable on PTO side of the engine.

2. Set the tester dial (**Figure 11**) to 45 and the switch (**Figure 11**) to LOW.

3. Turn the ignition switch ON, set the cutout and tether switches to ON and crank the engine by pulling the rewind starter handle.

4. If the engine starts, allow it to idle, check the tester's indicator light, then shut engine OFF.

5. Push the tester's reset button and repeat this test 2 more times.

6. If the tester's indicator lamp lights, the ignition system is OK. If tester's indicator lamp does not light, continue to *Test 3*.

Test 3 —CDI control unit test

1. Disconnect both connectors located between the CDI unit and the ignition high tension coil.

2. *Install a high tension ignition coil that is known to be good.* Install short jumper wires between the good ignition coil and the CDI unit, so the tester's wires can be connected to these two wires.

3. Connect the P test lead (**Figure 12**) to CDI unit's black wire (– terminal of ignition coil) and the N test lead (**Figure 12**) to the CDI unit's white/blue wire (+ terminal of the ignition coil). Refer to **Figure 14**.

4. Set the tester dial (**Figure 12**) to 85 and the switch (**Figure 12**) to LOW.

5. Turn the ignition switch ON, set the cutout and tether switches to ON and crank the engine by pulling the rewind starter handle.

6. If the engine starts, allow it to idle, check the tester's indicator light, then shut engine OFF.

7. Push the tester's reset button and repeat this test 2 more times.

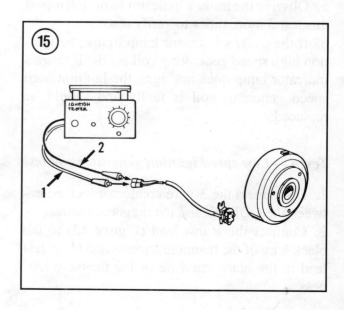

8. If the tester's indicator lamp lights, the CDI unit is OK, but the coil is faulty and should be replaced. If tester's indicator lamp does not light, continue to *Test 4*. If *Test 4* indicates that the ignition generator coil is OK, then the CDI unit should be suspected to be faulty.

Test 4 —Ignition generator coil test

1. Disconnect the 2-wire connector located between the CDI unit and the magneto harness.

2. Connect the N test lead (**Figure 13**) to the black/red wire of the magneto harness and the P test lead to the red wire of the magneto harness.

3. Set the tester dial to 85 and the switch to LOW.

4. Crank the engine by pulling the rewind starter handle and observe the tester's indicator lamp.

5. Repeat Step 4 at least twice to verify test.

6. If the tester's indicator lamp lights, the ignition generating coil is OK. If tester's indicator lamp does not light, the ignition generator coil is faulty and should be replaced.

Test 5 —Lighting coil test

1. Disconnect the wiring harness junction block at engine.

2. Connect the P test lead to one of the yellow wires and the N test lead to another (different) yellow wire.

3. Set the tester dial to 75 and switch to LOW.

4. Crank the engine by pulling the rewind starter handle and observe the tester's indicator lamp.

5. Repeat Step 4 at least 3 more times to verify test. Tests should be consistent.

6. If the tester's indicator lamp lights, the lighting coil is OK. If tester's indicator lamp does not light, the lighting coil is faulty and should be replaced.

1995 Engine Models 454, 467 & 670

The ignition system on these models uses a separate trigger coil just outside the flywheel (to the rear). A 2-wire plug with one white/yellow wire and one blue/yellow wire attaches the trigger coil to the CDI control unit. A 3-wire plug attaches the generator coil to the CDI control unit. This system uses components that are different from similar units and only parts designed for this system should be installed.

Test 1 —Ignition trigger coil test

1. Disconnect the 2-wire connector from the trigger coil to the CDI control unit.

2. Connect the P test lead (1, **Figure 15**) to the white/yellow wire from the trigger coil and N test lead (2, **Figure 15**) to the blue/yellow wire.

3. Set the tester dial to 35 and the switch to LOW.

4. Crank the engine by pulling the rewind starter handle and observe the tester's indicator lamp.

5. Repeat Step 4 at least twice more to verify test.

6. If the tester's indicator lamp lights, the ignition trigger coil is OK. If tester's indicator lamp does not light, the ignition trigger coil is improperly grounded or faulty.

Test 2 —High tension ignition coil output test

> *NOTE*
> *A squeeze clamp type paper clip about 20 mm (3/4 inch) long can be used as a test adapter to clamp over the high tension cable if the standard adapter is not available.*

1. Connect the N test lead (**Figure 11**) to the engine ground and the P test lead (**Figure 11**) to an adapter clipped to the high tension cable for the magneto side cylinder.

NOTE
Test indications may be different if test adapter is attached to spark plug cable on PTO side of engine.

2. Set the tester dial (**Figure 11**) to 45 and the switch (**Figure 11**) to LOW.

3. Turn ignition switch ON, set the cutout and tether switches to ON and crank the engine by pulling the rewind starter handle.

4. If the engine starts, allow it to idle, check the tester's indicator light, then shut engine OFF.

5. Push the tester's reset button and repeat this test 2 more times.

6. If the tester's indicator lamp lights, the ignition system is OK. If tester's indicator lamp does not light, continue to *Test 3*.

Test 3 —CDI control unit test

1. Disconnect both connectors located between the CDI unit and the ignition high tension coil.

2. *Install a high-tension ignition coil that is known to be good.* Install short jumper wires between the good ignition coil and the CDI unit, so the tester's wires can be connected to these two wires.

3. Connect the P test lead (**Figure 12**) to CDI unit's black wire (– terminal of ignition coil) and the N test lead (**Figure 12**) to the CDI unit's white/blue wire (+ terminal of the ignition coil). Refer to **Figure 14**.

4. Set the tester dial (**Figure 12**) to 85 and switch (**Figure 12**) to LOW.

5. Turn the ignition switch ON, set the cutout and tether switches to ON and crank the engine by pulling the rewind starter handle.

6. If the engine starts, allow it to idle, check the tester's indicator light, then shut engine OFF.

7. Push the tester's reset button and repeat this test 2 more times.

8. If the tester's indicator lamp lights, the CDI unit is OK, but the coil is faulty and should be replaced. If tester's indicator lamp does not light, continue to *Test 4*. If *Test 4* indicates that the

ignition generator coil is OK, then the CDI unit should be suspected to be faulty.

Test 4—Ignition generator coil test

1. Disconnect the 2-wire connector located between the CDI unit and the magneto harness.

2. Connect the N test lead (**Figure 13**) to the red wire of the magneto harness and the P test lead to the black/red wire of the magneto harness.

3. Set the tester dial to 85 and the switch to LOW.

4. Crank the engine by pulling the rewind starter handle and observe the tester's indicator lamp.

5. Repeat Step 4 at least twice to verify test.

6. If the tester's indicator lamp lights, the ignition generating coil is OK. If tester's indicator lamp does not light, the ignition generator coil is faulty and should be replaced.

Test 5 —Lighting coil test

1. Disconnect the wiring harness junction block at engine.

2. Connect the P test lead to one of the yellow wires and N test lead to another (different) yellow wire.

3. Set the tester dial to 75 and switch to LOW.

4. Crank the engine by pulling the rewind starter handle and observe the tester's indicator lamp.

5. Repeat Step 4 at least 3 more times to verify test. Tests should be consistent.

6. If the tester's indicator lamp lights, the lighting coil is OK. If tester's indicator lamp does not light, the lighting coil is faulty and should be replaced.

Ignition Component Resistance Test

An accurate ohmmeter is required to perform the following tests.

Ignition high tension coil

Refer to **Figure 16**.

1. Open the hood and locate the ignition high-tension coil. It is attached to the bulkhead.

2. Disconnect the 2 primary connectors from the high tension coil.

3. Check ignition coil primary resistance as follows:

a. If necessary, switch the ohmmeter to the R × 1 scale.

b. Measure resistance between the 2 primary terminals (black and white/blue). Primary terminals are marked "+" and "−" on later models as shown in **Figure 14**. Refer to **Table 1** for specifications.

c. Disconnect the meter leads.

4. Check ignition coil secondary resistance as follows:

a. Remove the spark plug cap (1, **Figure 16**) from the end of each high-tension cable.

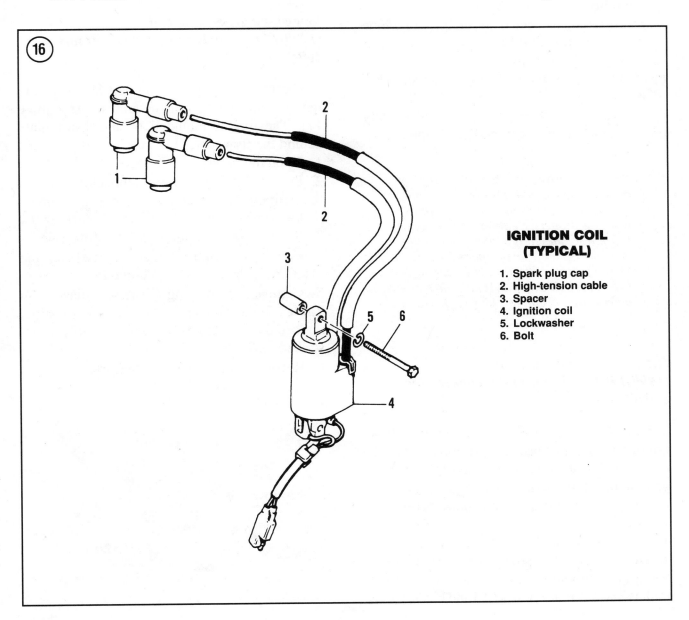

IGNITION COIL (TYPICAL)

1. Spark plug cap
2. High-tension cable
3. Spacer
4. Ignition coil
5. Lockwasher
6. Bolt

b. If necessary, switch the ohmmeter to the R × 1000 scale.

c. Measure resistance between the high-tension (spark plug) cables. Refer to **Table 1** for specifications.

5. Check ignition coil insulation as follows:

a. If necessary, switch the ohmmeter to the R × 1 scale.

b. Measure resistance between the white/blue connector wire and each high-tension (spark plug) cable. The meter should read infinity.

c. Measure resistance between the white/blue wire and the ignition coil core. The meter should read infinity.

6. If resistance of the coil is not as specified in Steps 3-5, the coil is probably faulty. Have the dealer recheck the coil to verify that coil is faulty before buying a replacement. See Chapter Nine.

> *NOTE*
> *Normal resistance in both the primary and secondary (high-tension) coil windings is not a guarantee that the unit is working properly; only an operational spark test can tell if a coil is producing adequate spark from the input voltage. A Ski-Doo dealer may have the equipment to test the coil's output. If not, substitute a known good coil to see if the problem fixed.*

High-speed generating coil (1990-1993 models with dual generating coils)

Some 1990-1993 models are equipped with an ignition system that uses 2 generating coils. The high-speed generating coil is part of the ignition generating coil assembly (A, **Figure 17**). The unit is mounted on the stator plate behind the flywheel.

1. Open the hood.

2. Disconnect the 3-prong connector between the ignition module and magneto. This connector has 3 wires: black, black/red and black/white.

3. Switch an ohmmeter to the R × 1 scale.

4. Connect the ohmmeter between the black/white and black/red magneto wires (**Figure 18**).

5. Compare the reading to the specification in **Table 2**. If the reading is not within specification, replace the high/low speed coil assembly as described in Chapter Nine.

6. Reconnect the 3-prong connector.

7. Close the hood.

Low-speed generating coil (1990-1993 models with dual generating coils)

The low-speed generating coil is part of the ignition generating coil assembly (A, **Figure 17**). The unit is mounted on the stator plate behind the flywheel.

1. Open the hood.

2. Disconnect the 3-prong connector between the ignition module and magneto. This connector has 3 wires: black, black/red and black/white.

3. Switch an ohmmeter to the R × 100 scale.

4. Connect the ohmmeter between the black and black/red magneto wires (**Figure 18**).

5. Compare the reading to the specification in **Table 2**. If the reading is not within specification, replace the high/low speed coil assembly as described in Chapter Nine.

6. Reconnect the 3-prong connector.

7. Close the hood.

Ignition generating coil
(1990-1992 models with single coil)

The ignition generating coil on some 1990-1992 models with a single coil is mounted on the stator plate behind the flywheel.

1. Open the hood.

2. Disconnect the 2-prong connector between the ignition module and magneto. This connector has 2 wires: black and black/red.

3. Switch an ohmmeter to the R × 100 scale.

4. Connect the ohmmeter between the black and black/red magneto wires (**Figure 18**).

5. Compare the reading to the specification in **Table 2**. If the reading is not within specification, replace the generating coil assembly as described in Chapter Nine.

6. Reconnect the 2-prong connector.

7. Close the hood.

Ignition generating stator coil
(1993-on except 1993 model with 583 engine)

The ignition generating coil is incorporated in the stator of these models. The stator also includes the lighting coil and is located behind the flywheel.

1. Open the hood.

2. Disconnect the 3-prong connector between the ignition module and magneto. This connector has 3 wires: black, black/red and red.

3. Connect the ohmmeter between the black and black/red wires.

4. Compare the reading to the specification in **Table 2**. If the reading is not within specification, replace the generating coil assembly as described in Chapter Nine.

5. Reconnect the 3-prong connector.

6. Close the hood.

Trigger coil

A separate ignition trigger coil is used on all 1993 and later models, except the 1993 Formula Plus X model. The trigger coil is located just outside the flywheel (to the rear). A 2-wire plug with 1 white/yellow wire and 1 blue/yellow wire attaches the trigger coil to the CDI control unit.

1. Open the hood.

2. Disconnect the 2-prong connector located between the CDI control unit and the ignition trigger coil. This connector has 2 wires: white/yellow and blue/yellow.

3. Connect an ohmmeter between the white/yellow and blue/yellow trigger coil wires.

4. Compare the reading to the specification in **Table 3**. If the reading is not within specification, replace the generating coil assembly as described in Chapter Nine.

5. Reconnect the 2-prong connector.

6. Close the hood.

Lighting coil

All 1990-1992 models and 1993 model with 583 engine

The lighting coil on these models is shown at B, **Figure 17**. The lighting coil is mounted on the stator plate behind the flywheel.

1. Open the hood.

2. Disconnect the yellow and yellow/black lighting coil wires from the voltage regulator.

3. Switch an ohmmeter to the R × 1 scale.

4. Attach the ohmmeter between the yellow/black and yellow lighting coil wires (**Figure 18**).

5. Compare the reading to the specification in **Table 4**. If the reading is not within specification, replace the lighting coil assembly as described in Chapter Nine.

6. Reconnect the wire connectors.

7. Close the hood.

1993 467, 582 & 670 engine models and all 1994-on models

The lighting coil on these models is incorporated in the stator. The stator on these models also includes the ignition generating coil and is located behind the flywheel.

1. Open the hood.

2. Disconnect the 2 yellow lighting coil wires from the regulator.

3. Switch an ohmmeter to the R × 1 scale.

4. Attach the ohmmeter between the 2 yellow lighting coil wires.

5. Compare the reading to the specification in **Table 4**. If the reading is not within specification, replace the lighting coil assembly as described in Chapter Nine.

6. Reconnect the wire connectors.

7. Close the hood.

VOLTAGE REGULATOR

If you are experiencing blown bulbs or if all of the lights are dim (filaments barely light), test the voltage regulator (**Figure 19**) as follows. In addition, check the bulb filament; an overcharged condition will usually melt the filament rather then break it.

1. Position the snowmobile so the ski tips are placed against a stationary object. Then raise the rear of the snowmobile so the track is clear of the ground.

2. Open the hood and secure it so it cannot fall.

3. Set the voltmeter to the 25 volt AC scale, then connect one of the voltmeter leads to a good ground.

NOTE
Do not disconnect voltmeter leads when testing voltage output.

4. Connect the other voltmeter lead to the voltage regulator yellow wire.

WARNING
When performing the following steps, ensure that the track area is clear and that no one walks behind the track or serious injuries may result.

WARNING
Never lean into the snowmobile's engine compartment while wearing a scarf or other loose clothing when the engine is running or when attempting to start the engine. If any clothing should catch in the drive belt or clutch, severe injury or death could occur. Make sure the pulley guard is in place.

5. Have an assistant start the engine. When starting the engine, do not use the throttle to increase the engine speed more than necessary.

6. Slowly increase the engine rpm and observe the voltmeter reading. If the voltmeter indicates less than 12.5 volts or more than 15 volts, replace the voltage regulator. See Chapter Nine.

7. Turn the engine off and disconnect the voltmeter.

8. Close the hood and lower the snowmobile track to the ground.

FUEL SYSTEM

Many snowmobile owners automatically assume that the carburetor or Electronic Fuel Injection (EFI) is at fault if the engine does not run properly. Fuel system problems are not uncommon, but most are caused by an empty tank, a plugged fuel filter, malfunctioning fuel pump, or sour, deteriorated or contaminated fuel. Changing the carburetor or EFI adjustments will not correct for these problems and will only compound the problem.

Fuel system troubleshooting should start at the gas tank and work through the system, reserving the carburetor or injector as the final point. **Figure 20** provides a series of symptoms and causes that can be useful in localizing fuel system problems.

Fuel enrichment systems, such as the starting primer, can also present problems. If the primer is not used properly or if it is not functioning correctly, the result could be either a flooded or lean fuel condition. A lean condition can be caused by a cracked or loose primer hose.

Identifying Fuel System Problems

The following check list can be used to help identify rich and lean fuel conditions. The more extreme the problem, the more exaggerated the symptoms.

If the engine is running rich, one or more of the following conditions may be noticed:

a. The spark plug(s) foul often. Sometimes this condition has been masked by installing spark plugs of a hotter heat range.

b. The engine misses and runs rough when operating under a load.

c. Exhaust smoke is excessive when the throttle is opened.

d. When the throttle open, the exhaust will sound choked or dull. Stopping the snowmobile and trying to clear the exhaust by holding the throttle open does not change the sound.

If the engine is running lean, one or more of the following conditions may be noticed:

a. The firing end of the spark plugs become very white or blistered in appearance. Sometimes spark plugs of a colder heat range have been installed to mask the problem.

b. The engine overheats.

c. Acceleration is slower.

d. Obvious performance flat spots are felt during operation. These feel much like the engine is trying to run out of gas.

e. Engine power is reduced.

f. At full throttle, engine rpm will not hold steady.

ENGINE

Engine problems are generally symptoms of something wrong in another system, such as ignition, fuel or starting. If properly maintained and serviced, the engine should experience no problems other than those caused by age and wear.

Overheating and Lack of Lubrication

Overheating and lack of lubrication will cause major engine mechanical damage. Make sure the cooling system isn't damaged and the oil injection tank is always filled. Make sure that cooling fluid contains antifreeze mixed in the proper ratio to protect at the temperatures encountered. Check to be sure that the thermostat is opening correctly. Incorrect ignition timing, a faulty cooling system or an excessively lean fuel mixture can also cause the engine to overheat.

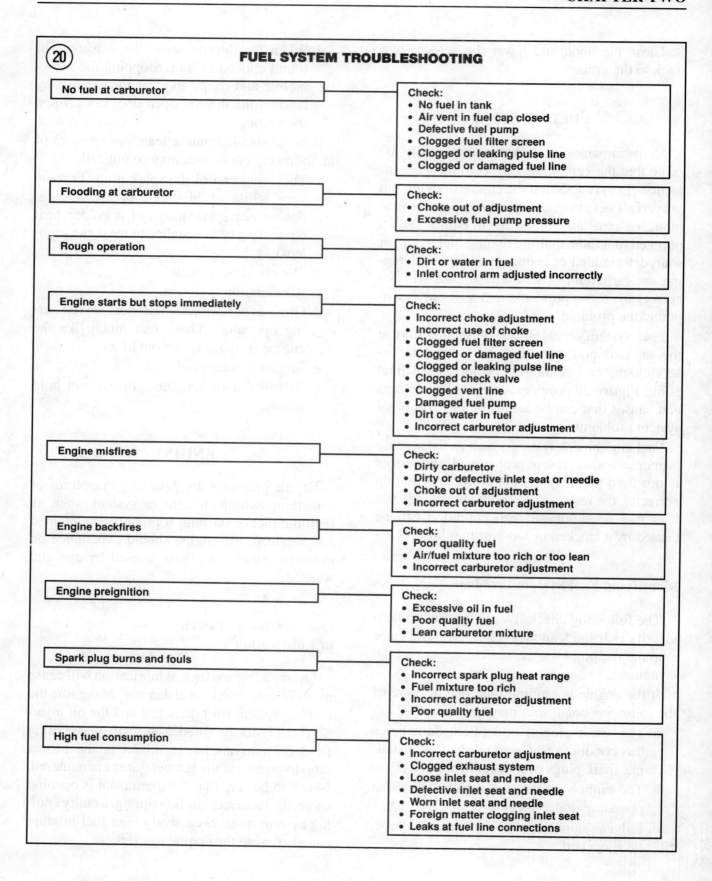

FUEL SYSTEM TROUBLESHOOTING

No fuel at carburetor

Check:
- No fuel in tank
- Air vent in fuel cap closed
- Defective fuel pump
- Clogged fuel filter screen
- Clogged or leaking pulse line
- Clogged or damaged fuel line

Flooding at carburetor

Check:
- Choke out of adjustment
- Excessive fuel pump pressure

Rough operation

Check:
- Dirt or water in fuel
- Inlet control arm adjusted incorrectly

Engine starts but stops immediately

Check:
- Incorrect choke adjustment
- Incorrect use of choke
- Clogged fuel filter screen
- Clogged or damaged fuel line
- Clogged or leaking pulse line
- Clogged check valve
- Clogged vent line
- Damaged fuel pump
- Dirt or water in fuel
- Incorrect carburetor adjustment

Engine misfires

Check:
- Dirty carburetor
- Dirty or defective inlet seat or needle
- Choke out of adjustment
- Incorrect carburetor adjustment

Engine backfires

Check:
- Poor quality fuel
- Air/fuel mixture too rich or too lean
- Incorrect carburetor adjustment

Engine preignition

Check:
- Excessive oil in fuel
- Poor quality fuel
- Lean carburetor mixture

Spark plug burns and fouls

Check:
- Incorrect spark plug heat range
- Fuel mixture too rich
- Incorrect carburetor adjustment
- Poor quality fuel

High fuel consumption

Check:
- Incorrect carburetor adjustment
- Clogged exhaust system
- Loose inlet seat and needle
- Defective inlet seat and needle
- Worn inlet seat and needle
- Foreign matter clogging inlet seat
- Leaks at fuel line connections

Preignition

Preignition is the premature burning of fuel and is caused by hot spots in the combustion chamber (**Figure 21**). The fuel actually ignites before it is supposed to. Glowing deposits in the combustion chamber, inadequate cooling or overheated spark plugs can all cause preignition. This is first noticed in the form of a power loss but will eventually result in damage to the internal parts of the engine because of higher combustion chamber temperatures.

Detonation

Commonly called "spark knock" or "fuel knock," detonation is the violent explosion of fuel in the combustion chamber instead of the controlled burning and expansion that occurs during normal combustion (**Figure 22**). Detonation causes excessive combustion pressure which can cause severe mechanical damage. Use of low octane gasoline is a common cause of detonation, but detonation can still occur even if high octane gasoline is used.

Some causes of detonation are improper ignition timing, lean fuel mixture, inadequate engine cooling, cross-firing of spark plugs, or the excessive accumulation of deposits on pistons and combustion chambers. If the engine has been modified, the compression ratio may be too high or a piston with an improperly designed squish area may be installed.

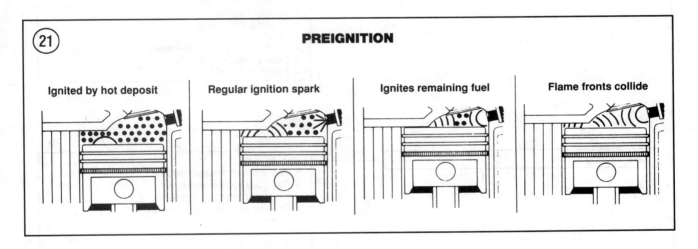

(21) PREIGNITION

Ignited by hot deposit   Regular ignition spark   Ignites remaining fuel   Flame fronts collide

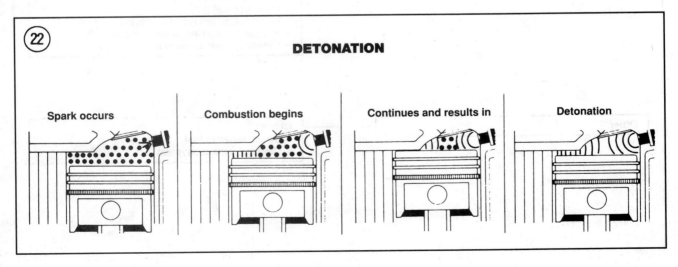

(22) DETONATION

Spark occurs   Combustion begins   Continues and results in   Detonation

㉓

LOW ENGINE POWER

Ignition system trouble

Check:
- Faulty ignition coil
- Incorrect ignition timing
- Incorrect spark plug heat range
- Loose wiring connectors

Fuel system trouble

Check:
- Contaminated fuel filter
- Contaminated fuel filter screen
- Throttle valve does not open fully
- Clogged high speed nozzle
- Clogged pulse line
- Leaking pulse line
- Insufficient fuel supply
- Faulty check valve diaphragm
- Faulty regulator diaphragm
- Faulty pulse diaphragm

Overheating

Check:
- See *Ignition system trouble*
- See *Fuel system trouble*
- Incorrect ignition timing
- Excessive carbon buildup in combustion chamber
- Incorrect fuel/oil mixture
- Incorrect oil type
- Incorrect fuel type
- Incorrect carburetor adjustment
- Clogged or leaking cooling system
- Clogged exhaust system

Other

Check:
- Dirt or water in fuel
- Clogged exhaust system

Since the snowmobile engine is relatively noisy, detonation may not be noticed, especially at high engine speed when wind noise is also present. Often, unnoticed detonation is the cause of engine damage that occurs for no apparent reason.

Poor Idling

A poor idle can be caused by improper fuel mixture adjustment, incorrect timing or ignition system malfunctions. On models with carburetors, check the carburetor pulse and vent lines for an obstruction. Also check for loose carburetor mounting bolts or a faulty carburetor flange gasket.

Misfiring

Misfiring can result from a dirty spark plug or damaged spark plug wire. If misfiring occurs only under heavy load, as when accelerating, it is usually caused by a defective spark plug. Check for fuel contamination.

Flat Spots

If the engine seems to die momentarily when the throttle is opened and then recover, check for a dirty carburetor, improperly adjusted fuel mixture or contaminated fuel. The fuel mixture may be too rich, but usually the low speed mixture is adjusted too lean.

Power Loss

Several factors can cause a lack of power and speed. Problems in the fuel system to check for are clogged fuel filter, air leaks in a fuel line between the tank and the fuel pump, a faulty fuel pump or leaking primer lines. Make sure that the throttle slide operates properly.

Check the ignition timing at full advance with the engine running as described in Chapter Three. This test will allow you to make sure that the ignition system is advancing correctly. If the ignition timing is correct when set statically (engine not running), but incorrect when checked dynamically, there may be a problem with an ignition component. Preignition or detonation will also result in a power loss.

A piston or cylinder that is galling, incorrect piston clearance or worn or sticky piston rings may be responsible. Look for loose bolts, defective gaskets or leaking mating surfaces on the cylinder head, cylinder or crankcase. Also check the crankshaft seals. Refer to *Two-Stroke Pressure Testing* in this chapter.

Exhaust fumes leaking within the engine compartment can slow and even stop the engine.

Refer to **Figure 23** for a general listing of engine troubles.

Piston Seizure

Piston seizure or galling is the transfer of metal from the piston to the cylinder bore. Overheating caused by excessive friction causes piston seizure. Excessive friction can be caused by pistons with incorrect bore clearance, piston rings with improper end gap or a compression leak. Incorrect type of oil, lack of oil or an incorrectly operating oil injection pump will also result in excessive friction and overheating. Incorrect spark plug (wrong heat range), incorrect ignition timing or overheating from any cause may result in piston seizure.

A noticeable reduction of speed may be your first sign of impending seizure while immediate stoppage indicates full lockup. A noise called "top end rattle" is often an early sign of seizure.

When diagnosing piston seizure, the pistons themselves can be used to troubleshoot and determine the failure cause. High cylinder temperatures normally cause seizure above the piston

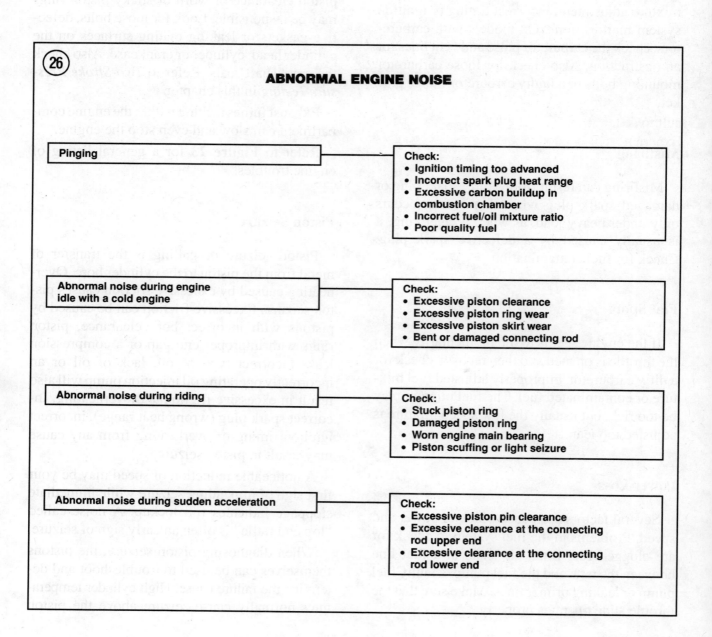

ABNORMAL ENGINE NOISE

Pinging — Check:
- Ignition timing too advanced
- Incorrect spark plug heat range
- Excessive carbon buildup in combustion chamber
- Incorrect fuel/oil mixture ratio
- Poor quality fuel

Abnormal noise during engine idle with a cold engine — Check:
- Excessive piston clearance
- Excessive piston ring wear
- Excessive piston skirt wear
- Bent or damaged connecting rod

Abnormal noise during riding — Check:
- Stuck piston ring
- Damaged piston ring
- Worn engine main bearing
- Piston scuffing or light seizure

Abnormal noise during sudden acceleration — Check:
- Excessive piston pin clearance
- Excessive clearance at the connecting rod upper end
- Excessive clearance at the connecting rod lower end

rings while seizure below the piston rings is usually caused by a lack of proper lubrication.

See **Figure 24** and **Figure 25** for examples of piston seizure.

Excessive Vibrations

Excessive vibration may be caused by loose engine, suspension or steering mount bolts.

Engine Noises

A change in the sound is often the first clue that the rider notices indicating that something may be wrong with the engine. Noises are difficult to differentiate and even harder to describe. Experienced is needed to diagnose sounds accurately (**Figure 26**).

TWO-STROKE PRESSURE TESTING

Sometimes an older or high-hour 2-stroke engine may be hard to start and generally runs poorly for no apparent reason. The fuel and ignition systems are functioning properly and a compression test indicates the engine's upper end is in acceptable condition.

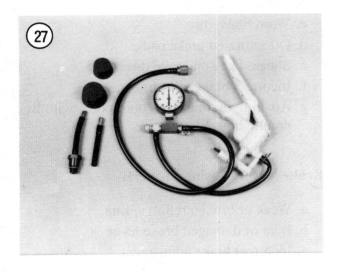

A conventional compression test, however, does *not* show a lack of primary (crankcase) compression. In a 2-stroke engine, the crankcase must be alternately under pressure and vacuum. After the piston closes the intake port, further downward movement of the piston causes the trapped mixture to be pressurized so it can rush quickly into the cylinder when the scavenging ports are opened. Upward piston movement lowers the pressure (creates a vacuum) in the crankcase, drawing the fuel/air mixture in from the carburetor or EFI system.

> *NOTE*
> *The operational sequence of a 2-stroke engine is illustrated in Chapter One under* **Engine Principles**.

If crankcase seals or cylinder base gaskets leak, the crankcase cannot hold either pressure or vacuum and proper engine operation is impossible. Any other source of leakage such as porous or cracked crankcase castings will result in the same conditions.

It is possible to test for and isolate engine crankcase leaks. The test is simple but requires special equipment. A typical 2-stroke pressure test kit is shown in **Figure 27**. Briefly, what is done is seal off all engine openings, then apply air pressure. If the engine does not hold air, a leak or leaks is indicated. Then it is only necessary to locate and repair the leaks.

The following procedure describes a typical pressure test.

> *NOTE*
> *Because of the labyrinth seal at the center of the crankshaft, the cylinders cannot be checked individually. When one cylinder is pressurized, the other cylinder is also pressurized. All openings to both cylinders must be blocked before applying pressure during testing.*

1. Remove the carburetors or EFI fuel system as described in Chapter Six or Chapter Seven.
2. Insert a plug tightly in the intake manifold.

3. Remove the exhaust pipes and block off the exhaust ports, using suitable adapters and fittings.

4. Remove one spark plug and install the pressure gauge adaptor into the spark plug hole. Connect the pressurizing lever and gauge to the installed adapter, then squeeze the lever until the gauge indicates approximately 9 psi (62 kPa).

5. Observe the pressure gauge. If the engine is in good condition, the pressure should not drop more than 1 1/2 to 2 psi (10-14 kPa) in several minutes. Any pressure loss of 1 psi (7 kPa) in one minute indicates serious sealing problems.

Before condemning the engine, first be sure that there are no leaks in the test equipment or sealing plugs. If the equipment shows no signs of leakage, go over the entire engine carefully. Large leaks can be heard; smaller ones can be found by going over every possible leakage source with a small brush and soap suds solution. Possible leakage points are listed below:

a. Crankshaft seals.
b. Spark plug(s).
c. Cylinder head joint.
d. Cylinder base joint.
e. Carburetor base joint.
f. Crankcase joint.
g. Rotary valve cover gasket.

POWER TRAIN

The following items provide a starting point from which to troubleshoot power train malfunctions. The possible causes for each malfunction are listed in a logical sequence.

Drive Belt Not Operating Smoothly in Primary Sheave

a. Drive sheave face is rough, grooved, pitted or scored.
b. Defective drive belt.

Uneven Drive Belt Wear

a. Misaligned primary and secondary sheaves.
b. Loose engine mounts.

Glazed Drive Belt

a. Excessive slippage caused by stuck or frozen track.
b. Engine idle speed too high.

Drive Belt Too Tight at Idle

a. Engine idle speed too high.
b. Incorrect sheave distance.
c. Incorrect belt length.

Drive Belt Edge Cord Failure

a. Misaligned primary and secondary sheaves.
b. Loose engine mounts.

Brake Not Holding Properly

a. Incorrect brake cable adjustment.
b. Worn brake pads.
c. Worn brake disc.
d. Oil saturated brake pads.
e. Sheared key on brake disc.
f. Incorrect brake adjustment.
g. Air in hydraulic lines on models with hydraulic brakes.

Brake Not Releasing Properly

a. Weak or broken return spring.
b. Bent or damaged brake lever.
c. Incorrect brake adjustment.

Excessive Chaincase Noise

a. Incorrect chain tension.
b. Excessive chain stretch.
c. Worn sprocket teeth.
d. Damaged chain and/or sprockets.

Chain Slippage

a. Incorrect chain tension.
b. Excessive chain stretch.
c. Worn sprocket teeth.

Leaking Chaincase

a. Loose chaincase cover mounting bolts.
b. Damaged chaincase cover gasket.
c. Damaged chaincase oil seal(s).
d. Cracked or broken chaincase.

Rapid Chain and Sprocket Wear

a. Insufficient chaincase oil level.
b. Broken chain tensioner.
c. Misaligned sprockets.

Drive Clutch Engages Before Engagement rpm

a. Worn spring.
b. Incorrect weight.

Drive Clutch Engages After Engagement rpm

a. Incorrect spring.
b. Worn or damaged secondary sheave buttons.

Erratic Shifting

a. Worn rollers and bushings.
b. Scuffed or damaged weights.

c. Dirty primary sheave assembly.
d. Worn or damaged secondary sheave buttons.

Engine Bogs During Engagement

a. Incorrect secondary sheave width adjustment.
b. Drive belt worn too thin.
c. Incorrect sheave distance.

Primary or Secondary Sheave Sticks

a. Damaged sheave assembly.
b. Moveable sheave damaged.
c. Dirty sheave assembly.

SKIS AND STEERING

The following items provide a starting point from which to troubleshoot ski and steering malfunctions. Some possible causes for each malfunction are listed in a logical sequence.

Loose Steering

a. Loose steering post bushing.
b. Loose steering post or steering column fasteners.
c. Loose tie rod ends.
d. Worn spindle bushings.
e. Stripped spindle splines.

Unequal Steering

a. Improperly adjusted tie rods.
b. Improperly installed steering arms.
c. Damaged steering components.

Rapid Ski Wear

a. Skis misaligned.

b. Worn out ski wear rods (skags).

TRACK ASSEMBLY

The following items provide a starting point from which to troubleshoot track assembly malfunctions. Also refer to *Track Wear Analysis* in this chapter.

Frayed Track Edge

a. Incorrect track alignment.
b. Track contacts rivets in tunnel area (incorrect rivets previously installed).

Track Grooved on Inner Surface

a. Track too tight.
b. Frozen rear idler shaft bearing.

Track Drive Ratcheting

a. Track too loose.
b. Drive sprockets misaligned.
c. Damaged drive sprockets.

Rear Idlers Turning on Shaft

Frozen rear idler shaft bearings.

Table 1 IGNITION HIGH TENSION COIL		
	Primary resistance	**Secondary resistance ***
1990		
583 (before serial No. 3 827 467)	0.23-0.43 ohms	3.85-7.15 K ohms
Other engine models	0.34-0.62 ohms	9-15 K ohms
1991-1992	0.34-0.62 ohms	9-15 K ohms
583 & 670 engine models	0.23-0.43 ohms	3.85-7.15 K ohms
Other engine models	0.34-0.62 ohms	9-15 K ohms
1993		
583 engine models	0.23-0.43 ohms	3.85-7.15 K ohms
Other engine models	0.3-0.7 ohms	8-16 K ohms
1994-1995	0.3-0.7 ohms	8-16 K ohms
* Spark plug cap removed		

2

Table 2 IGNITION GENERATING COIL

	Resistance
1990	
583 (before Serial No. 3 827 467)	
Single coil	40-76 ohms
Other engine models	
Low speed coil	120-180 ohms
High speed coil	2.8-4.2 ohms
1991	
MACH 1 X (643)	
Low speed coil	120-180 ohms
High speed coil	2.8-4.2 ohms
Other engine models	
Single coil	40-76 ohms
1992	
583, 643 & 670 engine models	
Low speed coil	120-180 ohms
High speed coil	2.8-4.2 ohms
467 & 582 engine models	
Single coil	40-76 ohms
1993	
583 engine models	
Low speed coil	120-180 ohms
High speed coil	2.8-4.2 ohms
Formula MX Z (467 Z engine)	
Stator coil (red - bk/red)	10-17 ohms
467, 582 & 670 engine models	
Stator coil (red - bk/red)	10-17 ohms
1994	
Stator coil (red - bk/red)	10-17 ohms
1995	
Stator coil (red - bk/red)	10-17 ohms

Table 3 IGNITION TRIGGER COIL

	Resistance
1993	
Formula MX Z (467 Z engine) (bl/y - w/y)	190-300 ohms
467, 582 & 670 engine models (bl/y - w/y)	190-300 ohms
1994-1995 (all models)	190-300 ohms

Table 4 LIGHTING COIL

	Resistance
1990-1991	0.05-0.6 ohms
1990	
583 (before SN. 3 827 467)	0.21-0.31 ohms
Other engine models	0.05-0.6 ohms
1991	
MACH 1 X (643)	0.21-0.31 ohms
Other engine models	0.05-0.6 ohms
1992	
583, 643 & 670 engine models	0.21-0.31 ohms
467 & 582 engine models	0.05-0.6 ohms
1993	
Formula MX Z (467 Z)	0.20-0.35 ohms
583 engine models	0.21-0.31 ohms
Other engine models	0.20-0.35 ohms
1994-1995 (all models)	0.20-0.35 ohms

Chapter Three

Lubrication, Maintenance and Tune-up

This chapter covers the regular maintenance required to keep your snowmobile in top shape. Regular, careful maintenance is the best guarantee for a trouble-free, long lasting vehicle. Snowmobiles are high-performance vehicles that demand proper lubrication, maintenance and tune-ups to maintain the high level of performance, extend engine life and extract the maximum economy of operation.

You can do your own lubrication, maintenance and tune-ups if you follow the correct procedures and use common sense. Always remember that engine damage can result from improper tuning and adjustment. In addition, where special tools or testers are called for during a particular maintenance or adjustment procedure, the tool should be used or you should refer service to a qualified dealer or repair shop.

The following information is based on recommendations from Ski-Doo that will help you keep your snowmobile operating at its peak level.

Tables 1-13 are at the end of the chapter.

NOTE
Be sure to follow the correct procedure and specifications for your specific model and year. Also use the correct quantity and type of fluid as indicated in the tables.

PRE-RIDE CHECKS

Check the machine thoroughly before each ride. Check vital fluids daily or before each ride to ensure proper operation and prevent severe component damage.

BREAK-IN PROCEDURE

Following cylinder servicing such as boring, honing and new rings, and major lower end work, the engine should be broken in just as if it were new. The performance and service life of the engine depends greatly on a careful and sensible break-in.

For the first 10-15 hours of operation, no more than 3/4 throttle should be used and the speed should be varied as much as possible. Prolonged steady running at one speed, no matter how moderate, is to be avoided, as is hard acceleration. Wet snow conditions should also be avoided during break-in.

To ensure adequate engine lubrication during break-in, add 500 cc of Bombardier Injection Oil (part No. 496 0133 00) to the first tank of gas. Use this oil *together* with the oil supplied by the injection system. Throughout the break-in period, check the oil injection reservoir tank to make sure the injection system is working (oil level diminishing).

After the initial 10-15 hours, check all engine and chassis fasteners for tightness. If the snowmobile is going to be used in extreme conditions, you may want to increase the break-in a few hours. After break-in, retighten the cylinder head nuts as described in this chapter and perform the 10-hour inspection as described in the following section.

NOTE
After the break-in is complete, install new spark plugs as described in this chapter.

10-HOUR INSPECTION

Perform this inspection after the first 10 hours of operation or 30 days after purchase, whichever comes first. The 10-hour inspection is listed in **Table 2**. The 10-hour inspection should be repeated whenever the engine top- or bottom-end has been overhauled or the engine removed from the frame. Likewise, chassis and steering inspection procedures should be performed after major service has been performed on these components.

Periodic maintenance procedures are listed in **Table 3**.

LUBRICATION

WARNING
A serious fire hazard always exists around gasoline. Do not allow any smoking in areas where fuel is being mixed or while refueling your machine. Always have a fire extinguisher, rated for gasoline and electrical fires, within reach just to play it safe.

Proper Fuel Selection

The Rotax 2-stroke engines used in Ski-Doo snowmobiles are lubricated by oil that circulates through the crankcase and eventually into the combustion chamber with the fuel. The oil is eventually burned with the fuel and expelled through the exhaust. The various components of the engine are lubricated by the oil as it clings to the various parts as it passes through the crankcase and cylinders. All models are equipped with an oil injection system. Pre-mixing oil with the fuel is not required on any of the models covered in this manual except during engine break-in. See *Break-In* in this chapter.

Table 4 lists fuel recommendations that should be followed to prevent engine knock and ensure proper operation.

Engine Oil Tank

An oil injection system is used on all models. During engine operation, oil is automatically

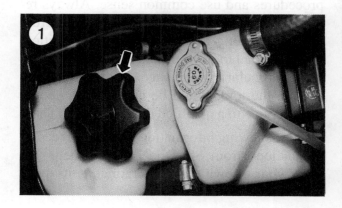

injected into the engine at a variable ratio depending on engine speed.

Check the oil level in the reservoir tank (**Figure 1**, typical) daily and each time the snowmobile is being refueled.

The oil tank is equipped with a oil level sensor that is connected to the injection oil level pilot lamp on the instrument panel (**Figure 2**, typical). When the oil level in the tank reaches a specified low point, the pilot lamp will light. Add oil as soon as possible when the low oil pilot light comes on.

NOTE
*The oil injection level pilot lamp (**Figure 2**) also lights whenever the brake lever is operated. If the lamp does not light during brake operation, replace the lamp as described in Chapter Nine.*

When the oil level is low, perform the following.

1. Open the hood.

2. Remove the oil tank fill cap (**Figure 1**) and pour in the required amount of 2-stroke injection oil specified in **Table 5**. Fill the tank until the oil

3

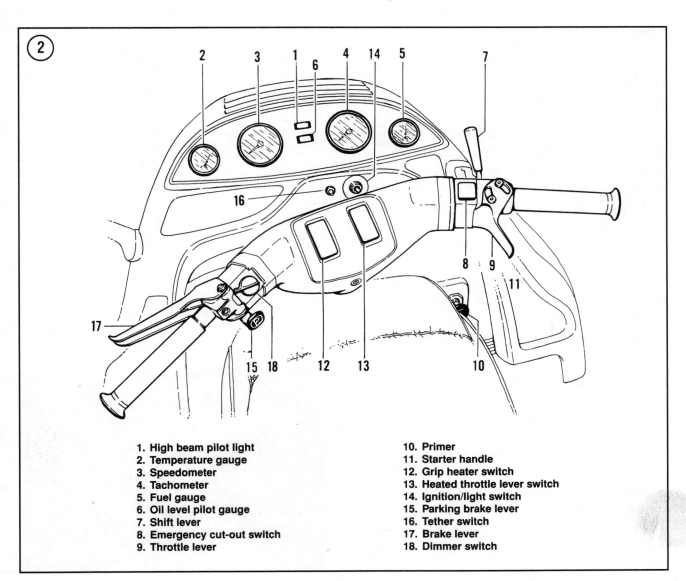

1. High beam pilot light
2. Temperature gauge
3. Speedometer
4. Tachometer
5. Fuel gauge
6. Oil level pilot gauge
7. Shift lever
8. Emergency cut-out switch
9. Throttle lever
10. Primer
11. Starter handle
12. Grip heater switch
13. Heated throttle lever switch
14. Ignition/light switch
15. Parking brake lever
16. Tether switch
17. Brake lever
18. Dimmer switch

level is approximately 13 mm (1/2 in.) from the top of the transparent tank.

3. Reinstall the fill cap and close the hood.

Chaincase Oil

The oil in the chain housing lubricates the chain and sprockets.

Always use one type and brand of oil. Different types or brands will often vary slightly in their composition and a mixture of the two may not lubricate as well as either alone.

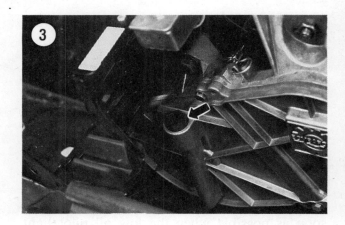

Chaincase oil level check

The chain housing oil level is checked with the dipstick (**Figure 3**).

1. Park the snowmobile on a level surface. Open the hood.

2. Unscrew and remove the dipstick (**Figure 3**) from the chaincase cover. Wipe the dipstick and insert it back into the chaincase. Do not screw the dipstick back into the cover.

3. Lift the dipstick out of the chaincase and check the oil level on the dipstick. The oil level should be between the upper and lower marks (**Figure 4**).

4. If the oil level is low, top off with a chaincase oil recommended in **Table 5**. Do not overfill. Recheck the oil level.

5. Reinstall the dipstick. Tighten it securely.

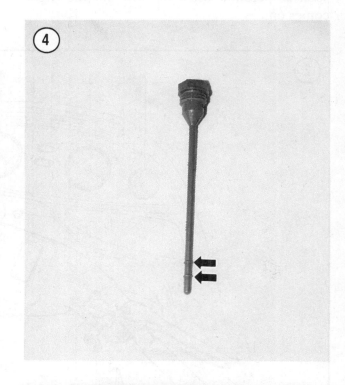

Changing chaincase oil

Oil in the chaincase should be changed once each year.

1. Park the snowmobile on a level surface.

2. Open the hood.

3. Remove the exhaust pipe and muffler as described in Chapter Eight.

4. Place an old carpet scrap or several shop cloths under the chaincase cover to absorb spilled oil.

NOTE
*The chaincase is filled with oil and the cover on models produced before 1993 is not equipped with a drain plug. Oil can be drained from 1993 and later models by removing the drain plug (**Figure 5**). To drain oil from the chaincase on earlier models, the cover (**Figure 6**) must be removed. Try to catch as much of the spilled oil in the shop cloths as possible.*

5A. On 1993 and later models, remove the drain plug (**Figure 5**) and drain oil from the chaincase. The cover can be removed from the chaincase for inspection and cleaning if desired.

5B. To remove the chaincase cover, proceed as follows:

a. Remove the screws and washers attaching the cover (**Figure 6**) to the chaincase.

b. Remove the cover and O-ring.

c. Clean the chaincase cover thoroughly. Remove as much oil from the bottom of the chaincase as possible.

d. Inspect the chaincase cover O-ring and replace if necessary.

6. Clean up as much oil as possible with the shop cloths.

NOTE
Store the oil soaked shop cloths in a suitable container until they can be cleaned.

7A. If the drain plug was removed, proceed as follows:

a. Inspect the magnet in the drain plug.

b. Clean and reinstall the plug.

7B. If cover was removed, proceed as follows:

a. Install the sealing O-ring.

b. Reinstall the chaincase cover (**Figure 6**), attaching screws and washers.

c. Tighten the screws securely.

8. Remove the chaincase dipstick (**Figure 3**).

9. Insert a funnel into the dipstick hole and fill the chain housing with the correct type (**Table 5**) and quantity (**Table 6**) of chaincase oil.

10. Check the oil level as described in the previous procedure.

Jackshaft Lubrication
(Brake Disc and Secondary Sheave)

The brake disc and secondary sheave should be lubricated so that they can slide freely on the jackshaft. Apply a spray penetrating lubricant from at the points indicated in **Figure 7**.

CAUTION
Do not over lubricate. Excessive lubrication can cause brake pad or drive belt contamination.

Drive Axle

Lubricate the drive axle with a low-temperature grease (**Table 5**) at the fitting shown in

Figure 8. The guard for the speedometer cable located on the left side is removed in **Figure 8** for clarity. It is not necessary to remove the guard to lubricate the left side and the right side does not have a guard.

Steering and Front Suspension Lubrication

Lubricate the steering and suspension points indicated in **Figure 9** and **Figure 10** monthly or after every 40 hours of operation. If the snowmobile is operated under severe service conditions or in wet snow, perform this service more frequently. Refer to Chapter Fifteen for component removal and installation.

Rear Suspension Lubrication

Lubricate the rear suspension with a low-temperature grease monthly or after every 40 hours of operation. If the snowmobile is operated under severe service conditions or in wet snow, perform this service more frequently. Refer to Chapter Sixteen for suspension removal and installation procedures. See **Figures 11-13** for lubrication points.

WEEKLY OR EVERY 150 MILES (240 KM) MAINTENANCE

Maintenance intervals are specified in **Table 3**.

Drive Belt Check

Check the drive belt (**Figure 14**) for cracks, fraying or unusual wear as described in Chapter Thirteen. Replace the drive belt if its width is less than specified in Chapter Thirteen.

Ski and Ski Runner Check

Check the skis (**Figure 15**) for cracks, bending or other damage. Raise the front of the snowmobile so the the skis clear the ground. Check ski

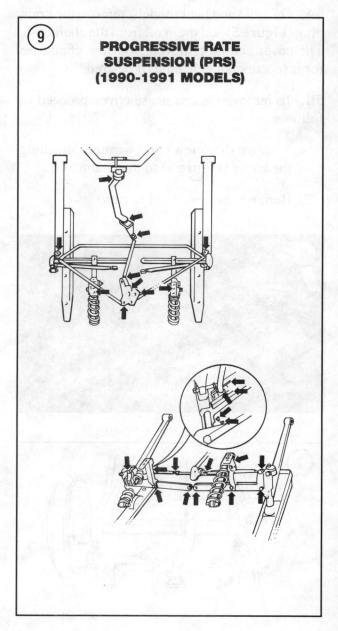

PROGRESSIVE RATE SUSPENSION (PRS) (1990-1991 MODELS)

movement by pivoting both skis up and down; skis should pivot smoothly without binding. If a ski is tight, refer to Chapter Fifteen for ski removal, installation and ski pivot bolt tightness.

Excessively worn or damaged ski runners reduce handling performance and can cause wear to the bottom of the ski. Because track and snow conditions determine runner wear, they should be inspected often. Check the ski runners for wear (**Figure 16**) and replace them if they are cracked or more than half worn at any point. Refer to Chapter Fifteen.

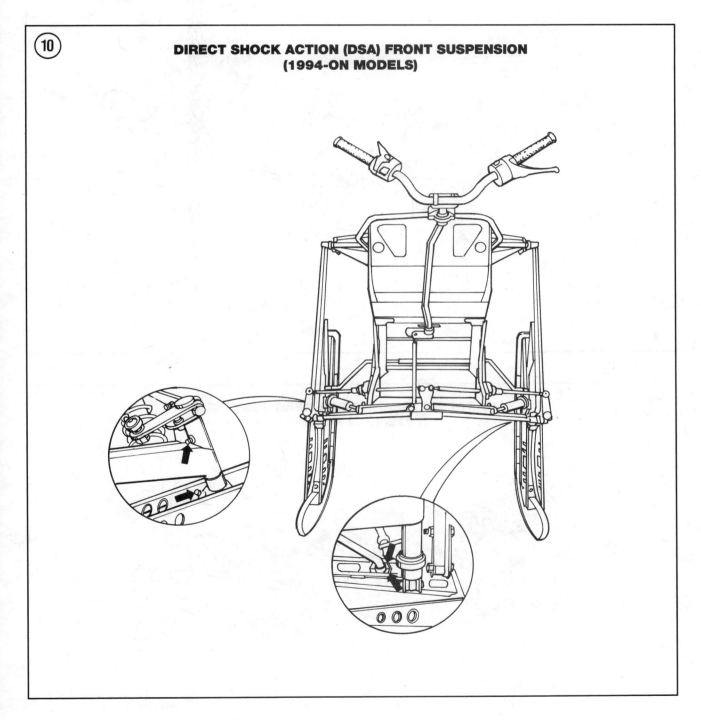

⑩   **DIRECT SHOCK ACTION (DSA) FRONT SUSPENSION**
                        (1994-ON MODELS)

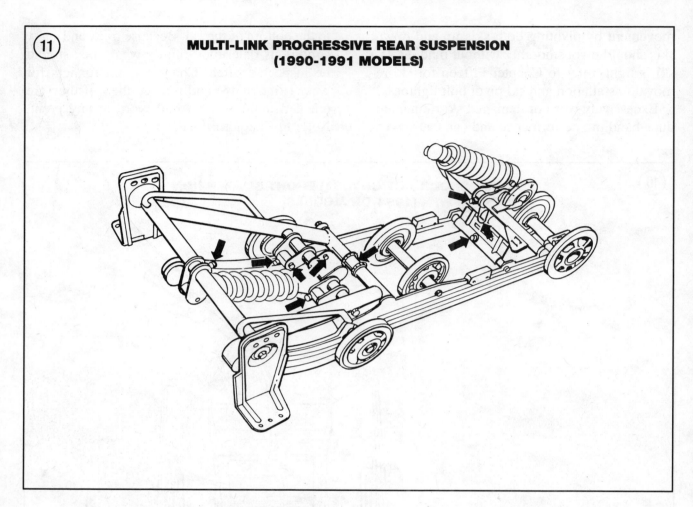

MULTI-LINK PROGRESSIVE REAR SUSPENSION
(1990-1991 MODELS)

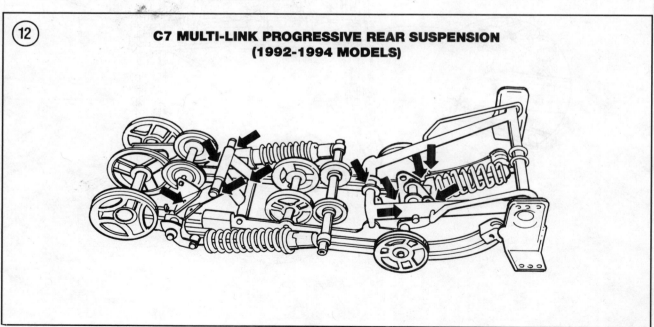

C7 MULTI-LINK PROGRESSIVE REAR SUSPENSION
(1992-1994 MODELS)

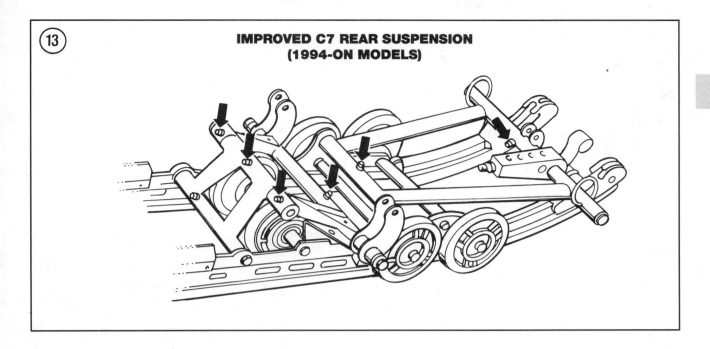

**IMPROVED C7 REAR SUSPENSION
(1994-ON MODELS)**

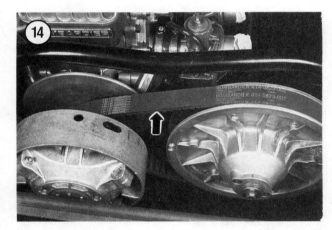

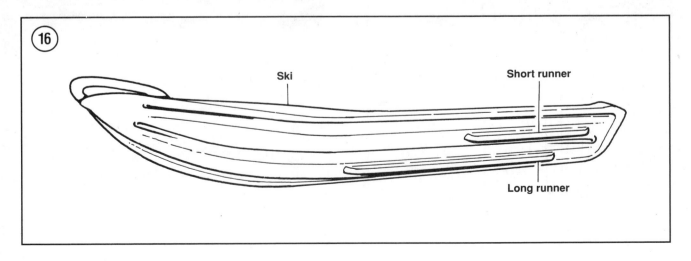

Ski

Short runner

Long runner

Brake Pad Wear Check

Replace the brake pads if the fixed brake pad measures 1 mm (1/32 in.) or less from the inner caliper half as shown in **Figure 17**. Refer to Chapter Fourteen for brake service to both mechanical and hydraulic units (**Figure 18** or **Figure 19**).

MONTHLY OR EVERY 500 MILES (800 KM)

Brake Adjustment

All models covered in this manual are equipped with a self-adjusting brake mechanism. Check and adjust the brake as follows:

1. Apply the brake firmly and measure the distance from the brake lever to the handlebar grip as shown in **Figure 20**. The distance should be approximately 13 mm (1/2 in.).

2. If the distance measured in Step 1 is incorrect, squeeze the brake lever strongly several times to actuate the self-adjusting mechanism. Recheck the measurement.

3. If the distance cannot be corrected by squeezing the brake lever (Step 2), check the brake assembly as described in Chapter Fourteen.

NOTE
If brake adjustment is difficult or if you are unsure about its operation, refer adjustment to a Ski-Doo dealer.

Spark Plugs

Check the spark plugs periodically for firing tip condition and electrode gap. Refer to spark plug service under *Tune-Up* in this chapter.

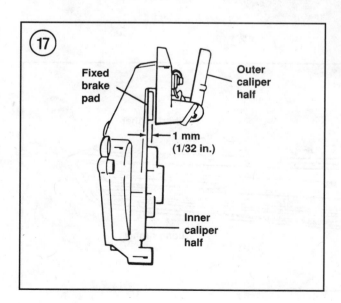

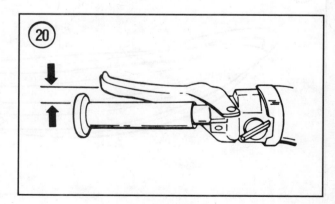

Drive Chain Adjustment

The drive chain adjuster mechanism consists of a chain tensioner block, roller, adjust bolt and hair pin (**Figure 21** or **Figure 22**). Chain tension is maintained by monitoring free play at the brake disc. The adjust bolt (A, **Figure 23** or A, **Figure 24**) threads into the chain tensioner block and is used to adjust roller (B, **Figure 23** or B, **Figure 24**) tension against the drive chain (C, **Figure 23** or C, **Figure 24**). The hair pin (D, **Figure 23** or D, **Figure 24**) locks the adjust bolt in position after the bolt and chaincase lock holes are aligned.

Excessive free play will cause excessive and premature chain and sprocket wear.

The drive chain can be adjusted without removing the chaincase cover.

1. Start the engine and run the snowmobile forward slightly. Turn the engine off.

2. Open the hood.

3. Remove the hair pin (A, **Figure 25** or A, **Figure 26**) from the drive chain adjust bolt located on the right side.

4. Turn adjust the bolt (B, **Figure 25** or B, **Figure 26**) *clockwise* by hand until it stops.

5. Turn the adjust bolt *counterclockwise* until the hair pin will enter the locking hole in the adjust bolt.

6. Install the hair pin to lock the adjustment.

NOTE
Figure 26 shows the chain adjuster assembly with the chaincase cover removed. It is not necessary to remove the cover when performing this procedure. The chaincase shown is not a reversing model, but they are similar.

7. Turn the brake disc (**Figure 27**) *clockwise* to remove free play, then turn the brake disc *counterclockwise* and measure the free play. The free play should be within 3-5 mm (1/8-13/64 in.). If the free play is incorrect and the adjust bolt is correctly tightened, remove the chaincase and

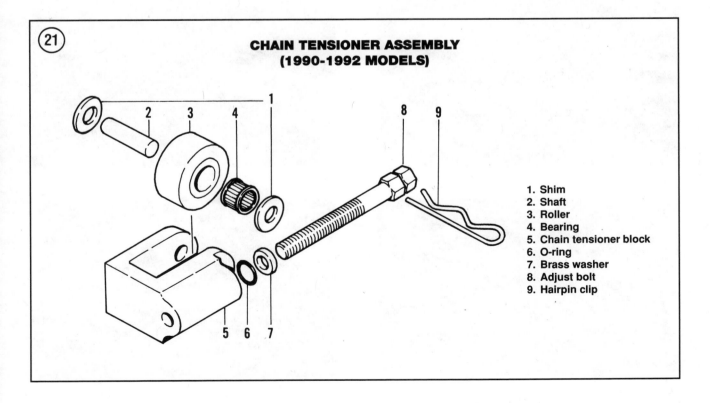

(21) **CHAIN TENSIONER ASSEMBLY**
(1990-1992 MODELS)

1. Shim
2. Shaft
3. Roller
4. Bearing
5. Chain tensioner block
6. O-ring
7. Brass washer
8. Adjust bolt
9. Hairpin clip

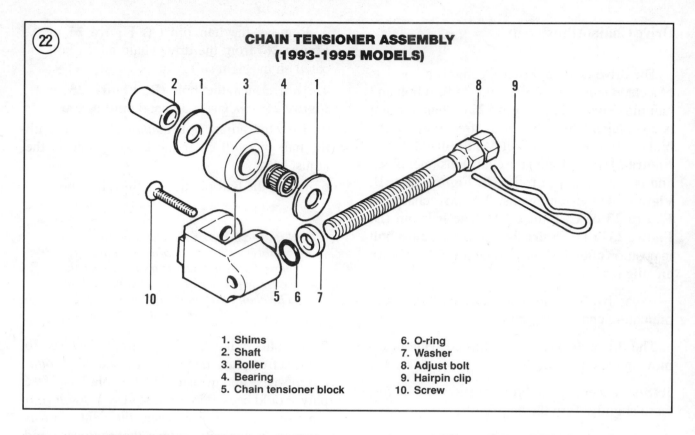

**CHAIN TENSIONER ASSEMBLY
(1993-1995 MODELS)**

1. Shims
2. Shaft
3. Roller
4. Bearing
5. Chain tensioner block
6. O-ring
7. Washer
8. Adjust bolt
9. Hairpin clip
10. Screw

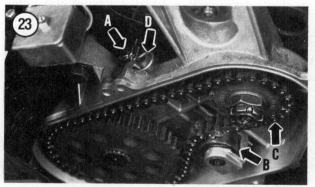

inspect the tensioner assembly and drive chain assembly as described in Chapter Fourteen.

Exhaust System

The exhaust system is a vital link to the performance and operation of the Ski-Doo engine. Check the exhaust system from the cylinder exhaust port to the muffler for:

a. Damaged or leaking gaskets.
b. Loose or missing fasteners.
c. Cracked, dented or otherwise damaged components.

Refer to Chapter Eight for cleaning, repair and other service to the exhaust system.

Air Filter Cleaning

All models are equipped with an air filter at the air intake silencer. Service the air filter as follows.

> *CAUTION*
> *Operating the engine without the air filter or modification to the air intake system may result in engine damage. Any changes in the air intake system will also alter the fuel mixture adjustment.*

1. Open the hood.
2. Remove the air filter (**Figure 28** or **Figure 29**) from the air intake silencer.
3. The filter should be free of all snow and water contamination. If necessary, clean the filter with solvent and blow dry with compressed air. Do not use heat in an attempt to shorten the drying time. If the air filter is torn or otherwise damaged, install a new filter.
4. When the air filter is thoroughly dry, carefully install it so it fits snugly in the air intake silencer opening.

> *NOTE*
> *Do not leave the hood open during a snowfall where snow can collect on and block the air filter element. If you must work in the engine compartment during these conditions, cover the air filter.*

Oil Injection Oil Filter Inspection/Replacement

An inline oil filter (**Figure 30**) is installed between the injection oil tank and the oil pump. A clamp is used on each end of the filter. The oil filter is installed to prevent contaminants from entering the pump and obstructing oil passages or causing the pump to stick.

> *CAUTION*
> *An oil filter that is contaminated and clogged will also prevent oil from reaching the engine. Change the filter if contamination can be seen or is suspected. Engine seizure from lack of oil is more difficult to repair than installing a new filter.*

Inspect the oil filter frequently (at least once a month) for contamination buildup or other obstruction. If the oil filter is contaminated, replace it and check the reservoir tank. The connecting lines and oil system reservoir tank should be removed, cleaned and checked for contamination or damage. After the system has been cleaned, install a new oil filter, fill the reservoir with new approved oil, and bleed the oil pump as described in Chapter Ten to make sure that oil is being delivered to the engine.

When replacing the oil filter, note the following:

a. Place a cloth underneath the oil filter to absorb oil spilled when the filter is removed.

b. Loosen or remove the hose clamps from the filter nipples.

c. Detach both hoses from the filter.

d. Check the hose clamps for fatigue or damage. Install new clamps if required.

e. Attach hoses to the new filter.

f. Install the clamps over each hose and filter nipple. Tighten the clamps securely.

g. Fill the reservoir with new approved oil.

h. Bleed the oil injection pump as described in Chapter Ten.

i. Remove and safely discard the cloth used to catch oil.

Wire Harness, Control Cables and Hose Lines

All wiring, cables and hoses should be inspected for proper routing. If necessary, secure loose components with cable ties. Replace damaged components as required.

Primary Sheave Adjustment

Refer to Chapter Thirteen.

Track Inspection

Inspect the track as described in Chapter Sixteen.

Track Adjustment

The track is subject to high torque loads which may cause the track to stretch and wear. Check the track adjustment frequently as part of a routine, maintenance schedule. Failure to maintain correct track tension and alignment will reduce performance and will wear the track prematurely. Track adjustments include track tension and alignment.

Tension adjustment

Correct track tension is important because a loose track will slap on the bottom of the tunnel and wear the track, tunnel and heat exchangers. A loose track can also ratchet on the drive sprockets and damage both the track and sprockets.

A track that is too tight will rapidly wear the slider shoe material and the idler wheels. Performance will also be reduced because of increased friction and drag on the system.

NOTE
Ride the snowmobile in snow for approximately 15-20 minutes before adjusting track tension.

Measure track tension as follows:

1. Raise the snowmobile with a suitable lift so the track is clear of the ground.
2. Clean ice, snow and dirt from the track and suspension.
3. Attach a spring scale to the track at approximately the middle of the slider shoe (**Figure 31**). Pull the scale to deflect the track away from the slider shoe until a force of 7.3 kg. (16 lbs.) is indicated by the scale. Measure the distance between the slider shoe and the inside of the track. Refer to **Table 13** for the correct deflection.
5. If the measured deflection is incorrect, adjust track tension as follows:
   a. Loosen both rear idler wheel retaining bolts (A, **Figure 32**).
   b. Loosen both axle adjuster locknuts (B, **Figure 32**).
   c. Turn both adjusters (C, **Figure 32**) in or out equally to adjust the track. Tighten lock nuts (B, **Figure 32**) when adjustment is complete.
   d. Apply the recommended amount of force and recheck the adjustment as described in Step 3 and Step 4.
   e. Tighten the rear idler wheel bolt (A, **Figure 32**) to the torque specification in **Table 7**.
6. After checking track tension, check *Track alignment* as described in this chapter.

Track alignment

Track alignment is related to track tension and should be checked and adjusted when the tension is checked and adjusted. If the track is misaligned, the rear idler wheels, drive sprocket lugs and track lugs will wear rapidly. The resistance between the track and the sides of the wheels will reduce snowmobile performance.

1. Adjust the *Track tension* as described in this chapter.
2. Position the machine on its skis so the ski tips are against a wall or other immovable barrier.

3. Elevate and support the machine so that the track is completely clear of the ground and free to rotate.

WARNING
Don't stand behind or in front of the machine when the engine is running, and take care to keep hands, feet and clothing away from the track when it is moving.

4. Start the engine and apply just enough throttle to turn the track several complete revolutions. Then shut off the engine and allow the track to coast to a stop. Don't stop it with the brake.

5. Check the alignment of the slider shoes and the track lugs (**Figure 33**).

6. If the slider shoes are equal distance from the lugs and the openings in the track are centered with the slider shoes (**Figure 33**), the alignment is correct.

7. If the track is offset (closer to the slider shoes on one side), alignment should be adjusted as follows:

  a. Loosen both rear idler wheel bolts (A, **Figure 32**) and both lock nuts (b, **Figure 32**).

  b. If the track is offset to the left, tighten the left adjuster bolt (C, **Figure 32**) and loosen the right one equally.

  c. If the track is offset to the right, tighten the right adjuster bolt and loosen the left one equally.

  d. Repeat Steps 4 and 5 to recheck alignment. If alignment is still not correct, repeat Step 7, then Steps 4 and 5 until the track is properly aligned.

  e. Tighten the rear idler wheel bolt to the torque specification in **Table 7**.

8. Recheck track tension as described in this chapter after making any changes to the adjuster bolts (C, **Figure 32**).

Slide Suspension Inspection

Inspect the suspension system for loose, damaged or missing components. Refer to Chapter Sixteen.

Steering Inspection

Check the steering assembly monthly. Ski alignment cannot be maintained with bent or

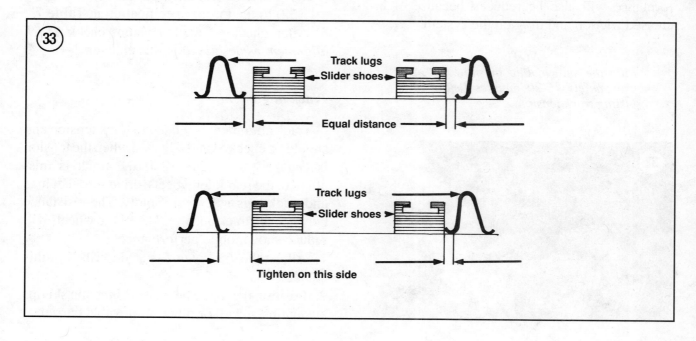

otherwise damaged steering components or with loose or missing fasteners. Refer to Chapter Fifteen.

Ski Alignment

Check ski alignment at the beginning of each season, if a steering component is replaced, or if control is a problem. Ski alignment should also be checked if a ski experiences a hard side impact. Refer to Chapter Fifteen for complete ski alignment procedures.

General Inspection

Refer to *General Inspection and Maintenance* in this chapter.

ONCE A YEAR OR EVERY 2,000 MILES (3,200 KM)

Engine Mounts and Fasteners

Loose engine mount screws (**Figure 34**) will cause incorrect clutch alignment. Check the front and rear engine mounting screws to make sure they are tight. See **Figure 35** or **Figure 36**, as appropriate. Check all accessible engine assembly screws and nuts for tightness. Tighten all screws and nuts to the torque specification in **Table 7**.

NOTE
If the engine mount screws are loose, check clutch alignment as described in Chapter Thirteen.

Cylinder Head Torque

Refer to *Tune-up* in this chapter.

Ignition Timing

Refer to *Tune-up* in this chapter.

Carburetor Adjustment

Refer to *Tune-up* in this chapter.

Throttle Cable Routing

The single throttle cable that begins at the thumb control is attached to 3 cables by a junction block. The 3 branched cables are connected to each carburetor (or EFI throttle) and the oil injection pump. Check the throttle cable from the thumb throttle to the carburetor (A, **Figure 37**) and oil pump (B, **Figure 37**) for proper routing. Check the cable ends for fraying or splitting that could cause the cable to break or stick in the housing.

Oil Pump Adjustment

The oil pump injects lubricating oil into the engine and the amount of oil is determined by throttle position. Control cable adjustment is necessary because cables will wear and stretch during normal use. Incorrect cable adjustment can cause too little or too much oil and result in engine seizure and poor performance.

Check the oil pump cable adjustment once a year or whenever the throttle cable is disconnected or replaced.

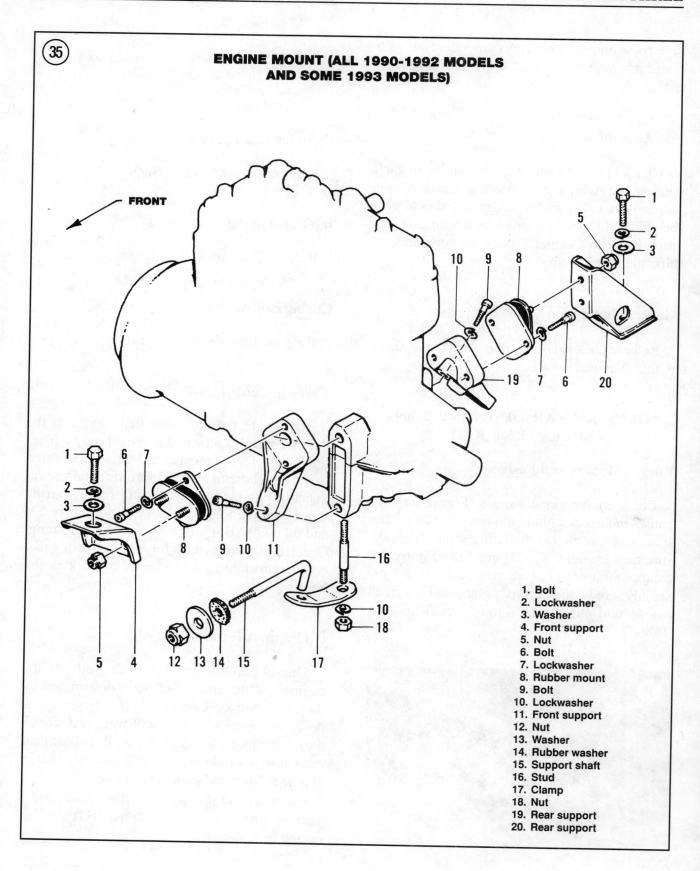

ENGINE MOUNT (ALL 1990-1992 MODELS AND SOME 1993 MODELS)

1. Bolt
2. Lockwasher
3. Washer
4. Front support
5. Nut
6. Bolt
7. Lockwasher
8. Rubber mount
9. Bolt
10. Lockwasher
11. Front support
12. Nut
13. Washer
14. Rubber washer
15. Support shaft
16. Stud
17. Clamp
18. Nut
19. Rear support
20. Rear support

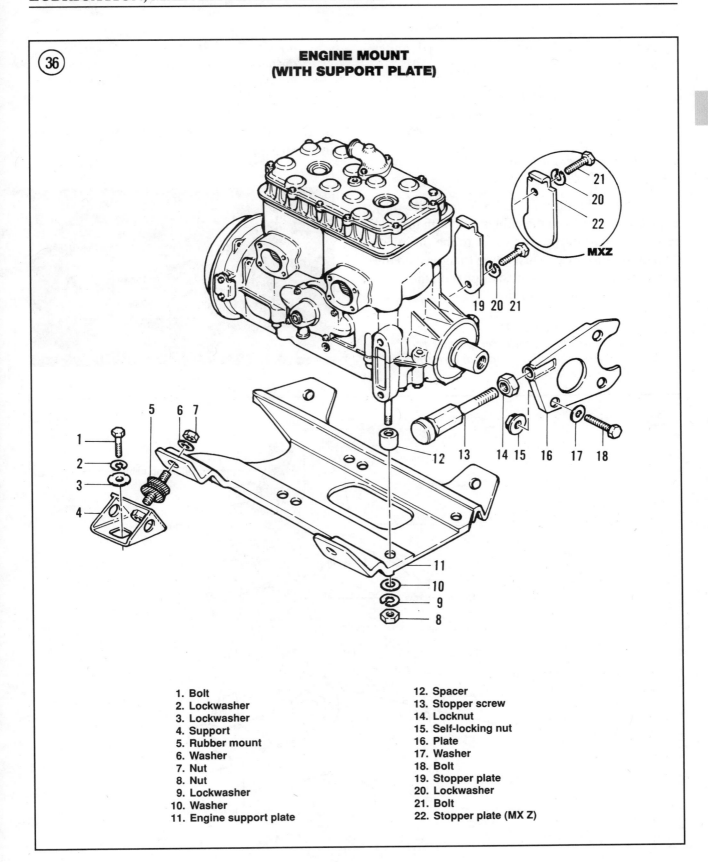

36 ENGINE MOUNT
(WITH SUPPORT PLATE)

MXZ

3

1. Bolt
2. Lockwasher
3. Lockwasher
4. Support
5. Rubber mount
6. Washer
7. Nut
8. Nut
9. Lockwasher
10. Washer
11. Engine support plate
12. Spacer
13. Stopper screw
14. Locknut
15. Self-locking nut
16. Plate
17. Washer
18. Bolt
19. Stopper plate
20. Lockwasher
21. Bolt
22. Stopper plate (MX Z)

1. Adjust the carburetor as described under *Tune-up* in this chapter.

> *CAUTION*
> *If the carburetor is not adjusted before adjusting the oil pump, engine damage may occur. The oil injection pump operation must be synchronized with the carburetor opening.*

2. Press the thumb throttle lever until free play is just removed from the cables and both throttle levers begin to move. The cable to the oil injection pump should also just begin to move and the mark on the pump lever must align with the mark on the pump housing (**Figure 38**).

> *CAUTION*
> *It is important that all free play is removed from the cables, but that throttles are not moved. If it is necessary to move the throttles to align the marks on pump, the oil injection control cable must be adjusted.*

3. If the adjustment marks do not align as shown in **Figure 38**:

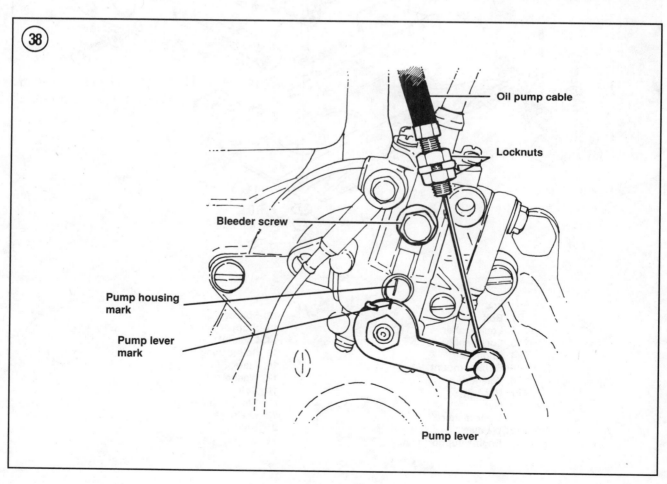

a. Loosen the cable adjuster locknuts (**Figure 38**).

b. Reposition the cable until the 2 marks align.

c. Tighten the locknuts and recheck the adjustment.

Headlight Beam

Refer to Chapter Nine.

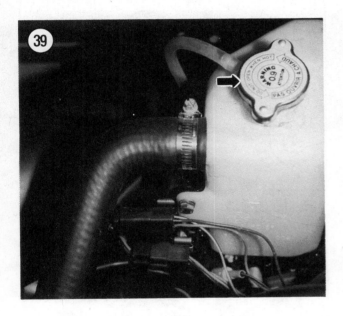

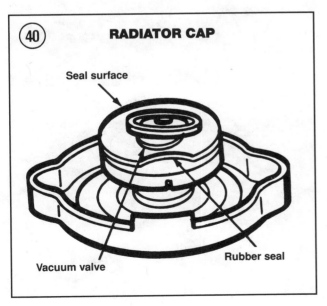

RADIATOR CAP

Seal surface

Vacuum valve

Rubber seal

Cooling System Inspection

> *WARNING*
> *Never remove the radiator cap (**Figure 39**), coolant drain screws or disconnect any hose while the engine is hot. Scalding fluid and steam may be blown out under pressure and cause serious injury.*

Once a year, or whenever troubleshooting the cooling system, the following items should be checked. If you do not have the test equipment, the tests can be done by a Ski-Doo dealer, radiator shop or service station.

1. Loosen the radiator cap to its first detent and release the system pressure, then turn the cap to its second detent and remove it from the radiator. See **Figure 39**.

2. Check the rubber washers on the radiator cap (**Figure 40**) for tears or cracks. Check for a bent or distorted cap. Raise the vacuum valve and rubber seal and rinse the cap under warm tap water to flush away any loose rust or dirt particles.

3. Inspect the radiator cap neck seat on the coolant tank for dents, distortion or contamination. Wipe the sealing surface with a clean cloth to remove any rust or dirt.

> *CAUTION*
> *Do not exceed 89.6 kPa (13 psi) when performing Steps 4 and 5 or damage to the cooling system will occur.*

4. Have the radiator cap pressure tested (**Figure 41**). The specified radiator cap relief pressure is 90 kPa (13 psi). The cap must be able to sustain this pressure for 6 seconds. Replace the radiator cap if it does not hold pressure.

5. Leave the radiator cap off and have the entire cooling system pressure tested. The entire cooling system should be pressurized to 90 kPa (13 psi). The system must be able to hold this pressure for 10 seconds. Replace or repair any components that fail this test.

6. Check all cooling system hoses for damage or deterioration. Replace any hose that is ques-

tionable. Make sure all hose clamps (**Figure 42**) are tight.

7. Check the heat exchangers (**Figure 43**) for cracks or damage. Replace if necessary, as described in Chapter Eleven.

Coolant Check

> *WARNING*
> *Do not remove the radiator cap (**Figure 39**) when the engine is hot.*

1. Park the snowmobile on level ground.
2. Open the hood.
3. Loosen the radiator cap to its first detent and release the system pressure, then turn the cap to its second detent and remove it from the radiator. See **Figure 39**.
4. Check the level in the coolant tank. If the coolant level is not 60 mm (2 3/8 in.) from the top of the coolant tank (**Figure 44**), add coolant as follows.
5. If the level is low, add a sufficient amount of antifreeze and water (in a 60/40 ratio) through the radiator cap opening as described under *Coolant*.
6. Reinstall the radiator cap (**Figure 39**).

Coolant

Only a high quality ethylene glycol based coolant compounded for aluminum engines should be used. Mix the coolant with water in a 60/40 ratio. Coolant capacity is listed in **Table 6**. When mixing antifreeze with water, make sure to use only soft or distilled water. Distilled water can be purchased at supermarkets in gallon containers. Do not use tap or saltwater because it will damage engine parts.

> *CAUTION*
> *Always mix coolant in the proper ratio for the coldest temperature in your area. Antifreeze alone is more likely to freeze*

at a higher temperature than a 60/40 mixture of antifreeze and water.

Coolant Change

The cooling system should be completely drained and refilled once a year (preferably before off-season storage).

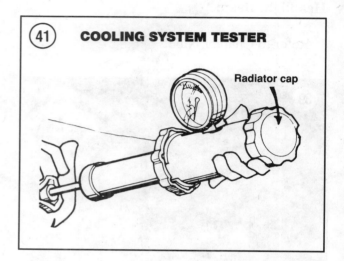

41) COOLING SYSTEM TESTER

Radiator cap

CAUTION
Use only a high quality ethylene glycol antifreeze specifically labeled for use with aluminum engines. Do not use an alcohol-based antifreeze.

The following procedure must be performed when the engine is *cold*.

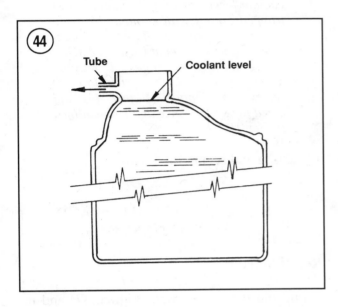

CAUTION
Be careful not to spill antifreeze on painted surfaces as it may damage the surface. Wash immediately with soapy water and rinse thoroughly with clean water.

1. Park the snowmobile on a level surface.
2. Open the hood.

WARNING
*Do not remove the radiator cap (**Figure 39**) when the engine is hot.*

3. Loosen the radiator cap to its first detent and release the system pressure, then turn the cap to its second detent and remove it from the radiator. See **Figure 39**.
4. Use a primer pump and a suitable length of hose to siphon the coolant from the coolant tank and the engine into a suitable container (**Figure 45**).

NOTE
The siphon hose should be long enough to reach through the coolant tank deep into the lower hose. The lower hose is curved and the hose must be flexible enough to follow the hose.

WARNING
Do not siphon coolant with your mouth and a hose. The coolant mixture is poisonous and ingestion of even a very small amount may cause sickness. Observe warning labels on antifreeze containers. Animals are attracted to antifreeze so make sure you discard used antifreeze in a safe and suitable manner; do not store antifreeze in an open container.

WARNING
The EPA has classified ethylene glycol as an environmental toxic waste, which cannot be legally flushed down a drain or poured on the ground. Treat antifreeze that is to be discarded as you treat motor oil. Put it in a suitable container and dispose of it according to local regulations.

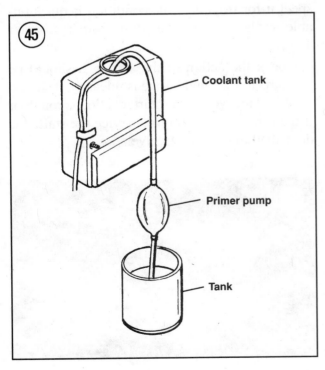

WARNING
Spilled antifreeze is very slippery on concrete floors. Wipe up spilled anti-freeze as soon as possible.

5. Remove the engine bleed plug(s) from the coolant housing and the cylinder head (**Figure 46**, typical) and raise the rear of the snowmobile with a jack to allow the heat exchangers to drain.

6. Lower the snowmobile to the ground after the coolant has finished draining. Do not reinstall the bleed screw.

7. Remove the siphon pump when the tank is empty and as much coolant has been removed as possible.

8. Additional coolant can be removed by detaching hoses and removing the coolant recovery tank. Reinstall the recovery tank and hoses if they were removed.

9. Rinse spilled coolant from the engine and engine compartment with clean water.

NOTE
All models do not have bleed plugs (Figure 46) in both the cylinder head and the coolant fitting as shown.

10. Pour a 60/40 mixture of antifreeze and distilled water into the coolant tank until it begins to flow from the hole for the bleed plug(s) (**Figure 46**). Reinstall the bleed plug(s) and tighten securely. Continue to add coolant until the level reaches 60 mm (2 3/8 in.) below the top of the coolant tank (**Figure 44**).

11. Start the engine and allow it to idle until it reaches operating temperature. When the thermostat opens and the coolant begins to circulate, allow the engine to idle for a few more minutes.

12. Turn the engine off and check the coolant freezing level with an antifreeze checker. Make sure the freezing level exceeds the coldest temperatures in your area.

13. If the coolant level has lowered, add coolant to maintain the correct level in the filler neck (Step 10). If the coolant level dropped significantly, you may want to start the engine and allow it to idle again with the radiator cap removed. Continue to add coolant until the coolant level stabilizes, then turn the engine off and install the radiator cap.

NOTE
After flushing the cooling system, the coolant level may drop when pockets of trapped air fill with coolant. To avoid operating the engine with a low coolant level, check the level at least once again before starting the engine. It may be necessary to allow the system to cool, remove bleed plugs (Figure 46) and bleed the system once again as outlined in Step 10.

14. Close and secure the hood.

GENERAL INSPECTION AND MAINTENANCE

Recoil Starter

Pull out the starter rope (**Figure 47**) and inspect it for fraying. If its condition is questionable, replace the rope as described in Chapter Twelve.

Check the action of the starter. It should be smooth, and when the rope is released, it should return all the way. If the starter action is rough or if the rope does not return, service the starter as described in Chapter Twelve.

Body Inspection

Repair or replace all damaged body panels.

Body Fasteners

Tighten any loose body bolts. Replace loose rivets by first drilling out the old rivet, then installing a new one with a pop riveter. This tool,

along with an assortment of rivets, is available through many hardware and auto parts stores. Follow the manufacturer's instructions for installing rivets.

Check all welded joints for cracks and damage. Damaged welded joints should be repaired by a competent welding shop.

Drive Assembly

Refer to Chapter Four for drive assembly tuning and adjustment. Refer to Chapter Thirteen for drive assembly service.

Guide Wheel Inspection

Inspect the rubber on the guide wheels for wear and damage (**Figure 48**). Replace the wheels if they are in poor condition. Refer to Chapter Sixteen.

Drive Axle Sprockets

Inspect the teeth on the drive axle sprockets for wear and damage (**Figure 49**). If the sprockets are damaged, replace them as described in Chapter Sixteen.

Fuel Tank and Lines

Inspect the fuel tank for cracks and abrasions. If the tank is damaged or leaking, replace it before returning the unit to service. See Chapter Six or Chapter Seven.

Fuel Tank Cleaning

The fuel tank should be removed and thoroughly flushed once a season. Refer to Chapter Six or Seven.

Oil Tank

Inspect the oil tank for cracks, abrasions or leaks. Replace the tank if its condition is in doubt.

Electrical System

All of the switches should be checked for proper operation. Refer to Chapter Nine.

Electrical Connectors

Inspect the high-tension leads to the spark plugs (**Figure 50**) for cracks and breaks in the insulation and replace the leads if they are not perfect. Breaks in the insulation allow the spark to arc to ground and will impair engine performance.

Check primary ignition wiring and lighting wiring for damaged insulation. Usually minor damage can be repaired by wrapping the damaged area with electrical insulating tape. If insulation damage is extensive, the damaged wires should be replaced.

Abnormal Engine Noise

> *WARNING*
> *Never lean into the snowmobile's engine compartment while wearing a scarf or other loose clothing when the engine is running or when anyone is attempting to start the engine. If the scarf or clothing should catch in the drive belt or clutch, severe injury could occur. Make sure the belt guard is in place.*

Open the hood, then start the engine and listen for abnormal noises. Often the first indication of trouble is a change in sound. An unusual rattle might indicate a loose fastener that can be easily repaired or the first indications of severe engine damage. With familiarity of the machine and practice, you will be able to identify most new sounds. Periodic inspection for abnormal engine noises can prevent engine failure later on.

Oil and Fuel Lines

Inspect the oil and fuel lines for loose connections and damage. Tighten all connections and replace any lines that are damaged or cracked.

Pulse Hose

The pulse hose(s) between the engine crankcase and the fuel pump(s) should be inspected at the beginning of each season for cracks or other damage. Worn or damaged hoses will cause air leaks that result in intermittent operating problems. Check the pulse hose(s) for loose connections or damaged hose clamps. Replace pulse hose(s) and clamps when necessary.

ENGINE TUNE-UP

The number of definitions of the term "tune-up" is probably equal to the number of people defining it. For the purposes of this book, a tune-up is general adjustment and maintenance to insure peak engine performance.

The following paragraphs discuss the different parts of a tune-up which should be performed in the order given. Have the new parts on hand before you begin.

To perform a tune-up on your snowmobile, you need the following tools and equipment:

a. 14 mm spark plug wrench.
b. Socket wrench and assorted sockets.
c. Phillips head screwdriver.
d. Spark plug feeler gauge and gap adjusting tool.
e. Dial indicator.
f. Flywheel puller.
g. Compression gauge.

Cylinder and Cylinder Head Nuts

The engine must be at room temperature for this procedure.
1. Open the hood.
2. Tighten each cylinder head screw or nut in a crisscross pattern to the tightening torque in **Table 7**. Refer to **Figure 51**.

Cylinder Compression

A cylinder compression check is one of the quickest ways to check the internal condition of the engine's upper end. It's a good idea to check compression at each tune-up, record the compression of each cylinder, then compare the current compression with test results from earlier tune-ups. The first step is to write the measured compression of each cylinder and the date, so that it can be compared with tests recorded at the next tune-up. A gradual change probably indicates normal wear. A sudden drop in compression, however, may indicate a developing problem.

1. Elevate and support the machine so the track is completely off the ground and free to rotate. Start and run the engine until it warms to normal operating temperature, then turn the engine off.

> *WARNING*
> *Don't stand behind or in front of the machine when the engine is running, and take care to keep hands, feet and clothing away from the track when it is turning.*

> *CAUTION*
> *To prevent expensive engine damage, refer to **Spark Plug Removal/Cleaning** in this chapter before removing the spark plugs in Step 2.*

2. Remove both spark plugs. Insert the plugs in the caps and ground both plugs to the cylinder head or exhaust pipe.

> *CAUTION*
> *If the plugs are not grounded during the compression test, the ignition system could be damaged.*

3. Screw a compression gauge into one spark plug hole or, if you have a press-in type gauge, hold it firmly in position.

4. Check that the emergency cutout switch is in the OFF position.

5. Hold the throttle wide open and crank the engine several revolutions until the gauge gives its highest reading. Record the reading, indicating the cylinder (MAG end or PTO end). Remove the pressure tester and relieve the pressure valve.

6. Repeat Steps 3-5 for the opposite cylinder.

7. There should be no more than a 10% difference in compression between cylinders.

8. If the compression is very low, a ring is probably broken or there is hole in the piston.

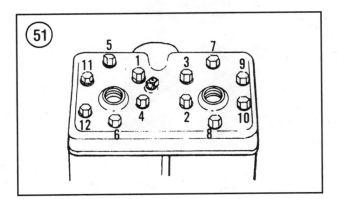

SPARK PLUG CONDITIONS

NORMAL

GAP BRIDGED

CARBON FOULED

OVERHEATED

OIL FOULED

SUSTAINED PREIGNITION

Correct Spark Plug Heat Range

The proper spark plug is very important in obtaining maximum performance and reliability. The condition of a used spark plug can tell a trained mechanic a lot about engine condition and carburetion.

Select plugs of the heat range designed for the loads and conditions under which the snowmobile will be run. Use of spark plugs with incorrect heat ranges can result in a seized piston, scored cylinder wall, or damaged piston crown.

In general, use hot plugs for low speeds and low temperatures. Use cold plugs for high speeds, high engine loads and high temperatures. The plugs should operate hot enough to burn off unwanted deposits, but not so hot that they burn themselves or cause preignition. The insulator of a spark plug that is the correct heat range will be

a light tan color after the engine has operated for awhile. See **Figure 52**.

The reach (length) of a plug is also important. A shorter than normal plug will cause hard starting, reduced engine performance and carbon buildup on the exposed cylinder head threads. A spark plug that is longer than normal might interfere with the piston or may cause overheating. Physical damage to the piston or overheating often results in severe engine damage. Refer to **Figure 53**. If the spark plug extends into the combustion chamber as shown by the *Too long* view in **Figure 53**, carbon buildup on the exposed threads may prevent the spark plug from being removed. Forcing the spark plug out will probably damage the threads in the cylinder head.

The recommended spark plug for the various models is listed in **Table 8**. It may be desirable to install spark plugs of slightly different heat range than listed to match operating conditions.

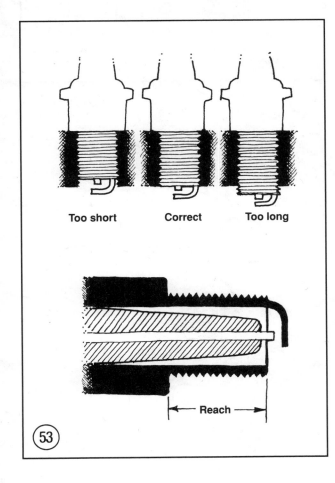

Too short   Correct   Too long

Reach

53

Spark Plug Removal/Cleaning

1. Grasp the spark plug lead as near the plug as possible and pull it from the plug. If the spark plug cap **Figure 50** is stuck to the plug, twist the cap slightly to break it loose.

CAUTION
The dirt could fall into the cylinder when the plug is removed, causing serious engine damage.

2. Use compressed air to blow away any dirt that has accumulated next to the spark plug base.

NOTE
If the plug is difficult to remove, apply penetrating oil, like WD-40 or Liquid Wrench, around the base of the plug and let it soak. If the plug is still difficult to remove, reapply the penetrating oil as necessary.

3. Remove the spark plug with a spark plug wrench.

4. Inspect the plug carefully. Look for a broken center porcelain, excessively eroded electrodes, excessive carbon buildup or oil fouling. See **Figure 52**.

Gapping and Installing the Plug

The gap between the electrodes of a new spark plug should be carefully set before installing. A specific gap is necessary to ensure a reliable, consistent spark. Use a special spark plug gapping tool to bend the ground electrode and a wire feeler gauge to measure gap between electrodes.

> *NOTE*
> *Never try to close the spark plug gap by tapping the spark plug on a solid surface. This can damage the plug internally. Always use the special tool to open or close the gap. Be careful not to bend the electrode enough to brake to weaken it.*

1. Insert a wire feeler gauge between the center and side electrode (**Figure 54**). The correct gap is listed in **Table 8**. If the gap is correct, you will feel a slight drag as you pull the wire through. If there is no drag, or the gauge won't pass through, bend the side (ground) electrode with a gapping tool (**Figure 55**) to set the proper gap.

2. Apply antiseize to the plug threads before installing the spark plug.

> *NOTE*
> *Antiseize can be purchased at most automotive parts stores.*

3. Screw the spark plug in by hand until it seats. Very little effort should be required. If force is necessary, the threads are dirty or the plug cross-threaded. Unscrew the plug, clean the threads and try again.

4. Use a spark plug wrench and tighten the plug an additional 1/4 to 1/2 turn after the gasket has made contact with the head. If you are installing

an old, regapped plug and reusing the old gasket, only tighten an additional 1/4 turn.

> *CAUTION*
> *Do not overtighten. This will only squash the gasket and destroy its sealing ability. This could cause compression leakage around the base of the plug. It is*

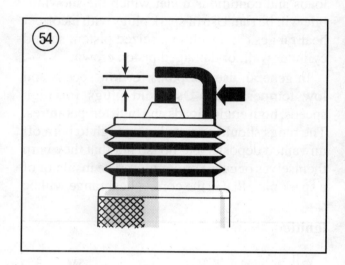

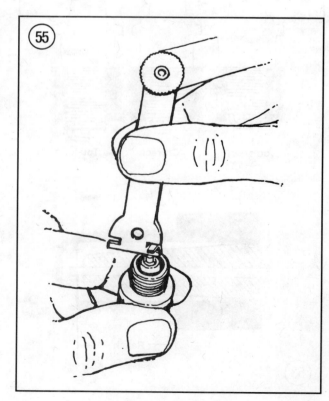

also important to tighten the spark plug sufficiently to provide a good seal. If the plug is too loose, hot exhaust gasses will pass around the threads and eventually make the plug difficult to remove without damaging threads in cylinder head.

5. Install the spark plug wires. Make sure they snap onto the top of the plugs tightly.

CAUTION
Make sure the spark plug wire is located away from the exhaust pipe.

Reading Spark Plugs

Much information about engine and spark plug performance can be determined by careful examination of the spark plugs. Refer to Chapter Four.

Ignition Timing

All models are equipped with a breakerless capacitor discharge ignition (CDI). The ignition system is much less susceptible to failures caused by dirt, moisture and wear than conventional breaker-point ignition.

Ski-Doo recommends a 2-step procedure when checking ignition timing—static timing and dynamic timing.

Static timing of Bombardier engines requires the use of an accurate dial indicator to determine top dead center (TDC) of the piston before making any timing adjustment. TDC is determined

by removing the spark plug and installing the dial indicator in the plug opening. The static timing method is used to verify the flywheel timing marks before using a timing light to check ignition timing. The static timing procedure can be used for the following:

   a. Verify factory timing marks.
   b. Detect a broken or missing flywheel Woodruff key.
   c. Detect a twisted crankshaft.
   d. To scribe timing marks on a new flywheel.
   e. On models with a separate trigger coil, setting initial timing.

Dynamic engine timing uses a timing light connected to the MAG side spark plug lead. As the engine is cranked or run, the light flashes each time the spark plug fires. When the light is pointed at the moving flywheel, the mark on the flywheel appears to stand still. The flywheel mark should align with the stationary timing pointer on the engine.

Static Timing Check

1. Open the hood.
2. Remove the drive belt as described in Chapter Thirteen.
3. Remove both spark plugs as described in this chapter.
4. Remove the crankcase inspection plug (**Figure 56**).
5. Install and position a dial indicator as follows:
   a. Screw the extension onto a dial indicator and insert the dial indicator into the adapter (**Figure 57**).
   b. Screw the dial indicator adaptor into the cylinder head (**Figure 58**) on the MAG side. Do not lock the dial indicator in the adapter at this time.
   c. Rotate the flywheel (by turning the primary sheave) until the dial indicator rises all the way up in its holder (piston is approaching top dead center). Then slide the indicator far enough into the holder to obtain a reading.

d. Lightly tighten the set screw on the dial indicator adaptor to secure the dial gauge.

e. Rotate the flywheel until the dial gauge stops and reverses direction. This is top dead center. Zero the dial gauge by aligning the zero with the indicator needle (**Figure 59**).

f. Tighten the set screw on the dial indicator adaptor securely.

6. Rotate the crankshaft clockwise (viewed from the right-hand side) until the gauge needle has made approximately 3 revolutions. Then carefully turn the crankshaft clockwise until the gauge indicates that the piston is the correct distance before top dead center as indicated in **Table 9**.

7. View the timing marks through the hole in the crankcase (**Figure 60** or **Figure 61**). The marks should be aligned. If not, perform the following:

a. Scribe a new mark on the flywheel that aligns with the crankcase center mark shown in **Figure 60** or **Figure 61**. This mark will be used as the reference when using the timing light.

b. Repeat the timing procedure to check the accuracy of the new mark.

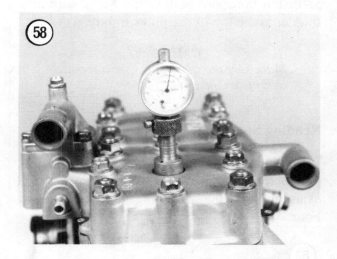

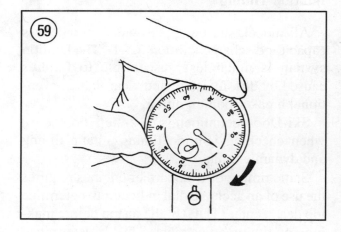

57

Base
Set screw
Plunger
Adapter
Extension

8. Remove the gauge and adapter. Install the spark plugs and connect the high-tension leads.

9. Reinstall the drive belt (Chapter Thirteen).

Trigger Coil Initial Timing (Models So Equipped)

Initial timing can be set for models which have a separate trigger coil. Refer to *static timing check* in this chapter to make sure that the flywheel is correctly installed, the timing mark is correctly located on the flywheel and to position the flywheel for setting the trigger coil initial timing. Proceed as follows:

1. Position the crankshaft and flywheel at timing position as described for *Static timing check* in this chapter.

2. The small bump in the center of the trigger coil (**Figure 62** or **Figure 63**) should be aligned with a mark next to the protrusion on the flywheel (**Figure 64**).

3. If the protrusion is not aligned with center of the trigger coil, loosen the 2 screws attaching the trigger coil, move the trigger coil, then tighten the screws.

4. Perform the *Dynamic Timing Check* as described in this chapter and adjust timing as described in *Setting Ignition Timing*.

Dynamic Timing Check

1. Open the hood.

2. Perform the *Static Timing Check* in this chapter to make sure that flywheel is correctly installed and timing mark is correctly positioned.

3. Connect a stroboscopic timing light according to its manufacturer's instructions to the MAG side spark plug lead (**Figure 65**).

4. Connect a tachometer according to its manufacturer's instructions.

5. Position the machine, on its skis, so the tips of the skis are against a wall or other immovable barrier. Elevate and support the machine so the

track is completely clear of the ground and free to rotate.

> *WARNING*
> *Don't allow anyone to stand behind or in front of the machine when the engine is running, and take care to keep hands, feet and clothing away from the track when it is running.*

> *NOTE*
> *Because ignition components are temperature sensitive, check ignition timing when the engine is cold.*

6. Start the engine and turn the headlight ON.

7. Allow the engine to idle for approximately 10-15 seconds, then run the engine at 6,000 rpm briefly and point the timing light at the crankcase timing inspection hole (**Figure 60** or **Figure 63**). The timing light will flash, appearing to stop the timing mark at the instant of ignition.

8. The flywheel timing mark will be aligned with the center mark of the hole, if ignition timing is correct.

9. If the timing mark is not correctly aligned, the ignition timing should be adjusted. Refer to *Setting Ignition Timing* in this chapter.

10. Turn the engine off and lower the snowmobile to the ground.

11. When ignition timing is correct, remove the timing light and tachometer. Install all of the covers that were removed (**Figure 66**).

Setting Ignition Timing

The ignition must occur at a specific time for the engine to perform at its optimum level. The procedure for changing the ignition timing is not the same for all engine models. Refer to **Table 10** for the type of ignition installed on your specific model, then refer to the appropriate following paragraphs.

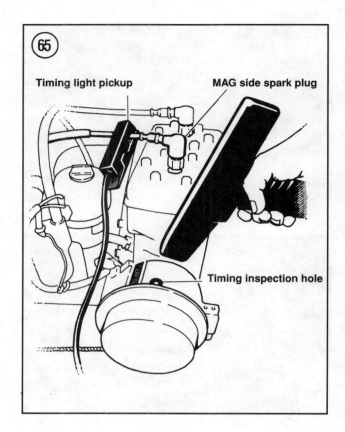

Timing light pickup   MAG side spark plug

Timing inspection hole

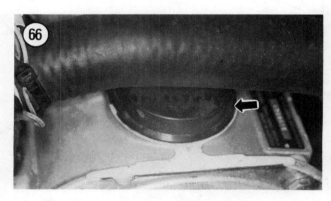

Models without separate trigger coil

This type of ignition is used on all 1990-1992 models. It is also used on the 1993 Formula Plus X equipped with a 583 model engine. Refer to **Figure 67**. Some of these models have one ignition generating coil, while others have dual (one low speed, one high speed) ignition generating

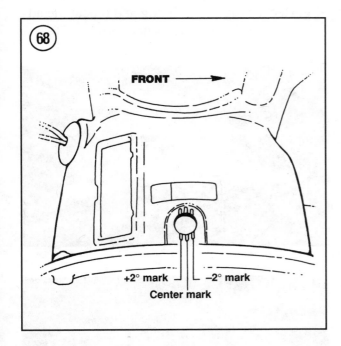

coils. Refer to the following for changing the ignition timing for these models.

1. Before changing the ignition timing, refer to *Static Timing Check* in this chapter to make sure the marks are correctly located on the flywheel and the flywheel is correctly installed. After making sure the marks are correct, perform the *Dynamic Timing Check* as outlined in this chapter. Leave the timing light attached.

2. Remove the recoil starter assembly as described in Chapter Twelve.

3. Remove the starter pulley and flywheel as described in Chapter Nine.

4. Ignition timing is changed by moving the stator plate (A, **Figure 67**). Note the following:

   a. The mark on either side of the center crankcase mark indicates 2° of crankshaft rotation. See **Figure 68**.

   b. If the flywheel mark is aligned with the crankcase mark on the right (**Figure 68**), ignition timing is retarded.

   c. If the flywheel mark is aligned with the crankcase mark on the left (**Figure 68**), ignition timing is advanced.

   d. To change ignition timing, loosen the 2 screws (B, **Figure 67**) retaining the stator plate. Turn the stator plate counterclockwise to advance or clockwise to retard ignition timing (**Figure 69**).

   e. Tighten the stator plate retaining screws.

   f. Reinstall the flywheel, starter pulley and recoil starter assembly.

   g. Recheck ignition timing, and repeat the adjustment procedure as necessary.

Models with a separate trigger mounted at side of the flywheel

This type of ignition is used on 1993 models with 467 and 582 engines, 1994 models with 467, 582 and 583 engines, and 1995 models with 467 engine. The separate trigger coil is attached to the engine crankcase outside and at the side (rear) of the flywheel (**Figure 70**). Refer to the

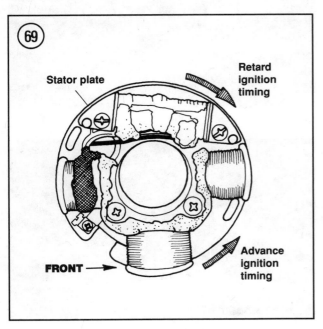

following for changing the ignition timing on these models.

1. Before changing the ignition timing, refer to *Static Timing Check* in this chapter to make sure the marks are correctly located on the flywheel and the flywheel is correctly installed. After making sure the marks are correct, perform the *Dynamic Timing Check* as outlined in this chapter. Leave the timing light attached.

2. Remove the recoil starter assembly as described in Chapter Twelve.

3. Ignition timing is changed by moving the trigger coil (A, **Figure 70**). Note the following:

   a. The mark on either side of the center crankcase mark indicates 2° of crankshaft rotation. See **Figure 71**.

   b. If the flywheel mark is aligned with the crankcase mark on the right (B, **Figure 71**), ignition timing is retarded.

   c. If the flywheel mark was aligned with the crankcase mark on the left (A, **Figure 71**), ignition timing is advanced.

   d. To change ignition timing, loosen the 2 screws (B, **Figure 70**) retaining the trigger coil. Move the trigger coil counterclockwise to advance or clockwise to retard ignition timing.

   e. Tighten the trigger coil retaining screws.

   f. Reinstall the recoil starter assembly.

   g. Recheck ignition timing and repeat the adjustment procedure as necessary.

Models with a separate trigger coil mounted at the top of the flywheel

This type of ignition is used on in 1993, 1994, and 1995 models with 670 engines and 1995 models with 454 engine. The separate trigger coil is attached to the engine crankcase just above the flywheel (**Figure 72**). Refer to the following for changing the ignition timing for these models.

1. Before changing the ignition timing, refer to *Static Timing Check* in this chapter to make sure the marks are correctly located on the flywheel and the flywheel is correctly installed. After making sure the marks are correct, perform the *Dynamic Timing Check* as outlined in this chapter. Leave the timing light attached.

2. Remove the cover (**Figure 66**) from the trigger coil.

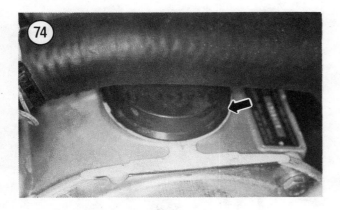

3. Ignition timing is changed by moving the trigger coil (**Figure 73**). Note the following:

   a. If the flywheel mark is positioned to the left (rear) of the crankcase mark, the timing is advanced. See A, **Figure 73**.

   b. If the flywheel mark is positioned to the right (front) of the crankcase mark, the timing is retarded. See B, **Figure 73**.

   c. To change ignition timing, loosen the 2 screws (C, **Figure 73**) retaining the trigger coil. Move the trigger coil counterclockwise to advance or clockwise to retard ignition timing.

   d. Tighten the trigger coil retaining screws.

   e. Recheck ignition timing and repeat the adjustment procedure as necessary.

   f. Install the cover (**Figure 74**).

Carburetor Adjustment

Refer to Chapter Seven for adjusting the Electronic Fuel Injection (EFI) on 1993 Formula Plus EFI models.

Idle mixture

Adjustment of the pilot air screw controls the fuel and air mixture at idle speed. Turning the pilot air screw (**Figure 75**) clockwise reduces the amount of air and enrichens the mixture.

1. Open the hood.

2. Locate the pilot air screws (**Figure 75**) on the side of each carburetor.

3. Turn both pilot air screws in (clockwise) until they lightly seat.

4. Back the pilot air screws out the number of turns specified in **Table 11**.

> *CAUTION*
> *Do not use the pilot air screws to attempt to set engine idle speed. Pilot air screws must be set as specified or an excessively lean mixture and subsequent engine damage may result.*

Synchronization

For maximum engine performance, both cylinders must work equally. If one cylinder's throttle opens earlier, that cylinder will be required to work harder. This will cause poor acceleration, rough engine performance and engine overheating. For proper carburetor synchronization, both slides must begin to lift at exactly the same time and continue to be open the same amount throughout their operating range.

Carburetor synchronization should be checked at each tune-up or whenever the engine suffers from reduced performance.

1. Open the hood.

2. Remove the air intake silencer (**Figure 76**, typical).

3. Back out both carburetor idle speed screws (**Figure 77**) so the carburetor valves drop all the way to the bottom.

4. Turn one carburetor idle speed screw (**Figure 77**) clockwise until it just touches the carburetor slide. Then turn the idle speed screw 2 turns clockwise.

5. Repeat Step 4 for the opposite carburetor.

6. Use a strong rubber band and clamp the throttle lever to the handlebar grip in the wide-open throttle position.

> *NOTE*
> *Make sure the throttle lever is held in the wide open position. This will insure maximum performance during engine operation.*

7. Loosen the locknut securing the adjuster at the top of each carburetor (**Figure 78**). Feel inside the carburetor bore to see if the cutout portion on the throttle valve is *flush* with the inside of the carburetor bore as indicated in **Figure 79**. If necessary, turn the adjuster (**Figure 79**) as required to position the throttle valve flush with the top of the carburetor bore. Tighten the locknut and recheck the throttle valve position.

8. Repeat Step 7 for the other carburetor.

9. Remove the rubber band clamp from handlebar and allow the throttle to return to the idle position.

3

CAUTION
Maintaining throttle cable free play is
critical to prevent throttle cable damage.

10. Operate the throttle lever a few times, then hold the throttle lever wide open. Pull the throttle cable or push the throttle valve up with your fingers to make sure the cable has some free play when wide open. There should be 1.5 mm (1/16 in.) free play. If necessary, loosen the locknut (**Figure 78**) and turn the adjuster (**Figure 79**) to

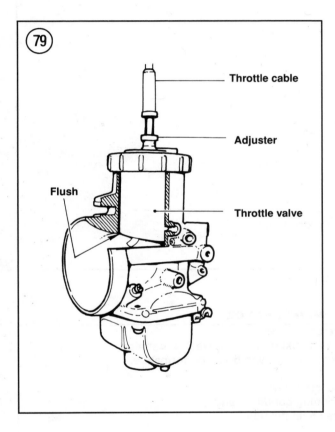

(79)

Throttle cable

Adjuster

Flush

Throttle valve

obtain correct free play. Recheck synchronization.

11. After completing carburetor synchronization, perform the *Oil Pump Adjustment* procedure in this chapter.

12. Reinstall the air intake silencer.

13. Start the engine and warm to operating temperature. Check idle speed (see **Table 12**). If necessary, turn both idle speed adjustment screws (**Figure 77**) equal amounts to obtain specified idle speed.

CAUTION
*Do not use the pilot air screws (**Figure** 75) to change the engine idle speed. Pilot air screws must be set as described in this chapter or the engine may be damaged by an excessively lean mixture.*

Idle speed

1. Open the hood.

2. Connect a tachometer according to the tool manufacturer's instructions.

NOTE
When turning the throttle stop screw in Step 3, turn the screws on both carburetors the same amount.

3. Set the engine idle speed by turning both carburetor's throttle stop screws (**Figure 77**) exactly the same amount. Turn the stop screws in to increase or out to decrease idle speed. Refer to **Table 12** for the correct idle speed for your model.

Table 1 WEEKLY INSPECTION

Check coolant level.
Check injection system oil level.
Check chaincase oil level.

Table 2 INITIAL 10 HOUR INSPECTION

Check coolant level.
Check injection system oil level.
Check chaincase oil level.
Check drive chain tension.
Retorque cylinder head.
Check engine mount tightness.
Check exhaust system fasteners.
Check ignition timing.
Check spark plug condition and gap.
Check carburetor adjustment.
Check oil injection pump adjustment.
Check brake pad wear and brake performance.
Check ski alignment and adjustment.
Retighten the handlebar bolts.
Retighten the steering arm bolts.
Retighten rear axle screw.
Inspect the drive belt.
Check sheave alignment.
Check driven sheave preload.
Inspect track for wear or damage.
Check track tension and alignment.
Perform all steering, suspension and drive axle lubrication procedures.
Check light operation.
Check all switches for proper operation.

Table 3 PERIODIC MAINTENANCE

Weekly or every 150 miles (240 km)	Check drive belt condition.
	Inspect skis and ski runners for wear or damage.
	Check brake pad wear and brake performance.
Monthly or every 500 miles (800 km)	Check brake adjustment.
	Check spark plug condition and gap.
	Adjust drive chain tension.
	Clean the air filter.
	Inspect the oil injection oil filter for contamination. Replace oil filter when necessary.
	Inspect all wiring harness, control cable and hose assemblies for incorrect routing and missing fasteners.
	Check the primary sheave for correct adjustment.
	Check track condition.
	Check track tension and alignment and adjust if necessary.
	Check all suspension components for missing fasteners and excessive play.
	Check all steering components for missing fasteners and excessive play.
	(continued)

3

Table 3 PERIODIC MAINTENANCE (continued)

Monthly or every 500 miles (800 km) (continued)	Check steering adjustments and adjust if necessary. Check exhaust system for missing or damaged components and fasteners. Check all fasteners for tightness. Check all wiring for chafing or other damage. Check all electrical connectors for looseness or damage. Perform general inspection
Once a year or every 2000 miles (3,200 km)	Check torque of engine mount bolts. Retorque cylinder head. Check all control cables for routing and damage. Check ignition timing. Adjust carburetors. Adjust oil injection pump*. Check headlight beam aim. Check cooling system hoses for looseness or damage. Replace coolant.

* The carburetors must always be adjusted before adjusting the oil injection pump.

Table 4 FUEL RECOMMENDATIONS

1995 MACH 1 670	Super unleaded (91 octane)
All models except MACH 1	Regular unleaded (87 octane)

Table 5 RECOMMENDED LUBRICANTS

Item	Lubricant type
Countershaft bearing, hub bearings, bogie wheels, ski legs, idler bearings, leaf spring cushion pads, etc.	A
Oil seal interior lips	A
Engine injection oil	B
Chaincase	C

Lubricant legend:
   A. Bombardier bearing grease or equivalent multipurpose lithium base grease for use through a temperature range of $-40°$ to $95°$ C ($-40°$ to $200°$ F). This grease will be referred to as a "low temperature grease" throughout this manual.
   B. Bombardier injection oil or equivalent. Injection oil must flow at $-40°$ C ($-40°$ F).
   C. Bombardier chaincase oil or equivalent. Make sure equivalent oil provides lubrication at low temperatures.
   * WD-40 can be used as a general lubricant.

Table 6 APPROXIMATE REFILL CAPACITY

Chaincase		
1990-1992	200 cc	7 oz.
1993-1995	350 cc	12 oz.
		(continued)

Table 6 APPROXIMATE REFILL CAPACITY (continued)

Oil injection reservoir		
1990-1993	2.9 L	98 oz.
1994		
Formula STX, GT, MACH 1	2.9 L	98 oz.
Other models	4.1 L	138.7 oz.
1995		
MX Z	2.55 L	86 oz.
Other models	4.1 L	138.7 oz.
Cooling system		
1990-1991	4.2 L	142 oz.
1993		
MX Z	4.7 L	159 oz.
Other models	4.2 L	142 oz.
1994		
Formula MX, MX Z, ST, Z	4.7 L	159 oz.
Summit 470 HAC, 583 HAC	4.7 L	159 oz.
Other models	4.2 L	142 oz.
1995		
Formula STX LT	5.0 L	169 oz.
Summit 583, 670	5.0 L	169 oz.
Grand Touring models	5.0 L	169 oz.
Other models	4.7 L	159 oz.
Fuel tank		
1990	40.9 L	10.8 gal.
1991 without electric start	40.9 L	10.8 gal.
1991 electric start models	33 L	8.7 gal.
1992	35.3 L	9.3 gal.
1993		
MX Z	42.1 L	11.1 gal.
Formula Plus EFI	45.3 L	12 gal.
Other models	35.3 L	9.3 gal.
1994		
Formula MX Z	39.0 L	10.3 gal.
MACH 1, GT models	35.3 L	12 gal.
Other models	42.1 L	11.1 gal.
1995		
MX Z	37.0 L	9.8 gal.
Other models	42.1 L	11.1 gal.

Table 7 MAINTENANCE TIGHTENING TORQUES

	N·m	ft.-lb.
Crankcase nuts or screws		
1990		
M6	10	7.5
M8	22	16
1991-on		
M6	10	7.5
M8	24	17
M10	38	28
Cylinder base screws or nuts		
1990-1991	22	16
1992-on	30	22

(continued)

Table 7 MAINTENANCE TIGHTENING TORQUES (continued)

	N·m	ft.-lb.
Cylinder head		
1990-1991		
All models	22	16
1992		
467 & 582 engines		
Cylinder head	30	22
Head cover	10	7.5
583, 643 & 670 engines	22	16
1993		
467 & 582 engines		
Cylinder head	30	22
Head cover	10	7.5
583 & 670 engines	22	16
1994-on		
467 & 582 engines		
Cylinder head	30	22
Head cover	10	7.5
454, 583 & 670 engines	22	16
Engine mounts		
1990-on		
M10 screws	48	35
M10 nuts	38	28
M8 Allen screws	25	18
M8 nuts	25	18
Exhaust valve screws		
454, 583, 643 & 670 engines	10	7.5
Exhaust manifold screws or nuts		
1990-1992		
467 engine model	21	15
536 engine model	25	18
583 engine model	10	7.5
1993		
467 engine model	25	18
582 & 583 engines	25	18
583 engine model	25	18
1994-on		
467 & 582 engines	25	18
454, 583 & 670 engines	10	7.5
Flywheel nut		
1990-1994		
643 & 670 engines	125	92
Other engine models	105	77
1995		
467, 582 & 583	105	77
454, 583HAC, 670	125	92
Rear idler wheel bolts	48	35
Rotary valve cover	22	16

Table 8 SPARK PLUGS

Model	Plug type	Gap mm (in.)
All models	NGK BR9ES	0.45 (0.018)

Table 9 IGNITION TIMING (WITH DIAL INDICATOR)

	mm (BTDC)	in. (BTDC)
1990		
Formula MX & MX LT	2.51	0.099
Formula Plus & Plus LT	2.18	0.086
Formula MACH 1 & MACH 1 XTC	1.75	0.069
1991		
Formula MX, MX E, MX X, MX XTC & MX XTC E	2.53	0.100
Formula Plus, Plus E, Plus X, Plus XTC & Plus XTC E	2.18	0.086
Formula MACH 1 & MACH 1 XTC	1.90	0.075
Formula MACH 1 X	1.90	0.075
1992		
Formula MX & MX XTC R	2.29	0.090
Formula Plus, Plus E, Plus XTC & Plus XTC E	2.18	0.086
Formula Plus X	1.88	0.074
Formula MACH 1 & MACH 1 XTC	1.90	0.075
Formula MACH 1 X	1.93	0.076
Formula MACH 1 XTC II	1.90	0.075
1993		
Formula MX, MX XTC R & MX Z	2.29	0.090
Formula Plus, Plus E, Plus XTC & Formula Plus EFI	2.18	0.086
Formula Plus X	1.88	0.074
Formula MACH 1 & MACH 1 XTC	1.93	0.076
Formula Grand Touring	2.18	0.090
1994		
Formula MX, MX Z, MX Z X, Summit 470 HAC & Formula ST	2.08	0.082
Formula STX, Formula STX II, Summit 583 HAC & Formula Z	1.75	0.069
MACH 1	1.93	0.076
Grand Touring & Grand Touring XTC	2.18	0.086
Grand Touring SE	1.93	0.076
1995		
MX	2.29	0.090
MX Z	1.48	0.058
Formula SS	1.93	0.076
Formula STX	1.75	0.069
Formula STX (LT)	1.75	0.069
Summit 583	1.75	0.069
Summit 670	1.93	0.076
Formula Z	1.75	0.069
MACH 1	1.93	0.076
Grand Touring 470	2.29	0.090
Grand Touring 580	2.18	0.086
Grand Touring SE	1.93	0.076

Table 10 IGNITION TIMING TYPE

1990-1992	Without trigger coil
1993	
Engine models 467 & 582	Trigger coil at side
Engine models 583	Without trigger coil
Engine model 670	Trigger coil on top
1994	
Engine models 467, 582 & 583	Trigger coil at side
Engine model 670	Trigger coil on top
1995	
Engine model 467 (470)	Trigger coil at side
Engine models 454 & 670	Trigger coil on top

Table 11 CARBURETOR PILOT AIR SCREW ADJUSTMENT

	Turns out from lightly seated*
1990	
Formula MX & MX LT (467)	1 1/2 turns
Formula Plus & Plus LT (536)	1 1/2 turns
Formula MACH 1 MACH 1 XTC (583)	1 1/2 turns
1991	
Formula MX, MX E, MX XTC & MX XTC E (467)	1 1/2 turns
Formula MX X (467)	1 1/2 turns
Formula Plus, Plus E, Plus XTC & Plus XTC E (536)	1 1/2 turns
Formula Plus X (536)	1 1/2 turns
Formula MACH 1 & XTC (643)	2 turns
Formula MACH 1 X (643)	1 1/2 turns
1992	
Formula MX & MX XTC R (467)	1 1/2 turns
Formula Plus, Plus E, Plus XTC & XTC E (582)	1 1/2 turns
Formula Plus X (583)	1 1/2 turns
Formula MACH 1, MACH 1 XTC &	
MACH 1 XTC II (643)	2 turns
Formula MACH 1 X (670)	2 turns
1993	
Formula MX &, MX XTC R (467)	1 1/2 turns
Formula MX Z (467)	1 1/3 turns
Formula Plus, Plus E & Plus XTC (582)	1 1/2 turns
Formula Plus X (583)	1 1/2 turns
Formula MACH 1 & MACH 1 XTC (670)	2 3/4 turns
Formula Grand Touring (582)	1 1/2 turns
1994	
Formula MX & MX Z (467)	3/4 turn
Summit 470 (470 HAC)	1 5/8 turns
Formula MX Z X (467)	
Formula ST (467)	3/4 turn
Formula STX & STX II (583)	1 turn
Formula Z (583)	3/4 turn
Summit 583 HAC	2 1/4 turns
MACH 1 & Grand Touring SE (670)	3/4 turn
Grand Touring & Grand Touring XTC (582)	1 1/4 turns
1995	
MX (467)	1 turn
MX Z (454)	1/2 turn

(continued)

Table 11 CARBURETOR PILOT AIR SCREW ADJUSTMENT (continued)

	Turns out from lightly seated*
1995 (continued)	
Formula SS (670)	1 turn
Formula STX (583)	1 1/2 turns
Summit 583	1 turn
Summit 670	1 1/8 turns
Formula STX (LT) (583)	1 1/2 turns
Formula Z (583)	1 turn
MACH 1 (670)	1 turn
Grand Touring 470(467)	1 turn
Grand Touring 580 (582)	1 1/4 turns
Grand Touring SE (670)	1 1/8 turns

* The listed number indicates the recommended initial setting and is usually correct within ± 1/8 turn.

Table 12 ENGINE IDLE SPEED

1990-1992	
All models	1,800-2,000 rpm
1993	
Formula MX Z (467)	1,500-1,700 rpm
All other models	1,800-2,000 rpm
1994	
Formula MX & MX Z (467)	1,600-1,800 rpm
Summit 470 (470 HAC)	1,500-1,700 rpm
Formula MX Z X (467)	1,600-1,800 rpm
Formula ST (467)	1,600-1,800 rpm
Formula STX & STX II (583)	1,800-2,000 rpm
Formula Z (583)	1,500-1,800 rpm
Summit 583 HAC	1,800-2,000 rpm
MACH 1 & Grand Touring SE (670)	1,800-2,000 rpm
Grand Touring & Grand Touring XTC (582)	1,800-2,000 rpm
1995	
MX (467), MX Z (454) & Grand Touring 470(467)	1,600-1,800 rpm
All other models	1,800-2,000 rpm

Table 13 TRACK SPECIFICATIONS

Year Model	Force Kg.	(lb.)	Deflection mm	(in.)
1990				
All models	7.3	(16)	40	(1 9/16)
1991				
MACH 1	7.3	(16)	30	(1 3/16)
Other models	7.3	(16)	40	(1 9/16)
1992				
All models	7.3	(16)	40	(1 9/16)
1993				
Formula MX Z	7.3	(16)	45-50	(1 3/4-1 31/32)
Other models	7.3	(16)	40-45	(1 9/16-1 3/4)
1994				
Grand Touring & MACH 1	7.3	(16)	40-45	(1 9/16-1 3/4)
Other models	7.3	(16)	45-50	(1 3/4-1 31/32)
1995				
All models	7.3	(16)	45-50	(1 3/4-1 31/32)

Chapter Four

High Altitude and Rear Suspension Adjustment

If the snowmobile is to deliver its maximum efficiency and peak performance, the engine and chassis must be properly adjusted to the conditions in which it is being operated. This chapter describes carburetor changes for different altitudes and adjustments to the rear suspension for different snow conditions.

Basic tune-up procedures are described in Chapter Three. **Tables 1-10** are found at the end of the chapter.

CARBURETOR TUNING

Ski-Doo snowmobiles are tuned at the factory for sea level conditions. However, when the snowmobile is operated at a higher altitude, engine performance will drop because of a change in air density. At sea level, the air is much denser than the air at 10,000 ft. (3048 m). You should figure on a 3% loss of power output for every 1,000 ft. (305 m) of elevation change (increase). This decrease in power is caused by a drop in cylinder pressure and a change in the fuel/air ratio. For example, an engine that produces 40 horsepower at sea level will produce approximately 38.8 horsepower at 1,000 ft. (305 m). At 10,000 ft. (3048 m), the engine produces 29.5 horsepower. With sea level jetting, the engine would run extremely rich at 10,000 ft. (3048 m).

Conversely, if the carburetors are adjusted for proper operation at 10,000 ft. (3048 m) altitude, the engine would run lean when operated at lower altitudes. Lean conditions reduce performance, but also lead to overheating and detonation, which can both result in severe engine damage.

Air temperature must also be considered when jetting the carburetor. For example, the carburetors are set at the factory to run at temperatures of 32 - –4° F (0 - –20° C) at sea level. If the snowmobile is to be operated under conditions other than those specified, the carburetors must be adjusted accordingly.

Figure 1 illustrates the different carburetor circuits and how they overlap during engine operation.

Before changing carburetor jets, make the following adjustments as described in Chapter Three:

a. Throttle cable, pilot screw, idle speed and carburetor synchronization.

b. Oil pump adjustment.

> *NOTE*
> *Changes in port shape and smoothness, or installing a different expansion chamber or carburetor, will also require jetting changes because these factors alter the engine's ability to breathe. Aftermarket equipment manufacturers often include a tech sheet listing suitable jetting changes to correspond to their equipment or modification. This information should be taken into account along with altitude and temperature conditions previously mentioned.*

> *NOTE*
> *It is important to note that the following jetting procedures should be used as guidelines only. Individual adjustments will vary because of altitude, temperature and snow conditions. The condition of the spark plugs should be used as the determining factor when changing jets and adjusting the carburetor.*

Carburetor Adjustment

Refer to **Table 1** for recommended standard jet size originally installed in your model. It may be necessary to reduce the jet size when the snowmobile is going to be run at high altitude. Replace jets as required. Refer to Chapter Six for carburetor removal and disassembly.

Low-speed tuning

The pilot jet and pilot air screw control the fuel mixture from idle to about 1/4 throttle (**Figure 1**). In addition, the pilot air screw controls mixture adjustment when the throttle is opened from idle to the full-open position quickly and when the engine is run at half-throttle. Note the following when adjusting the pilot air screw:

a. Turning the pilot air screw clockwise enrichens the fuel mixture.

b. Turning the pilot air screw counterclockwise leans the fuel mixture.

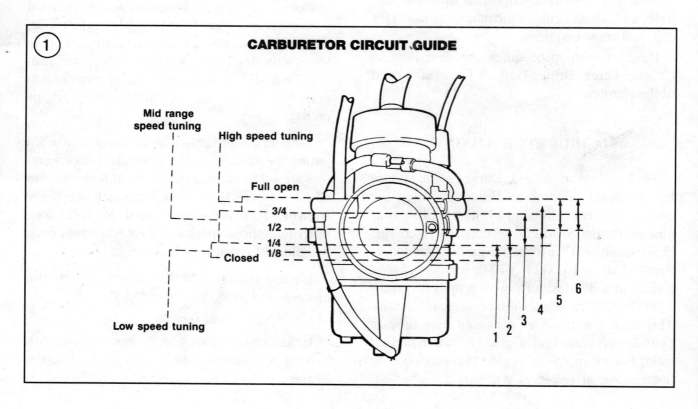

① **CARBURETOR CIRCUIT GUIDE**

Mid range speed tuning
High speed tuning
Full open
3/4
1/2
1/4
Closed
1/8
Low speed tuning
1 2 3 4 5 6

c. Pilot jets are identified by number. Pilot jets with larger numbers will flow more fuel than jets with smaller numbers. Installing jets with larger numbers will richen the fuel mixture.

d. When operating the snowmobile in relatively warm weather or at a higher altitude, turn the pilot air screw counterclockwise. When operating the snowmobile in excessively cold weather conditions, turn the pilot air screw clockwise.

1. Open the hood.

NOTE
Figure 2 shows the carburetor removed for clarity.

2. Locate the pilot air screws on the side of each carburetor (**Figure 2**).

3. Turn both pilot air screws in until they lightly seat. Then back the screws out the number of turns specified in **Table 2** for your model.

4. Start the engine and allow it to warm up to normal operating temperature.

NOTE
Figure 3 shows the carburetor removed for clarity.

5. Adjust the throttle stop screw (**Figure 3**) until the engine is idling at the rpm listed for your model in **Table 3**. Then slowly turn the pilot air screws (**Figure 2**) counterclockwise. (Turning the pilot air screws counterclockwise will lean the fuel mixture.) Continue to turn the pilot air screws counterclockwise until the highest engine speed is reached. When the highest speed is reached, adjust the throttle stop screw (**Figure 3**) to set the idle speed to the specification listed in **Table 3**.

6. Operate the engine and check performance. If the engine performance is off at high-altitudes or in extremely cold areas or if the off-idle pickup is poor, install larger pilot jets. Refer to Chapter Six for carburetor removal and disassembly.

7. After replacing the pilot jets, repeat Steps 2-6.

Mid-range tuning

The jet needle controls the mixture at medium speeds, from approximately 1/4 to 3/4 throttle (**Figure 1**). The jet needle has 2 operating ends. The top of the needle has 5 evenly spaced circlip grooves (**Figure 4**). The bottom half of the needle is tapered; this portion extends into the needle jet. While the jet needle is fixed into position by the circlip, fuel cannot flow through the space between the needle jet and jet needle until the throttle valve is raised approximately 1/4 open. When the throttle valve is raised, the tapered portion of the jet needle moves out of the needle jet (**Figure 5**). The grooves in the upper end of the jet needle permit adjustment of the mid-range mixture ratio. Installing the clip in a higher groove will lower the needle deeper in the jet, causing the mixture to be leaner. Installing the

4

clip in a lower groove will raise the needle and will result in a richer mixture.

1. Open the hood.

> *NOTE*
> *Prior to removing the top cap, thoroughly clean the area around it so that no dirt can fall into the carburetor.*

2. Unscrew and remove the carburetor top cap (**Figure 6**) and pull the throttle valve assembly (**Figure 7**) from the carburetor.

3. Remove the jet needle (**Figure 8**) from the throttle valve.

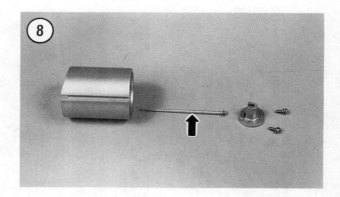

Adjustment positions

Lean

Rich

Jet needle

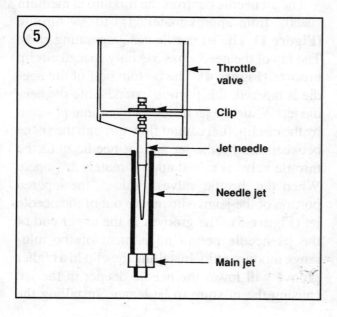

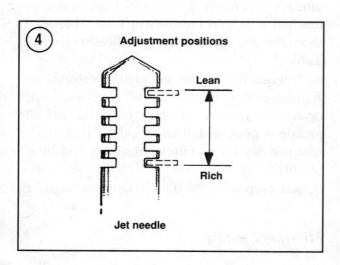

Throttle valve

Clip

Jet needle

Needle jet

Main jet

NOTE
Some models have a washer installed on the jet needle. Don't lose it when removing the jet needle.

4. Note the position of the clip (**Figure 4**) before removing it. Remove the clip and reposition it on the jet needle. Make sure the clip seats in the needle groove completely.

5. Reverse to install. Make sure the O-ring in the cap is positioned correctly (**Figure 9**) before installing the cap.

High-speed tuning

The main jet controls the mixture from 3/4 to full throttle and has some effect at lesser throttle openings (**Figure 1**). Each main jet is stamped with a number. Larger numbers provide a richer mixture and smaller numbers a leaner mixture.

Refer to **Table 1** for standard size main jet originally installed.

When operating the snowmobile in relatively warm weather or at a higher altitude, a smaller main jet should be used. When operating the snowmobile in excessively cold weather conditions, install a larger main jet.

CAUTION
The information given in Step 1 for determining main jet sizes should be used as a guideline only. Because of variables that exist with each individual machine, the spark plug condition should be used as the determining factor. When in doubt, always jet on the rich side.

1. After determining the altitude and temperature range that the snowmobile will be operated in, refer to the portion of **Figure 10** that allows

---

(10) **CARBURETOR MAIN JET CORRECTION CHART**

ALTITUDE	TEMPERATURE °F (°C)							
feet (meters)	–60 (–50)	–40 (–40)	–20 (–30)	0 (–20)	14 (–10)	32 (0)	50 (10)	70 (20)
0 – Sea level	250	240	230	220	210	200	190	180
2,000 (600)	240	230	220	210	200	190	180	170
4,000 (1,200)	220	210	210	200	190	180	170	160
6,000 (1,800)	210	200	200	190	180	170	160	155
8,000 (2,400)	200	195	190	180	170	160	155	150
10,000 (3,000)	195	185	180	170	160	155	150	145

ALTITUDE	TEMPERATURE °F (°C)							
feet (meters)	–60 (–50)	–40 (–40)	–20 (–30)	0 (–20)	14 (–10)	32 (0)	50 (10)	70 (20)
0 – Sea level	260	250	240	230	220	220	210	195
2,000 (600)	250	240	230	220	210	200	195	190
4,000 (1,200)	230	220	210	210	200	195	190	180
6,000 (1,800)	220	210	200	200	185	180	175	170
8,000 (2,400)	210	200	195	190	175	170	170	160
10,000 (3,000)	200	195	185	180	160	155	150	140

ALTITUDE	TEMPERATURE °F (°C)							
feet (meters)	–60 (–50)	–40 (–40)	–20 (–30)	0 (–20)	14 (–10)	32 (0)	50 (10)	70 (20)
0 – Sea level	270	260	250	240	230	230	220	200
2,000 (600)	260	250	240	230	220	210	200	190
4,000 (1,200)	240	230	220	210	210	200	190	180
6,000 (1,800)	230	220	210	200	195	190	180	170
8,000 (2,400)	220	210	200	195	185	175	170	160
10,000 (3,000)	210	200	185	175	165	160	150	140

(continued)

(10) (continued)

ALTITUDE	TEMPERATURE °F (°C)							
feet (meters)	–60 (–50)	–40 (–40)	–20 (–30)	0 (–20)	14 (–10)	32 (0)	50 (10)	70 (20)
0 – Sea level	280	270	260	250	240	240	230	220
2,000 (600)	270	260	250	240	230	220	210	200
4,000 (1,200)	250	240	230	220	210	210	200	190
6,000 (1,800)	240	230	220	210	200	195	190	180
8,000 (2,400)	230	210	200	190	195	185	175	165
10,000 (3,000)	210	200	190	180	175	165	160	150

ALTITUDE	TEMPERATURE °F (°C)							
feet (meters)	–60 (–50)	–40 (–40)	–20 (–30)	0 (–20)	14 (–10)	32 (0)	50 (10)	70 (20)
0 – Sea level	290	280	270	260	250	250	240	230
2,000 (600)	280	270	260	250	240	240	230	220
4,000 (1,200)	260	260	250	240	230	230	220	210
6,000 (1,800)	250	230	220	210	200	200	190	180
8,000 (2,400)	240	210	200	190	185	175	170	160
10,000 (3,000)	220	200	190	180	175	165	160	150

ALTITUDE	TEMPERATURE °F (°C)							
feet (meters)	–60 (–50)	–40 (–40)	–20 (–30)	0 (–20)	14 (–10)	32 (0)	50 (10)	70 (20)
0 – Sea level	300	290	280	270	260	250	230	210
2,000 (600)	290	280	270	260	250	240	210	200
4,000 (1,200)	270	260	250	240	230	220	200	195
6,000 (1,800)	260	250	240	230	220	210	195	175
8,000 (2,400)	250	240	230	220	210	200	175	170
10,000 (3,000)	230	220	210	200	190	180	170	160

ALTITUDE	TEMPERATURE °F (°C)							
feet (meters)	–60 (–50)	–40 (–40)	–20 (–30)	0 (–20)	14 (–10)	32 (0)	50 (10)	70 (20)
0 – Sea level	310	300	290	280	270	260	250	240
2,000 (600)	300	290	280	270	260	250	240	230
4,000 (1,200)	290	280	270	260	250	240	230	220
6,000 (1,800)	280	270	260	250	240	230	220	210
8,000 (2,400)	270	260	250	240	230	220	210	200
10,000 (3,000)	260	250	240	230	220	210	200	190

ALTITUDE	TEMPERATURE °F (°C)							
feet (meters)	–60 (–50)	–40 (–40)	–20 (–30)	0 (–20)	14 (–10)	32 (0)	50 (10)	70 (20)
0 – Sea level	320	310	300	290	280	270	260	250
2,000 (600)	310	300	290	280	270	260	250	240
4,000 (1,200)	300	290	280	270	260	250	240	230
6,000 (1,800)	290	280	270	260	250	240	230	220
8,000 (2,400)	280	270	260	250	240	230	220	210
10,000 (3,000)	270	260	250	240	230	220	210	200

(continued)

(continued)

ALTITUDE	TEMPERATURE °F (°C)							
feet (meters)	−60 (−50)	−40 (−40)	−20 (−30)	0 (−20)	14 (−10)	32 (0)	50 (10)	70 (20)
0 – Sea level	330	320	310	300	290	280	270	260
2,000 (600)	320	310	300	290	280	270	260	250
4,000 (1,200)	310	300	290	280	270	260	250	240
6,000 (1,800)	300	290	280	270	260	250	240	230
8,000 (2,400)	290	280	270	260	250	240	230	220
10,000 (3,000)	280	270	260	250	240	230	220	210

ALTITUDE	TEMPERATURE °F (°C)							
feet (meters)	−60 (−50)	−40 (−40)	−20 (−30)	0 (−20)	14 (−10)	32 (0)	50 (10)	70 (20)
0 – Sea level	350	340	330	320	310	300	290	280
2,000 (600)	340	330	320	310	300	290	280	270
4,000 (1,200)	330	320	310	300	290	280	270	260
6,000 (1,800)	320	310	300	290	280	270	260	250
8,000 (2,400)	310	300	290	280	270	260	250	240
10,000 (3,000)	300	290	280	270	260	250	240	230

ALTITUDE	TEMPERATURE °F (°C)							
feet (meters)	−60 (−50)	−40 (−40)	−20 (−30)	0 (−20)	14 (−10)	32 (0)	50 (10)	70 (20)
0 – Sea level	360	350	340	330	320	310	300	290
2,000 (600)	350	340	330	320	310	300	290	280
4,000 (1,200)	340	330	320	310	300	290	280	270
6,000 (1,800)	330	320	310	300	290	280	270	260
8,000 (2,400)	320	310	300	290	280	270	260	250
10,000 (3,000)	310	300	290	280	270	260	250	240

ALTITUDE	TEMPERATURE °F (°C)							
feet (meters)	−60 (−50)	−40 (−40)	−20 (−30)	0 (−20)	14 (−10)	32 (0)	50 (10)	70 (20)
0 – Sea level	370	360	350	340	330	320	310	300
2,000 (600)	360	350	340	330	320	310	300	290
4,000 (1,200)	350	340	330	320	310	300	290	280
6,000 (1,800)	340	330	320	310	300	290	280	270
8,000 (2,400)	330	320	310	300	290	280	270	260
10,000 (3,000)	320	310	300	290	280	270	260	250

ALTITUDE	TEMPERATURE °F (°C)							
feet (meters)	−60 (−50)	−40 (−40)	−20 (−30)	0 (−20)	14 (−10)	32 (0)	50 (10)	70 (20)
0 – Sea level	380	370	360	350	340	330	320	310
2,000 (600)	370	360	350	340	330	320	310	300
4,000 (1,200)	360	350	340	330	320	310	300	290
6,000 (1,800)	350	340	330	320	310	300	290	280
8,000 (2,400)	340	330	320	310	300	290	280	270
10,000 (3,000)	330	320	310	300	290	280	270	260

(continued)

4

⑩ (continued)

ALTITUDE	TEMPERATURE °F (°C)							
feet (meters)	–60 (–50)	–40 (–40)	–20 (–30)	0 (–20)	14 (–10)	32 (0)	50 (10)	70 (20)
0 – Sea level	390	380	370	360	350	340	330	320
2,000 (600)	380	370	360	350	340	330	320	310
4,000 (1,200)	370	360	350	340	330	320	310	300
6,000 (1,800)	360	350	340	330	320	310	300	290
8,000 (2,400)	350	340	330	320	310	300	290	280
10,000 (3,000)	340	330	320	310	300	290	280	270

ALTITUDE	TEMPERATURE °F (°C)							
feet (meters)	–60 (–50)	–40 (–40)	–20 (–30)	0 (–20)	14 (–10)	32 (0)	50 (10)	70 (20)
0 – Sea level	400	390	380	370	360	350	340	330
2,000 (600)	390	380	370	360	350	340	330	320
4,000 (1,200)	380	370	360	350	340	330	320	310
6,000 (1,800)	370	360	350	340	330	320	310	300
8,000 (2,400)	360	350	340	330	320	310	300	290
10,000 (3,000)	350	340	330	320	310	300	290	280

ALTITUDE	TEMPERATURE °F (°C)							
feet (meters)	–60 (–50)	–40 (–40)	–20 (–30)	0 (–20)	14 (–10)	32 (0)	50 (10)	70 (20)
0 – Sea level	410	400	390	380	370	360	350	340
2,000 (600)	400	390	380	370	360	350	340	330
4,000 (1,200)	390	380	370	360	350	340	330	320
6,000 (1,800)	380	370	360	350	340	330	320	310
8,000 (2,400)	370	360	350	340	330	320	310	300
10,000 (3,000)	360	350	340	330	320	310	300	290

ALTITUDE	TEMPERATURE °F (°C)							
feet (meters)	–60 (–50)	–40 (–40)	–20 (–30)	0 (–20)	14 (–10)	32 (0)	50 (10)	70 (20)
0 – Sea level	420	410	400	390	380	370	360	350
2,000 (600)	410	400	390	380	370	360	350	340
4,000 (1,200)	400	390	380	370	360	350	340	330
6,000 (1,800)	390	380	370	360	350	340	330	320
8,000 (2,400)	380	370	360	350	340	330	320	310
10,000 (3,000)	370	360	350	340	330	320	310	300

ALTITUDE	TEMPERATURE °F (°C)							
feet (meters)	–60 (–50)	–40 (–40)	–20 (–30)	0 (–20)	14 (–10)	32 (0)	50 (10)	70 (20)
0 – Sea level	430	420	410	400	390	380	370	360
2,000 (600)	420	410	400	390	380	370	360	350
4,000 (1,200)	410	400	390	380	370	360	350	340
6,000 (1,800)	400	390	380	370	360	350	340	330
8,000 (2,400)	390	380	370	360	350	340	330	320
10,000 (3,000)	380	370	360	350	340	330	320	310

(continued)

(continued)

ALTITUDE	TEMPERATURE °F (°C)							
feet (meters)	–60 (–50)	–40 (–40)	–20 (–30)	0 (–20)	14 (–10)	32 (0)	50 (10)	70 (20)
0 – Sea level	450	440	430	**420**	410	400	390	380
2,000 (600)	440	430	420	410	400	390	380	370
4,000 (1,200)	430	420	410	400	390	380	370	360
6,000 (1,800)	420	410	400	390	380	370	360	350
8,000 (2,400)	410	400	390	380	370	360	350	340
10,000 (3,000)	400	390	380	370	360	350	340	330

ALTITUDE	TEMPERATURE °F (°C)							
feet (meters)	–60 (–50)	–40 (–40)	–20 (–30)	0 (–20)	14 (–10)	32 (0)	50 (10)	70 (20)
0 – Sea level	470	460	450	**440**	430	420	410	400
2,000 (600)	460	450	440	430	420	410	400	390
4,000 (1,200)	450	440	430	420	410	400	390	380
6,000 (1,800)	440	430	420	410	400	390	380	370
8,000 (2,400)	430	420	410	400	390	380	370	360
10,000 (3,000)	420	410	400	390	380	370	360	350

ALTITUDE	TEMPERATURE °F (°C)							
feet (meters)	–60 (–50)	–40 (–40)	–20 (–30)	0 (–20)	14 (–10)	32 (0)	50 (10)	70 (20)
0 – Sea level	510	500	490	**480**	470	460	450	440
2,000 (600)	500	490	480	470	460	450	440	430
4,000 (1,200)	490	480	470	460	450	440	430	420
6,000 (1,800)	480	470	460	450	440	430	420	410
8,000 (2,400)	470	460	450	440	430	420	410	400
10,000 (3,000)	460	450	440	430	420	410	400	390

ALTITUDE	TEMPERATURE °F (°C)							
feet (meters)	–60 (–50)	–40 (–40)	–20 (–30)	0 (–20)	14 (–10)	32 (0)	50 (10)	70 (20)
0 – Sea level	520	510	500	**490**	480	470	460	450
2,000 (600)	510	500	490	480	470	460	450	440
4,000 (1,200)	500	490	480	470	460	450	440	430
6,000 (1,800)	490	480	470	460	450	440	430	420
8,000 (2,400)	480	470	460	450	440	430	420	410
10,000 (3,000)	470	460	450	440	430	420	410	400

ALTITUDE	TEMPERATURE °F (°C)							
feet (meters)	–60 (–50)	–40 (–40)	–20 (–30)	0 (–20)	14 (–10)	32 (0)	50 (10)	70 (20)
0 – Sea level	610	600	590	**580**	570	560	550	540
2,000 (600)	600	590	580	570	560	550	540	530
4,000 (1,200)	590	580	570	560	550	540	530	520
6,000 (1,800)	580	570	560	550	540	530	520	510
8,000 (2,400)	570	560	550	540	530	520	510	500
10,000 (3,000)	560	550	540	530	520	510	500	490

4

you to compute the necessary jet changes as follows:

   a. Refer to **Table 1** to determine the standard size of main jet for your model.

   b. Find the standard size main jet listed for your snowmobile at sea level and at 0° F (–20° C) in **Figure 10** (white numbers on black).

   c. Cross reference the corrected size for the altitude and temperature in which your snowmobile will be operating.

   d. For example, if the standard size listed for your model is 220 (when operating at 0° F and sea level), then if operating at 14° F and 4,000 ft. (1,219 m) altitude the approximate size of the main jet is 195.

> *CAUTION*
> *The sizes listed in the Correction Chart are approximate and should only be used as a guide. It is still important to analyze the spark plugs to be sure the fuel-to-air ratio is correct and not too lean.*

2. Refer to Chapter Six for carburetor removal and installation. Then replace main jets as required.

3. Reinstall the carburetor as described in Chapter Six.

> *CAUTION*
> *Do not run the engine without the air intake silencer installed as engine seizure may result.*

> *WARNING*
> *If you are taking spark plug readings, the engine will be HOT! Use caution because the fuel in the float bowl will spill out when the main jet cover is removed from the bottom of the float bowl. Have a fire extinguisher and an assistant standing by when performing this procedure.*

4. Run the snowmobile at high speed and then stop the engine.

5. Open the hood and remove the spark plugs. Read the spark plugs as described in this chapter.

6. Reinstall the spark plugs.

7. If it is necessary to change main jets, perform the following:

   a. Remove the carburetor as described in Chapter Six.

   b. Remove the float bowl (**Figure 11**).

   c. Remove and replace the main jet (**Figure 12**).

   d. Reinstall the float bowl. Make sure the float bowl gasket is in place and not torn or damaged.

   e. Repeat for the opposite carburetor.

   f. Reinstall the carburetors as described in Chapter Six.

   g. Make sure the throttle cables work smoothly before starting the engine.

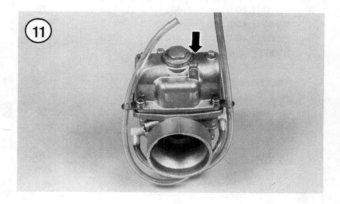

Reading Spark Plugs

Because the firing end of a spark plug operates in the combustion chamber, it reflects the operating condition of the engine. Much information about engine and spark plug performance can be determined by careful examination of the spark plug. This information is more valid after performing the following steps. Refer to **Figure 13**.

1. Ride the snowmobile a short distance at full throttle.

2. Turn the ignition switch to the OFF position before closing the throttle, coast and brake to a stop.

3. Remove the spark plugs and examine them. Refer to **Figure 13**.

Normal condition

If the plug has a light tan-or gray-colored deposit and no abnormal gap wear or erosion, good engine carburetion and ignition condition are indicated. The plug in use is of the proper heat range and may be serviced and returned to use.

Carbon fouled

Soft, dry, sooty deposits covering the entire firing end of the plug are evidence of incomplete combustion. Even though the firing end of the plug is dry, the plug's insulation decreases. An electrical path is formed that lowers the voltage from the ignition sysstem. Engine misfiring is a sign of carbon fouling. Carbon fouling can be caused by one or more of the following:

a. Too rich fuel mixture (incorrect jetting).

b. Spark plug heat range too cold.

c. Over-retarded ignition timing.

d. Ignition component failure.

e. Low engine compression.

Oil fouled

The tip of an oil fouled plug has a black insulator tip, a damp oily film over the firing end and a carbon layer over the entire nose. The electrodes will not be worn. Common causes for this condition are:

a. Too much oil in the fuel (incorrect jetting or incorrect oil pump adjustment).

b. Wrong type of oil.

c. Ignition component failure.

d. Spark plug heat range too cold.

e. Engine still being broken in.

Oil fouled spark plugs may be cleaned in an emergency, but it is better to replace them. It is important to correct the cause of fouling before the engine is returned to service.

Gap bridging

Plugs with this condition exhibit gaps shorted by combustion deposits between the electrodes. If this condition is encountered, check for an improper oil type, excessive carbon in combustion chamber or a clogged exhaust port and pipe. Be sure to locate and correct the cause of this condition.

Overheating

Badly worn electrodes and premature gap wear and signs of overheating, along with a gray or white "blistered" porcelain insulator surface. The most common cause for this condition is using a spark plug of the wrong heat range (too hot). If you have not changed to a hotter spark plug and the plug is overheated, consider the following causes:

a. Lean fuel mixture (incorect main jet or incorrect oil pump adjustmenet).

b. Ignition timing too advanced.

c. Cooling system malfunction.

d. Engine air leak.

4

13

SPARK PLUG CONDITIONS

NORMAL

GAP BRIDGED

CARBON FOULED

OVERHEATED

OIL FOULED

SUSTAINED PREIGNITION

e. Improper spark plug installation (overtightening).

f. No spark plug gasket.

Worn out

Corrosive gases formed by combustion and high voltage sparks have eroded the electrodes. Spark plugs in this condition require more voltage to fire under hard acceleration. Replace with a new spark plug.

Preignition

If the electrodes are melted, preignition is almost certainly the cause. Check for carburetor mounting or intake manifold leaks and overadvanced ignition timing. It is also possible that a plug of the wrong heat range (too hot) is being used. Find the cause of the preignition before returning the engine into service.

HIGH-ALTITUDE CLUTCH TUNING

Standard clutch and drive specifications are listed in **Tables 4-7**. When the snowmobile is operated at an altitude of more than 4,000 ft. (1,200 m), it may be necessary to adjust the clutch to compensate for engine power loss. If the clutch is not adjusted, the engine may bog down when the belt engages. The engine is also easier to bog when running in deep snow. Both conditions can lead to premature drive belt failure.

Refer to Chapter Thirteen for complete clutch service procedures.

GEARING

Depending upon altitude, snow and track conditions, a different gear ratio may be required. Snow conditions that offer few rough sections require a higher gear ratio. Less optimum snow conditions or more rugged terrain require a lower gear ratio. Refer to the standard gear ratio chart in **Table 8**. Replacement sprockets and chains can be purchased through Ski-Doo dealers. Refer to Chapter Fourteen for sprocket and chain replacement procedures.

SUSPENSION ADJUSTMENT

The suspension can be adjusted to accommodate rider weight and snow conditions.

Correct suspension adjustment is arrived at largely through a matter of trial-and-error "tuning." There are several fundamental points that must be understood and applied before the suspension can be successfully adjusted to your needs.

Ski pressure—the load on the skis relative to the load on the track—is the primary factor controlling handling performance. If the ski pressure is too light, the front of the machine tends to float and steering control becomes vague, with the machine tending to drive straight ahead rather than turn, and wander when running straight at steady throttle.

On the other hand, if ski pressure is too heavy, the machine tends to plow during cornering and the skis dig in during straight line running rather than stay on top of the snow.

Ski pressure for one snow condition is not necessarily good for another condition. For instance, if the surface is very hard and offers little steering traction, added ski pressure—to permit the skis to "bite" into the snow—is desirable. Also, the hard surface will support the skis and not allow them to penetrate when the machine is running in a straight line under power.

On the other hand, if the surface is soft and tacky, lighter ski pressure is desirable to prevent the skis from sinking into the snow. Also, the increased traction afforded by the snow will allow the skis to turn with light pressure.

It's apparent, then, that good suspension adjustment involves a through analysis relating to ski pressure versus conditions. The suspension has been set at the factory to work in most conditions encountered by general riding. However, when the snowmobile is operated in varying or more difficult conditions, the suspension should be adjusted. It is important to remember that suspension tuning is a compromise. An adjustment that works well in one situation may not work as well in another.

Front spring preload
(all models without HPG shocks)

The front spring (**Figure 14**) is provided with 5 preload positions. See **Figure 15**. The No. 1 position is soft and the No. 5 position hard. The No. 1 position may be sufficient with light load and smooth terrain, while the No. 5 position reduces bottoming over large bumps with a heaver rider. The spring preload is changed by rotating the cam at the end of each spring. Use the adjustment key (or wrench) to turn the cam. The adjusting cam may be located at the upper end of the shock absorber on some models.

Front suspension spring preload
(models with HPG nitrogen charged shocks)

The front suspension shock absorber spring is provided with adjusting nuts to adjust spring preload. See **Figure 16**. Initial setting for the first preload ring is 85.5 mm (3.11/32 in.) from the end as shown at A, **Figure 16**.

After setting the position of the first preload ring, tighten the second ring nut against the first to lock it in place. Be sure to also check the pressure of the nitrogen charge. Charge should be 2070 kPa (300 psi). Install the cap (B, **Figure 16**) over the Schrader valve.

CAUTION
Use a suitable, regulated nitrogen filling tank, regulator, gauge, hose and fittings to charge the shock with gas. If suitable

equipment is not available, take the shock to a Ski-Doo dealer.

Rear suspension spring preload
(all models without HPG shocks)

The rear suspension is provided with three shock absorbers, each equipped with a spring. The spring located at the front center of the rear suspension is refered to as the center unit. The two shock absorbers located at the rear of the rear suspension are refered to as the rear units.

The *center* unit is provided with 5 preload positions. See **Figure 17**. The No. 1 position is soft and the No. 5 position hard. The No. 1

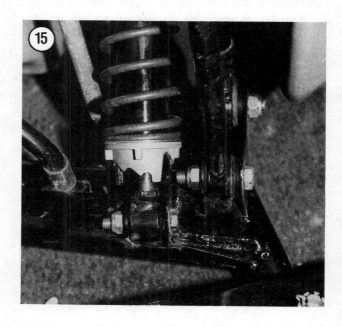

position works well when riding over small bumps and provides more positive steering. The No. 5 position reduces bottoming over large bumps but steering is reduced. The spring preload is changed by rotating the cams at the end of the spring. To adjust the front shock preload, remove the front shock as described in Chapter Sixteen. Use the adjustment key to turn the shock ring.

The *rear* units are also provided with 5 preload positions. See **Figure 18**. The No. 1 position is soft and the No. 5 position hard. Always adjust both shocks to the same preload position. Initial preload adjustment can be set according to rider weight. Note the following:

a. Up to 140 lbs. (64 kg): Position No. 1.

b. 140 lbs. (64 kg) to 160 lbs. (73 kg): Position No. 2.

c. 160 lbs. (73 kg) to 180 lbs. (82 kg): Position No. 3.

d. 180 lbs. (82 kg) and up: Position No. 4 or No. 5.

The suspension should collapse about 38 mm (1 1/2 in.) with a rider on the seat. After adjusting spring preload according to rider weight, consider track and speed conditions. Flat track conditions and low speeds require a smaller preload position. High terrain and fast speed conditions require a higher preload position.

If you are having difficulty adjusting the suspension with the stock spring, different spring rates are available from Ski-Doo dealers.

The rear spring preload is changed by rotating the cams (**Figure 18**) at the end of the spring.

Rear suspension spring preload (models with HPG nitrogen charged shocks)

The rear suspension is provided with three shock absorbers, each equipped with a spring. The spring located at the front center of the rear suspension is refered to as the center unit. The two shock absorbers located at the rear of the rear suspension are refered to as the rear units.

The *center* unit is provided with adjusting nuts to adjust spring preload. See **Figure 19**. Initial setting for the first preload ring is 104 mm (4.0 in.) from the end as shown at A, **Figure 19**.

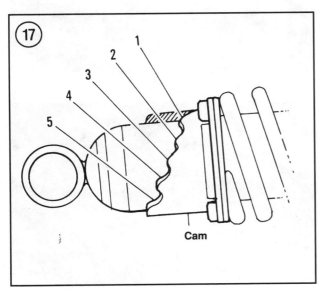

Cam

Spring preload is softer when distance (A, **Figure 19**) is less than the standard setting. The softer settings may work well when riding over small bumps at moderate speed and will provides more positive steering (because of increased ski ground pressure. Spring preload is more firm when distance (A, **Figure 19**) is longer than the standard setting. The firm settings may reduce bottoming over large bumps on rough trails. The firm settings will also reduce steering effort, but steering will be less positive. After setting the position of the first preload ring, tighten the second ring nut against the first to lock it in place. Be sure to also check the pressure of the nitrogen charge. Charge should be 2070 kPa (300 psi). Install the cap (B, **Figure 19**) over the Schrader valve.

> *CAUTION*
> *Use a suitable, regulated nitrogen filling tank, regulator, gauge, hose and fittings to charge the shock with gas. If suitable equipment is not available, take the shock to a Ski-Doo dealer.*

The rear shock absorbers (**Figure 20**) are also provided with adjusting nuts to adjust spring preload. Always adjust both shocks to the same preload position. Initial setting for the first preload ring is 78 mm (3.0 in.) from the end as shown at A, **Figure 20**. Spring preload is softer when distance (A, **Figure 20**) is less than the standard setting. The softer settings may reduce ski ground pressure. Spring preload is more firm when distance (A, **Figure 20**) is longer than the standard setting. The firm settings will lift the rear of the vehicle and increase rear suspension travel. The firm settings will also increase ski ground pressure.

After setting the position of the first preload ring, tighten the second ring nut against the first to lock it in place. Be sure to also check the pressure of the nitrogen charge. Charge should be 2070 kPa (300 psi). Install the cap over the Schrader valve.

Nitrogen Charged Shock Absorber

The shock absorber **Figure 19** used on some models is gas charged, rebuildable and (to some degree internally) adjustable.

Models With HPG Nitrogen Charged Shocks
Disassembly/Adjustment

Refer to **Figure 21**. Service to these nitrogen filled shock absorbers requires the use of a suitable, regulated nitrogen filling tank, regulator, gauge, hose and fittings to charge the shock with gas. If suitable equipment is not available, take the shock to a Ski-Doo dealer.

1. Remove the spring from the shock absorber as described in Chapter Fifteen or Chapter Sixteen.

2. Clean all components thoroughly in solvent and allow to dry.

3. Clamp the end of the damper body (3, **Figure 21**) in a soft jawed vise.

4. Use a 32 mm open end wrench to unscrew the seal assembly (14, **Figure 21**).

CAUTION
*Use care to prevent damage to the piston (10, **Figure 21**) by dragging it against the threads at the end of the body. Removing the piston assembly slowly will also reduce the amount of oil spilled during removal.*

5. Withdraw the piston and rod assembly slowly from the damper body.

WARNING
Be careful when using compressed air to remove the floating piston. Catch the floating piston in a cushion of shop towels to prevent damage to the piston.

6. Use compressed air introduced through the opening in the bottom of the damper body to blow the floating piston (4, **Figure 21**) from the body.

7. Clamp the end of the damper rod (15, **Figure 21**) in a soft jawed vise.

8. Remove the self locking retaining nut (5, **Figure 21**).

CAUTION
*The seal located in the assembly (14, **Figure 21**) will be damaged if removed from the rod and replacement parts may not be available. The seal does not need to be removed to change compression or rebound shims, so removal is not recommended.*

9. Carefully withdraw all parts from the rod and arrange in the sequence removed.

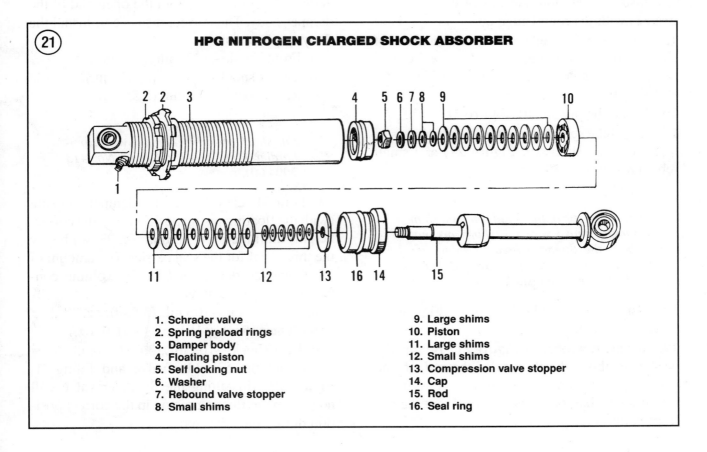

HPG NITROGEN CHARGED SHOCK ABSORBER

21

1. Schrader valve
2. Spring preload rings
3. Damper body
4. Floating piston
5. Self locking nut
6. Washer
7. Rebound valve stopper
8. Small shims
9. Large shims
10. Piston
11. Large shims
12. Small shims
13. Compression valve stopper
14. Cap
15. Rod
16. Seal ring

10. Check the runout of the rod (15, **Figure 21**) between V-blocks. Install a new shock absorber if runout exceeds 0.025 mm (0.001 in.).

11. Refer to **Table 5** and the following to select the thickness of shims (8, 9, 11 and 12, **Figure 21**).

  a. Be reluctant to deviate from the suggested shim selections listed in **Table 5**.

  b. The thickness of shims (8 and 9, **Figure 21**) controls rebound dampening.

  c. The thickness of shims (11 and 12 **Figure 21**) controls compression dampening.

  d. Both the diameter and thickness of the shims controls dampening.

12. If a new seal (14, **Figure 21**) is being installed over the rod, use a seal protector (part No. 529 0265 00).

13. Lubricate and install the O-ring (16, **Figure 21**) into its groove. Make sure the O-ring is not twisted or damaged.

14. Install the compression valve stop (13, **Figure 21**) with the round edge up.

15. Install the selected number and thickness of small compression shims (12, **Figure 21**) and large compression shims (11, **Figure 21**). Refer to **Table 10**.

16. Install the piston (10, **Figure 21**).

17. Install the selected number and thickness of large rebound shims (9, **Figure 21**) and small rebound shims (8, **Figure 21**).

NOTE
Check the top of the small rebound shim stack to make sure the shims are not above the threaded area. If shims are above the threads on rod, too many shims have been installed.

18. Install the rebound valve stop (7, **Figure 21**) with the rounded edge down.

19. Install the washer (6, **Figure 21**). Be sure the washer is above the threads of the rod. If one washer is not enough, it may be necessary to install more than one washer to prevent the nut from bottoming.

NOTE
*The self locking qualities of the nut (5, **Figure 21**) will be reduced with each use. Install a new nut after installing 4 times.*

20. Install the self locking nut (5, **Figure 21**) Tighten the nut to 11-13 N•m (96-108 in.-lb.) torque.

21. Lubricate the inside of the damper body (3, **Figure 21**) with molykote GN paste (part No. 413 7037 00).

22. Use the special guide (part No. 529 0266 00) and insert the floating piston (4, **Figure 21**) into the damper body.

NOTE
The floating piston separates the air from the shock oil and it must be positioned correctly so the correct amount of oil can be determined.

23. Push the floating piston into the bore until it is the correct distance from the open end of the damper body. The correct distance to install the floating piston is:

  a. Front shock—143 mm (5.62 in.).

  b. Center shock—140 mm (5.51 in.).

  c. Rear shock—141 mm (5.55 in.).

NOTE
Fill shock absorber damper with Bombardier HPG shock oil (part No. 413 7094 00).

24. Pour shock oil into the damper housing (with the floating piston positioned at the correct height) until the oil is 10 mm (0.393 in.) below the threads of for the seal carrier. The amount of oil should be determined by the volume contained, but will be about:

  a. Front shock—106 mL (3.58 fl. oz.).

  b. Center shock—101 mL (3.41 fl. oz.).

  c. Rear shock—103 mL (3.48 fl. oz.).

25. Install the Schrader valve and fitting (1, **Figure 21**). Installing the Schrader valve will help keep the floating piston in the correct position during the next steps.

NOTE
Push the damper piston into housing bore slowly. Be careful to not damage the piston seal on the threaded housing, do not force the floating piston to move, and do not force oil from the housing bore. The small passages in the piston and shims should fill with oil as the assembly is installed. Be careful not to trap air in the system.

26. Oil the damper piston sealing ring, then install the assembled piston, rod and damperer

shims into the damper housing. It may be necessary to move the piston up then down to force air through the piston assembly when installing. The piston should be below the level of the oil and should allow room to install the seal carrier.

27. Check the level of the oil, which should at least be above the lower threads of in the housing. Some oil may be forced out, but it is important that air is not trapped in the system. If oil is too low, it may be necessary to add oil.

28. Thread the seal carrier into the housing bore and tighten to 88-98 N•m (64-72 ft.-lb.) torque.

Stopper Strap

High-performance 1993 and later models are equipped with one or two stopper straps. See **Figure 22**. On models so equipped, the stopper strap or straps are designed to control weight transfer during acceleration. When the belt(s) are longer, the track lead angle can be greater and more weight will be transfered to the track, resulting in better traction. When the belt(s) are shorter, the track lead angle will be less, allowing less weight transfer, but will also result in more positive steering control. It is important that both straps, on models with 2 straps, be adjusted to the same length.

Limiter Screw Adjustment

On models so equipped, the limiter screw (**Figure 23**) controls weight transfer during acceleration. Adjustment is provided by changing the length of the limiter screw with the adjust nut. Note the following:

a. To provide less ski pressure and more speed, adjust the nut so it is *further away* from the cotter pin (or end of screw).

b. To provide more ski pressure and more steering stability, adjust the nut so it is *closer* to the cotter pin (or end of screw).

Table 1 CARBURETOR APPLICATION

Year model	Main jet	Needle jet	Float setting
1990			
Formula MX & MX LT (467)			
PTO side (VM 34-352A)	220	159 P-4	22-24 mm
Magneto side (VM 34-353A)	240	159 P-4	22-24 mm
Formula Plus & Plus LT (536)			
Both Carbs. (VM 34-381)	250	159 Q-4	22-24 mm
Formula MACH 1 MACH 1 XTC (583)			
PTO side (VM 38-214)	340	480 P-4	16-18 mm
Magneto side (VM 38-215)	360	480 P-2	16-18 mm
1991			
Formula MX, MX E, MX XTC & MX XTC E (467)			
PTO side (VM 34-352A)	230	159 P-6	23-25 mm
Magneto side (VM 34-353A)	240	159 P-4	23-25 mm
Formula MX X (467)			
PTO side (VM 38-239)	390	480 P-4	16-18 mm
Magneto side (VM 38-240)	400	480 P-4	16-18 mm
Formula Plus, Plus E, Plus XTC & Plus XTC E (536)			
PTO side (VM 34-408)	260	159 Q-6	23-25 mm
Magneto side (VM 34-409)	260	159 Q-6	23-25 mm
Formula Plus X (536)			
PTO side (VM 38-231)	360	480 P-4	16-18 mm
Magneto side (VM 38-215)	360	480 P-2	16-18 mm
Formula MACH 1 & XTC (643)			
PTO side (VM 40-48C)	400	224-BB-0	17-19 mm
Magneto side (VM 40-49C)	420	224-BB-0	17-19 mm
Formula MACH 1 X (643)			
PTO side (VM 44-27A)	580	224-BB-0	17-19 mm
Magneto side (VM 44-26A)	480	224-BB-0	17-19 mm
1992			
Formula MX & MX XTC R (467)			
PTO side (VM 34-352B)	230	159 P-6	23-25 mm
Magneto side (VM 34-353A)	240	159 P-4	23-25 mm
Formula Plus, Plus E, Plus XTC & XTC E (582)			
PTO side (VM 34-413A)	280	159 Q-6	23-25 mm
Magneto side (VM 34-414B)	300	159 Q-8	23-25 mm
Formula Plus X (583)			
PTO side (VM 38-231)	360	480 P-4	16-18 mm
Magneto side (VM 38-250)	380	480 P-2	16-18 mm
Formula MACH 1, MACH 1 XTC & MACH 1 XTC II (643)			
PTO side (VM 40-48D)	420	224-BB-0	17-19 mm
Magneto side (VM 40-49D)	440	224-BB-0	17-19 mm
Formula MACH 1 X (670)			
PTO side (VM 44)	560	224-BB-0	17-19 mm
Magneto side (VM 44)	520	224-BB-0	17-19 mm
1993			
Formula MX &, MX XTC R (467)			
PTO side (VM 34-352B)	230	159 P-6	23-25 mm
Magneto side (VM 34-353A)	240	159 P-4	23-25 mm

(continued)

Table 1 CARBURETOR APPLICATION (continued)

Year model	Main jet	Needle jet	Float setting
1993 (continued)			
Formula MX Z (467)			
PTO side (VM 34-426)	330	159 P-4	23-25 mm
Magneto side (VM 34-427A)	360	159 P-4	23-25 mm
Formula Plus, Plus E & Plus XTC (582)			
PTO side (VM 38-254)	380	480 P-4	17-19 mm
Magneto side (VM 38-255)	400	480 P-4	17-19 mm
Formula Plus X (583)			
PTO side (VM 38-260)	360	480 P-2	17-19 mm
Magneto side (VM 38-261)	390	480 P-2	17-19 mm
Formula MACH 1 & MACH 1 XTC (670)			
PTO side (VM 40-54)	420	224 AA5	17-19 mm
Magneto side (VM 40-551)	440	224 AA5	17-19 mm
Formula Grand Touring (582)			
PTO side (VM 38-260)	360	480 P-2	17-19 mm
Magneto side (VM 38-261)	390	480 P-2	17-19 mm
1994			
Formula MX & MX Z (467)			
PTO side (VM 34-433)	290	159 N-4	24 mm
Magneto side (VM 34-434)	280	159 N-4	24 mm
Summit 470 (470 HAC)			
PTO side (VM 34-426)	380	159 O-2	24 mm
Magneto side (VM 34-427A)	400	159 O-2	24 mm
Formula MX Z X (467)			
PTO side (VM 34-433)	300	159 O-2	24 mm
Magneto side (VM 34-434)	300	159 O-2	24 mm
Formula ST (467)			
PTO side (VM 34-433)	290	159 N-4	24 mm
Magneto side (VM 34-434)	280	159 N-4	24 mm
Formula STX & STX II (583)			
PTO side (VM 38-274)	340	480 P-6	18.1 mm
Magneto side (VM 38-275)	350	480 P-6	18.1 mm
Formula Z (583)			
PTO side (VM 40-63)	360	224 AA-6	18.1 mm
Magneto side (VM 40-64)	360	224 AA-6	18.1 mm
Summit 583 HAC			
PTO side (VM 38-278)	490	480 Q-4	18.1 mm
Magneto side (VM 38-279)	490	480 Q-4	18.1 mm
MACH 1 & Grand Touring SE (670)			
PTO side (VM 40-57)	370	224 AA-4	18.1 mm
Magneto side (VM 40-58)	390	224 AA-4	18.1 mm
Grand Touring & Grand Touring XTC (582)			
PTO side (VM 34-254A)	350	480 P-4	18.1 mm
Magneto side (VM 34-255A)	360	480 P-4	18.1 mm
1995			
MX (467)			
PTO side (VM 34-433)	290	159 N-4	23.9 mm
Magneto side (VM 34-434)	280	159 N-4	23.9 mm
MX Z (454)			
Both (VM 34-448)	270	159 N-6	23.9 mm

(continued)

4

Table 1 CARBURETOR APPLICATION (continued)

Year model	Main jet	Needle jet	Float setting
1995 (continued)			
Formula SS (670)			
PTO side (VM 40-71)	360	224 AA-3	18.1 mm
Magneto side (VM 40-72)	370	224 AA-3	18.1 mm
Formula STX (583)			
PTO side (VM 38-291)	320	480 P-0	18.1 mm
Magneto side (VM 38-292)	330	480 P-0	18.1 mm
Formula STX (LT) (583)			
PTO side (VM 38-291)	320	480 P-0	18.1 mm
Magneto side (VM 38-292)	330	480 P-0	18.1 mm
Summit 583			
PTO side (VM 38-289)	380	480 P-6	19.6 mm
Magneto side (VM 38-290)	380	480 P-6	19.6 mm
Summit 670			
PTO side (VM 40-67)	420	224 AA-4	19.6 mm
Magneto side (VM 40-68)	420	224 AA-4	19.6 mm
Formula Z (583)			
Both (VM 40-69)	340	224 AA-6	18.1 mm
MACH 1 (670)			
PTO side (VM 44-30)	430	224 AA-7	17-19 mm
Magneto side (VM44-31)	410	224 AA-7	17-19 mm
Grand Touring 470(467)			
PTO side (VM 34-433)	290	159 N-4	23.9 mm
Magneto side (VM 34-434)	280	159 N-4	23.9 mm
Grand Touring 580 (582)			
PTO side (VM 38-293)	360	480 O-4	18.1 mm
Magneto side (VM 38-294)	370	480 O-4	18.1 mm
Grand Touring SE (670)			
PTO side (VM 40-71)	360	224 AA-3	18.1 mm
Magneto side (VM 40-72)	370	224 AA-3	18.1 mm

Table 2 CARBURETOR PILOT AIR SCREW ADJUSTMENT

	Turns out from lightly seated*
1990	
Formula MX & MX LT (467)	1 1/2 turns
Formula Plus & Plus LT (536)	1 1/2 turns
Formula MACH 1 MACH 1 XTC (583)	1 1/2 turns
1991	
Formula MX, MX E, MX XTC & MX XTC E (467)	1 1/2 turns
Formula MX X (467)	1 1/2 turns
Formula Plus, Plus E, Plus XTC & Plus XTC E (536)	1 1/2 turns
Formula Plus X (536)	1 1/2 turns
Formula MACH 1 & XTC (643)	2 turns
Formula MACH 1 X (643)	1 1/2 turns
1992	
Formula MX & MX XTC R (467)	1 1/2 turns
Formula Plus, Plus E, Plus XTC & XTC E (582)	1 1/2 turns
(continued)	

Table 2 CARBURETOR PILOT AIR SCREW ADJUSTMENT (continued)

	Turns out from lightly seated*
1992 (continued)	
Formula Plus X (583)	1 1/2 turns
Formula MACH 1, MACH 1 XTC &	
MACH 1 XTC II (643)	2 turns
Formula MACH 1 X (670)	turns
1993	
Formula MX &, MX XTC R (467)	1 1/2 turns
Formula MX Z (467)	1 1/3 turns
Formula Plus, Plus E &	
Plus XTC (582)	1 1/2 turns
Formula Plus X (583)	1 1/2 turns
Formula MACH 1 & MACH 1 XTC (670)	2 3/4 turns
Formula Grand Touring (582)	1 1/2 turns
1994	
Formula MX & MX Z (467)	3/4 turn
Summit 470 (470 HAC)	1 5/8 turns
Formula MX Z X (467)	
Formula ST (467)	3/4 turn
Formula STX & STX II (583)	1 turn
Formula Z (583)	3/4 turn
Summit 583 HAC	2 1/4 turns
MACH 1 & Grand Touring SE (670)	3/4 turn
Grand Touring & Grand Touring XTC (582)	1 1/4 turns
1995	
MX (467)	1 turn
MX Z (454)	1/2 turn
Formula SS (670)	1 turn
Formula STX (583)	1 1/2 turns
Summit 583	1 turn
Summit 670	1 1/8 turns
Formula STX (LT) (583)	1 1/2 turns
Formula Z (583)	1 turn
MACH 1 (670)	1 turn
Grand Touring 470(467)	1 turn
Grand Touring 580 (582)	1 1/4 turns
Grand Touring SE (670)	1 1/8 turns

* The listed number indicates the recommended initial setting and is usually correct within ± 1/8 turn.

Table 3 ENGINE IDLE SPEED

1990	
Formula MX & MX LT (467)	1,800-2,000 rpm
Formula Plus & Plus LT (536)	1,800-2,000 rpm
Formula MACH 1 MACH 1 XTC (583)	1,800-2,000 rpm
1991	
All models	1,800-2,000 rpm
1992	
Formula MX & MX XTC R (467)	1,800-2,000 rpm
Formula Plus, Plus E, Plus XTC &	
XTC E (582)	1,800-2,000 rpm

(continued)

Table 3 ENGINE IDLE SPEED (continued)

1992 (continued)	
Formula Plus X (583)	1,800-2,000 rpm
Formula MACH 1, MACH 1 XTC, MACH 1 XTC II (643)	1,800-2,000 rpm
Formula MACH 1 X (670)	1,800-2,000 rpm
1993	
Formula MX &, MX XTC R (467)	1,800-2,000 rpm
Formula MX Z (467)	1,500-1,700 rpm
Formula Plus, Plus E & Plus XTC (582)	1,800-2,000 rpm
Formula Plus X (583)	1,800-2,000 rpm
Formula MACH 1 & MACH 1 XTC (670)	1,800-2,000 rpm
Formula Grand Touring (582)	1,800-2,000 rpm
1994	
Formula MX & MX Z (467)	1,600-1,800 rpm
Summit 470 (470 HAC)	1,500-1,700 rpm
Formula MX Z X (467)	
Formula ST (467)	1,600-1,800 rpm
Formula STX & STX II (583)	1,800-2,000 rpm
Formula Z (583)	1,500-1,800 rpm
Summit 583 HAC	1,800-2,000 rpm
MACH 1 & Grand Touring SE (670)	1,800-2,000 rpm
Grand Touring & Grand Touring XTC (582)	1,800-2,000 rpm
1995	
MX (467)	1,600-1,800 rpm
MX Z (454)	1,600-1,800 rpm
Formula SS (670)	1,800-2,000 rpm
Formula STX (583)	1,800-2,000 rpm
Formula STX (LT) (583)	1,800-2,000 rpm
Summit 583	1,800-2,000 rpm
Summit 670	1,800-2,000 rpm
Formula Z (583)	1,800-2,000 rpm
MACH 1 (670)	1,800-2,000 rpm
Grand Touring 470 (467)	1,600-1,800 rpm
Grand Touring 580 (582)	1,800-2,000 rpm
Grand Touring SE (670)	1,800-2,000 rpm

Table 4 DRIVE SYSTEM SPECIFICATIONS

Model	Engagement rpm	Drive belt width (new)	Drive belt deflection
1990			
MX & MX LT	3500-3700	34.9 mm (1.37 in.)	32 mm @ 6.8 kg (1.26 in. @ 15 lb.)
Plus models	3400-3600	34.9 mm (1.37 in.)	32 mm @ 6.8 kg (1.26 in. @ 15 lb.)
MACH 1	2400-2600	34.9 mm (1.37 in.)	32 mm @ 6.8 kg (1.26 in. @ 15 lb.)
1991			
MX	3500-3600	34.9 mm (1.37 in.)	32 mm @ 6.8 kg (1.26 in. @ 15 lb.)
Plus models	3400-3600	34.9 mm (1.37 in.)	32 mm @ 6.8 kg (1.26 in. @ 15 lb.)
MACH 1	3300-3400	34.9 mm (1.37 in.)	32 mm @ 6.8 kg (1.26 in. @ 15 lb.)

(continued)

Table 4 DRIVE SYSTEM SPECIFICATIONS (continued)

Model	Engagement rpm	Drive belt width (new)	Drive belt deflection
1992			
MX	3500-3600	34.5 mm (1.36 in.)	32 mm @ 6.8 kg (1.26 in. @ 15 lb.)
Plus	3400-3600	34.5 mm (1.36 in.)	32 mm @ 6.8 kg (1.26 in. @ 15 lb.)
MACH 1	3300-3400	34.9 mm (1.37 in.)	32 mm @ 6.8 kg (1.26 in. @ 15 lb.)
1993			
MX Z	3300-3500	34.5 mm (1.36 in.)	32 mm @ 6.8 kg (1.26 in. @ 15 lb.)
Other MX models	3500-3600	34.5 mm (1.36 in.)	32 mm @ 6.8 kg (1.26 in. @ 15 lb.)
Plus EFI	3300-3500	34.5 mm (1.36 in.)	32 mm @ 6.8 kg (1.26 in. @ 15 lb.)
Other Plus models	3400-3500	34.5 mm (1.36 in.)	32 mm @ 6.8 kg (1.26 in. @ 15 lb.)
MACH 1	3500-3600	34.5 mm (1.36 in.)	32 mm @ 6.8 kg (1.26 in. @ 15 lb.)
1994			
MX	3300-3500	34.5 mm (1.36 in.)	32 mm @ 6.8 kg (1.26 in. @ 15 lb.)
MX Z	3400-3600	34.5 mm (1.36 in.)	32 mm @ 6.8 kg (1.26 in. @ 15 lb.)
Formula ST	3300-3500	34.5 mm (1.36 in.)	32 mm @ 6.8 kg (1.26 in. @ 15 lb.)
Formula STX	3400-3600	34.9 mm (1.37 in.)	32 mm @ 6.8 kg (1.26 in. @ 15 lb.)
Formula Z	3700-3900	34.9 mm (1.37 in.)	32 mm @ 6.8 kg (1.26 in. @ 15 lb.)
Summit 470	3700-3900	34.5 mm (1.36 in.)	32 mm @ 6.8 kg (1.26 in. @ 15 lb.)
Summit 583	3700-3900	34.9 mm (1.37 in.)	32 mm @ 6.8 kg (1.26 in. @ 15 lb.)
Grand Touring	3300-3500	34.5 mm (1.36 in.)	32 mm @ 6.8 kg (1.26 in. @ 15 lb.)
Grand Touring XTC	3300-3500	34.5 mm (1.36 in.)	32 mm @ 6.8 kg (1.26 in. @ 15 lb.)
Grand Touring SE	3400-3600	34.5 mm (1.36 in.)	32 mm @ 6.8 kg (1.26 in. @ 15 lb.)
MACH 1	3400-3600	34.5 mm (1.36 in.)	32 mm @ 6.8 kg (1.26 in. @ 15 lb.)
Grand Touring SE	3400-3600	34.5 mm (1.36 in.)	32 mm @ 6.8 kg (1.26 in. @ 15 lb.)
1995			
MX	3400-3600	34.3 mm (1.35 in.)	32 mm @ 6.8 kg (1.26 in. @ 15 lb.)
Grand Touring SE	3400-3600	34.5 mm (1.36 in.)	32 mm @ 6.8 kg (1.26 in. @ 15 lb.)
MX Z	4300-4500	34.9 mm (1.37 in.)	32 mm @ 6.8 kg (1.26 in. @ 15 lb.)
STX	3400-3600	34.9 mm (1.37 in.)	32 mm @ 6.8 kg (1.26 in. @ 15 lb.)

(continued)

4

Table 4 DRIVE SYSTEM SPECIFICATIONS (continued)

Model	Engagement rpm	Drive belt width (new)	Drive belt deflection
1995 (continued)			
STX LT	3100-3300	34.9 mm (1.37 in.)	32 mm @ 6.8 kg (1.26 in. @ 15 lb.)
Formula SS	3400-3600	35.2 mm (1.39 in.)	32 mm @ 6.8 kg (1.26 in. @ 15 lb.)
Formula Z	3700-3900	34.9 mm (1.37 in.)	32 mm @ 6.8 kg (1.26 in. @ 15 lb.)
Summit 583	3700-3900	34.9 mm (1.37 in.)	32 mm @ 6.8 kg (1.26 in. @ 15 lb.)
Summit 670	3800-4000	35.2 mm (1.39 in.)	32 mm @ 6.8 kg (1.26 in. @ 15 lb.)
Grand Touring 470	3400-3600	34.3 mm (1.35 in.)	32 mm @ 6.8 kg (1.26 in. @ 15 lb.)
Grand Touring 580	3100-3300	34.9 mm (1.37 in.)	32 mm @ 6.8 kg (1.26 in. @ 15 lb.)
Grand Touring SE	3400-3600	35.2 mm (1.39 in.)	32 mm @ 6.8 kg (1.26 in. @ 15 lb.)
MACH 1	4400-4600	35.2 mm (1.39 in.)	32 mm @ 6.8 kg (1.26 in. @ 15 lb.)

Table 5 PULLEY ALIGNMENT

Model	Distance between pulleys Z	Offset X	Offset Y
1990-1992	26-27 mm (1.024-1.063 in.)	35.6-36.4 mm (1.40-1.43 in.)	*
1993			
Formula MX Z	15.5-16.5 mm (1.024-1.063 in.)	34.6-35.4 mm (1.36-1.39 in.)	**
Other models	26-27 mm (1.024-1.063 in.)	35.6-36.4 mm (1.40-1.43 in.)	*
1994			
Grand Touring	15.5-16.5 mm (1.024-1.063 in.)	34.5-35.5 mm (1.36-1.40 in.)	**
MACH 1	15.5-16.5 mm (1.024-1.063 in.)	34.5-35.5 mm (1.36-1.40 in.)	**
Other models	26-27 mm (1.024-1.063 in.)	35.6-36.4 mm (1.40-1.43 in.)	**
1995	15.5-16.5 mm (1.024-1.063 in.)	34.5-35.5 mm (1.36-1.40 in.)	**

* Measured offset Y should be 0.75-1.5 mm (0.030-0.060 in.) greater than measured offset X.
** Measured offset Y should be 1.0-2.0 mm (0.040-0.080 in.) greater than measured offset X.

Table 6 DRIVE PULLEY SPRING SPECIFICATIONS

Model	Spring free length mm (in.)	Spring color code
1990		
MX	113.6-116.6 (4.47-4.59)	Blue/Yellow
Plus	131.1-134.1 (5.16-5.28)	Blue/Orange
MACH 1	82.6-85.6 (3.25-3.37)	Red/Blue
1991		
MX	113.6-116.6 (4.47-4.59)	Blue/Yellow
Plus	131.1-134.1 (5.16-5.28)	Blue/Orange
MACH 1	96.8-99.8 (3.81-3.93)	Yellow/Yellow
1992		
MX	128.2-130.2 (5.05-5.13)	White
Plus X	104.2-107.2 (4.10-4.22)	Blue/Green
Other Plus models	98.3-101.3 (3.87-3.99)	Blue/Blue
MACH 1 X	142.8-145.8 (5.62-5.74)	Pink/Green
MACH 1	96.8-99.8 (3.81-3.93)	Yellow/Yellow
1993		
MX Z	98.3-101.3 (3.87-3.99)	Blue/Blue
Other MX models	128.2-130.2 (5.05-5.13)	White
Plus X	104.2-107.2 (4.10-4.22)	Purple/Purple
Other Plus models	131.1-134.1 (5.16-5.28)	Blue/Orange
Grand Touring	131.1-134.1 (5.16-5.28)	Blue/Orange
MACH 1	98.3-101.3 (3.87-3.99)	Blue/Blue
1994		
MX	92-95 (3.62-3.74)	Blue
MX Z	113.6-116.6 (4.47-4.59)	Blue/Yellow
STX	104.2-107.2 (4.10-4.22)	Blue/Green
Formula Z	120.5-123.5 (4.74-4.86)	Yellow
Summit 470 & 583	104.2-107.2 (4.10-4.22)	Purple/Purple
Grand Touring SE	98.3-101.3 (3.87-3.99)	Blue/Blue

(continued)

Table 6 DRIVE PULLEY SPRING SPECIFICATIONS (continued)

Model	Spring free length mm (in.)	Spring color code
1994 (continued)		
Other GT models	131.1-134.1 (5.16-5.28)	Blue/Orange
MACH 1	98.3-101.3 (3.87-3.99)	Blue/Blue
1995		
MX	113.6-116.6 (4.47-4.59)	Blue/Yellow
MX Z	123-126 (4.84-4.96)	Pink/White
STX	104.2-107.2 (4.10-4.22)	Blue/Green
STX LT	92.5-95.5 (3.64-3.76)	Yellow/Green
Formula SS	104.2-107.2 (4.10-4.22)	Blue/Green
Formula Z	120.5-123.5 (4.74-4.86)	Yellow
Summit 583	104.2-107.2 (4.10-4.22)	Violet/Violet
Summit 670	120.5-123.5) (4.74-4.86)	Yellow
Grand Touring 470	92-95 (3.62-3.74)	Blue/Pink
Grand Touring 580	153.2-156.2 (6.03-6.15)	Pink/Violet
Grand Touring SE	104.2-107.2 (4.10-4.22)	Yellow/Orange
MACH 1	123-126 (4.84-4.96)	Pink/White

Table 7 DRIVEN PULLEY SPECIFICATIONS

Model	Spring preload kg (lb.)	Cam angle degrees
1990		
MX & Plus	6.3-6.5 (13.9-14.3)	NA
MACH 1	7.3 (16.1)	NA
1991		
MX & Plus	6.3-6.5 (13.9-14.3)	NA
MACH 1	7.3 (16.1)	NA
1992		
MX	6.3-6.5 (13.9-14.3)	NA
Plus	7.3 (16.1)	NA
MACH 1	7.3 (16.1)	NA
1993		
MX Z	4.6-5.9 (10-13)	NA
Other MX models	4.8-6.2 (10.6-13.6)	NA
Plus	4.1-5.4 (9-12)	NA
Grand Touring	4.1-5.4 (9-12)	NA
MACH 1	4.6-5.9 (10-13)	NA

(continued)

Table 7 DRIVEN PULLEY SPECIFICATIONS (continued)

Model	Spring preload kg (lb.)	Cam angle degrees
1994		
MX	4.1-5.6 (9.0-12.3)	NA
MX Z	5.5-7.0 (12.1-15.4)	NA
STX	5.5-7.0 (12.1-15.4)	NA
Formula Z	5.5-7.0 (12.1-15.4)	NA
Summit 470 & 583	5.5-7.0 (12.1-15.4)	NA
Grand Touring	4.1-5.6 (9.0-12.3)	NA
MACH 1	4.1-5.6 (9.0-12.3)	NA
1995		
MX	5.5-7.0 (12.1-15.4)	44
MX Z	5.5-7.0 (12.1-15.4)	44
STX	5.5-7.0 (12.1-15.4)	50
STX LT	5.5-7.0 (12.1-15.4)	44
Formula SS	5.5-7.0 (12.1-15.4)	47
Formula Z	5.5-7.0 (12.1-15.4)	50
Summit 583	5.5-7.0 (12.1-15.4)	44
Summit 670	5.5-7.0 (12.1-15.4)	47
Grand Touring 470	5.5-7.0 (12.1-15.4)	44
Grand Touring 580	5.5-7.0 (12.1-15.4)	50
Grand Touring SE	5.5-7.0 (12.1-15.4)	47
MACH 1	5.5-7.0 (12.1-15.4)	47

Table 8 DRIVE CHAIN SPECIFICATIONS

Model	Chain pitch* and length	Chain drive ratio
1990		
Formula MX	3/8-72	22:44
Formula MX LT	3/8-72	22:44
Formula Plus	3/8-68	20:38
Formula Plus LT	3/8-68	20:38
Formula MACH 1	3/8-70	22:40
Formula MACH 1 XTC	3/8-70	22:40
1991		
Formula MX	3/8-74	22:44
Formula MX E	3/8-74	26:44
Formula MX X	3/8-74	26:44
Formula MX XTC	3/8-74	26:44
Formula MX XTC E	3/8-74	26:44
Formula Plus	3/8-70	22:40
Formula Plus E	3/8-70	22:40
Formula Plus X	3/8-70	22:40
Formula Plus XTC	3/8-70	22:40
Formula Plus XTC E	3/8-70	22:40
Formula MACH 1	3/8-74	26:44
Formula MACH 1 X	3/8-74	26:44
Formula MACH 1 XTC	3/8-74	26:44

(continued)

Table 8 DRIVE CHAIN SPECIFICATIONS (continued)

Model	Chain pitch* and length	Chain drive ratio
1992		
Formula MX	3/8-72	22:44
Formula MX XTC R	3/8-72	22:44
Formula Plus	3/8-70	23:40
Formula Plus E	3/8-70	23:40
Formula Plus XTC	3/8-70	22:40
Formula Plus XTC E	3/8-70	22:40
Formula Plus X	3/8-70	23:40
Formula MACH 1	3/8-74	26:44
Formula MACH 1 X	3/8-70	23:40
Formula MACH 1 XTC	3/8-74	24:44
1993		
Formula MX	3/8-72	26:44
Formula MX XTC R	3/8-70	22:44
Formula MX Z	3/8-74	24:44
Formula Plus	3/8-74	25:44
Formula Plus E	3/8-74	25:44
Formula Plus XTC	3/8-72	23:44
Formula Plus EFI	3/8-74	25:44
Formula Plus X	3/8W-74	25:44
Formula MACH 1	3/8W-74	25:44
Formula MACH 1 XTC	3/8W-74	25:44
Formula Grand Touring	3/8W-74	25:44
1994		
Formula MX	3/8-74	23:44
Formula MX Z	3/8W-74	23:44
Summit 470	3/8-72	22:44
Formula ST	3/8-72	23:44
Formula STX	3/8-74	25:44
Summit 583	3/8-72	23:44
Formula Z	3/8-74	25:44
MACH 1	3/8W-74	26:44
Grand Touring	3/8W-74	25:44
Grand Touring XTC	3/8W-72	23:44
Grand Touring SE	3/8W-74	26:44
1995		
MX	3/8-72	23:44
MX Z	3/8W-72	23:44
Formula SS	3/8W-74	26:44
Formula STX	3/8-74	25:44
Summit 583	3/8-72	23:44
Summit 670	3/8-74	25:44
Formula Z	3/8-74	25:44
MACH 1	3/8W-74	26:44
Grand Touring 470	3/8W-72	23:44
Grand Touring 580	3/8W-74	25:44
Grand Touring SE	3/8W-74	26:44

* All models use 3/8 in. pitch silent chain. Some 1993 and later models are equipped with chain that is wider than other models. The wide chain is 13 links wide, while the other chain is made of 11 links. Chain should not be shortened, lengthened or substituted. Only the original type of chain is recommended.

Table 9 GAS FILLED SHOCK ABSORBER SPECIFICATIONS

Front suspension—	
Distance A, **Figure 19**	85.5 mm (3.11/32 in.)
Nitrogen charge pressure	2070 kPa (300 psi)
Rear suspension—	
Center shock	
Distance A, **Figure 22**	104 mm (4.0 in.)
Nitrogen charge pressure	2070 kPa (300 psi)
Rear shocks	
Distance A, **Figure 23**	78 mm (3.0 in.)
Nitrogen charge pressure	2070 kPa (300 psi)

Table 10 NITROGEN FILLED SHOCK SPECIFICATIONS

	Standard	Trail	Cross country
Front shock			
Piston slits	4	4	4
Compression shims	8-30 mm × 0.152 mm	8-30 mm × 0.152 mm	6-30 mm × 0.152 mm
	2-15 mm × 0.114 mm	2-15 mm × 0.114 mm	1-24 mm × 0.114 mm
			1-21 mm × 0.114 mm
Rebound shims	8-26 mm × 0.203 mm	8-26 mm × 0.203 mm	12-26mm× 0.203 mm
	2-12 mm × 0.203 mm	1-12 mm × 0.203 mm	1-16 mm × 0.203 mm
Center shock			
Piston slits	6	6	0
Compression shims	9-30 mm × 0.152 mm	9-30 mm × 0.152 mm	12-30 mm × 0.203 mm
	2-15 mm × 0.114 mm	2-15 mm × 0.114 mm	1-24 mm × 0.114 mm
			1-21 mm × 0.114 mm
Rebound shims	8-26 mm × 0.203 mm	8-26 mm × 0.203 mm	12-26mm × 0.203 mm
	2-15 mm × 0.114 mm	1-15 mm × 0.114 mm	1-16 mm × 0.203 mm
Rear shock			
Piston slits	6	6	2
Compression shims	8-30 mm × 0.203 mm	8-30 mm × 0.203 mm	7-30 mm × 0.203 mm
	6-15 mm × 0.114 mm	6-15 mm × 0.114 mm	1-24 mm × 0.114 mm
			1-20 mm × 0.152 mm
Rebound shims	10-26 mm × 0.203 mm	10-26 mm × 0.152 mm	10-26mm × 0.203 mm
	2-15 mm × 0.114 mm	2-15 mm × 0.114 mm	1-20 mm × 0.203 mm

4

Chapter Five

Engine

All of the Ski-Doo snowmobiles covered in this manual are equipped with a Rotax rotary valve, water-cooled 2-stroke parallel twin engine. The Rotax engines are equipped with ball-type main crankshaft bearings and needle bearings on both ends of the connecting rods. Crankshaft components are available as individual parts. However, other than to replace the outer seals, it is recommended that the crankshaft work be entrusted to a dealer or other competent engine specialist.

This chapter covers information to provide top-end service as well as crankcase disassembly and crankshaft service.

Work on the snowmobile engine requires considerable mechanical ability. You should carefully consider your own capabilities before attempting any operation involving major disassembly of the engine.

Much of the labor charge for dealer repairs involves the removal and disassembly of other parts to reach the defective component. Even if you decide not to tackle the entire engine overhaul after studying the text and illustrations in this chapter, it may be cheaper to perform the preliminary operations yourself and then take the engine to your dealer. Since dealers have lengthy waiting lists for service (especially during the fall and winter season), this practice can reduce the length of time your snowmobile is in the shop. If you have done much of the preliminary work, your repairs can be scheduled and performed much quicker.

Engine identification numbers are listed in **Table 1**. General engine specifications are listed in **Table 2**. Engine service specifications are listed in **Tables 3-9**. **Tables 1-11** are found at the end of the chapter.

ENGINE NUMBER IDENTIFICATION

Bombardier uses a series of 3 numbers to identify Ski-Doo snowmobiles engines. Refer to **Table 1** for model listing and engine number identification.

ENGINE LUBRICATION

The engine is normally lubricated by the oil injection system. Refer to Chapter Ten for servicing the oil injection pump. Lubrication of a new or rebuilt engine may be initially supplemented by adding oil to the fuel used to power the engine. Refer to Chapter Three for *Break-In Procedure*.

SERVICE PRECAUTIONS

Whenever you work on your Ski-Doo, there are several precautions that should be followed

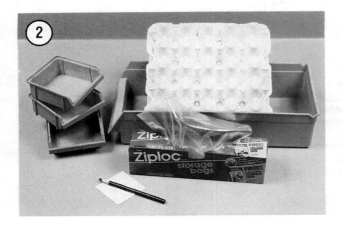

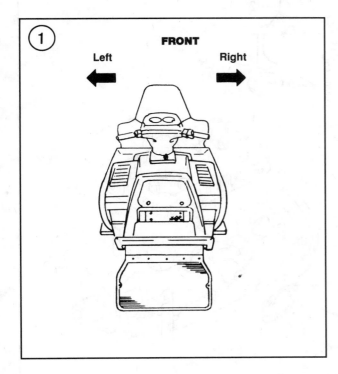

to help with disassembly, inspection, and reassembly.

1. In the text there is frequent mention of the left-hand and right-hand side of the engine. This refers to the engine as it is mounted in the frame, not as it sits on your workbench. See **Figure 1**.

2. Always replace a worn or damaged fastener with one of the same size, type and torque requirements. Make sure to identify each screw before replacing it with another. Screw threads should be lubricated with engine oil, unless otherwise specified, before torque is applied. If a tightening torque is not listed in **Table 11** at the end of this chapter, refer to the torque and fastener information in Chapter One.

3. Use special tools where noted. In some cases, it may be possible to perform the procedure with makeshift tools, but this procedure is not recommended. The use of makeshift tools can damage the components and may cause serious personal injury. Special snowmobile tools may be purchased through any Ski-Doo dealer. Other tools can be purchased through your dealer, or from a motorcycle or automotive accessory store. When purchasing tools from an automotive accessory dealer or store, remember that all threaded parts that screw into the engine must have metric threads.

4. Before removing the first screw or nut, to prevent frustration during assembly, get a number of boxes, plastic bags and containers (**Figure 2**). Use these containers to separate and organize the parts as they are removed. Also have a roll of masking tape and a permanent, waterproof marking pen to label each part or assembly. If your snowmobile was purchased second hand and it appears that some of the wiring may have been changed or replaced, label each electrical connection before separating it.

5. Use a vise with protective jaws to hold parts. If protective jaws are not available, insert wooden blocks on each side of the part(s) before clamping it in the vise.

③

EXHAUST SYSTEM
(TYPICAL, 1990-1993 MODEL WITH SINGLE EXHAUST)

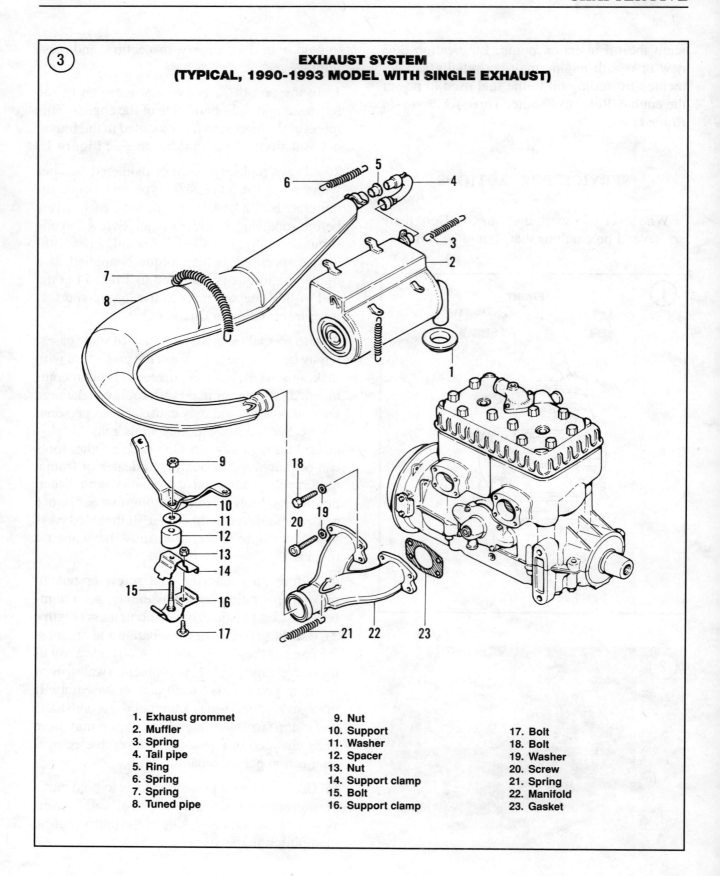

1. Exhaust grommet
2. Muffler
3. Spring
4. Tail pipe
5. Ring
6. Spring
7. Spring
8. Tuned pipe

9. Nut
10. Support
11. Washer
12. Spacer
13. Nut
14. Support clamp
15. Bolt
16. Support clamp

17. Bolt
18. Bolt
19. Washer
20. Screw
21. Spring
22. Manifold
23. Gasket

6. Remove and install pressed-on parts with an appropriate mandrel, support and hydraulic press. **Do not** try to pry, hammer or otherwise force them on or off.

7. Refer to **Table 11** at the end of the chapter for torque specifications. Proper torque is essential to enssure long life and satisfactory service from snowmobile components.

8. Discard all O-rings and oil seals during disassembly. Apply a small amount of heat resistant grease to the inner lips of each oil seal to prevent damage when the engine is first started.

9. Keep a record of all shims as they are removed. As soon as the shims are removed, inspect them for damage and write down their thickness and location.

10. Work in an area where there is sufficient lighting and room for component storage.

SERVICING ENGINE IN FRAME

Some of the components can be serviced while the engine is mounted in the snowmobile:
  a. Cylinder head.
  b. Cylinder.
  c. Piston.
  d. Carburetor.
  e. Magneto.
  f. Oil pump.
  g. Recoil starter.
  h. Drive clutch assembly (primary sheave).

ENGINE REMOVAL

Engine removal and crankcase separation is required for repair of the bottom end (crankshaft, connecting rods and bearings).

1. Open the hood, unplug the harness from the headlight, then free the harness from the hood. Disconnect the hood restraining cable and have an assistant support the hood. Remove the screws that attach the hood hinge to the chassis, then lift off the hood. Set the hood out of the way to prevent it from being damaged.

2. See **Figures 3-5** as appropriate for your model. Remove the exhaust assembly as follows:
  a. Disconnect the springs (**Figure 6**, typical) that hold the exhaust pipe(s) to the muffler.
  b. Remove the tailpipe and muffler (**Figure 7**, typical).
  c. Disconnect the spring that attaches the exhaust pipe(s) to the support (**Figure 8**).
  d. Disconnect the springs that hold the exhaust pipe(s) to the manifold (**Figure 9**) or exhaust socket (**Figure 10**), then remove the exhaust pipe(s).

3. Remove the drive belt as described in Chapter Thirteen.

4. Remove the primary sheave as described in Chapter Thirteen.

5. Drain the cooling system as described under *Coolant Change* in Chapter Three.

6. Remove the recoil starter as described in Chapter Twelve.

7. Remove the air silencer as described in Chapter Six or Chapter Seven.

8A. On models with carburetors, observe the following:
  a. Unscrew the carburetor caps (A, **Figure 11**) and withdraw the throttle valves (slides) from the carburetors. Be careful that you do not damage the jet needles.

> *CAUTION*
> *It is not necessary to remove the throttle slides and caps from the cables unless service to these parts is required. Tie the cables, caps and throttle slides back, out of the way to protect them from damage if they remain attached.*

  b. Detach the fuel primer hoses (**Figure 12**) from each carburetor.

8B. On 1993 Formula Plus EFI models, detach the vacuum lines, electrical connectors, fuel lines and throttle cable (**Figure 13**) from the EFI system.

9. Disconnect the oil injection control cable from the oil pump (**Figure 14**).

5

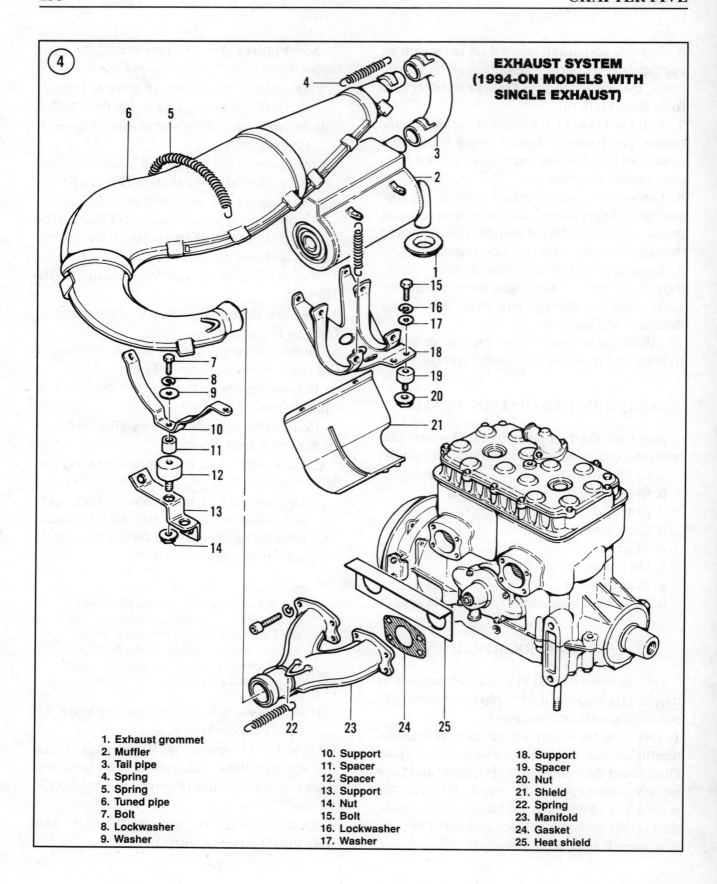

④

**EXHAUST SYSTEM
(1994-ON MODELS WITH
SINGLE EXHAUST)**

1. Exhaust grommet
2. Muffler
3. Tail pipe
4. Spring
5. Spring
6. Tuned pipe
7. Bolt
8. Lockwasher
9. Washer
10. Support
11. Spacer
12. Spacer
13. Support
14. Nut
15. Bolt
16. Lockwasher
17. Washer
18. Support
19. Spacer
20. Nut
21. Shield
22. Spring
23. Manifold
24. Gasket
25. Heat shield

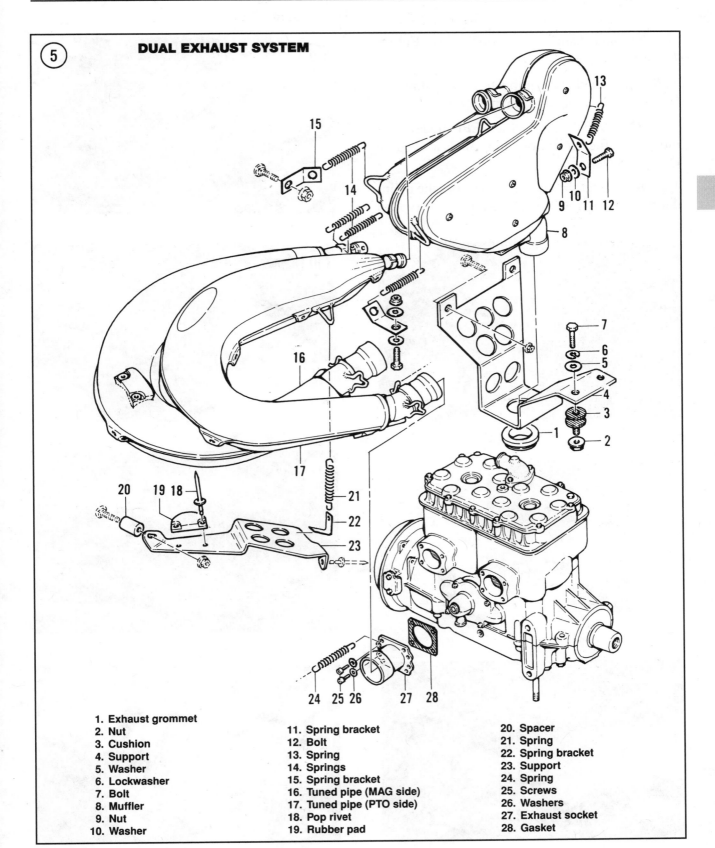

⑤ **DUAL EXHAUST SYSTEM**

5

1. Exhaust grommet
2. Nut
3. Cushion
4. Support
5. Washer
6. Lockwasher
7. Bolt
8. Muffler
9. Nut
10. Washer

11. Spring bracket
12. Bolt
13. Spring
14. Springs
15. Spring bracket
16. Tuned pipe (MAG side)
17. Tuned pipe (PTO side)
18. Pop rivet
19. Rubber pad

20. Spacer
21. Spring
22. Spring bracket
23. Support
24. Spring
25. Screws
26. Washers
27. Exhaust socket
28. Gasket

10. Disconnect and plug the oil hose (B, **Figure 11**) at the oil pump.

11A. On models so equipped, remove the carburetors as described in Chapter Six.

11B. On 1993 Formula Plus EFI models, remove the fuel injection unit as described in Chapter Seven.

12. Disconnect the coolant hose from the cylinder head. **Figure 15** and **Figure 16** show typical

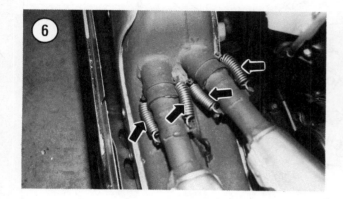

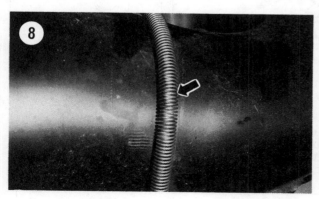

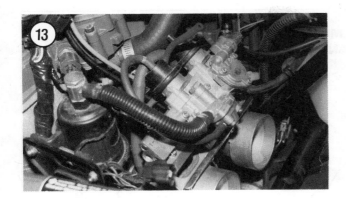

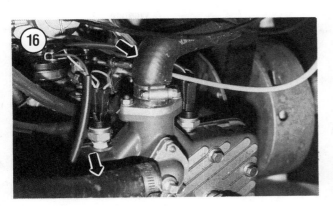

hose connections. Some models have 1 hose attached to the cylinder head (**Figure 15**) and other models have 2 hoses attached (**Figure 16**).

13. Disconnect the fuel pump impulse hose (**Figure 17**) from the crankcase fitting.

14. Disconnect the electrical connectors (**Figure 18**) from the CDI unit.

15. Disconnect both spark plug cables from the spark plugs.

16. If necessary, the engine top end (cylinder heads, pistons, and cylinder blocks) can be removed before removing the engine from the frame. Refer to *Cylinder* in this chapter.

5

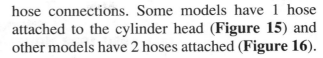

> *NOTE*
> *Because of the number of bushings, washers and rubber dampers used on the engine bracket assemblies, refer to Figure 19, Figure 20 or Figure 21 when performing Step 17 and Step 18.*

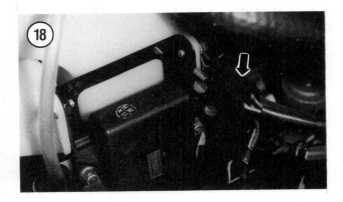

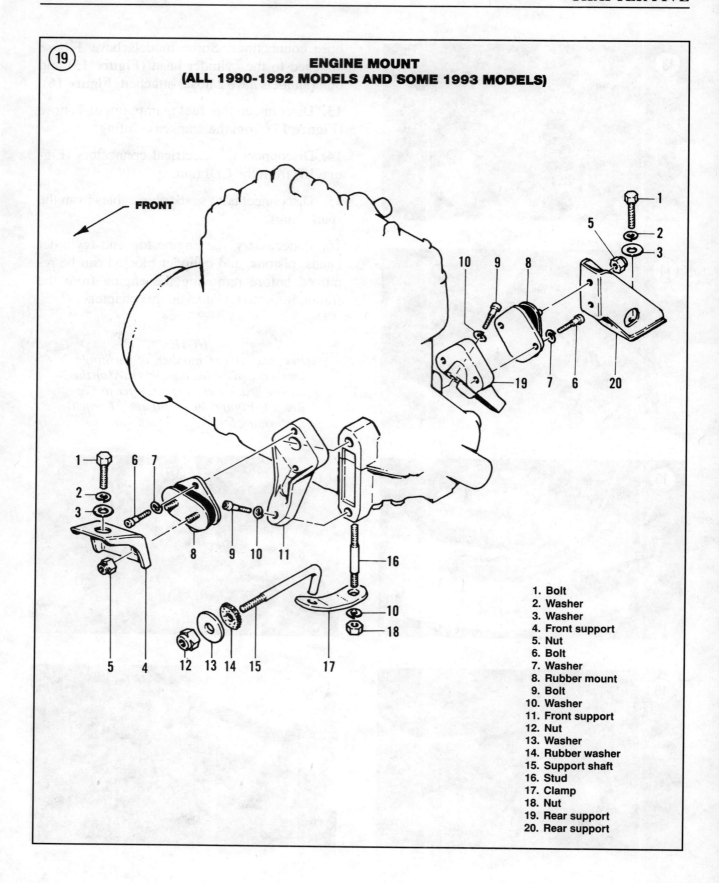

19

ENGINE MOUNT
(ALL 1990-1992 MODELS AND SOME 1993 MODELS)

FRONT

1. Bolt
2. Washer
3. Washer
4. Front support
5. Nut
6. Bolt
7. Washer
8. Rubber mount
9. Bolt
10. Washer
11. Front support
12. Nut
13. Washer
14. Rubber washer
15. Support shaft
16. Stud
17. Clamp
18. Nut
19. Rear support
20. Rear support

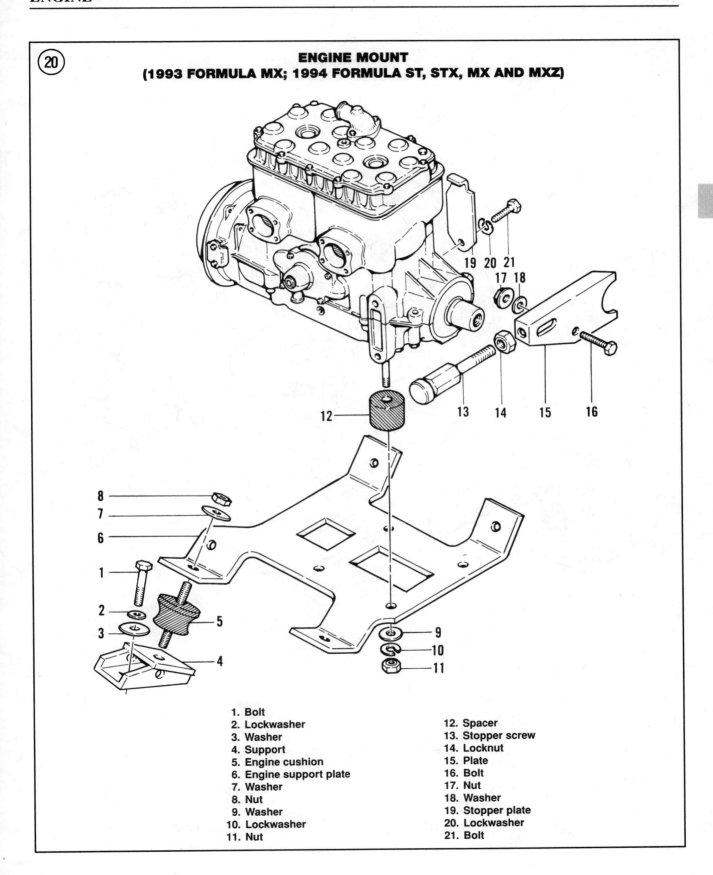

ENGINE MOUNT
(1993 FORMULA MX; 1994 FORMULA ST, STX, MX AND MXZ)

1. Bolt
2. Lockwasher
3. Washer
4. Support
5. Engine cushion
6. Engine support plate
7. Washer
8. Nut
9. Washer
10. Lockwasher
11. Nut
12. Spacer
13. Stopper screw
14. Locknut
15. Plate
16. Bolt
17. Nut
18. Washer
19. Stopper plate
20. Lockwasher
21. Bolt

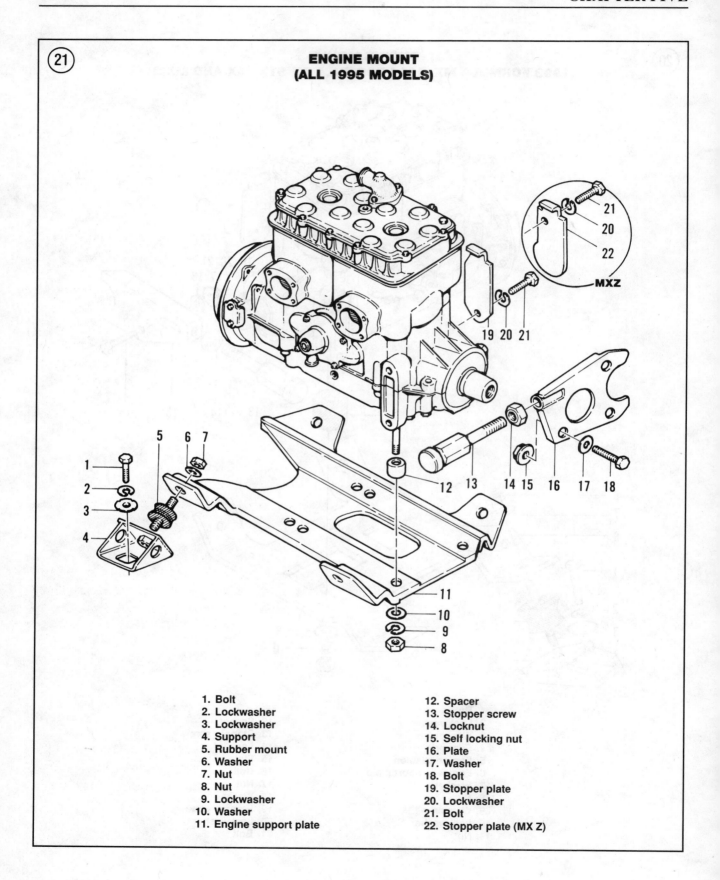

**ENGINE MOUNT
(ALL 1995 MODELS)**

1. Bolt
2. Lockwasher
3. Lockwasher
4. Support
5. Rubber mount
6. Washer
7. Nut
8. Nut
9. Lockwasher
10. Washer
11. Engine support plate
12. Spacer
13. Stopper screw
14. Locknut
15. Self locking nut
16. Plate
17. Washer
18. Bolt
19. Stopper plate
20. Lockwasher
21. Bolt
22. Stopper plate (MX Z)

17. Loosen and remove the engine torque rod nut (**Figure 22**) and disconnect the torque rod from the engine clamp.

18. Loosen the front and rear engine bracket bolts (**Figure 23**). Remove the nuts and washers from the front engine rubber mounts, then remove the nuts and washers from the rear rubber mounts.

19. Check to make sure all of the wiring and hoses have been disconnected from the engine.

20. With at least 1 assistant, lift the engine up and remove it from the frame. Carry it **Figure 24** to a workbench for further disassembly.

ENGINE MOUNTS

Removal/Installation

The engine mounts and supports are a critical part of the snowmobile drive train. Damaged or loose engine mounts will allow the engine to shift or pull out of alignment during operation. This condition will cause primary and secondary sheave misalignment that will result in drive belt wear and reduced performance. The engine mount and support assembly should be inspected carefully whenever the engine is removed from the frame or if clutch misalignment is a problem.

Refer to **Figures 19-21** when performing this procedure.

All 1990-1992 models, all 1993 models (except Formula MX and MXZ and 1994 Grand Touring and MACH 1 models

Refer to **Figure 19**.

1. To ease installation, mark each of the engine mounts, supports and rubber mounts for position during removal. Refer to **Figure 24**.

> *NOTE*
> *Different length bolts are used to hold the mounts and supports. Identify bolts as they are removed and store accordingly so they can be installed in the same location.*

2. Unbolt and remove the front engine mounts, rubber mounts and engine supports (**Figure 25**).

3. Remove the engine torque rod clamp (**Figure 26**) from the left-hand side of the engine.

4. Unbolt and remove the rear engine mounts, rubber mounts and engine supports (**Figure 27**).

5

5. Installation is the reverse of these steps. Observe the following:

a. Check the engine mounts, rubber mounts and engine supports for cracks or damage. Inspect the rubber mounts for separation or other damage.

b. Check all of the engine and support mount bolts for damaged threads. Replace damaged bolts with the same grade, because replacement bolts that are weaker will loosen and allow the engine to slip.

c. Inspect the washers for splitting or other damage.

d. Check threads of the tapped holes in the crankcase (**Figure 28**) for damaged threads or debris buildup. Clean threads with a suitable size metric tap. If Loctite was previously used, make sure to remove all traces of Loctite residue before reinstalling bolts.

e. Check the front and rear engine mount brackets in the frame for cracks or other of damage. Check the bracket tapped holes for thread damage or debris buildup. Clean threads as described in substep d.

f. Replace worn or damaged parts as required.

g. Tighten the engine mount, rubber mount and support bolts to the torque specification in **Table 11**.

1993 Formula MX, 1994 Formula ST, STX, MX and MX Z, and all 1995 models

Refer to **Figure 20** for 1993 Formula MX, 1994 Formula ST, STX, MX and MX Z models. Refer to **Figure 21** for all 1995 models.

1. To ease installation, mark each of the engine mounts (**Figure 29**), supports and rubber mounts for position during removal.

> *NOTE*
> *Different length bolts are used to hold the mounts and supports. Identify bolts as they are removed and store accordingly so they can be installed in the same location.*

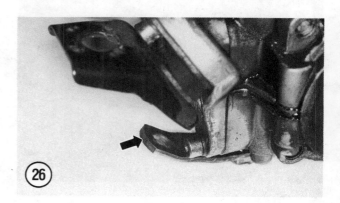

2. Unbolt and remove the front engine mounts, rubber mounts and engine support (**Figure 30**).

3. Unbolt and remove the rear engine mounts, rubber mounts and engine supports (A, **Figure 31**).

NOTE
It is not necessary to alter the adjustment of the stopper (B, Figure 31) to remove and install the engine.

4. Install new mounts by carefully reversing the removal steps. Observe the following:

  a. Check the engine mounts, rubber mounts and engine support for cracks or damage. Inspect the rubber mounts for separation or other damage. If required, the engine support (**Figure 20** or **Figure 21**) can be unbolted and removed from the engine. Make sure to reinstall spacers and tighten retaining nuts to the torque specified in **Table 11**.

  b. Check all of the engine and support mount bolts and studs for damaged threads. Replace damaged bolts with the same grade of bolt. Bolts that are weaker will loosen and allow the engine to slip.

  c. Inspect all washers for splitting or other damage.

  d. Check threads of all tapped holes in the crankcase for damaged threads or debris buildup. If necessary, clean threads with a suitable size metric tap. If Loctite was previously used, make sure to remove all traces of Loctite residue before reinstalling bolts.

  e. Check the front and rear engine mount brackets and the surrounding area of the frame for cracks or other signs of damage. Check the bracket tapped holes for thread damage or debris buildup. Clean threads as described in substep d.

  f. Replace worn or damaged parts as required.

  g. Tighten the engine mount, rubber mount and support bolts to the torque specification in **Table 11**.

  h. Refer to Chapter Thirteen for drive belt alignment and distance adjustment. The stopper (B, **Figure 31**) is used to adjust the center-to-center distance of the drive pulleys.

5

ENGINE INSTALLATION

1. Clean the engine compartment and wash with clean water.

2. Clean all of the exposed electrical connectors with an electrical contact cleaner.

3. Before installing the engine, inspect components which are difficult to view when the engine is installed. Observe the following:

   a. Check all of the coolant hoses and the hose connections for looseness or damage. Make sure the hose clamps are tight. Many of the coolant hoses are preshaped and should only be replaced with duplicates of the originals. When replacing any coolant hose, make sure it is positioned correctly.

   b. Check all of the steering component tightening torques as described in Chapter Fifteen. Check the steering shaft clamp (A, **Figure 32**, typical) for tightness.

   c. Check the fuel pump (B, **Figure 32**) mounting screws for tightness. Check the fuel pump outlet and pulse hoses for age deterioration, cracks or other damage; replace damaged hoses as required.

4. Examine the engine mounts and supports as described in this chapter.

5. Check inside the frame for any object that may interfere with engine installation. Make sure wiring harnesses are routed and secured properly.

6. Install the front and rear engine supports and mounts onto the engine as described in this chapter.

7. With the help of an assistant, place the engine partway into position on the frame.

NOTE
To ease installation of the coolant hoses in the following steps, coat the inside of the hose where it slides on the mating joint with antifreeze.

8. It is easier to connect the lower coolant hose to the water pump before the engine is completely lowered onto the frame. Attach the coolant hose to the water pump and secure the end of the hose with a clamp. Make sure the hose is not twisted and that the clamp will not contact the frame when the engine is lowered in the frame. When the hose is securely attached, lower the engine onto the frame brackets. Check the hose clamp to make sure it is away from the frame.

9. On engines equipped with the torque rod (15, **Figure 19**), connect the engine torque rod to the clamp on the left-hand side of the engine.

10. Install, but do not tighten the engine mount bolts.

11. Install the primary sheave and drive belt as described in Chapter Thirteen.

12. Align the engine/clutch assembly as described in Chapter Thirteen. Tighten the engine mount bolts to the torque specified in **Table 11**.

13. Install any engine top end components that are still removed.

14. Attach the spark plug cables to the spark plugs.

15. Reconnect all electrical connectors.

16. Reconnect the pulse hose to the crankcase and secure the hose with the metal clamp. Several different fuel pumps have been used, but the pulse hose (C, **Figure 32**) routes crankcase pulses to the center of the fuel pump.

17. Attach the coolant hose(s) to the cylinder head and secure with a hose clamp.

18. Attach the hose from the oil injection tank to the oil pump.

19. Connect the oil injection control cable to the oil pump (**Figure 14**).

CAUTION
Do not adjust the oil injection control cable until after the carburetors have been synchronized as described in Chapter Three.

20A. On models with carburetors, install the throttle slides and caps to the carburetors. If the carburetors were removed, reinstall them as described in Chapter Six.

NOTE
The left and right carburetors on some models are different; while the left and right carburetors may be identical on other models, but with different jetting. Make sure to follow the identification and installation information given in Chapter Six.

20B. On 1993 Formula Plus EFI models, attach the vacuum lines, electrical connectors, fuel lines and throttle cable to the EFI system. Refer to Chapter Seven for installing the fuel injection unit.

21. On models with carburetors, refer to the *Synchronization* procedure described in Chapter Three.

22. Adjust the oil injection control cable as described in Chapter Three.

23. Bleed the oil injection pump as described in Chapter Ten.

24. Install the air silencer as described in Chapter Six or Chapter Seven.

25. Install the recoil starter assembly as described in Chapter Twelve. Check starter operation.

26. Refill the cooling system as described in Chapter Eleven.

27. Install the exhaust pipe and muffler. See **Figures 3-5**. Make sure all springs are properly attached and none of the exhaust components are binding.

28. Install the engine hood. Reconnect the headlight electrical connector.

ENGINE TOP END

The engine top end consists of the cylinder head, cylinder blocks, pistons, piston rings, piston pins and the connecting rod small-end bearings.

The engine top end can be serviced with the engine installed in the frame. However the following service procedures are shown with the engine removed for clarity.

Refer to the illustration for your model when servicing the engine top end.
  a. **Figure 33**: Engine 454.
  b. **Figure 34**: Engine 467.
  c. **Figure 35**: Engine 536.
  d. **Figure 36**: Engine 582.
  e. **Figure 37**: Engine 583.
  f. **Figure 38**: Engine 643.
  g. **Figure 39**: Engine 670.

Cylinder Head
Removal/Installation

CAUTION
To prevent warpage and damage to any component, remove the cylinder heads only when the engine has cooled to room temperature. Never pry the cylinder head or cylinder head cover while trying to remove it.

NOTE
*If the engine is being disassembled for inspection procedures, check the compression as described in Chapter Three **before** disassembly.*

1. If the engine is mounted in the frame, perform the following:
  a. Open the engine hood, unplug the harness from the headlight and free the harness from the hood. Disconnect the hood restraining cable and have an assistant sup-

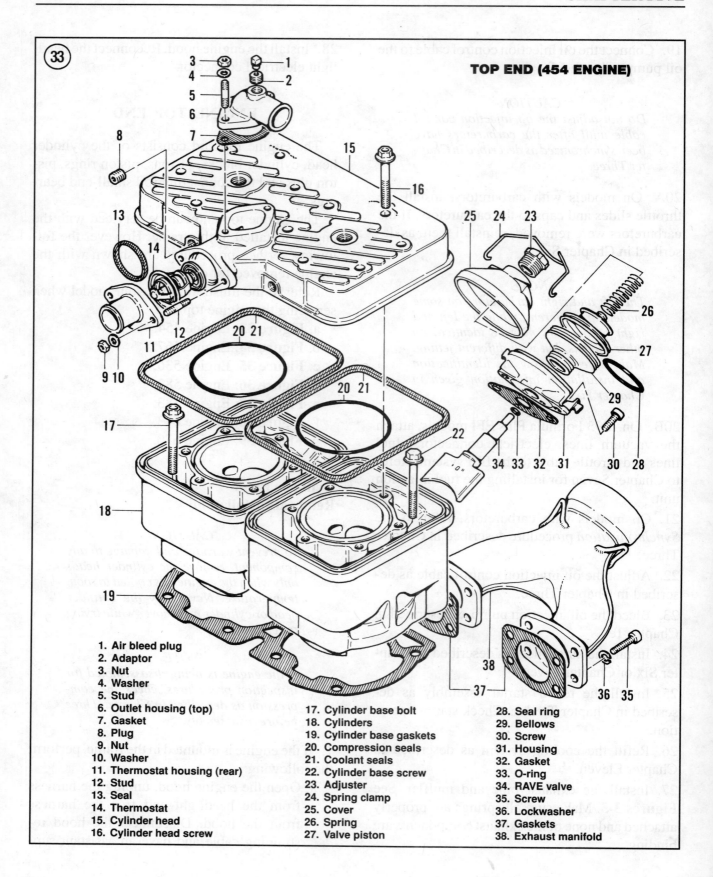

33

TOP END (454 ENGINE)

1. Air bleed plug
2. Adaptor
3. Nut
4. Washer
5. Stud
6. Outlet housing (top)
7. Gasket
8. Plug
9. Nut
10. Washer
11. Thermostat housing (rear)
12. Stud
13. Seal
14. Thermostat
15. Cylinder head
16. Cylinder head screw
17. Cylinder base bolt
18. Cylinders
19. Cylinder base gaskets
20. Compression seals
21. Coolant seals
22. Cylinder base screw
23. Adjuster
24. Spring clamp
25. Cover
26. Spring
27. Valve piston
28. Seal ring
29. Bellows
30. Screw
31. Housing
32. Gasket
33. O-ring
34. RAVE valve
35. Screw
36. Lockwasher
37. Gaskets
38. Exhaust manifold

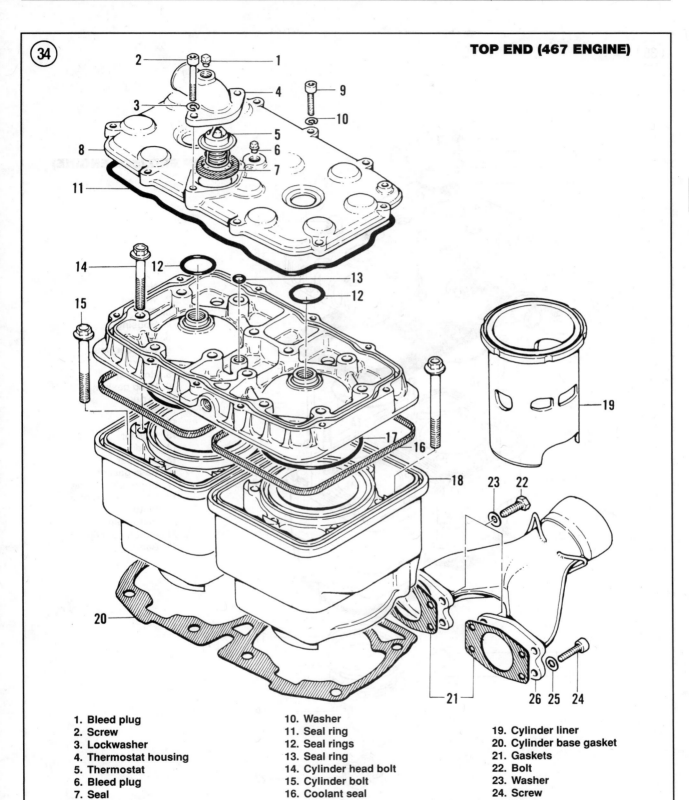

③④ **TOP END (467 ENGINE)**

5

1. Bleed plug
2. Screw
3. Lockwasher
4. Thermostat housing
5. Thermostat
6. Bleed plug
7. Seal
8. Cylinder head cover
9. Cover screw
10. Washer
11. Seal ring
12. Seal rings
13. Seal ring
14. Cylinder head bolt
15. Cylinder bolt
16. Coolant seal
17. Compression seal
18. Cylinder
19. Cylinder liner
20. Cylinder base gasket
21. Gaskets
22. Bolt
23. Washer
24. Screw
25. Washer
26. Exhaust manifold

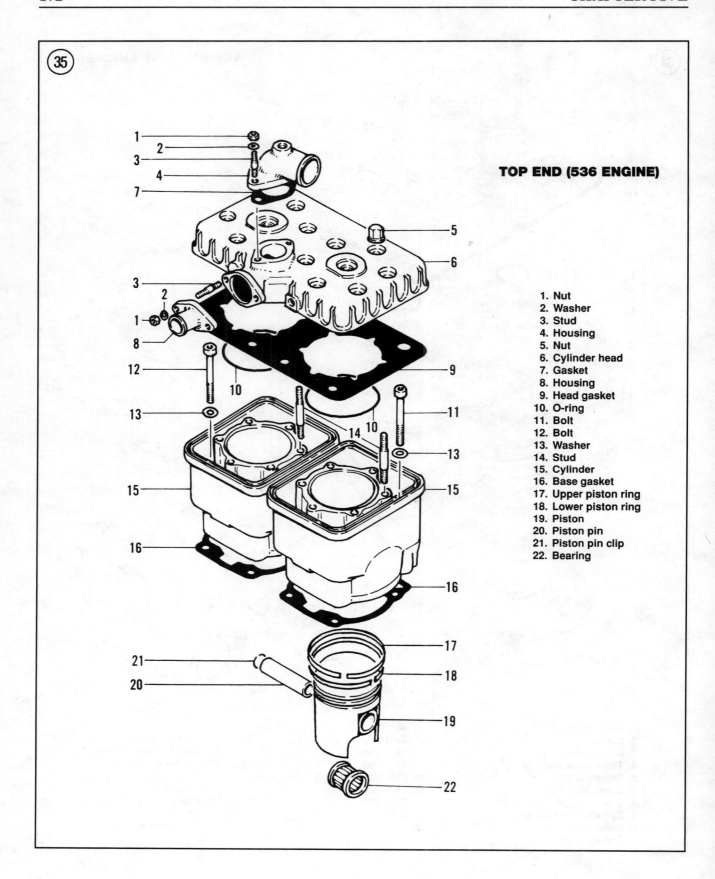

TOP END (536 ENGINE)

1. Nut
2. Washer
3. Stud
4. Housing
5. Nut
6. Cylinder head
7. Gasket
8. Housing
9. Head gasket
10. O-ring
11. Bolt
12. Bolt
13. Washer
14. Stud
15. Cylinder
16. Base gasket
17. Upper piston ring
18. Lower piston ring
19. Piston
20. Piston pin
21. Piston pin clip
22. Bearing

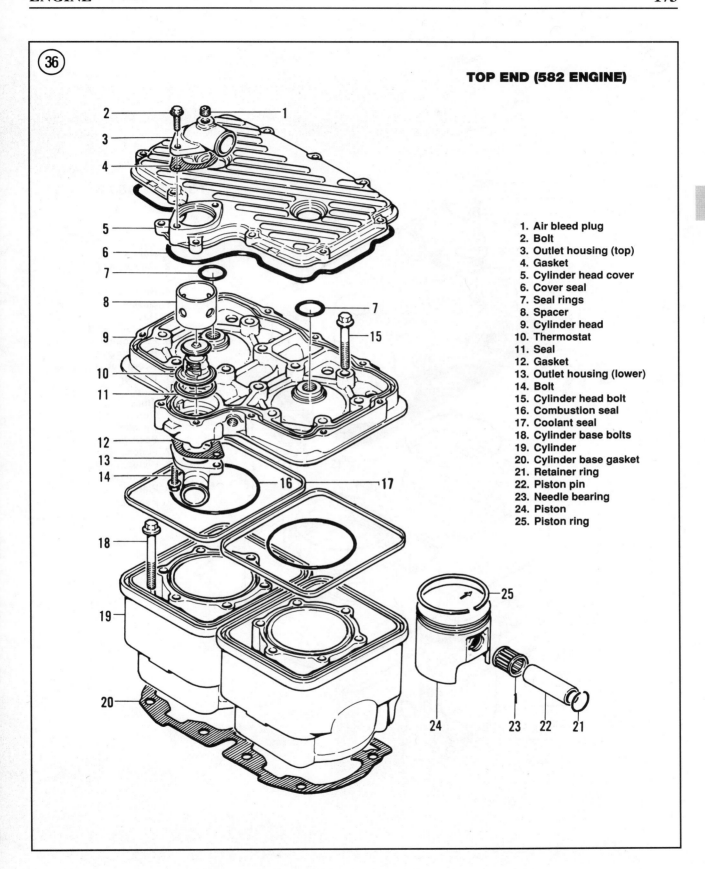

TOP END (582 ENGINE)

1. Air bleed plug
2. Bolt
3. Outlet housing (top)
4. Gasket
5. Cylinder head cover
6. Cover seal
7. Seal rings
8. Spacer
9. Cylinder head
10. Thermostat
11. Seal
12. Gasket
13. Outlet housing (lower)
14. Bolt
15. Cylinder head bolt
16. Combustion seal
17. Coolant seal
18. Cylinder base bolts
19. Cylinder
20. Cylinder base gasket
21. Retainer ring
22. Piston pin
23. Needle bearing
24. Piston
25. Piston ring

5

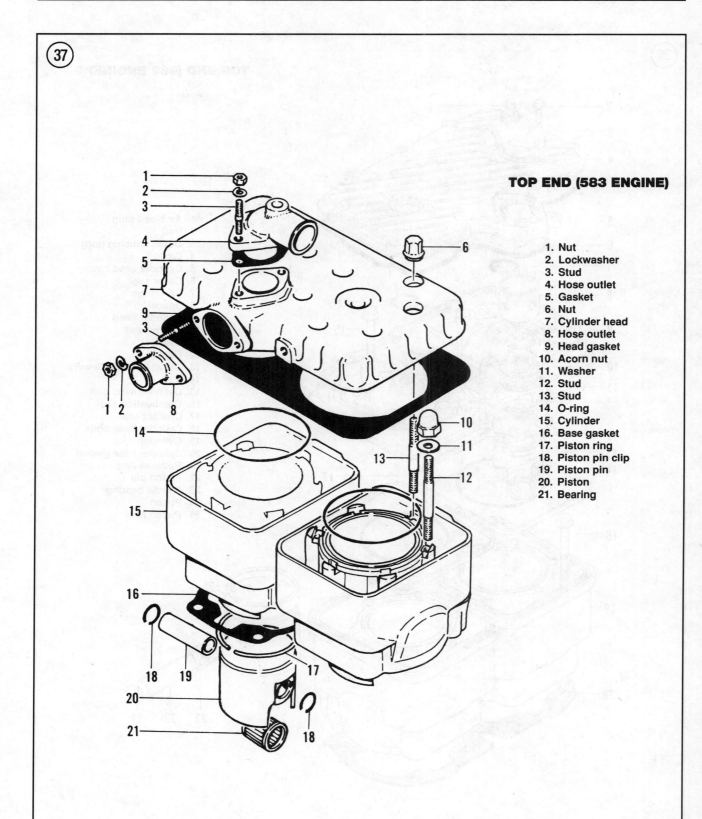

(37)

TOP END (583 ENGINE)

1. Nut
2. Lockwasher
3. Stud
4. Hose outlet
5. Gasket
6. Nut
7. Cylinder head
8. Hose outlet
9. Head gasket
10. Acorn nut
11. Washer
12. Stud
13. Stud
14. O-ring
15. Cylinder
16. Base gasket
17. Piston ring
18. Piston pin clip
19. Piston pin
20. Piston
21. Bearing

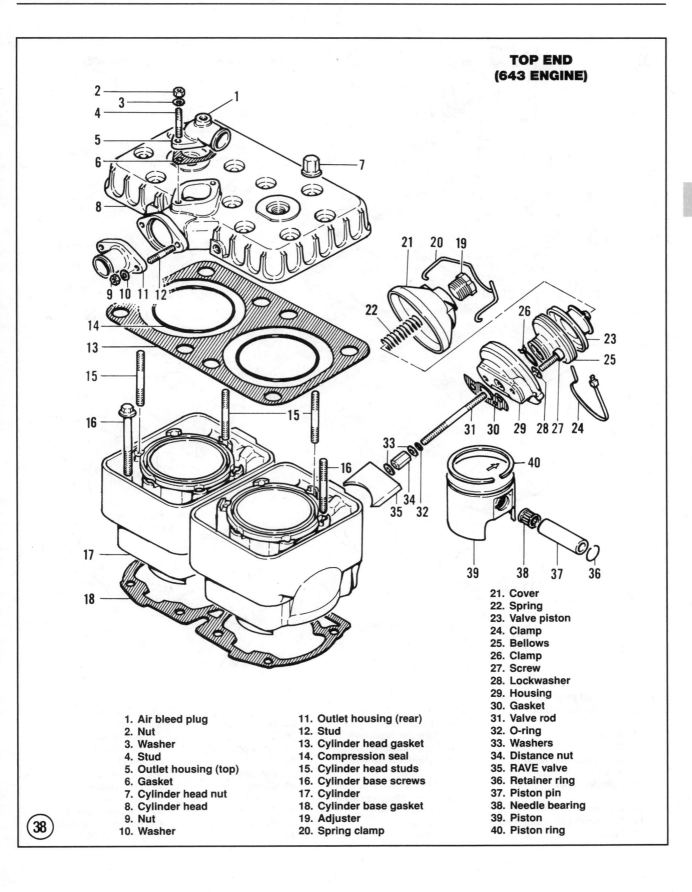

**TOP END
(643 ENGINE)**

5

1. Air bleed plug
2. Nut
3. Washer
4. Stud
5. Outlet housing (top)
6. Gasket
7. Cylinder head nut
8. Cylinder head
9. Nut
10. Washer

11. Outlet housing (rear)
12. Stud
13. Cylinder head gasket
14. Compression seal
15. Cylinder head studs
16. Cylinder base screws
17. Cylinder
18. Cylinder base gasket
19. Adjuster
20. Spring clamp

21. Cover
22. Spring
23. Valve piston
24. Clamp
25. Bellows
26. Clamp
27. Screw
28. Lockwasher
29. Housing
30. Gasket
31. Valve rod
32. O-ring
33. Washers
34. Distance nut
35. RAVE valve
36. Retainer ring
37. Piston pin
38. Needle bearing
39. Piston
40. Piston ring

38

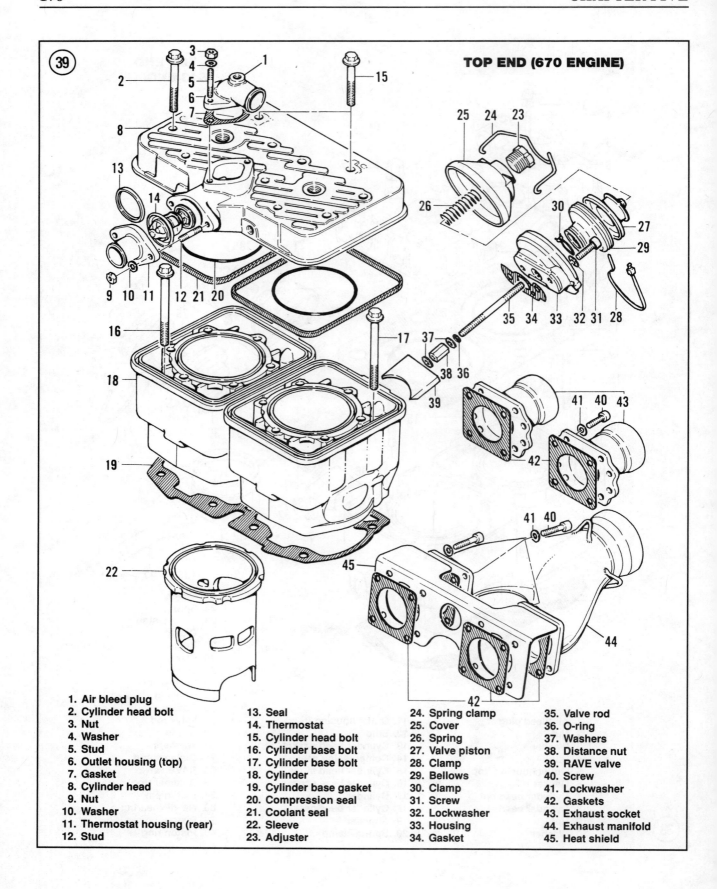

39   **TOP END (670 ENGINE)**

1. Air bleed plug
2. Cylinder head bolt
3. Nut
4. Washer
5. Stud
6. Outlet housing (top)
7. Gasket
8. Cylinder head
9. Nut
10. Washer
11. Thermostat housing (rear)
12. Stud
13. Seal
14. Thermostat
15. Cylinder head bolt
16. Cylinder base bolt
17. Cylinder base bolt
18. Cylinder
19. Cylinder base gasket
20. Compression seal
21. Coolant seal
22. Sleeve
23. Adjuster
24. Spring clamp
25. Cover
26. Spring
27. Valve piston
28. Clamp
29. Bellows
30. Clamp
31. Screw
32. Lockwasher
33. Housing
34. Gasket
35. Valve rod
36. O-ring
37. Washers
38. Distance nut
39. RAVE valve
40. Screw
41. Lockwasher
42. Gaskets
43. Exhaust socket
44. Exhaust manifold
45. Heat shield

port the hood while you remove the screws that attach the hood hinge to the chassis. Remove the hood and set it out of the way to prevent it from being damaged.

b. Drain the cooling system as described in Chapter Three.

c. Loosen the hose clamp (A, **Figure 40** or A, **Figure 41**), then disconnect the coolant hose(s) from the cylinder head.

d. Disconnect both spark plug cables from the spark plugs.

NOTE
It may be necessary to remove the air silencer to gain access 1 cylinder head mounting fastener. If so, remove the air silencer as described in Chapter Six or Chapter Seven.

2. Loosen, but do not remove, the spark plugs so they can be removed later.

3. On 467 and 582 engines, carefully remove the 12 screws (B, **Figure 40**) attaching the cylinder head cover to the cylinder head. Loosen the cover by tapping around the outer edge with a rubber or plastic mallet, then carefully remove the cover.

4A. On 467 and 582 engines, loosen the cylinder head retaining screws (**Figure 42**) in a crisscross pattern.

4B. On all models except 467 and 582, loosen the cylinder head retaining screws or nuts (B, **Figure 41**) in a crisscross pattern.

5. Loosen the cylinder head by tapping around the perimeter with a rubber or plastic mallet, then remove the cylinder head.

6. Remove and discard the cylinder head gaskets. Refer to **Figures 33-39**.

7. Lay a rag over the open cylinders to prevent dirt from falling into the cylinders or water passages.

8. Inspect the cylinder head as described in this chapter.

NOTE
*While the cylinder head is removed, check the retaining studs (**Figure 43**) or screws for stripped threads or other damage. Make sure that studs are tight in cylinder threads. Check the condition of threads (**Figure 44**) for the cylinder head and cylinder head cover retaining screws. If necessary, remove the cylinder*

and replace damaged studs or repair damaged threads as described in this chapter.

NOTE
*On all 467 engines and 1993-on 582 engines, alignment pins must be installed as shown in **Figure 45** to protect the cylinder head seal rings from being damaged while installing the cylinder head.*

9. Install the head gaskets as follows:
   a. *454, 467, 582 and 670*: Install the inner (A, **Figure 46**) and outer (B, **Figure 46**) O-rings into the cylinder O-ring grooves. Check that each O-ring seats squarely in the groove.
   b. *536, 583 and 643*: Install the inner O-ring in the cylinder groove (**Figure 47**). Install the cylinder head and gasket so that the row of large holes (**Figure 48**) is on the front (exhaust side) and the row of smaller holes is on the opposite (inlet) side.

10. Install the cylinder head so the thermostat mounting area faces to the rear (inlet side) of the engine. See **Figures 33-39**.

11. Lubricate the threads of cylinder head retaining studs or screws and install finger tight.

CAUTION
On models with acorn nuts attaching the cylinder head, it is important to make sure that the stud does not bottom in the nut. If you replaced the cylinder studs and one or more acorn nuts bottom out,

the stud was not installed deep enough or the wrong end of the stud was threaded into the cylinder. Refer to **Cylinder Head Stud Replacement** in this chapter for the correct procedure. If you are still having problems, install a washer underneath the nut until you can reposition or replace the stud. Make sure that the stud is not pulling out of the lower end.

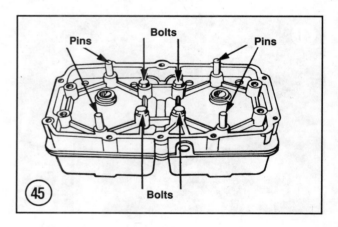

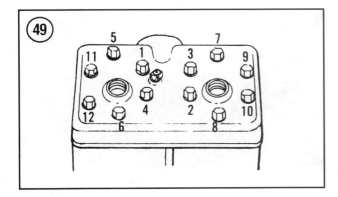

12. Tighten the retaining screws or nuts in the sequence shown in **Figure 49** to the torque specification in **Table 11**.

13. On models with a cylinder head cover observe the following:

   a. Install the O-rings (A, **Figure 50**) around the spark plug holes. Install the large perimeter O-ring (B, **Figure 50**).

   NOTE
   *Some engines that have the cylinder head cover may not have the hole that is sealed by the small O-ring in the center of the cylinder head shown in C, **Figure 50**.*

   b. Install the small O-ring (C, **Figure 50**) on models so equipped.

   c. Install the cylinder head cover and tighten the screws in a crisscross pattern to the torque listed in **Table 11**.

14. Set the gap and install the spark plugs as described in Chapter Three.

15. If the engine is installed in the frame, perform the following:

   a. Connect the spark plug cables to the spark plugs.

   b. Connect the coolant hoses to the cylinder head. **Figure 40** and **Figure 41** show a typical installations.

   c. Refill the cooling system as described in Chapter Three.

   d. Reinstall the engine hood.

Inspection

1. Wipe away any soft deposits from the cylinder head (**Figure 51**). Carefully remove hard deposits with a wire brush or a soft metal scraper. Be careful not to gouge the aluminum surfaces. Burrs created from improper cleaning might cause preignition.

   NOTE
   Always use an aluminum thread fluid or kerosene on the thread chaser and cylin-

der head threads when performing Step 2.

2. With the spark plug removed, check the spark plug threads (**Figure 52**) in the cylinder head for carbon buildup or cracking. The carbon can be removed with a 14 mm spark plug chaser. After cleaning the threads, reinstall the spark plug and make sure it can be installed all the way (**Figure 53**).

3. Use a straightedge and feeler gauge to measure the flatness of the cylinder head (**Figure 54**). Remove small imperfections or slight warpage by resurfacing the cylinder head as follows:

   a. Tape a piece of 400-600 grit wet emery sandpaper to a piece of thick plate glass or surface plate (**Figure 55**).

   b. Slowly resurface the head by moving it in a figure-eight pattern on the sandpaper (**Figure 56**).

   c. Rotate the head several times to avoid removing too much material from one side. Check progress often with the straightedge and feeler gauge (**Figure 54**).

   d. If the cylinder head warpage still exceeds the service limit, have the head resurfaced by a machine shop familiar with snowmobile and motorcycle service. Note that removing material from the cylinder head mating surface will change the compression ratio and clearance of the squish area around the outside edge.

4. Check the cylinder head water passages (**Figure 57**) for coolant residue and sludge buildup. Clean passages thoroughly with solvent and allow to dry thoroughly.

5. Wash the cylinder head in soap and hot water and rinse thoroughly before installation.

CYLINDER

An aluminum cylinder block is used with a cast iron liner (sleeve). On most models, the cylinder liner can be bored and oversize pistons

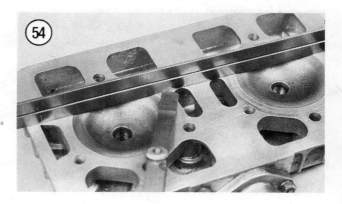

and rings installed to correct for severe wear. New standard size cylinder liners are available that can be installed by a competent machine shop. Before removing or reboring a cylinder liner, be sure to check availability.

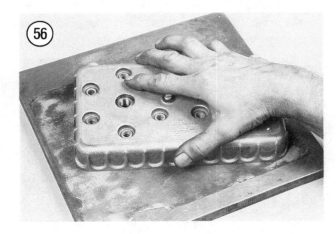

Refer to illustration for your model when servicing the cylinder.

   a. **Figure 33**: Engine 454.
   b. **Figure 34**: Engine 467.
   c. **Figure 35**: Engine 536.
   d. **Figure 36**: Engine 582.
   e. **Figure 37**: Engine 583.
   f. **Figure 38**: Engine 643.
   g. **Figure 39**: Engine 670.

5

Removal

1. Remove the cylinder head as described in this chapter.

2. If the engine is installed in the frame, remove the muffler and exhaust pipe(s) as described in Chapter Eight.

3A. On engines with a Y-type exhaust manifold, unbolt and remove the manifold from both cylinders.

3B. On engines with separate exhaust pipes for each cylinder, unbolt the exhaust socket from each cylinder.

> *NOTE*
> *Some models are equipped with a heat deflector that is unbolted with the exhaust manifold. Gaskets are located on both sides of the exhaust deflector.*

4A. On 1990 MACH 1 and MACH 1 XTC models, gradually loosen the 4 acorn nuts attaching each cylinder to the crankcase in a crisscross pattern. Then remove the nuts (**Figure 58**) and washers (**Figure 59**).

4B. The cylinders on all models except 1990 models with 583 engine, are attached to the crankcase with bolts. Remove the 4 bolts from inside the cylinder's water passage.

> *NOTE*
> *Both cylinders must be reinstalled in their original mounting positions. Mark the left cylinder "PTO" and the right cylinder "MAG" before removal.*

5. Rotate the engine until one piston is at the bottom of its stroke, then pull the cylinder (**Figure 60**) straight up, away from the piston.

6. Repeat procedure to remove the other cylinder.

7. Remove and discard the cylinder base gasket.

8. Cover the openings in the crankcase around the connecting rods with clean rags to keep dirt and loose parts from entering the crankcase.

9. *454, 583, 643 and 670*: Cylinders for these engines are equipped with the Rotax Automatic Variable Exhaust (RAVE) system. If necessary, remove and service the RAVE assembly as described in this chapter.

Inspection

Cylinder measurement requires a precision inside micrometer or bore gauge. If you don't have the right tools, have your dealer or a machine shop measure the parts.

1. Remove all gasket residue from the bottom (**Figure 61**) gasket surface.

2. Clean the cylinder O-ring groove (**Figure 62**) with a scribe or other sharp tool.

3. Clean all gasket residue from the exhaust manifold sealing area (A, **Figure 63**) of the cylinder.

> *NOTE*
> *On 454, 583, 643 and 670 models, remove the RAVE valve before cleaning the exhaust port in Step 4. Remove the RAVE valve as described in this chapter.*

4. Use a soft scraper or a wire brush to remove all carbon deposits from the exhaust port (B, **Figure 63**).

> *CAUTION*
> *When cleaning the exhaust port in Step 4, do not allow the wire brush or scraper to slip inside the cylinder and damage the cylinder liner. Be especially careful if using power equipment, such as a rotating wire brush and an electric drill.*

5. Wash the cylinder with hot soapy water, then rinse with water to remove loose dirt and carbon particles before attempting to measure the cylinder bore. Measurements may be incorrect if the cylinder is not cleaned thoroughly.

6. Measure the cylinder bore diameter as described under *Piston/Cylinder Clearance Check* in this chapter.

5

NOTE
If the cylinder diameters are within specification, it is possible to buy and install new standard size pistons without reboring. New pistons will take up some of the excessive piston-to-cylinder clearance. However, do not install new stand-

ard size pistons in a cylinder that is worn past the wear limit.

7. If the cylinder is not worn past the service limit, check the bore carefully for scratches or gouges that require reconditioning.

NOTE
If a partial piston seizure occurred prior to tearing down the engine, aluminum from the piston(s) may be stuck to the cylinder(s). A machine shop can safely remove this aluminum transfer; however, if the cylinder is scored, it must be bored oversize.

8. Check all threaded holes in the cylinder block for thread damage. Minor damage can be cleaned up with a suitable metric tap. Refer to Chapter One for information pertaining to threads, fasteners and repair tools. If damage is severe, a thread insert should be installed.

9. Check the studs (C, **Figure 63**) for stripped threads or other damage. If necessary, replace studs as described in this chapter.

10. After the cylinder has been serviced, wash the bore with hot soapy water. This is the only way to clean the fine grit material left from the bore or honing job from the cylinder wall. After washing, run a clean white cloth through the cylinder. The cylinder and the white cloth should show no traces of grit or other debris. If still dirty, the cylinder wall must be rewashed. After the cylinder is thoroughly cleaned, lubricate the cylinder wall with clean engine oil to prevent the iron cylinder liners from rusting.

CAUTION
A combination of soap and water is the only solution that will completely clean the cylinder wall. Kerosene and similar solvents will drive the fine grit into crevices and porous surfaces. Grit left in the cylinder will act as a grinding compound and cause premature wear to the new rings.

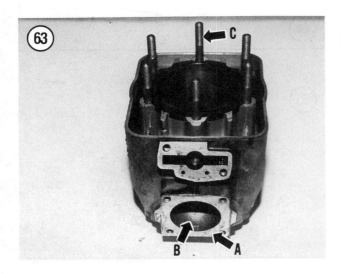

Cylinder Stud Replacement

Damaged or dirty threaded holes or studs will prevent parts from fitting together as tightly as they should, allowing combustion gases to escape. This will reduce engine performance and cause engine damage. When an acorn nut is used, a specified stud length (**Figure 64**) must be maintained to prevent the nut from bottoming on the stud before it is properly torqued. Replace damaged studs as follows:

A tube of Loctite 242 (blue), 2 nuts, 2 wrenches and a new stud is required during this procedure.

1. Thread 2 nuts onto the damaged cylinder stud. Then tighten the 2 nuts against each other so that they are locked.

NOTE
If the threads of the damaged stud do not allow installation of the 2 nuts, you can remove the stud with a pair of locking pliers.

2. Turn the bottom nut and stud counterclockwise to unscrew the stud.

3. Clean the threaded hole in the cylinder with solvent or electrical contact cleaner and allow to thoroughly dry.

NOTE
*When installing the new stud, install it so that the end with the shorter thread is screwed into the threaded hole of the cylinder. Refer to **Figure 64**.*

4. Install 2 nuts on the longer threads of the new stud as in Step 1 and tighten to make sure they are locked together securely.

5. Coat the shorter threads of the new stud with Loctite 242 (blue).

6. Turn the top nut and stud clockwise to screw the new stud in securely. Measure the distance (**Figure 65**) from the cylinder surface to the top of the installed stud. The stud height should be 43 mm (1.70 in.). If not, reposition the stud as necessary.

7. Remove the nuts and repeat for each stud as required.

8. Follow Loctite's directions on cure time before assembling the component.

Installation

The cylinders must be properly aligned during installation so the holes in the cylinder head will align with the cylinder studs or threaded holes in cylinder blocks. Ski-Doo offers special aligning tools for this purpose. The following procedure

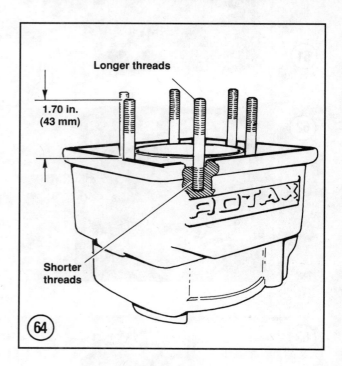

describes cylinder installation and alignment with and without the special tools. If you purchase the aligning tools, make sure to purchase the correct tools for your engine.

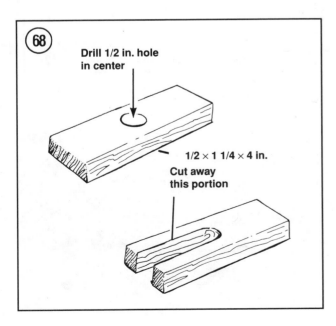

1. *454, 583, 643 and 670 engines*: Install the RAVE assembly, if previously removed, as described in this chapter.

2. Clean the cylinder bore as described under *Inspection* in this chapter.

3. Make sure the top surface of the crankcase and the bottom cylinder surface are clean prior to installation.

4. Install new base gaskets (**Figure 66**).

> *NOTE*
> *Check the pistons to make sure the piston pin clips are installed and correctly positioned with their gaps toward the bottom.*

5. Make sure the end gaps of the piston rings are aligned with the locating pins in the ring grooves (**Figure 67**). Oil the piston rings and the inside of the cylinder bores lightly with engine oil.

6. Place a piston holding tool under one piston and turn the crankshaft until the piston is down firmly against the tool. This will make cylinder installation easier.

> *NOTE*
> *You can make this tool from wood as shown in **Figure 68**.*

> *NOTE*
> *When installing, make sure to install the cylinder previously marked PTO on the left-hand side. If the cylinders were rebored, make sure to match the cylinder with its individual piston.*

7. Align the cylinder with the piston so the exhaust port faces toward the front of the engine. Install the cylinder, compressing each piston ring with your fingers as the cylinder slides over it. When the both rings are in the cylinder, slide the cylinder down and remove the piston holding tool. Slide the cylinder all the way down against the gasket and crankcase. Make sure the base of the cylinder is fully seated against the crankcase.

8. Repeat Step 7 to install the other cylinder.

9A. *454 engine models:* Install and align the cylinders as follows:

a. Install the special screws that attach the cylinder bases to the crankcase and tighten the bolts finger tight. The shorter bolts are for the exhaust side.

b. Attach the special cylinder aligning tool to the exhaust flanges as shown in **Figure 69**. If the special alignment tool is not available, the exhaust manifold can be temporarily attached to the cylinder flanges to align the cylinders.

c. Check alignment by temporarily fitting the cylinder head without gaskets or seals, then turning the engine crankshaft one turn. Remove the cylinder head when you are confident that the cylinders are aligned.

NOTE
Hold onto the crankcase when tightening the cylinder retaining screws in sub-step d. Do not hold onto the cylinders for support when tightening.

d. Remove the cylinder base bolts one at a time, coat threads with Loctite 242 thread lock, then reinstall the bolts. Tighten the bolts in the sequence shown in **Figure 70** to the torque listed in **Table 11**. Refer to (**Figure 71**).

9B. *467 engines and 582 engines of 1993-on models:* Install and align the cylinders as follows:

a. Install the special screws that attach the cylinder bases to the crankcase and tighten the screws finger tight.

b. Use a feeler gauge as shown in **Figure 72** to set the gap between the cylinders to 0.43 mm (0.017 in.). Make sure that gap is the same all the way across the cylinders.

c. Install alignment pins in the 4 positions shown in **Figure 45** and temporarily install the cylinder head over the alignment pins. Be sure that it is not necessary to move the cylinders to install the cylinder head over the alignment pins, then remove the cylinder head.

NOTE
Hold onto the crankcase when tightening the cylinder retaining bolts in sub-step d. Do not hold onto the cylinders for support when tightening.

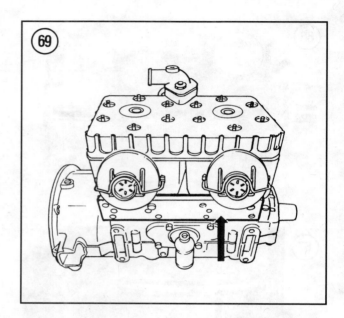

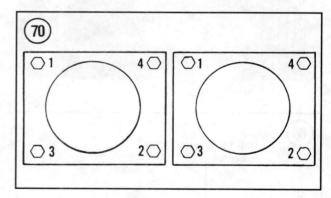

d. Remove the cylinder base bolts one at a time, coat threads with Loctite 242 thread lock, then reinstall the bolts. Tighten the screws in the sequence shown in **Figure 70** to the torque listed in **Table 11**. Refer to (**Figure 71**).

9C. *All 1990 536 and 583 engine models:* Install and align the cylinders as follows:

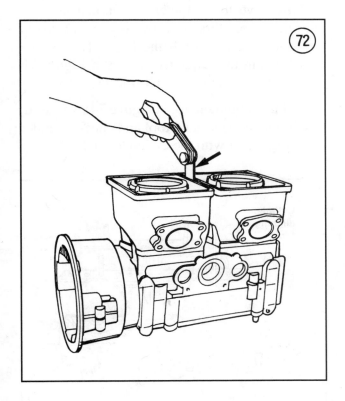

a. Install the washers (**Figure 59**) and nuts (**Figure 58**) on all of the cylinder retaining studs.

b. Tighten all of the cylinder retaining nuts finger tight.

c. Turn the crankshaft 1 revolution and allow cylinders to move slightly into alignment.

d. Attach the special alignment tool to the cylinder head studs as shown in **Figure 73** or install the cylinder head (upside down with spark plugs removed) onto the cylinder head retaining studs and turn the crankshaft again.

e. Install the exhaust manifold or special alignment tool as shown in **Figure 69** and secure it with its mounting screws finger tight.

f. Turn the crankshaft once again to align cylinders.

NOTE
Hold onto the crankcase when tightening the cylinder retaining nuts in substep g. Do not hold onto the cylinders for support when tightening.

g. Remove the cylinder head and tighten the cylinder nuts in a crisscross pattern (**Figure 70**) to the torque specification in **Table 11**. See **Figure 71**.

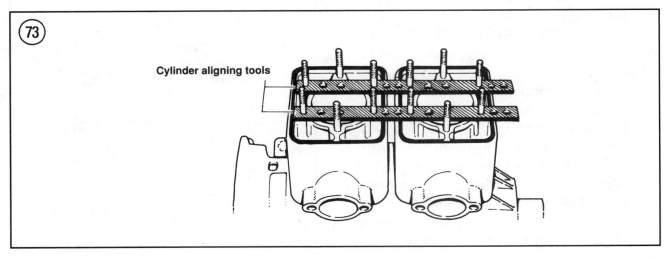

Cylinder aligning tools

h. If the alignment tool (**Figure 73**) was used, remove the special tool and check cylinder alignment with the cylinder head.

i. Remove the special alignment tool (**Figure 69**) or exhaust manifold.

9D. *1994-on 583 engine models:* Install and align the cylinders as follows:

a. Install the special screws that attach the cylinder bases to the crankcase and tighten the screws finger tight. The shorter screws are for the exhaust side.

b. Attach the special cylinder aligning tool to the exhaust flanges as shown in **Figure 69**. If the special alignment tool is not available, the exhaust manifold can be temporarily attached to the cylinder flanges to align the cylinders.

c. Check alignment by temporarily fitting the cylinder head without gaskets or seals, then turning the engine crankshaft one turn. Remove the cylinder head when you are confident that the cylinders are aligned.

NOTE
Hold onto the crankcase when tightening the cylinder retaining bolts in sub-step d. Do not hold onto the cylinders for support when tightening.

d. Remove the cylinder base bolts one at a time, coat the threads with Loctite 242 thread lock, then reinstall the bolts. Tighten the bolts in the sequence shown in **Figure 70** to the torque listed in **Table 11**.

9E. *643 engine models:* Install and align cylinders as follows:

a. Install the special screws that attach the cylinder bases to the crankcase and tighten the screws finger tight.

b. Attach the special alignment tool to the cylinder head studs as shown in **Figure 74** or temporarily install the cylinder head onto the cylinder head retaining studs.

c. Install the exhaust manifold or special alignment tool as shown in **Figure 69** and

secure it with its mounting screws tightened to the torque specified in **Table 11**.

NOTE
Hold onto the crankcase when tightening the cylinder retaining bolts in sub-step d. Do not hold onto the cylinders for support when tightening.

d. Remove the cylinder base bolts one at a time, coat threads with Loctite 242 thread lock, then reinstall the bolts. Tighten the bolts in the sequence shown in **Figure 70** to the torque listed in **Table 11**.

e. If the alignment tool (**Figure 74**) was used, remove the special tool and check cylinder alignment with the cylinder head.

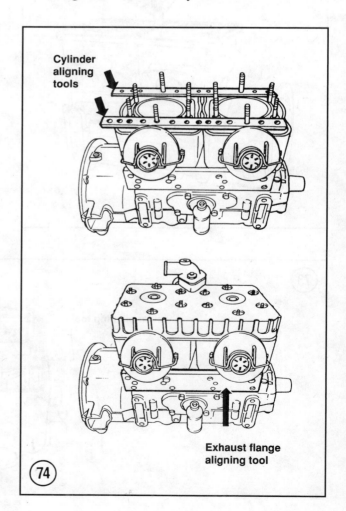

Cylinder aligning tools

Exhaust flange aligning tool

74

f. Remove the special alignment tool (**Figure 74**) or exhaust manifold.

9F. *670 engine models:* Install and align the cylinders as follows:

a. Install the special screws that attach the cylinder bases to the crankcase and tighten the screws finger tight. The shorter screws are for the exhaust side.

b. Use a feeler gauge as shown in **Figure 72** to set the gap between the cylinders to 0.43 mm (0.017 in.). Make sure that gap is the same all the way across the cylinders.

c. Install alignment pins in the 4 outer positions similar to the positions shown in **Figure 45** (typical).

d. Temporarily install the cylinder head over the alignment pins. Be sure that it is not necessary to move the cylinders to install the cylinder head over the alignment pins, then remove the cylinder head.

NOTE
Hold onto the crankcase when tightening the cylinder retaining screws in substep e. Do not hold onto the cylinders for support when tightening.

e. Remove the cylinder base bolts one at a time, coat threads with Loctite 242 thread lock, then reinstall the bolts. Tighten the bolts in the sequence shown in **Figure 70** to the torque listed in **Table 11**. Refer to (**Figure 71**).

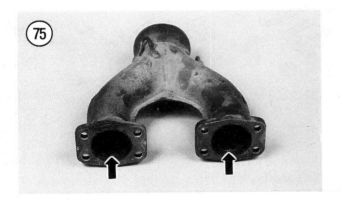

NOTE
*Do not remove the alignment pins **Figure 45**) until after cylinder head is installed.*

NOTE
*Before installing the exhaust manifold, check the ports and passages in the manifold for carbon buildup (**Figure 75**). If carbon buildup is severe, clean the ports as described under **Exhaust System** in Chapter Eight.*

10A. On engines with Y-manifold, but *without a heat shield*, install the exhaust manifold with new gaskets. Install the manifold screws and washers and tighten to the torque specification in **Table 11**.

10B. On engines *with a heat shield* partially covering the exhaust manifold, install the heat shield and exhaust manifold assembly in the following order:

a. Position gaskets against the cylinder ports.

b. Position the heat shield so that the bend faces away from the cylinders as shown in **Figure 4**.

c. Install two more gaskets.

d. Install the exhaust manifold.

e. Install the manifold screws and washers.

f. Tighten exhaust screws to the torque specification in **Table 11**.

10C. On engines *with individual exhaust pipes*, install the exhaust socket for each exhaust pipe using a new gasket. Tighten the retaining screws to the torque specified in **Table 11**.

11. Install the cylinder head as described in this chapter.

12. Install the exhaust pipe and muffler as described in Chapter Eight.

13. If new components were installed or if the cylinders were bored or honed, the engine must be broken-in as if it were new. Refer to *Break-In Procedure* in Chapter Three.

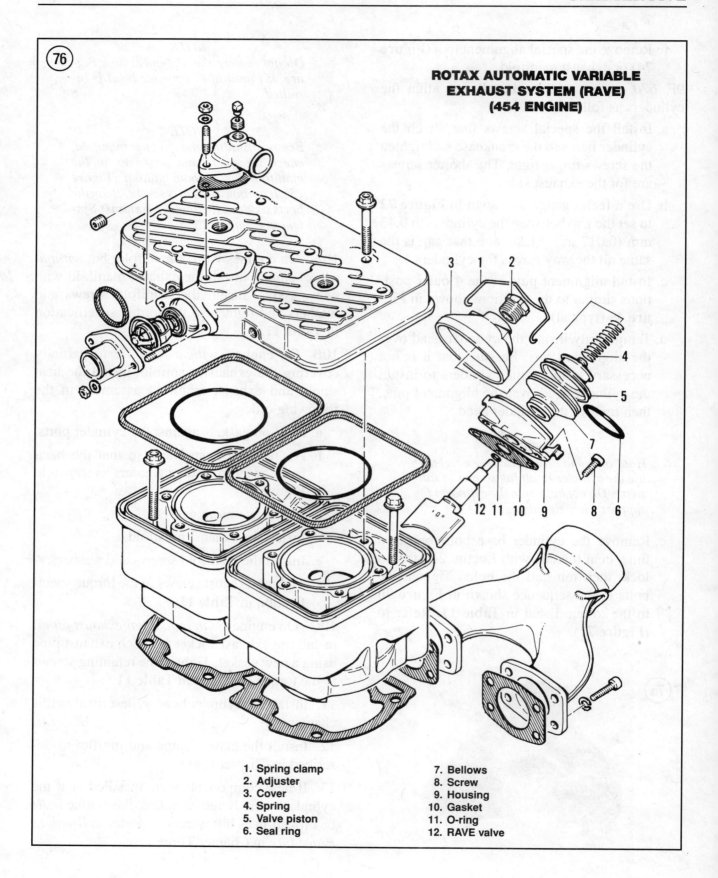

(76)

**ROTAX AUTOMATIC VARIABLE
EXHAUST SYSTEM (RAVE)
(454 ENGINE)**

1. Spring clamp
2. Adjuster
3. Cover
4. Spring
5. Valve piston
6. Seal ring
7. Bellows
8. Screw
9. Housing
10. Gasket
11. O-ring
12. RAVE valve

ROTAX AUTOMATIC VARIABLE EXHAUST (RAVE) (454, 583, 643 AND 670 ENGINES)

These engines are equipped with the Rotax Automatic Variable Exhaust (RAVE). Refer to **Figure 76** or **Figure 77** when performing procedures in this section. The RAVE assembly for 454 engines (**Figure 77**) is slightly different from other models, but the service procedure is similar for all models.

Removal

The RAVE assembly can be removed with the engine mounted in the snowmobile. Illustrations for this procedure show the cylinder removed for clarity.

1. Pry the spring clip (A, **Figure 78**) away from the cover (B, **Figure 78**) and remove the cover.
2. Remove the spring (**Figure 79**).
3. Unscrew and remove the valve piston (**Figure 80**).

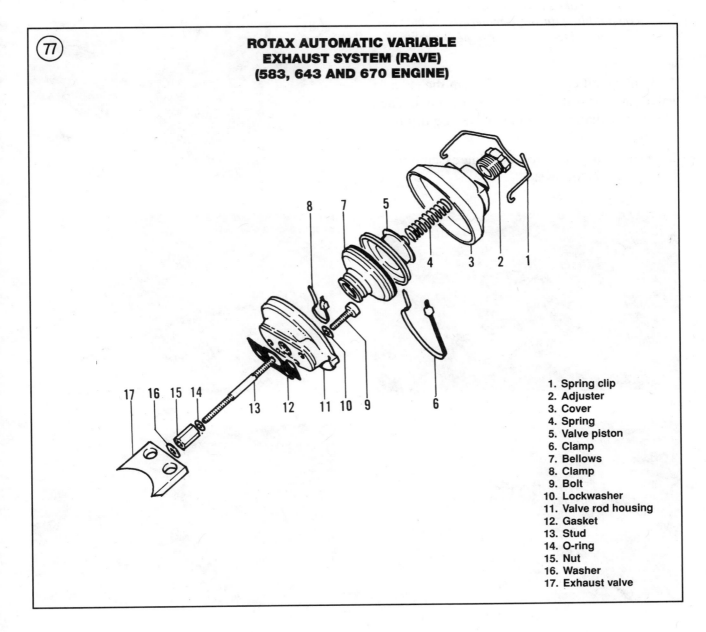

ROTAX AUTOMATIC VARIABLE EXHAUST SYSTEM (RAVE) (583, 643 AND 670 ENGINE)

1. Spring clip
2. Adjuster
3. Cover
4. Spring
5. Valve piston
6. Clamp
7. Bellows
8. Clamp
9. Bolt
10. Lockwasher
11. Valve rod housing
12. Gasket
13. Stud
14. O-ring
15. Nut
16. Washer
17. Exhaust valve

4. Remove the screws holding the valve rod housing onto the cylinder block (**Figure 81**). Remove the valve rod housing (**Figure 82**).

5. Remove the gasket (**Figure 83**).

6. Remove the exhaust valve (**Figure 84**).

Inspection

> *CAUTION*
> *Before cleaning plastic or rubber components, make sure the cleaning agent is compatible with these materials. Some types of solvents can cause permanent damage.*

1. Remove all carbon residue from the exhaust valve and the valve port in the cylinder. Then clean the exhaust valve in solvent and dry thoroughly.

2. Inspect the valve rod housing assembly (A, **Figure 85**) as follows:

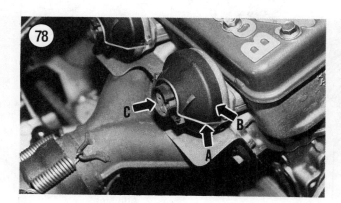

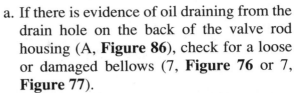

a. If there is evidence of oil draining from the drain hole on the back of the valve rod housing (A, **Figure 86**), check for a loose or damaged bellows (7, **Figure 76** or 7, **Figure 77**).

b. Check the bellows (B, **Figure 85**) for splitting or other damage. If the bellows is damaged, replace it by removing it from the valve rod housing. When installing the bellows, secure it with a new cable tie (6, **Figure 76**).

c. Check the passages in the valve rod housing (B, **Figure 86**) and cylinder (**Figure 87**) for buildup of residue. Clean passages with a piece of wire or other tool that won't enlarge or otherwise damage the opening.

3. Visually check the exhaust valve (**Figure 88**) for cracks, deep scoring, excessive wear, heat discoloration or other damage.

4. Check the O-ring (B, **Figure 89**) for heat deterioration that shows up as cracks or splitting.

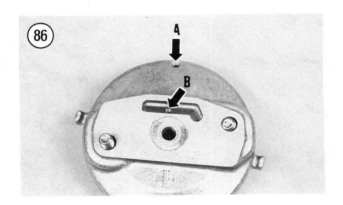

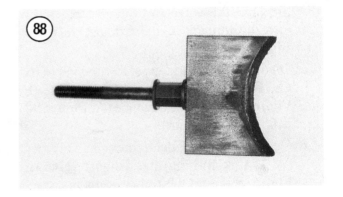

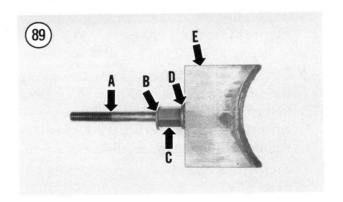

5. If necessary, service the exhaust valve as follows:

   a. Slide the O-ring (B, **Figure 89**) from the valve rod.

   b. On 583, 643 and 670 engine models, secure the exhaust valve (E, **Figure 89**) in a soft-jawed vise. Unscrew the valve rod (C, **Figure 89**) from the exhaust valve and remove the washer (D, **Figure 89**). Separate the nut from the valve rod.

   c. Replace worn or damaged parts. Remove all Loctite residue from the valve rod, nut and exhaust valve.

   d. On 583, 643 and 670 engine models, screw the nut (C, **Figure 89**) onto the longer threaded end of the valve rod (A, **Figure 89**) with the notched end of the nut facing away from the valve and washer (C, **Figure 89**). Turn the nut onto the valve rod until it stops. Slide the washer (D, **Figure 89**) over the valve rod until it rests against the nut (C, **Figure 89**). Apply high-temperature Loctite onto the valve rod threads that screw into the threads of the exhaust valve (E, **Figure 89**).

   e. On 583 engine models, screw the valve rod (A, **Figure 89**) into the exhaust valve (E, **Figure 89**) until the distance (A, **Figure 90**) is 63 mm (2.480 in.).

   f. On 643 engine models, screw the valve rod (A, **Figure 89**) into the exhaust valve (E, **Figure 89**) until the rod bottoms out.

   g. On 670 engine models, screw the valve rod (A, **Figure 89**) into the exhaust valve (E, **Figure 89**) until the distance (A, **Figure 90**) is 59.5 mm (2.3425 in.).

   h. On 583, 643 and 670 engine models, secure the exhaust valve in a soft-jawed vise and tighten the nut (C, **Figure 89**) securely against the exhaust valve (E, **Figure 89**) without disturbing the set distance.

   i. On all models, install a new O-ring (B, **Figure 89**) over the valve rod.

6. Inspect the spring (**Figure 91**) for fatigue or breakage. If the spring is too weak, the RAVE valve will open too soon and there will be a mid-range hesitation. If a spring that is too strong has been substituted, the engine will not be able to reach full rpm. Springs have been used with different wire sizes, but free length should be as follows:

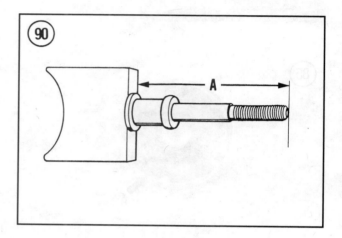

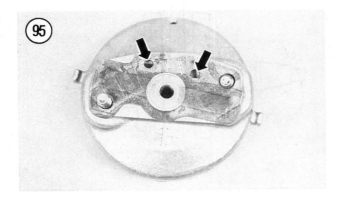

a. On 1990-1993 models with 583, 643 or 670 engine models, the free length of the spring (**Figure 91**) should be 48.5 mm (1 29/32 in.).

b. On 1994-on models with 583 and 670 engine models, the free length of the spring (**Figure 91**) should be 38.0 mm (1 1/2 in.).

c. On 1995 models with 454 engine models, the free length of the spring (**Figure 91**) should be 48.5 mm (1 29/32 in.).

7. Inspect the valve piston (**Figure 92**) for wear, cracks, distortion or other damage.

8. Inspect the cover (A, **Figure 93**) for wear, cracks, distortion or other damage. Check the adjustment screw (B, **Figure 93**) for cracks or damage.

9. Replace all worn or damaged parts.

Assembly

Prior to assembly, perform the *Inspection* procedure to make sure all worn or defective parts have been repaired or replaced. All parts should be thoroughly cleaned before installation or assembly.

1. Insert the exhaust valve into the cylinder port so that the longer tapered side of the valve faces down (**Figure 84**). Push the valve in all the way (**Figure 94**).

> *NOTE*
> *It is important that the valve moves freely. If the valve sticks, determine the cause before proceeding.*

2. Install a new gasket (**Figure 83**) so that all of the holes in the gasket align with the passages at the bottom of the valve rod housing. See **Figure 95**.

3. Align the valve rod housing (**Figure 82**) with the gasket (**Figure 83**) and install the 2 housing screws. Tighten the screws securely (**Figure 96**).

> *NOTE*
> *Make sure the screws installed in Step 3 do not damage the gasket.*

5

4. Thread the valve piston (**Figure 80**) completely onto the valve rod by hand, until it bottoms.

5. Install the spring (**Figure 79**) and cover (B, **Figure 78**). Secure the cover with the spring clip (A, **Figure 78**).

6. Turn the adjustment screw (C, **Figure 78**) by hand until it bottoms.

PISTON, PISTON PIN, AND PISTON RINGS

The piston is made of an aluminum alloy. The piston pin is a precision fit and is held in place by a clip at each end. A caged needle bearing is used at the small end of the connecting rod.

Refer to illustration for your model when servicing the piston assembly.

    a. **Figure 33**: Engine 454.
    b. **Figure 34**: Engine 467.
    c. **Figure 35**: Engine 536.
    d. **Figure 36**: Engine 582.
    e. **Figure 37**: Engine 583.
    f. **Figure 38**: Engine 643.
    g. **Figure 39**: Engine 670.

Piston and Piston Ring Removal

1. Remove the cylinder head and cylinder as described in this chapter.

2. Identify the pistons by marking the piston crowns (**Figure 97**) either "PTO" (left side) and "MAG" (right side). In addition, keep each piston together with its own pin, bearing and piston rings to avoid confusion during reassembly.

3. Before removing the piston, hold the rod tightly and rock the piston as shown in **Figure 98**. Do not confuse any rocking motion with the normal side-to-side sliding motion. Rocking indicates wear on the piston pin, needle bearing, piston pin bore, or a combination of all three.

NOTE
Wrap a clean shop cloth under the piston so that the clip will not fall into the crankcase.

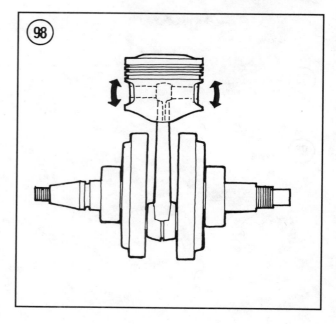

WARNING
Safety glasses should be worn when per-forming Step 4.

4. Remove the piston pin clip from the outside of the piston (**Figure 99**) with needlenose pliers. Hold your thumb over one edge of the clip when removing it to prevent it from springing out.

5. Use a proper size wooden dowel or socket extension and push the pin from the piston.

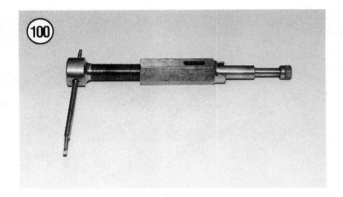

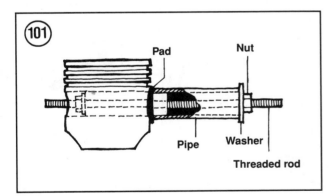

CAUTION
If the engine ran hot or seized, the piston pin may be difficult to remove, but do not drive the piston pin from the piston. Hammering will damage the piston, needle bearing and connecting rod. If the piston pin will not push out by hand, remove it as described in Step 6.

6. If the piston pin is tight, use special tool (part No. 529 0290 00) shown in **Figure 100** or fabricate the tool shown in **Figure 101**. Assemble the tool onto the piston and pull the piston pin from the piston. Make sure to install a pad between the piston and piece of pipe to prevent scoring the side of the piston.

7. Lift the piston from the connecting rod.

8. Remove the needle bearing from the connecting rod (**Figure 102**).

9. Repeat the removal procedure for the other piston.

10. If the pistons are going to remain off for some time, cover the end of each rod with a piece of foam insulation tube, or shop cloth to protect it.

NOTE
Always remove the top piston ring first.

11. Remove the upper ring by spreading the ends with your thumbs just enough to slide it up over the piston (**Figure 103**). Repeat for the lower ring.

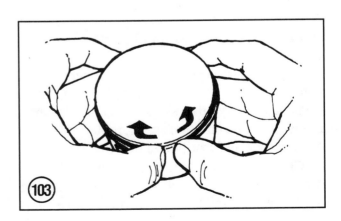

Piston (Wrist) Pin and Needle Bearing Inspection

1. Clean the needle bearing (**Figure 102**) in clean solvent to prevent contamination and dry thoroughly. Use a magnifying glass and inspect the bearing cage for cracks at the corners of the needle slots and inspect the needles themselves for cracking. Install a new bearing if it is questionable in any way.

2. Check the piston pin (**Figure 104**) for wear, scoring or cracks. Replace the piston pin if necessary.

3. Oil the needle bearing and pin and install them in the connecting rod. Rotate the pin slowly and check for play (**Figure 105**). If any play exists, check the condition of the connecting rod bore carefully. Install a new piston pin and bearing if the rod bore is in good condition. If the connecting rod bore shows evidence of damage, replace the connecting rods as described in this chapter.

4. Oil the piston pin and install it in the piston pin hole (**Figure 106**). Check for up and down play between the pin and piston. There should be no noticeable play. If play is noticeable, replace the piston pin and/or piston.

> *CAUTION*
> *If there are signs of piston seizure or overheating, replace the piston pins and bearings as a set (**Figure 107**). These parts are weakened from excessive heat and may fail later.*

Connecting Rod Inspection

1. Wipe the piston pin bore in the connecting rod with a clean rag and check it for galling, scratches, or any other signs of wear or damage. If any of these conditions exist, replace the connecting rods as described in this chapter.

2. Check the connecting rod big end axial play. You can make a quick check by simply rocking the connecting rod back and forth (**Figure 108**).

If there is more than a very slight rocking motion (some side-to-side sliding is normal), you should measure the connecting rod axial play with a feeler gauge. Measure between the side of the crankshaft and the washer. **Figure 109** shows the measurement being taken with the crankshaft removed for clarity. If the play exceeds the specified wear limit (**Tables 3-9**), the crankshaft must be rebuilt.

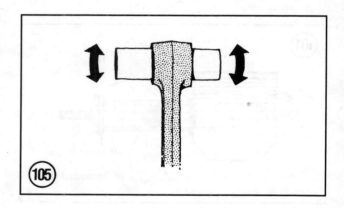

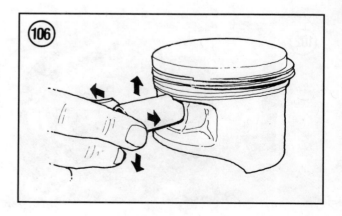

Piston and Ring Inspection

1. Carefully check the piston for cracks at the top edge of the transfer cutaways (**Figure 110**). Replace the piston if any cracks are found. Check the piston skirt (**Figure 111**) for brown

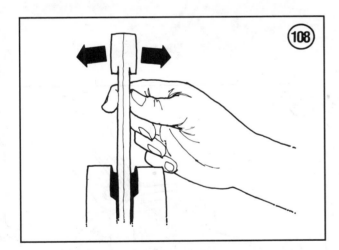

varnish buildup. More than a slight amount is an indication of worn or sticking rings which should be replaced. Be sure to clean the piston carefully before installing new rings.

2. Check the piston skirt for galling and abrasion which may have resulted from piston seizure. If light galling is present, smooth the affected area with No. 400 emery paper and oil or a fine oilstone. If galling is severe or if the piston is deeply scored, replace it.

3. If the piston is damaged, it is important to pinpoint the cause so the failure will not repeat after engine assembly. Refer to the following when checking damaged pistons:

   a. If the piston damage is contained to the area above the piston pin bore, the engine is probably overheating. Seizure or galling conditions contained to the area below the piston pin bore is usually caused by a lack of lubrication, rather than overheating.

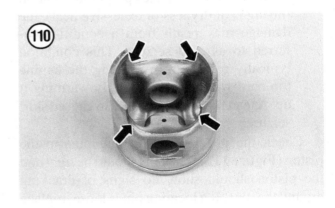

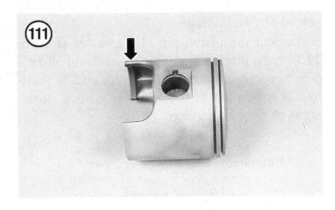

5

b. If the piston has seized and appears very dry (apparent lack of oil or lubrication on the piston), a lean fuel mixture probably caused the overheating. Overheating can result from incorrect jetting, air leaks or over advanced ignition timing.

c. Preignition will cause a sand-blasted appearance on the piston crown. This condition is discussed in Chapter Two.

d. If the piston damage is confined to the exhaust port area on the front of the piston, look for incorrect jetting (too lean) or over advanced ignition timing.

e. If the piston has a melted pocket starting in the crown or if there is a hole in the piston crown, the engine is running too lean. This may be caused by incorrect jetting, an air leak or over advanced ignition timing. A spark plug that is too hot can also cause this type of piston damage.

f. If the piston is seized around the skirt but the dome color indicates proper lubrication (no signs of dryness or excessive heat), the damage may result from a condition referred to as cold seizure. This condition typically results from running the engine too hard without first properly warming it up. A lean fuel mixture can also caused skirt seizure.

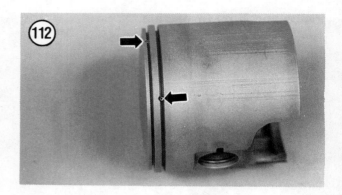

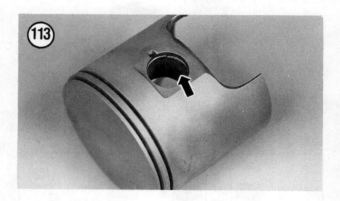

4. Check the piston ring locating pins in the piston (**Figure 112**). The pins should be tight and the piston should show no signs of cracking around the pins. If a locating pin is loose, replace the piston. A loose pin will fall out and cause severe engine damage.

5. Inspect the piston pin clip grooves (**Figure 113**) in the piston for damage that could allow a clip to come out and cause severe engine damage. Replace the piston if either groove shows signs of wear or damage.

NOTE
Maintaining proper piston ring end gap helps ensure peak engine performance. Excessive ring end gap reduces engine

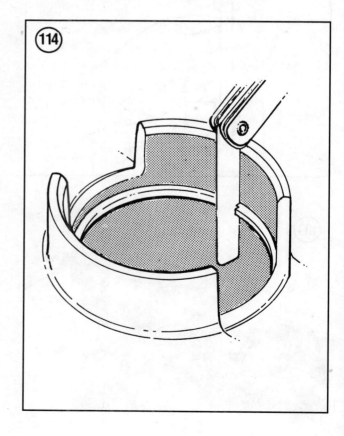

performance and may cause overheating. Insufficient ring end gap will cause the ring ends to butt together and break the ring, resulting in severe engine damage.

6. Measure piston ring end gap as follows. Position a ring in the bottom of the cylinder, then push it into the cylinder with the crown of the

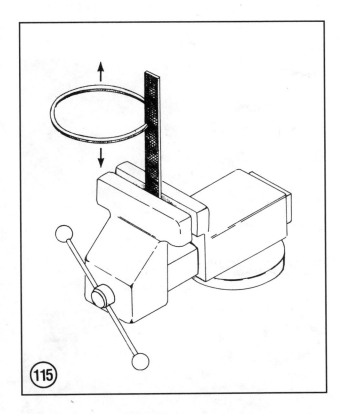

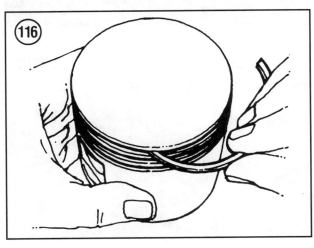

piston until the ring is just below the transfer ports. Using the piston to move the ring ensures that the ring is square in the cylinder bore. Measure the end gap with a flat feeler gauge (**Figure 114**) and compare to the wear limit in the appropriate table (**Tables 3-9**). If the gap is greater than specified, replace the rings as a set.

NOTE
*When installing new rings, measure the end gap as described in Step 6. If the gap is less than specified, make sure you have the correct piston rings. If the replacement rings are correct but the end gap is too small, carefully file the ends with a fine cut file until the gap is correct (**Figure 115**). Insufficient gap will allow the ends to butt together and break the ring, which may in turn cause severe piston and cylinder damage.*

CAUTION
*A old ring can be broken and used to clean carbon from the ring groove as shown in **Figure 116**. Be careful to remove only carbon from the grooves and do not cut into the soft aluminum of the piston. If the grooves are damaged by cleaning, a new piston should be installed.*

7. Carefully remove all carbon buildup from the ring grooves. Inspect the piston for missing, broken or cracked ring lands. Inspect the grooves carefully for cleanliness and for the absence of burrs or nicks. Recondition or replace the piston if necessary.

8A. The top piston ring on all models is a semi-trapezoidal type and its side clearance cannot be checked as described in Step 8B. Be sure the groove is clean and not damaged. Be sure the ring is new or undamaged and the end gap is correct when checked in Step 6.

8B. The second (bottom) ring on 454, 467, 536 and 670 engine models is rectangular and the side clearance in its groove should be checked as follows. Install the bottom ring in its groove and measure the groove clearance with a flat feeler gauge (**Figure 117**). Compare to the specification in **Table 3**, **Table 4**, **Table 5**, or **Table 9**. If the clearance is greater than specified, the rings must be replaced as a set. If the clearance is excessive with a new ring, replace the piston.

9. Inspect the condition of the piston crown (**Figure 118**). Normal carbon buildup can be removed with a wire brush or scraper. If the piston shows signs of overheating, pitting or other abnormal conditions, the engine may be experiencing preignition or detonation; both conditions are discussed in Chapter Two.

CAUTION
Do not wire brush piston skirts or ring lands. The wire brush removes aluminum that will increase piston clearance. The brush also rounds the corners of the ring lands which result in decreased support for the piston rings.

10. If the piston checked out okay after performing these inspection procedures, measure the piston outside diameter as described under *Piston/Cylinder Clearance* in this chapter.

11. If new piston rings are required, the cylinders should be honed before assembling the engine. Refer to *Cylinder Honing* in this chapter.

Piston/Cylinder Clearance

The following procedure requires the use of highly specialized and expensive measuring tools. If such equipment is not readily available, have the measurements performed by a dealer or machine shop. Always replace both pistons as a set.

1. Measure the outside diameter of the piston with a micrometer approximately 16 mm (5/8 in.) above the bottom of the piston skirt, at a 90° angle to the piston pin (**Figure 119**). If the diameter exceeds the wear limit in **Tables 3-9**, install new pistons.

NOTE
Always install new rings when installing a new piston.

2. Clean the cylinder block completely. Wash the cylinder bore with soap and water to remove oil and carbon particles. The cylinder bore must be cleaned thoroughly before attempting any measurement to prevent incorrect readings.

3. Measure the cylinder bore with a bore gauge or telescoping gauge (**Figure 120**). Measure the

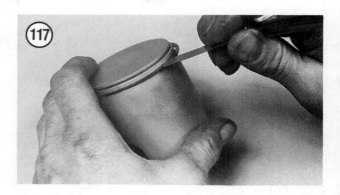

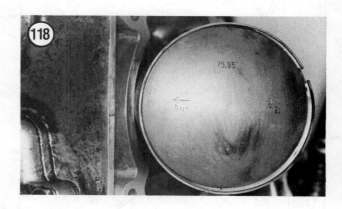

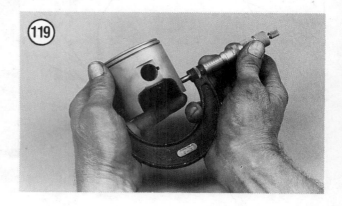

cylinder bore at 3 vertical locations in the cylinder, aligned with the piston pin and at 90° to the pin as shown in **Figure 121**. If the bore is greater than specification (**Tables 3-9**), the cylinders must be rebored to the next oversize and new pistons and rings installed. If the cylinder has already been bored oversize or if damage is too deep, a new cylinder must be installed.

NOTE
*Be sure to have the new pistons **before** boring the cylinders oversize so the pistons can be measured. The cylinders must be bored to match the pistons. Piston-to-cylinder clearance is specified in **Tables 3-9**.*

4. Piston clearance is the difference between the maximum piston diameter and the minimum cylinder diameter. If the clearance of a used

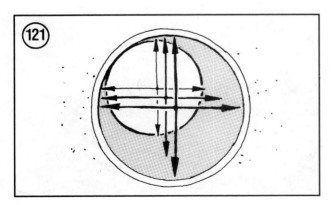

cylinder and piston exceeds the specification in **Tables 3-9**, the cylinders should be rebored and new pistons and rings installed. If the cylinder has already been bored oversize, a new cylinder must be installed.

Cylinder Honing

The surface condition of a worn cylinder bore is normally very shiny and smooth. If you install new piston rings in a cylinder with minimum wear, the rings will not seat properly and engine performance and longevity will suffer. Cylinder honing, often referred to as deglazing, is required every time new piston rings are installed. The surface is slightly roughed up by honing the cylinder to provide a textured or crosshatched surface. This surface finish controls initial wear of the new rings and helps them to seat and seal properly. Cylinder preparation by honing can be performed by a Ski-Doo dealer or independent repair shop. The cost of having the cylinder honed by a dealer is usually minimal compared to the cost of purchasing a hone and doing the job yourself. If you choose to hone the cylinder yourself, follow the instructions of the hone manufacturer closely.

CAUTION
*After a cylinder has been reconditioned by boring or honing, the bore must be properly cleaned with soap and water to remove all material left from the machining operation. Refer to **Inspection** under **Cylinder** in this chapter. Improper cleaning will not remove all of the machining residue, resulting in rapid wear of the new pistons and rings.*

Piston Installation

1. Prior to assembly, perform the inspection procedure to make sure all worn or defective parts have been cleaned or replaced. All parts should

be thoroughly cleaned before installation or assembly.

2. Lubricate the piston pin needle bearing with oil and install it in the connecting rod (**Figure 122**).

3. Oil the piston pin and install it in the piston until the end extends slightly beyond the inside of the boss (**Figure 123**).

4. Place the piston over the connecting rod with the "AUS" and arrow on the piston crown pointing toward the front (exhaust side) of the engine as shown in **Figure 124**. This is essential so the piston ring ends will be correctly positioned and will not catch in the ports. Align the piston pin with the bearing and push the pin into the piston until it is even with the piston pin clip grooves.

CAUTION
*If the piston pin will not slide in the piston smoothly with hand pressure, use the home-made tool described under **Piston Removal** to install the piston pin (**Figure 100**). The pipe is not used when installing the pin. Instead, insert the threaded rod through the piston pin, pin bearing, connecting rod and piston. A small washer and nut should be on threaded rod at the end which extends from the piston pin. Slide a large washer onto the opposite end of the threaded rod next to the piston. Install the nut next to the large washer and tighten it to pull the piston pin into the piston. Do not use excessive force. If it is difficult to move the piston pin, make sure the pin is not*

catching on the needle bearing in the connecting rod.

5. Install *new* piston pin clips (**Figure 125**), making sure they are completely seated in their grooves. It is important to have the opening in the clips facing down. See **Figure 126**.

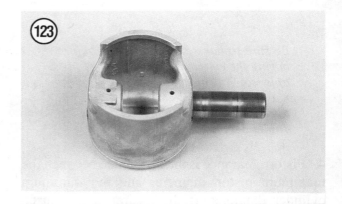

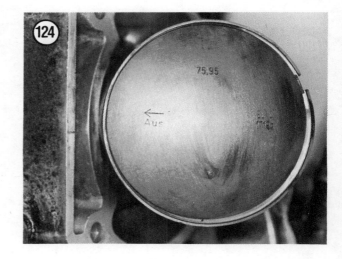

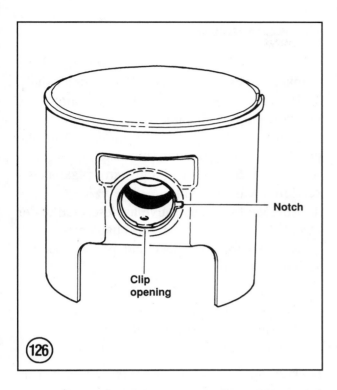

(126)

Notch

Clip
opening

(127)

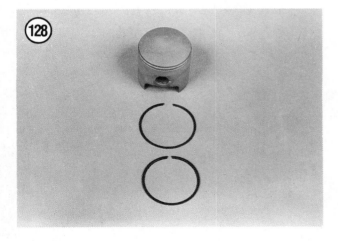

(128)

NOTE
Figure 127 *shows piston pin clips being installed with the Ski-Doo piston pin retainer clip installer (part No. 529 0086 00). This tool ensures positive installation without distorting or damaging the clip.*

CAUTION
Always install new piston pin clips. Clips must snap securely into the piston grooves. A weak or improperly installed clip could disengage during engine operation and cause severe engine damage.

6. Check the installation by rocking the piston back and forth around the pin. It should rotate freely.

7A. *454, 467, 536 and 670 engine models*: See **Figure 128**. Install the bottom piston ring first, then the top ring. Make sure that the rings are installed with the manufacturer's mark toward the top of the piston. Spread the ends of the ring carefully with your thumbs and slip the ring gently over the top of the piston. If reinstalling used rings, install them in the original grooves.

7B. *582, 583 and 643 engine models*: Install the piston ring by spreading the ends of the ring with your thumbs and slipping the ring over the top of the piston. See **Figure 129**.

8. Make sure the ring(s) are free to enter the groove(s) all the way around the circumference and that the ends are aligned with the locating pins. See **Figure 129** or **Figure 130**.

(129)

5

9. If new components are installed, the engine must be broken-in as if it were new. Refer to *Break-In Procedure* in Chapter Three.

CRANKCASE, CRANKSHAFT AND ROTARY VALVE

Disassembling the crankcase (splitting the case halves) and removal of the crankshaft assembly requires engine removal from the snowmobile. The cylinder head, cylinders and other attached assemblies can be removed with the engine in the sled, before removing the engine.

The diecast, thin wall aluminum alloy crankcase (**Figure 131**) is precision machined in 2 halves and is easily damaged. To avoid damage to the crankcase, do not hammer or pry on any of the interior or exterior walls. The crankcase halves are sold only as a matched set and if one half of the crankcase is damaged, both must be replaced. The crankcase halves are bolted together and aligned with dowel pins. The crankcase is assembled without a gasket, using only Loctite Gasket Eliminator 515 to seal the joint between the halves.

Crankshaft service includes disassembly of the crankshaft, replacement of unsatisfactory parts and accurate crankshaft alignment. Special measuring and alignment tools, a hydraulic press and experience are necessary to disassemble, assemble and accurately align the crankshaft assembly. Components of the crankshaft are available as individual parts; however, service should only be entrusted to a trained dealer or engine specialist. You can save considerable expense by disassembling the engine and taking the crankshaft to the dealer for his precision service.

The specifications and procedures which follow are presented to facilitate a complete, step-by-step major lower end overhaul that can be followed when completely reconditioning the engine.

Crankcase Disassembly

This procedure describes disassembly of the crankcase halves and removal of the crankshaft.
1. Remove the engine from the snowmobile as described in this chapter.
2. Remove all of the engine mounts from the crankcase as described in this chapter.
3. Remove the flywheel and stator plate as described in Chapter Nine.
4. Remove the rotary valve as described under *Rotary Valve and Shaft* in this chapter.
5. Remove the cylinders and pistons, as described in this chapter.

CAUTION
Do not damage the crankcase studs when performing the following procedures.

6. Turn the crankcase assembly so that it rests upside-down as shown in **Figure 132**.
7. Loosen the crankcase screws in 2 or more stages, reversing the sequence shown in **Figure 133**. Remove all of the crankcase screws.
8. Tap on the large screw bosses (**Figure 134**) with a soft mallet to separate the crankcase halves, then lift the bottom case half from the top half.

CAUTION
Make sure that you have removed all the fasteners. If the cases are hard to separate, check for any fasteners you may have missed. Do not pry the cases apart

CRANKCASE

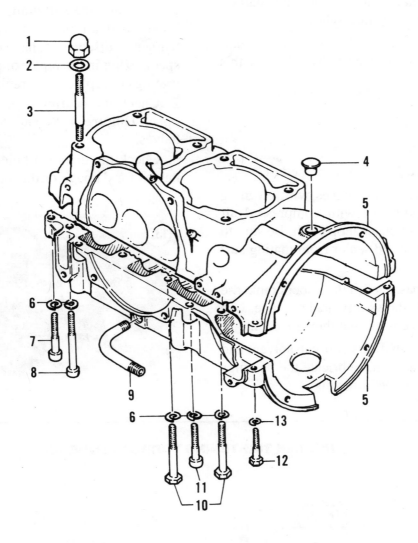

1. Acorn nut
2. Washer
3. Stud
4. Plug
5. Upper case half
6. Lower case half
7. Lockwasher
8. Bolt
9. Bolt
10. Tube
11. Bolt
12. Bolt
13. Bolt
14. Washer

5

with a screwdriver or any other sharp tool, otherwise the sealing surface will be damaged.

9. Remove the crankshaft (**Figure 135**) from the upper crankcase half. Support the crankshaft on the workbench so it cannot roll off.

10. If necessary, remove the rotary valve shaft as described under *Rotary Valve Shaft* in this chapter.

Cleaning

Refer to **Figure 131** for this procedure.

1. Clean both crankcase halves with cleaning solvent. Thoroughly dry with compressed air and wipe off with a clean shop cloth. Be sure to remove all traces of old sealer from mating surfaces.

2. Clean the oil passages in the upper crankcase half. **Figure 136**, shows a typical passage. Use compressed air to ensure that they are clean.

3. Clean the crankshaft assembly in solvent and dry with compressed air. Lubricate the bearings with engine oil to prevent rusting.

Crankcase Inspection

Refer to **Figure 131** for this procedure.

1. Carefully inspect the case halves (**Figure 137**) for cracks and fractures. Also check the areas around the stiffening ribs, around bearing bosses and all of the threaded holes. If any damage is discovered, have it repaired by a shop specializing in the repair of precision aluminum castings or replace the crankcase.

2. Check the bearing support area of both the upper (**Figure 138**) and lower (**Figure 139**) halves.

3. Check the threaded holes in both crankcase halves for damage or dirt buildup. If necessary,

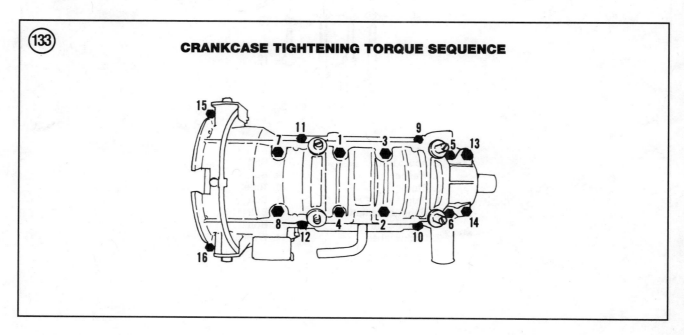

CRANKCASE TIGHTENING TORQUE SEQUENCE

(134)

(135)

(136)

(137)

clean or repair the threads with a suitable size metric tap. Coat the tap threads with kerosene or aluminum tap fluid before use.

4. On model so equipped, check the upper crankcase studs (**Figure 140**) for thread damage. If necessary, replace damaged studs as described under *Crankcase Stud Replacement* in this chapter.

5. Check the oil seal grooves (**Figure 141**) in the upper and lower crankcase halves for cracks or damage.

5

(138)

(139)

(140)

6. Inspect the rotary valve oil seal and bearing as described under *Rotary Valve Shaft* in this chapter.

7. Check the rotary valve machined surface on the upper and lower crankcase halves (**Figure 142**). Check the surface for gouges or other damage that would indicate rotary valve or rotary valve shaft damage.

8. Inspect the rotary valve as described in this chapter.

9. If there is any doubt as to the condition of the crankcase halves, and they cannot be repaired, replace the crankcase halves as a set.

Crankcase Stud Replacement

On 1990 583 engine models, the cylinders are attached to the crankcase with studs and acorn nuts. Damaged crankcase studs will prevent the cylinders from being properly tightened and this will cause engine damage.

Because acorn nuts are used to attach the cylinder, the crankcase studs must be installed to a specified length (**Figure 143**) and the stud must be secured with Loctite 242 (blue) threadlocker.

1. Thread two nuts onto the damaged stud. Then tighten the 2 nuts against each other so that they are locked.

NOTE
If the threads of the damaged stud do not allow installation of the 2 nuts, remove the stud with a pair of locking pliers.

2. Turn the bottom nut counterclockwise and unscrew the stud.

3. Clean the threads with solvent or electrical contact cleaner and allow to thoroughly dry.

4. Install 2 nuts on the top half of the new stud as in Step 1. Make sure they are locked together securely.

5. Coat the bottom threads of the new stud with Loctite 242 (blue).

6. Turn the top nut clockwise and screw the new stud in until the distance from the top of the

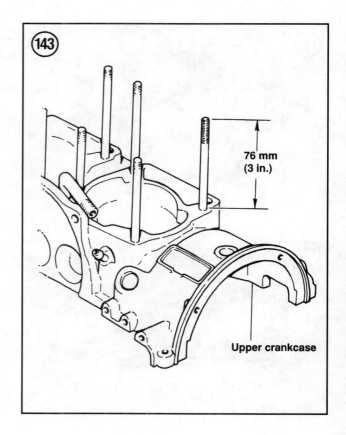

76 mm
(3 in.)

Upper crankcase

installed stud to the crankcase (**Figure 143**) is 76 mm (3 in.). If incorrect, reposition the stud as necessary.

7. Remove the nuts and repeat for each stud as required.

8. Allow sufficient time for threadlocker to cure before installing the cylinders. Follow Loctite's directions.

Crankshaft Inspection

Refer to **Figure 144** or **Figure 145** for this procedure.

1. Check the left- (**Figure 146**) and right-hand (**Figure 147** or **Figure 148**) crankshaft oil seals. Replace the seals if damaged.

5

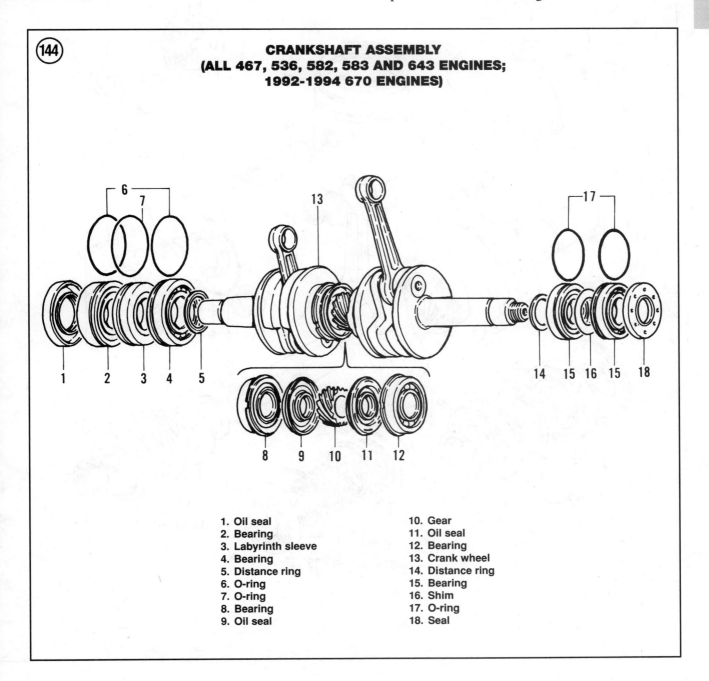

CRANKSHAFT ASSEMBLY
(ALL 467, 536, 582, 583 AND 643 ENGINES;
1992-1994 670 ENGINES)

1. Oil seal
2. Bearing
3. Labyrinth sleeve
4. Bearing
5. Distance ring
6. O-ring
7. O-ring
8. Bearing
9. Oil seal
10. Gear
11. Oil seal
12. Bearing
13. Crank wheel
14. Distance ring
15. Bearing
16. Shim
17. O-ring
18. Seal

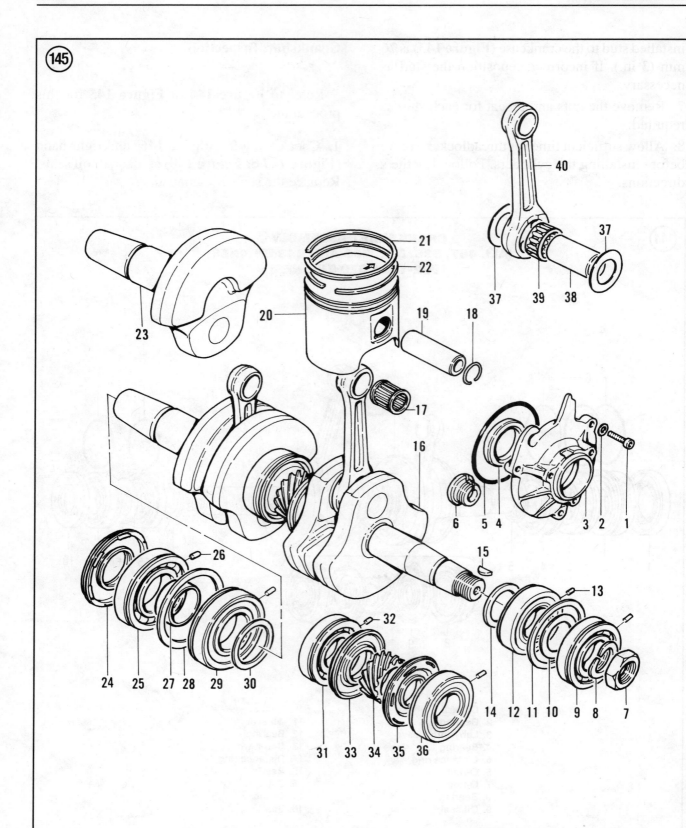

CRANKSHAFT ASSEMBLY
(1995 454 AND 670 ENGINES)

1. Screw
2. Washer
3. Armature plate
4. Seal
5. O-ring
6. Grommet
7. Nut
8. Lockwasher
9. Ball bearing
10. Washer
11. Shim
12. Ball bearing
13. Dowel pin
14. Spacer
15. Woodruff key
16. Crankshaft
17. Needle bearing
18. Retainer ring
19. Piston pin
20. Piston
21. Top ring
22. Second ring
23. Crankshaft drive end
24. Oil seal
25. Ball bearing
26. Dowel pin
27. Spacer
28. Ring
29. Ball bearing
30. Spacer
31. Ball bearing
32. Dowel pin
33. Oil seal
34. Central drive gear
35. Oil seal
36. Ball bearing
37. Side washers
38. Crankpin
39. Big end roller bearing
40. Connecting rod

NOTE
A set of V-blocks can be made of hard-wood to perform the check described in Step 2.

2. Inspect the connecting rod small-end (**Figure 149**) and big-end (**Figure 150**) for excessive heat discoloration or other damage. Position the

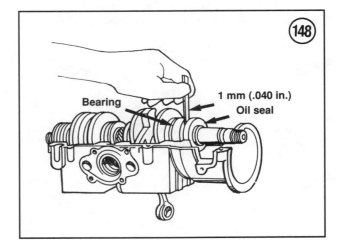

crankshaft on V-blocks and spin the connecting rod by hand, while checking for excessive noise or roughness.

3. Check connecting rod big-end axial play (side clearance) with a feeler gauge. Insert the gauge between the crankshaft and the connecting rod as shown in **Figure 151**. If the play meets or exceeds the service limit, the big-end bearings and connecting rod must be replaced. See **Tables 3-9** for service limit for your specific engine.

4. Repeat Steps 2 and 3 for the other connecting rod.

5. Carefully examine the condition of the crankshaft ball bearings (A, **Figure 152**). Clean the bearings with solvent and allow to dry thoroughly. Oil each bearing, then check it by rolling the bearing by hand. Make sure that it turns quietly and smoothly. There must not be any rough spots or apparent radial play. Defective bearings must be replaced.

6. Inspect the central gear (**Figure 153**) for cracks, deep scoring or excessive wear. If the central gear is damaged, check the gear on the rotary valve shaft for damage. Even if one gear appears damaged while the other appears okay, replace *both* gears.

> *NOTE*
> *The bearings installed on the outside of the crank wheels can be replaced as described under **Crankshaft Bearing Replacement** in this chapter. To replace the bearings, seals and central gear installed between the crank wheels, the*

crankshaft must be disassembled; refer service to a qualified dealer or crankshaft specialist.

7. Support the crankshaft by placing it onto 2 precision V-blocks located at the main bearing surfaces and check runout with a dial indicator as shown in **Figure 154**. The dial indicator must be positioned at the points indicated in **Figure**

154. Turn the crankshaft slowly and observe the indicator reading. The maximum difference recorded is crankshaft runout. If the runout at any position exceeds the service limit, (**Tables 3-9**), the crankshaft should be serviced by a dealer or crankshaft specialist.

NOTE
Do not check crankshaft runout with the crankshaft placed between centers. V-blocks must be used as described in Step 7.

8. Check the crankshaft threads (**Figure 155**) for stripping, cross-threading or other damage. Have threads repaired by a dealer or machine shop.

9. Check the key seat (C, **Figure 152**) for cracks or other damage. If the key seat is damaged, refer service to a dealer or machine shop.

10. If the crankshaft exceeded any of the service limits in Steps 3 or 4 or if one or more bearings are worn or damaged, have the crankshaft rebuilt by a dealer or crankshaft specialist.

11. Replace all of the bearing and labyrinth sleeve O-rings (B, **Figure 152**) before reinstalling the crankshaft. Notice that 3 different size O-rings are used (**Figure 144**) on some models. When purchasing new O-rings, have the parts manager identify O-ring position.

12. Check the rotary valve clearance as described under *Rotary Valve Inspection* in this chapter.

5

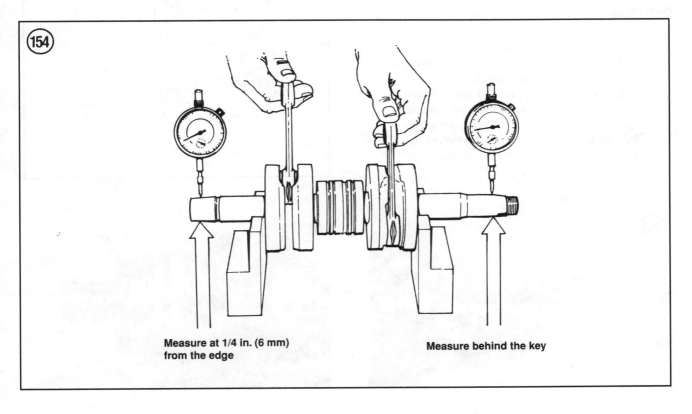

Measure at 1/4 in. (6 mm) from the edge

Measure behind the key

Crankshaft Bearing Replacement

Replace the outer crankshaft bearings and the labyrinth sleeve as follows. The Ski-Doo puller assembly (part No. 420 8762 98) (**Figure 156**) or equivalent is required to remove the bearings and sleeve.

> *CAUTION*
> *When using the Ski-Doo puller (or equivalent puller) to remove the bearings in Step 1, place a protective cap over the end of the crankshaft (**Figure 156**) to prevent the puller screw from damaging the end of the crankshaft.*

1. Using the puller assembly, remove the left- (**Figure 157** or **Figure 158**) and right-hand (**Figure 159** or **Figure 160**) bearing assemblies.

2. Clean the crankshaft bearing area with solvent or electrical contact cleaner and thoroughly dry.

3. Coat both crankshaft bearing areas with antiseize lubricant (part No. 413 7010 00) or equivalent.

> *NOTE*
> *Different bearings are used as main bearings at specific locations on the crankshaft. See **Figure 144** and **Figure 145**. When you purchase the replacement bearings, have the parts manager identify each bearing and its position on the crankshaft. It is critical that the bearings are properly installed.*

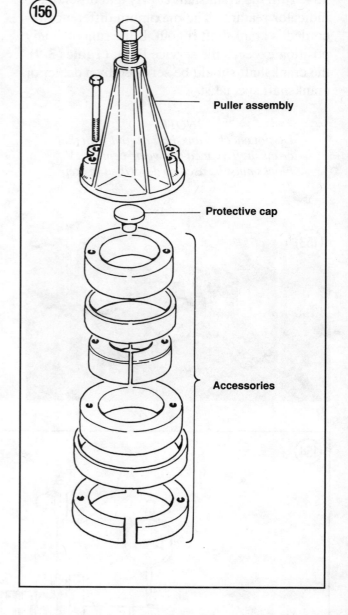

Puller assembly

Protective cap

Accessories

NOTE
Ski-Doo recommends that the bearings be heated to 75° C (167° F) in oil before installation. Completely read Step 4 through before heating and installing bearings. During bearing installation, the crankshaft should be supported se-curely so that the bearings can be installed quickly. If a bearing cools and tightens on the crankshaft before it is completely installed, remove the bearing with the puller and reheat.

4. Install the bearings and labyrinth sleeve as follows:

   a. Lay the bearings on a clean lint free surface in the order of assembly.

   b. On all except 1995 454 and 670 engine models, refer to **Figure 157** and **Figure 159** when installing the bearings and labyrinth sleeve. On 1995 454 and 670 engine models, refer to **Figure 158** and **Figure 160** when installing the bearings and retaining disk. On all models, make sure that the bearing and sleeve O-ring grooves are positioned in the direction shown.

5

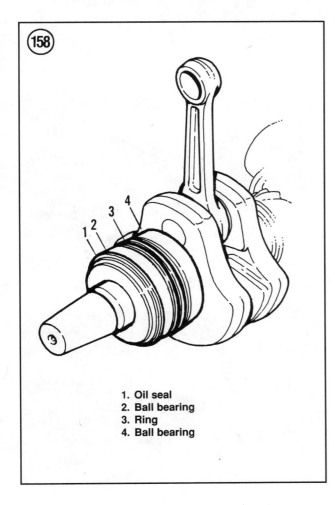

1. Oil seal
2. Ball bearing
3. Ring
4. Ball bearing

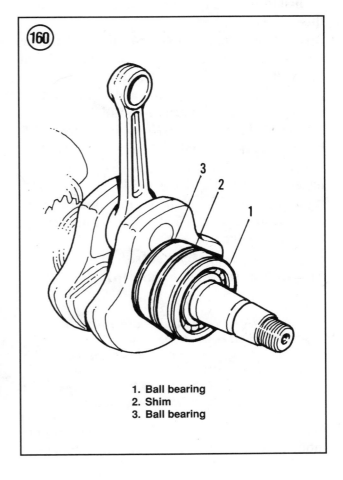

1. Ball bearing
2. Shim
3. Ball bearing

NOTE
If the bearings are installed with the O-rings grooves incorrectly aligned, the O-rings will not align properly with the grooves in the upper and lower crankcase halves.

c. Refer to *Shrink Fit* under *Ball Bearing Replacement* in Chapter One.

d. Heat and install the bearings and labyrinth sleeve. Refer to **Figure 144**, **Figure 157** and **Figure 159** or **Figure 145**, **Figure 158** and **Figure 160** during installation.

e. After the bearings have cooled, install the bearing and labyrinth sleeve O-rings.

Crankshaft Installation

Refer to **Figure 144** or **Figure 145** for this procedure.

1. Install the rotary valve shaft as described in this chapter.

2A. On all except 1995 454 and 670 engine models, fill both of the outer crankshaft oil seal lip cavities with a low-temperature lithium base grease, then install the left- and right-hand oil seals as shown in **Figures 146-148**.

2B. On 1995 454 and 670 engine models, fill both of the outer crankshaft oil seal lip cavities with a low-temperature lithium base grease, then install the left-side (**Figure 146**) oil seal. The right side oil seal is installed in the armature plate on these models, which is installed after assembling the crankcase.

3. Support the upper crankcase half by its crankcase studs as shown in **Figure 161**.

NOTE
Step 4A or 4B describes crankshaft installation; however, because of the number of separate procedures required during installation, read all of the procedures included in Step 4A or 4B before actually installing the crankshaft.

4A. On all *except* 1995 454 and 670 engine models, align the crankshaft with the upper

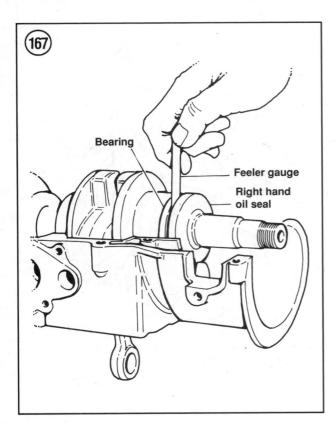

crankcase half and install the crankshaft (**Figure 162**). Note the following:

a. Make sure that the left-hand outer crankshaft oil seal ring and the O-rings fit into the crankcase grooves as shown in **Figure 163**.

b. Make sure that the crankshaft gear (**Figure 164**) meshes properly with the rotary valve shaft gear.

c. Check that the 2 center bearing clips and oil seal ring fit into the crankcase grooves as shown in **Figure 165**.

d. Make sure that the 2 right-hand bearing O-rings fit into the crankcase grooves as shown at A, **Figure 166**.

CAUTION
The bearing-to-oil seal gap set in sub-step e provides room for bearing lubrication. If the gap is not set, bearing failure may result.

e. Position the right-hand oil seal (B, **Figure 166**) so that there is a 1 mm (0.040 in.) gap between the oil seal and bearing. Check the gap with a feeler gauge as shown in **Figure 167**.

4B. On 1995 454 and 670 engine models, align the crankshaft with the upper crankcase half and install the crankshaft (**Figure 168**). Note the following:

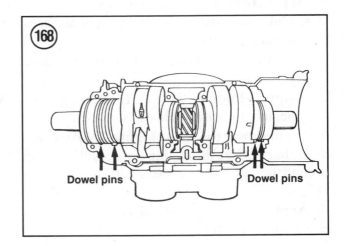

a. Make sure that the left-hand outer crankshaft oil seal ring and the O-rings fit into the crankcase grooves as shown in **Figure 169**.

b. Make sure that the crankshaft gear (**Figure 164**) meshes properly with the rotary valve shaft gear.

c. Check that the 2 center bearing clips and oil seal ring fit into the crankcase grooves as shown in **Figure 165**.

d. Make sure that the 2 right-hand bearing O-rings fit into the crankcase grooves as shown in **Figure 170**.

e. Check to be sure that all of the bearing alignment dowels are engaging the notches on the exhaust side of crankcase as shown in **Figure 168**.

5. Recheck Steps of 4A or 4B before proceeding with assembling the crankcase.

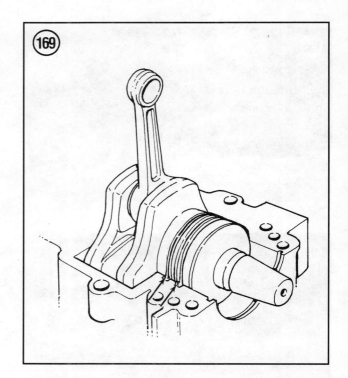

Crankcase Assembly

1. Install the crankshaft in the upper crankcase half as described in this chapter.

2. Oil the crankshaft gear and the bottom end bearings with injection oil.

> *NOTE*
> *Follow the manufacturer's directions when applying primer and crankcase sealer in Step 3.*

3. Apply crankcase sealer as follows:

a. Make sure the crankcase mating surfaces are completely clean.

b. Apply Loctite Primer N to both crankcase surfaces.

c. Apply Loctite Gasket Eliminator 515 Sealant to both crankcase surfaces.

4. Put the lower case half (**Figure 171**) onto the upper half. Check the mating surfaces all the way around the case halves to make sure they are even (**Figure 172**).

5. Apply a light coat of oil to the crankcase screw threads before installing them.

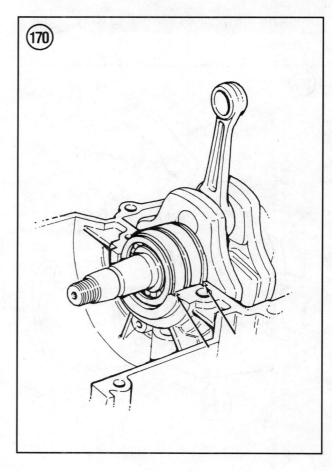

6. Install the crankcase screws and tighten by hand.

7. On 1995 454 and 670 engine models, install the armature plate (**Figure 173**) with the crankshaft right-side seal installed. Use a new O-ring and tighten retaining screws by hand before tightening the crankcase screws.

8. Torque the crankcase screws in 2-steps in the sequence shown in **Figure 174**. Refer to **Table 11** for torque specifications.

CAUTION
While tightening the crankcase fasteners, make frequent checks to ensure that the crankshaft turns freely and that the crankshaft locating rings and crankcase dowel pins fit into place in the case halves.

9. Check again that the crankshaft turns freely. If it is binding, separate the crankcase halves and determine the cause of the problem.

10. On 1995 454 and 670 engine models, coat threads of the armature plate retaining screws with Loctite 242, then tighten screws securely.

11. Turn the engine right side up.

12. Coat the crank pins and connecting rod bearings liberally with 2-stroke engine oil. Squirt the same oil into the main bearings though the oil delivery holes located in the transfer ports.

13. Install the engine top end as described in this chapter.

14. Install the rotary valve and impeller as described in this chapter.

15A. On all *except* 1995 454 and 670 engine models, install the stator plate and flywheel as described in Chapter Nine.

15B. On 1995 454 and 670 engine models, install the stator, trigger coil and flywheel as described in Chapter Nine.

16. Install the engine mounts as described in this chapter.

17. Instal the engine in the frame as described in this chapter.

18. If new components were installed, the engine must be broken-in as if it were new. Refer to *Break-In Procedure* in Chapter Three.

ROTARY VALVE AND SHAFT

Refer to **Figure 175** or **Figure 176** when performing the procedures in this section.

Rotary Valve Removal

The rotary valve can be removed with the engine mounted in the snowmobile. This procedure is shown with the engine removed for clarity.

1. If the engine is mounted in the snowmobile, perform the following:

   a. Remove the carburetors as described in Chapter Six or the fuel injection unit as described in Chapter Seven.

   b. Disconnect the oil injection hose from the oil pump, then plug the hose to prevent oil leakage and contamination.

   c. Disconnect the oil pump control cable from the oil pump.

NOTE
It is not necessary to remove the oil pump from the rotary valve cover in Step 2. If service to the oil pump is required, refer to Chapter Ten.

2. Remove the screws holding the rotary valve cover to the crankcase. Remove the rotary valve cover (**Figure 177**) and its O-ring.

NOTE
The rotary valve is asymmetrical. Mark the valve and shaft with a felt tip pen to assist valve installation.

3. Remove the rotary valve (**Figure 178**).

4. If necessary, remove the rotary valve shaft as described in this chapter.

Inspection

1. Inspect the rotary valve (**Figure 179**) for cracks, splitting or other damage. Replace the rotary valve if necessary.

2. Whenever the crankcase is disassembled, check the rotary valve clearance as follows:

   a. With the crankcase disassembled, install the rotary valve onto the end of the rotary valve shaft (**Figure 180**).

   b. Install the rotary valve cover without its O-ring. Install the cover retaining screws and tighten the cover securely.

   c. Insert a feeler gauge between the rotary valve and the upper crankcase (**Figure 180**). If the clearance is not within 0.27-0.40 mm (0.011-0.016 in.), check the rotary valve, crankcase and rotary valve cover for damage.

Rotary Valve Timing

The upper crankcase on most models has a ridge mark (**Figure 181**) that can be used for

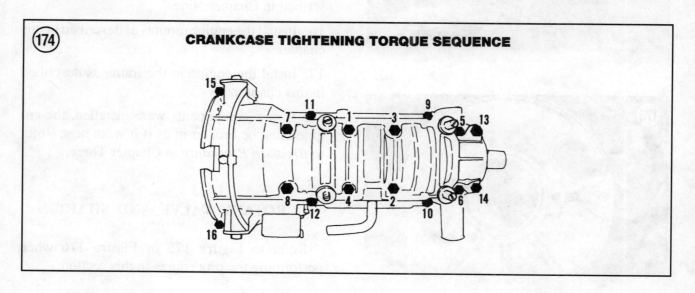

(174)   **CRANKCASE TIGHTENING TORQUE SEQUENCE**

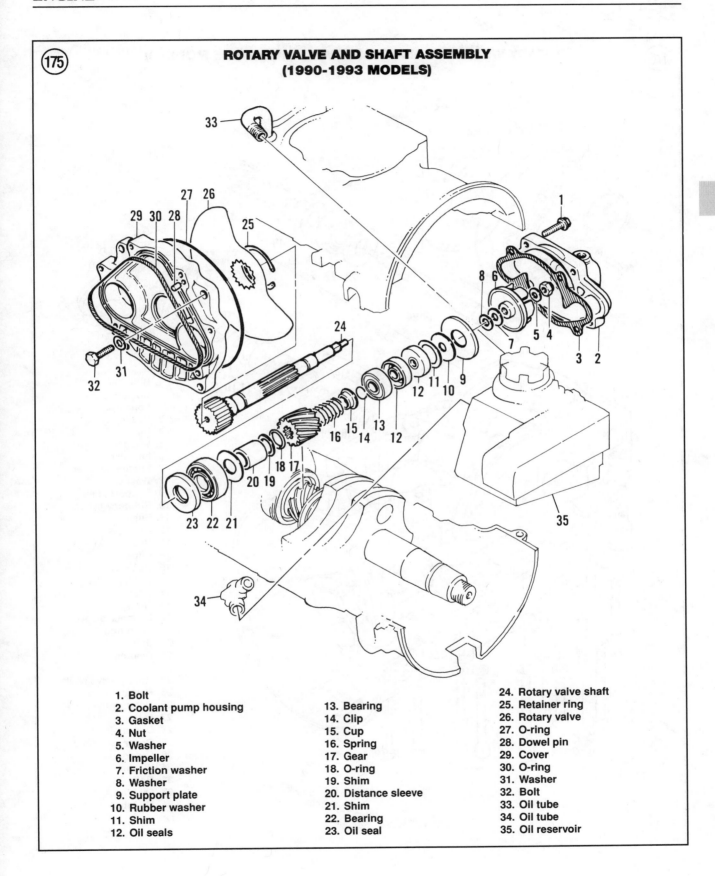

**ROTARY VALVE AND SHAFT ASSEMBLY
(1990-1993 MODELS)**

1. Bolt
2. Coolant pump housing
3. Gasket
4. Nut
5. Washer
6. Impeller
7. Friction washer
8. Washer
9. Support plate
10. Rubber washer
11. Shim
12. Oil seals
13. Bearing
14. Clip
15. Cup
16. Spring
17. Gear
18. O-ring
19. Shim
20. Distance sleeve
21. Shim
22. Bearing
23. Oil seal
24. Rotary valve shaft
25. Retainer ring
26. Rotary valve
27. O-ring
28. Dowel pin
29. Cover
30. O-ring
31. Washer
32. Bolt
33. Oil tube
34. Oil tube
35. Oil reservoir

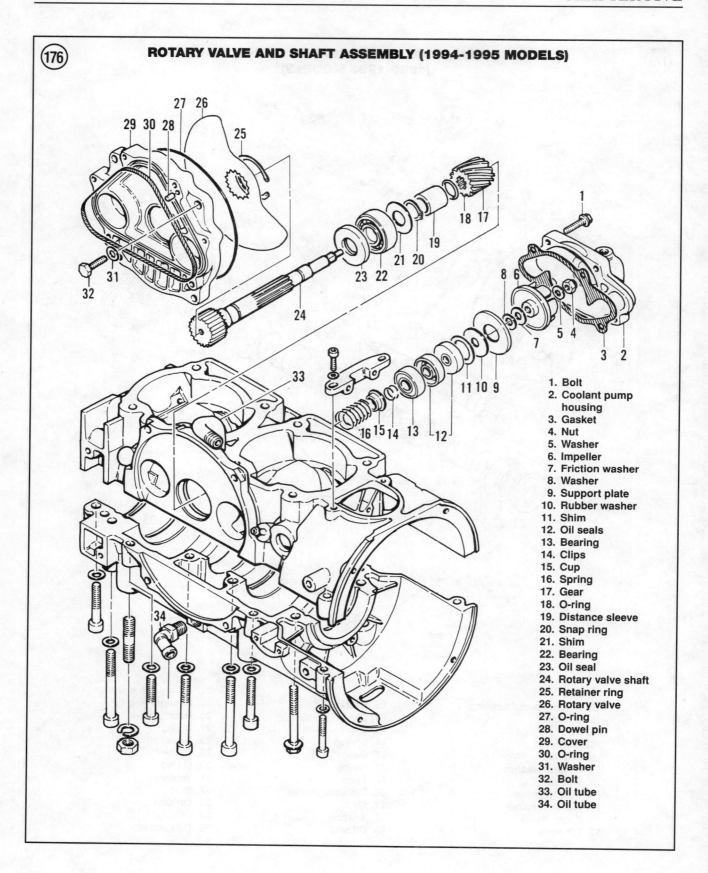

176

ROTARY VALVE AND SHAFT ASSEMBLY (1994-1995 MODELS)

1. Bolt
2. Coolant pump housing
3. Gasket
4. Nut
5. Washer
6. Impeller
7. Friction washer
8. Washer
9. Support plate
10. Rubber washer
11. Shim
12. Oil seals
13. Bearing
14. Clips
15. Cup
16. Spring
17. Gear
18. O-ring
19. Distance sleeve
20. Snap ring
21. Shim
22. Bearing
23. Oil seal
24. Rotary valve shaft
25. Retainer ring
26. Rotary valve
27. O-ring
28. Dowel pin
29. Cover
30. O-ring
31. Washer
32. Bolt
33. Oil tube
34. Oil tube

rotary valve installation. If the crankcase has a ridge mark, install the rotary valve as described under *Rotary Valve Installation*. If the crankcase does not have a ridge mark or if you are installing a different or modified rotary valve, a dial indicator and degree wheel are required to correctly position the valve.

1. Install the rotary valve shaft, if previously removed, as described in this chapter.

2. Install the engine top end assembly, if previously removed.

> *NOTE*
> *Do not attempt to use the timing pin to locate top dead center for the right side cylinder. Use the following or similar procedure.*

3. Find top dead center (TDC) for the right (MAG) side cylinder as follows:

  a. Remove both spark plugs as described in Chapter Three.

> *NOTE*
> *Removal of both spark plugs will make turning the crankshaft easier and smoother.*

  b. Screw the extension onto a dial indicator and insert the dial indicator into the adapter.

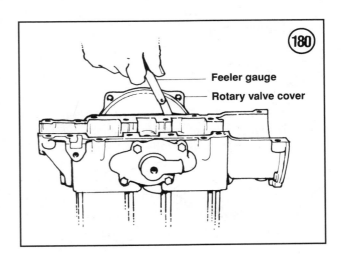

Feeler gauge
Rotary valve cover

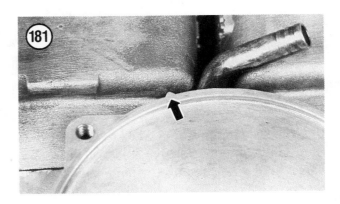

5

c. Screw the dial indicator adaptor into the cylinder head (**Figure 182**) on the MAG side. Do not lock the dial indicator in the adapter at this time.

NOTE
Remove the drive belt, if necessary, before performing substep d.

d. Rotate the flywheel (by turning the primary sheave) until the dial indicator rises all the way up in its holder (piston is approaching top dead center). Then slide the indicator far enough into the holder to obtain a reading.

e. Lightly tighten the set screw on the dial indicator adaptor to secure the dial gauge.

f. Rotate the flywheel until the dial on the gauge stops and reverses direction. This is top dead center. Zero the dial gauge by aligning the zero with the indicator needle (**Figure 183**).

g. Tighten the set screw on the dial indicator adaptor securely.

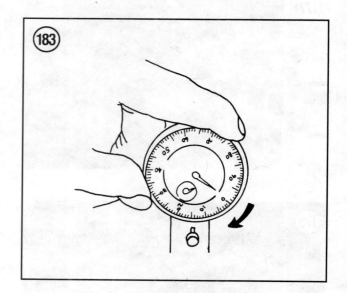

NOTE
A degree wheel (part No. 414 3529 00) designed for use with these engines is available from Ski-Doo dealers.

4. Set the engine at TDC as described in Step 3, then install a degree wheel onto the rotary valve shaft with the 360-0° mark aligned with the lower edge of the right (MAG) side inlet port.

NOTE
*When performing Step 5, refer to **Table 10** for rotary valve opening degrees for your engine model.*

5. Mark the crankcase as shown in **Figure 184** at the location (in degrees) listed as "Opening BTDC" in **Table 10**.

6. With the engine still at TDC as described in Step 3, reposition the degree wheel on the rotary valve shaft with the 360-0° mark aligned with the top edge of the right (MAG) side inlet port.

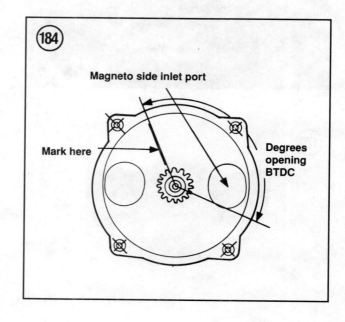

Magneto side inlet port

Mark here

Degrees opening BTDC

NOTE
*When performing Step 7, refer to **Table 10** for rotary valve closing degrees for your engine model.*

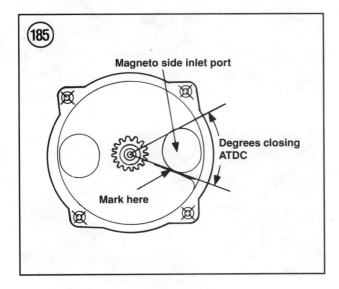

Magneto side inlet port

Degrees closing ATDC

Mark here

7. Mark the crankcase as shown in **Figure 185** at the location (in degrees) listed as "Closing ATDC" in **Table 10**.

8. Position the rotary valve on the gear (**Figure 186**) so its edges align with both marks made in Step 5 and Step 7.

NOTE
The rotary valve is asymmetrical. If marks do not align, turn valve over to determine which position provides the more accurate timing.

9. For the remainder of installation, refer to *Rotary Valve Installation* Step 6 and following after determining correct installation of the rotary valve.

Rotary Valve Installation

Coat the rotary valve with engine oil before final assembly.

1. Install the rotary valve shaft, if previously removed, as described in this chapter.

2. Install the engine top end assembly, if previously removed.

3. Find top dead center as described under *Rotary Valve Timing* in this chapter.

4. Locate the ridge mark on the upper crankcase. See **Figure 181**.

5. Position the rotary valve on the gear (**Figure 186**) so the valve edge aligns with the ridge mark as shown in **Figure 187**.

NOTE
The rotary valve is asymmetrical. If the marks do not align, turn valve over to determine which position provides the more accurate timing.

NOTE
*If your crankcase does not have a ridge mark, install rotary valve as described under **Rotary Valve Timing** in this chapter.*

6. Install the O-ring into the groove in the rotary valve cover (**Figure 188**).

7. Install the rotary valve cover (**Figure 177**). Install the cover retaining screws and tighten to the torque specification in **Table 11**.

8. Reverse Steps 1 and 2 under *Rotary Valve Removal* to complete installation.

Rotary Valve Shaft Removal

Refer to **Figure 175** or **Figure 176** for this procedure.

1. Remove the engine from the snowmobile as described in this chapter.

2. Remove the rotary valve as described in this chapter.

3. Remove the screws attaching the water pump cover (**Figure 189**, typical) to the crankcase. Remove the water pump cover and gasket (**Figure 190**).

4. Remove the impeller assembly as follows:

   a. Remove the impeller nut (**Figure 191**).

   b. Remove the washer (**Figure 192**).

   c. Carefully pull the impeller (**Figure 193**) from the rotary valve shaft.

   d. Remove the serrated (friction) washer (**Figure 194**).

> *NOTE*
> *The washer removed in substep e (**Figure 195**) is different from the one shown in **Figure 192**. Do not switch them during reassembly.*

   e. Remove the washer (**Figure 195**).

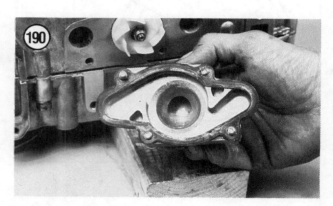

5. Split the crankcase and remove the crankshaft as described in this chapter.

6. Remove the snap ring from the rotary valve side with snap ring pliers (**Figure 196**).

> *CAUTION*
> *The end of the rotary valve and coolant pump can be easily damaged during removal in Step 7. Special pusher tool (part No. 420 8766 12) that protects the end of the shaft is available from Ski-Doo dealers.*

7. Carefully tap the rotary valve shaft from the crankcase from the exhaust side. Remove the rotary valve shaft (**Figure 197**).

Rotary Valve Shaft
Crankcase Bearing and Seal Replacement

Refer to **Figure 175** or **Figure 176** for this procedure. Removal and installation of bearings and seals is easier if the appropriate special tools are available. Read the complete procedure through before beginning disassembly. If you are not equipped with the special tools, it may be better to have a Ski-Doo dealer install those parts.

1. Use the seal pusher (part No. 420 8765 12) (**Figure 198**) to drive the bearing, seals, shim, rubber washer and support plate from the upper crankcase. See **Figure 199**.

2. Before cleaning the crankcase, check the drain hole (**Figure 200**) in the crankcase for oil

5

or coolant leakage. If oil or coolant residue is present, the oil seal or the coolant seal was leaking.

3. Clean the bearing bore in the crankcase with solvent and thoroughly dry.

4. Check the bearing/seal area in the crankcase for cracks or other damage.

5. Hold the bearing outer race and turn the inner race by hand (**Figure 201**). Check for roughness or excessive noise. Replace the bearing if necessary.

NOTE
*Install the bearing in Step 6 so that the shielded side (**Figure 202**) faces toward the rotary valve.*

6. Place the ball bearing against the bearing bore as shown in **Figure 203**, then use the bearing pusher (part No. 420 8765 00) to drive the bearing into the crankcase (**Figure 204**). The bearing should seat against the crankcase shoulder (**Figure 205**).

NOTE
Use the seal pushers (part Nos. 420 8765 12 and 420 8770 50) when installing the oil seal and coolant seal in Step 7.

7. Install the oil seal and coolant seal as follows:

a. Coat the lips of the first (oil) seal with Molykote 111 (or equivalent) and align the seal with the crankcase so the *closed* side faces out. Drive the oil seal into the crank-

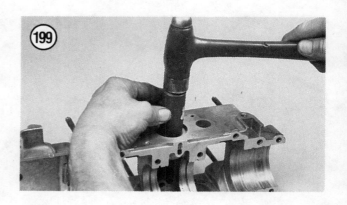

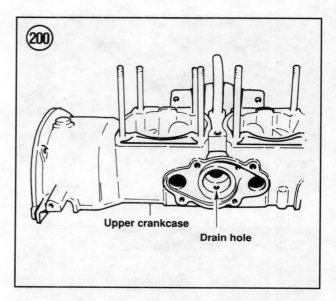

Upper crankcase   Drain hole

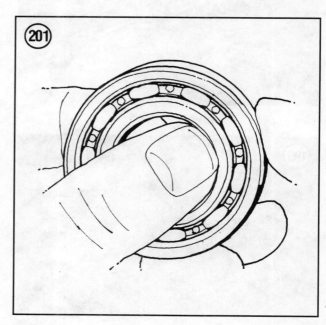

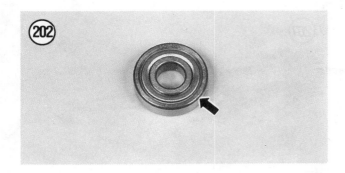

case until it seats against the bearing (**Figure 199**).

NOTE
*If the special seal pusher is not available, be sure the drain hole in the crankcase (**Figure 200**) is not covered.*

b. Coat the lips of the second (coolant) seal with Molykote 111 (or equivalent) and align the seal with the crankcase so that the *open* side faces out. Drive the oil seal into the crankcase using seal pusher (part No. 420 8770 50).

c. Install the shim (11, **Figure 175** or **Figure 176**) so it rests against the coolant seal.

d. Fill the area outside the seal with Molykote 111 (or equivalent).

e. Install the rubber washer.

f. Install the support plate using pusher (part No. 529 0207 00) with the flange toward impeller (out).

Rotary Valve Shaft Inspection

Refer to **Figure 206** for this procedure.

1. Check the bearings (A, **Figure 206**) for roughness or excessive noise.

2. Inspect gears and splines (B, **Figure 206**) for cracks, deep scoring or excessive wear.

3. Check the lip of oil seal (C, **Figure 206**) for cuts or other damage.

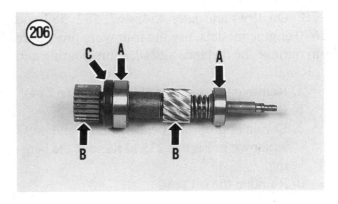

4. Replace worn or damaged parts as described under *Rotary Valve Shaft Disassembly/Reassembly* in this chapter.

Rotary Valve Shaft Disassembly/Reassembly

A press is required to disassemble and reassemble the rotary valve shaft. Read the complete procedure through before beginning disassembly. If you do not have the necessary special tools, refer service to a Ski-Doo dealer.

NOTE
Use special tool (part No. 529 0235 00) to compress the spring while removing the clip as described in Step 1.

1. Compress spring by pressing against the cup (**Figure 207**) and remove the snap ring (**Figure 208**) from the end of the rotary valve shaft.
2. Remove the spring retainer cup (**Figure 209**).
3. Remove the spring (**Figure 210**).
4. Remove the gear (**Figure 211**).
5. Remove the O-ring (**Figure 212**).
6. Remove the shim (**Figure 213**).
7A. On 1993 and earlier 467, 536, 582, 583 and 643 engine models, use the following procedure to remove the distance sleeve, shim, bearing and oil seal.

    a. Heat the distance sleeve (**Figure 214**) with a torch to break the Loctite bond.

    b. Use an appropriate bearing puller and press as shown in **Figure 215** to remove the distance sleeve, shim and bearing.

    c. Remove the oil seal.

7B. On 1994 and later 454, 467, 582, 583 and 670 engine models, use the following procedure to remove the distance sleeve, shim, bearing and oil seal.

    a. Remove the distance sleeve (**Figure 214**).

    b. Remove the snap ring and shim.

    c. Use an appropriate bearing puller and press as shown in **Figure 215** to remove the bearing.

    d. Remove the oil seal.

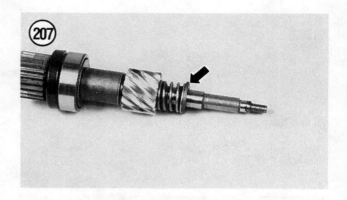

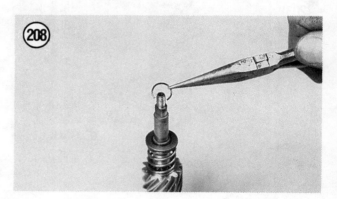

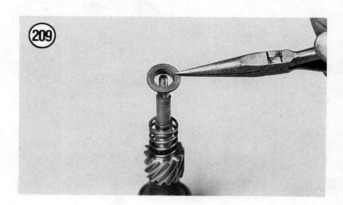

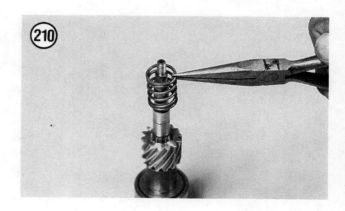

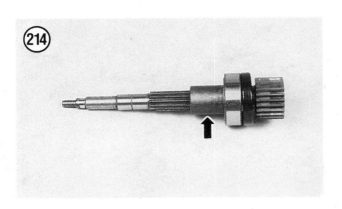

8. Clean all parts in solvent and thoroughly dry.

9A. On 1993 and earlier 467, 536, 582, 583 and 643 engine models, install the oil seal, bearing, shim and distance sleeve as follows:

 a. Fill the oil seal lip with a low-temperature lithium base grease.

 b. Install the oil seal (**Figure 216**) so the shield side faces toward the rotary valve.

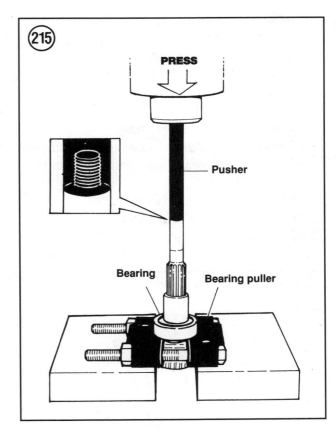

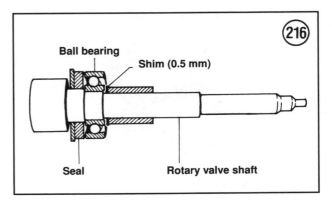

c. Apply Loctite RC 609 to the inside of the distance sleeve.

d. Use a press as shown in **Figure 217** to install the bearing, shim and distance sleeve.

e. Install the shim (**Figure 213**).

9B. On 1994 and later 454, 467, 582, 583 and 670 engine models, use the following procedure to install oil seal, bearing, shim and distance sleeve.

a. Fill the oil seal lip with a low-temperature lithium base grease.

b. Install the oil seal (**Figure 216**) so the shield side faces toward the rotary valve.

c. Use a press as shown in **Figure 217** to install the bearing.

d. Install shim and snap ring.

e. Install the distance sleeve with its counterbore facing toward the installed snap ring and bearing.

10. Install a new O-ring (**Figure 212**).

11. Install the gear (**Figure 211**).

12. Install the spring (**Figure 210**).

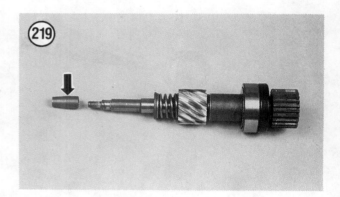

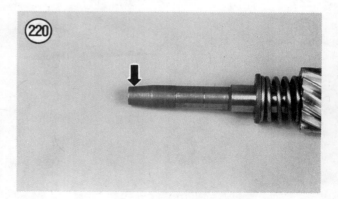

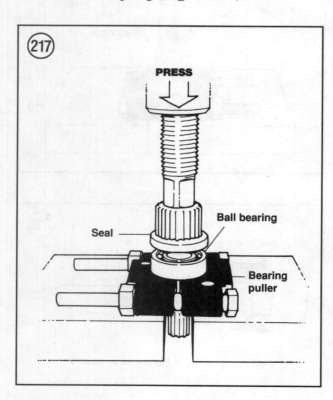

13. Install the spring retainer cup (**Figure 209**).
14. Compress the cup and install the snap ring (**Figure 208**). Make sure the snap ring seats in the rotary valve shaft completely (**Figure 207**).

Impeller Inspection

Inspect the impeller (**Figure 218**) for cracks or other damage. Replace if necessary.

Rotary Valve Shaft Installation

To prevent oil seal damage, the seal protector sleeve (part No. 420 8769 80) (**Figure 219**) must be installed onto the end of the rotary valve shaft. See **Figure 220**.

1. Install the seal protector sleeve onto the end of the rotary valve shaft (**Figure 220**).

2. Coat the seal sleeve with a low-temperature lithium base grease and insert the rotary valve shaft into the upper crankcase (**Figure 221**). Push the shaft into the crankcase until it stops (**Figure 222**). Then use the rotary valve seal pusher (part No. 420 8766 07) (**Figure 223**) to drive the rotary valve shaft, seal and bearing all the way into the crankcase. See **Figure 224**. Remove the seal sleeve from the end of the rotary valve shaft (**Figure 225**).

3. Secure the rotary valve shaft with the snap ring (**Figure 226**). Make sure the snap ring seats in the crankcase groove completely.

5

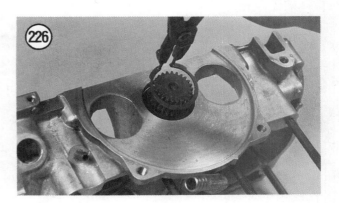

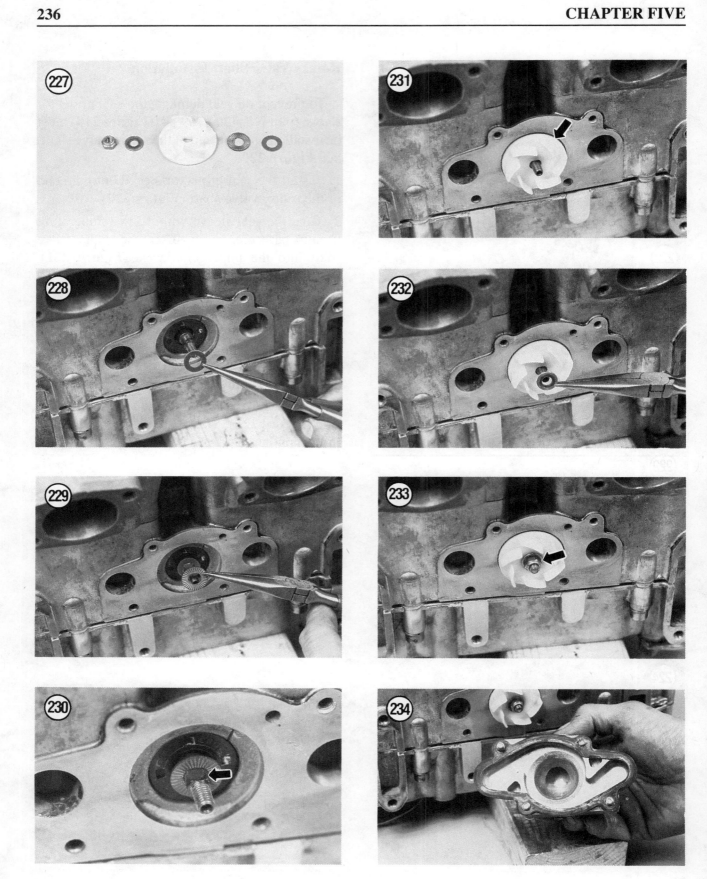

4. Install the crankshaft and assemble the crankcases as described in this chapter.

5. Install the impeller assembly (**Figure 227**) as follows:

  a. Install the small thrust washer (**Figure 228**).

  b. Install the serrated friction washer (**Figure 229**) with its grooves facing toward the outside.

  c. Align the flat on the impeller with the flat on the shaft (**Figure 230**) and install the impeller. See **Figure 231**.

  d. Install the washer (**Figure 232**).

  e. Install a new impeller nut (**Figure 233**). Tighten the nut securely.

  f. Install the water pump cover with a new gasket (**Figure 234**). Tighten the cover retaining screws securely.

5

Table 1 ENGINE NUMBER IDENTIFICATION

Year model	Engine number
1990	
Formula MX & MX LT	467
Formula Plus & Plus LT	536
Formula MACH 1 & MACH 1 XTC	583
1991	
Formula MX, MX E, MX X, MX XTC & MX XTC E	467
Formula Plus, Plus E, Plus X, Plus XTC & Plus XTC E	536
Formula MACH 1, MACH 1 X & MACH 1 XTC	643
1992	
Formula MX & MX XTC R	467
Formula Plus, Plus E, Plus XTC & Plus XTC E	582
Formula Plus X	583
Formula MACH 1, MACH 1 XTC & MACH 1 XTC II	643
Formula MACH 1 X	670
1993	
Formula MX, MX (2) & MX XTC R	467
Formula MX Z	467 (Z)
Formula Plus, Plus (2), Plus E, Plus XTC & Plus EFI	582
Formula Plus X	643
Formula MACH 1, MACH 1 (2) & MACH 1 XTC	670
Formula Grand Touring	582

(continued)

Table 1 ENGINE NUMBER IDENTIFICATION (continued)

Year model	Engine number
1994	
Formula MX, MX Z, MX Z X & ST	467
Summit 470 HAC	467HAC
Formula STX, STX II & Z	583
Summit 583 HAC	583HAC
MACH 1	670
Grand Touring & Grand Touring XTC	582
Grand Touring SE	670
1995	
MX & Grand Touring 470	467
MX Z	454
Formula SS	670
Formula STX, STX (LT) & Z	583
Summit 583	583HAC
Summit 670	670HAC
MACH 1 & Grand Touring SE	670
Grand Touring 580	582

Table 2 GENERAL ENGINE SPECIFICATIONS

Bore		
454	67.5 mm	(2.658 in.)
467	69.5 mm	(2.736 in.)
536	72.0 mm	(2.835 in.)
582, 583 & 583HAC	76.0 mm	(2.992 in.)
643	76.0 mm	(2.992 in.)
670	78.0 mm	(2.736 in.)
Stroke		
454	61.0 mm	(2.402 in.)
467	61.0 mm	(2.402 in.)
536	64.0 mm	(2.520 in.)
582, 583 & 583HAC	64.0 mm	(2.520 in.)
643	68.0 mm	(2.677 in.)
670	70.0 mm	(2.756 in.)
Displacement		
454	436.6 cc	(26.6 cu. in.)
467	462.7 cc	(28.2 cu. in.)
536	521.2 cc	(31.8 cu. in.)
582, 583 & 583HAC	580.7 cc	(35.4 cu. in.)
643	616.9 cc	(37.6 cu. in.)
670	668.7 cc	(40.8 cu. in.)
Compression ratio		
454	6.6:1	
467	6.8-7.3:1	
536	6.1:1	
582	6.70-7.5:1	
583 & 583HAC	5.2-7.1:1	
643	6.3:1	
670	6.0-6.4:15-3	

(continued)

Table 3 454 ENGINE SERVICE SPECIFICATIONS

	Desired mm (in.)	Wear limit mm (in.)
Cylinder		
Taper	–	0.08 (0.003)
Out-of-round	–	0.05 (0.002)
Piston-to-cylinder		
Clearance	0.11-0.135 (0.0043-0.0053)	0.20 (0.008)
Piston ring end gap	0.20-0.35 (0.008-0.014)	1.00 (0.039)
Piston ring groove		
Clearance	0.040-0.100 (0.0016-0.0039)	0.20 (0.008)
Connecting rod big end		
Axial play	0.40-0.75 (0.016-0.029)	1.20 (0.047)
Crankshaft end play	0.10-0.30 (0.004-0.012)	--
Crankshaft deflection*		
PTO end	–	0.06 (0.002)
Magneto end	–	0.03 (0.001)
Rotary valve to crankcase		
Clearance	–	0.27-0.40 (0.011-0.016)

* Support crankshaft in V blocks at location of the end main bearings and measure deflection about 3 mm (1/8 in.) from the end of the crankshaft or 86 mm (3.386 in.) from V block at PTO end. Measure deflection midway between the keyway and the first thread at magneto end.

Table 4 467 ENGINE SERVICE SPECIFICATIONS

	Desired mm (in.)	Wear limit mm (in.)
Cylinder		
Taper	–	0.08 (0.003)
Out-of-round	–	0.05 (0.002)
Piston-to-cylinder clearance		
1990-1994	0.10-0.12 (0.0039-0.0047)	0.20 (0.008)
Piston ring end gap		
1990-1994	0.20-0.35 (0.008-0.014)	1.00 (0.039)
Piston ring groove clearance		
1990-1994	0.04-0.11 (0.002-0.004)	0.20 (0.008)
	(continued)	

5

Table 4 467 ENGINE SERVICE SPECIFICATIONS (continued)

	Desired mm (in.)	Wear limit mm (in.)
Connecting rod big end axial play		
1990	0.40 (0.016)	1.20 (0.047)
1991-1994	0.40-0.75 (0.016-0.029)	1.20 (0.047)
Crankshaft end play		
1990-1994	0.10-0.30 (0.004-0.012)	–
Crankshaft deflection		
1990-1991*	–	0.08 (0.003)
1992-1994**		
PTO end	–	0.06 (0.002)
Magneto end	–	0.03 (0.001)
Rotary valve to crankcase clearance		
1990-1994	–	0.27-0.40 (0.011-0.016)

* Support crankshaft in V blocks at location of the end main bearings and measure deflection 6 mm (1/4 in.) from PTO end and midway between the keyway and the first thread at magneto end.

** Support crankshaft in V blocks at location of the end main bearings and measure deflection about 3 mm (1/8 in.) from the end of the crankshaft or 86 mm (3.386 in.) from V block at PTO end. Measure deflection midway between the keyway and the first thread at magneto end.

Table 5 536 ENGINE SERVICE SPECIFICATIONS

	Specification mm (in.)	Wear limit mm (in.)
Cylinder		
Taper	–	0.08 (0.0031)
Out-of-round	–	0.05 (0.0020)
Piston-to-cylinder clearance		
1990	0.09-0.10 (0.0035-0.0039)	0.20 (0.008)
1991	0.09-0.11 (0.0035-0.0043)	0.20 (0.008)
Piston ring end gap	0.20-0.35 (0.008-0.014)	1.00 (0.0039)
Piston ring groove clearance	0.04-0.11 (0.002-0.004)	0.20 (0.008)
Connecting rod big end axial play	0.40 (0.016)	1.20 (0.047)
Crankshaft end play	0.10-1.00 (0.004-0.040)	–
	(continued)	

Table 5 536 ENGINE SERVICE SPECIFICATIONS (continued)

	Specification mm (in.)	Wear limit mm (in.)
Crankshaft deflection*	–	0.08 (0.003)
Rotary valve to crankcase clearance	–	0.27-0.48 (0.011-0.019)

* Support crankshaft in V blocks at location of the end main bearings and measure deflection 6 mm (1/4 in.) from PTO end and midway between the keyway and the first thread at magneto end.

Table 6 582 ENGINE SERVICE SPECIFICATIONS

	Specification mm (in.)	Wear limit mm (in.)
Cylinder		
Taper	–	0.08 (0.003)
Out-of-round	–	0.05 (0.002)
Piston-to-cylinder clearance	0.05-0.07 (0.0020-0.0028)	0.15 (0.0059)
Piston ring end gap	0.25-0.40 (0.010-0.016)	1.00 (0.039)
Piston ring groove clearance	0.043-0.083 (0.0017-0.0033)	0.160 (0.0063)
Connecting rod big end axial play	0.40-0.75 (0.016-0.029)	1.2 (0.047)
Crankshaft end play	–	0.10-0.30 (0.004-0.012)
Crankshaft deflection*		
PTO end	–	0.06 (0.002)
Magneto end	–	0.03 (0.001)
Rotary valve to crankcase clearance	0.27 (0.011)	0.48 (0.019)

* Support crankshaft in V blocks at location of the end main bearings and measure deflection about 3 mm (1/8 in.) from the end of the crankshaft or 86 mm (3.386 in.) from V block at PTO end. Measure deflection midway between the keyway and the first thread at magneto end.

Table 7 583 ENGINE SERVICE SPECIFICATIONS

	Specification mm (in.)	Wear limit mm (in.)
Cylinder		
Taper	–	0.08 (0.003)
Out-of-round	–	0.05 (0.002)
	(continued)	

Table 7 583 ENGINE SERVICE SPECIFICATIONS (continued)

	Specification mm (in.)	Wear limit mm (in.)
Piston-to-cylinder clearance		
1990	0.11-0.13 (0.0043-0.0051)	0.20 (0.0079)
1993-1994	0.04-0.05 (0.0016-0.0020)	0.15 (0.0059)
Piston ring end gap	0.20-0.35 (0.008-0.014)	1.00 (0.039)
Piston ring groove clearance		
1990	0.04-0.11 (0.002-0.004)	0.20 (0.008)
1993-1994	0.04-0.10 (0.0016-0.0039)	0.20 (0.008)
Connecting rod big end axial play		
1990, 1993-1994	0.40 (0.016)	1.2 (0.047)
Crankshaft end play	–	0.10-0.30 (0.004-0.012)
Crankshaft deflection		
1990*	–	0.08 (0.003)
1992-1994**		
PTO end	–	0.06 (0.002)
Magneto end	–	0.03 (0.001)
Rotary valve to crankcase clearance		
1990, 1993-1994	0.27 (0.011)	0.48 (0.019)

* Support crankshaft in V blocks at location of the end main bearings and measure deflection 6 mm (1/4 in.) from PTO end and midway between the keyway and the first thread at magneto end.
** Support crankshaft in V blocks at location of the end main bearings and measure deflection about 3 mm (1/8 in.) from the end of the crankshaft or 86 mm (3.386 in.) from V block at PTO end. Measure deflection midway between the keyway and the first thread at magneto end.

Table 8 643 ENGINE SERVICE SPECIFICATIONS

	Specification mm (in.)	Wear limit mm (in.)
Cylinder		
Taper	–	0.08 (0.003)
Out-of-round	–	0.05 (0.002)
Piston-to-cylinder clearance	0.05-0.07 (0.0020-0.0028)	0.20 (0.008)
Piston ring end gap		
1991-1992	0.20-0.35 (0.008-0.014)	1.00 (0.039)
Piston ring groove clearance	0.04-0.11 (0.002-0.004)	0.20 (0.008)
	(continued)	

Table 8 643 ENGINE SERVICE SPECIFICATIONS (continued)

	Specification mm (in.)	Wear limit mm (in.)
Connecting rod big end axial play	0.39-0.74 (0.015-0.029)	1.2 (0.047)
Crankshaft end play	–	0.10-0.30 (0.004-0.012)
Crankshaft deflection*	–	0.08 (0.0031)
Rotary valve to crankcase clearance 1991-1992	–	0.3-0.5 (0.012-0.020)

* Support crankshaft in V blocks at location of the end main bearings and measure deflection 6 mm (1/4 in.) from PTO end and midway between the keyway and the first thread at magneto end.

Table 9 670 ENGINE SERVICE SPECIFICATIONS

	Specification mm (in.)	Wear limit mm (in.)
Cylinder		
Taper	–	0.08 (0.003)
Out-of-round	–	0.05 (0.002)
Piston-to-cylinder clearance		
1993	0.05-0.07 (0.0016-0.0020)	0.15 (0.0059)
1994	0.07-0.09 (0.0028-0.0035)	0.15 (0.0059)
Piston ring end gap	0.25-0.40 (0.010-0.016)	1.00 (0.039)
Piston ring groove clearance	0.030-0.062 (0.0012-0.0024)	0.20 (0.008)
Connecting rod big end axial play	0.40-0.75 (0.016-0.029)	1.2 (0.047)
Crankshaft end play	–	0.10-0.30 (0.004-0.012)
Crankshaft deflection		
1993*		
PTO end	–	0.063 (0.0024)
Magneto end	–	0.03 (0.0012)
1994*		
PTO end	–	0.06 (0.002)
Magneto end	–	0.03 (0.001)
(continued)		

Table 9 670 ENGINE SERVICE SPECIFICATIONS (continued)

	Specification mm (in.)	Wear limit mm (in.)
Rotary valve to crankcase clearance		
1993	–	0.27-0.48 (0.011-0.019)
1994	–	0.27-0.40 (0.011-0.016)

* Support crankshaft in V blocks at location of the end main bearings and measure deflection about 3 mm (1/8 in.) from the PTO end of the crankshaft or 100 mm (3.937 in.) from V block at PTO end. Measure deflection midway between the keyway and the first thread at magneto end.

Table 10 ROTARY VALVE TIMING

	Opening BTDC	Closing ATDC
1990		
467 engine models	132°	52°
536 engine models	117°	52°
536 (Formula Plus 500)	134°	69°
583 engine models	140°	68°
1991		
467 Formula MX X	143°	66°
Other 467 engines	132°	52°
536 Formula Plus X	134°	69°
Other 536 engines	137°	61°
636 Formula MACH 1 X	146°	75°
Other 643 engines	142°	70°
1992		
467 engine models	132°	52°
582 engine models	129.5°	69.5°
583 Formula Plus X	141.5°	69.5°
643 engine models	144°	72°
670 MACH 1 X	146°	75°
1993		
467 engine models	132°	52°
582 engine models	129.5°	69.5°
583 Plus X	141.5°	69.5°
670 engine models	146°	75°
1994		
467 MX Z X	145°	65°
Other 467 engines	132°	52°
582 engine models	134°	65°
583HAC Engines	132°	52°
Other 583 engines	134°	65°
670 engine models	144°	72°

(continued)

5

Table 10 ROTARY VALVE TIMING (continued)

	Opening BTDC	Closing ATDC
1995		
454 MX Z	145.5°	64°
467 engine models	132°	52°
582 engine models	129.5°	69.5°
583HAC engines	134°	65°
Other 583 engines	140°	71°
670 MACH 1 model	145°	76°
Other 670 engines	144°	72°

Table 11 ENGINE TIGHTENING TORQUES

	N·m	ft.-lb.
Cylinder head bolts or nuts		
1990-1991		
All models	22	16
1992		
467 & 582 engines		
Cylinder head	30	22
Head cover	10	7.5
583, 643 & 670 engines	22	16
1993		
467 & 582 engines		
Cylinder head	30	22
Head cover	10	7.5
583 & 670 engines	22	16
1994-on		
467 & 582 engines		
Cylinder head	30	22
Head cover	10	7.5
454, 583 & 670 engines	22	16
Cylinder base bolts or nuts		
1990-1991	22	16
1992-on	30	22
Crankcase nuts or bolts		
1990		
M6	10	7.5
M8	22	16
1991-on		
M6	10	7.5
M8	24	17
M10	38	28
Exhaust valve bolts		
454, 583, 643 & 670 engines	10	7.5

(continued)

Table 11 ENGINE TIGHTENING TORQUES (continued)

	N·m	ft.-lb.
Exhaust manifold bolts or nuts		
1990-1992		
467 engine model	21	15
536 engine model	25	18
583 engine model	10	7.5
1993		
467, 582 & 583 engines	25	18
1994-on		
467 & 582 engines	25	18
454, 583 & 670 engines	10	7.5
Flywheel nut		
1990-1994		
643 & 670 engines	125	92
Other engine models	105	77
1995		
467, 582 & 583	105	77
454, 583HAC, 670	125	92
Engine mounts		
1990-on		
M10 bolts	48	35
M10 nuts	38	28
M8 Allen bolts and nuts	25	18
Rotary valve cover	22	16

Chapter Six

Fuel System—Carbureted Models

The fuel system consists of the fuel tank, fuel pump, carburetors and the air silencer. This chapter includes service procedures for all parts of the carbureted fuel system. There are differences among the different models, which are noted in the service procedures and tables.

Carburetor specifications are listed in **Tables 1-3** at the end of the chapter.

AIR SILENCER

The air silencer typical of all 1990-1993 models, 1994 MACH 1 and 1994 Grand Touring models is shown in **Figure 1**. The air silencer typical of 1994 Formula (MX, MXZ, MXZ X, ST, STX and Z) models and all 1995 models is shown in **Figure 2**. The air silencer, sometimes referred to as the air box, should be inspected periodically for cleanliness and cracks.

> *CAUTION*
> *Never run the engine with the air silencer removed. Running without the air silencer or air filters will lean the fuel mixture (too much air - not enough fuel) and may result in engine seizure. The air silencer and filters must be installed during carburetor adjustments.*

Removal/Installation

Refer to **Figure 3** for all 1990-1993 models, 1994 MACH 1 and 1994 Grand Touring models. Refer to **Figure 4** for 1994 Formula (MX, MXZ, MXZ X, ST, STX and Z) models and all 1995 models.
1. Open the hood.
2. If so equipped, loosen the inlet boot clamps at the carburetors.
3. Detach the inlet hoses from the air silencer.
4. Remove the screws attaching the air silencer. Check for anything that would interfere with air silencer removal.
5. Remove the air silencer (**Figure 3** or **Figure 4**).
6. Cover the carburetors to prevent the entrance of dirt or moisture while the air silencer is removed.
7. Install by reversing the procedure. Be sure the air inlet hoses are properly attached to the carburetors and to the air silencer.

Inspection

Clean the air silencer box thoroughly and check for cracks or other damage. Cracks in the air silencer box should be repaired before reinstalling.

CARBURETOR

All models except the 1993 Formula Plus EFI are equipped with 2 slide type carburetors. Refer to *Fuel Injection System* in this chapter to service an EFI model.

Refer to **Tables 1-3** for carburetor application, identification and specifications.

Carburetor Operation

For proper operation, a gasoline engine must be supplied with fuel and air mixed in proper proportions. A mixture in which there is too much fuel is said to be rich. A lean mixture is one that has insufficient fuel. The hand operated primer pump, though not part of the carburetor, is used to squirt additional fuel into the incoming fuel and air mixture and thus enrich the mixture for cold starting. A carburetor that is operating correctly and properly adjusted will supply the proper mixture of air and fuel at various engine speeds and under a wide range of operating conditions.

The carburetors installed on these models contain several major systems. A float and float valve mechanism are used to maintain a constant fuel level in the float bowl. The idle mixture system controls the amount of fuel at low engine speeds. The main fuel system controls the amount of fuel at high speeds. At intermediate engine speeds, the fuel is controlled by the needle jet and its jet needle.

Float Mechanism

The carburetor is equipped with a float actuated, needle and seat type fuel inlet valve. The inlet valve (**Figure 5**) is attached to the float and moves up and down with the float. Up and down movement of the inlet valve opens and closes the fuel flow into the float bowl, maintaining a steady flow of fuel and a consistent fuel level in the float bowl. The fuel is supplied to the carburetor by a pulse operated diaphragm type fuel pump.

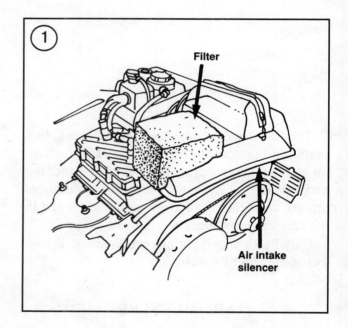

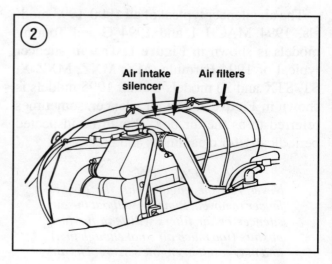

③ **AIR SILENCER ASSEMBLY**
ALL 1990-1993 MODELS; 1994 MACH I AND GRAND TOURING MODELS)

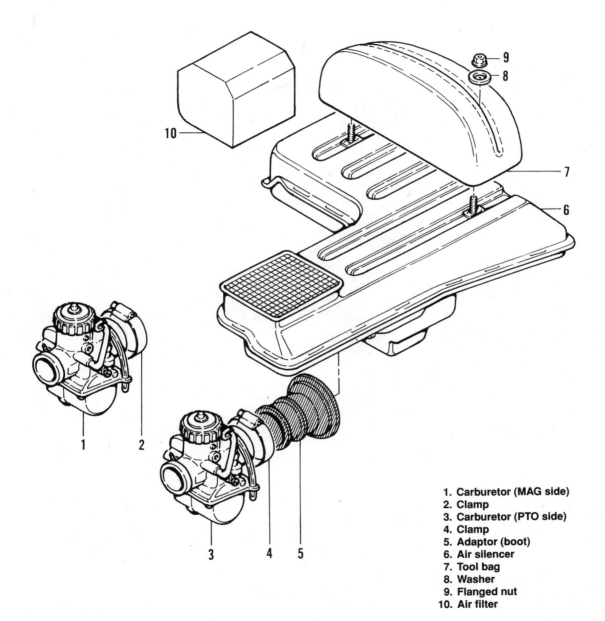

1. Carburetor (MAG side)
2. Clamp
3. Carburetor (PTO side)
4. Clamp
5. Adaptor (boot)
6. Air silencer
7. Tool bag
8. Washer
9. Flanged nut
10. Air filter

6

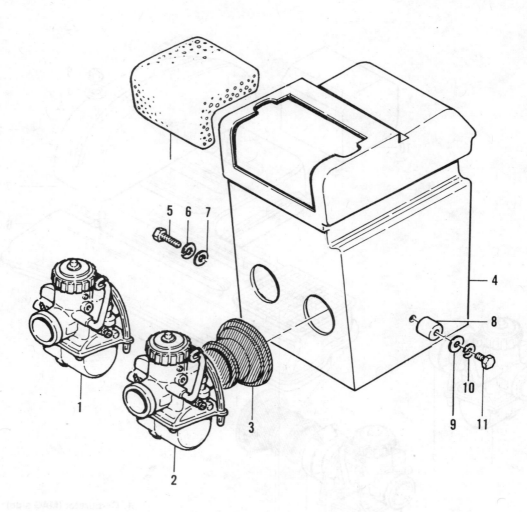

**AIR SILENCER ASSEMBLY
(1994 FORMULA MX, MXZ, MXZX, ST, STX AND Z MODELS; ALL 1995 MODELS)**

1. Carburetor (MAG side)
2. Carburetor (PTO side)
3. Adaptor (boot)
4. Air silencer
5. Bolt
6. Lockwasher
7. Washer
8. Spacer
9. Washer
10. Lockwasher
11. Bolt

④

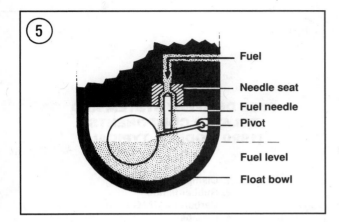

5

Fuel

Needle seat

Fuel needle

Pivot

Fuel level

Float bowl

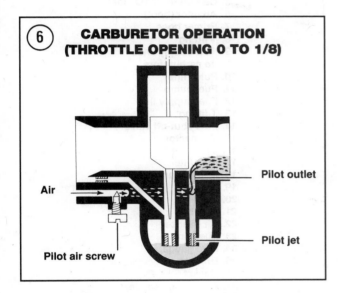

6

CARBURETOR OPERATION
(THROTTLE OPENING 0 TO 1/8)

Air

Pilot outlet

Pilot jet

Pilot air screw

Idle, Intermediate and Main Fuel Systems

The purpose of the carburetor is to atomize fuel and mix it in correct proportions with air entering the engine through the air intake, throughout the entire speed range. At small throttle openings (from idle to about 1/8 open), only a small amount of fuel is mixed with a small amount of air. A typical idle mixture system is shown in **Figure 6**. The pilot air screw shown in **Figure 6** controls a small amount of air mixed with fuel from the pilot jet. Opening the pilot air screw (sometimes called an idle mixture needle) permits more air to enter the idle mixture system and leans the mixture.

As the throttle is opened further, more air enters the engine around the throttle slide as shown in **Figure 7** and **Figure 8**. Fuel is drawn into the air stream from between the needle jet and the jet needle.

When the throttle is completely open, the amount of fuel drawn into the air stream is limited by the size of the main jet (**Figure 9**).

None of these changes from the idle mixture circuit to the intermediate (needle) range to high speed (main jet) is abrupt, but is transitional.

6

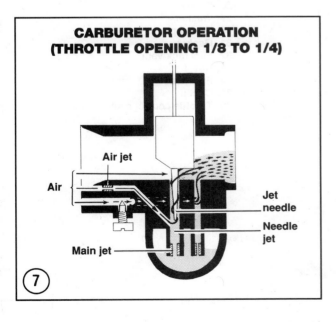

CARBURETOR OPERATION
(THROTTLE OPENING 1/8 TO 1/4)

Air jet

Air

Jet needle

Needle jet

Main jet

7

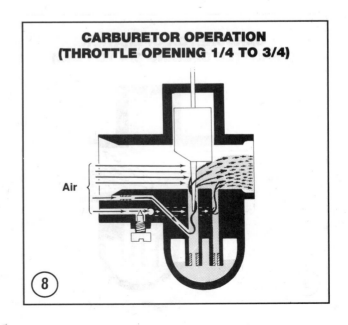

CARBURETOR OPERATION
(THROTTLE OPENING 1/4 TO 3/4)

Air

8

Starting Enrichment

A hand operated fuel primer located on the right side of the cowl is used to enrichen the fuel/air mixture for cold starting. When cold, the primer should be pushed 2-3 times before starting.

Carburetor
Removal/Installation

1. Open the hood.
2. Remove the air silencer (**Figure 3** or **Figure 4**) as described in this chapter.

> *NOTE*
> *Carburetors are often different for the left and right sides. Mark the carburetors to indicate which carburetor is installed on the magneto side, before removing either carburetor. A simple way is to apply a colored mark to the rotary valve cover near the mounting flange for the right (magneto) side carburetor. Then apply a similar identification mark to magneto side carburetor.*

3. Label the hoses at the carburetors. Refer to **Figures 10-15**. Loosen the metal hose clamps

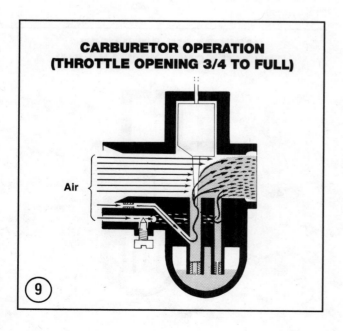

CARBURETOR OPERATION
(THROTTLE OPENING 3/4 TO FULL)

Air

9

FUEL DELIVERY SYSTEM AND RELATED COMPONENTS (1990 MODELS, TYPICAL)

1. Clamps
2. Rubber flange
3. Carburetor (MAG side)
4. Clamps
5. Carburetor (PTO side)
6. Adaptor (boot)
7. Primer hose
8. T fitting
9. Fuel supply lines to carburetors
10. Pulse line
11. Fuel pump
12. Fuel supply line
13. T fitting
14. Fuel shut-off valve
15. Connector
16. Grommet
17. Fuel filter
18. Primer pump
19. Air filter
20. Boot
21. Tool bag
22. Air silencer
23. Fuel tank
24. Fuel gauge
25. Bracket
26. Gasket
27. Fuel gauge sender
28. Screw
29. Washer
30. Fuel cap
31. Gasket
32. Fuel tank vent
33. Nut
34. Fuel hose
35. Circlip
36. Throttle control cable

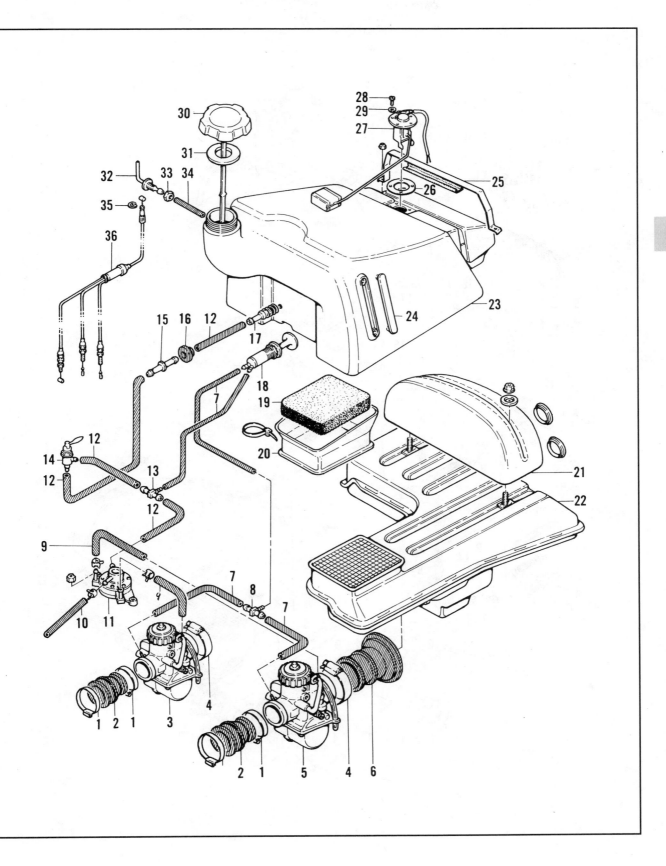

6

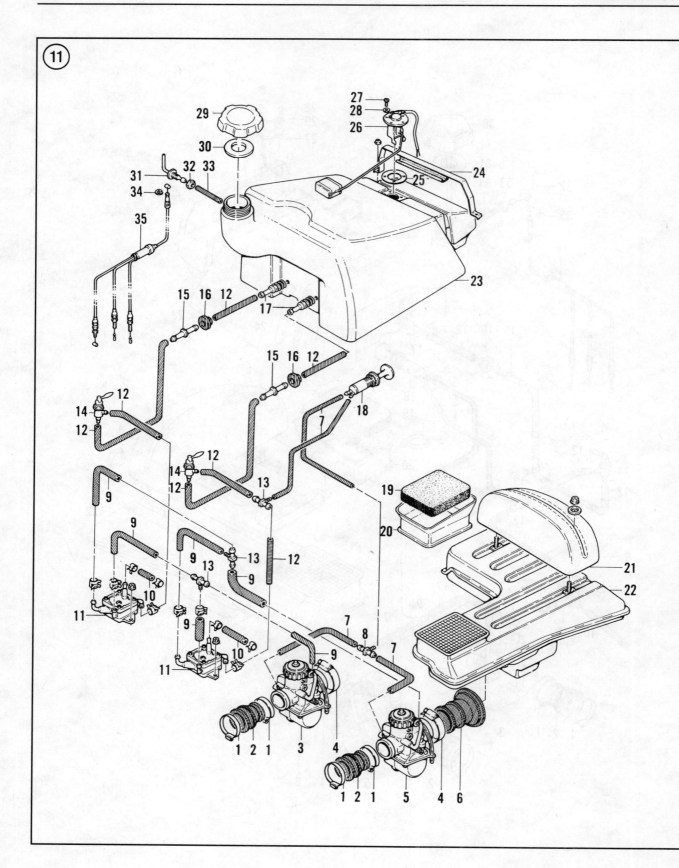

6

FUEL DELIVERY SYSTEM AND RELATED COMPONENTS
(1991-1994 MODELS EQUIPPED WITH DUAL FUEL PUMPS)

1. Clamps
2. Rubber flange
3. Carburetor (MAG side)
4. Clamps
5. Carburetor (PTO side)
6. Adaptor (boot)
7. Primer hose
8. T fitting
9. Fuel supply lines
   to carburetors
10. Pulse lines
11. Fuel pumps
12. Fuel supply lines
13. T fittings
14. Fuel shut-off valves
15. Connectors
16. Grommets
17. Fuel filters
18. Primer pump
19. Air filter
20. Boot
21. Tool bag
22. Air silencer
23. Fuel tank
24. Bracket
25. Gasket
26. Fuel gauge sender
27. Screw
28. Washer
29. Fuel cap
30. Gasket
31. Fuel tank vent
32. Nut
33. Fuel hose
34. Circlip
35. Throttle control cable

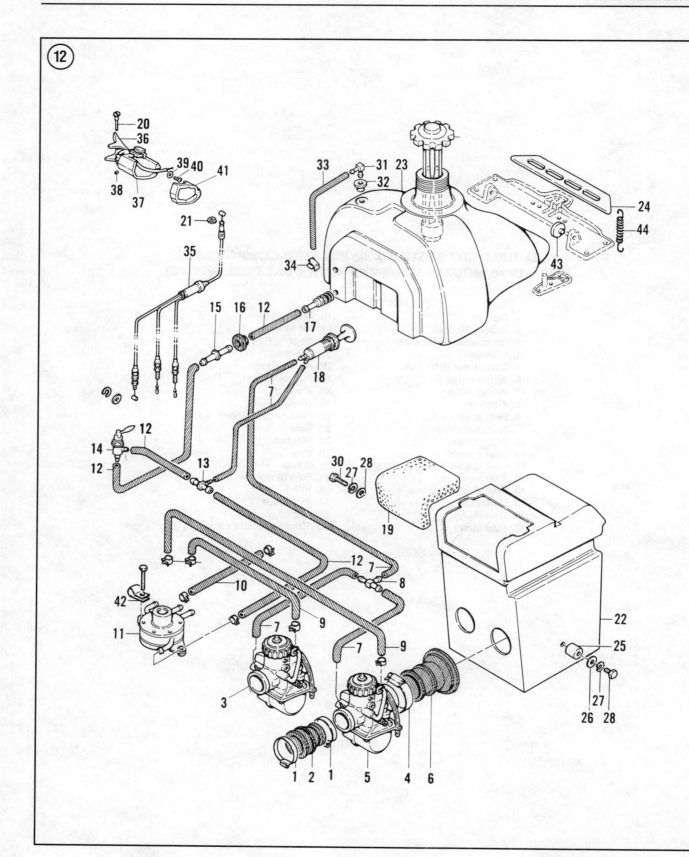

FUEL DELIVERY SYSTEM AND RELATED COMPONENTS
(1993-ON FORMULA MX, 1994 ST AND 1994-ON FORMULA MXZ)

1. Clamps
2. Rubber flange
3. Carburetor (MAG side)
4. Clamps
5. Carburetor (PTO side)
6. Adaptor (boot)
7. Primer hose
8. T fitting
9. Fuel supply lines
   to carburetors
10. Pulse line
11. Fuel pump
12. Fuel supply lines
13. T fitting
14. Fuel shut-off valve
15. Connector
16. Grommet
17. Fuel filter
18. Primer pump
19. Air filter
20. Bolt
21. Circlip
22. Air silencer
23. Fuel tank
24. Bracket
25. Spacer
26. Washer
27. Lockwasher
28. Bolt
29. Fuel cap & gauge
30. Bolt
31. Fuel tank vent
32. Grommet
33. Vent hose
34. Clip
35. Throttle control cable
36. Throttle lever
37. Stop switch
38. Set screw
39. Washer
40. Screw
41. Adapter
42. Clamp
43. Bumper
44. Spring

6

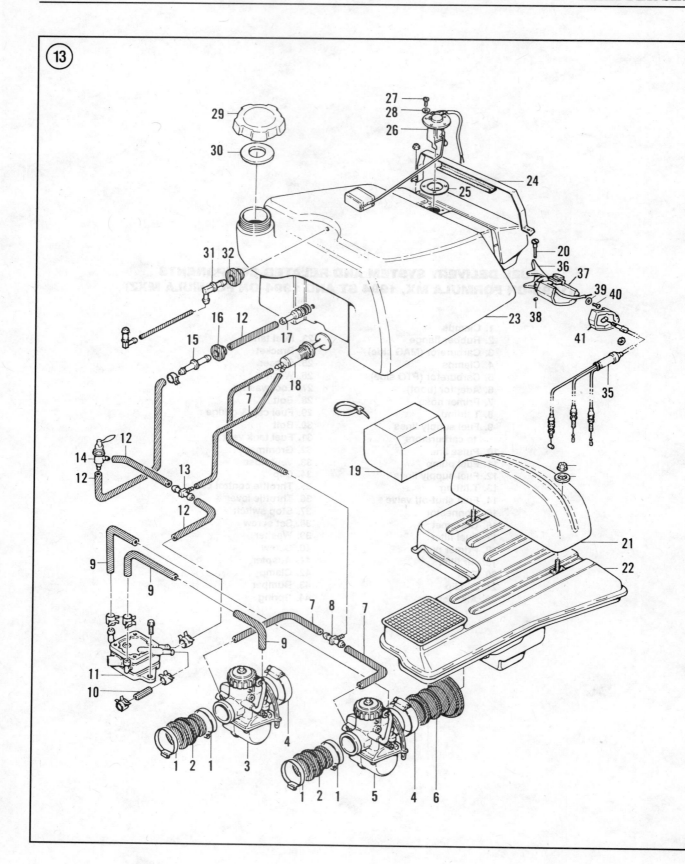

FUEL DELIVERY SYSTEM AND RELATED COMPONENTS
(1993 FORMULA PLUS, PLUS E, PLUS XTC, MX AND MX XTR; 1994 MACH I, GT AND GTX XTC MODELS)

1. Clamps
2. Rubber flange
3. Carburetor (MAG side)
4. Clamps
5. Carburetor (PTO side)
6. Adaptor (boot)
7. Primer hose
8. T fitting
9. Fuel supply lines to carburetors
10. Pulse line
11. Fuel pump
12. Fuel supply lines
13. T fitting
14. Fuel shut-off valve
15. Connector
16. Grommets
17. Fuel filter
18. Primer pump
19. Air filter
20. Bolt
21. Tool bag
22. Air silencer
23. Fuel tank
24. Bracket
25. Gasket
26. Fuel gauge sender
27. Screw
28. Washer
29. Fuel cap
30. Gasket
31. Fuel tank vent
32. Grommet
33. Vent hose
34. Elbow
35. Throttle control cable
36. Throttle lever
37. Stop switch
38. Set screw
39. Washer
40. Screw
41. Adapter

6

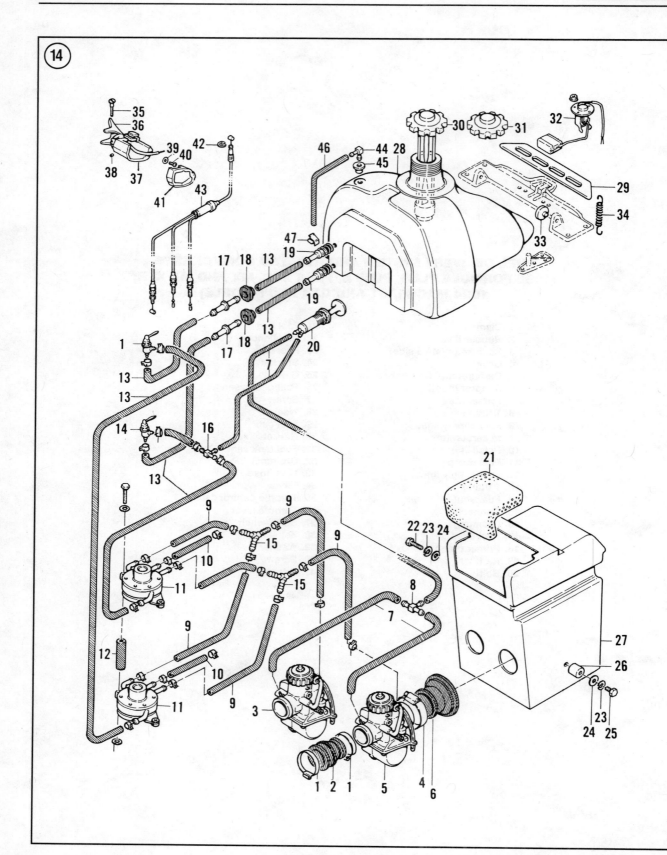

FUEL DELIVERY SYSTEM AND RELATED COMPONENTS
(1994 FORMULA STX, STX II AND Z MODELS)

1. Clamps
2. Rubber flange
3. Carburetor (MAG side)
4. Clamps
5. Carburetor (PTO side)
6. Adaptor (boot)
7. Primer hose
8. T fitting
9. Fuel supply lines
   to carburetors
10. Pulse lines
11. Fuel pumps
12. Spacer
13. Fuel supply lines
14. Fuel shut-off valve
15. Y fittings
16. T fitting
17. Connectors
18. Grommet
19. Fuel filter
20. Primer pump
21. Air filter
22. Bolt
23. Lockwasher
24. Washer
25. Bolt
26. Spacer
27. Air silencer
28. Fuel tank
29. Bracket
30. Fuel cap & gauge
31. Fuel cap
32. Fuel gauge sender
33. Bumper
34. Spring
35. Bolt
36. Throttle lever
37. Stop switch
38. Set screw
39. Washer
40. Screw
41. Adapter
42. Circlip
43. Throttle control cable
44. Fuel tank vent
45. Grommet
46. Vent hose
47. Clip

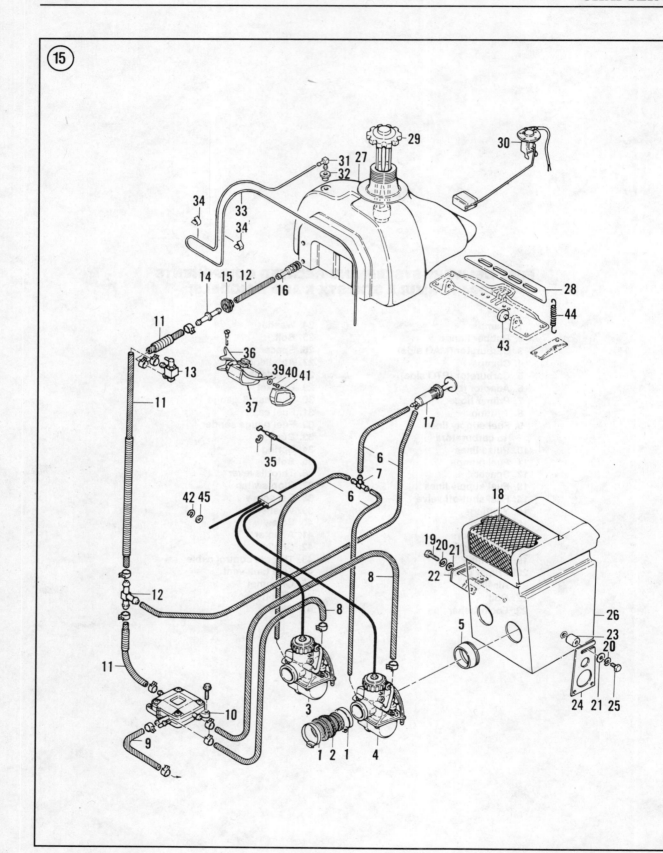

6

FUEL DELIVERY SYSTEM AND RELATED COMPONENTS
(1995 FORMULA SS AND MACH I MODELS)

1. Clamps
2. Rubber flange
3. Carburetor (MAG side)
4. Carburetor (PTO side)
5. Adaptor
6. Primer hose
7. T fitting
8. Fuel supply lines
   to carburetors
9. Pulse line
10. Fuel pump
12. Fuel supply lines
12. T fitting
13. Fuel shut-off valve
14. Connector
15. Grommet
16. Fuel filter
17. Primer pump
18. Air filter
19. Bolt
20. Lockwashers
21. Washer
22. Bracket
23. Spacer
24. Bracket
25. Bolt
26. Air silencer
27. Fuel tank
28. Bracket
29. Fuel cap & gauge
30. Fuel gauge sender
31. Fuel tank vent
32. Grommet
33. Vent hose
34. Clips
35. Throttle control cable
36. Throttle lever
37. Stop switch
38. Set screw
39. Washer
40. Screw
41. Adapter
42. Circlip
43. Bumper
44. Spring
45. Washer

before disconnecting the hoses. Plug the hoses to prevent fuel leakage and contamination.

4. Loosen the carburetor caps (**Figure 16** and remove the throttle slide assemblies from the carburetor bodies.

> *CAUTION*
> *Handle the slide carefully to prevent scratching or otherwise damaging the slide and needle jet. If it is not necessary to remove the throttle slide or other parts from the throttle cable, wrap the assembly in a plastic bag and attach it to the handlebar to reduce chance of damage.*

5. Loosen the hose clamps at the intake manifold.

6. Remove the carburetors.

7. Installation is the reverse of these steps.

8. Install the carburetors in their original locations. The *NOTE* before Step 3 in this procedure suggests one method of identifying the original location before removing. **Table 1** will assist in identifying the location of the original carburetors.

9. Make initial adjustments to the carburetors as described in Chapter Three. Initial idle mixture setting is listed in **Table 2**.

10. Adjust the oil pump control cable as described in Chapter Three.

11. Make sure the fuel hoses are properly connected. Secure the fuel hoses with new clamps.

> *WARNING*
> *Do not start the engine if the fuel hoses are leaking.*

12. Make sure the boots and clamps between carburetors and the manifold are properly installed. Tighten the clamps.

13. Make sure the boots and clamps between carburetors and the air silencer are installed securely to prevent an air leak.

14. Make final adjustments to the carburetors as described in Chapter Three. The idle speed setting is listed in **Table 3**.

Carburetor to Intake Manifold Boots

The boots between the intake manifold and the carburetors should be inspected frequently for looseness or damage that would allow air leakage. Air leaks between the carburetor and the engine can result in a lean fuel mixture. Apply a light coat of RTV sealant to the manifold tubes (**Figure 17**) before attaching the boots.

Carburetor Application

The carburetors used on these models are similar but differences occur between carburetors used on the left and right cylinders. Refer to **Table 1** for original application.

Disassembly

Refer to **Figure 18** for this procedure.

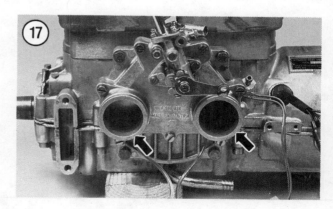

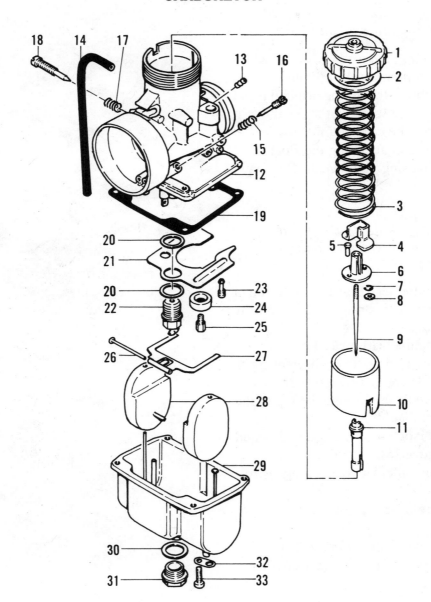

CARBURETOR

6

1. Cap
2. Seal
3. Spring
4. Retainer
5. Screw
6. Retainer
7. E-clip
8. Spacer
9. Jet needle
10. Throttle valve
11. Needle jet

12. Housing
13. Nipple
14. Hose
15. Spring
16. Pilot air screw
17. Spring
18. Throttle stop screw
19. Gasket
20. Washer
21. Baffle plate
22. Needle valve assembly

23. Pilot jet
24. Baffle ring
25. Main jet
26. Pivot pin
27. Float arm
28. Floats
29. Float bowl
30. Gasket
31. Plug
32. Hose guide
33. Screw

NOTE
Because the jetting between the PTO and MAG side carburetors are different, store the components in separate boxes.

1. Before removing, count the turns while screwing the pilot air screw (idle mixture needle) in until it seats lightly. Record the original exact position, then back the screw out and remove it and the spring from the carburetor.

2. Remove the screws attaching the float bowl to the carburetor housing. Remove the float bowl (**Figure 19**).

CAUTION
The pilot jet is easily damaged if the wrong size screwdriver is used to remove or install the jet.

3. Remove the pilot jet (**Figure 20**) using a flat-tip screwdriver with straight sides that fits the slot in jet correctly.

4. Remove the main jet (**Figure 21**).

5. Remove the baffle ring. Two different types have been used (**Figure 22** or **Figure 23**).

6. Remove the needle jet through the top of the carburetor (**Figure 24**).

7. Remove the pivot pin (A, **Figure 25**) and pivot arm (B, **Figure 25**).

8. Remove the fuel inlet valve assembly as follows:
   a. Remove the clip (**Figure 26**), if so equipped.
   b. Remove the inlet valve (**Figure 27**).
   c. Remove the inlet valve seat (**Figure 28**).

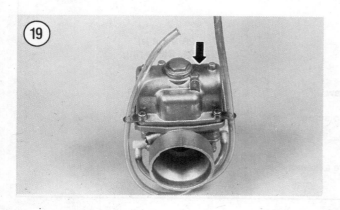

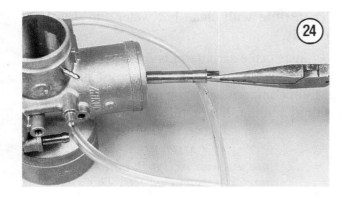

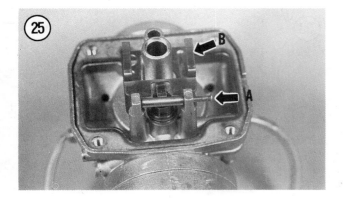

d. Remove the washer (**Figure 29**).

e. Remove the baffle plate (**Figure 30**).

f. Remove the washer (**Figure 31**).

9. Remove the float bowl gasket (**Figure 32**).

10. Clean and inspect the carburetor assembly as described in this chapter.

Assembly

Refer to **Figure 18** for this procedure.

1. Install a new float bowl gasket (**Figure 32**), if the old gasket is damaged.

2. Install the inlet valve assembly as follows:

NOTE
Replace the sealing washers during assembly.

a. Install the first washer (**Figure 31**).

b. Install the baffle plate (**Figure 30**).

c. Install the second washer (**Figure 29**).

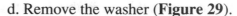

6

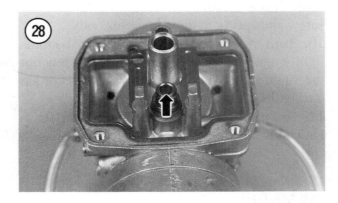

d. Install and tighten the inlet valve seat (**Figure 28**).

e. Install the fuel inlet valve with its tapered end inside, against the valve seat (**Figure 27**).

f. Install the retaining clip, (**Figure 26**) if so equipped.

3. Install the float arm (B, **Figure 25**) and the pivot pin (A, **Figure 25**). Push the pin in fully.

4. Install the needle jet (**Figure 24**) so the notch in the bottom aligns with the pin in the needle jet bore. Refer to **Figure 33**.

5. Install the baffle ring (**Figure 22** or **Figure 23**).

6. Install the main jet and tighten it securely (**Figure 21**).

7. Install the pilot jet (**Figure 20**) using a suitable screwdriver. Tighten the pilot jet securely.

8. Install the floats, then install the float bowl. See **Figure 19**. Tighten the attaching screws securely.

9. Slide the locking spring onto the pilot air screw (idle mixture needle), then install the screw and spring in the carburetor body.

10. Turn the pilot air screw in until it bottoms lightly against its seat, then back the screw out the same number of turns that were recorded during disassembly.

11. Adjust the carburetors as described in Chapter Three.

**Cleaning/Inspection
(All Models)**

Most commercial carburetor cleaners will damage rubber O-rings, seals and plastic parts. Be sure that all rubber and plastic parts are removed before using a harsh cleaner.

1. Clean the carburetor castings and metal parts with aerosol solvent and a brush. Spray the aerosol solvent on the casting and scrub off any gum or varnish with a small bristle brush.

2. After cleaning the castings and metal parts, wash them thoroughly in hot water and soap.

Then rinse with clean hot water and dry thoroughly.

3. Inspect the carburetor body and float bowl for fine cracks, erosion or evidence of fuel leaks. Minor damage can be repaired with an epoxy or liquid aluminum type filler.

CAUTION
Do not use wire or a drill bit to clean carburetor passages or jets. This can

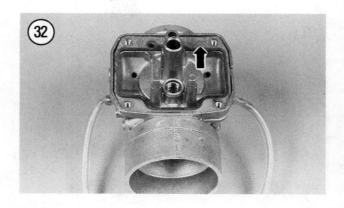

enlarge the passages and change the carburetor calibration. If a passage or jet is severely clogged, use a piece of broom straw to clean it.

4. Use a spray cleaner to remove varnish from the jets, then blow compressed air through the jets to dry and make sure that passages are open.

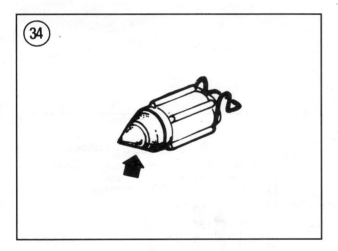

5. Inspect the tip (**Figure 34**) of the fuel inlet valve for wear or damage. Replace the valve and seat as a set if they are less than perfect.

NOTE
A damaged float valve will result in flooding of the carburetor float chamber and impair performance. In addition, accumulation of raw gasoline in the engine compartment presents a severe fire hazard.

6. Inspect the tapered end of the pilot air screw for scoring and replace it if less than perfect.

7. Inspect the jets for internal damage and damaged threads. Replace any jet that is less than perfect. Make certain replacement jets are the same size as the originals.

CAUTION
The jets must be completely clean. The residue that builds up on jets is often nearly clear and shiny. Some small holes may appear to be clean but may be completely blocked. Inspect all jets and internal passages carefully and critically. Any burring, roughness, abrasion or distortion could also cause a lean mixture that may result in major engine damage.

8. Check the movement of the float arm on the pivot pin. It must move freely without binding.

9. O-ring seals tend to become hardened after prolonged use and exposure to heat and, therefore, lose their ability to seal properly. Inspect all O-rings and replace if necessary.

10. Check the floats (**Figure 35**) for fuel saturation, deterioration or excessive wear where they contact the float arm. If the floats are in good condition, check them for leakage as follows. Fill the float bowl with water and push the floats down. There should be no signs of bubbles. Replace the floats if necessary.

Float Height
Check and Adjustment

1. Remove the float bowl as described in this chapter.

2. Remove the float bowl gasket.

3. Invert the carburetor. Allow the float arm to contact the fuel inlet valve, but don't compress the spring-loaded plunger located in the valve.

4. Measure the distance from the float arm to the float bowl gasket surface (**Figure 36**). Refer to **Table 1** for the recommended float height.

5. If the float height is incorrect, remove the float pin (A, **Figure 25**) and baffle plate (B, **Figure 25**). Bend the tang on the end of the plate to adjust.

6. Reinstall the plate and pin. Recheck the float height adjustment.

7. Install the float bowl as described in this chapter.

Jet Needle/Throttle Valve
Removal/Installation

A typical jet needle/throttle valve assembly is shown in **Figure 37**.

1. Unscrew the carburetor cap and pull the throttle valve from the carburetor.

2. Push the throttle valve up onto the end of the throttle cable, against the spring. Then detach the cable from the retainer.

3. Remove the screws attaching the retainer plate to the throttle valve and remove the plate.

4. Remove the jet needle.

5. Installation is the reverse of these steps. Note the following:

   a. Carburetor tuning is described in Chapter Four.

   b. Some models have a nylon washer installed between the jet needle E-clip and throttle valve (**Figure 38**). During reassembly, make sure the nylon washer is installed.

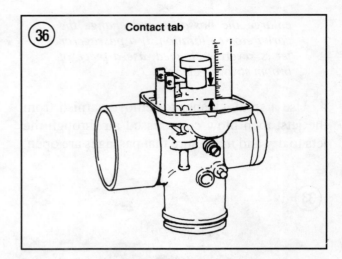

36 Contact tab

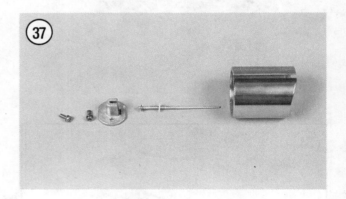

37

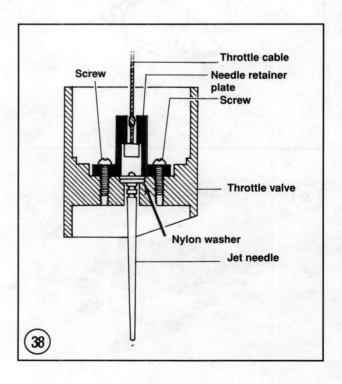

38

Throttle cable
Needle retainer plate
Screw
Throttle valve
Nylon washer
Jet needle
Screw

6

CAUTION
Failure to install the nylon washer might
cause engine seizure.

c. When inserting the throttle valve into the carburetor, align the groove in the throttle valve with the pin in the carburetor bore while also aligning the jet needle with the opening of the needle jet.

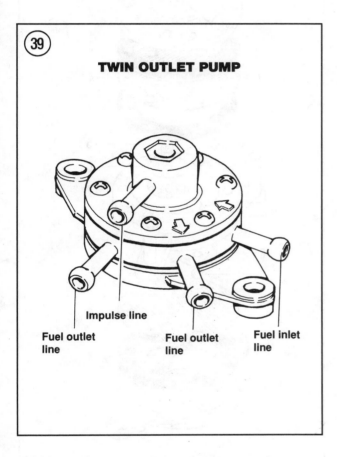

TWIN OUTLET PUMP

Impulse line

Fuel outlet line

Fuel outlet line

Fuel inlet line

FUEL PUMP

Removal/Installation

Different types of fuel pumps have been used, but all are basically the same. Refer to **Figures 10-15** for routing the pulse lines from the crankcase, fuel inlet lines from the tank and fuel output (pressure) lines to the carburetors. Some models are equipped with two separate fuel pumps as shown in **Figure 11**.

1. Open the hood.
2. Remove the air silencer as described in this chapter.

NOTE
To remove the wire hose clamps in Step 3, squeeze the ends together with pliers, then slide the clamp from the fuel fitting. Do not pull the hoses off until after removing the clamps or you may damage the ends of the hose.

3. Label the hoses at the fuel pump (**Figure 39**) then disconnect them. Plug the hoses to prevent fuel leakage or contamination.
4. Remove the bolts holding the fuel pump to the bulkhead and remove the fuel pump (**Figure 40**).
5. Replace the wire hose clamps if they have lost tension.
6. Installation is the reverse of these steps. Reconnect the hoses according to the identification marks made before disassembly.

Disassembly/Assembly

Refer to **Figure 41** for this procedure. Some fuel pumps may appear to be different from the one shown, but operation and service is similar. Repair parts are not available for all models of fuel pumps.

1. Plug the 4 pump body fuel fittings and clean the pump in solvent. Dry thoroughly.
2. Test the pump outlet check valve by sucking and blowing through one of the outlet openings

(block other outlet opening). See **Figure 39** for typical outlet identification. You should be able to draw air though the valve but not blow air through it.

3. Test the pump inlet check valve by sucking and blowing through the inlet opening. You should be able to blow through the valve, but not draw air through it.

4. Replace the check valves if they do not operate as specified in Step 2 or Step 3.

5. Remove the screws holding the covers to each side of the pump body. Separate the covers from the body.

6. Remove the diaphragms and gaskets. Inspect the diaphragms and gaskets for holes, tears or deterioration. Discard the gaskets.

NOTE
Do not remove the valve holders and valves unless new valves are available and replacement is required. Do not re-install valves that were previously used.

7. Remove the valve holders and valves. Discard the valves.

8. Clean and inspect the pump components as described in this chapter.

9. Install new valves as follows:

    a. Align the new valve with its seat. Make sure the valve is flat.

    b. Lubricate the tip of the valve holder with a drop of oil. Then push the holder through the valve with a pin punch or rod with a diameter of 2.5 mm (3/32 in.) as shown in **Figure 42**.

    c. Repeat for both valves.

10. Install the diaphragms and gaskets in the order shown in **Figure 41**. Secure the pump with the screws.

11. Repeat Step 2 and Step 3 to test the check valves after installation.

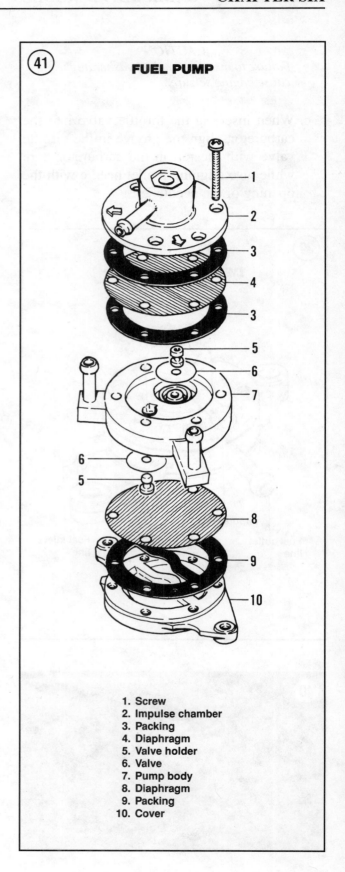

41   **FUEL PUMP**

1. Screw
2. Impulse chamber
3. Packing
4. Diaphragm
5. Valve holder
6. Valve
7. Pump body
8. Diaphragm
9. Packing
10. Cover

Cleaning and Inspection

1. Clean the pump body and covers in solvent, then dry with compressed air.

2. Check body condition. Make sure the valve seats provide a flat contact area for the valve disc. Replace the pump assembly if the body is cracked.

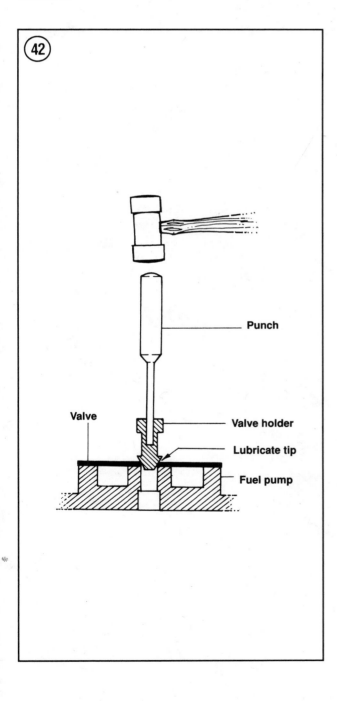

Punch

Valve

Valve holder

Lubricate tip

Fuel pump

3. Check diaphragms for holes or tearing. Replace the diaphragms if hard or otherwise damaged.

FUEL TANK

Removal/Installation

Refer to **Figures 43-48** for this procedure.

1. Remove the seat and center cover.

2. Label and disconnect all hoses from the fuel tank. Plug the hoses to prevent leakage.

3. Remove the fuel tank mounting bolts and remove the fuel tank.

4. Installation is the reverse of these steps. Check all hose connections for leaks. When mounting fuel tank, position the fuel tank mounting bracket so the tank has 1.6 mm (1/16 in.) of clearance for expansion.

Cleaning/Inspection

WARNING
Clean the fuel tank in an open area away from all sources of flames or sparks.

1. Pour old gasoline from the tank into a sealable container manufactured specifically for gasoline storage.

2. Pour about 1 qt. (0.9 L) of fresh gasoline into the tank and slosh it around for several minutes to loosen sediment. Then pour the contents into a sealable container.

3. Examine the tank for cracks and abrasions, particularly at points where the tank contacts the body. Areas that rub can be protected and cushioned by coating them with a silicone sealer and allowing it to dry before installing the tank. If abrasion is extensive or if the tank is leaking, replace it.

6

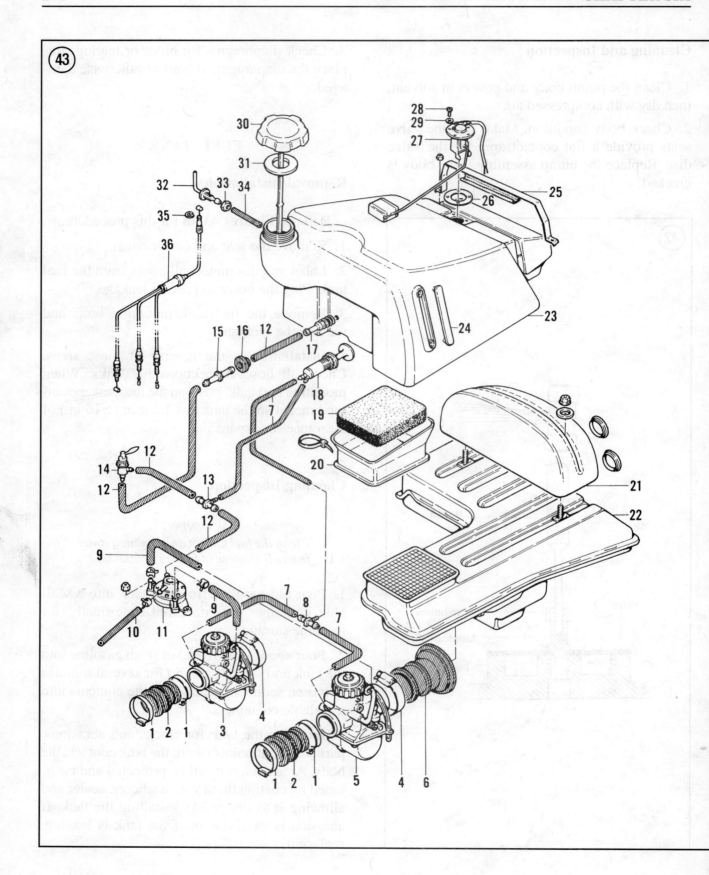

FUEL DELIVERY SYSTEM AND RELATED COMPONENTS
(ALL 1990 MODELS)

1. Clamps
2. Rubber flange
3. Carburetor (MAG side)
4. Clamps
5. Carburetor (PTO side)
6. Adaptor (boot)
7. Primer hose
8. T fitting
9. Fuel supply lines
    to carburetors
10. Pulse line
11. Fuel pump
12. Fuel supply line
13. T fitting
14. Fuel shut-off valve
15. Connector
16. Grommet
17. Fuel filter
18. Primer pump
19. Air filter
20. Boot
21. Tool bag
22. Air silencer
23. Fuel tank
24. Fuel gauge
25. Bracket
26. Gasket
27. Fuel gauge sender
28. Screw
29. Washer
30. Fuel cap
31. Gasket
32. Fuel tank vent
33. Nut
34. Fuel hose
35. Circlip
36. Throttle control cable

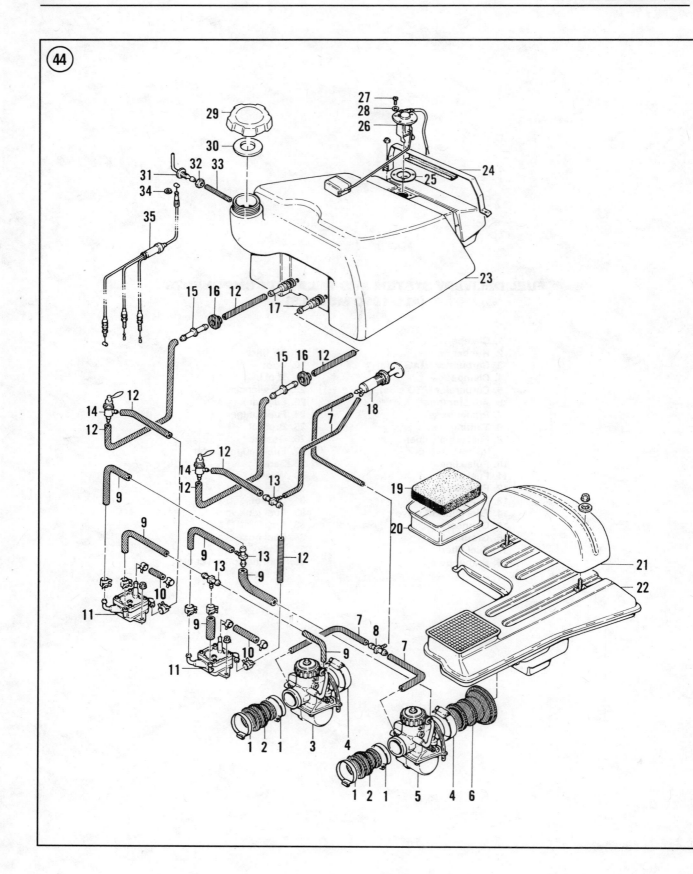

FUEL DELIVERY SYSTEM AND RELATED COMPONENTS
(1991-1994 MODELS EQUIPPED WITH DUAL FUEL PUMPS)

1. Clamps
2. Rubber flange
3. Carburetor (MAG side)
4. Clamps
5. Carburetor (PTO side)
6. Adaptor (boot)
7. Primer hose
8. T fitting
9. Fuel supply lines to carburetors
10. Pulse lines
11. Fuel pumps
12. Fuel supply lines
13. T fittings
14. Fuel shut-off valves
15. Connectors
16. Grommets
17. Fuel filters
18. Primer pump
19. Air filter
20. Boot
21. Tool bag
22. Air silencer
23. Fuel tank
24. Bracket
25. Gasket
26. Fuel gauge sender
27. Screw
28. Washer
29. Fuel cap
30. Gasket
31. Fuel tank vent
32. Nut
33. Fuel hose
34. Circlip
35. Throttle control cable

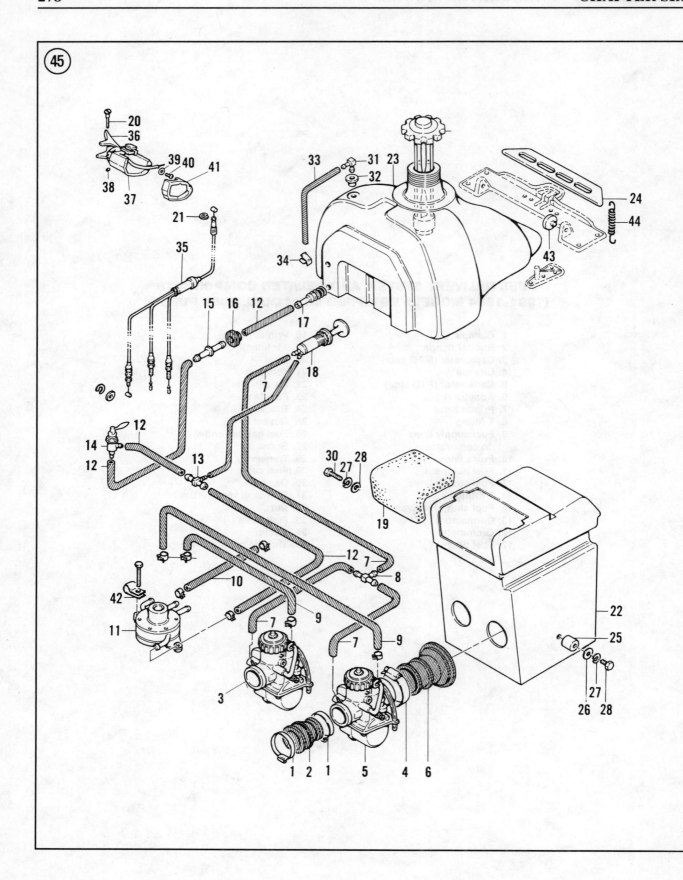

FUEL DELIVERY SYSTEM AND RELATED COMPONENTS
(1993-ON FORMULA MX; 1994 ST AND 1994-ON FORMULA MXZ MODELS)

1. Clamps
2. Rubber flange
3. Carburetor (MAG side)
4. Clamps
5. Carburetor (PTO side)
6. Adaptor (boot)
7. Primer hose
8. T fitting
9. Fuel supply lines to carburetors
10. Pulse line
11. Fuel pump
12. Fuel supply lines
13. T fitting
14. Fuel shut-off valve
15. Connector
16. Grommet
17. Fuel filter
18. Primer pump
19. Air filter
20. Bolt
21. Circlip
22. Air silencer
23. Fuel tank
24. Bracket
25. Spacer
26. Washer
27. Lockwasher
28. Bolt
29. Fuel cap & gauge
30. Bolt
31. Fuel tank vent
32. Grommet
33. Vent hose
34. Clip
35. Throttle control cable
36. Throttle lever
37. Stop switch
38. Set screw
39. Washer
40. Screw
41. Adapter
42. Clamp
43. Bumper
44. Spring

6

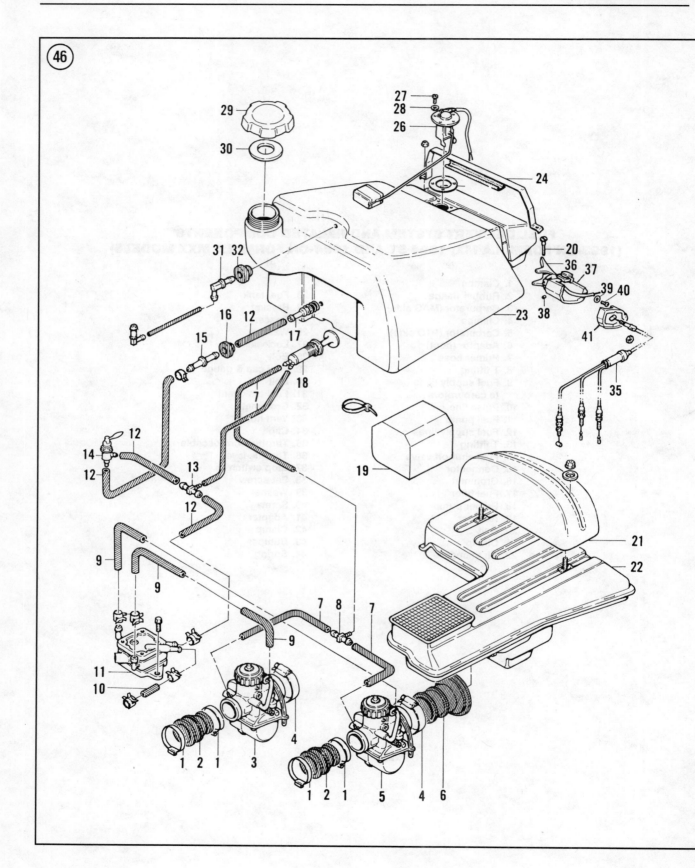

6

FUEL DELIVERY SYSTEM AND RELATED COMPONENTS
(1993 FORMULA PLUS, PLUS E, PLUS XTC, MX, MX XTR AND GT; 1994 MACH I, GT AND GT XTC MODELS)

1. Clamps
2. Rubber flange
3. Carburetor (MAG side)
4. Clamps
5. Carburetor (PTO side)
6. Adaptor (boot)
7. Primer hose
8. T fitting
9. Fuel supply lines to carburetors
10. Pulse line
11. Fuel pump
12. Fuel supply lines
13. T fitting
14. Fuel shut-off valve
15. Connector
16. Grommets
17. Fuel filter
18. Primer pump
19. Air filter
20. Bolt
21. Tool bag
22. Air silencer
23. Fuel tank
24. Bracket
25. Gasket
26. Fuel gauge sender
27. Screw
28. Washer
29. Fuel cap
30. Gasket
31. Fuel tank vent
32. Grommet
33. Vent hose
34. Elbow
35. Throttle control cable
36. Throttle lever
37. Stop switch
38. Set screw
39. Washer
40. Screw
41. Adapter

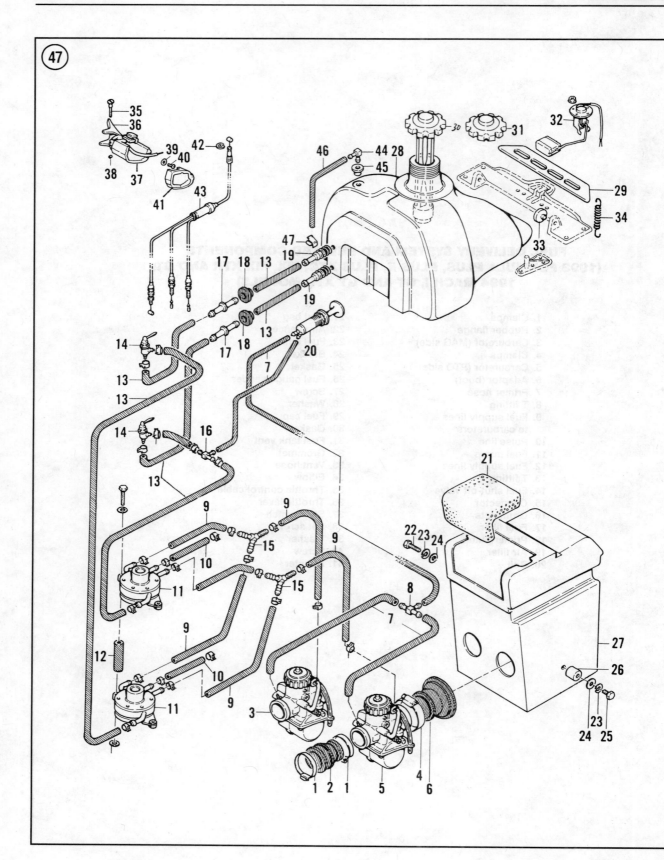

FUEL DELIVERY SYSTEM AND RELATED COMPONENTS
(1994 FORMULA STX, STX II AND Z MODELS)

1. Clamps
2. Rubber flange
3. Carburetor (MAG side)
4. Clamps
5. Carburetor (PTO side)
6. Adaptor (boot)
7. Primer hose
8. T fitting
9. Fuel supply lines to carburetors
10. Pulse lines
11. Fuel pumps
12. Spacer
13. Fuel supply lines
14. Fuel shut-off valve
15. Y fittings
16. T fitting
17. Connectors
18. Grommet
19. Fuel filter
20. Primer pump
21. Air filter
22. Bolt
23. Lockwasher
24. Washer
25. Bolt
26. Spacer
27. Air silencer
28. Fuel tank
29. Bracket
30. Fuel cap & gauge
31. Fuel cap
32. Fuel gauge sender
33. Bumper
34. Spring
35. Bolt
36. Throttle lever
37. Stop switch
38. Set screw
39. Washer
40. Screw
41. Adapter
42. Circlip
43. Throttle control cable
44. Fuel tank vent
45. Grommet
46. Vent hose
47. Clip

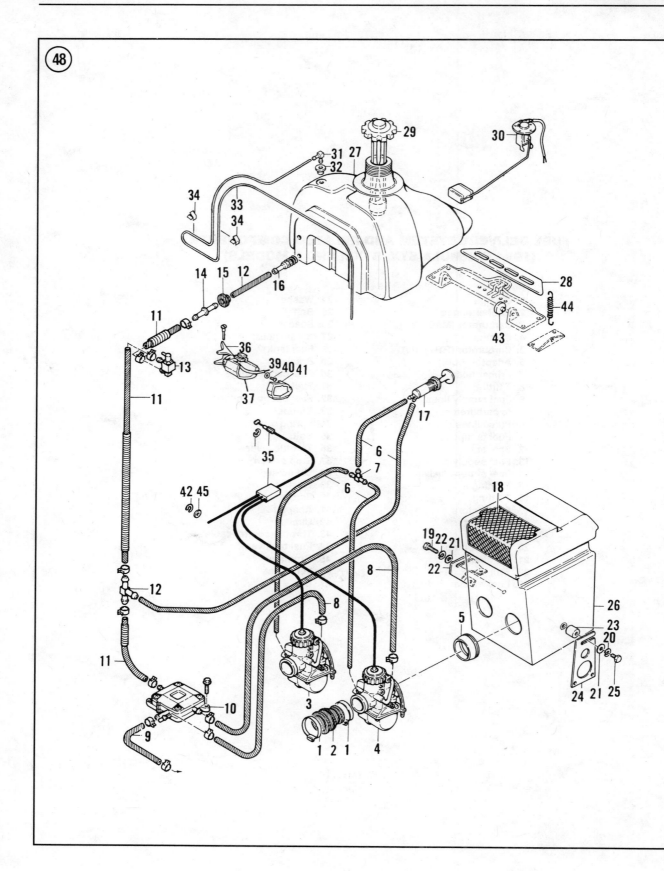

6

FUEL DELIVERY SYSTEM AND RELATED COMPONENTS
(1995 FORMULA SS AND MACH I MODELS)

1. Clamps
2. Rubber flange
3. Carburetor (MAG side)
4. Carburetor (PTO side)
5. Adaptor
6. Primer hose
7. T fitting
8. Fuel supply lines
   to carburetors
9. Pulse line
10. Fuel pump
12. Fuel supply lines
12. T fitting
13. Fuel shut-off valve
14. Connector
15. Grommet
16. Fuel filter
17. Primer pump
18. Air filter
19. Bolt
20. Lockwashers
21. Washer
22. Bracket
23. Spacer
24. Bracket
25. Bolt
26. Air silencer
27. Fuel tank
28. Bracket
29. Fuel cap & gauge
30. Fuel gauge sender
31. Fuel tank vent
32. Grommet
33. Vent hose
34. Clips
35. Throttle control cable
36. Throttle lever
37. Stop switch
38. Set screw
39. Washer
40. Screw
41. Adapter
42. Circlip
43. Bumper
44. Spring
45. Washer

FUEL VALVE

Removal/Installation

To remove the fuel valve, first disconnect the hoses from the fuel valve shown in **Figures 43-48**. Remove the mounting bracket, then remove the valve. During installation, make sure the lever stoppers are positioned so the inner tip of the fuel valve lever contacts the stoppers while in the closed or open position. Because vibration could accidentally close the fuel valve during engine operation, the stoppers hold the valve ON. **Figure 49** shows proper adjustment of the stoppers with the lever in the closed and open position. If necessary, bend the stoppers by hand until their position is correct.

THROTTLE CABLE REPLACEMENT

When replacing the throttle cable, note the following:

a. Make sure the circlip is installed at the upper cable end as shown in **Figure 50**.

b. Adjust the carburetors as described in Chapter Three. See *Synchronization*.

c. Adjust the oil injection cable as described in Chapter Three.

d. Operate the throttle lever to make sure the carburetor throttle slides operate correctly.

e. Check cable routing.

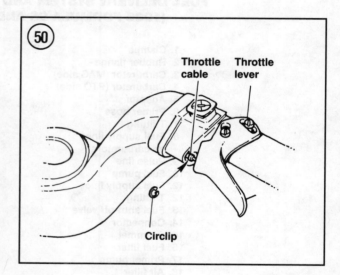

Throttle cable   Throttle lever

Circlip

Table 1 CARBURETOR APPLICATION

Year/model	Main jet	Needle jet	Float setting
1990			
Formula MX & MX LT (467)			
PTO side (VM 34-352A)	220	159 P-4	22-24 mm
Magneto side (VM 34-353A)	240	159 P-4	22-24 mm
Formula Plus & Plus LT (536)			
Both carbs. (VM 34-381)	250	159 Q-4	22-24 mm
Formula MACH 1 MACH 1 XTC (583)			
PTO side (VM 38-214)	340	480 P-4	16-18 mm
Magneto side (VM 38-215)	360	480 P-2	16-18 mm
1991			
Formula MX, MX E, MX XTC & MX XTC E (467)			
PTO side (VM 34-352A)	230	159 P-6	23-25 mm
Magneto side (VM 34-353A)	240	159 P-4	23-25 mm
Formula MX X (467)			
PTO side (VM 38-239)	390	480 P-4	16-18 mm
Magneto side (VM 38-240)	400	480 P-4	16-18 mm
Formula Plus, Plus E, Plus XTC & Plus XTC E (536)			
PTO side (VM 34-408)	260	159 Q-6	23-25 mm
Magneto side (VM 34-409)	260	159 Q-6	23-25 mm
Formula Plus X (536)			
PTO side (VM 38-231)	360	480 P-4	16-18 mm
Magneto side (VM 38-215)	360	480 P-2	16-18 mm
Formula MACH 1 & XTC (643)			
PTO side (VM 40-48C)	400	224-BB-0	17-19 mm
Magneto side (VM 40-49C)	420	224-BB-0	17-19 mm
Formula MACH 1 X (643)			
PTO side (VM 44-27A)	580	224-BB-0	17-19 mm
Magneto side (VM 44-26A)	480	224-BB-0	17-19 mm
1992			
Formula MX & MX XTC R (467)			
PTO side (VM 34-352B)	230	159 P-6	23-25 mm
Magneto side (VM 34-353A)	240	159 P-4	23-25 mm
Formula Plus, Plus E, Plus XTC & XTC E (582)			
PTO side (VM 34-413A)	280	159 Q-6	23-25 mm
Magneto side (VM 34-414B)	300	159 Q-8	23-25 mm
Formula Plus X (583)			
PTO side (VM 38-231)	360	480 P-4	16-18 mm
Magneto side (VM 38-250)	380	480 P-2	16-18 mm
Formula MACH 1, MACH 1 XTC & MACH 1 XTC II (643)			
PTO side (VM 40-48D)	420	224-BB-0	17-19 mm
Magneto side (VM 40-49D)	440	224-BB-0	17-19 mm
Formula MACH 1 X (670)			
PTO side (VM 44)	560	224-BB-0	17-19 mm
Magneto side (VM 44)	520	224-BB-0	17-19 mm
1993			
Formula MX &, MX XTC R (467)			
PTO side (VM 34-352B)	230	159 P-6	23-25 mm
Magneto side (VM 34-353A)	240	159 P-4	23-25 mm

(continued)

6

Table 1 CARBURETOR APPLICATION (continued)

Year/model	Main jet	Needle jet	Float setting
1993 (continued)			
Formula MX Z (467)			
PTO side (VM 34-426)	330	159 P-4	23-25 mm
Magneto side (VM 34-427A)	360	159 P-4	23-25 mm
Formula Plus, Plus E & Plus XTC (582)			
PTO side (VM 38-254)	380	480 P-4	17-19 mm
Magneto side (VM 38-255)	400	480 P-4	17-19 mm
Formula Plus X (583)			
PTO side (VM 38-260)	360	480 P-2	17-19 mm
Magneto side (VM 38-261)	390	480 P-2	17-19 mm
Formula MACH 1 & MACH 1 XTC (670)			
PTO side (VM 40-54)	420	224 AA5	17-19 mm
Magneto side (VM 40-551)	440	224 AA5	17-19 mm
Formula Grand Touring (582)			
PTO side (VM 38-260)	360	480 P-2	17-19 mm
Magneto side (VM 38-261)	390	480 P-2	17-19 mm
1994			
Formula MX & MX Z (467)			
PTO side (VM 34-433)	290	159 N-4	24 mm
Magneto side (VM 34-434)	280	159 N-4	24 mm
Summit 470 (470 HAC)			
PTO side (VM 34-426)	380	159 O-2	24 mm
Magneto side (VM 34-427A)	400	159 O-2	24 mm
Formula MX Z X (467)			
PTO side (VM 34-433)	300	159 O-2	24 mm
Magneto side (VM 34-434)	300	159 O-2	24 mm
Formula ST (467)			
PTO side (VM 34-433)	290	159 N-4	24 mm
Magneto side (VM 34-434)	280	159 N-4	24 mm
Formula STX & STX II (583)			
PTO side (VM 38-274)	340	480 P-6	18.1 mm
Magneto side (VM 38-275)	350	480 P-6	18.1 mm
Formula Z (583)			
PTO side (VM 40-63)	360	224 AA-6	18.1 mm
Magneto side (VM 40-64)	360	224 AA-6	18.1 mm
Summit 583 HAC			
PTO side (VM 38-278)	490	480 Q-4	18.1 mm
Magneto side (VM 38-279)	490	480 Q-4	18.1 mm
MACH 1 & Grand Touring SE (670)			
PTO side (VM 40-57)	370	224 AA-4	18.1 mm
Magneto side (VM 40-58)	390	224 AA-4	18.1 mm
Grand Touring & Grand Touring XTC (582)			
PTO side (VM 34-254A)	350	480 P-4	18.1 mm
Magneto side (VM 34-255A)	360	480 P-4	18.1 mm
1995			
MX (467)			
PTO side (VM 34-433)	290	159 N-4	23.9 mm
Magneto side (VM 34-434)	280	159 N-4	23.9 mm
MX Z (454)			
Both (VM 34-448)	270	159 N-6	23.9 mm
Formula SS (670)			
PTO side (VM 40-71)	360	224 AA-3	18.1 mm
Magneto side (VM 40-72)	370	224 AA-3	18.1 mm

(continued)

Table 1 CARBURETOR APPLICATION (continued)

Year/model	Main jet	Needle jet	Float setting
1995 (continued)			
Formula STX (583)			
PTO side (VM 38-291)	320	480 P-0	18.1 mm
Magneto side (VM 38-292)	330	480 P-0	18.1 mm
Formula STX (LT) (583)			
PTO side (VM 38-291)	320	480 P-0	18.1 mm
Magneto side (VM 38-292)	330	480 P-0	18.1 mm
Summit 583			
PTO side (VM 38-289)	380	480 P-6	19.6 mm
Magneto side (VM 38-290)	380	480 P-6	19.6 mm
Summit 670			
PTO side (VM 40-67)	420	224 AA-4	19.6 mm
Magneto side (VM 40-68)	420	224 AA-4	19.6 mm
Formula Z (583)			
Both (VM 40-69)	340	224 AA-6	18.1 mm
MACH 1 (670)			
PTO side (VM 44-30)	430	224 AA-7	17-19 mm
Magneto side (VM44-31)	410	224 AA-7	17-19 mm
Grand Touring 470(467)			
PTO side (VM 34-433)	290	159 N-4	23.9 mm
Magneto side (VM 34-434)	280	159 N-4	23.9 mm
Grand Touring 580 (582)			
PTO side (VM 38-293)	360	480 O-4	18.1 mm
Magneto side (VM 38-294)	370	480 O-4	18.1 mm
Grand Touring SE (670)			
PTO side (VM 40-71)	360	224 AA-3	18.1 mm
Magneto side (VM 40-72)	370	224 AA-3	18.1 mm

6

Table 2 CARBURETOR PILOT AIR SCREW ADJUSTMENT

	Turns out*
1990	
Formula MX & MX LT (467)	1 1/2 turns
Formula Plus & Plus LT (536)	1 1/2 turns
Formula MACH 1 MACH 1 XTC (583)	1 1/2 turns
1991	
Formula MX, MX E, MX XTC & MX XTC E (467)	1 1/2 turns
Formula MX X (467)	1 1/2 turns
Formula Plus, Plus E, Plus XTC & Plus XTC E (536)	1 1/2 turns
Formula Plus X (536)	1 1/2 turns
Formula MACH 1 & XTC (643)	2 turns
Formula MACH 1 X (643)	1 1/2 turns
1992	
Formula MX & MX XTC R (467)	1 1/2 turns
Formula Plus, Plus E, Plus XTC & XTC E (582)	1 1/2 turns
Formula Plus X (583)	1 1/2 turns
Formula MACH 1, MACH 1 XTC & MACH 1 XTC II (643)	2 turns
Formula MACH 1 X (670)	turns

(continued)

Table 2 CARBURETOR PILOT AIR SCREW ADJUSTMENT (continued)

	Turns out*
1993	
Formula MX &, MX XTC R (467)	1 1/2 turns
Formula MX Z (467)	1 1/3 turns
Formula Plus, Plus E & Plus XTC (582)	1 1/2 turns
Formula Plus X (583)	1 1/2 turns
Formula MACH 1 & MACH 1 XTC (670)	2 3/4 turns
Formula Grand Touring (582)	1 1/2 turns
1994	
Formula MX & MX Z (467)	3/4 turn
Summit 470 (470 HAC)	1 5/8 turns
Formula MX Z X (467) & Formula ST (467)	3/4 turn
Formula STX & STX II (583)	1 turn
Formula Z (583)	3/4 turn
Summit 583 HAC	2 1/4 turns
MACH 1 & Grand Touring SE (670)	3/4 turn
Grand Touring & Grand Touring XTC (582)	1 1/4 turns
1995	
MX (467)	1 turn
MX Z (454)	1/2 turn
Formula SS (670)	1 turn
Formula STX (583)	1 1/2 turns
Summit 583	1 turn
Summit 670	1 1/8 turns
Formula STX (LT) (583)	1 1/2 turns
Formula Z (583)	1 turn
MACH 1 (670)	1 turn
Grand Touring 470(467)	1 turn
Grand Touring 580 (582)	1 1/4 turns
Grand Touring SE (670)	1 1/8 turns

* The listed number indicates the recommended initial setting and is usually correct within ± 1/8 turn.

Table 3 ENGINE IDLE SPEED

1990	
Formula MX & MX LT (467)	1,800-2,000 rpm
Formula Plus & Plus LT (536)	1,800-2,000 rpm
Formula MACH 1 MACH 1 XTC (583)	1,800-2,000 rpm
1991	
All models	1,800-2,000 rpm
1992	
Formula MX & MX XTC R (467)	1,800-2,000 rpm
Formula Plus, Plus E, Plus XTC & XTC E (582)	1,800-2,000 rpm
Formula Plus X (583)	1,800-2,000 rpm
Formula MACH 1, MACH 1 XTC,	
MACH 1 XTC II (643)	1,800-2,000 rpm
Formula MACH 1 X (670)	1,800-2,000 rpm
1993	
Formula MX &, MX XTC R (467)	1,800-2,000 rpm
Formula MX Z (467)	1,500-1,700 rpm
Formula Plus, Plus E & Plus XTC (582)	1,800-2,000 rpm

(continued)

Table 3 CARBURETOR IDLE SPEED (continued)

1993 (continued)	
Formula Plus X (583)	1,800-2,000 rpm
Formula MACH 1 & MACH 1 XTC (670)	1,800-2,000 rpm
Formula Grand Touring (582)	1,800-2,000 rpm
1994	
Formula MX & MX Z (467)	1,600-1,800 rpm
Summit 470 (470 HAC)	1,500-1,700 rpm
Formula MX Z X (467), Formula ST (467)	1,600-1,800 rpm
Formula STX & STX II (583)	1,800-2,000 rpm
Formula Z (583)	1,500-1,800 rpm
Summit 583 HAC	1,800-2,000 rpm
MACH 1 & Grand Touring SE (670)	1,800-2,000 rpm
Grand Touring & Grand Touring XTC (582)	1,800-2,000 rpm
1995	
MX (467)	1,600-1,800 rpm
MX Z (454)	1,600-1,800 rpm
Formula SS (670)	1,800-2,000 rpm
Formula STX (583)	1,800-2,000 rpm
Formula STX (LT) (583)	1,800-2,000 rpm
Summit 583	1,800-2,000 rpm
Summit 670	1,800-2,000 rpm
Formula Z (583)	1,800-2,000 rpm
MACH 1 (670)	1,800-2,000 rpm
Grand Touring 470 (467)	1,600-1,800 rpm
Grand Touring 580 (582)	1,800-2,000 rpm
Grand Touring SE (670)	1,800-2,000 rpm

6

Chapter Seven

Fuel System—Fuel Injected Models

For proper operation, a gasoline engine must be supplied with fuel and air mixed in proper proportions. A mixture in which there is too much fuel is said to be rich. A lean mixture is one that has insufficient fuel for efficient combustion.

Electronic fuel injection is used on 1993 Formula Plus EFI models. The system is also called Self Fuel Control Injection or SFCI. The fuel injection system consists of the following subsystems: air flow system, fuel flow system, electronic control system and electrical system.

A fuel system that is operating correctly and properly adjusted will supply the proper mixture of air and fuel at all engine speeds and under a wide range of operating conditions.

This chapter includes service procedures for all parts (**Figure 1**) of the fuel system. Specifications are listed in **Tables 1-3** at the end of the chapter.

WARNING
Gasoline is highly flammable. Always exercise extreme care when working around gasoline and work in a well-ventilated area, away from any flames, sparks or other possible ignition source.

Prevent spills by being prepared to plug any disconnected hoses. Clean up any spilled gasoline immediately. Sparks or other accidental ignition sources are possible even when care is taken, so be prepared for an emergency.

CAUTION
*The system contains components that should **NOT** be disassembled and the system should **NEVER** be modified in any way either by changing or removal of components. Refer to the following precautions whenever testing or servicing the Electronic Fuel Injection system.*

a. Be reluctant to change any adjustments to the system. Follow recommended procedures carefully after determining that adjustment is indicated. Be careful not to change any fuel system adjustments in an attempt to correct a different problem.

b. Do not disassemble the Electronic Control Unit (ECU).

c. Do not disassemble, change or substitute any of the system's sensors. Each is specifically designed to function in balance with other components within the EFI system.

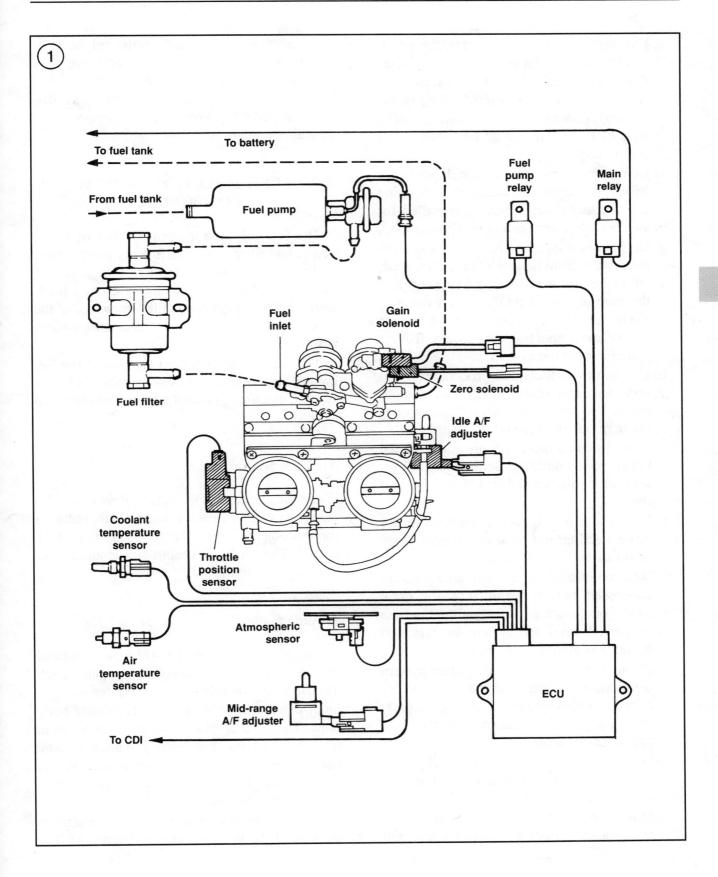

① To fuel tank

To battery

From fuel tank

Fuel pump

Fuel pump relay

Main relay

7

Fuel inlet

Gain solenoid

Fuel filter

Zero solenoid

Idle A/F adjuster

Coolant temperature sensor

Throttle position sensor

Air temperature sensor

Atmospheric sensor

Mid-range A/F adjuster

ECU

To CDI

d. Use only parts recommended by the manufacturer and available from your Ski-Doo dealer when replacing a defective part.

e. Always install new O-rings, sealing washers and gaskets when assembling. Make sure there are no air or fuel leaks after assembling.

f. Do not touch any of the terminals with your hands or attempt to clean terminals using any product except cleaners specified for electronic connectors and components.

g. Do not disconnect the battery or any electrical wires from fuel injection components while the engine is running. Make sure that the main key switch is OFF, then disconnect the negative battery cable from the battery, before disconnecting any wires from a component of the system.

h. Use approved tools and procedures when removing and installing system components. Use care to prevent damaging parts while removing or installing them.

i. Make sure that fuel hoses are not restricted either accidentally or deliberately. Never attempt to restrict or block a fuel hose or line.

j. Be prepared to plug fuel system lines before disconnecting any hose or removing any component.

k. Be sure that all fuel lines and other parts are connected before turning ON the main switch or operating the fuel pump. Fuel can be forced from the system quickly and gasoline is extremely flammable.

l. Do not use compressed air to clean system components. Control of the fuel and air mixture is managed by balancing the pressure of the two. The sensitive components can be easily damaged.

m. Do not operate the system (or fuel pump) dry. The fuel provides both cooling and lubrication for some parts.

n. Make sure the components of the system are protected from both mechanical and electrical shocks. Impacts that might occur in an accident or while servicing may physically break printed circuits or other small components. Static electricity discharged when you touch a component can also damage parts.

FUEL INJECTION SYSTEM COMPONENTS

The fuel injection system consists of a fuel pump, fuel filters, one fuel injector per cylinder, fuel supply pipe, fuel pressure regulator, throttle housing assembly and electronic control hardware. Refer to **Figures 1-3** for drawings of the fuel delivery system and the electronic control system.

The fuel injection system consists of the following subsystems: air flow system, fuel flow system, electronic control system and electrical system.

Air Flow System

Air for the air/fuel mixture is drawn into the engine by engine vacuum. The air filter removes foreign objects before the air enters the intake system. Throttle bodies control the amount of air entering each cylinder.

Throttle bodies

Individual throttle bodies (**Figure 1**) control the amount of air entering the engine. Each throttle body controls the air intake for one cylinder using a throttle plate in the throttle body bore. The throttle plates move in response to movement of the handlebar mounted throttle control lever. Adjustment screws are used to synchronize throttle plate movement so both cylinders perform equally.

A throttle position sensor (TPS) is located on the side of the throttle housing (**Figure 1**). The electronic control unit (ECU) receives a signal from the TPS to determine throttle position.

Fuel Flow System

The fuel flow system consists of the fuel tank, fuel pump, fuel filters, fuel supply gallery, pressure regulators and fuel injectors. Refer to **Figures 1-3**.

Fuel pump

The roller vane type pump uses an electric motor and is attached to the tunnel behind the engine. Fuel is used to lubricate and cool the pump. A fine mesh screen in the fuel tank pickup prevents the entrance of foreign material into the pump.

CAUTION
Running the engine without fuel supplied to the fuel pump may damage the fuel pump.

Filters

Fuel is drawn through a filter at the end of the pick-up hose in the fuel tank before it enters the fuel pump. After leaving the fuel pump, the pressurized fuel passes through a canister filter. A final filter is inserted in the fuel inlet fitting of the pressure switching valve.

Fuel pressure regulator assembly

The fuel pump supplies pressurized fuel to the pressure regulator. The pressure regulator assembly includes the pressure switching valve, control regulator, base regulator and load control regulator. The gain and zero solenoids are also attached to the regulator body. The gain and zero solenoids are available separately.

Excess fuel returns to the fuel tank through the hose connection attached to the fuel gallery. The

injector nozzles and the regulator assembly are attached to the fuel gallery.

A "T" vacuum hose connects the load control regulator and the pressure switching valve to manifold vacuum. Rapid changes in manifold vacuum, such as caused by opening or closing the throttle quickly, will be sensed and the air/fuel mixture altered to prevent an excessively rich or lean mixture.

Fuel injector

A fuel injector for each cylinder directs fuel into the throttle bore just behind the throttle plate. The volume of fuel injected is determined by the injector open time period, which is controlled by the ECU.

Electronic Control System

The electronic control system consists of the fuel injection electronic control unit, throttle position sensor, intake air temperature sensor, engine temperature sensor, barometric pressure sensor, engine speed (rpm) sensor, gain solenoid and zero solenoid. Refer to **Figures 1-3**.

Electronic control unit

The electronic control unit (ECU) manages the amount of fuel injected to maintain optimum performance under all speed ranges and load conditions. The electronic circuits in the ECU receive information from the input sensors and devices, then determines the optimum air/fuel mixture. Sensors provide information concerning engine temperature, intake air temperature and throttle position. The ECU monitors engine speed through a wire connected to the ignition CDI module. A barometric pressure sensor located in the ECU case provides information on barometric pressure so the ECU can adjust the air/fuel mixture for different altitudes. The ECU

7

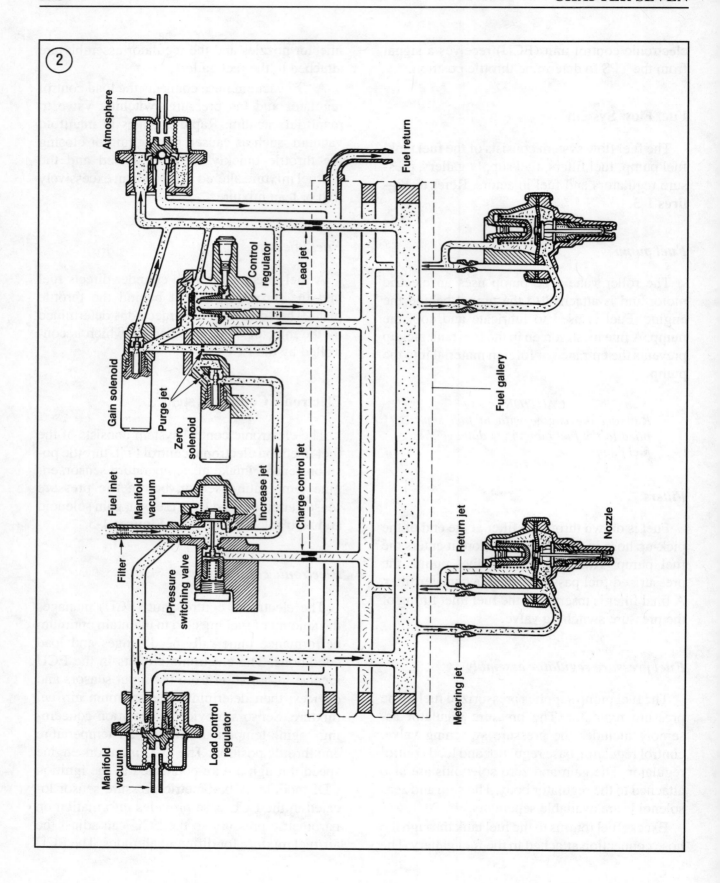

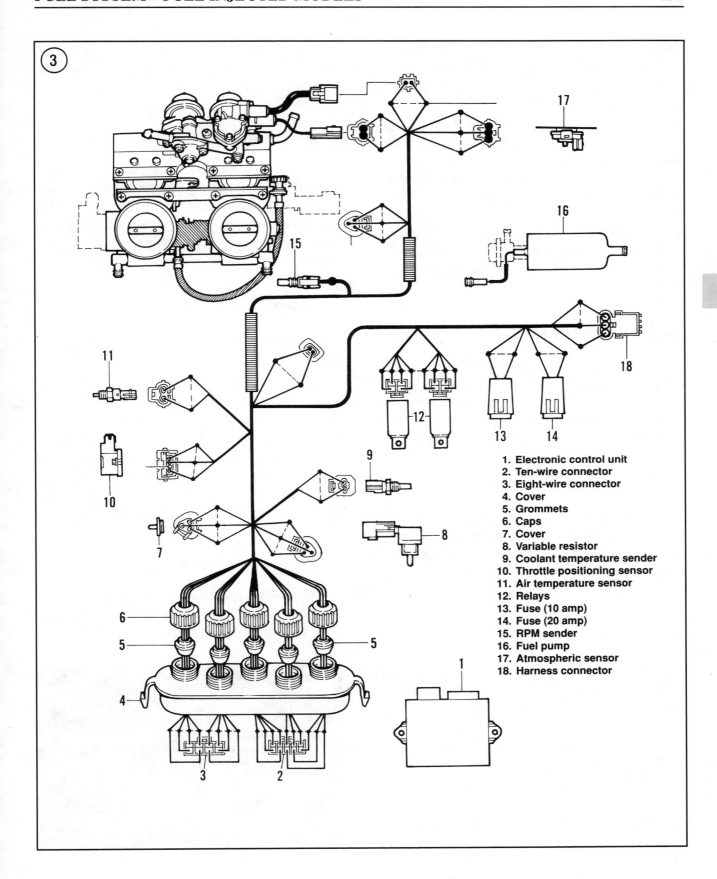

1. Electronic control unit
2. Ten-wire connector
3. Eight-wire connector
4. Cover
5. Grommets
6. Caps
7. Cover
8. Variable resistor
9. Coolant temperature sender
10. Throttle positioning sensor
11. Air temperature sensor
12. Relays
13. Fuse (10 amp)
14. Fuse (20 amp)
15. RPM sender
16. Fuel pump
17. Atmospheric sensor
18. Harness connector

7

controls the amount of fuel injected by controlling the gain solenoid and zero solenoid.

The ECU receives signals from the sensors to monitor performance while the engine is running, then compares current input data with the reference data in the computer chip. For instance, if signal from a sensor is outside of the range for normal operation, the ECU determines that a problem exists. If the ECU finds a problem, it enters a "fail-safe" mode and enriches the air/fuel mixture. The ECU signals the possible problem by flashing the amber monitor light on the instrument panel in a coded sequence. Refer to **Table 1**.

Throttle position sensor

The throttle position sensor (TPS) is a variable resistance device located on the end of the throttle shaft (**Figure 1**). Throttle movement changes sensor resistance. The sensor sends the position of the throttle plate to the ECU.

Intake air temperature sensor

The air temperature sensor is a variable resistance device located in the front of the air silencer that changes resistance in relation to the intake air temperature. The sensor sends a signal of the air temperature to the ECU.

Barometric pressure sensor

The atmospheric pressure sensor is located under the console, in the center. The sensor measures barometric pressure for use by the ECU.

Coolant temperature sensor

The engine temperature sensor is located in the cooling chamber of the cylinder head. The sensor is the variable resistance type that changes resistance when temperature changes. The sensor sends a signal of the coolant temperature to the ECU.

Zero solenoid and gain solenoid

The amount of fuel delivered is controlled electrically by opening the zero and gain solenoids. The two solenoids are attached to the regulator body and each is available separately. The signal for the zero and gain solenoids are both provided by the ECU.

Electrical System

Several electrical components make up the electrical system in the electronic fuel injection system.

Fuses

A 30 amp main fuse is located between the battery and the ignition switch. Two additional fuses (one 10 amp and one 20 amp) are located under the console, behind the air silencer.

Main relay and fuel pump relay

The relays control power to the fuel pump and the ECU. The relays are located under the console, behind the air silencer.

TESTING AND TROUBLESHOOTING

The first step in troubleshooting the EFI system is to observe the amber monitor (diagnostic) light on the dash(**Figure 4**). If the monitor light glows OFF and ON, during normal use, trouble is indicated. The duration of the light may be either short or long. A series of illumination pulses becomes a trouble code. Refer to **Table 1** for determining the possible causes of the indicated trouble codes.

NOTE
The trouble codes only identify problem areas, not specific components. A problem may lie with a sensor, faulty wiring, bad connection or internal ECU circuit. The trouble codes are generated by the ECU, so they identify only electrical problems recognized by ECU. Other problems, such as mechanical problems or fuel delivery problems, may not be correctly recognized and trigger an ECU trouble code unrelated to the actual problem.

Fuel Pump

A quick check to determine if the fuel pump is receiving power is to turn the ignition ON and listen for the pump to run. The pump, attached to the tunnel at the rear of the engine, should produce audible noise. The pump relay will stop current to the pump after about 3 seconds and the main relay will shut the whole system down after about 30 seconds. If the pump does not make any noise upon starting, disconnect the electrical plug to the pump and check to be sure that battery current is available at the connector. If electrical current is never available at the plug, check the relays for proper operation.

NOTE
If the machine is not used for a long period, the fuel pump may stick due to residue from evaporated gasoline. At-tempt to free the pump by lightly tapping it with a soft-faced hammer.

Pressure at the inlet of the fuel pressure regulator assembly should be 243-253 kPa (34.3-36.7 psi). The fuel pump volume and pressure can usually be considered sufficient if the pump operates and delivers fuel. If insufficient volume or pressure is suspected, be sure to inspect the fuel tank pickup filter and the canister filter. Debris in the tank may adhere to the pickup during operation, then float free when fuel flow stops. The final filter, inserted in the fuel inlet fitting of the pressure switching valve, should also be checked if suspected.

Fuel Pressure

Fuel pressure is regulated by the base regulator, load control regulator and the regulator of the switching valve. Pressures can be checked using the special manifold tool (part No. 529 0222 00) and 3 pressure gauges (**Figure 5**). Testing and adjusting should only be done by an authorized Ski-Doo dealer.

1. Detach the connector from the zero solenoid (**Figure 5**).
2. Attach a test wire to the gain solenoid connector, then attach this test wire to the positive terminal of the 12 volt battery.
3. With the zero solenoid energized as described in Step 2, observe pressures as follows:
   a. Pressure at gauge 1, **Figure 5** should be 231-253 kPa (33.4-36.6 psi).
   b. Pressure at gauge 2, **Figure 5** should be 159-175 kPa (23-25.4 psi).
   c. Pressure at the center gauge 3, **Figure 5** should be 17-33 kPa (2.5-4.8 psi) less than the pressure measured at gauge 1, **Figure 5**.

Fuel Delivery

The amount of fuel sprayed from the injectors under controlled conditions in a specific time can

7

be used to isolate some problems. To check, proceed as follows.

1. Remove the fuel injectors, gallery and pressure regulator assembly from the engine as described in this chapter.

2. Install a sufficiently long section of hose between the fuel pump outlet to the fuel inlet fitting on the pressure regulator assembly.

3. Install a sufficiently long section of hose between the fuel gallery outlet fitting and the return hose to the fuel tank.

NOTE
Leave electrical connections detached during the test.

4. Position a graduated beaker or similar measuring device in front of each injection nozzle to catch the fuel that will be sprayed.

5. Turn on the ignition switch and check for spray or leakage. The injectors should not spray until battery voltage is applied to the gain solenoid. The gain or zero solenoid may be leaking if the nozzles begin to spray.

6. Attach a test wire to the connector from the gain solenoid, then connect this wire to the positive terminal of the 12 volt battery. Fuel should begin to spray from the nozzles when the battery voltage is connected.

7. Disconnect the 12 volt test wire from the battery and clean all fuel from the beakers.

NOTE
Be prepared to connect, then disconnect the 12 volt supply wire from the battery for a specific amount of time. Specified injection time is 15 seconds, so this is the usual increment of time used. Time can

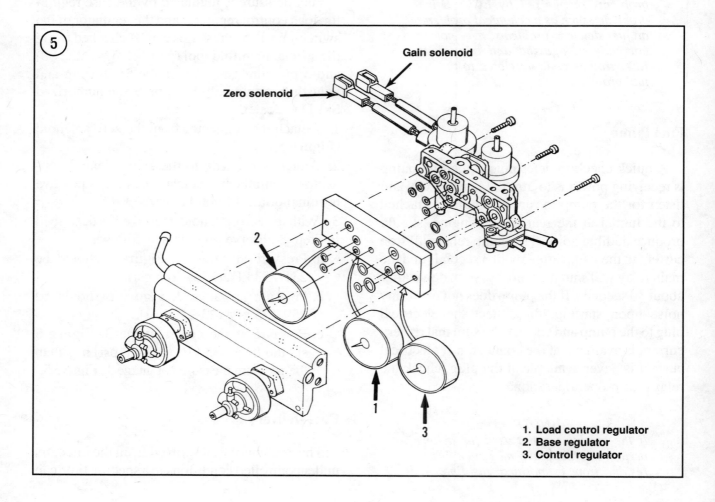

⑤

Gain solenoid

Zero solenoid

1. Load control regulator
2. Base regulator
3. Control regulator

be easily increased to 30 seconds and the volume sprayed should be doubled.

8. Connect the 12 volt supply wire to the battery and measure the amount of fuel sprayed from each nozzle.

9. Each nozzle should spray 108 ml in 15 seconds.

10. If injection is intermittent or an incorrect volume, some possible causes are:

a. If volume sprayed is too low, make sure to check that all 3 filters are clean and that the battery is fully charged.

b. If volume sprayed is too high, check the metering jets (7, **Figure 6**). Refer to Disassembly and Assembly steps for the *Fuel*

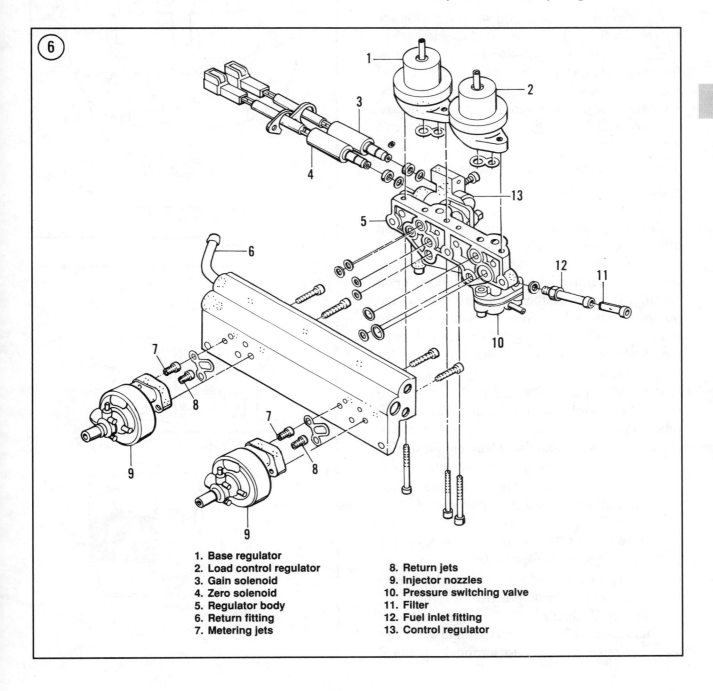

1. Base regulator
2. Load control regulator
3. Gain solenoid
4. Zero solenoid
5. Regulator body
6. Return fitting
7. Metering jets
8. Return jets
9. Injector nozzles
10. Pressure switching valve
11. Filter
12. Fuel inlet fitting
13. Control regulator

Pressure Regulator, Gallery and Nozzles Assembly in this chapter.

c. Intermittent operation may be caused by poor electrical test connections or dirt in the system causing sticking.

Zero and Gain Solenoids

Coils in the zero and gain solenoids (**Figure 6**) should have 45-55 ohms resistance when checked at 20-30° C (68-86° F). Resistance of the solenoids can be checked at the electrical connectors, without removing them from the regulator body. The solenoids may be electrically okay, but leak when checking the system's *Fuel Delivery*.

Relays

The pump relay will stop current to the pump after about three seconds and the main relay will shut down the whole system after about 30 seconds. If the pump does not make any noise upon starting, disconnect the electrical plug to the pump and check to be sure that battery voltage is available at the connector. If battery voltage is not available at the plug, check the relays for proper operation.

Both relays are alike and both are located under the console behind the air silencer. The relays can be checked using an ohmmeter to check resistance across the terminals (**Figure 7**).

a. With no power applied to the relay, resistance between terminal 1, **Figure 7** and terminal 2, **Figure 7** should be within 50-70 ohms. There should be infinite resistance (no continuity) between terminal 3, **Figure 7** and terminal 4 **Figure 7**.

b. Apply 12 volts negative to terminal 1, **Figure 7** and 12 volts positive to terminal 2, **Figure 7**, then check continuity between terminal 3, **Figure 7** and terminal 4, **Figure 7**. Applying power to terminals 1 and 2

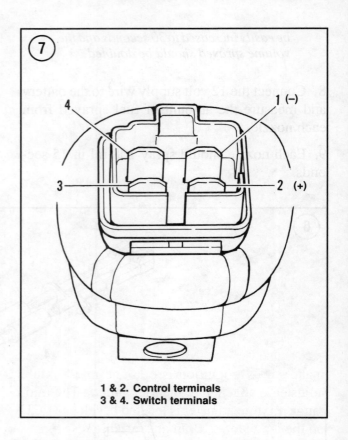

7

4   1 (−)

3   2 (+)

1 & 2. Control terminals
3 & 4. Switch terminals

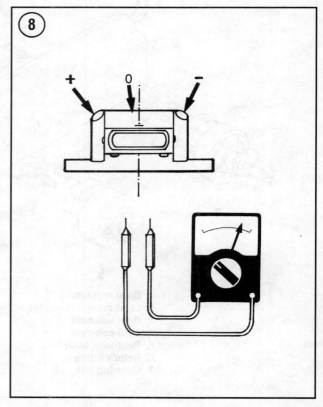

8

+   0   −

should close the connection resulting in continuity between terminals 3 and 4.

Throttle Position Sensor

Test the throttle position sensor (TPS), with the engine not running. Disconnect the electrical plug from the TPS and use an ohmmeter to read the resistance between the "0" and the "−" terminals. Refer to **Figure 8**. Resistance should be 500-600 ohms with throttle at idle. Open the throttle and measure the resistance again. Resistance should increase as the throttle is opened.

Fuel/Air Mixture Adjusters

To test the fuel/air mixture adjusters, first make sure the ignition is off. The idle mixture adjuster is attached to the fuel gallery. The mid-range mixture adjuster is located beside the ECU on the air silencer. Both are variable resistors.

1. Disconnect the electrical plug from the fuel/air adjuster.

NOTE
Identify the original setting of the adjuster screws before moving the screw to the positions for the tests. Mark the po-

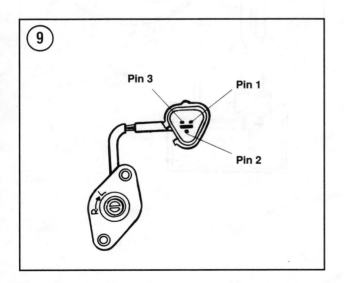

sition of the screw slot before moving the adjuster.

2. Turn the adjuster screw fully counterclockwise (full rich). The housing near the adjuster screw is marked with an arrow and an "R" to indicate rich.
3. Measure the resistance between pin 1, **Figure 9** and pin 2, **Figure 9** with an ohmmeter. Resistance should be 3,500 ohms or more.
4. Turn the adjuster screw fully clockwise. The housing near the adjuster screw is marked with an arrow and "L" to indicate lean.
5. Again measure the resistance between pin 1, **Figure 9** and pin 2, **Figure 9** with an ohmmeter. Resistance should be 500 ohms or less.
6. Measure the resistance between terminal 1, **Figure 9** and pin 3, **Figure 9** with an ohmmeter. Resistance should be 3,000 ohms or more regardless of where the adjuster screw is set.
7. If the resistance is not within the specified limits, install a new adjuster variable resistor.
8. Test the remaining adjuster assembly.
9. Set both adjusters as described in this chapter.

Coolant and Inlet Air Temperature Sensors

To test either the coolant temperature sensor or the inlet air temperature sensor, make sure the engine is not running and ignition is off.

1. Detach the electrical connector and remove the sensor.
2. Attach an ohmmeter to the sensor terminals and put the sensor in a container filled with water as shown in **Figure 10**.
3. Measure the temperature of the water and the resistance of the sensor.
4. Compare the measured temperature and resistance with the standard shown in **Table 2**.
5. Install a new sensor if test results are much different than indicated in **Table 2**.
6. Install new gaskets on the sensors when reinstalling.

7

Atmospheric Pressure Sensor

The atmospheric pressure sensor is located inside the waterproof case containing the ECU. To test the atmospheric pressure sensor, first make sure the ignition is off.

1. Open the waterproof case containing the ECU, so the electrical connectors are visible. Refer to **Figure 11**.

NOTE
Do not detach connectors from the ECU.

2. Set the multimeter to read DC voltage.

3. Attach the meter's positive (+) lead to the white/yellow wire at the No. 16 pin of the connector. Refer to **Figure 11**.

4. Attach the meter's negative (−) lead to the black/orange wire at the No. 9 pin of the connector. Refer to **Figure 11**.

5. Turn ON the ignition switch and check the DC voltage.

6. Compare the relationship of the indicated DC voltage and the present barometric pressure with the standard shown in **Table 3**.

7. Install a new sensor if test results are considerably different than indicated in **Table 3**.

8. Use new gaskets when reassembling.

COMPONENT SERVICE

Air Silencer

The air silencer, sometimes referred to as the air box, is shown in **Figure 12**.

Removal/installation

Refer to **Figure 12** for this procedure.

1. Open the hood.

2. Loosen the clamps attaching the inlet boot to the throttle bodies.

3. Detach the inlet hoses from the air silencer.

4. Remove the screws attaching the air silencer. Check for other components that would interfere with removal.

5. Remove the air silencer (**Figure 12**).

CAUTION
Never run the engine with the air silencer removed. Running without the air silencer or air filter will lean the fuel mixture (too much air - not enough fuel) and may result in engine seizure. The air silencer and filters must be installed during troubleshooting and adjustments.

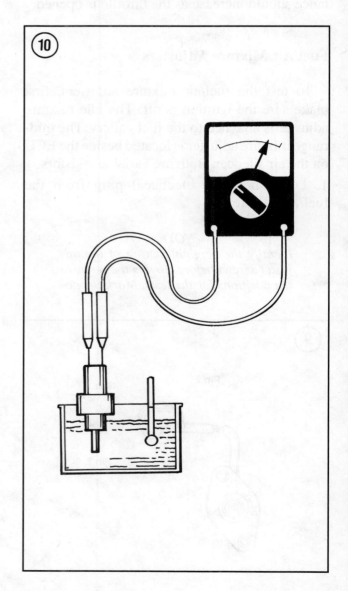

6. Cover the openings in throttle bodies to prevent the entrance of dirt or moisture while the air silencer is removed.

7. Install the air silencer by reversing this procedure. Be sure the air inlet boots and hoses are properly attached to the throttle bodies and the air silencer.

Inspection

Clean the air silencer box thoroughly and check for cracks or other damage. Cracks in the air silencer box must be repaired before reinstalling.

Fuel Tank

Removal/installation

1. Remove the seat and center cover.
2. Label and disconnect all hoses from the fuel tank. Plug the hoses to prevent leakage.
3. Remove the fuel tank mounting bolts and remove the fuel tank.
4. Installation is the reverse of these steps. Check all hose connections for leaks.

Cleaning/inspection

The fuel tank must be removed for cleaning and inspection.

7

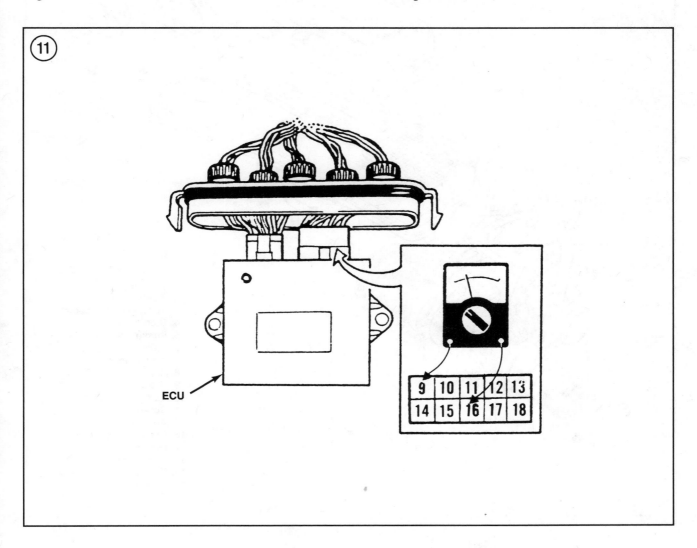

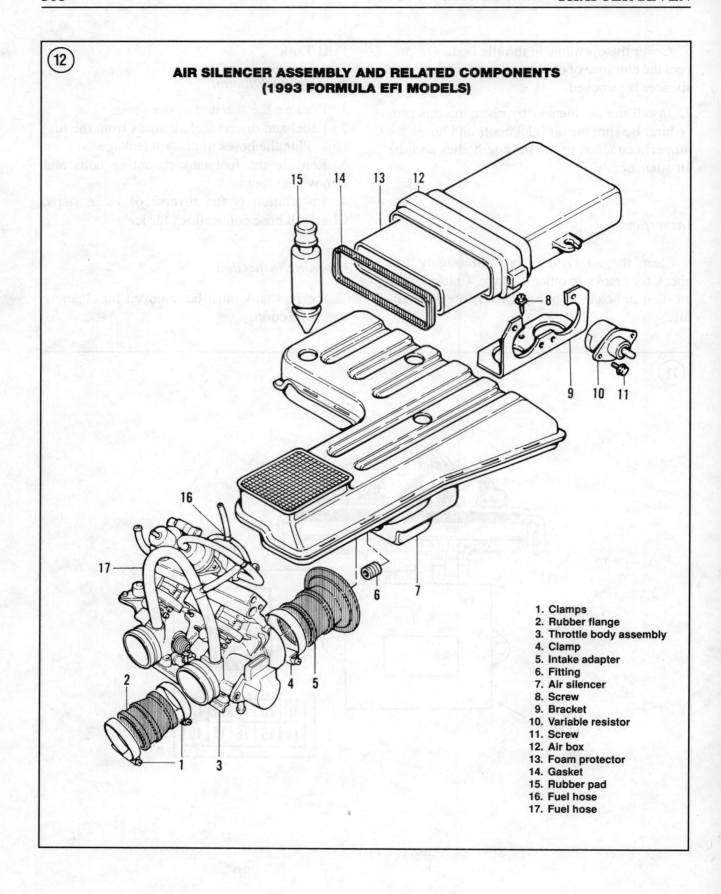

⑫

**AIR SILENCER ASSEMBLY AND RELATED COMPONENTS
(1993 FORMULA EFI MODELS)**

1. Clamps
2. Rubber flange
3. Throttle body assembly
4. Clamp
5. Intake adapter
6. Fitting
7. Air silencer
8. Screw
9. Bracket
10. Variable resistor
11. Screw
12. Air box
13. Foam protector
14. Gasket
15. Rubber pad
16. Fuel hose
17. Fuel hose

WARNING
Clean the fuel tank in an open area away from all sources of flames or sparks.

1. Pour old gasoline from the tank into a sealable container manufactured specifically for gasoline storage.

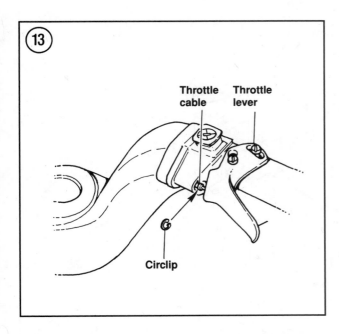

Throttle cable   Throttle lever

Circlip

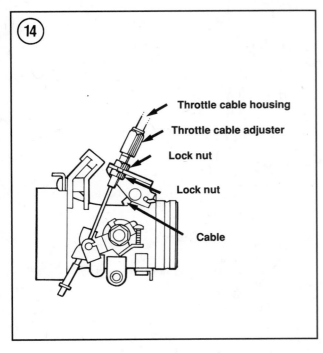

Throttle cable housing

Throttle cable adjuster

Lock nut

Lock nut

Cable

2. Pour about 1 qt. (0.9 L) of fresh gasoline into the tank and slosh it around for several minutes to loosen sediment. Then pour the contents into a sealable container.

3. Examine the tank for cracks and abrasions, particularly at points where the tank contacts the body. Areas that rub can be protected and cushioned by coating them with a silicone sealer and allowing it to dry before installing the tank. If abrasion is extensive or if the tank is leaking, replace it.

Throttle Cable

Replacement

The throttle cable uses a junction for branching to the separate throttle valves and the oil injection pump. When replacing the throttle cable, note the following:

a. Make sure the circlip is installed at the upper cable end as shown in **Figure 13**.

b. Adjust the throttle cable locknuts **Figure 14** so both throttle valves close simultaneously.

c. Adjust the oil injection cable as described in Chapter Three.

d. Operate the throttle lever to make sure the throttle valves operate correctly.

e. Check cable routing and make sure that engine speed does not increase when the steering is turned.

Fuel Pressure Regulator, Gallery and Nozzles Assembly

The fuel pump supplies pressurized fuel to the pressure regulator assembly. The pressure regulator assembly includes the pressure switching valve, control regulator, base regulator and load control regulator. The gain and zero solenoids are also attached to the regulator body. The gain and zero solenoids are available separately.

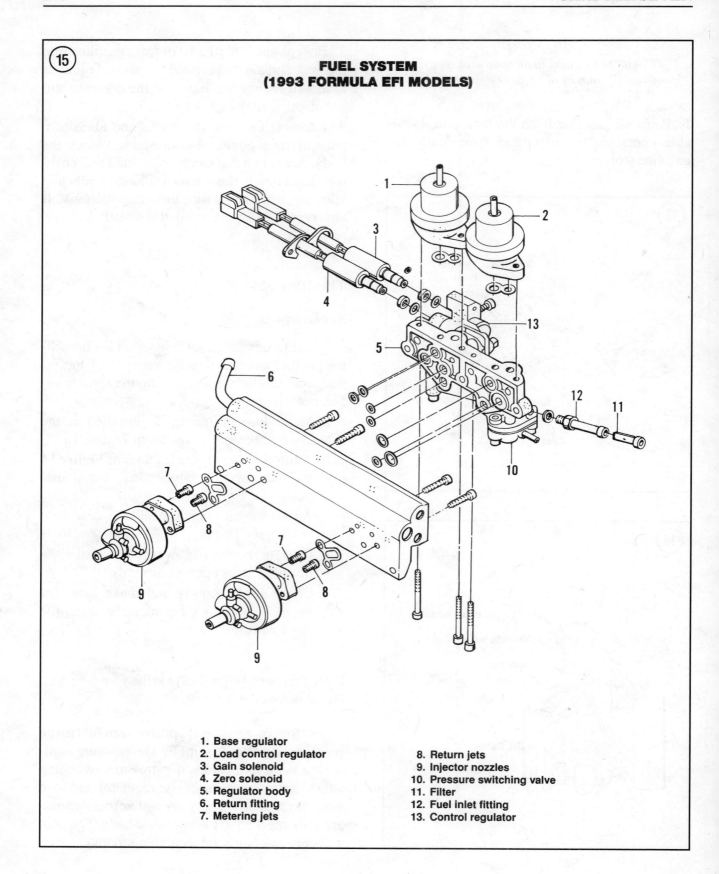

FUEL SYSTEM
(1993 FORMULA EFI MODELS)

1. Base regulator
2. Load control regulator
3. Gain solenoid
4. Zero solenoid
5. Regulator body
6. Return fitting
7. Metering jets
8. Return jets
9. Injector nozzles
10. Pressure switching valve
11. Filter
12. Fuel inlet fitting
13. Control regulator

Excess fuel returns to the fuel tank through the hose attached to the fuel gallery. The injector nozzles and the regulator assembly are attached to opposite sides of the fuel gallery. Refer to **Figure 15**.

Removal/installation

Refer to **Figure 15** for this procedure.

1. Open the hood.

> *WARNING*
> *Be prepared to plug fuel lines before fuel begins to leak from detached hoses. Fuel is a fire hazard and is also slippery.*

2. Detach fuel lines from the inlet fitting and the return fitting.

3. Mark the original location, then detach vacuum lines and electrical connectors that would interfere with removal.

4. Remove the four screws (A, **Figure 16**) attaching the regulator, fuel gallery and nozzles assembly to the throttle bodies.

> *CAUTION*
> *Clean dirt and foreign matter from the area around the fuel injectors and fuel supply pipe prior to removing the fuel injectors. Any dirt or foreign matter that falls into the fuel injector openings in the throttle body may cause engine damage.*

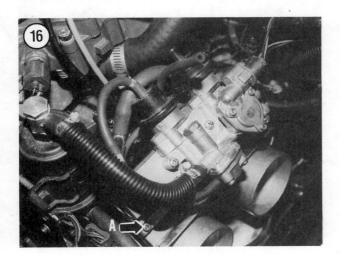

5. Lift the regulator, fuel gallery and nozzles from the throttle bodies.

6. Reinstall by reversing the procedure. Make sure that all seals are in good condition. Lubricate O-rings and seals with engine oil before assembling. Tighten retaining screws (A, **Figure 16**) to 3.5 N•m (30 in.-lb.).

> *WARNING*
> *Check for fuel system leaks before starting engine. Do not start the engine if there is the slightest gasoline leak. The smallest leak can cause a large fire.*

Disassembly and assembly

Refer to **Figure 15** for this procedure. The nozzles, fuel gallery, zero solenoid and gain solenoid are available separately. Be sure that all seals are in good condition when assembling.

> *CAUTION*
> *Most commercial carburetor cleaners will damage rubber O-rings, seals and plastic parts. Be sure that all rubber and plastic parts are removed before using a harsh cleaner.*

1. The zero and gain solenoids (**Figure 15**) can be withdrawn after removing the screw attaching the retainer plate to the body. Be sure that O-rings and seals are in good condition when assembling.

2. The base regulator and the load control regulator (**Figure 15**) can be unbolted and removed from the switching valve and body. These regulators are not available for service, except as an assembly with the switching valve body. The load control regulator is stamped "L" and is located on the left side. The load control regulator is also usually marked by yellow color.

3. The regulator assembly can be unbolted and separated from the fuel gallery. The regulator assembly, which includes the zero solenoid, gain solenoid, base regulator and load control regulator is available for service as a unit.

7

4. The nozzles (**Figure 15**) are available separately. The nozzles are attached to the fuel gallery with 2 screws. The return jet and metering jets (**Figure 15**) can be removed from the nozzles. Be sure that jet sizes are not changed by cleaning, reversing location, substitution or any other reason. Return jet is size No. 102.5 and metering jet is size No. 110. Make sure the seals are in good condition when attaching nozzles to the fuel gallery.

Fuel Pump

Removal/installation

The fuel pump must be serviced as a unit assembly. The fuel pump is attached to the tunnel at the rear of the engine.

1. Disconnect the negative battery lead.
2. Thoroughly clean the area around the fuel pump.
3. Detach the electrical connector to the fuel pump (**Figure 17**).
4. Depressurize the fuel injection system as described in this chapter.

> *NOTE*
> *Position rags to catch gasoline when disconnecting the fuel lines from the fuel pump.*

5. Disconnect the fuel hoses from the fuel pump and immediately plug all openings.

> *NOTE*
> *The fuel pump will contain gasoline. Be prepared to catch and drain gasoline from the fuel pump.*

6. Unscrew the fuel pump mounting screws and remove the fuel pump.
7. Reinstall the fuel pump by reversing removal steps while noting the following:

> *CAUTION*
> *Check for fuel leaks before starting the engine.*

8. After assembly is complete, turn the ignition switch ON, but do not start the engine. Turning on the ignition switch will energize the fuel pump, so that you can check for gasoline leaks.

> *WARNING*
> *Do not start the engine if there is the slightest gasoline leak. The smallest leak can cause a large fire.*

9. Start the engine and check again for leaks.

Electronic Control Unit (ECU)

Removal/installation

The ECU is located on the top of the air silencer. Individual components of the ECU are not available separately. The atmospheric sensor unit is contained in the same enclosure and is attached to electrical connector pins No. 9 and No. 16 (**Figure 11**).

> *CAUTION*
> *The ECU can be damaged by static electricity. Work in an environment that prevents static electricity. Ground yourself and the metal case of the ECU to prevent static discharges.*

1. Disconnect the negative battery lead.

2. Detach the box containing the ECU from the top of the air silencer as shown in **Figure 18**.
3. Open the enclosure and withdraw the ECU as shown in **Figure 19**.
4. Detach the electrical connectors from the ECU and remove the unit.
5. Attach the electrical connectors to the ECU.
6. Check the cover gasket and seals around the wires. The enclosure should be water tight when assembled.
7. Install the ECU enclosure cover and attach the enclosure to the top of the air silencer.
8. Reconnect the negative battery lead.

Throttle Position Sensor (TPS)
Removal/Installation

The throttle position sensor (TPS) is located on the end of the throttle shaft as shown in **Figure 20**.
1. Disconnect the TPS lead.
2. Unscrew the 2 mounting screws.
3. Carefully pull the sensor from the throttle shaft.
4. After installation, refer to *Adjustments* in this chapter to synchronize the TPS setting.

DEPRESSURIZING THE FUEL SYSTEM

The fuel system is pressurized to about 35 psi (242 kPa) while the engine is running. This pressure is maintained for some time after the engine is shut off. The system should be depressurized before any fuel line is disconnected.

> *CAUTION*
> *Do not attempt to depressurize the system by running the engine with no fuel in the fuel tank. Doing so may damage the fuel pump, which is lubricated and cooled by the fuel.*

There are several ways to depressurize the fuel system; 3 ways are presented in this procedure.

7

1. Relieving fuel pressure via the pressure regulator:

    a. With the engine stopped and ignition OFF, disconnect the pressure regulator vacuum hose from the throttle body. The hose can be detached from the T fitting (**Figure 21**) and a hose temporarily attached to the fitting for substep b.

    b. Apply vacuum to the vacuum hose using a suitable hand-operated vacuum pump like the Mity-Vac (available from auto parts suppliers). Applying vacuum opens the pressure regulator valve so fuel bleeds into fuel return hose thereby relieving fuel pressure.

2. Relieving fuel pressure by running engine:

    a. Start and run engine at idle.

    b. Disconnect electrical power to fuel pump by unplugging the connector.

    c. Allow the engine to idle until it stops. Sufficient fuel will be used to lower the pressure in the fuel system.

    d. After the engine stops, turn the ignition switch OFF and reconnect the fuel pump lead.

WARNING
Before depressurizing the fuel system using the procedure described in Step 3 (following), be sure to have a fire extinguisher rated for gasoline fires within reach. Do not smoke or allow anyone else to smoke near the area where gasoline will be spilled. Also, check for any open flames (water heater or clothes dryer gas pilots) that might ignite the spilled fuel. The work area must be well ventilated.

WARNING
The engine and exhaust system must be cold before depressurizing the fuel system as described in the following procedure. If possible, allow the machine to sit for several hours so the system can partially depressurize.

3. Relieving fuel pressure by disconnecting fuel hose.

    a. Disconnect the negative battery lead.

WARNING
Wear eye protection when disconnecting pressurized fuel lines.

    b. Use a shop rag to catch any expelled gasoline, while slowly loosening the fuel hose fitting (**Figure 22**) at the top of the fuel filter.

    c. Cover any open fuel lines.

    d. Wipe up any spilled fuel and properly discard gasoline-soaked rags.

ADJUSTMENTS

Idle Speed and Throttle Synchronization

For maximum engine performance, both cylinders must work equally. If one cylinder's throt-

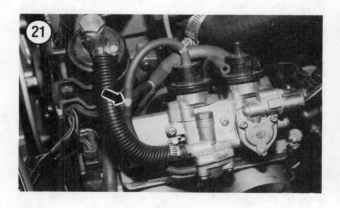

tle opens earlier, that cylinder will be required to work harder resulting in poor acceleration, rough performance and overheating. For proper synchronization, both throttle plates must begin to open at exactly the same time and continue to be open the same amount throughout their operating range.

Check throttle synchronization at each tune-up or if the engine suffers from reduced performance.

1. Open the hood.
2. Remove the air intake silencer.

CAUTION
Maintaining throttle cable free play is critical to prevent throttle cable damage.

3. Use a strong rubber band and clamp the throttle lever to the handlebar grip in the wide-open throttle position.

NOTE
Make sure the throttle lever is held in the wide-open position. This will ensure maximum performance during engine operation.

4. Loosen the locknuts securing the cable adjuster (**Figure 14**).
5. Pull the throttle cable housing (**Figure 14**) up with your fingers to make sure that the cable has some free play when wide open. There should be 1.5 mm (1/16 in.) free play. If necessary, loosen the locknuts (**Figure 14**) and turn the adjuster (**Figure 14**) to obtain the correct free play.

5. After adjusting the throttle maximum opening, perform the *Oil Pump Adjustment* procedure described in Chapter Three.
7. Connect a tachometer according to its manufacturer's instructions.
8. Start the engine and warm to operating temperature, then check idle speed. If necessary, turn the idle speed adjuster knob (A, **Figure 23**) to obtain 1,800-2,000 rpm.

Air/Fuel Mixture

The mixture is automatically controlled to compensate for varying operating conditions; however, the system also has variable resistors that can change idle and mid-range mixture. In most instances, the production setting for the air/fuel mixture will provide satisfactory engine performance; however, adjustment may be required to compensate for varying operating conditions.

The air/fuel mixture for engine speeds below 3,500 rpm can be adjusted slightly by setting the *idle mixture adjuster* shown at B, **Figure 23**.

  a. Operate the engine until it reaches normal operating temperature.
  b. Adjust idle speed to 2,000 rpm.
  c. Turn the idle mixture adjuster (B, **Figure 23**) as required to obtain maximum engine speed.
  d. Turn the idle mixture adjuster (B, **Figure 23**) counterclockwise an additional 1/16 turn. This setting will usually prevent the engine from bogging down and provide acceptable starting characteristics.

The air/fuel mixture in the mid-range can be adjusted by setting the *mid-range adjusting screw* (**Figure 24**) located on the top of the air silencer.

  a. Operate the engine until it reaches normal operating temperature.
  b. Run the snowmobile at about 3,500-4,500 rpm in conditions as near as possible to normal operating conditions.

7

c. Turn the mid-range mixture adjuster (**Figure 24**) as required to obtain the best mid-range performance.

d. It may be desirable to set the mid-range mixture adjuster (**Figure 24**) slightly richer (counterclockwise) to improve acceleration and reduce bogging down.

Synchronize TPS Setting

The throttle position sensor (TPS) has elongated mounting holes to allow some adjustment when installing. It may be necessary to synchronize the TPS with the throttle plates if the TPS has been replaced or moved during service.

1. Open the hood.

2. Back out the idle speed screw so the throttle plates are completely closed.

3. Set a multimeter to read DC voltage.

4. Attach the meter's positive (+) lead to the green/yellow wire at the No. 12 pin in the connector. Refer to **Figure 25**.

5. Attach the meter's negative (–) lead to the black/orange wire at the No. 9 pin in the connector. Refer to **Figure 25**.

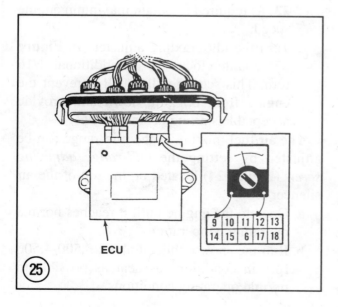

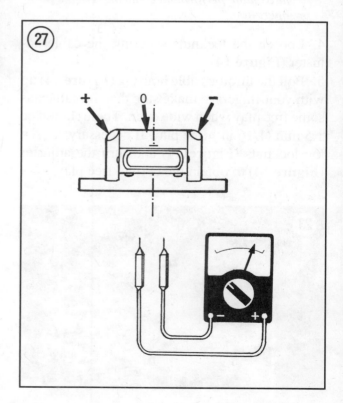

6. Turn ON the ignition switch and check the DC voltage.

7. The multimeter should indicate 0.1-0.3 DC volts.

8. If voltage is incorrect, loosen the TPS mounting screws (**Figure 26**), then reposition the TPS so the indicated voltage is correct. Tighten the 2 mounting screws to 3.5 N.m (30 in.-lb.) torque.

9. The idle speed stop screw **Figure 25** can be set initially by attaching an ohmmeter between the 0 terminal (**Figure 27**) and a good ground. Turn the idle speed stop screw until the indicated resistance is 500-600 ohms.

Tables 1-3 are on the following pages.

7

Table 1 ELECTRONIC FUEL INJECTION ERROR CODES

Monitor light symbol*	Possible cause
1 long, 1 short	The zero solenoid or connecting wires may be defective. The ECU may be defective, but this is less likely.
1 long, 2 short	The gain solenoid or connecting wires may be defective. The ECU may be defective, but this is less likely.
5 short	Battery voltage/charging voltage is too high, especially at high engine speeds. Check charging system. The ECU may be defective, but this is less likely.
2 long, 1 short	Throttle position sensor (TPS) or connecting wires may be defective. The ECU may be defective, but this is less likely.
2 long, 2 short	The water temperature sensor or connecting wiring may be defective. The ECU may be defective, but this is less likely.
2 long, 3 short	The air temperature sensor or connecting wiring may be defective. The ECU may be defective, but this is less likely.
2 long, 4 short	Battery voltage/charging voltage is too low. Check the charging system The ECU may also be defective, but this is less likely.
3 long, 1 short	Atmospheric pressure sensor or connecting wires may be defective. The ECU may be defective, but this is less likely.
3 long, 2 short	The air/fuel adjuster or connecting wires may be defective. The ECU may be defective, but this is less likely.
3 long, 3 short	The electronic control unit (ECU) may be defective.

* If the monitor light glows OFF and ON, during normal use, a trouble is indicated. The duration of the light may be either short or long as listed.

** Accessories or devices connected to the battery circuit may cause malfunctioning of the fuel injection system due to excessive current draw. Accessories must be connected to the appropriate circuit.

Table 2 TEMPERATURE SENSOR DESIRED SPECIFICATIONS

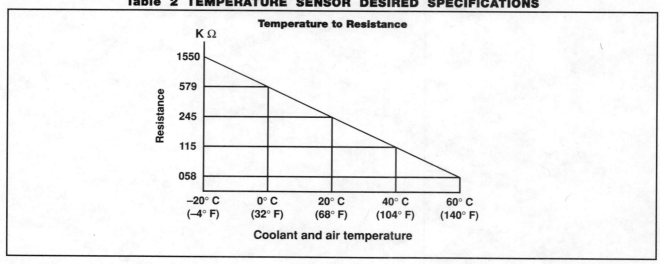

Table 3 ATMOSPHERIC PRESSURE SENSOR DESIRED SPECIFICATIONS

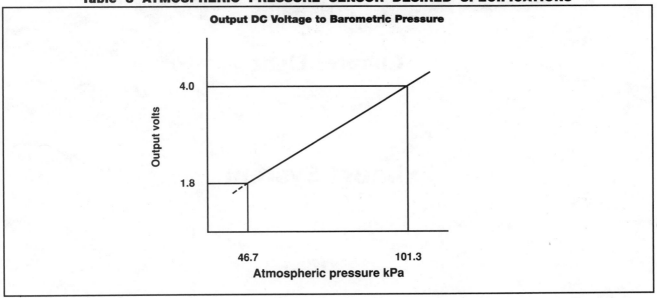

Chapter Eight

Exhaust System

The exhaust system consists of the exhaust manifold (or individual exhaust sockets), exhaust pipe(s) and a muffler.

This chapter includes service procedures for all parts of the exhaust systems.

Removal/Installation

Refer to **Figure 1** or **Figure 2** for this procedure.

1. Open the hood.

> *WARNING*
> *If the exhaust system is hot, wait until it cools before removing it.*

2. Detach the springs (**Figure 3**) that attach the muffler to the exhaust pipe. Disconnect the springs that retain the muffler.

3. Disconnect the long exhaust pipe spring (**Figure 4**).

4. Disconnect the springs that attach the exhaust pipe to the manifold (**Figure 5**) or exhaust socket.

5. Remove the exhaust pipe.

6. Remove the muffler and tailpipe (**Figure 6**).

7. Remove the bolts and washers holding the exhaust manifold or exhaust socket to the cylinders. Remove the exhaust manifold (**Figure 7**) or exhaust socket.

8. Examine the exhaust pipe and muffler (**Figure 8**) for cracks or other damage. Repair as described in this chapter.

9. Installation is the reverse of these steps.

10. Install new exhaust manifold gaskets.

11. Check the exhaust system for leaks after installation.

Cleaning

1. Clean all accessible exhaust passages with a blunt-roundnose tool.

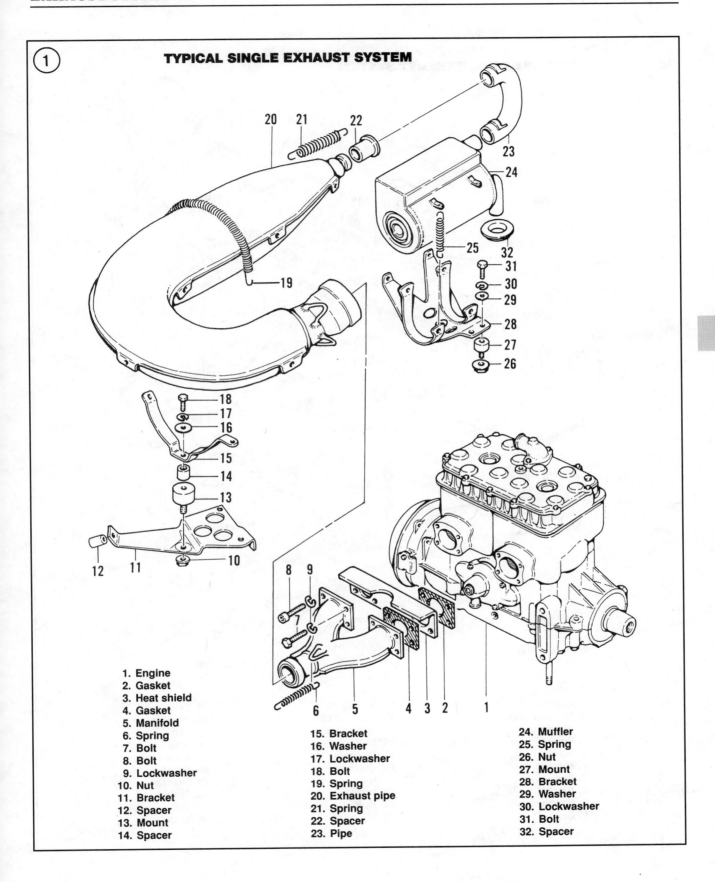

TYPICAL SINGLE EXHAUST SYSTEM

1. Engine
2. Gasket
3. Heat shield
4. Gasket
5. Manifold
6. Spring
7. Bolt
8. Bolt
9. Lockwasher
10. Nut
11. Bracket
12. Spacer
13. Mount
14. Spacer

15. Bracket
16. Washer
17. Lockwasher
18. Bolt
19. Spring
20. Exhaust pipe
21. Spring
22. Spacer
23. Pipe

24. Muffler
25. Spring
26. Nut
27. Mount
28. Bracket
29. Washer
30. Lockwasher
31. Bolt
32. Spacer

8

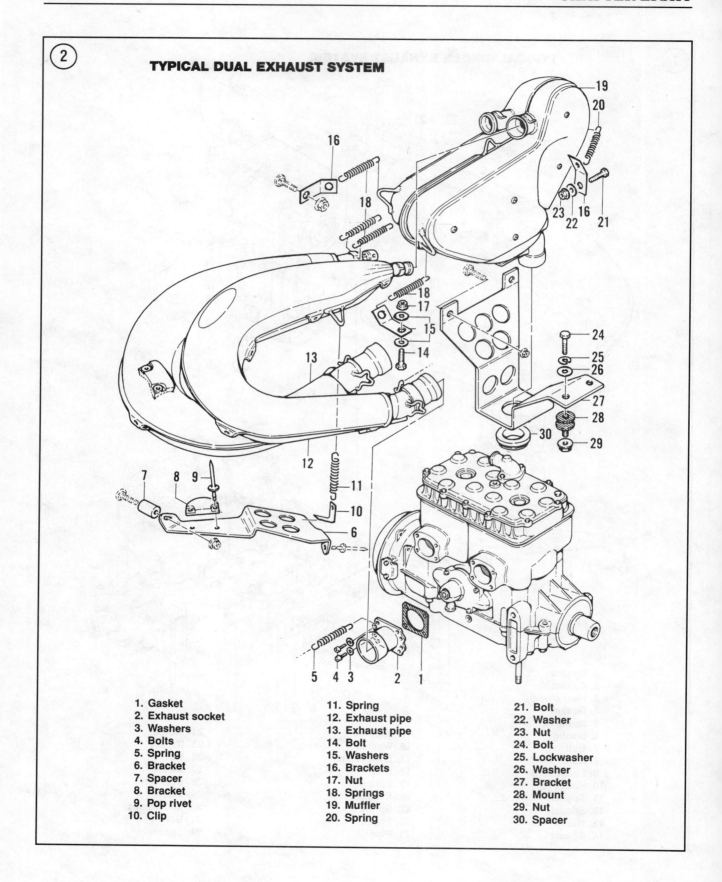

② **TYPICAL DUAL EXHAUST SYSTEM**

1. Gasket	11. Spring	21. Bolt
2. Exhaust socket	12. Exhaust pipe	22. Washer
3. Washers	13. Exhaust pipe	23. Nut
4. Bolts	14. Bolt	24. Bolt
5. Spring	15. Washers	25. Lockwasher
6. Bracket	16. Brackets	26. Washer
7. Spacer	17. Nut	27. Bracket
8. Bracket	18. Springs	28. Mount
9. Pop rivet	19. Muffler	29. Nut
10. Clip	20. Spring	30. Spacer

2. There are several ways to clean areas further down the pipe, including the following.

WARNING
When performing Step 3, do not start the drill until the cable is inserted into the pipe. At no time should the drill be running when the cable is free of the pipe. The whipping action of the cable could cause serious personal injury. Wear

8

heavy shop gloves and a face shield when using this equipment.

3. Chuck a section of discarded speedometer cable in an electric drill (**Figure 9**). Fray the loose end of the cable and insert the cable into the pipe. Operate the drill while moving the cable back and forth inside the pipe. Take your time and do a thorough job.

> *WARNING*
> *Make sure that all of the bearings or nuts are removed from the pipe when finished cleaning.*

4. Find several large ball bearings or nuts that will just fit into the exhaust pipe. Count the bearings or nuts as they are inserted into the pipe, then shake the pipe violently to break loose carbon that is inside.

5. Shake the large pieces out into a trash container.

EXHAUST SYSTEM REPAIR

A dent in the exhaust pipe will change the system's flow characteristics and may degrade performance. Minor damage can be easily repaired if you have welding equipment, some simple body tools, and a bodyman's slide hammer.

Small Dents

1. Drill a small hole in the center of the dent. Screw the end of the slide hammer into the hole.

2. Heat the area around the dent evenly with a torch.

3. When the dent is heated to a uniform orange-red color, operate the slide hammer to raise the dent.

4. When the dent is removed, unscrew the slide hammer and weld the drilled hole closed.

Large Dents

Large dents that are not crimped can be removed with heat and a slide hammer as previously described. However, several holes must be drilled along the center of the dent so that it can be pulled out evenly.

If the dent is sharply crimped along the edges, the affected section should be cut out with a hacksaw, straightened with a body dolly and hammered and welded back into place.

Before cutting the exhaust pipe apart, scribe alignment marks across the area to be cut to facilitate correct alignment when rewelding the pipe.

After the welding is completed, wire brush and clean all welds. Paint the entire pipe with a high-temperature paint to prevent rusting.

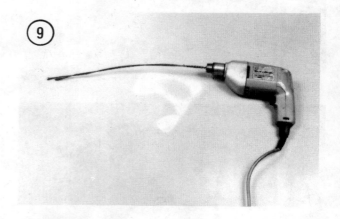
⑨

Chapter Nine

Electrical System

The electrical system includes the ignition, lighting, starting and other electrical accessory systems.

The ignition system used on all 1990-1992 models and 1993 models with a 583 engine is shown in **Figure 1**, typical. Some early models are equipped with two ignition generating coils and others have a single ignition generating coil (10, **Figure 1**).

The ignition system used on all 1993-on models except 1993 models with 583 engine is different from earlier models and is equipped with a separate ignition trigger coil.

This chapter provides service procedures for the ignition and electrical systems. Some electrical troubleshooting procedures are described in Chapter Two. Wiring diagrams are at the end of the book. **Tables 1-3** are located at the end of the chapter.

Some models are equipped with a battery and electric starter system. Procedures for servicing the starter motor are included in this chapter. The starter ring gear is attached to the primary drive pulley with 6 screws. Refer to Chapter Thirteen to remove the primary drive sheave.

FLYWHEEL AND STATOR ASSEMBLY (ALL 1990-1992 MODELS AND 1993 MODELS WITH 583 ENGINE)

All models use a capacitor discharge ignition system. Refer to **Figure 1**. The ignition system used on some of these models uses a dual generator coil, while other models use a single coil. The ignition dual generator coil is easily identified by the 2 sets of coil lamination (plates), 2 windings and 3 ignition generator wires (black, black/white and black/red). The ignition single generator coil is identified by only 1 set of coil lamination (plates), 1 winding and 2 ignition generator wires (black and white/blue). Each system uses components that are different from

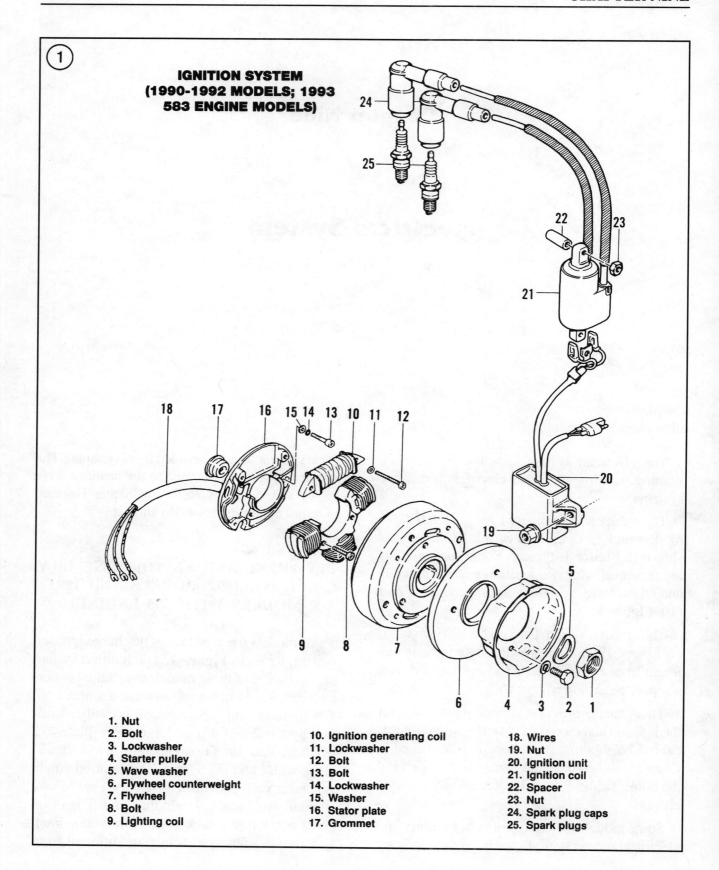

① IGNITION SYSTEM
(1990-1992 MODELS; 1993
583 ENGINE MODELS)

1. Nut
2. Bolt
3. Lockwasher
4. Starter pulley
5. Wave washer
6. Flywheel counterweight
7. Flywheel
8. Bolt
9. Lighting coil
10. Ignition generating coil
11. Lockwasher
12. Bolt
13. Bolt
14. Lockwasher
15. Washer
16. Stator plate
17. Grommet
18. Wires
19. Nut
20. Ignition unit
21. Ignition coil
22. Spacer
23. Nut
24. Spark plug caps
25. Spark plugs

other units and only parts designed for the specific system should be installed.

NOTE
Refer to Chapter Two for troubleshooting and test procedures.

Flywheel
Removal/Installation

The flywheel must be removed to service the stator coils. Flywheel replacement is usually necessary only if the magnets have been damaged by excessive heat or shock. Refer to **Figure 1** when performing this procedure.

1. Remove the muffler as described in Chapter Eight.

2. Remove the spark plug from the right (MAG) side of the engine. Pull the recoil starter to bring the MAG side piston to TDC. Reinstall the spark plug and reconnect the cap.

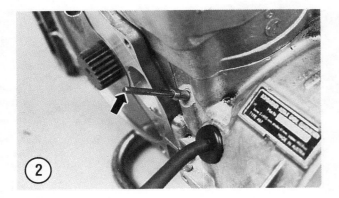

3. Remove the recoil starter housing as described in Chapter Twelve.

NOTE
The flywheel can be removed with the engine installed in the frame. The following photographs show the engine removed for clarity.

4. Detach the hose from the crankcase fitting for the fuel pump. This pulse hose fitting can be located by following the pulse hose from the fuel pump to the crankcase.

5. Insert the crankshaft locking tool (part No. 420 8766 40) through the pulse hose fitting and engage the tool with the crankshaft (**Figure 2**). After installing the tool, rotate the crankshaft slightly until the tool locks the crankshaft.

CAUTION
Do not attempt to use a substitute tool for the special crankshaft locking tool (part No. 420 8766 40) in Step 5. Substituting the tool may cause crankshaft damage, the substitute tool may bend and be difficult to remove or the tool may break off in the engine.

6. Remove the bolts and washers holding the starter pulley (A, **Figure 3**) to the flywheel. Remove the starter pulley.

7. Remove the flywheel counterweight (6, **Figure 1**), if so equipped.

NOTE
*The flywheel nut is secured with Loctite. To prevent thread damage, tap on the flywheel nut before attempting to loosen it in Step 8. **Do not** strike the flywheel.*

8. Loosen, then remove the flywheel nut and lockwasher.

9. Bolt the flywheel ring (A, **Figure 4**) (part No. 420 8766 55 or 420 8760 80) onto the face of the flywheel.

10. Thread the puller (B, **Figure 4**) (part No. 420 8760 65 or 529 0225 00) into the ring.

9

CAUTION
Do not heat or hammer the flywheel to remove it in Step 11. Heat may cause the flywheel to seize on the crankshaft and hammering can damage the flywheel or crankshaft bearings. If necessary to hit the puller bolt to loosen the flywheel from the crankshaft taper, be extremely careful.

11. Tighten the puller bolt (B, **Figure 4**) and break the flywheel free of the crankshaft taper. You may have to alternate hitting on the center puller bolt sharply with a hammer, then tightening the puller bolt. If the flywheel is extremely difficult to remove, have a Ski-Doo dealer remove it.

12. Remove the flywheel from the end of the crankshaft, then remove the puller from the flywheel.

13. Remove the Woodruff key from the flywheel (**Figure 5**).

NOTE
*Examine the magnets (**Figure 6**) for metal trash before installing the flywheel. Debris stuck to the magnets can damage the coils.*

14. Spray the flywheel and crankshaft tapers with a rust inhibitor, such as WD-40.

15. Place the Woodruff key in the crankshaft key slot (**Figure 5**). Position the flywheel (**Figure 7**) over the crankshaft with its key slot aligned with the key in the crankshaft.

16. Apply Loctite 242 (blue) to the flywheel nut threads and install the lockwasher and flywheel nut (B, **Figure 3**). Lock the crankshaft with same tool used during removal and tighten the flywheel nut (A, **Figure 8**) to the torque specification in **Table 1**.

17. Install the flywheel counterweight (if so equipped) by aligning the mark on the counterweight with the mark on the flywheel.

18. Install the starter pulley (A, **Figure 3**), washers and bolts. Tighten the bolts securely.

19. Remove the crankshaft locking tool from the pulse hose fitting (**Figure 2**).

20. Reinstall the recoil starter housing as described in Chapter Twelve.

21. If the engine is installed in the frame, observe the following:

a. Reconnect the pulse hose to the pulse nozzle on the crankcase. Secure the hose with the wire clip.

b. Reinstall the muffler as described in Chapter Eight.

Inspection

1. Check the flywheel carefully for cracks or breaks.

> *WARNING*
> *A cracked or chipped flywheel must be replaced. A damaged flywheel may fly apart at high rpm, causing severe engine*

damage. Do not attempt to repair a damaged flywheel.

2. Check the tapered bore of the flywheel and the crankshaft taper for signs of fretting or working.

3. Check the key slot in the flywheel (**Figure 9**) for cracks or other damage. Check the key slot in the crankshaft (**Figure 5**) for cracks or other damage.

4. Check the Woodruff key for cracks or damage.

5. Check the crankshaft and the flywheel nut threads for wear or damage.

6. Replace the flywheel, flywheel nut, crankshaft half and/or woodruff key as required.

7. Check the balancer (hydro-damper) attached to the flywheel on some models.

a. Install a new balancer if cracked or bent.

b. Install a new balancer if it makes a metallic ring when shaken.

c. Install a new balancer if oil is leaking.

Stator Plate
Removal/Installation

> *NOTE*
> *Refer to Chapter Two for troubleshooting and test procedures.*

1. Remove the flywheel as described in this chapter.

2. If the engine is installed in the frame, disconnect the stator wires from their electrical connectors.

3. Make a mark on the stator plate and crankcase for alignment during reassembly.

4. Remove the screws that attach the stator plate to the crankcase. Remove the grommet (B, **Figure 8**) and pull the wires through the opening while removing the stator plate (**Figure 10**).

5. Installation is the reverse of these steps. Observe the following.

9

a. Check the coil wires (**Figure 11**) for chafing or other damage. Replace the coil harness if necessary.

b. Check and adjust ignition timing as described in Chapter Three.

c. Make sure all electrical connections are tight and free from corrosion. Loose or corroded connections is often the cause of failure with electronic ignition systems.

Ignition Generating Coil Replacement

Some 1993 and earlier models are equipped with 2 ignition generating coils and others have a single ignition generating coil (10, **Figure 1**). The double coil has 3 wires and the single coil is identified by only 2 wires. If necessary, observe the following to replace either type of generating coil (A, **Figure 12**).

1. Remove the stator plate as described in this chapter.

2. Heat the back of the stator plate at the points shown at A, **Figure 13** to loosen the Loctite used to secure the coil screws. Do not exceed 200° F (93° C) when heating the screws.

> *CAUTION*
> *Protect the wire harness at the stator plate (**Figure 14**) when heating the screws in Step 2.*

3. Remove the Phillips screws holding the generating coil (A, **Figure 12**) to the stator plate.

4. Cut or unsolder the wires at the coil as close to the coil as possible.

5. Reverse to install the new coil. Observe the following:

a. Resolder the wires to the new coil terminals with rosin core solder.

b. Remove the shipping nuts from the new coil screws.

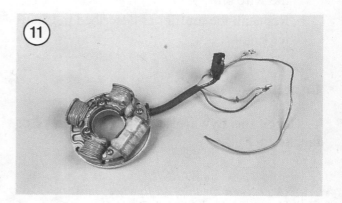

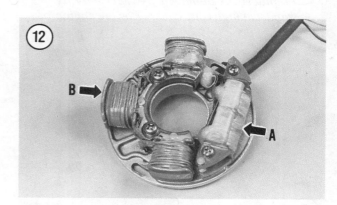

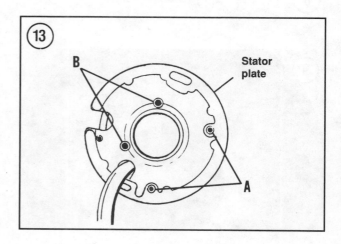

c. Position the new generating coil onto the stator plate.

d. Coat the new screws with Loctite 242 (blue) and install the screws. Place the centering tool (part No. 420 8769 22) over the coils

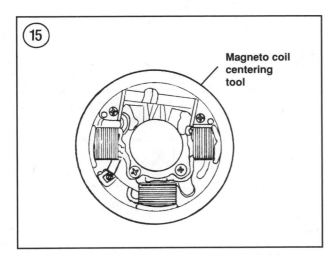

Magneto coil centering tool

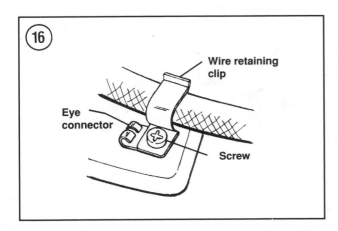

Wire retaining clip

Eye connector

Screw

(**Figure 15**) and tighten the generating coil screws.

Lighting Coil Replacement

If necessary, replace the lighting coil (B, **Figure 12**) as follows:

1. Remove the stator plate as described in this chapter.

2. Heat the back of the stator plate at the points shown at B, **Figure 13** to loosen the Loctite used to secure the coil screws. Do not exceed 200° F (93° C) when heating the screws.

CAUTION
*Protect the wire harness at the stator plate (**Figure 14**) when heating the screws in Step 2.*

3. Remove the Phillips screws holding the lighting coils (B, **Figure 12**) to the stator plate.

4. Remove the wire retaining clip from the stator plate (**Figure 16**).

5. Each lighting coil wire is protected by a harness tube (**Figure 17**). Observe the following to disconnect the coil wires from the main wire harness.

a. Pull the harness tubes toward the lighting coil to uncover the soldered joint.

b. Unsolder both coil wires.

c. Use rosin core solder when soldering wires in substep d.

d. Solder the lighting coil's white harness tube wire to the yellow wire. Refer to **Figure 17**.

e. Solder the lighting coil's black harness tube wire to the yellow/black wire. Refer to **Figure 17**.

6. Reverse to install the new coil. Observe the following:

a. Position the new lighting coil onto the stator plate.

b. Coat the new screws with Loctite 242 (blue) and install the screws. Place the centering tool (part No. 420 8769 22) over the coils

9

(**Figure 15**) and tighten the lighting coil screws.

c. Reattach the wire retaining clip as shown in **Figure 16**.

FLYWHEEL AND STATOR ASSEMBLY (ALL 1993-ON MODELS EXCEPT 1993 MODELS WITH 583 ENGINE)

All models use a capacitor discharge ignition system. Refer to **Figure 18**. The ignition system uses a separate trigger coil located just outside the flywheel (to the rear). A 2-wire plug attaches the trigger coil to the CDI control unit and a 3-wire plug attaches the ignition generator coil to the CDI control unit. This system uses components that are different from similar units, therefore, only parts designed for the specific model should be installed.

NOTE
Refer to Chapter Two for troubleshooting and test procedures.

Flywheel Removal/Installation

The flywheel must be removed to service the trigger coil or stator coils. Flywheel replacement is necessary if the magnets have been damaged by excessive heat or shock. Damage to the key slot and the taper is the most common reason for replacing the flywheel. Damage to the key slot or taper is usually caused by the retaining nut not tight enough. Refer to **Figure 18** when removing the flywheel.

1. Remove the muffler as described in Chapter Eight.

2. Remove the spark plug from the right (MAG) side of the engine. Pull the recoil starter to bring the MAG side piston to TDC. Reinstall the spark plug and reconnect the cap.

3. Remove the recoil starter housing as described in Chapter Twelve.

NOTE
The flywheel can be removed with the engine installed in the snowmobile. The

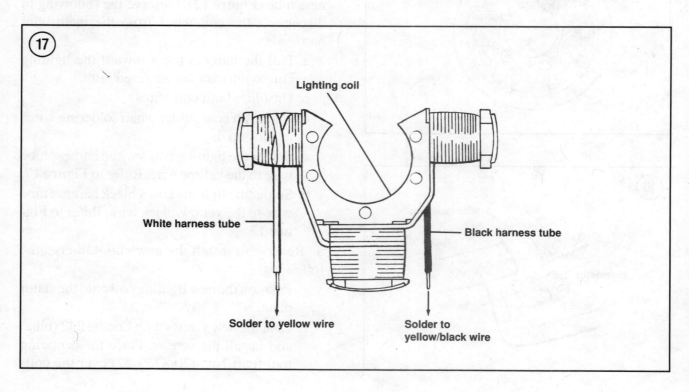

(17)

Lighting coil

White harness tube

Black harness tube

Solder to yellow wire

Solder to
yellow/black wire

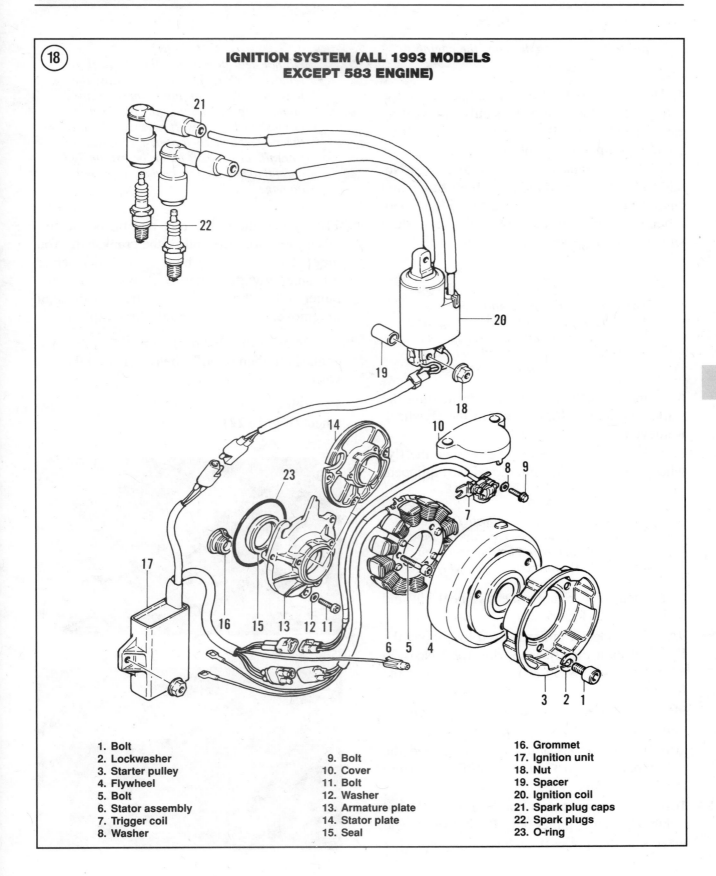

IGNITION SYSTEM (ALL 1993 MODELS EXCEPT 583 ENGINE)

1. Bolt
2. Lockwasher
3. Starter pulley
4. Flywheel
5. Bolt
6. Stator assembly
7. Trigger coil
8. Washer
9. Bolt
10. Cover
11. Bolt
12. Washer
13. Armature plate
14. Stator plate
15. Seal
16. Grommet
17. Ignition unit
18. Nut
19. Spacer
20. Ignition coil
21. Spark plug caps
22. Spark plugs
23. O-ring

9

following photographs show the engine removed for clarity.

4. Detach the pulse hose from the crankcase fitting for the fuel pump. This pulse hose fitting can be located by following the pulse hose from the fuel pump to the crankcase.

5. Insert the crankshaft locking tool (part No. 420 8766 40) through the pulse hose fitting and engage the tool with the crankshaft (**Figure 19**). After installing the tool, rotate the crankshaft slightly until the tool locks the crankshaft.

CAUTION
Do not use a substitute tool for the special crankshaft locking tool (part No. 420 8766 40) in Step 5. Substituting the tool may cause crankshaft damage, the tool may bend and be difficult to remove or the tool may break off in the engine.

6. Remove the bolts and washers holding the starter pulley (A, **Figure 20**) to the flywheel. Remove the starter pulley.

7. It may also be necessary to remove the flywheel counterweight from models so equipped.

NOTE
*The flywheel nut is secured with Loctite. To prevent thread damage, tap on the flywheel nut before attempting to loosen it in Step 8. **Do not** strike the flywheel.*

8. Loosen, then remove the flywheel nut and lockwasher (B, **Figure 20**).

9A. If the special puller is used to remove the flywheel, bolt the flywheel ring (part No. 420 8766 55 or 420 8760 80) onto the face of the flywheel.

9B. If a conventional puller is used, bolt the puller hub (A, **Figure 21**) to the flywheel.

10A. If the special puller is used, thread the puller (part No. 420 8760 65 or 529 0225 00) into the flywheel ring.

10B. If a conventional puller is used, hand tighten the center puller bolt (B, **Figure 21**) and make sure that puller is centered.

CAUTION
Do not heat or hammer the flywheel to remove it in Step 11. Heat may cause the flywheel to seize on the crankshaft and hammering can damage the flywheel or crankshaft bearings. If necessary to hit the puller bolt to loosen the flywheel from the crankshaft taper, be extremely careful to prevent flywheel or crankshaft damage.

11. Tighten the puller bolt and break the flywheel free from the end of the crankshaft. You may have to alternate hitting the puller center bolt sharply with a hammer, then tightening the puller bolt. If the flywheel is extremely difficult to remove, have a Ski-Doo dealer remove it.

12. Remove the flywheel from the end of the crankshaft, then remove the puller from the flywheel.

13. Remove the Woodruff key from the flywheel (**Figure 22**).

NOTE
*Examine the magnets (**Figure 23**) for metal trash before installing the flywheel. Debris stuck to the magnets can damage the coils.*

14. Examine the flywheel, coils and the end of the crankshaft before assembling.

CAUTION
The tapered bore in the flywheel and the matching tapered end of the crankshaft must be absolutely clean to seat correctly. Any dirt, burrs or other damage to the tapered surface must be removed before assembling. If the flywheel is not seated correctly, both the flywheel and the crankshaft will be damaged.

15. Clean the bore in the flywheel and the tapered end of the crankshaft. Spray the flywheel and crankshaft tapers with a rust inhibitor, such as WD-40.

16. Place the Woodruff key in the crankshaft key slot (**Figure 22**). Position the flywheel over the crankshaft with its key slot aligned with the key in the crankshaft.

CAUTION
Make sure that the retaining nut is properly tightened as described in Step 16. The key slot in the flywheel and crankshaft will be damaged if the retaining nut is not tightened properly. The tapered bore in flywheel and the tapered end of the crankshaft may also be damaged by improper tightening.

17. Apply Loctite 242 (blue) to the flywheel threads and install the lockwasher and flywheel nut (B, **Figure 20**). Lock the crankshaft with same tool used during removal and tighten the flywheel retaining nut to the torque specification in **Table 1**.

18. Install the flywheel counterweight (if so equipped) by aligning the mark on the counterweight with the mark on the flywheel.

19. Install the starter pulley (A, **Figure 20**), washers and bolts. Tighten the bolts securely.

20. Remove the crankshaft locking tool from the pulse hose fitting (**Figure 19**).

21. Reinstall the recoil starter housing as described in Chapter Twelve.

22. If the engine is installed in the snowmobile, observe the following:

9

a. Reconnect the pulse hose to the pulse fitting on the crankcase (**Figure 24**). Secure the hose with the clamp.

b. Reinstall the muffler as described in Chapter Eight.

Inspection

1. Check the flywheel carefully for cracks or breaks.

> *WARNING*
> *Cracked or chipped flywheel must be replaced. A damaged flywheel may fly apart at high rpm, causing severe engine damage. Do not attempt to repair a damaged flywheel.*

2. Check the tapered bore of the flywheel and the crankshaft taper for signs of fretting or working.

3. Check the key slot in the flywheel (**Figure 25**) for cracks or other damage. Check the key slot in the crankshaft (**Figure 22**) for cracks or other damage.

4. Check the Woodruff key for cracks or damage.

5. Check the crankshaft and flywheel nut threads for wear or damage.

6. Replace the flywheel, flywheel nut, crankshaft half and/or woodruff key as required.

7. Check the balancer (hydro-damper) attached to the flywheel on some models.

   a. Install a new balancer if cracked or bent.

   b. Install a new balancer if it makes a metallic ring when shaken.

   c. Install a new balancer if oil is leaking.

Stator (Armature) Coils
Removal/Installation

The ignition generator coil and the lighting coils are both attached to the stator plate. The stator plate on 454 and 670 models also contains the crankshaft seal. The coils must be removed

before the stator plate can be removed. The stator coils and stator plate must also be removed before the ignition trigger coil can, because the wires from the trigger coil are routed under the stator plate.

> *NOTE*
> *Refer to Chapter Two for coil troubleshooting and test procedures.*

1. Remove the flywheel as described in this chapter.

2. If the engine is installed in the snowmobile, disconnect wires from the stator at the electrical connectors.

3. Remove the screws (**Figure 26**) that attach the stator coils to the stator plate.

4. Remove the grommet from around the wires and pull the wires through the opening while removing the stator coils. Refer to **Figure 27**.

5. Check the coil wires for chafing or other damage. Replace the coil harness, if necessary.

6. On 454 and 670 engine models, observe the following:

   a. Check the condition of the crankshaft seal (15, **Figure 18**) and install a new seal as outlined in this chapter if it is questionable.

   b. Use new sealing ring (23, **Figure 18**) when reassembling.

7. Install by reversing the removal procedure, while observing the following.

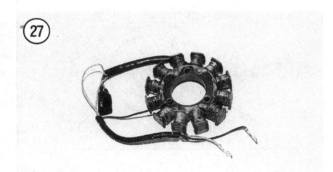

a. Check and adjust ignition timing as described in Chapter Three.

b. Make sure that wires are not pinched when assembling.

CAUTION
Do not coat wire terminals with silicone sealant. Contacts will corrode if silicone sealer is uses to water proof the connections.

c. Make sure all electrical connections are tight and free from corrosion. Coat contacts with dielectric grease, then attach electrical connectors. A loose or corroded connection is often the cause of electronic ignition system failure.

d. Be sure the grommet is correctly seated around the wires.

Stator Plate
Removal/Installation

The lighting coils and the ignition generating coil are attached to the stator plate. Observe the following to remove the stator assembly.

1. Remove the stator coils as described in this chapter.

2. Remove the screws attaching the stator plate (**Figure 28**) to the crankcase.

3. Reverse to install the stator plate.

Trigger Coil Replacement

The trigger coil is located outside the flywheel, but the attaching wires are routed under the stator plate. Observe the following to replace the trigger coil.

NOTE
It is not necessary to completely remove the stator plate, but it must be loose enough to remove the trigger coil wires from behind it.

9

1. Remove the stator plate as described in this chapter.

2. Remove the screws (**Figure 29**) attaching the trigger coil to the crankcase.

3. Withdraw the wires (**Figure 30**) from the hole and remove the trigger coil.

4. Reverse the procedure to install the new trigger coil.

5. Adjust the trigger coil air gap as follows:

   a. Rotate the flywheel until the protrusion is aligned with the trigger coil as shown in **Figure 31**.

   b. Use a feeler gauge to measure the clearance between the trigger coil and the flywheel protrusion.

   c. If clearance is not between 0.55-1.45 mm (0.022-0.057 in.), loosen the 2 screws attaching the trigger coil, reposition the coil and retighten the screws. Recheck clearance after tightening the screws.

   d. Check and adjust ignition timing as described in Chapter Three.

Crankshaft Seal Replacement

The stator plate on 454 and 670 engine models also contains the crankshaft seal. If this seal leaks, the engine will not run properly. To replace the seal, remove the stator assembly as described in this chapter. The old seal can be pressed from the stator plate and a new seal can be pressed into

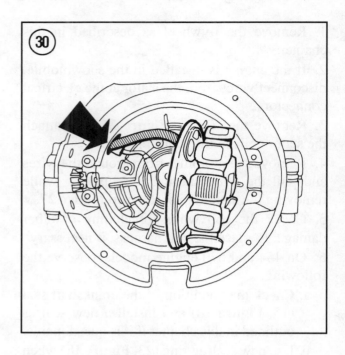

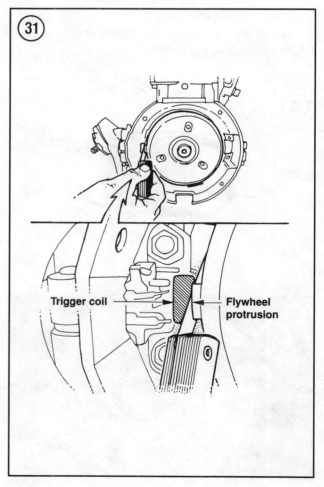

Trigger coil   Flywheel protrusion

the plate. Seal driver (part No. 420 8765 14) can be used to facilitate installation.

IGNITION COIL

Refer to **Figure 32** when performing procedures in this section.

Removal/Installation

1. Open the hood.

2. Disconnect the spark plug caps from the spark plugs (**Figure 33**).

3. Disconnect the ignition coil connector at the CDI box.

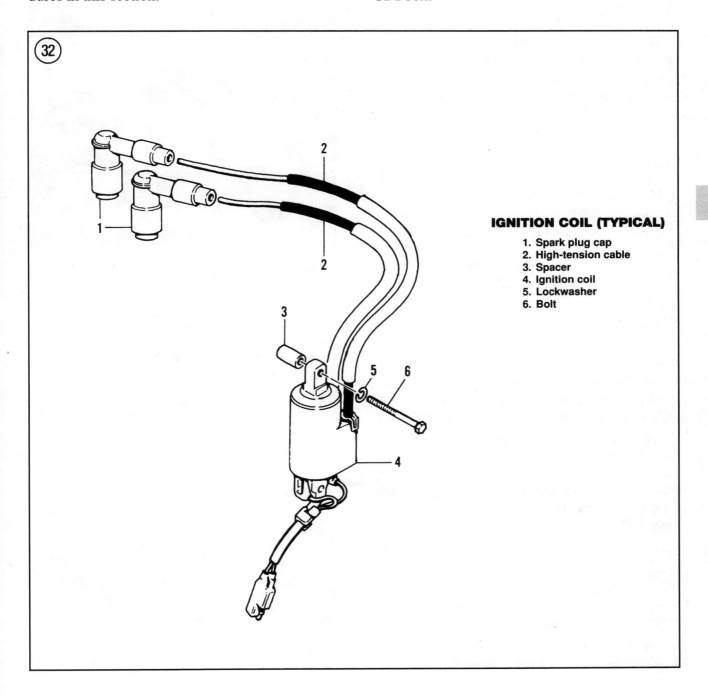

IGNITION COIL (TYPICAL)

1. Spark plug cap
2. High-tension cable
3. Spacer
4. Ignition coil
5. Lockwasher
6. Bolt

9

4. Remove the nuts holding the ignition coil (**Figure 34**) and remove the ignition coil. See **Figure 35**.

5. Installation is the reverse of these steps. Make sure all wire terminals are clean. Coat the terminals with dielectric grease before connecting.

Spark Plug Caps

The spark plug caps (**Figure 36**) can be replaced by pulling the old caps off of the coil's high tension wire. Reverse to install. Make sure the cap is pushed all the way on the high tension wire.

Testing

Refer to Chapter Two for testing and troubleshooting the ignition coils.

CDI BOX

Removal/Installation

1. Open the hood.

2. Disconnect the 2 connectors from the CDI box.

3. Locate the CDI box in the engine compartment. On some models, it may be necessary to remove the coolant tank. Remove the nuts holding the CDI box to its mounting bracket. Remove the CDI box. See **Figure 37**, typical.

4. Install by reversing these removal steps. Before attaching the electrical connectors to the unit, make sure the connectors are clean. Use electrical contact cleaner to clean the connectors.

VOLTAGE REGULATOR

The voltage regulator is attached to the vehicle frame (tunnel).

1. Disconnect the voltage regulator wires.

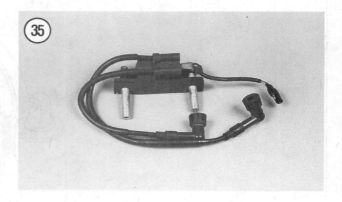

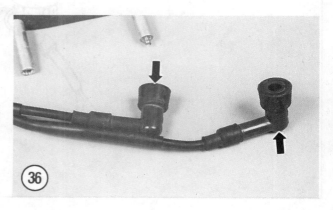

2. Remove the nut or the bolt and screw and remove the voltage regulator. See **Figure 38** (late model).

3. Installation is the reverse of these steps. Before connecting the wire connectors to the unit, make sure the connectors are clean of all dirt and moisture residue. Use electrical contact cleaner to clean the connectors.

Testing

Refer to Chapter Two for testing and troubleshooting the voltage regulator.

LIGHTING SYSTEM

The lighting system consists of the headlight, taillight/brakelight combination, meter illumination lights and pilot lamps. In the event of trouble with any light the first thing to check is the affected bulb itself. If the bulb is good, check all wiring and connections with a test light or ohmmeter. Replacement bulbs are listed in **Table 2**.

Headlight Replacement

> *CAUTION*
> *Most models are equipped with quartz-halogen bulbs (**Figure 39**). Do not touch the bulb glass with your fingers. Traces of oil from your fingers on the bulb will drastically reduce the life of the bulb. Clean any traces of oil from the bulb with cloth moistened in alcohol or lacquer thinner.*

> *WARNING*
> *If the headlight has just burned out or been recently turned off it will be **hot**. Don't touch the bulb until it cools off.*

Refer to **Figures 40-42**.
1. Open the hood.
2. Disconnect the electrical connector from the bulb.
3. Remove the rubber boot (**Figure 43**) and disconnect the bulb retainer clip. Remove the bulb.
4. Installation is the reverse of these steps. Make sure the bulb engages the bulb housing correctly.

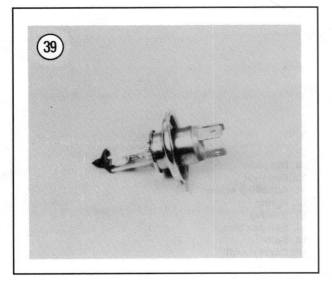

9

Headlight Adjustment

1. Park the snowmobile on a level surface 12 ft. 6 in. (381 cm) from a vertical wall (**Figure 44**).

> *NOTE*
> *A rider should be seated on the snowmobile when performing the following.*

2. Measure the distance from the floor to the center of the headlight lens (**Figure 44**). Make a mark on the wall the same distance from the floor. For instance, if the center of the headlight lens is 2 ft. (0.61 m) above the floor, mark A in **Figure 44** should also be 2 ft. (0.61 m) above the floor.

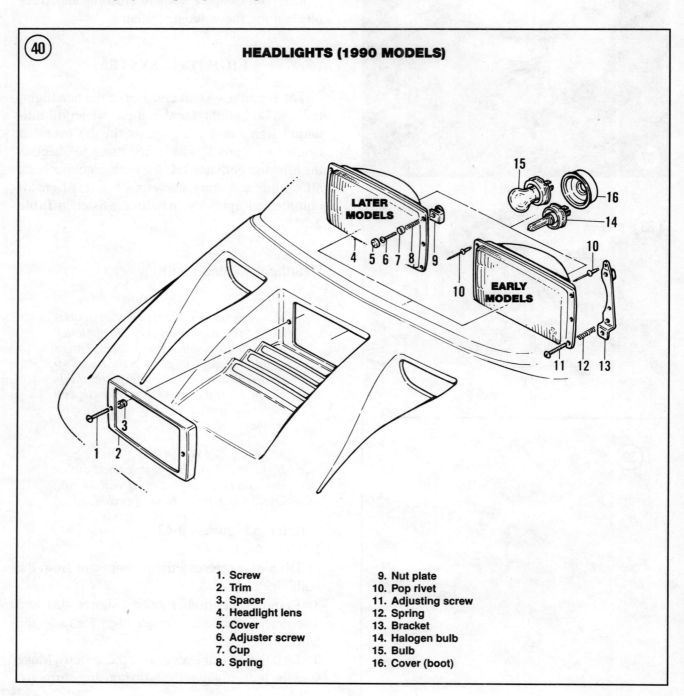

40 **HEADLIGHTS (1990 MODELS)**

LATER MODELS
EARLY MODELS

1. Screw
2. Trim
3. Spacer
4. Headlight lens
5. Cover
6. Adjuster screw
7. Cup
8. Spring
9. Nut plate
10. Pop rivet
11. Adjusting screw
12. Spring
13. Bracket
14. Halogen bulb
15. Bulb
16. Cover (boot)

3. Start the engine, turn on the headlight and set the beam selector to HIGH. Do not adjust the headlight beam with the selector set at LOw.

4. The most intense area of the beam on the wall should be 1 in. (25 mm) below the A mark (A, **Figure 44**) and aligned with the imaginary vertical centerline from the headlight to the wall.

5. To move the beam, turn the adjuster screws (**Figure 45**).

Taillight Bulb Replacement

1. Remove the taillight lens mounting screws and remove the lens (**Figure 46**).

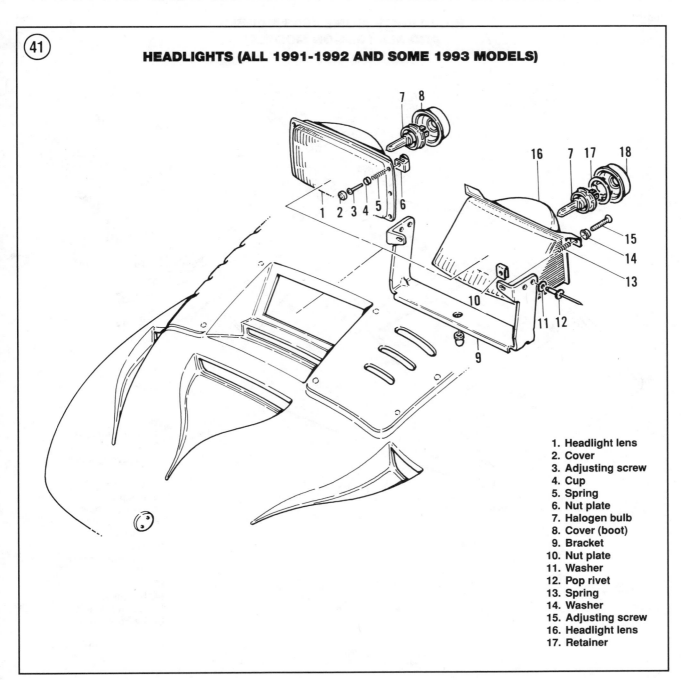

(41)

HEADLIGHTS (ALL 1991-1992 AND SOME 1993 MODELS)

1. Headlight lens
2. Cover
3. Adjusting screw
4. Cup
5. Spring
6. Nut plate
7. Halogen bulb
8. Cover (boot)
9. Bracket
10. Nut plate
11. Washer
12. Pop rivet
13. Spring
14. Washer
15. Adjusting screw
16. Headlight lens
17. Retainer

9

2. Turn the bulb counterclockwise and remove it (**Figure 47**).

3. Clean the lens in a mild detergent and check for cracks.

4. Installation is the reverse of these steps.

METER ASSEMBLY

The meter assembly consists of a speedometer, tachometer, fuel level gauge and temperature gauge (**Figure 48**, typical). The meters are installed in the hood (**Figure 49**).

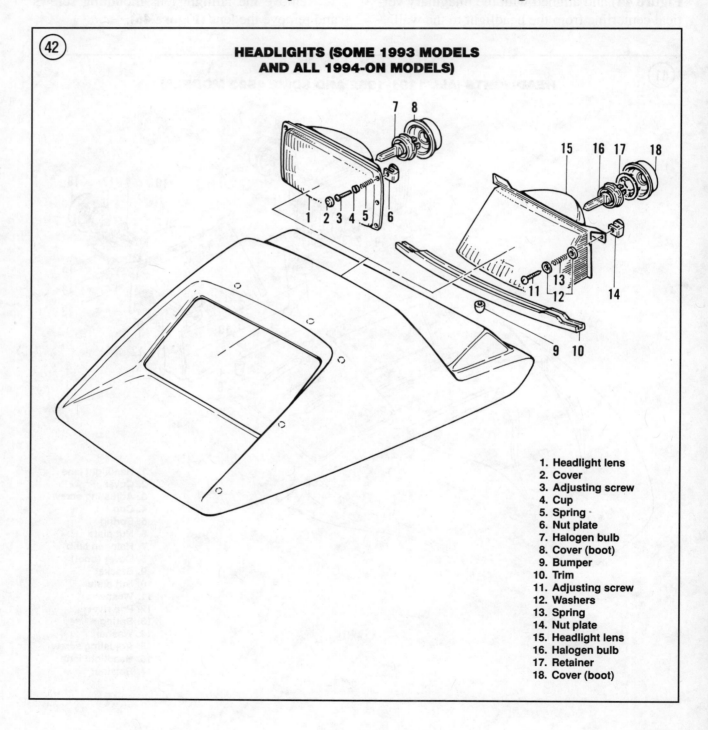

HEADLIGHTS (SOME 1993 MODELS AND ALL 1994-ON MODELS)

1. Headlight lens
2. Cover
3. Adjusting screw
4. Cup
5. Spring
6. Nut plate
7. Halogen bulb
8. Cover (boot)
9. Bumper
10. Trim
11. Adjusting screw
12. Washers
13. Spring
14. Nut plate
15. Headlight lens
16. Halogen bulb
17. Retainer
18. Cover (boot)

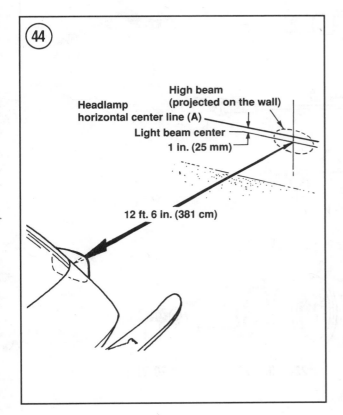

Bulb Replacement

1. Open the hood.

2. Locate the bulb socket at the affected meter assembly and pull the bulb socket out of the meter assembly. If necessary, remove the meter mounting bracket (**Figure 50**, typical) to gain access to the bulb socket. Replace the bulb.

3. Installation is the reverse of these steps.

Meter Removal/Installation

1. Open the hood.

2. Disconnect the electrical connectors from the affected meter.

3. Pull the bulb socket out of the meter assembly.

4. Disconnect the speedometer cable from the meter.

5. Remove the nuts securing the meter mounting bracket and remove the meter.

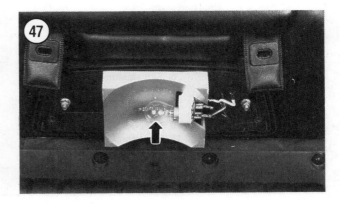

9

(48) METER ASSEMBLY

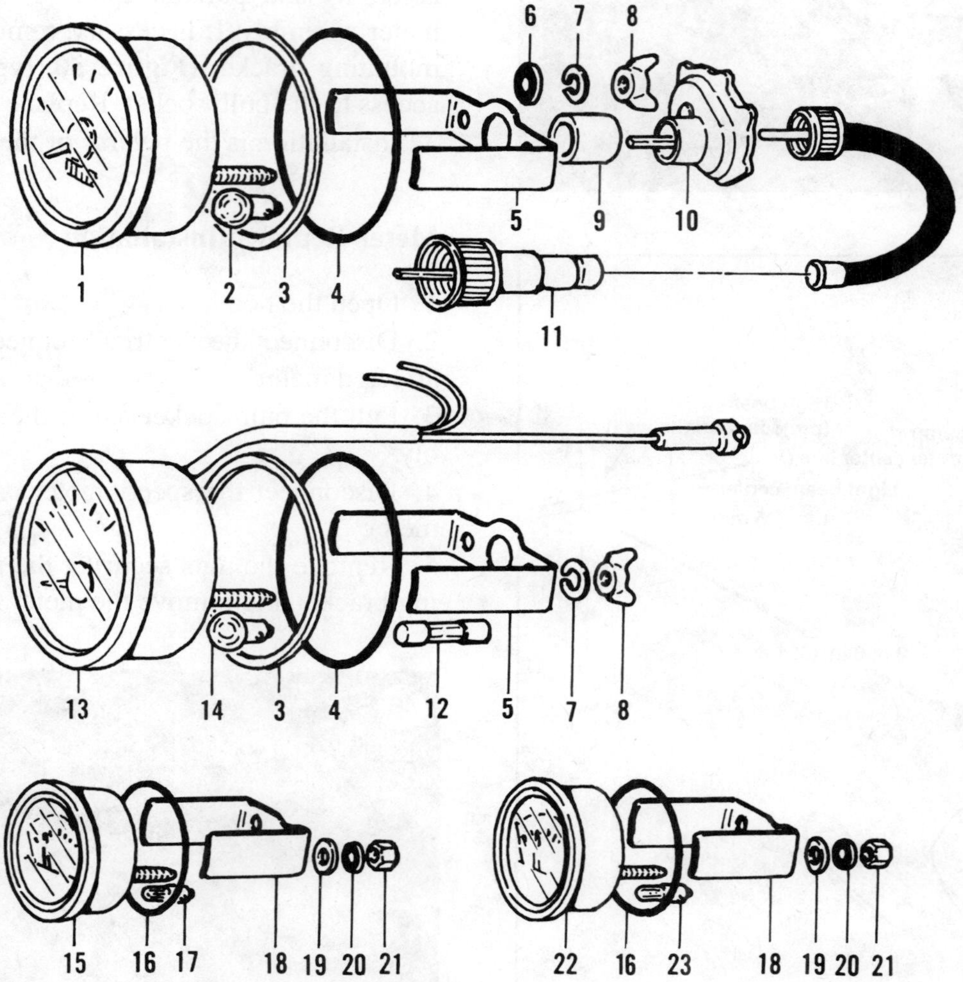

1. Speedometer
2. Bulb
3. O-ring
4. Retainer ring
5. Mounting bracket
6. Flat washer
7. Lockwasher
8. Wing nut
9. Spacer
10. Speedometer corrector
11. Speedometer cable
12. Fuse (tachometer equipped models only)
13. Tachometer (if so equipped)
14. Bulb (tachometer equipped models only)
15. Fuel level gauge
16. O-ring
17. Bulb
18. Mounting bracket
19. Flat washer
20. Lockwasher
21. Nut
22. Temperature gauge
23. Bulb

6. Installation is the reverse of these steps.

Tachometer Fuse

The tachometer is protected by a 0.1 amp fuse (**Figure 51**). If the tachometer stops during engine operation, remove the fuse and check its condition. Replace the fuse if necessary.

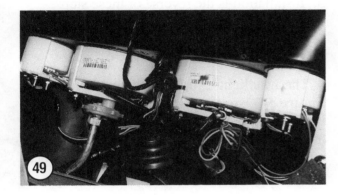

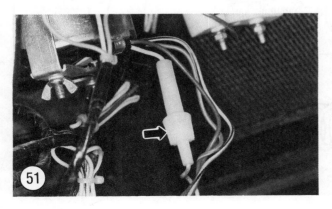

CAUTION
Never use a higher amperage fuse than specified and never substitute tinfoil or wire for a fuse. The fuse is designed to protect the gauge and substitution could result in tachometer damage in the event of an overload.

PILOT LAMPS

Several different indicator lights may be located on the dash or console. Service is similar for most of the lamps and usually limited to installing a new bulb. Some of the warning lamps may be connected to a wire from a sensor (sending unit).

High Beam Pilot Lamp

The high beam pilot lamp lights whenever the headlight is on HIGH beam. Replace the bulb if it does not light.
1. Open the hood.
2. Disconnect the electrical connector from the high beam pilot lamp and remove the pilot lamp.
3. Reverse to install. Check pilot lamp operation by turning the headlight to HIGH; the lamp should come on.

Oil Level Pilot Lamp

The oil tank is equipped with a oil level sensor that is wired to the injection oil level pilot lamp on the instrument panel. When the oil level in the tank reaches a specified low point, the pilot lamp will light.

The oil injection level pilot lamp lights whenever the brake lever is operated. If the lamp does not light during brake operation, replace the lamp as follows:
1. Open the hood.
2. Disconnect the electrical connector from the oil level pilot lamp and remove the pilot lamp.

9

3. Reverse to install. Check pilot lamp operation by applying the brake lever with the engine running; the lamp should come on.

SWITCHES

Switches can be tested for continuity with an ohmmeter (see Chapter One) or a self-powered test light at the switch connector plug by operating the switch in each of its operating positions and comparing results with the switch operation.

When testing switches, observe the following:

a. When separating any connector, pull on the connector housings, not the wires.

b. After locating a defective circuit, check the connectors to make sure they are clean, tight and properly joined. Check all wires going into a connector housing to make sure each wire is properly positioned and that the wire is not broken and that the terminal end is not loose.

c. When joining connectors, push them together until they click into place.

d. When replacing the handlebar switch assemblies, make sure the cables are routed

correctly so they will not crimp when the handlebar is turned from side to side.

Tether Switch Removal/Installation

Refer to **Figure 52**.
1. Disconnect the tether switch electrical connector.
2. Unscrew the tether switch and remove it.
3. Installation is the reverse of these steps.

Headlight Dimmer Switch

The headlight dimmer switch (**Figure 53** or **Figure 54**) is mounted in the brake lever housing. To replace the switch, disassemble the brake housing. Disconnect the switch connectors and remove the switch. Reverse the removal procedure to install.

Brake Light Switch

The brake light switch (**Figure 55** or **Figure 56**) is mounted in the brake lever housing. To

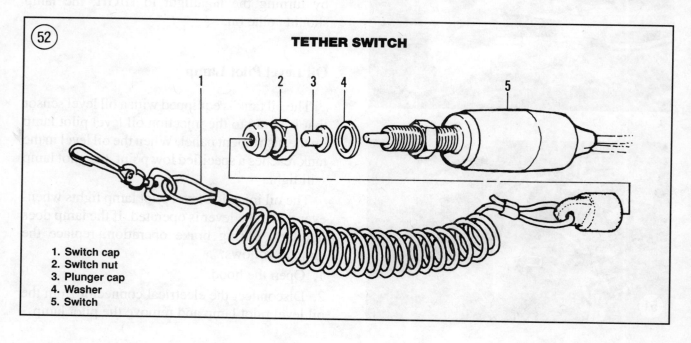

(52)   **TETHER SWITCH**

1. Switch cap
2. Switch nut
3. Plunger cap
4. Washer
5. Switch

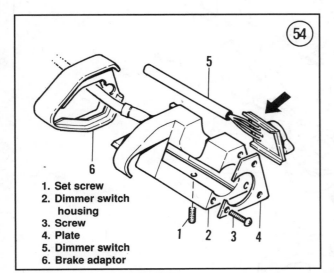

1. Set screw
2. Dimmer switch
   housing
3. Screw
4. Plate
5. Dimmer switch
6. Brake adaptor

replace the switch, disassemble the brake housing. Disconnect the switch connectors and remove the switch. Reverse the removal procedure to install.

Emergency Cutout (Kill) Switch

The emergency cutout switch (**Figure 57**) is mounted in the throttle housing. To replace the switch, disassemble the throttle housing. Disconnect the switch connectors and remove the switch. Reverse the removal procedure to install.

Ignition Switch

The ignition switch is mounted on the console. Refer to **Figure 58** if replacing the switch.

Temperature Sensor

The temperature sensor (**Figure 59**, typical) is mounted in the cylinder head. Some models are equipped with an overheat warning light, while

9

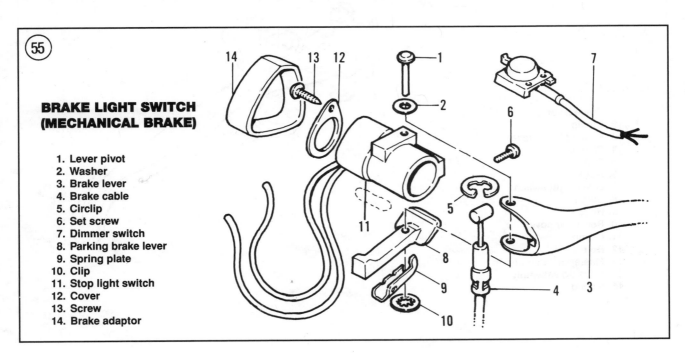

**BRAKE LIGHT SWITCH
(MECHANICAL BRAKE)**

1. Lever pivot
2. Washer
3. Brake lever
4. Brake cable
5. Circlip
6. Set screw
7. Dimmer switch
8. Parking brake lever
9. Spring plate
10. Clip
11. Stop light switch
12. Cover
13. Screw
14. Brake adaptor

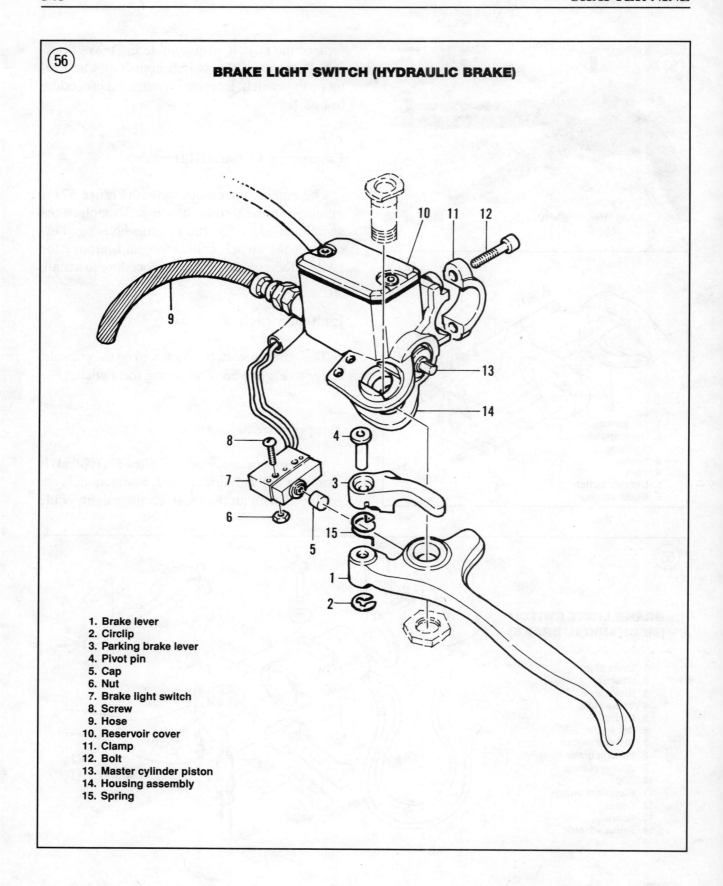

56

BRAKE LIGHT SWITCH (HYDRAULIC BRAKE)

1. Brake lever
2. Circlip
3. Parking brake lever
4. Pivot pin
5. Cap
6. Nut
7. Brake light switch
8. Screw
9. Hose
10. Reservoir cover
11. Clamp
12. Bolt
13. Master cylinder piston
14. Housing assembly
15. Spring

other models are equipped with a gauge. The light or gauge is located on the console.

> *WARNING*
> *Do not attempt to remove the temperature sensor (sending unit) while the engine and coolant is hot; serious burns may result. Make sure the engine and coolant has cooled before attempting to remove the sensor.*

To replace the temperature sensor, proceed as follows.

1. Detach the wires from the sensor.
2. Drain coolant or be prepared to catch the fluid that will leak when the sensor is removed.
3. Unscrew the sensor from the cylinder head.
4. Use sealer on threads of sensor and reverse the removal procedure to install.

FUEL LEVEL SENSOR

Some models are equipped with an electric fuel level gauge located in the instrument console. A sensor and float assembly, mounted in the fuel tank (**Figure 60** or **Figure 61**), sends an electrical signal to the fuel gauge.

To replace the fuel level sensor, observe the following:

1. Remove and drain the fuel tank as described in Chapter Six or Chapter Seven.

9

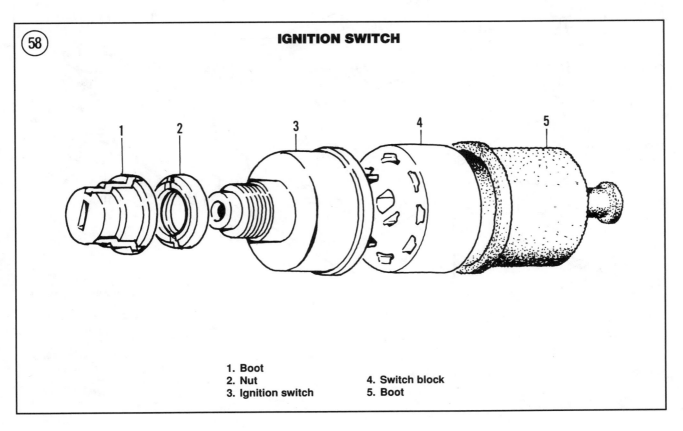

IGNITION SWITCH

1. Boot
2. Nut
3. Ignition switch
4. Switch block
5. Boot

2. Remove the screws and washers securing the sensor to the fuel tank.

3. Remove the sensor and gasket. Discard the gasket.

4. Reverse the removal procedure to install the fuel level sensor. Use a new gasket. Tighten the retaining screws in a crossing pattern first to 1 N•m (9 in.-lb.), then to 2.5 N•m (22 in.-lb.).

OIL LEVEL GAUGE

All models are equipped with a warning light on the instrument console to indicate when oil in

(59)

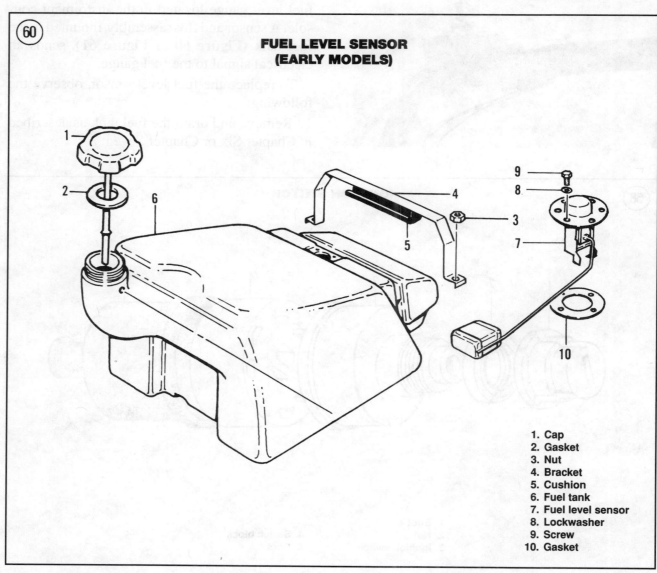

(60)

FUEL LEVEL SENSOR (EARLY MODELS)

1. Cap
2. Gasket
3. Nut
4. Bracket
5. Cushion
6. Fuel tank
7. Fuel level sensor
8. Lockwasher
9. Screw
10. Gasket

the engine oil reservoir reaches a dangerously low level. The sender is located in the oil tank as shown in **Figure 62** or **Figure 63**.

To replace the low oil level sender proceed as follows:

1. Open the hood

2. Disconnect the wires from the electrical connector.

3A. On models with the sender entering the top of the tank, pull the sender (5, **Figure 62**) from the tank.

3B. On models with the oil level sender integral with the tank outlet, first remove the tank, drain the oil, then pull the sender (13, **Figure 63**) from the tank.

4. On all models, the sender is installed by pushing it into place. The sealing grommet

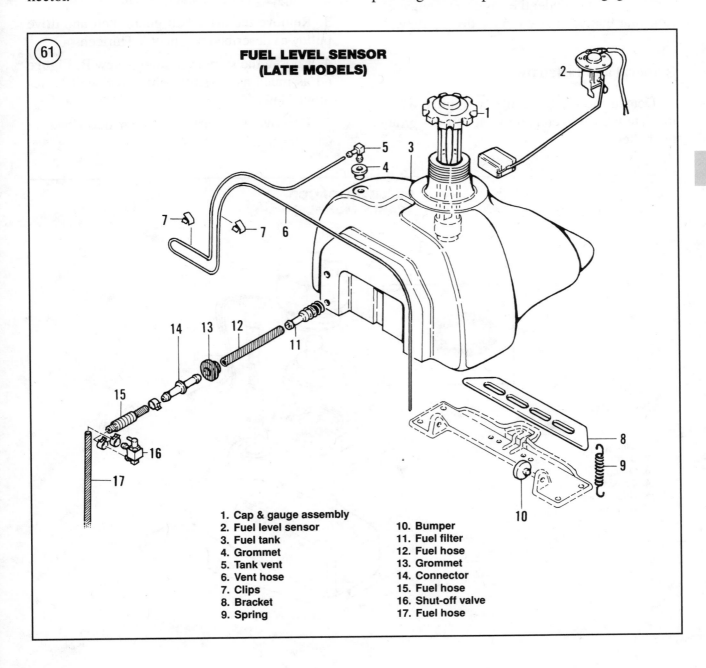

FUEL LEVEL SENSOR (LATE MODELS)

1. Cap & gauge assembly
2. Fuel level sensor
3. Fuel tank
4. Grommet
5. Tank vent
6. Vent hose
7. Clips
8. Bracket
9. Spring
10. Bumper
11. Fuel filter
12. Fuel hose
13. Grommet
14. Connector
15. Fuel hose
16. Shut-off valve
17. Fuel hose

9

(11, **Figure 63**), should be replaced if damaged or hard.

ELECTRIC STARTING MOTOR

The starter circuit includes the battery, starter relay and the starter motor. The starter switch is incorporated in the ignition key switch and the starter relay is attached to the starter. The electric starter is located under the engine and engages a ring gear that is attached to the drive pulley.

Removal and Installation

1. Detach the ground cable A, **Figure 64** and insulate the cable end so that it can not ground the battery.

WARNING
Electrical sparks or unplanned operation of an electrical device can cause injury. One method to make sure that the ground cable cannot accidentally make contact is to insulate the cable end with tape, hose or similar insulating cover. Another method is to remove the battery.

2. Remove the air intake silencer as described in Chapter Six or Chapter Seven.

3. Remove the drive belt guard, belt and drive pulley as described in Chapter Thirteen.

4. Loosen the starter retaining screw B, **Figure 64** as much as possible. The screw will be removed later.

5. Remove the carburetors as described in Chapter Six.

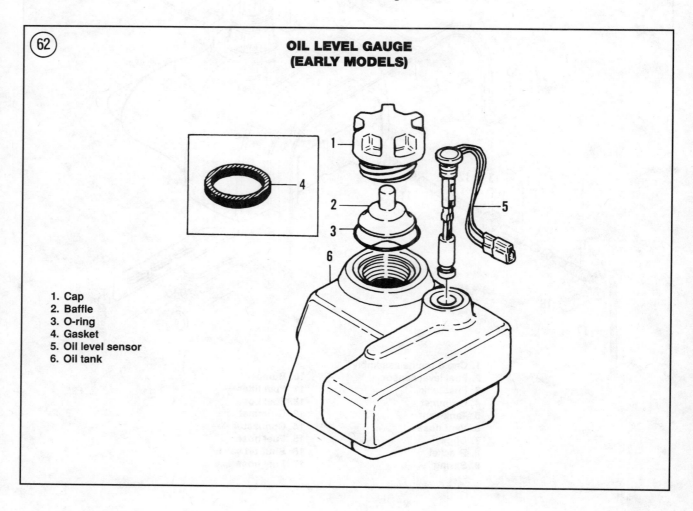

62

OIL LEVEL GAUGE (EARLY MODELS)

1
2
3
4
5
6

1. Cap
2. Baffle
3. O-ring
4. Gasket
5. Oil level sensor
6. Oil tank

6. Remove the exhaust pipe and muffler as described in Chapter Eight.

7. Unbolt and remove the heat shield from around the rewind starter.

8. Work through the locations where the exhaust pipe and air intake silencer were located and detach the tie rod from the steering column.

9. Move the disconnected end of the tie rod (A, **Figure 65**) toward the front.

10. Cut the tie wrap from around the cover protecting the starter electrical connections and remove the protective cover.

11. Detach the RED positive cable from the starter.

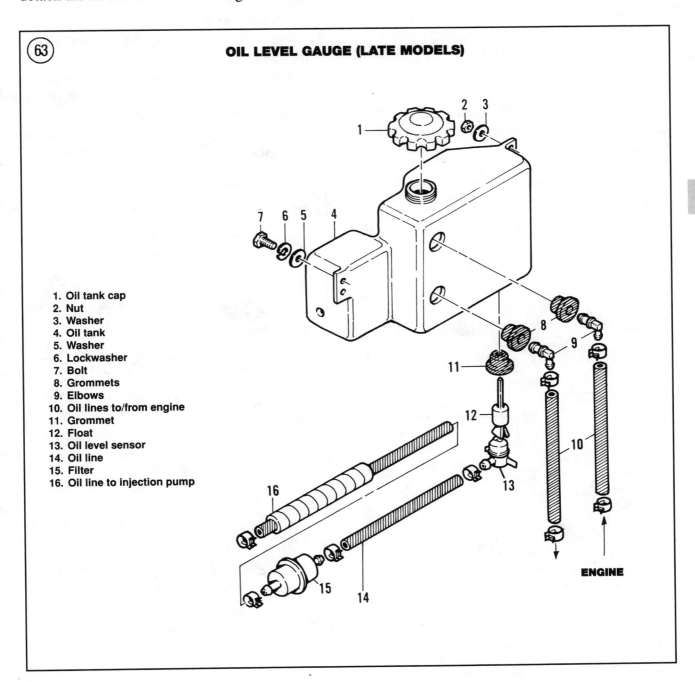

63

OIL LEVEL GAUGE (LATE MODELS)

1. Oil tank cap
2. Nut
3. Washer
4. Oil tank
5. Washer
6. Lockwasher
7. Bolt
8. Grommets
9. Elbows
10. Oil lines to/from engine
11. Grommet
12. Float
13. Oil level sensor
14. Oil line
15. Filter
16. Oil line to injection pump

ENGINE

9

NOTE
The screw B, Figure 65 is coated with Loctite. It may be necessary to heat the screw to soften the threadlock before the screw can be removed.

WARNING
Do not use an open flame to heat the screw removed in Step 12. Fuel vapors and fuel/oil residue will be in this area and will present a fire hazard that will almost certainly be ignited by an open flame. The manufacturer suggests heating the screw with a heat gun.

12. Remove the screw B, **Figure 65** that attaches the starter support bracket to the bottom of the engine.

13. Complete removal of the screw (B, **Figure 64**) loosened in Step 4. It is necessary to move the starter while removing screw.

14. Move the starter away from the engine and into the location previously occupied by the air silencer and carburetors.

15. Disconnect the red/green wire from the starter solenoid.

16. Lift the starter and solenoid out.

17. Reinstall by reversing the removal procedure, observing the following.

   a. Connect the red positive cable and the red/green cable to the starter before attaching the black ground cable.

   b. Install the wire protector cover and secure it with a tie wrap as shown in **Figure 66**.

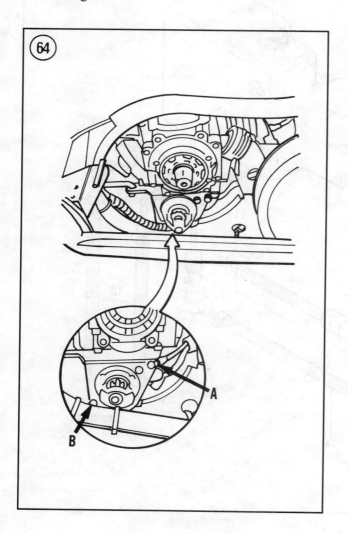

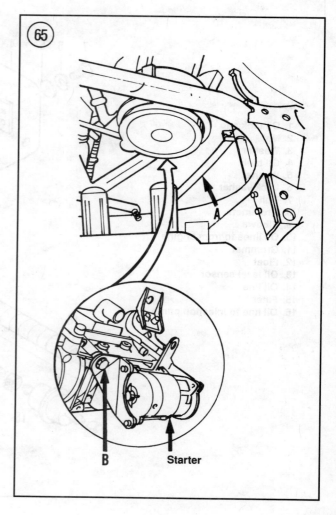

c. Coat the threads of the screw B, **Figure 65** with Loctite 271 before tightening.

d. Tighten the self-locking nut at the end of the steering tie rod to 53 N·m (39 ft.-lbs.).

Disassembly/Reassembly

Refer to **Figure 67** for this procedure.

1. Detach the bare wire between the starter and solenoid.

2. Remove the nuts attaching the starter solenoid to the starter.

3. Separate the solenoid from the starter by lifting the solenoid plunger out of the lever. The solenoid is only available as an assembly, so it should not be disassembled further.

4. Remove the bracket and long through bolts from starter, then separate the starter frame from the drive (nose) housing.

CAUTION
Be careful not to lose thrust washers, springs or other small parts when disassembling. Some parts may be propelled by spring pressure as parts are separated.

5. Separate the end cap and armature from the starter frame.

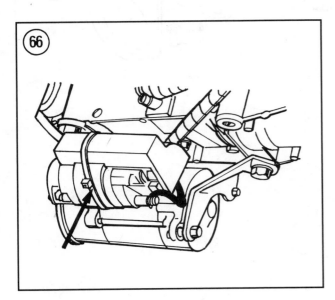

6. Separate the retainer halves (18, **Figure 67**) by inserting a screwdriver in the crack between them, then twisting the screwdriver.

7. Remove the clip (19, **Figure 67**), retainer half, drive pinion and clutch.

8. Clean and inspect all parts. Refer to **Table 3**.

9. Press new bushings in until flush with housings.

10. If new brushes are installed, observe the following:

a. Cut the wires off the old brushes close to the welded attachment.

CAUTION
Use care that solder does not fill the braided wire to the brushes. The braided wire must be flexible and once solder wicks into the braid, it cannot be removed. A heat sink (or needlenose pliers) can be clamped on the braided wire next to the crimped end to stop solder from flowing into the braided wire. Also, be careful not to damage any of the plastic pieces when soldering.

b. Crimp the plate over the connector and solder the crimped section carefully.

11. Before assembling, coat all bushing surfaces, thrust surfaces and sliding (splined) parts with G.E. Versilube G321.

12. Install the clutch and pinion on the armature shaft.

13. Slide the inner retainer half on the armature shaft and install the retaining clip.

14. Slide the outer retainer half on the armature shaft, then use 2 pliers to squeeze the retainer halves together over the retaining clip.

15. Install the outer thrust washer over the end of the armature shaft and lever fork into the shift collar.

16. Insert the armature, pinion, clutch and lever into the starter (nose) frame.

17. Slide the motor housing over the armature. The notched sections of the starter (nose) frame and the motor housing must fit together.

9

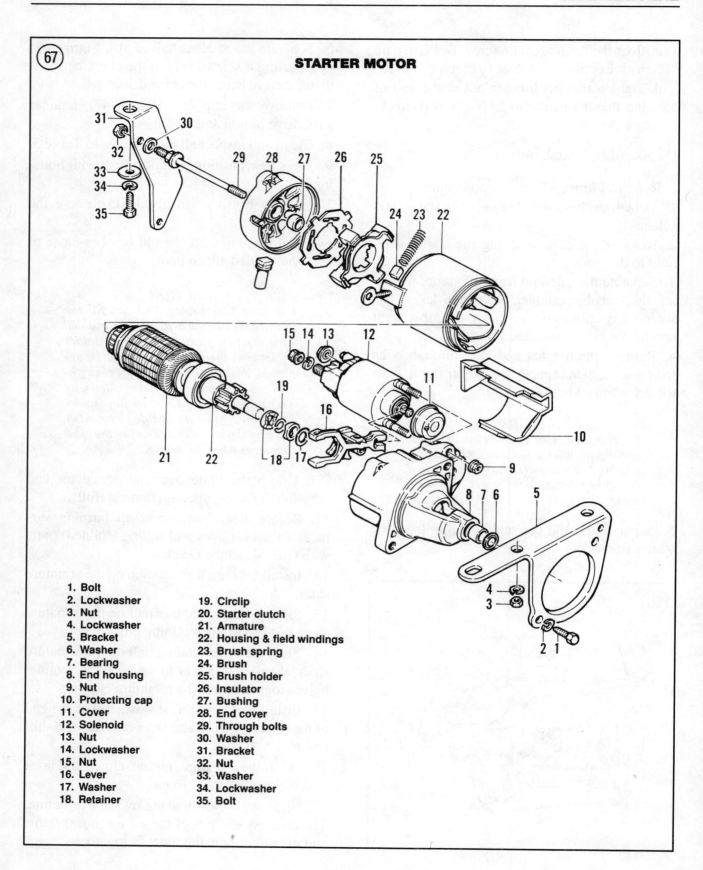

STARTER MOTOR

1. Bolt
2. Lockwasher
3. Nut
4. Lockwasher
5. Bracket
6. Washer
7. Bearing
8. End housing
9. Nut
10. Protecting cap
11. Cover
12. Solenoid
13. Nut
14. Lockwasher
15. Nut
16. Lever
17. Washer
18. Retainer
19. Circlip
20. Starter clutch
21. Armature
22. Housing & field windings
23. Brush spring
24. Brush
25. Brush holder
26. Insulator
27. Bushing
28. End cover
29. Through bolts
30. Washer
31. Bracket
32. Nut
33. Washer
34. Lockwasher
35. Bolt

18. Install the brush holder, then insert the brushes into position in the holder.

19. Compress the brush springs and insert them between the brushes and the closed end of the brush holder.

20. Position the insulator over the brushes and brush holder.

21. Install the end cap, making sure that the notched section of the motor housing and end cap fit together.

22. Install the 2 through bolts. Tighten through bolts after making sure that the end cap, motor housing and starter (nose) frame are properly aligned.

23. Install the solenoid, engaging the solenoid plunger with the engagement lever. The bare wire from the starter should be connected to the shorter stud on the solenoid.

24. Bench check the starter and solenoid. Make sure that the starter and solenoid operate properly before installing.

WIRING DIAGRAMS

Wiring diagrams are located at the end of this book.

9

Table 1 FLYWHEEL NUT TIGHTENING TORQUE

Engine models	N·m	ft.-lbs.
1990		
467, 536, 583	105	77
1991		
467	105	77
643	125	92
1992		
467, 582	105	77
583, 643, 670	125	92
1993		
467, 467(Z), 582	105	77
583, 670	125	92
1994		
467, 467 HAC	105	77
582, 583	105	77
670	125	92
1995		
454, 583 HAC	125	92
467, 582, 583	105	77
670, 670 HAC	125	92

Table 2 REPLACEMENT BULBS

	Wattage
Headlight	
1990 MX (std.)	60/60
1990 MX (opt.)	60/55 Halogen
All other models	60/55 Halogen
Taillight	
1990	8.3/26.9
1991	5/21
1992	NA
1993-1995	8/27
Instrument bulbs	
Tachometer & speedometer	
1991, 1992	5
1993 (except MX Z)	5
1993 Formula MX Z	2 × 3
1994 Grand Touring & MACH 1	5/5
1994 (except GT & MACH 1)	6/6
1995	2 × 3
Fuel & temp. gauge	
1990-1993	2
1994 MX, Summit	2
1994 Formula Z	3/3
1994 Grand Touring	2/2
1994 MACH 1	2/2
1995 (models so equipped)	3/3
Pilot lights	
EFI monitor	special
Heated grip	special
Heated thumb	special
High beam	special
Oil	special
Temperature	special

Table 3 STARTER SPECIFICATIONS

	mm	in.
Starter shaft		
Clearance in bushings	0.20	0.008
Brush spring length		
New	10	0.4
Minimum limit	6	0.236
Commutator minimum diameter	27	1.063

Chapter Ten

Oil Injection System

The most desirable fuel/oil ratio for snowmobile engines depends upon engine speed and load. Without oil injection, oil must be hand-mixed with gasoline. Since the mixture of gasoline and oil does not change, oil must be mixed at the highest ratio necessary to ensure sufficient lubrication at high engine speeds and load conditions. This ratio contains more oil than required to lubricate the engine properly at idle

speeds without load. The result is that the spark plug is sometimes oil fouled from too much oil.

With oil injection, the amount of oil is changed to provide the optimum amount to lubricate the engine while it is running at varying speeds and load conditions.

All models covered in this manual are equipped with an oil injection system. The system consists of an external oil tank (reservoir), oil injection hoses, control cable and a mechanical gear-driven pump with variable control. The oil pump control cable is attached to the control lever on the pump. The oil pump control cable is joined to the throttle control cable so they operate simultaneously.

This chapter covers complete oil injection system service.

SYSTEM COMPONENTS

The oil injection pump (**Figure 1**, typical) is mounted on the rotary valve cover. The oil pump gear is mounted to the oil pump. The pump gear engages the rotary valve shaft gear. The oil pump is connected to the throttle by a cable. An oil reservoir tank is mounted in the engine compartment (**Figure 2**, typical). Oil injection hoses connect the oil tank to the pump and connect the pump to the engine. A warning light on the dash indicates when oil in the reservoir becomes low.

OIL PUMP SERVICE

Oil Pump Bleeding

The oil lines and pump should always be filled with oil. Bleed air from the pump during pre-delivery service and whenever:

   a. The oil tank was allowed to become empty.

   b. Any oil injection hose was disconnected.

   c. The machine was on its side.

1. Make sure the oil tank is full. See Chapter Three.

2. Make sure all hoses are connected to the oil pump, engine and the oil reservoir tank.

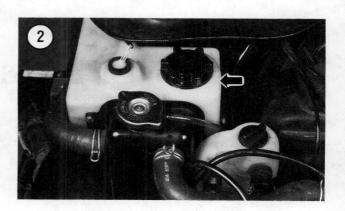

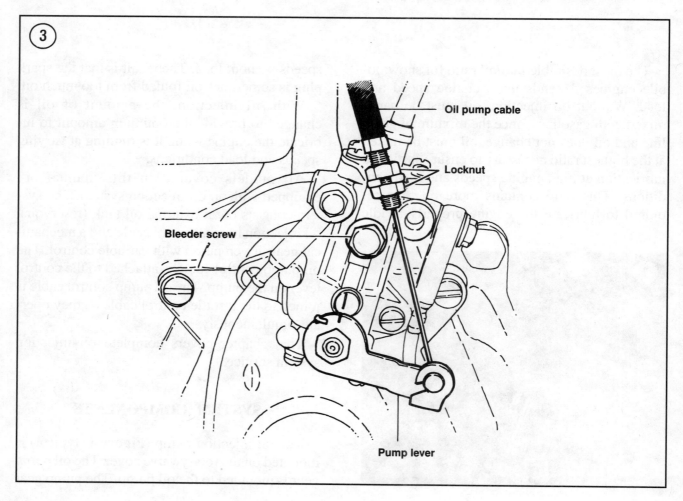

Oil pump cable

Locknut

Bleeder screw

Pump lever

3. *Main oil line*: To bleed the main oil line (line between the oil tank and pump):

   a. Loosen the bleeder screw (**Figure 3**) or the clamp on the upper hose attached to the side of the oil tank.

   b. Allow oil to bleed from the bleeder screw or the loosened hose until there are no air bubbles in any of the oil lines.

   c. Tighten the bleeder screw or hose clamp.

WARNING
***Never** lean into the snowmobile's engine compartment while wearing a scarf or other loose clothing when the engine is running or when attempting to start the engine. If the scarf or clothing should catch in the drive belt or clutch, severe injury or death could occur. Make sure the belt guard is in place.*

4. *Small oil lines*: To bleed the small oil lines (lines between oil pump and intake manifold) (A, **Figure 4**), start the engine and allow it to idle. Then hold the pump lever (B, **Figure 4**) in the fully-open position. When there are no air bubbles in the hoses, release the pump lever and turn the engine off.

NOTE
*****Figure 4** shows the carburetors and engine removed for clarity.*

COMPONENT REPLACEMENT

Oil Reservoir Tank Removal/Installation

Refer to **Figure 5** for early models or **Figure 6** for later models.

1. Open the hood.
2. Label the hoses at the tank before removal.

NOTE
Prevent oil in the tank from leaking during removal. If access to a hose is difficult, purchase hose with the same ID, block one end with a bolt and use this hose to plug the tank outlet port as the original hose is detached.

3. Remove the oil level gauge from the oil tank (**Figure 2**).
4. Remove the bolts holding the oil tank to the frame.
5. Lift the oil tank up slightly and disconnect the hoses from the tank. Plug the outlet ports to prevent oil leakage.
6. Installation is the reverse of these steps.
7. Bleed the oil pump as described in this chapter.

Oil Level Gauge

Refer to Chapter Nine.

Oil Hoses

New oil hoses should be installed if the old hoses become hard and brittle. When replacing damaged or worn oil hoses, be sure to install transparent hoses with the correct diameter. Non-transparent hoses will not allow you to visually inspect the hoses for air pockets or other blockage that could cause engine seizure. When reconnecting hoses, secure each hose end with a clamp.

10

OIL PUMP

Removal/Disassembly

This procedure describes procedures to remove the oil pump and gear assembly. Refer to **Figure 7** when performing this procedure.

1. If the engine is installed in the snowmobile, observe the following:

a. Remove the carburetors as described in Chapter Six or the fuel injection unit as described in Chapter Seven.

b. Disconnect the oil pump cable from the oil pump.

c. Disconnect the main oil hose from the oil pump.

2. Remove the screws holding the 2 rotary valve cover halves together and separate the covers.

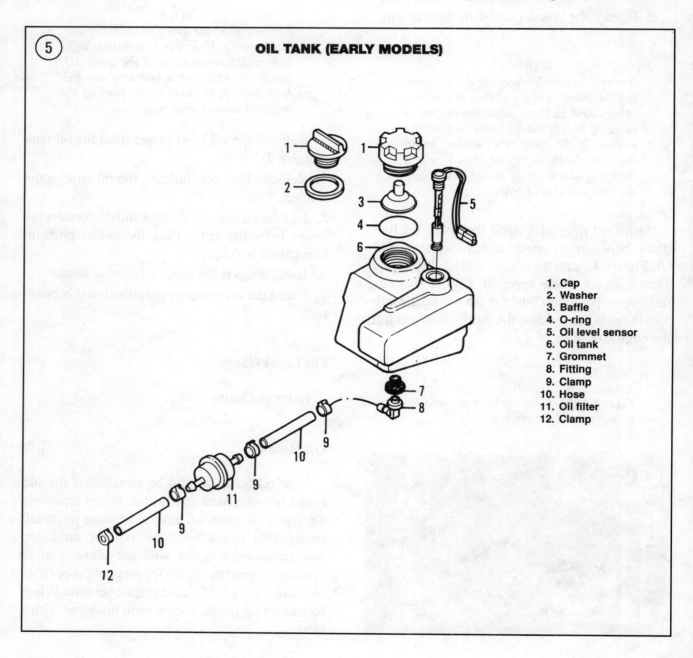

OIL TANK (EARLY MODELS)

1. Cap
2. Washer
3. Baffle
4. O-ring
5. Oil level sensor
6. Oil tank
7. Grommet
8. Fitting
9. Clamp
10. Hose
11. Oil filter
12. Clamp

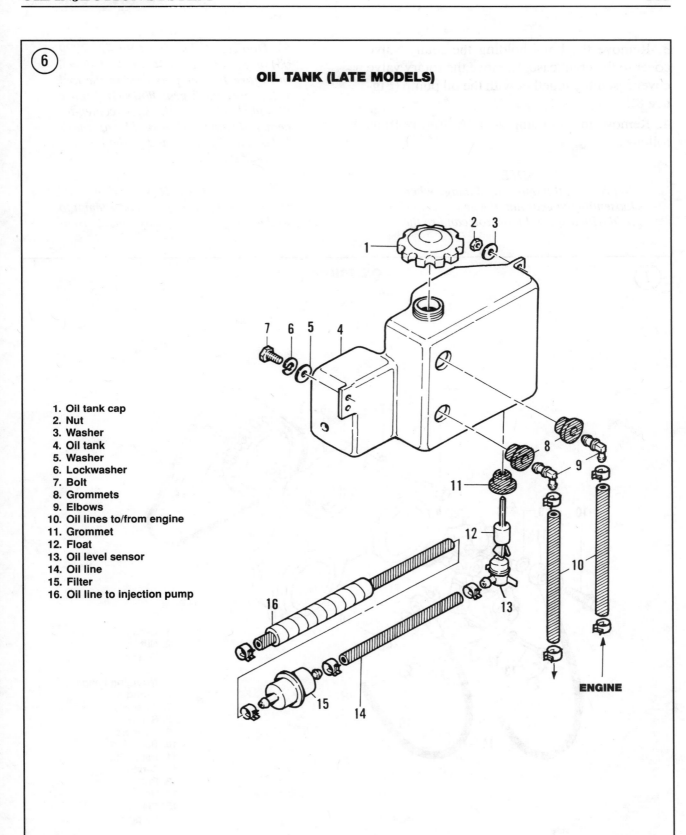

OIL TANK (LATE MODELS)

1. Oil tank cap
2. Nut
3. Washer
4. Oil tank
5. Washer
6. Lockwasher
7. Bolt
8. Grommets
9. Elbows
10. Oil lines to/from engine
11. Grommet
12. Float
13. Oil level sensor
14. Oil line
15. Filter
16. Oil line to injection pump

ENGINE

10

3. Remove the bolts holding the rotary valve cover to the crankcase. Remove the rotary valve cover assembly together with the oil pump (**Figure 8**).

4. Remove the oil pump gear (A, **Figure 9**) as follows:

NOTE
To prevent oil pump gear damage when loosening the gear nut, the gear must be held with a special tool. You can use the

*Ski-Doo gear holder (part No. 420 2779 05) or you can fabricate the tool shown in **Figure 10**. The pins used in the tool will fit into the 2 gear holes (B, **Figure 9**) and should have the same center-to-center distance (**Figure 11**) as the 2 holes. The 2 pins should fit the holes in the gear snugly.*

CAUTION
Do not use a pair of pliers or attempt to wedge the gear in any way when loosen-

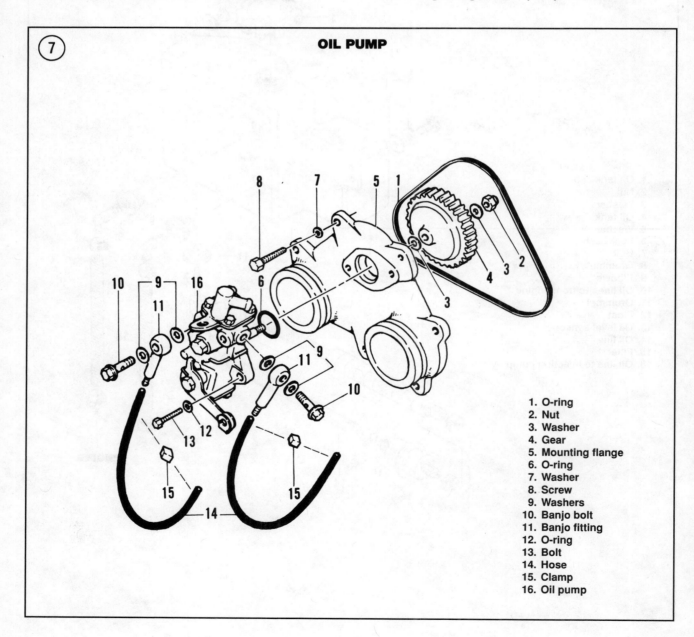

⑦ OIL PUMP

1. O-ring
2. Nut
3. Washer
4. Gear
5. Mounting flange
6. O-ring
7. Washer
8. Screw
9. Washers
10. Banjo bolt
11. Banjo fitting
12. O-ring
13. Bolt
14. Hose
15. Clamp
16. Oil pump

8

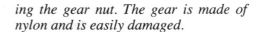

ing the gear nut. The gear is made of nylon and is easily damaged.

a. Hold the oil pump gear with the special tool and remove the gear nut (C, **Figure 9**).

b. Remove the washer (**Figure 12**).

c. Remove the gear (**Figure 13**).

d. Remove the washer (**Figure 14**).

5. Remove the screws (**Figure 15**) holding the oil pump to the outer cover and remove the oil pump.

9

12

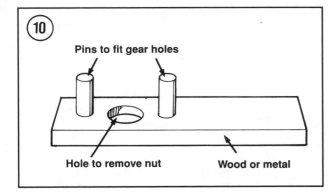

10

Pins to fit gear holes

Hole to remove nut   Wood or metal

13

11

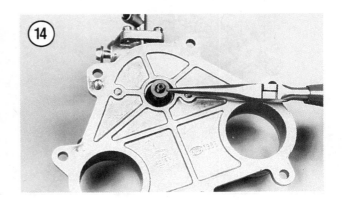

14

10

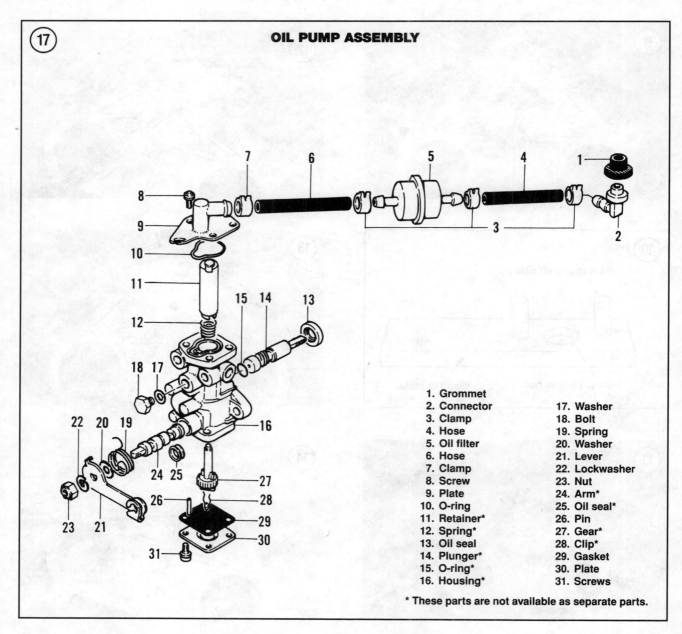

OIL PUMP ASSEMBLY

1. Grommet
2. Connector
3. Clamp
4. Hose
5. Oil filter
6. Hose
7. Clamp
8. Screw
9. Plate
10. O-ring
11. Retainer*
12. Spring*
13. Oil seal
14. Plunger*
15. O-ring*
16. Housing*
17. Washer
18. Bolt
19. Spring
20. Washer
21. Lever
22. Lockwasher
23. Nut
24. Arm*
25. Oil seal*
26. Pin
27. Gear*
28. Clip*
29. Gasket
30. Plate
31. Screws

* These parts are not available as separate parts.

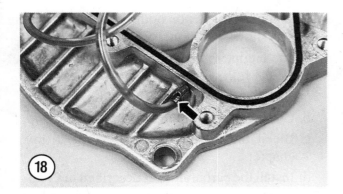

(18)

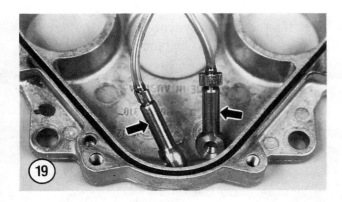

(19)

(20)

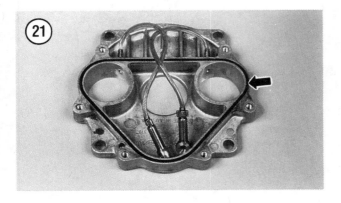

(21)

NOTE
*Do not lose or damage the pin (**Figure 16**). Some prefer to remove the pin so that it will not accidentally fall out.*

Inspection

1. It is generally not recommended to disassemble the oil pump. Many individual parts of the pump are not available. See **Figure 17**. If a non-replaceable part is damaged, the entire oil pump assembly must be replaced.

2. Check the oil hose fittings (**Figure 18**) for tightness.

3. Inspect the fittings (**Figure 19**) for contamination or damage. The fittings contain check valves which should permit oil to flow out, but not drain back.

4. Check the oil pump oil seal (**Figure 20**) for cuts or other damage. Replace the oil seal if it appears damaged or if there are signs of oil leakage.

5. Replace the cover O-ring (**Figure 21**) if it is crushed, cut or otherwise damaged.

6. Check the oil pump gear for cracks, excessive wear or other damage.

7. Inspect machined surfaces for burrs, cracks or other damage. Repair minor damage with a fine-cut file or oilstone.

8. Clean the banjo bolts (**Figure 22**) with solvent and dry thoroughly before reassembly.

9. Move the oil pump arm (**Figure 23**) and check for excessive tightness or other damage. Replace the oil pump if necessary.

NOTE
*Test oil pump operation by attaching a drill to the pump drive. The drill must rotate **counterclockwise** and the pump must always be supplied with oil. Do not rotate the pump dry. Oil should be pumped from both outlet fittings when the control lever is held in the maximum delivery position against spring pressure.*

10

Assembly/Installation

1. Install the oil pump and secure it with its mounting screws (**Figure 15**).
2. Install the oil pump gear as follows:
   a. Install the washer (**Figure 14**).
   b. Install the gear (**Figure 13**).
   c. Install the washer (**Figure 12**).
   d. Install and tighten the nut (C, **Figure 9**). Use the same tool used during disassembly to hold the gear when tightening the nut.
3. Install the O-ring and assemble the rotary valve cover halves and oil pump (**Figure 24**). Make sure to install the dowel pin (**Figure 16**). Install the cover screws and tighten securely.
4. If the rotary valve was removed, install and time it as described in Chapter Five.
5. Install the rotary valve cover (**Figure 14**). Install and tighten the cover screws securely.
6. Route the oil injection lines as shown in **Figure 25**. When installing the banjo bolts, make sure to place a washer on both sides of the banjo fitting as shown (9, **Figure 7**).
7. If the engine is installed in the snowmobile, observe the following:
   a. Connect the main oil hose to the oil pump.
   b. Connect the oil pump cable to the oil pump.
   c. Bleed the oil pump as described in this chapter.
   d. Install the carburetors as described in Chapter Six or the fuel injection unit as described in Chapter Seven.
   e. If so equipped, synchronize the carburetors as described in Chapter Three.
   f. Adjust the oil pump as described in Chapter Three.

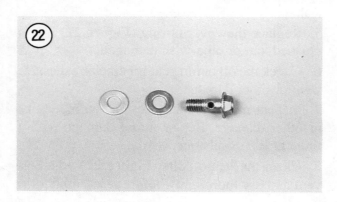

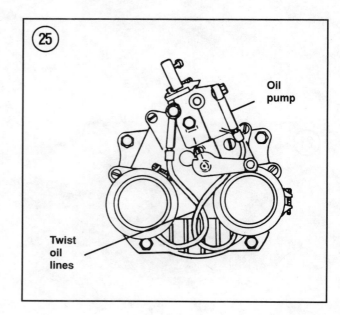

Chapter Eleven

Liquid Cooling System

The liquid cooling system is a closed system that consists of a pressure (radiator) cap, water pump, coolant reservoir tank, heat exchanger and hoses. See **Figures 1-7**. During operation the coolant heats up and expands, thus pressurizing the system.

Cooling system flushing procedures are provided in Chapter Three.

Table 1, located at the end of this chapter, lists cooling system specifications.

> *WARNING*
> *Do not remove the pressure (radiator) cap (**Figure 8**) when the engine is hot. The coolant is very hot and is under pressure. Severe scalding will result if the coolant comes in contact with your skin. The cooling system must be cooled prior to removing any component of the system.*

THERMOSTAT

Two different types of cooling systems are used.

The cooling system used on 454, 536, 582, 583 and 670 engines has 2 coolant outlets attached to the cylinder head (**Figure 9**). One outlet directs the coolant to the heat exchangers and the other outlet directs fluid to the coolant tank that has a pressure (radiator) cap. The thermostat for these models is located under the lower outlet fitting (**Figure 10**) that leads to the heat exchangers. When the engine is cool, the thermostat (**Figure 11**) stops the flow of coolant to the heat exchanger, but allows coolant to flow from the other fitting and circulate within the system. As the engine warms, the thermostat opens the passage to the heat exchangers and, at the same time, closes the other passage.

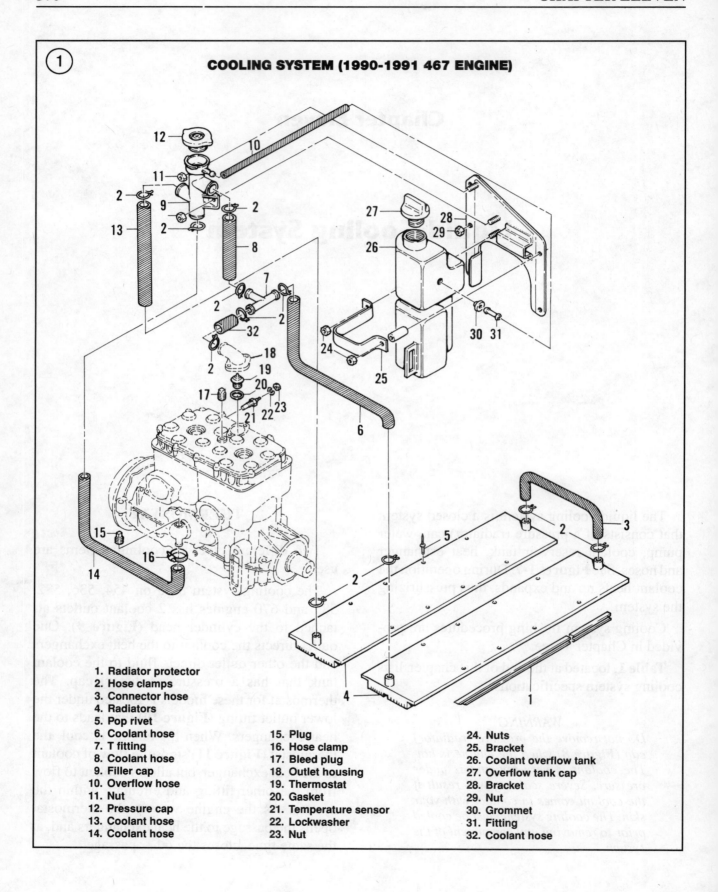

① **COOLING SYSTEM (1990-1991 467 ENGINE)**

1. Radiator protector
2. Hose clamps
3. Connector hose
4. Radiators
5. Pop rivet
6. Coolant hose
7. T fitting
8. Coolant hose
9. Filler cap
10. Overflow hose
11. Nut
12. Pressure cap
13. Coolant hose
14. Coolant hose
15. Plug
16. Hose clamp
17. Bleed plug
18. Outlet housing
19. Thermostat
20. Gasket
21. Temperature sensor
22. Lockwasher
23. Nut
24. Nuts
25. Bracket
26. Coolant overflow tank
27. Overflow tank cap
28. Bracket
29. Nut
30. Grommet
31. Fitting
32. Coolant hose

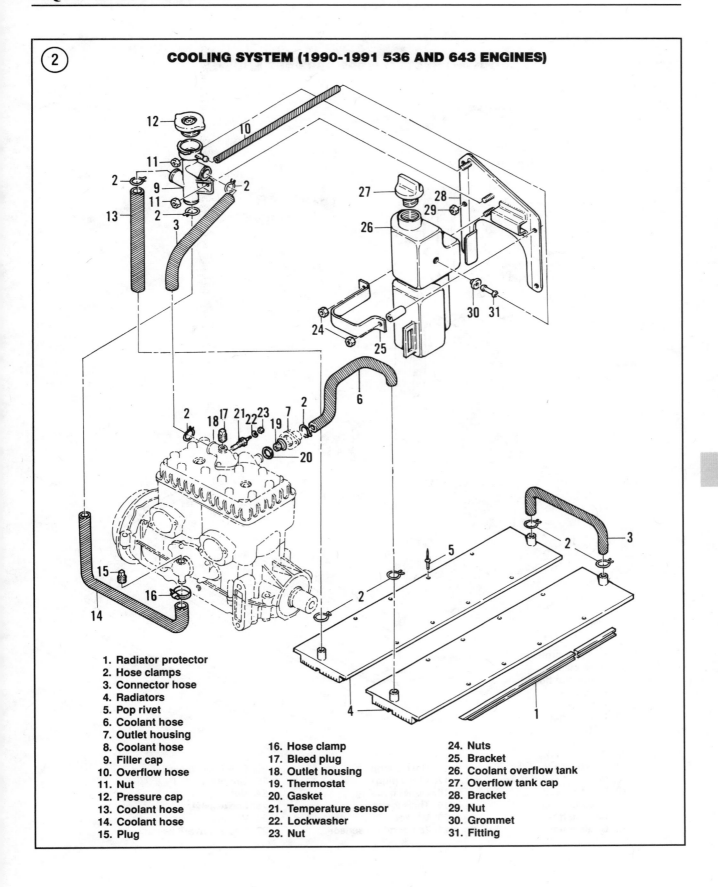

COOLING SYSTEM (1990-1991 536 AND 643 ENGINES)

1. Radiator protector
2. Hose clamps
3. Connector hose
4. Radiators
5. Pop rivet
6. Coolant hose
7. Outlet housing
8. Coolant hose
9. Filler cap
10. Overflow hose
11. Nut
12. Pressure cap
13. Coolant hose
14. Coolant hose
15. Plug

16. Hose clamp
17. Bleed plug
18. Outlet housing
19. Thermostat
20. Gasket
21. Temperature sensor
22. Lockwasher
23. Nut

24. Nuts
25. Bracket
26. Coolant overflow tank
27. Overflow tank cap
28. Bracket
29. Nut
30. Grommet
31. Fitting

11

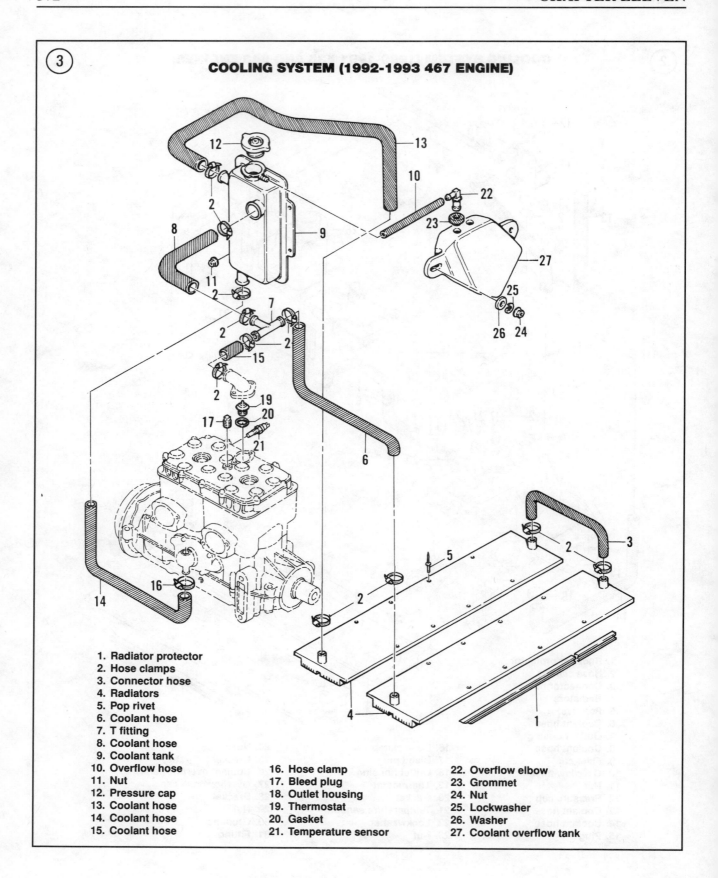

(3) **COOLING SYSTEM (1992-1993 467 ENGINE)**

1. Radiator protector
2. Hose clamps
3. Connector hose
4. Radiators
5. Pop rivet
6. Coolant hose
7. T fitting
8. Coolant hose
9. Coolant tank
10. Overflow hose
11. Nut
12. Pressure cap
13. Coolant hose
14. Coolant hose
15. Coolant hose
16. Hose clamp
17. Bleed plug
18. Outlet housing
19. Thermostat
20. Gasket
21. Temperature sensor
22. Overflow elbow
23. Grommet
24. Nut
25. Lockwasher
26. Washer
27. Coolant overflow tank

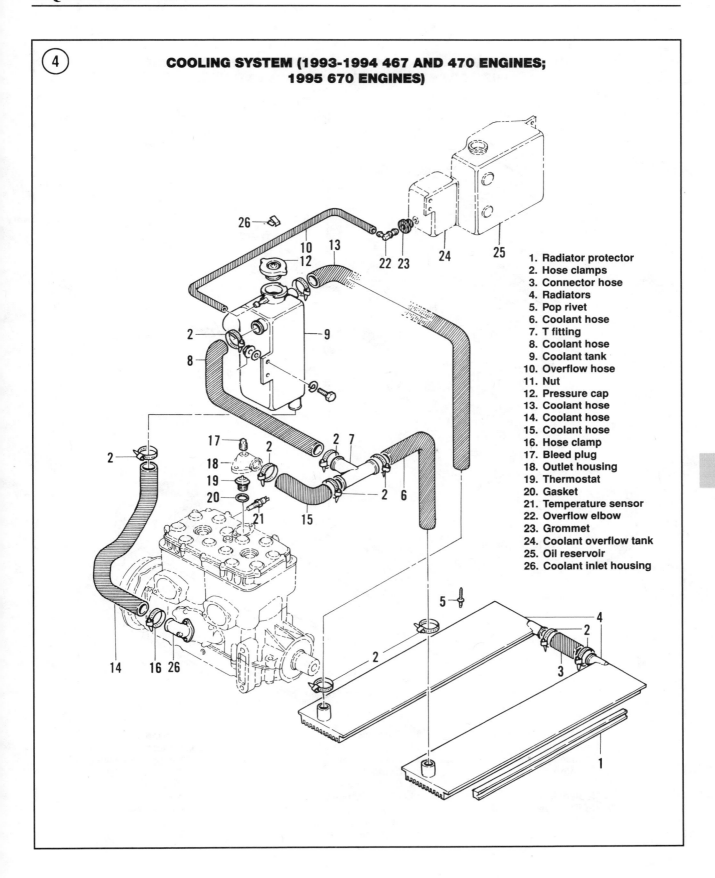

COOLING SYSTEM (1993-1994 467 AND 470 ENGINES; 1995 670 ENGINES)

1. Radiator protector
2. Hose clamps
3. Connector hose
4. Radiators
5. Pop rivet
6. Coolant hose
7. T fitting
8. Coolant hose
9. Coolant tank
10. Overflow hose
11. Nut
12. Pressure cap
13. Coolant hose
14. Coolant hose
15. Coolant hose
16. Hose clamp
17. Bleed plug
18. Outlet housing
19. Thermostat
20. Gasket
21. Temperature sensor
22. Overflow elbow
23. Grommet
24. Coolant overflow tank
25. Oil reservoir
26. Coolant inlet housing

11

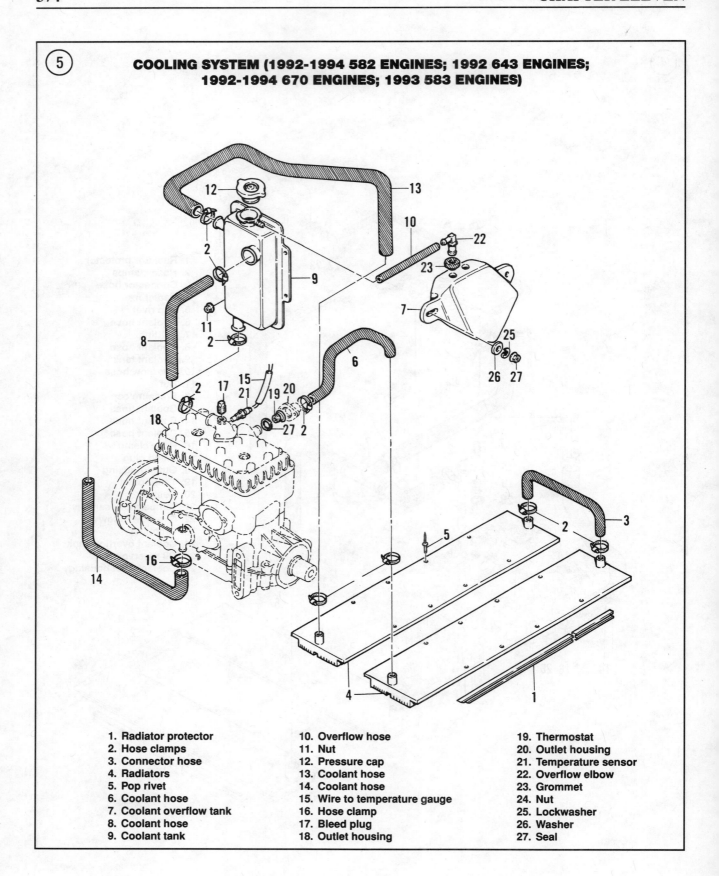

COOLING SYSTEM (1992-1994 582 ENGINES; 1992 643 ENGINES; 1992-1994 670 ENGINES; 1993 583 ENGINES)

1. Radiator protector
2. Hose clamps
3. Connector hose
4. Radiators
5. Pop rivet
6. Coolant hose
7. Coolant overflow tank
8. Coolant hose
9. Coolant tank
10. Overflow hose
11. Nut
12. Pressure cap
13. Coolant hose
14. Coolant hose
15. Wire to temperature gauge
16. Hose clamp
17. Bleed plug
18. Outlet housing
19. Thermostat
20. Outlet housing
21. Temperature sensor
22. Overflow elbow
23. Grommet
24. Nut
25. Lockwasher
26. Washer
27. Seal

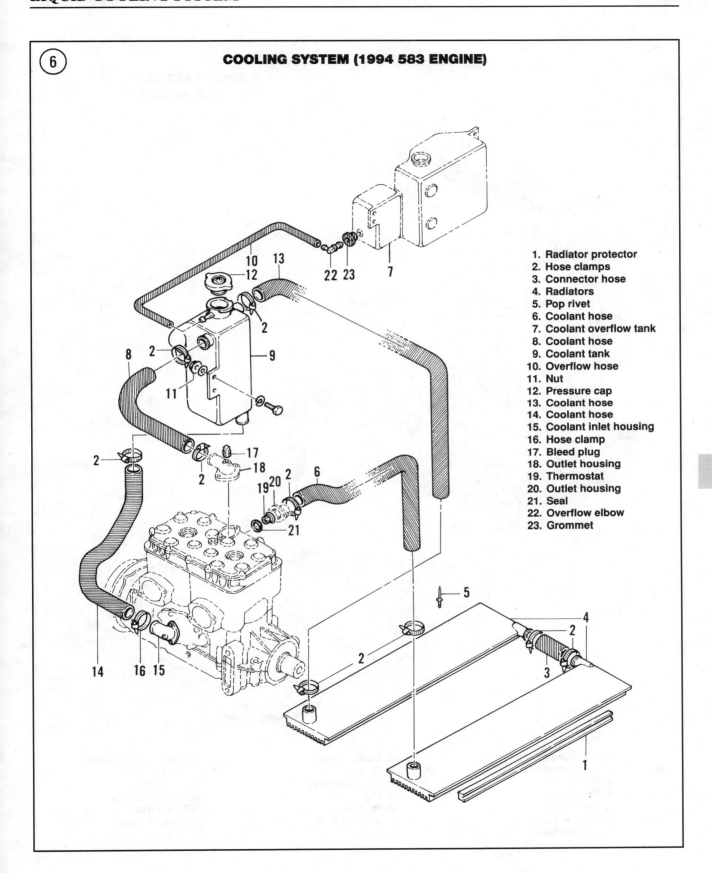

COOLING SYSTEM (1994 583 ENGINE)

1. Radiator protector
2. Hose clamps
3. Connector hose
4. Radiators
5. Pop rivet
6. Coolant hose
7. Coolant overflow tank
8. Coolant hose
9. Coolant tank
10. Overflow hose
11. Nut
12. Pressure cap
13. Coolant hose
14. Coolant hose
15. Coolant inlet housing
16. Hose clamp
17. Bleed plug
18. Outlet housing
19. Thermostat
20. Outlet housing
21. Seal
22. Overflow elbow
23. Grommet

11

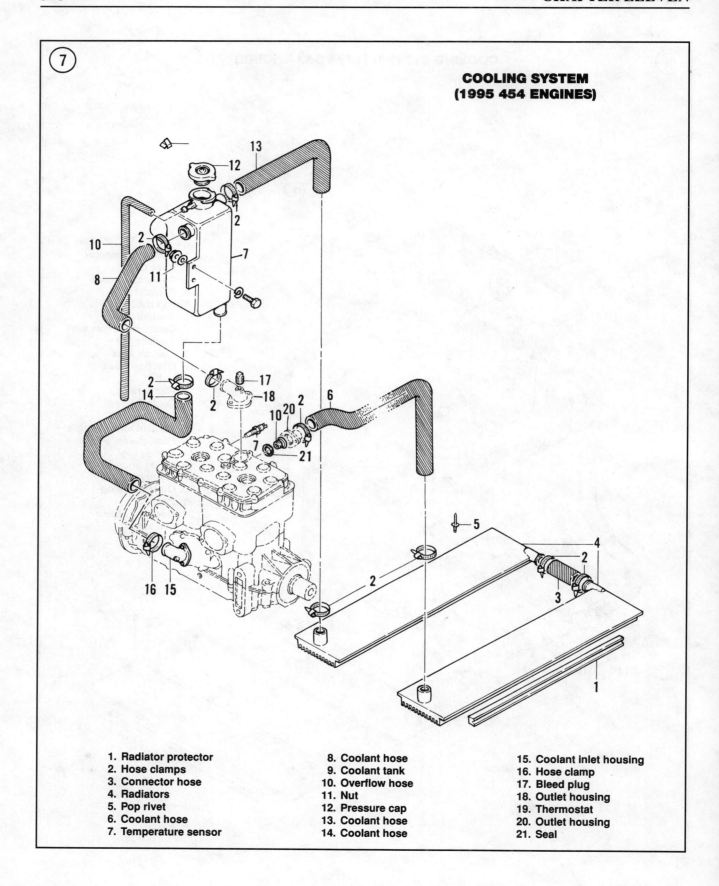

⑦

**COOLING SYSTEM
(1995 454 ENGINES)**

1. Radiator protector
2. Hose clamps
3. Connector hose
4. Radiators
5. Pop rivet
6. Coolant hose
7. Temperature sensor
8. Coolant hose
9. Coolant tank
10. Overflow hose
11. Nut
12. Pressure cap
13. Coolant hose
14. Coolant hose
15. Coolant inlet housing
16. Hose clamp
17. Bleed plug
18. Outlet housing
19. Thermostat
20. Outlet housing
21. Seal

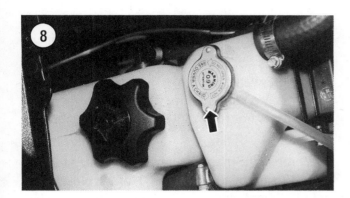

The cooling system used on 467, 470 and 643 engines (**Figure 12**) is equipped with a thermostat (**Figure 13**) that reduces coolant flow from the engine when cold. As the engine warms up, the thermostat gradually opens, allowing coolant to circulate through the system, including the heat exchangers. This system can be identified by having only 1 coolant outlet on the cylinder head.

CAUTION
Do not operate the engine without a thermostat. Removal of the thermostat may cause overcooling or in some cases may cause loss of coolant and overheating. The engine may be seriously damaged if it is operated either too hot or too cool. Also, be sure that the correct thermostat is installed.

11

Removal

1. Open the hood.

> *WARNING*
> *Make sure the engine is cool before pro-*
> *ceeding with Step 2. Severe scalding will*
> *result if hot coolant comes in contact*
> *with your skin.*

2. Drain the cooling system as described in Chapter Three.

3. Locate the outlet fitting(s) attached to the cylinder head. Engine models 467, 470 and 643 have only 1 coolant outlet fitting (**Figure 12**) attached to the cylinder head. Engine models 454, 536, 582, 583 and 670 have 2 fittings (**Figure 9**) attached to the cylinder head, but the thermostat is located under the lower fitting.

4. Loosen the hose clamp and disconnect the hose from the outlet fitting (**Figure 10**). Prop the hose up to prevent coolant loss.

5. Unbolt the outlet fitting and carefully separate the fitting from the cylinder head. Refer to **Figure 11** or **Figure 13**.

6. Remove the thermostat. See **Figures 1-7**.

Testing

Test the thermostat to ensure proper operation. Replace the thermostat if it remains open at normal room temperature or stays closed after the specified temperature has been reached during the test procedure.

1. Pour some water into a container that can be heated. Submerge the thermostat in the water and suspend a thermometer as shown in **Figure 14**. Use a thermometer that is rated higher than the test temperature (**Table 1**).

> *NOTE*
> *Suspend the thermostat with wire so it*
> *does not touch the sides or bottom of the*
> *pan.*

2. Heat the water until the thermostat starts to open. Check the water temperature on the ther-

mometer. It should be approximately 107° F (42° C). If the thermostat valve did not start to open at the temperature, replace it.

3. Let the water cool to 10° *under* the thermostat's rated opening temperature. If the thermostat valve is not fully closed at this temperature, replace it.

4. Remove the thermostat from the water and let it cool to room temperature. Hold it close to a light bulb and check for leakage. If light can be seen at more than 1 or 2 tiny points around the

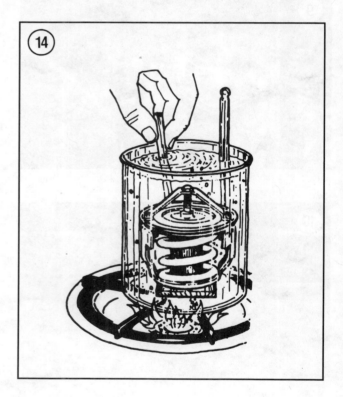

edge of the valve, the thermostat is defective and should be replaced.

Installation

Refer to **Figures 1-7**.

1. If a new thermostat is being installed, test it as described in this chapter.

2. Place the thermostat into the cylinder head as shown in **Figures 1-7** and install the outlet fittings.

3. Install the hoses and secure with the hose clamps.

4. Refill the cooling system as described in Chapter Three.

WATER PUMP

The water pump impeller is mounted on the rotary valve shaft under the cover (**Figure 15**) located on front of the crankcase. Refer to Chapter Five for service procedures.

HEAT EXCHANGER

Removal/Installation

Refer to **Figures 1-7**.

1. Drain the cooling system as described in Chapter Three.

2. Remove the engine as described in Chapter Five.

3. Remove the rear suspension, track and front axle as described in Chapter Sixteen.

4. Loosen the hose clamps and remove the 2 hoses from inside the engine compartment.

5. Remove the seat.

6. Loosen the hose clamps and remove the 2 hoses from the top of the tunnel.

7. Turn the machine on its side.

8. Remove the bolts holding the front of the heat exchanger to the frame.

9. Drill out the rivets holding the side and rear of the heat exchanger to the frame. Remove the heat exchanger assembly.

10. Inspect the hoses as described under *Hoses* in this chapter.

11. Installation is the reverse of these steps. Observe the following:

    a. Use new rivets when installing the side and rear of the heat exchanger.

    b. Replace worn or damaged water hoses.

    c. Replace fatigued or damaged hose clamps.

    d. Refill the cooling system as described in Chapter Three.

HOSES

Hoses deteriorate with age and should be replaced periodically or if they show signs of cracking or leakage. To be safe, replace the hoses every 2 years. Loss of coolant will cause the engine to overheat and result in severe damage.

Whenever any component of the cooling system is removed, inspect the hoses(s) and determine if replacement is necessary.

Inspection

1. Check all cooling hoses for flexibility and softness after the engine has cooled. A hose that is brittle or hard must be replaced. Also check hoses for cracks, abrasions, cuts or other conditions that might cause a leak.

2. With the engine hot, examine the hoses for swelling along the entire hose length. Eventually a hose will rupture if softened by oil or heat.

3. Check clamps and the condition of the hose under and around the hose clamps for possible leakage.

Replacement

Hose replacement should be performed when the engine is cool.

11

1. Drain the cooling system as described under *Coolant Change* in Chapter Three.

NOTE
Make sure to note the routing and any clamps that support the hoses.

2. Loosen the hose clamps from the hose to be replaced. Slide the clamps along the hose and out of the way.

3. Twist the hose end to break the seal and remove it from the connecting joint. If the hose has been on for some time, it may have become fused to the joint. If so, cut the hose parallel to the joint connections with a knife or razor. The hose then can be carefully pried loose with a screwdriver.

CAUTION
Excessive force applied to the hose during removal could damage the connecting joint.

4. Examine the connecting joint for cracks or other damage. Repair or replace parts as re-

quired. If the joint is okay, remove rust with sandpaper.

5. Inspect the hose clamps and replace as necessary.

6. Slide the hose clamps over the outside of hose and install the hose to the inlet and outlet connecting joint. Make sure the hose clears all obstructions and is routed properly.

NOTE
If it is difficult to install a hose on a joint, soak the end of the hose in hot water for approximately 2 minutes. This will soften the hose and ease installation.

7. With the hose positioned correctly on the joint, position the clamps back away from the end of the hose slightly. Tighten the clamps securely, but not so much that the hose is damaged.

8. Refill the cooling system as described under *Coolant Change* in Chapter Three. Start the engine and check for leaks. Retighten hose clamps as necessary.

Chapter Twelve

Recoil Starter

All models are equipped with a rope-operated recoil starter. The starter is mounted in a housing that is bolted onto the engine next to the flywheel. Pulling the rope handle turns the starter sheave and moves the drive pawl out. The drive pawl engages the starter pulley attached to the flywheel and continued rotation of the starter sheave turns the engine. When the rope handle is released, the spring inside the assembly rewinds the sheave and wraps the rope around the sheave.

Rewind starters are relatively trouble free; a broken or frayed rope is the most common malfunction. This chapter covers removal and installation of the starter assembly, starter pulley, rope and rewind spring.

Refer to Chapter Nine for service to the electric starter used on some models.

Starter Housing
Removal/Installation

1. Open the hood.
2. Pull the starter handle out (**Figure 1**), untie the knot (**Figure 2**) and remove the handle—don't release the rope yet. After removing the handle, tie a knot in the end of the rope to temporarily stop the rope from retracting into the starter housing. Release the starter rope slowly until it is held by the temporary knot.
3. Remove the screws attaching the starter housing to the engine, then remove the starter housing (**Figure 3**).
4. Installation is the reverse of these steps. Observe the following.
5. Position the starter housing with the rope exit correctly aligned toward the rear (**Figure 3**).

Install the housing retaining screws and tighten securely.

6. Thread the starter rope back through its original path and out the hole in the cowl.

7. Untie the knot at the end of the rope and feed the rope through the handle (**Figure 1**). Tie a knot in the end of the rope as shown in **Figure 4**. Operate the starter assembly to make sure it works properly. Check the path of the rope through the engine compartment to make sure it is not kinked or interfering with any other component.

Starter Pulley
Removal/Installation

The starter pulley (3, **Figure 5**) is attached to the flywheel. The starter pulley can be removed with the engine installed in the snowmobile. This procedure is shown with the engine removed for clarity.

1. Open the hood assembly.

2. Remove the recoil starter assembly as described in this chapter.

3. If the engine is installed in the snowmobile, disconnect the fuel pump pulse hose from the crankcase fitting. Refer to **Figure 6**.

4. Insert the crankshaft locking tool (part No. 420 8766 40) through the pulse hose fitting and engage the tool with the crankshaft (**Figure 6**). After installing the tool, rotate the crankshaft until the tool locks the crankshaft.

Rope knot

Handle

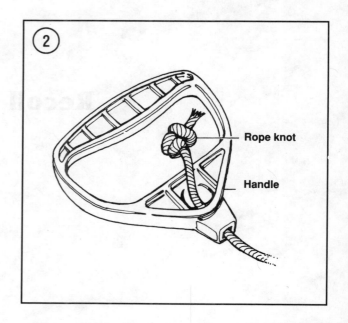

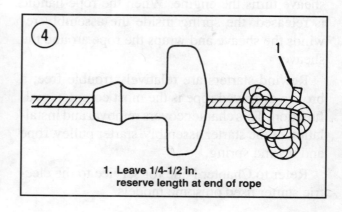

1. Leave 1/4-1/2 in. reserve length at end of rope

5. Remove the screws and lock washers attaching the starter pulley (**Figure 7**) to the flywheel. Remove the starter pulley.

6. Remove the flywheel counterweight (2, **Figure 5**), if so equipped.

7. Installation is the reverse of these steps. Observe the following.

8. Install the flywheel counterweight (if so equipped), aligning the mark on the counterweight with the mark on the flywheel.

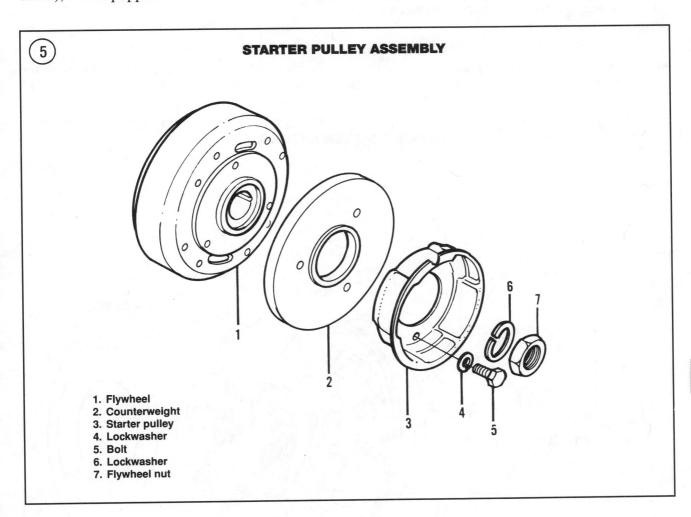

STARTER PULLEY ASSEMBLY

1. Flywheel
2. Counterweight
3. Starter pulley
4. Lockwasher
5. Bolt
6. Lockwasher
7. Flywheel nut

12

9. Install the starter pulley (3, **Figure 5**), lock-washers and screws. Tighten the retaining screws securely.

10. Remove the crankshaft locking tool from the pulse hose fitting (**Figure 6**).

11. Reinstall the recoil starter housing as described in this chapter.

12. If the engine is installed in the snowmobile, attach the pulse hose to the fitting on the crankcase. Secure the hose with the wire clip.

Starter Housing Disassembly

This procedure describes complete disassembly of the recoil starter housing. Refer to **Figure 8** for this procedure.

1. Remove the recoil starter housing as described in this chapter.

2. Hold the starter rope securely and remove the temporary knot tied in the rope.

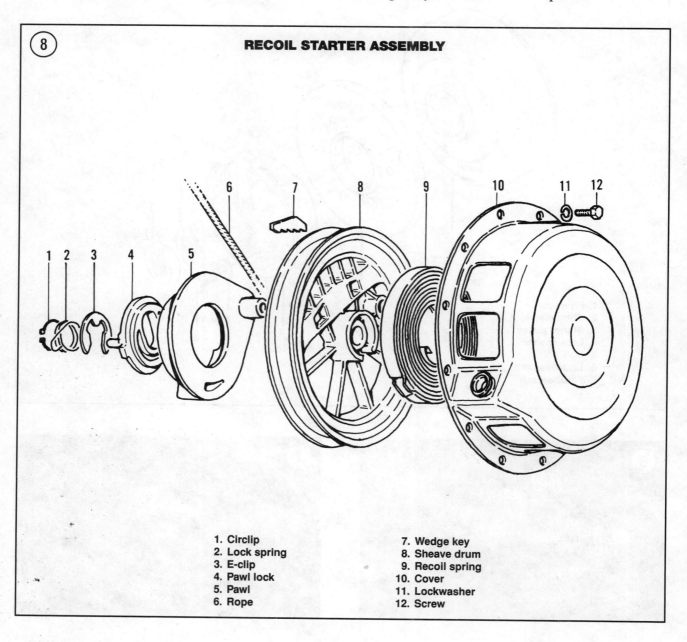

8 **RECOIL STARTER ASSEMBLY**

1. Circlip
2. Lock spring
3. E-clip
4. Pawl lock
5. Pawl
6. Rope
7. Wedge key
8. Sheave drum
9. Recoil spring
10. Cover
11. Lockwasher
12. Screw

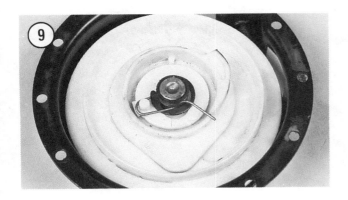

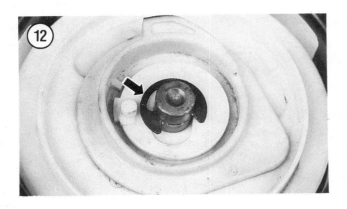

3. Hold the starter sheave (8, **Figure 8**) to keep it from turning, release the starter rope and allow the sheave to turn slowly until it stops.

4. Turn the starter assembly so the sheave assembly faces up as shown in **Figure 9** and remove the snap ring from the housing post groove (**Figure 10**).

5. Remove the lock spring (**Figure 11**).

6. Remove the E-clip from the housing post groove (**Figure 12**).

7. Remove the pawl lock (**Figure 13**) and pawl (**Figure 14**).

8. Remove the sheave (**Figure 15**) and rope assembly from the starter housing.

9. If the rope is being replaced, use a screwdriver or similar tool to slide the wedge key (7, **Figure 8**) to release the rope.

WARNING
The rewind spring will usually remain in the cavity of the housing, but it may unwind suddenly and violently. Uncon-

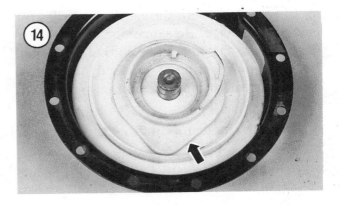

12

trolled unwinding can cause in serious personal injury. Wear hand and eye protection while removing and installing the spring.

10. Place the rewind housing assembly on the floor with the closed side up. Tap lightly on the top of the housing while holding it tightly against the floor and allow the spring to fall from the housing. The spring will unwind inside the housing. The spring housing (**Figure 16**) will also be removed on 1990-1992 models.

Starter Housing Inspection

NOTE
Before cleaning plastic components, make sure the cleaning agent is compatible with plastic. Some types of solvents can permanently damage the plastic pieces.

1. Clean all parts thoroughly and allow to dry.

2. Inspect the starter post (**Figure 17**) for cracks, deep scoring or excessive wear. Check the grooves in the post for damage. Replace the housing if the starter post is damaged.

3. Check the pawl (A, **Figure 18**) and pawl lock (B, **Figure 18**) for cracks or other damage. Replace damaged parts as required.

4. Check the sheave drum (**Figure 19**) for cracks or damage.

5. Check the recoil spring (**Figure 20**) for cracks or damage. Breakage often occurs near the attachments points at the ends of the spring. Install a new spring if cracked or broken. Reshaping ends or similar repairs are not recommended.

6. Check the starter rope for fraying, splitting or breakage.

7. Replace any parts that are in questionable condition.

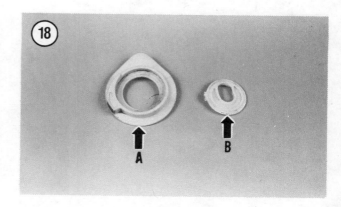

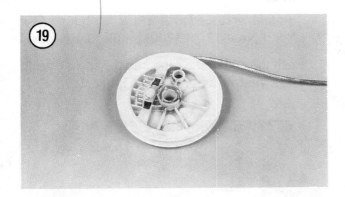

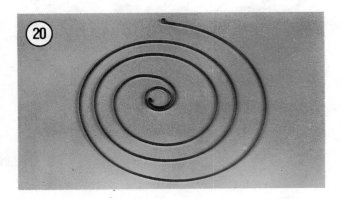

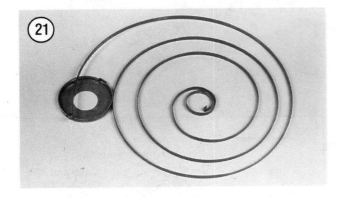

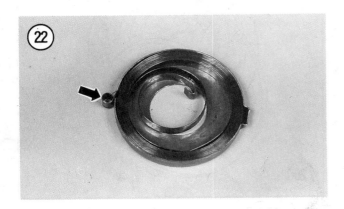

Starter Housing Assembly

Refer to **Figure 8** for this procedure.

WARNING
Wear hand and eye protection while installing the recoil spring.

NOTE
The recoil starter spring used on 1990-1992 models is installed in a spring guide before installation into the starter housing. The spring is wound clockwise into the spring guide on 1990-1992 models so equipped. The spring is wound directly into starter housing on 1993-on models and in the opposite (counterclockwise) direction. Refer to Step 1A for 1990-1992 models or to Step 1B for later models.

1A. Install the recoil spring (**Figure 20**) for 1990-1992 models, as follows:

  a. Lubricate the rewind spring and the cavity of the starter housing with a silicone compound grease.

NOTE
Improper or insufficient lubrication will cause parts of the rewind starter, including springs, to fail. Do not use Molykote G-n (part No. 413 70 3700) on the rewind spring and do not use silicone grease on the lock spring. The starter should be removed, cleaned and lubricated occasionally as a part of regular maintenance.

  b. Hook the outer spring loop over the notch in the spring guide as shown in **Figure 21**.

  c. Wind the spring **clockwise** until the spring is completely installed in spring guide. Refer to **Figure 22**.

  d. Lubricate the starter post and spring cavity (**Figure 23**) in the starter housing with a silicone compound grease. Do not use Molykote G-n (part No. 413 70 3700) on the starter post.

12

e. Align the outer spring loop with the guide notch in the starter housing and install the spring/guide assembly. Make sure the spring outer loop (A, **Figure 24**) and the spring guide latch (B, **Figure 24**) are installed as shown.

NOTE
The recoil starter spring used on 1993-on models is installed directly into the starter housing. Refer to Step 1A for earlier models.

1B. Install the recoil spring (**Figure 25**) for 1993-on models, as follows:

a. Lubricate the rewind spring and the cavity of the starter housing with a silicone compound grease.

NOTE
Improper or insufficient lubrication will cause parts of the rewind starter, including springs, to fail. Do not use Molykote G-n (part No. 413 70 3700) on the rewind spring. The starter should be removed, cleaned and lubricated occasionally as a part of regular maintenance.

b. Hook the outer spring loop over the notch in the housing as shown in **Figure 26**.
c. Wind the spring **counterclockwise** until the spring is completely installed in the cavity of housing. Refer to **Figure 27**.
d. Lubricate the starter post and spring guide in the starter housing with a silicone com-

pound grease. Do not use Molykote G-n (part No. 413 70 3700) on the starter post.

2. Push the end of the rope into the sheave drum past the window as shown in **Figure 28**.

24

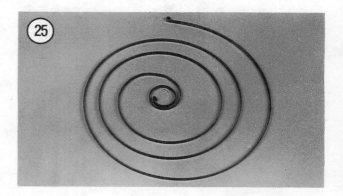
25

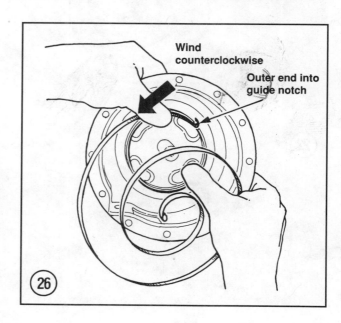
Wind counterclockwise

Outer end into guide notch

26

23

NOTE
*If the rope exited the sheave drum window as shown in **Figure 29**, push it back into the sheave drum as shown in **Figure 28**.*

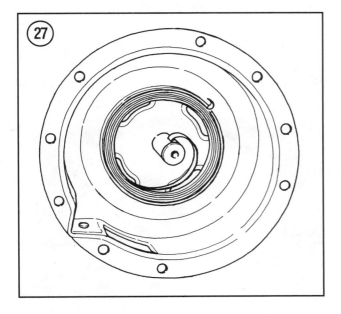

3. Insert the wedge key into the sheave drum. Then lock the end of the rope with the key by wedging the key against the rope as shown in **Figure 30**. Pull the rope to seat the key.

4. Wind the rope onto the sheave drum. All of the rope should be wrapped around the sheave drum (in the pulley groove).

5. Align the inner hook of the recoil spring with notch on the sheave drum (**Figure 31**) and install the sheave drum. Twist the sheave drum slightly to make sure the drum and end of the spring are engaged.

6. Preload the recoil spring as follows:

    a. Wind the sheave drum **counterclockwise** 1 turn, against the pressure of the rewind spring. Keep the rope coiled tightly around the sheave drum.

    b. Continue turning the sheave drum counterclockwise until the free end of the rope is aligned with the hole in the housing for the rope.

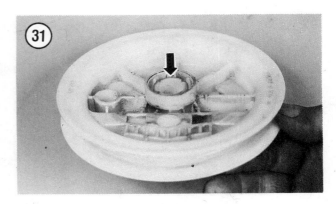

12

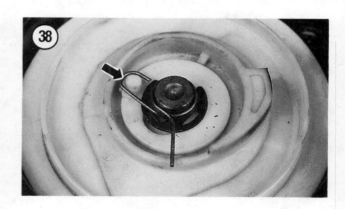

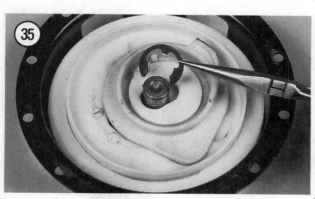

c. Pull the rope partway from the hole and tie a knot in the rope to keep it from winding back into the housing. Refer to **Figure 32**.

NOTE
The procedure outlined in the preceeding steps will preload the rewind spring slightly more than 1 turn. This should be sufficient if the rope was coiled tightly around the sheave drum before preloading the rewind spring.

7. Align the post on the pawl with the hole in the sheave drum and install the pawl (**Figure 33**).

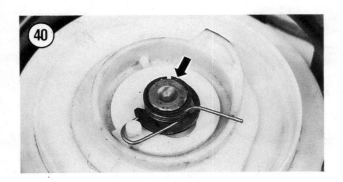

8. Install the pawl lock (**Figure 34**).

9. Install the E-clip (**Figure 35**) into the lower post groove. Make sure the E-clip engages the groove completely (**Figure 36**).

10. Install the lock spring (**Figure 37**) over the post so that the end of the spring fits over the pawl lock arm as shown in **Figure 38**.

CAUTION
Do not use silicone compound grease or standard multipurpose grease on the lock spring. Using anything except Molykote G-n paste (part No. 413 70 3700) may cause the lock spring to vibrate off in operation.

11. Lubricate the lock spring with Molykote G-n paste.

12. Install the circlip (**Figure 39**) so it seats in the upper post groove. Make sure the circlips seats in the post groove completely (**Figure 40**).

13. Operate the recoil starter to make sure the sheave assembly works smoothly and returns properly.

12

Chapter Thirteen

Drive System

The drive train consists of a drive pulley (sheave) mounted on the left end of the engine crankshaft, a driven pulley (sheave) mounted on the left end of a jackshaft (countershaft) and a drive belt connecting the two pulleys. The jackshaft drives the chaincase, which contains a drive chain and reduction sprockets. A brake disc is also located near the right end of the jackshaft. The chaincase contains a speed reduction on all models; it also contains the reverse gears on models so equipped. A drive axle (shaft) fitted with track drive sprockets exits from the chaincase. This chapter describes complete procedures for the primary and secondary pulley components. Service to the chaincase, jackshaft and brake are described in Chapter Fourteen.

General drive belt specifications are listed in **Table 1**. **Tables 1-4** are at the end of the chapter.

WARNING
Never lean into a snowmobile's engine compartment while wearing a scarf or other loose clothing when the engine is running or when attempting to start the engine. If the scarf or clothing should catch in the drive system, severe injury or death could occur. Make sure the belt guard is always in place.

DRIVE UNIT

Torque is transferred from the engine crankshaft to the jackshaft (countershaft) by a centrifugally actuated, variable pulley type of transmission. The transmission or drive unit automatically changes the drive ratio to permit the machine to move from idle to maximum speed. Major components are the drive pulley assembly, driven pulley assembly and drive belt (**Figure 1**).

The drive and driven pulleys are basically 2 variable diameter pulleys that automatically vary the amount of reduction. Changes in the reduction ratio are possible by moving the sides of the pulleys closer together or further apart. Changing the gap between the sides of the pulley causes the belt to move up or down in the pulley groove, changing the effective diameter of the pulley. These changes in pulley diameter adjust to correspond with the prevailing load and speed conditions. See **Figure 2**.

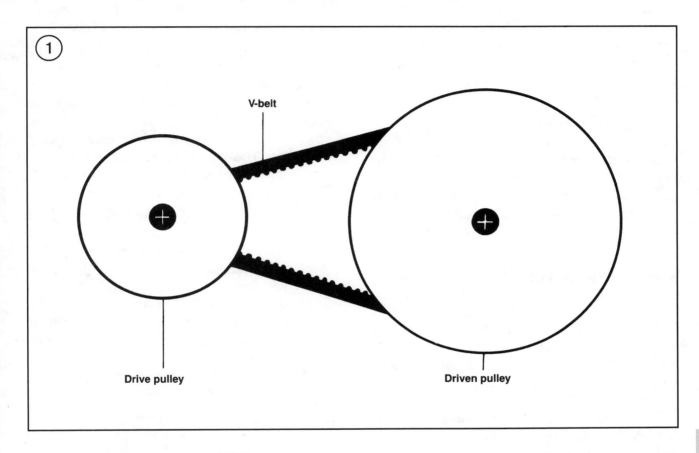

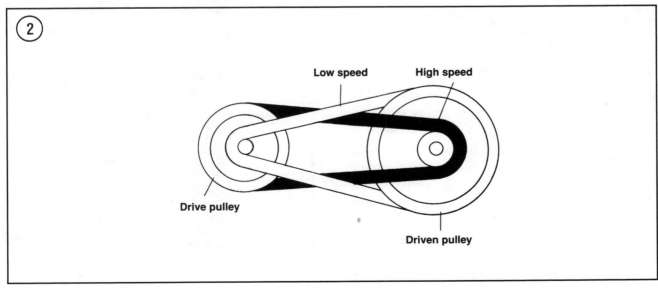

The shift sequence is determined by a combination of engine torque and engine rpm. When track resistance (or load) increases, such as when going up hill, the pulleys change the reduction ratio; engine rpm will remain nearly the same but the vehicle's speed drops. When track resistance decreases, the pulleys automatically shift toward a higher ratio; engine rpm remains the same but the vehicle's speed will increase.

DRIVE PULLEY ASSEMBLY

Major components of the drive pulley assembly are the sliding pulley half (sheave), fixed pulley half (sheave), weight levers, weight ramps, primary spring and V-belt. The V-belt connects the drive and driven pulleys (**Figure 1**).

Fixed and Sliding Pulley Halves

The sides of the pulleys are made of mild steel and the belt surfaces are precision machined to a smooth taper. The pulleys are carefully balanced to prevent vibration. The tapered surfaces of the pulleys match the V-belt gripping surface (**Figure 3**).

The drive pulley assembly is mounted on the left end of the engine crankshaft. When the engine is at idle or stopped, the fixed and sliding halves of the pulley are held apart by the primary spring. At slow idle speed or when the engine is stopped, the groove should be wide enough for the V-belt to drop down between the sides of the pulley. There is no engagement because the width of the belt is *less* than the space between the sides of the drive pulley.

When the engine speed is increased from idle, centrifugal force causes the weight levers mounted on the sliding half of the drive pulley to swing out. When centrifugal force of the weights is sufficient to overcome the pressure of the primary spring, the sliding half of the pulley is moved closer to the fixed half. This movement narrows the groove between the pulley halves

until the sides of the pulley grip the belt. The point at which the pulley grips the belt is called the engagement rpm. Refer to **Table 1** for the recommended engagement rpm for specific models. At low speed, the belt will be located as shown at the low-speed position in **Figure 2**.

As engine rpm is increased, centrifugal force causes the weights of the drive pulley to swing further out and force the sliding half of the pulley closer to the fixed half. As the groove of the drive pulley becomes narrower, the V-belt is forced upward in the groove toward the outer edge of the pulley. The V-belt is forced deeper into the groove of the driven pulley as indicated by the high-speed position of the belt in **Figure 2**.

Though not part of the drive pulley, it should be noted that the release (secondary) spring of the driven pulley forces the sides of the pulley together. Pressure against the sides of the driven pulley will force the sliding half away from the fixed side. Movement of the weight levers in the drive pulley will force the pulley halves together and the belt will move to the outer diameter of

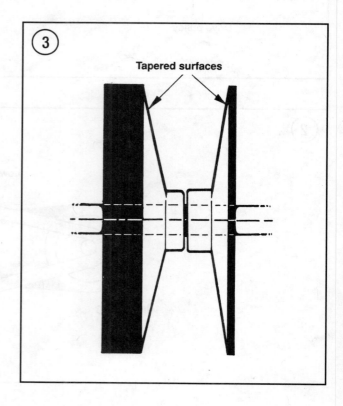

③ Tapered surfaces

the drive pulley. At the same time the belt will force the sides of the driven pulley apart so that it can operate deeper in the groove.

Drive Pulley Spring

The clutch release spring of the drive pulley controls engagement speed. If a lighter spring is installed, the belt will engage at a lower engine rpm. If a heavier spring is installed, the engine speed (rpm) will have to be higher to overcome spring pressure and allow engagement.

Centrifugal Weight Levers

As previously noted, weighted levers in the drive pulley react to engine speed and swing out. Rollers on the ends of the weighted levers press against the weight ramps to move the sliding half of the drive pulley. Centrifugal force causes the weights to swing out as the speed of the engine increases. Movement of the weighted levers and the sliding half of the pulley is opposed by the pressure of the primary spring. Until engine speed reaches the engagement rpm, the weights have not yet moved the sliding half of the pulley enough to engage the belt. The force excerted by the weighted levers is controlled by engine rpm. The faster the crankshaft rotates, the farther the weights pivot out. Movement of the sliding half of the drive pulley is controlled by the shape of the weight ramps.

DRIVEN PULLEY

Major components of the driven pulley assembly are the sliding half, fixed half, release (secondary) spring and cam bracket. The pulley halves are made of mild steel. The belt surfaces are machined to a smooth tapered surface. The tapered surfaces of the pulley halves matches the V-belt gripping surface (**Figure 4**).

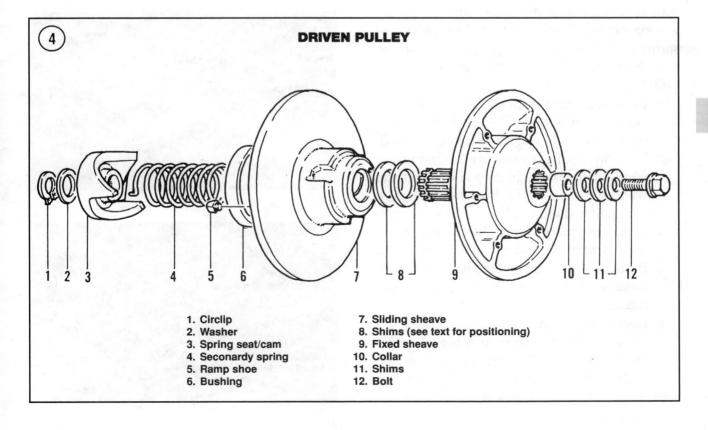

④ DRIVEN PULLEY

1. Circlip
2. Washer
3. Spring seat/cam
4. Seconardy spring
5. Ramp shoe
6. Bushing
7. Sliding sheave
8. Shims (see text for positioning)
9. Fixed sheave
10. Collar
11. Shims
12. Bolt

13

The drive pulley assembly is mounted on the left end of the jackshaft (countershaft). The chaincase is located on the right end of the jackshaft. When the engine is stopped or at idle, the driven pulley assembly is held in its low speed position by tension from the secondary (release) spring (**Figure 4**).

The driven pulley is a torque sensitive unit. If the snowmobile encounters an increased load condition, the cam bracket forces the driven pulley to downshift by moving the driven pulley halves closer together. The speed of the snowmobile will slow, but the engine will continue to run at a high rpm. By sensing load conditions and shifting accordingly, the engine can continue to operate in its peak power range.

Release Spring

The release spring located in the driven pulley assembly helps determine the shifting pattern. The spring is also used to keep the torque sensing cam in contact with the slider buttons. Spring tension can be changed by installing a different spring or by repositioning the end of the spring in different holes drilled in the cam. Observe the following:

a. Increasing release spring tension will prevent the belt from moving to a higher speed position until the engine speed is increased. If the drive pulley moves to a faster ratio too soon, engine rpm will drop and the engine will begin to bog down. For peak efficiency, the engine should operate within its optimum peak power range. Increasing spring tension may prevent upshifting too early. By not shifting up, the engine should continue to operate within its peak power range.

b. Decreasing secondary spring tension allows the belt to move to a higher speed position at a lower engine rpm. The engine will not operate as efficiently if it is running faster than its peak power range. Decreas-

ing spring tension allows adjustment so that the drive system will shift into a higher ratio sooner to match the engine power.

The torque sensing cam angle will have more effect on the shifting sequence under heavy load than the release spring tension, but both are adjustable.

Torque Sensing Cam Angle

The drive pulley spring tension and the torque sensing cam angle work together to control how easily the driven pulley will shift to a faster speed ratio. The cam pushes against the sliding pulley. If the cam angle is steep, the pulleys will shift to a faster speed ratio sooner and will not be as responsive to increases in load. Conversely, low cam angles will exert more side pressure and will slow shifts until the load is reduced and speeds are higher.

DRIVE BELT

The drive belt transmits power from the drive pulley to the driven pulley. The belt provides a vital link in the operation and performance of the snowmobile. To insure top performance, the drive pulley, drive belt and driven pulley must be matched to each other and to the snowmobile model. The correct size drive belt must be installed, because belt width and length are critical

to proper operation. Belt wear affects clutch operation and shifting characteristics. Since normal wear changes the width of the belt, it must be frequently adjusted as described in this chapter. See **Table 1** for the width of a new drive belt for your snowmobile.

With general use, there is no specific mileage or time limit on belt life. Belt life is directly related to maintenance and the type of snowmobile operation. The belt should be inspected at the intervals listed in Chapter Three. Early belt failure (200 miles or less) is abnormal and the cause should be determined to prevent subsequent damage.

> *WARNING*
> *Never lean into the snowmobile's engine compartment while wearing a scarf or other loose clothing when the engine is running or when attempting to start the engine. If the scarf or clothing should catch in the drive belt or clutch, severe injury or death could occur. Do not run the engine with the belt guard removed (Figure 5).*

Removal/Installation

1. Open the hood.
2. Remove the pins (**Figure 6**) and remove the drive belt guard (**Figure 7**).
3. Check the drive belt for its manufacturer's markings (**Figure 8**) so that during installation it will run in the correct direction. If the belt is not marked, draw an arrow on the belt facing forward or install a new belt.
4. Push against the driven pulley (A, **Figure 9**) and rotate it clockwise to separate the pulley halves. Then roll the belt (B, **Figure 9**) over the driven pulley and remove it.
5. Inspect the drive belt as described in this chapter.
6. Perform the *Drive Belt Alignment* as described in this chapter.
7. Reverse Steps 1-4 and install the drive belt. If installing the original belt, make sure to install it

13

so that the manufacturer's marks on the belt (or those made before removal) face in the same direction (forward). When installing a new belt, install it so that you can read the belt identification marks while standing on the left-hand side of the machine and looking into the engine compartment (**Figure 8**).

Inspection

Inspect the drive belt weekly or every 150 miles (240 km) of operation.

1. Remove the drive belt as described in this chapter.

2. Measure the width of the drive belt at its widest point (**Figure 10**). Replace the belt if the width is 3.0 (1/8 in.) less than the new width listed in **Table 1**.

3. Visually inspect the belt for the following conditions:

   a. *Frayed edge:* Check the sides of the belt for a frayed edge cord (**Figure 11**). This indicates drive belt misalignment. Drive belt misalignment can be caused by incorrect pulley alignment and loose engine mounting bolts.

   b. *Worn narrow in one section:* Examine the belt for a section that is worn narrower in one section (**Figure 12**). This condition is

caused by excessive belt slippage due to a stuck track or a too high engine idle speed.

   c. *Belt disintegration:* Drive belt disintegration (**Figure 13**) is caused by severe belt wear or misalignment. Disintegration can also be caused by the use of an incorrect belt.

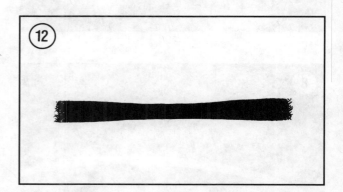

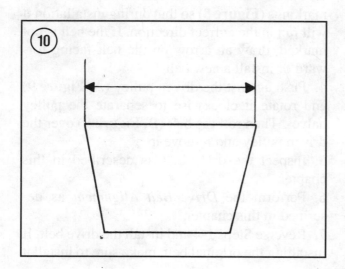

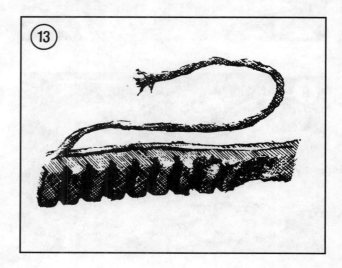

d. *Sheared cogs:* Sheared cogs as shown in **Figure 14** are usually caused by violent drive pulley engagement. This is an indication of a defective or improperly installed drive pulley.

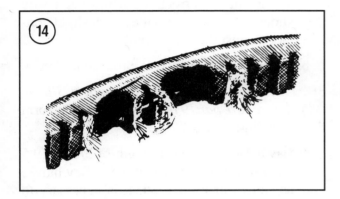

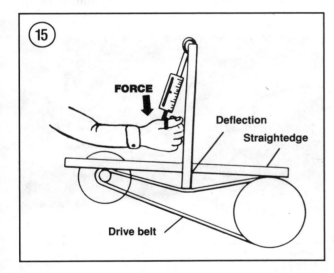

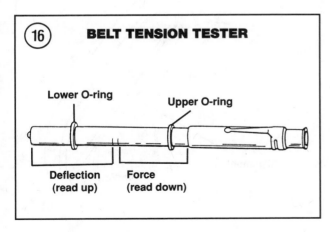

4. Replace a worn or damaged belt immediately. Always carry a spare belt (**Figure 7**) on your snowmobile for emergency purposes.

Drive Belt Deflection

Perform this procedure whenever a new drive belt is installed.

1. Check drive belt alignment as described in this chapter.

2A. A wooden stick and a spring scale are required for this procedure. Check belt deflection as follows:

a. Position a ruler on the drive belt for reference.

b. Using a stick and a spring scale, apply 15 lb. (6.8 kg) of pressure to the center of the belt as shown in **Figure 15**. Belt deflection should be within the specification in **Table 1**.

c. If deflection is incorrect, perform Step 3.

2B. The Ski-Doo belt tension tester (**Figure 16**) is required for this procedure. Check belt deflection as follows:

a. Position the lower tester O-ring to the belt deflection measurement for your model. See **Table 1**. Then position the upper tester O-ring to zero on the force scale.

b. Place the end of the tester on the drive belt and push the tester down until the lower O-ring is flush with the edge of the ruler. See **Figure 17**. Read the force scale reading at the top edge of the upper O-ring. It should read 15 lb. (6.8 kg).

c. If force scale reading is incorrect, perform Step 3.

3. To change belt tension, turn the Allen screws on the driven pulley (**Figure 18**) 1/4 turn and recheck belt deflection. Observe the following:

a. To tighten belt tension, turn the Allen screws counterclockwise.

b. To loosen belt tension, turn the Allen screws clockwise.

13

c. Turn Allen screws equally in 1/4-turn increments.

d. After making adjustment, rotate the driven pulley to help seat the belt in the pulley grooves. Then recheck adjustment.

Drive Belt Alignment

The center-to-center distance from the drive pulley to the driven pulley and the offset of the pulleys must be correctly maintained for good performance and long belt life.

Correct center-to-center distance ensures correct belt tension and reduction ratio. If the center-to-center distance is too short, the shift ratio will be too narrow. If the center-to-center distance is too long, the drive belt will be pulled down too deep in the driven pulley groove too soon. The machine will not pull strongly because the pulleys are shifting too quickly towards the 1:1 ratio.

1. Adjust track tension as described in Chapter Three.

2. Remove the drive belt as described in this chapter.

3A. *Checking pulley alignment with Ski-Doo alignment bar (part No. 529 0071 00)*. Perform the following:

a. Place the alignment bar into the clutch assembly as shown in **Figure 19**. Clutch alignment is correct when the bar easily slides over the drive pulley with slight contact against the driven pulley.

b. If alignment is incorrect, proceed to Step 4.

3B. *Checking pulley alignment with a 3/8 in. (9.5 mm) square bar 19 in. (48 cm) long*. Perform the following:

a. Lay a 19 in. (48 cm) length of 3/8 in. (9.5 mm) square bar between the pulley halves as shown in **Figure 20**. It is necessary to turn and push the driven pulley half to open

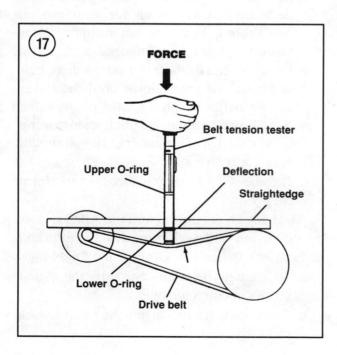

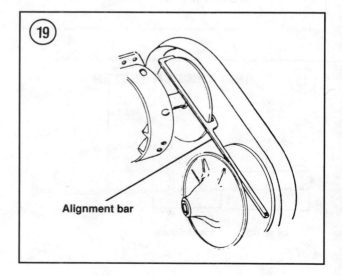

it for placement of the square bar. When bar is in place, release the pulley.

b. Check pulley offset and distance as specified in **Figure 20**. Refer to **Table 2** for specifications.

c. If alignment is incorrect, proceed to Step 4.

4A. *Pulley distance adjustment:* If distance Z in **Figure 20** is incorrect, perform the following:

a. Loosen the engine torque rod nut (**Figure 21**, 3) and the engine mount nuts (**Figure 22**).

b. Reposition engine until distance Z (**Figure 20**) is correct.

c. Tighten engine mount nuts to the torque specifications in Chapter Five.

d. Tighten torque rod nut **Figure 23** so that nut seats against washer. Do not overtighten as overtightening will cause pulley misalignment.

4B. *Pulley alignment adjustment:* If pulley offset X in **Figure 20** is incorrect, perform the following:

a. Remove the driven pulley bolt (**Figure 24**) as described in this chapter. Don't lose the washers on the bolt (**Figure 25**).

b. Remove the driven pulley (**Figure 26**).

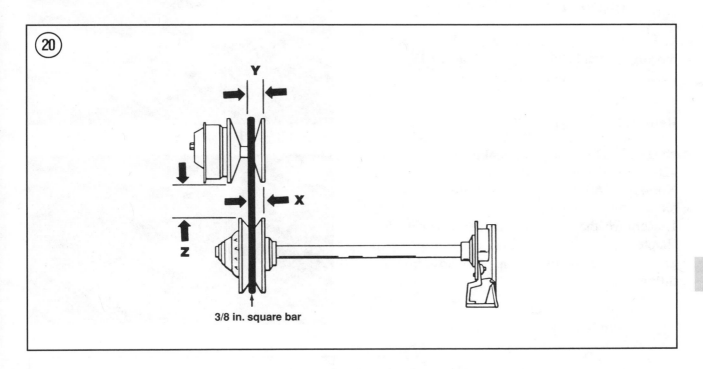

20

Y

X

Z

3/8 in. square bar

13

21

22

c. Adjust offset by adding or removing shims placed between driven pulley and the jackshaft (countershaft) bearing support (**Figure 27**).

d. Reinstall the driven pulley and recheck the offset. If the offset is incorrect, repeat ths procedure as necessary.

e. After adjusting the pulley offset, perform the *Driven Pulley Free Play* as described in this chapter.

5. Reinstall the drive belt as described in this chapter.

DRIVE PULLEY SERVICE

The drive pulley is mounted on the left end of the engine crankshaft. Refer to **Figure 28** when performing procedures in this section.

Removal

The Ski-Doo crankshaft locking tool (part No. 420 8766 40) and the drive pulley puller (part No. 420 4760 30) (**Figure 29**) are required to remove the drive pulley.

1. Remove the drive belt as described in this chapter.

2. Disconnect the fuel pump pulse hose from its fitting at the crankcase.

NOTE
Figure 30 shows the engine removed for clarity.

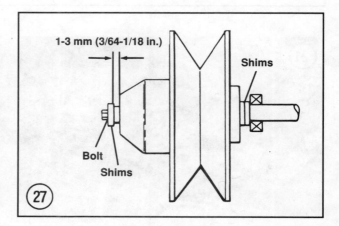

1-3 mm (3/64-1/18 in.)

Shims

Bolt

Shims

⓲

DRIVE PULLEY ASSEMBLY

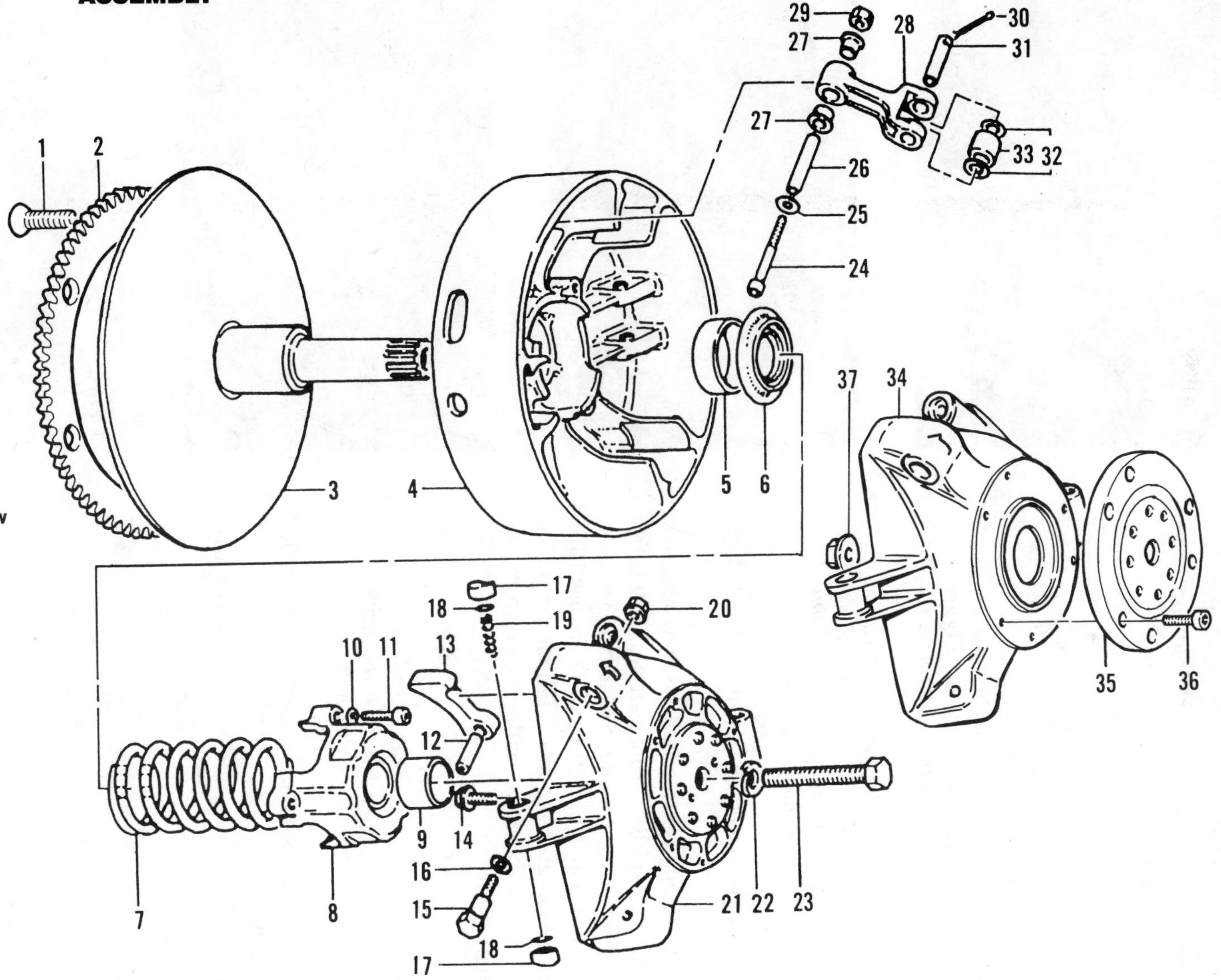

1. Screws
2. Starter ring gear
3. Pulley inner half
4. Pulley outer half
5. Bushing
6. Spring seat
7. Spring
8. Spring cover
9. Bushing
10. Washer
11. Screw
12. Tube
13. Weight
14. Bolt
15. Calibration screw
16. Washer
17. Slider shoe
18. O-ring
19. Spring
20. Nut
21. Governor cup
22. Lockwasher
23. Bolt
24. Bolt
25. Washer
26. Bushing
27. Bushing
28. Lever
29. Nut
30. Cotter pin
31. Pin
32. Roller
33. Roller
34. Governor cup
    (some models)
35. Plate
36. Bolt
37. Nut

13

3. Use the special clutch holding tool (part No. 529 0064 00) or equivalent to hold the drive pulley while using the puller in Step 5.

> *NOTE*
> *The special crankshaft locking tool (part No. 420 8766 40) is used to hold the crankshaft. Insert the locking tool through the pulse hose fitting and engage the tool with the crankshaft (**Figure 30**). After installing the tool, rotate the crankshaft slightly until the tool locks the crankshaft. Be careful not to break or bend the locking tool and be careful not to damage the crankshaft when using this method of holding the crankshaft.*

4. Loosen and remove the bolt and washer (**Figure 30**).

5. Install the appropriate puller screw (**Figure 31**) through the pulley. Tool part No. 529 0079 00 is used for 467, 536, 582, 583 and 643 engine models. Tool part No. 529 0224 00 is used for 454 and 670 engine models. Tighten the puller screw to break the drive pulley loose from the crankshaft taper.

> *NOTE*
> *It may be necessary to rap sharply on the head of the puller to shock the drive pulley loose from the crankshaft.*

6. When the drive pulley is loose, remove the puller screw.

7. Remove the drive pulley assembly (**Figure 32**.

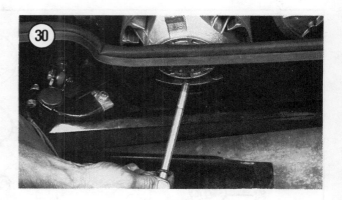

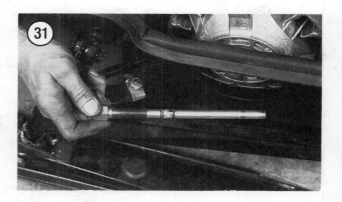

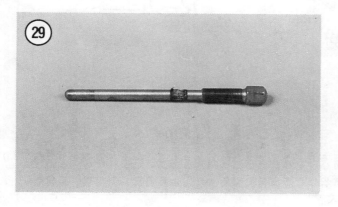

Disassembly

> *WARNING*
> *The drive pulley is under spring pressure. Attempting to disassemble or reassemble the drive pulley without the use of the specified special tools may cause severe personal injury. If you do not have access to the necessary tools, have the service performed by a dealer or other snowmobile mechanic.*

1. Thread the puller (part No. 420 4760 30) approximately 13 mm (1/2 in.) into the inner half (**Figure 33**). Then hold the pulley by the outer half and knock the puller to disengage the inner half. See **Figure 34**.

2. Remove the governor cup (**Figure 35**) as follows:

    a. Lift the governor cup up until the slider shoes rise to their highest position in their guides.

    b. Place the fork (part No. 529 0055 00) over the slider shoes (**Figure 36**) and remove the governor cup assembly.

> *NOTE*
> *The Ski-Doo puller (part No. 420 4760 30), spacer (part No. 529 0054 00) and cover (part No. 529 0056 00) are required for the following procedure.*

3. Remove the spring cover assembly (**Figure 37**) as follows:

    a. Assemble the special tools as shown in **Figure 38**. Make sure the puller is screwed in all the way.

    b. Remove the 3 Allen screws evenly to slowly release spring pressure from the spring cover.

    c. When spring pressure is fully released, remove the special tools.

    d. Remove the spring cover (**Figure 39**) and spring (**Figure 40**).

4. Separate the inner and outer half assemblies (**Figure 41**).

5. Remove the spring seat (**Figure 42**).

13

6. Disassemble the governor cup assembly (**Figure 43**) as follows:

    a. Remove the forks installed during removal (**Figure 44**).

    b. Remove a slider shoe (**Figure 45**).

    c. Remove an O-ring (**Figure 46**).

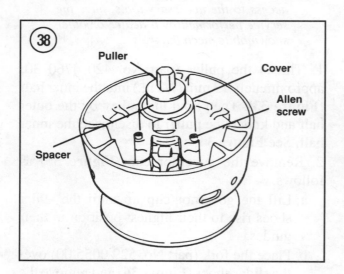

d. Remove the spring (**Figure 47**).

e. Remove the opposite slider shoe (**Figure 48**) and O-ring (**Figure 49**).

f. Repeat for remaining slider shoe assemblies.

7. Remove the weight ramps (**Figure 50**) from the outer half assembly as follows:

   a. Remove the 2 screws (**Figure 51**) holding each weight ramp in place.

13

b. Remove the weight ramp (**Figure 52**).

c. Repeat for the remaining weight ramps.

8. Remove the calibration screw (**Figure 53**) as follows:

a. Locate and mark the position of the calibration screw (**Figure 53**). Its original position is needed for reassembly.

b. Loosen and remove the calibration screw nut (**Figure 54**).

c. Remove the calibration screw and washer (**Figure 55**).

d. Repeat for the remaining calibration screws.

9. Remove the lever and bushing assembly (**Figure 56**) as follows:

a. Loosen the Allen bolt (A, **Figure 57**) and remove the nut (B, **Figure 57**).

b. Slide the bolt (**Figure 58**) through the slot in the outer half assembly and remove it. See **Figure 59**.

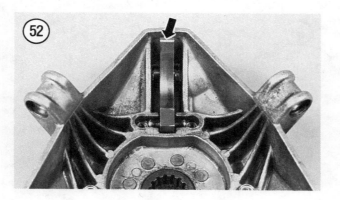

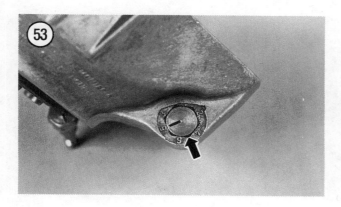

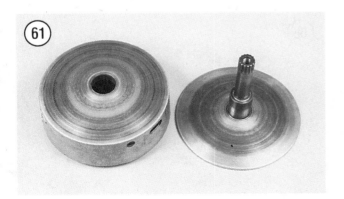

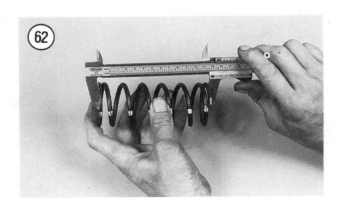

c. Remove the lever and bushing assembly (**Figure 60**).

d. Repeat for the remaining lever and bushing assemblies.

Inspection

> *CAUTION*
> *Step 1 describes cleaning of the drive pulley assembly. Do not clean the rollers and weight levers with solvent as solvent will damage the Duralon bushings.*

1. Clean all parts, except the rollers and weight levers, thoroughly in solvent. Wipe the rollers and weight levers with a rag.

2. Remove all Loctite residue from all threads.

3. Check the pulley halves (**Figure 61**) for cracks or damage.

4. Check the drive belt surfaces of the pulleys for rubber or rust buildup. For proper operation, the surfaces must be *clean*. Remove rubber or rust debris with a fine grade steel wool. Clean with a piece of lint-free cloth.

5. Check the drive pulley spring for cracks or distortion. If the spring appears okay, measure its free length with a vernier caliper (**Figure 62**). Replace the spring if its free length is shorter than the length specified in **Table 3**. Replace the spring with one of the same color code.

6. Check the slider shoe assembly (**Figure 63**) as follows:

13

a. Check the slider shoes for wear. If there is no groove visible in the top of a slider shoe, replace the slider shoes as a set.

b. Check the O-rings for cracks or other damage. Replace if necessary.

c. Check the spring for cracks, breakage or fatigue.

7. Check the weight ramps (**Figure 64**) for cracks or other damage.

8. Check the calibration screws (**Figure 65**) for cracks or other damage.

9. Check the lever and roller assembly (**Figure 66**) for damage. If the roller and/or bushing are damaged, replace them as follows:

a. Remove the cotter pin (**Figure 67**).

b. Withdraw the bushing (**Figure 68**) and remove the bushing and thrust washers. See **Figure 69**.

c. Replace worn or damaged parts.

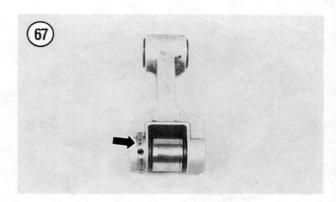

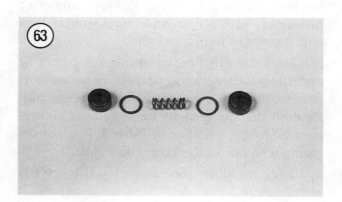

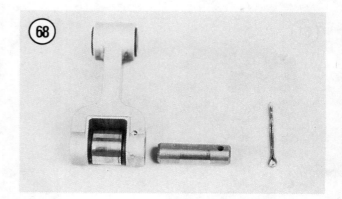

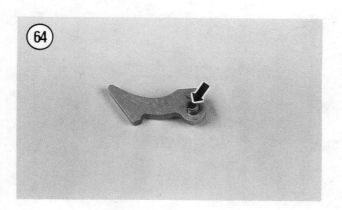

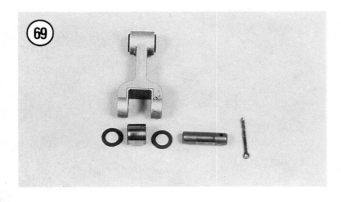

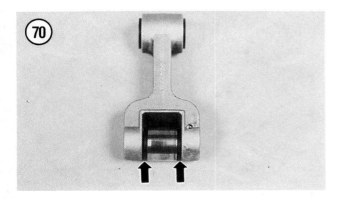

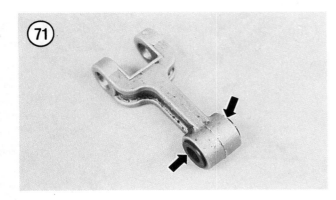

d. Assemble by reversing these steps. Make sure to install a thrust washer on both sides of the roller (**Figure 70**).

10. Check the 2 flange bushings in the top of the lever assembly (**Figure 71**). If the bushings appear worn or cracked, replace them. When installing new bushings, align them carefully with the lever and press into place.

NOTE
If the replacement bushings are made of black plastic, ream the bushings with a No. O letter drill after the new bushings have been installed in the lever assembly.

11. Inspect the Kahrlon bushing in the spring cover assembly (**Figure 72**). If the Kahrlon coating is worn from the bushing, replace the bushing as follows:

a. Place the spring cover in a press bed so that the arms on the cover face up as shown in **Figure 73**.

b. Press the bushing from the spring cover.

c. Clean the outer half assembly with ethyl alcohol.

d. Coat the outside of a new bushing with Loctite 609. Then press the bushing into the spring cover so that the bushing is flush with the cover as shown in **Figure 73**.

e. Flare the bushing on the outer spring cover side (**Figure 72**) to help prevent it from loosening in the cover.

12. Inspect the Kahrlon bushing in the outer half assembly (**Figure 74**). If the Kahrlon coating is

13

worn from the bushing, replace the bushing as follows:

> *NOTE*
> *Special tools are required to correctly install the bushing. If you do not have access to the special tools, have the bushing replaced by a Ski-Doo dealer.*

a. Press the old bushing from the outer half assembly.

b. Clean the outer half assembly with ethyl alcohol.

c. Coat the outside of the new bushing with Loctite 609. Then press the bushing into the outer half so that there is the same amount of clearance between the outer bushing edge and the outer half on both sides of the bushing.

d. Place the Ski-Doo outer flare tool (part No. 529 0060 00) on the bushing at the point shown in **Figure 75**. Then press the flare tool with a press to flare the bushing. Knock the flare tool from the bushing.

e. Place the Ski-Doo inner flare tool (part No. 529 0061 00) on the bushing at the point shown in **Figure 74**. Then press the flare tool with a press to flare the bushing. Knock the flare tool from the bushing.

13. Replace any part(s) in questionable condition.

Reassembly

Refer to **Figure 28** for this procedure.

> *CAUTION*
> *The drive pulley is assembled dry. Do not lubricate any component.*

1. Install the calibration screw (**Figure 76**) as follows:

a. Install the washer on the inside of the governor cup and install the calibration screw (**Figure 77**).

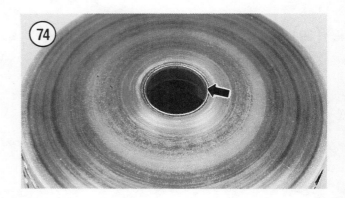

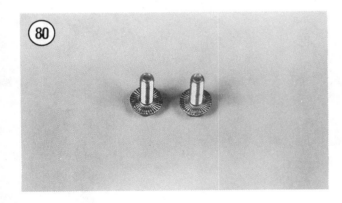

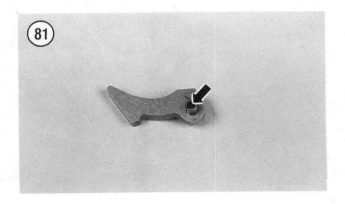

b. Set the calibration screw to the same number setting recorded during removal.

c. Install the nut (**Figure 78**) and tighten securely.

d. Repeat for each calibration screw.

2. Install the weight ramps (**Figure 64**) as follows:

   a. Place the weight ramp in the governor cup (**Figure 79**).

NOTE
*The bolts used to secure the weight ramps have serrated flanges (**Figure 80**). Make sure to install the correct type bolts.*

NOTE
*If replacement dowel pins are installed in the weight ramps (**Figure 81**), position the pins so that the open slot will face against the bolts when the bolts are tightened against the pins in substep b.*

   b. Install the bolts and tighten to 10 N·m (89 in.-lbs.). See **Figure 82**.

   c. Repeat for each weight ramp.

3. Install the lever and bushing assembly (**Figure 66**) as follows:

   a. Place the 3 lever assemblies in the outer half assembly so that the cotter pins face as shown in **Figure 83**. In addition, the head of the cotter pins must face up as shown in **Figure 84**.

13

b. Install the Allen bolt (**Figure 85**) and nut. Tighten the Allen bolt to 12 N•m (106 in.-lb.)

c. Make sure the bushings move freely.

d. Repeat for each lever assembly.

4. Install the slider shoes (**Figure 86**) as follows:

NOTE
When installing the slider shoes, install them so that the groove in the shoe face is positioned vertically.

a. Install the first O-ring (**Figure 87**) and slider shoe (**Figure 88**).

b. Install the spring (**Figure 89**).

c. Install the second O-ring (**Figure 90**) and slider shoe (**Figure 91**).

d. Repeat for each slider shoe assembly.

e. Install the fork (part No. 529 0055 00) over each slider shoe assembly as shown in **Figure 92**.

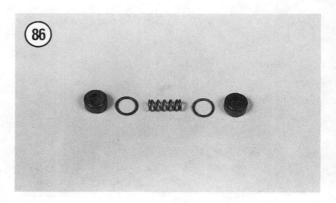

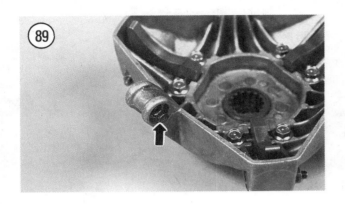

5. Install the spring seat in the outer half assembly (**Figure 93**).

6. Install the spring (**Figure 94**).

7. Align the arrow on the spring cover (**Figure 95**) with the arrow on the outer half and install the spring cover. See **Figure 96**.

8. Slide the outer half assembly over the inner half assembly (**Figure 97**).

13

9. Install the 3 Allen screws (**Figure 98**) and tighten evenly until the spring cover is installed. Tighten the screws securely. If necessary, use the puller assembly to compress the spring cover when installing the Allen bolts.

10. With the forks installed over the slider shoes as shown in **Figure 92**, place the governor cap over the outer half assembly so that the arrow on the governor cap aligns with the arrow on the outer half assembly. See **Figure 99**.

11. Remove the forks and push the governor cup down so that its splines engage with the inner half shaft splines.

> *CAUTION*
> *Make sure the governor cup splines engage with the inner half shaft splines.*

Installation

> *CAUTION*
> *Do not install any antiseize lubricant on the crankshaft taper when installing the drive pulley assembly.*

1. Clean the crankshaft taper with lacquer thinner or electrical contact cleaner.

2. Slide the drive pulley (**Figure 100**) onto the crankshaft.

3. Install the drive pulley bolt and lockwasher (**Figure 101**).

> *CAUTION*
> *When replacing the drive pulley bolt lockwasher, always use a Ski-Doo factory replacement lockwasher.*

4. Secure the crankshaft with the same tool used during disassembly or use a suitable holding tool as shown in **Figure 102**.

5. Tighten the drive pulley bolt as follows:

   a. Tighten the drive pulley bolt to 105 N•m (77 ft.-lb.).

   b. Remove the crankshaft locking tool and reconnect the fuel pump pulse hose.

   c. Install the drive belt as described in this chapter.

d. Close the shroud and raise the rear of the snowmobile so the track clears the ground.

e. Start and run the engine. Apply the brake 2 to 3 times and turn the engine off.

f. Reinstall the crankshaft locking tool.

g. Loosen the drive pulley bolt to 85 N·m (63 ft.-lb.). Then retighten to 95 N·m (70 ft.-lb.)

h. Remove the crankshaft locking tool and reconnect the fuel pump hose.

i. Lower the snowmobile to the ground.

NOTE
After 10 hours of operation, recheck the drive pulley bolt for tightness.

Drive Pulley Adjustment

The drive pulley calibration screw (**Figure 77**) can be changed to best suit high engine speed depending on altitude, temperature and track conditions. Observe the following:

a. The stock calibration screw position is No. 3.

b. Each number changes engine speed by approximately 200 rpm.

c. Lower numbers will decrease engine speed whereas high numbers will increase engine speed. For example, if the calibration screw is changed from No. 3 to No. 4, engine speed is increased approximately 200 rpm.

NOTE
Do not remove the calibration screw locknut when performing the following procedure as the washer on the inside of the clutch assembly may fall out.

1. Loosen the calibration screw locknut (**Figure 78**) just enough to allow the calibration screw to be turned.

2. Turn the calibration screw to the desired position number.

3. Turn all 3 calibration screws to the same position number.

4. Tighten the locknut securely.

DRIVEN PULLEY SERVICE

The driven pulley is mounted onto the left-hand side of the jackshaft. Refer to **Figure 103** or **Figure 104** when performing procedures in this section.

13

Removal

1. Remove the drive belt as described in this chapter.
2. Apply the parking brake to lock the jackshaft.
3. Loosen and remove the driven pulley bolt (**Figure 105**) and extension. Don't lose the shims on the end of the bolt (**Figure 106**).
4. Remove the driven pulley (**Figure 107**).
5. Remove the key (**Figure 108**).

> *NOTE*
> *The shim(s) (**Figure 109**) installed on the jackshaft behind the driven pulley are used to adjust pulley offset. Do not remove the shims unless jackshaft service is required. Make sure to install the same shims before driven pulley installation.*

Installation

1. Make sure the offset shims are installed on the jackshaft (**Figure 109**).

2. Apply a low-temperature grease to the splines in the driven pulley.

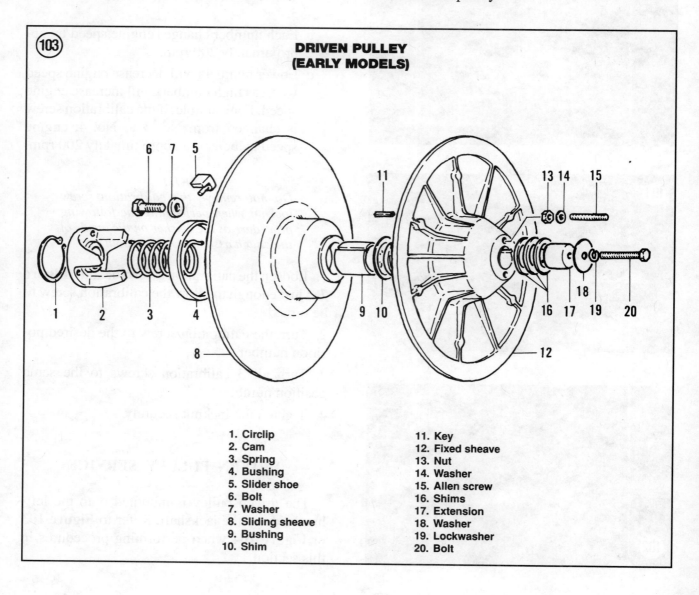

(103)

**DRIVEN PULLEY
(EARLY MODELS)**

1. Circlip
2. Cam
3. Spring
4. Bushing
5. Slider shoe
6. Bolt
7. Washer
8. Sliding sheave
9. Bushing
10. Shim
11. Key
12. Fixed sheave
13. Nut
14. Washer
15. Allen screw
16. Shims
17. Extension
18. Washer
19. Lockwasher
20. Bolt

DRIVEN PULLEY (LATE MODELS)

1. Circlip
2. Cam
3. Spring
4. Bushing
5. Slider shoe
6. Bolt
7. Washer
8. Sliding pulley half
9. Bushing
10. Shim
11. Key
12. Fixed pulley half
13. Nut
14. Washer
15. Allen screw
16. Shims
17. Extension
18. Washer
19. Lockwasher
20. Bolt
21. Bolt
22. Ring
23. Cup
24. Bolt

13

3. Slide the driven pulley onto the jackshaft (**Figure 107**).

4. Install the driven pulley bolt and the original number of shims (**Figure 106**). Tighten the bolt to 25 N•m (18 ft.-lb.). Apply the parking brake to lock the jackshaft when tightening the driven pulley bolt.

5. Check the driven pulley free play adjustment as described in this chapter.

6. Install the drive belt as described in this chapter.

Driven Pulley Free Play Adjustment

1. Remove the drive belt as described in this chapter.

2. Insert a 9.5 mm (3/8 in.) square bar between the driven pulley pulley halves.

3. The driven pulley must have side clearance after it is installed on the jackshaft and the retaining bolt is tightened securely. Check free play by moving the pulley back and forth by hand or by measuring the clearance between the driven pulley and washer with a feeler gauge. The pulley must have 1-3 mm (3/64-1/8 in.) axial clearance (**Figure 110**).

4. If the axial clearance is incorrect, proceed to Step 5.

5. Apply the parking brake to lock the jackshaft.

6. Loosen and remove the driven pulley bolt (**Figure 105**).

7. Adjust the driven pulley free play by adding or subtracting the number of shims on the extension (**Figure 106**). Adding shims decreases free play while removing shims increases it. Shims can be purchased through Ski-Doo dealers.

8. Install the driven pulley bolt and the new number of shims (**Figure 106**). Tighten the bolt to 25 N•m (18 ft.-lb.).

9. Recheck the driven pulley free play. If the free play is not within specifications, repeat this procedure until the free play is correct.

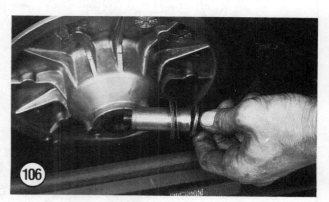

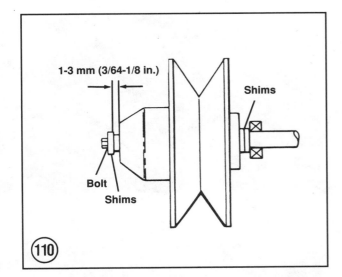

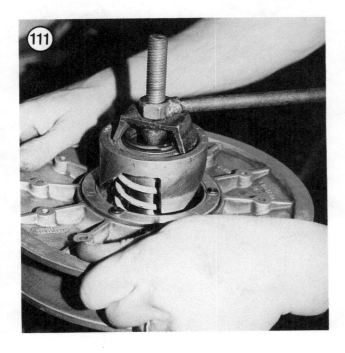

Disassembly

WARNING
The driven pulley is under spring pressure. Hold the driven pulley securely when removing the circlip in Step 1.

NOTE
*Compress the driven pulley spring using special tools (part No. 529 0151 00) as shown in **Figure 111** to hold the parts of the driven pulley and compress the outer cam while disassembling.*

1. Compress the outer cam (A, **Figure 112**) and remove the circlip (B, **Figure 112**).

NOTE
*The outer cam (A, **Figure 112**) is equipped with 6 holes for spring adjustment. Record the hole number before removing the outer cam in Step 2.*

2. Remove the cam (**Figure 113**).
3. Remove the spring (**Figure 114**).

13

4. Remove the key (**Figure 115**).

5. Separate the sliding and fixed halves (**Figure 116**).

6. Remove the washer (**Figure 117**).

Inspection

1. Clean the driven pulley assembly in solvent.

2. Check the belt drive surfaces of the pulley halves (**Figure 116**) for cracks, deep scoring or excessive wear.

3. Check the belt drive surfaces of the pulley halves for rubber or rust buildup. For proper operation, the pulley surfaces must be *clean*. Remove rubber or rust debris with a fine grade steel wool. Wipe off with a lint free cloth.

4. The nylon ramp shoes (**Figure 118**) provide a sliding surface between the cam and the driven pulley. The nylon pads rub against aluminum and wear is usually minimal. If a ramp shoe is gouged or damaged, smooth the surface with emery cloth; do not use a file. If a ramp shoe cannot be repaired, replace all the ramp shoes as a set. If ramp shoes appear okay, measure slope thickness with a vernier caliper as shown in **Figure 119**. Replace the ramp shoes as a set if any one shoe measures 1 mm (0.039 in.) or less. Install the ramp shoes so that they face in the direction shown in **Figure 118**.

5. Check the driven pulley spring (**Figure 120**) for cracks or distortion. Replace the spring if necessary. When replacing the driven pulley spring, purchase a new spring with the same color code.

> *NOTE*
> *Failure of the driven pulley spring may be caused by metal fatigue resulting from the constant twisting action. The driven pulley will open quicker than it should if the spring has weakened. This condition can be noticed when riding in mountain areas or deep snow; the machine will drive slower and have much less pulling power. Because it is difficult to gauge spring wear, you should replace the*

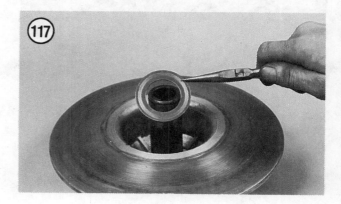

(118)

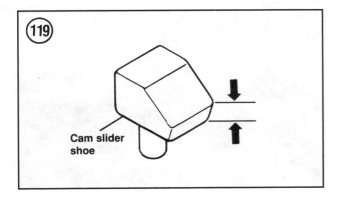

(119)

Cam slider
shoe

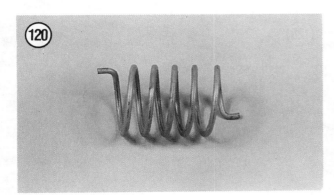

(120)

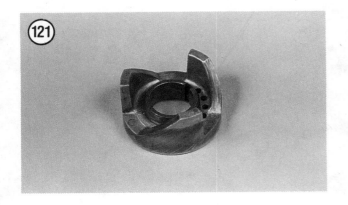

(121)

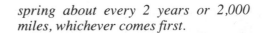

spring about every 2 years or 2,000 miles, whichever comes first.

6. Check the cam ramps (**Figure 121**) for scoring, gouging or other damage. Smooth the ramp area with #400 wet-or-dry sandpaper. If the ramp area is severely damaged, replace the spring seat.

7. Inspect the bushing (A, **Figure 122**) for wear or damage. If necessary, replace the bushing as follows:

    a. Remove the 3 bolts (B, **Figure 122**) holding the bushing in place.

    b. Remove the bushing with a press.

    c. Apply Loctite 609 onto the outside of the bushing.

    d. Align the new bushing bolt notches with the pulley half and press the bushing into the bore.

    e. Install and tighten the bushing bolts.

8. Inspect the bushing in the sliding pulley (**Figure 123**) for wear or damage. If necessary replace the bushing as follows:

(122)

13

(123)

a. Press the old bushing from the pulley.

b. Press the new busing into the pulley.

Assembly

> *NOTE*
> *Assembly is easier if the special tool (part No. 529 0151 00) is used as shown in Figures 124-127 to help hold the parts of the driven pulley while assembling.*

1. Place the fixed half of the pulley on the workbench so that the shaft faces up (**Figure 128**).

2. Install the washer (**Figure 117**) over shaft.

3. Install the sliding half of the pulley (**Figure 129**) over the fixed half of the pulley so that the belt surfaces face together.

4. Install the key (**Figure 115**) in the shaft.

5. Install the spring (**Figure 114**) so that one end of spring engages the hole in the pulley.

NOTE
*For normal reassembly, hook the spring in the same hole of the cam that was used before disassembly. The cam is equipped with 6 holes for spring adjustment (**Figure 113**).*

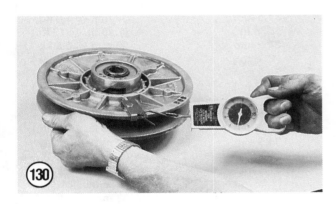

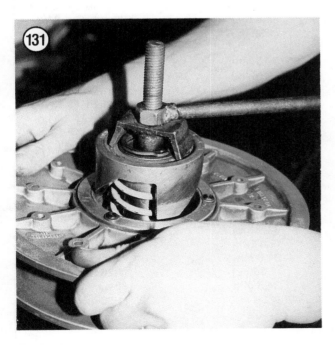

6. Hook the other end of the spring in one of the holes in the cam and slide the cam over the key and the shaft. See **Figure 112**.

7. Hold the fixed half of the pulley, then twist the sliding pulley half counterclockwise to preload the spring. Correct preload is listed in **Table 4**.

8. Compress the cam and spring enough to install the snap ring.

9. Make sure the circlip seats completely in the pulley shaft groove.

10. Check and adjust spring preload as follows:

    a. Attach a spring scale to the sliding half of the pulley with the Ski-Doo spring scale hook (part No. 529 0065 00) or equivalent. See **Figure 130**.

    b. Hold the fixed half of the pulley to prevent it from moving and pull the spring scale attached to the sliding half as shown in **Figure 131**. Read the spring scale when the pulley just begins to move. The recommended standard spring preload is listed in **Table 4**.

    c. It may be necessary to reposition the spring in the cam holes (**Figure 132**) until preload is correct. Adjust spring preload by first removing the cam, relocating the end of the spring as described in Step 6, then repeating Steps 7-9.

11. Install the driven pulley as described in this chapter.

13

Table 1 DRIVE SYSTEM SPECIFICATIONS

Model	Engagement rpm	Drive belt width (new)	Drive belt deflection
1990			
MX & MX LT	3,500-3,700	34.9 mm (1.37 in.)	32 mm @ 6.8 kg (1.26 in. @ 15 lb.)
Plus models	3,400-3,600	34.9 mm (1.37 in.)	32 mm @ 6.8 kg (1.26 in. @ 15 lb.)
MACH 1	2,400-2,600	34.9 mm (1.37 in.)	32 mm @ 6.8 kg (1.26 in. @ 15 lb.)
1991			
MX	3,500-3,600	34.9 mm (1.37 in.)	32 mm @ 6.8 kg (1.26 in. @ 15 lb.)
Plus models	3,400-3,600	34.9 mm (1.37 in.)	32 mm @ 6.8 kg (1.26 in. @ 15 lb.)
MACH 1	3,300-3,400	34.9 mm (1.37 in.)	32 mm @ 6.8 kg (1.26 in. @ 15 lb.)
1992			
MX	3,500-3,600	34.5 mm (1.36 in.)	32 mm @ 6.8 kg (1.26 in. @ 15 lb.)
Plus	3,400-3,600	34.5 mm (1.36 in.)	32 mm @ 6.8 kg (1.26 in. @ 15 lb.)
MACH 1	3,300-3,400	34.9 mm (1.37 in.)	32 mm @ 6.8 kg (1.26 in. @ 15 lb.)
1993			
MX Z	3,300-3,500	34.5 mm (1.36 in.)	32 mm @ 6.8 kg (1.26 in. @ 15 lb.)
Other MX models	3,500-3,600	34.5 mm (1.36 in.)	32 mm @ 6.8 kg (1.26 in. @ 15 lb.)
Plus EFI	3,300-3,500	34.5 mm (1.36 in.)	32 mm @ 6.8 kg (1.26 in. @ 15 lb.)
Other Plus models	3,400-3,500	34.5 mm (1.36 in.)	32 mm @ 6.8 kg (1.26 in. @ 15 lb.)
MACH 1	3,500-3,600	34.5 mm (1.36 in.)	32 mm @ 6.8 kg (1.26 in. @ 15 lb.)
1994			
MX	3,300-3,500	34.5 mm (1.36 in.)	32 mm @ 6.8 kg (1.26 in. @ 15 lb.)
MX Z	3,400-3,600	34.5 mm (1.36 in.)	32 mm @ 6.8 kg (1.26 in. @ 15 lb.)
Formula ST	3,300-3,500	34.5 mm (1.36 in.)	32 mm @ 6.8 kg (1.26 in. @ 15 lb.)
Formula STX	3,400-3,600	34.9 mm (1.37 in.)	32 mm @ 6.8 kg (1.26 in. @ 15 lb.)
Formula Z	3,700-3,900	34.9 mm (1.37 in.)	32 mm @ 6.8 kg (1.26 in. @ 15 lb.)
Summit 470	3,700-3,900	34.5 mm (1.36 in.)	32 mm @ 6.8 kg (1.26 in. @ 15 lb.)
Summit 583	3,700-3,900	34.9 mm (1.37 in.)	32 mm @ 6.8 kg (1.26 in. @ 15 lb.)
Grand Touring	3,300-3,500	34.5 mm (1.36 in.)	32 mm @ 6.8 kg (1.26 in. @ 15 lb.)
Grand Touring XTC	3,300-3,500	34.5 mm (1.36 in.)	32 mm @ 6.8 kg (1.26 in. @ 15 lb.)

(continued)

Table 1 DRIVE SYSTEM SPECIFICATIONS (continued)

Model	Engagement rpm	Drive belt width (new)	Drive belt deflection
1994 (continued)			
Grand Touring SE	3,400-3,600	34.5 mm (1.36 in.)	32 mm @ 6.8 kg (1.26 in. @ 15 lb.)
MACH 1	3,400-3,600	34.5 mm (1.36 in.)	32 mm @ 6.8 kg (1.26 in. @ 15 lb.)
Grand Touring SE	3,400-3,600	34.5 mm (1.36 in.)	32 mm @ 6.8 kg (1.26 in. @ 15 lb.)
1995			
MX	3,400-3,600	34.3 mm (1.35 in.)	32 mm @ 6.8 kg (1.26 in. @ 15 lb.)
Grand Touring SE	3,400-3,600	34.5 mm (1.36 in.)	32 mm @ 6.8 kg (1.26 in. @ 15 lb.)
MX Z	4,300-4,500	34.9 mm (1.37 in.)	32 mm @ 6.8 kg (1.26 in. @ 15 lb.)
STX	3,400-3,600	34.9 mm (1.37 in.)	32 mm @ 6.8 kg (1.26 in. @ 15 lb.)
STX LT	3,100-3,300	34.9 mm (1.37 in.)	32 mm @ 6.8 kg (1.26 in. @ 15 lb.)
Formula SS	3,400-3,600	35.2 mm (1.39 in.)	32 mm @ 6.8 kg (1.26 in. @ 15 lb.)
Formula Z	3,700-3,900	34.9 mm (1.37 in.)	32 mm @ 6.8 kg (1.26 in. @ 15 lb.)
Summit 583	3,700-3,900	34.9 mm (1.37 in.)	32 mm @ 6.8 kg (1.26 in. @ 15 lb.)
Summit 670	3,800-4,000	35.2 mm (1.39 in.)	32 mm @ 6.8 kg (1.26 in. @ 15 lb.)
Grand Touring 470	3,400-3,600	34.3 mm (1.35 in.)	32 mm @ 6.8 kg (1.26 in. @ 15 lb.)
Grand Touring 580	3,100-3,300	34.9 mm (1.37 in.)	32 mm @ 6.8 kg (1.26 in. @ 15 lb.)
Grand Touring SE	3,400-3,600	35.2 mm (1.39 in.)	32 mm @ 6.8 kg (1.26 in. @ 15 lb.)
MACH 1	4,400-4,600	35.2 mm (1.39 in.)	32 mm @ 6.8 kg (1.26 in. @ 15 lb.)

13

Table 2 PULLEY ALIGNMENT

Model	Distance between pulleys Z	Offset X	Offset Y
1990-1992	26-27 mm (1.024-1.063 in.)	35.6-36.4 mm (1.40-1.43 in.)	*
1993			
Formula MX Z	15.5-16.5 mm (1.024-1.063 in.)	34.6-35.4 mm (1.36-1.39 in.)	**
Other models	26-27 mm (1.024-1.063 in.)	35.6-36.4 mm (1.40-1.43 in.)	*

(continued)

Table 2 PULLEY ALIGNMENT (continued)

Model	Distance between pulleys Z	Offset X	Offset Y
1994			
Grand Touring	15.5-16.5 mm (1.024-1.063 in.)	34.5-35.5 mm (1.36-1.40 in.)	**
MACH 1	15.5-16.5 mm (1.024-1.063 in.)	34.5-35.5 mm (1.36-1.40 in.)	**
Other models	26-27 mm (1.024-1.063 in.)	35.6-36.4 mm (1.40-1.43 in.)	**
1995	15.5-16.5 mm (1.024-1.063 in.)	34.5-35.5 mm (1.36-1.40 in.)	**

* Measured offset Y should be 0.75-1.5 mm (0.030-0.060 in.) greater than measured offset X.
** Measured offset Y should be 1.0-2.0 mm (0.040-0.080 in.) greater than measured offset X.

Table 3 DRIVE PULLEY SPRING SPECIFICATIONS

Model	Spring free length mm (in.)	Spring color code
1990		
MX	113.6-116.6 (4.47-4.59)	Blue/Yellow
Plus	131.1-134.1 (5.16-5.28)	Blue/Orange
MACH 1	82.6-85.6 (3.25-3.37)	Red/Blue
1991		
MX	113.6-116.6 (4.47-4.59)	Blue/Yellow
Plus	131.1-134.1 (5.16-5.28)	Blue/Orange
MACH 1	96.8-99.8 (3.81-3.93)	Yellow/Yellow
1992		
MX	128.2-130.2 (5.05-5.13)	White
Plus X	104.2-107.2 (4.10-4.22)	Blue/Green
Other Plus models	98.3-101.3 (3.87-3.99)	Blue/Blue
MACH 1 X	142.8-145.8 (5.62-5.74)	Pink/Green
MACH 1	96.8-99.8 (3.81-3.93)	Yellow/Yellow
1993		
MX Z	98.3-101.3 (3.87-3.99)	Blue/Blue
Other MX models	128.2-130.2 (5.05-5.13)	White

(continued)

Table 3 DRIVE PULLEY SPRING SPECIFICATIONS (continued)

Model	Spring free length mm (in.)	Spring color code
1993 (continued)		
Plus X	104.2-107.2 (4.10-4.22)	Purple/Purple
Other Plus models	131.1-134.1 (5.16-5.28)	Blue/Orange
Grand Touring	131.1-134.1 (5.16-5.28)	Blue/Orange
MACH 1	98.3-101.3 (3.87-3.99)	Blue/Blue
1994		
MX	92-95 (3.62-3.74)	Blue
MX Z	113.6-116.6 (4.47-4.59)	Blue/Yellow
STX	104.2-107.2 (4.10-4.22)	Blue/Green
Formula Z	120.5-123.5 (4.74-4.86)	Yellow
Summit 470 & 583	104.2-107.2 (4.10-4.22)	Purple/Purple
Grand Touring SE	98.3-101.3 (3.87-3.99)	Blue/Blue
Other GT models	131.1-134.1 (5.16-5.28)	Blue/Orange
MACH 1	98.3-101.3 (3.87-3.99)	Blue/Blue
1995		
MX	113.6-116.6 (4.47-4.59)	Blue/Yellow
MX Z	123-126 (4.84-4.96)	Pink/White
STX	104.2-107.2 (4.10-4.22)	Blue/Green
STX LT	92.5-95.5 (3.64-3.76)	Yellow/Green
Formula SS	104.2-107.2 (4.10-4.22)	Blue/Green
Formula Z	120.5-123.5 (4.74-4.86)	Yellow
Summit 583	104.2-107.2 (4.10-4.22)	Violet/Violet
Summit 670	120.5-123.5 (4.74-4.86)	Yellow
Grand Touring 470	92-95 (3.62-3.74)	Blue/Pink
Grand Touring 580	153.2-156.2 (6.03-6.15)	Pink/Violet
Grand Touring SE	104.2-107.2 (4.10-4.22)	Yellow/Orange
MACH 1	123-126 (4.84-4.96)	Pink/White

13

Table 4 DRIVEN PULLEY SPECIFICATIONS

Model	Spring preload kg (lb.)	Cam angle degrees
1990		
MX & Plus	6.3-6.5 (13.9-14.3)	NA
MACH 1	7.3 (16.1)	NA
1991		
MX & Plus	6.3-6.5 (13.9-14.3)	NA
MACH 1	7.3 (16.1)	NA
1992		
MX	6.3-6.5 (13.9-14.3)	NA
Plus	7.3 (16.1)	NA
MACH 1	7.3 (16.1)	NA
1993		
MX Z	4.6-5.9 (10-13)	NA
Other MX models	4.8-6.2 (10.6-13.6)	NA
Plus	4.1-5.4 (9-12)	NA
Grand Touring	4.1-5.4 (9-12)	NA
MACH 1	4.6-5.9 (10-13)	NA
1994		
MX	4.1-5.6 (9.0-12.3)	NA
MX Z	5.5-7.0 (12.1-15.4)	NA
STX	5.5-7.0 (12.1-15.4)	NA
Formula Z	5.5-7.0 (12.1-15.4)	NA
Summit 470 & 583	5.5-7.0 (12.1-15.4)	NA
Grand Touring	4.1-5.6 (9.0-12.3)	NA
MACH 1	4.1-5.6 (9.0-12.3)	NA
1995		
MX	5.5-7.0 (12.1-15.4)	44
MX Z	5.5-7.0 (12.1-15.4)	44
STX	5.5-7.0 (12.1-15.4)	50
STX LT	5.5-7.0 (12.1-15.4)	44
Formula SS	5.5-7.0 (12.1-15.4)	47
Formula Z	5.5-7.0 (12.1-15.4)	50
Summit 583	5.5-7.0 (12.1-15.4)	44
Summit 670	5.5-7.0 (12.1-15.4)	47
Grand Touring 470	5.5-7.0 (12.1-15.4)	44
Grand Touring 580	5.5-7.0 (12.1-15.4)	50
Grand Touring SE	5.5-7.0 (12.1-15.4)	47
MACH 1	5.5-7.0 (12.1-15.4)	47

Chapter Fourteen

Brake, Jackshaft, Chaincase and Drive Axle

This chapter describes service procedures for the brake, jackshaft (countershaft), chaincase and drive axle. **Tables 1-3** are at the end of the chapter.

DRIVE CHAIN AND SPROCKETS (1990-1992 MODELS WITHOUT REVERSE)

Removal

Refer to **Figure 1** when performing this procedure.

1. Open the hood.

2. Remove the exhaust pipe and muffler as described in Chapter Eight.

3. Place shops rags under the chaincase cover to absorb any spilled oil.

NOTE
The chaincase is filled with oil and oil will spill when the chaincase cover is removed. Use rags to absorb as much spilled oil as possible.

4. Remove the screws attaching the chaincase cover (**Figure 2**) to the chaincase. Remove the cover and gasket. Discard the gasket.

5. Clean up as much oil as possible before proceeding with the removal.

6. Loosen chain tension as follows:
   a. Remove the pin (A, **Figure 3**).
   b. Turn the adjust bolt (B, **Figure 3**) counterclockwise and loosen chain tension.
   c. Make sure the chain tension is completely loose.

7. Remove the cotter pin from the end of the jackshaft (**Figure 4**). Do not reuse this cotter pin.

8. Have an assistant apply the front brake. Then loosen the drive sprocket nut (**Figure 4**).

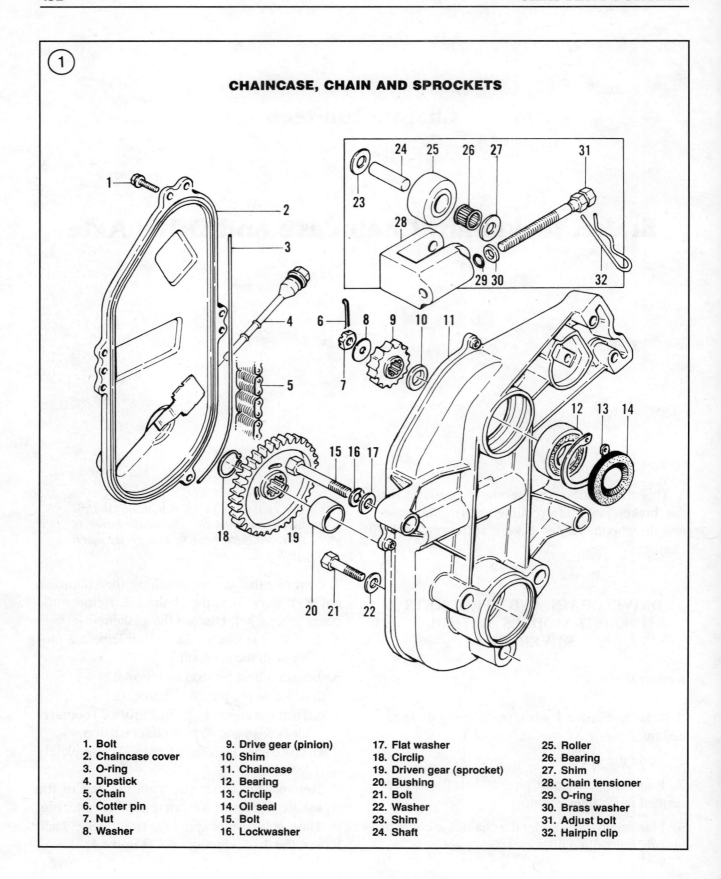

①

CHAINCASE, CHAIN AND SPROCKETS

1. Bolt	9. Drive gear (pinion)	17. Flat washer	25. Roller
2. Chaincase cover	10. Shim	18. Circlip	26. Bearing
3. O-ring	11. Chaincase	19. Driven gear (sprocket)	27. Shim
4. Dipstick	12. Bearing	20. Bushing	28. Chain tensioner
5. Chain	13. Circlip	21. Bolt	29. O-ring
6. Cotter pin	14. Oil seal	22. Washer	30. Brass washer
7. Nut	15. Bolt	23. Shim	31. Adjust bolt
8. Washer	16. Lockwasher	24. Shaft	32. Hairpin clip

9. Remove the driven sprocket circlip (**Figure 5**).

10. Remove the drive sprocket nut (**Figure 6**) and washer (**Figure 7**).

11. Remove the chain and sprockets (**Figure 8**) as an assembly. See **Figure 9**.

12. Remove the spacer from the jackshaft (**Figure 10**).

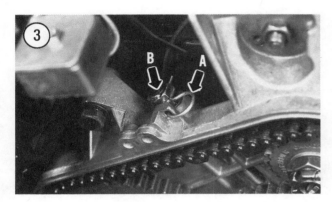

14

13. Remove the spacer from the drive axle (**Figure 11**).

Inspection

Refer to **Figure 1** for this procedure. Drive chain specifications are listed in **Table 1**.

1. Clean all components thoroughly in solvent. Remove any gasket residue from the cover and housing machined surfaces.

2. Inspect the drive and driven sprockets (**Figure 12**) for cracks, deep scoring, excessive wear or tooth damage. Check the splines for the same abnormal conditions.

3. Check the chain (**Figure 13**) for cracks, excessive wear or pin breakage.

4. If the sprockets and/or chain are severely worn or damaged, replace all 3 components as a set.

5. Check the chain tensioner for wear and damage. If you have to replace the chain and sprockets because of severe wear or damage, the chain tensioner gear should also be replaced.

6. Disassemble the chain tensioner. Refer to **Figure 1**. Check the bearing for damage. Replace if necessary. Reverse to assemble and install the tensioner.

7. Check the cover (**Figure 14**) for cracks, warpage or other damage.

Installation

Refer to **Figure 1** for this procedure.

1. Install the spacer on the drive axle (**Figure 11**).

2. Install the spacer on the jackshaft (**Figure 10**).

3. Lubricate the ends of the jackshaft and drive axle with the gear oil recommended in Chapter Three.

> *NOTE*
> *When installing the sprockets in Step 4, fit the sprockets onto the drive chain so*

*that the stamped sprocket number faces out (**Figure 15**).*

4. Install the chain and sprockets (**Figure 9**) as an assembly. See **Figure 8**.

5. Install the drive sprocket washer (**Figure 7**) and nut (**Figure 6**).

6. Install the driven sprocket circlip (**Figure 5**). Make sure the circlip seats in the drive axle groove completely.

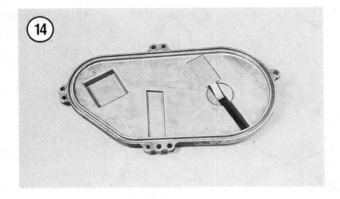

7. Lock the front brake. Then tighten the drive sprocket nut to 53 N•m (39 ft.-lb.). Install a *new* cotter pin through the jackshaft and bend the ends over to lock it. See **Figure 4**.

8. Install the chaincase cover together with the O-ring. Make sure the O-ring fits in the cover groove completely. Install the cover and its attaching screws. Tighten the screws securely.

9. Adjust the chain tension as described in Chapter Three.

10. Fill the chaincase with the amount and type of gear oil specified in Chapter Three.

11. Install the exhaust pipe and muffler as described in Chapter Eight.

12. Close and secure the hood.

DRIVE CHAIN AND SPROCKETS (1993-1995 MODELS WITHOUT REVERSE)

Removal

Refer to **Figure 16** when performing this procedure.

1. Open the hood.

2. Remove the exhaust pipe and muffler as described in Chapter Eight.

3. Place shop rags under the chaincase cover to absorb any spilled oil.

> *NOTE*
> *All of the chaincase oil will not be removed by draining. When the chaincase cover is removed, use the rags to absorb as much spilled oil as possible.*

4. Remove the drain plug (**Figure 17**) and drain oil from the chaincase as described in Chapter Three.

5. Remove the screws attaching the cover to the chaincase. Remove the cover and O-ring, then discard the O-ring. Install a new O-ring when assembling.

6. Clean up as much oil as possible before proceeding with the removal.

14

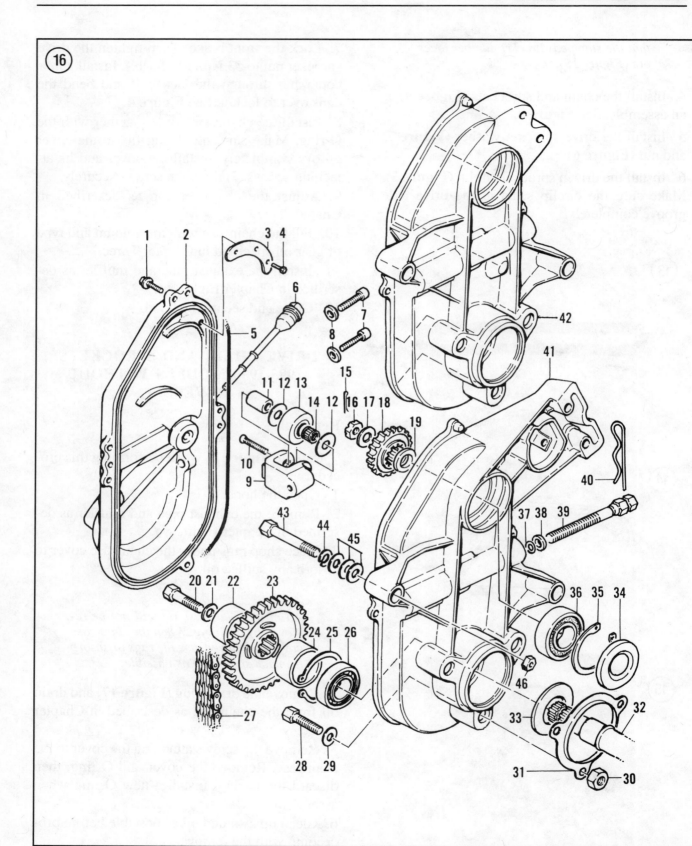

CHAINCASE, CHAIN AND SPROCKETS
(1993-1995 MODELS WITHOUT REVERSE)

1. Bolt
2. Cover
3. Oil deflector
4. Screw
5. O-ring
6. Dipstick
7. Allen screws
8. Washer
9. Tensioner block
10. Screw
11. Bushing
12. Washers
13. Roller
14. Roller bearing
15. Cotter pin
16. Castellated nut
17. Washer
18. Sprocket
19. Shim
20. Bolt
21. Lockwasher
22. Cap
23. Sprocket
24. Spacer
25. Circlip
26. Ball bearing
27. Chain
28. Bolt
29. Washer
30. Nut
31. Protector
32. Drive shaft
33. Oil seal
34. Oil seal
35. Circlip
36. Ball bearing
37. O-ring
38. Washer
39. Adjuster bolt
40. Hairpin clip
41. Chaincase
42. Chaincase (used on some models)
43. Bolt
44. Lockwasher
45. Shims
46. Nut

14

7. Loosen chain tension as follows:
   a. Remove the pin (A, **Figure 18**).
   b. Turn the adjust bolt (B, **Figure 18**) counter-clockwise and loosen chain tension.
   c. Check that chain tension is completely loose.

8. Remove the cotter pin from the end of the jackshaft (**Figure 19**). Do not reuse this cotter pin.

9. Have an assistant apply the front brake. Then loosen the drive sprocket nut (**Figure 19**).

10. Remove the screw (**Figure 20**), cap and lockwasher that attaches the driven sprocket to the drive axle.

11. Remove the drive sprocket retaining nut and washer (**Figure 19**).

12. Slide both sprockets from the shafts, then remove the chain and both sprockets as an assembly.

13. Remove the spacer from the jackshaft.

14. Remove the spacer from the drive axle.

Inspection

Refer to **Figure 16** for this procedure. Drive chain specifications are listed in **Table 1**.

1. Clean all components thoroughly in solvent. Remove any gasket residue from the cover and housing machined surfaces.

2. Inspect the drive and driven sprockets (**Figure 12**) for cracks, deep scoring, excessive wear or tooth damage. Check the splines for the same abnormal conditions.

3. Check the chain for cracks, excessive wear or pin breakage.

NOTE
*The chain and sprockets on some models are wider than other models with the same number of teeth. If new sprockets and chain are installed, be sure to install the same type as originally installed. Chain size listed in **Table 1** is followed by a "W" for models with the wider chain.*

4. If the sprockets and/or chain are severely worn or damaged, replace all 3 components as a set.

5. Check the chain tensioner for wear and damage. If you have to replace the chain and sprockets because of severe wear or damage, the chain tensioner gear should also be replaced.

6. Disassemble the chain tensioner (**Figure 16**). Check the bearing for damage and replace worn

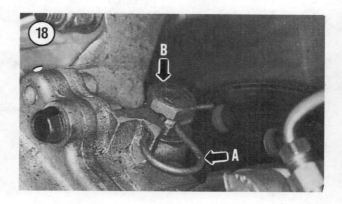

parts as necessary. Reverse the disassembly procedure to assemble and install the tensioner.

7. Check the cover (**Figure 14**) for cracks, warpage or other damage.

Installation

Refer to **Figure 16** for this procedure.

1. Install the spacer on the drive axle (**Figure 11**, typical).

2. Install the spacer on the jackshaft (**Figure 10**, typical).

3. Lubricate the ends of the jackshaft and drive axle with the gear oil recommended in Chapter Three.

NOTE
When installing the sprockets in Step 4, fit the sprockets onto the drive chain so the stamped markings (Figure 21) on sprocket face out.

4. Install the chain and both sprockets onto the jackshaft and drive axle as an assembly.

5. Install the drive sprocket washer (17, **Figure 16**) and nut (16, **Figure 16**).

6. Apply Loctite 242 to the threads of sprocket retaining screw (20, **Figure 16**), then install the cap (22, **Figure 16**), washer and retaining screw. Tighten screw securely.

7. Lock the front brake, then tighten the drive sprocket nut (**Figure 19**) to 53 N•m (39 ft.-lb.). Align holes by tightening if necessary. Install a *new* cotter pin and bend the ends of the cotter pin over against the nut.

8. Install the chaincase cover together with the O-ring. Make sure the O-ring fits in the cover groove completely. Install the cover and its attaching screws. Tighten the screws securely.

9. Adjust the chain tension as described in Chapter Three.

10. Fill the chaincase with the amount and type of gear oil specified in Chapter Three.

11. Install the exhaust pipe and muffler as described in Chapter Eight.

12. Close and secure the hood.

DRIVE CHAIN AND SPROCKETS (1993-1995 MODELS WITH REVERSE)

Removal

Refer to **Figure 22** when performing this procedure.

1. Open the hood.

2. Remove the exhaust pipe and muffler as described in Chapter Eight.

3. Place a number of shops rags underneath the chaincase cover.

NOTE
All of the chaincase oil will not be removed by draining. When the chaincase cover is removed, use the rags to absorb as much spilled oil as possible.

14

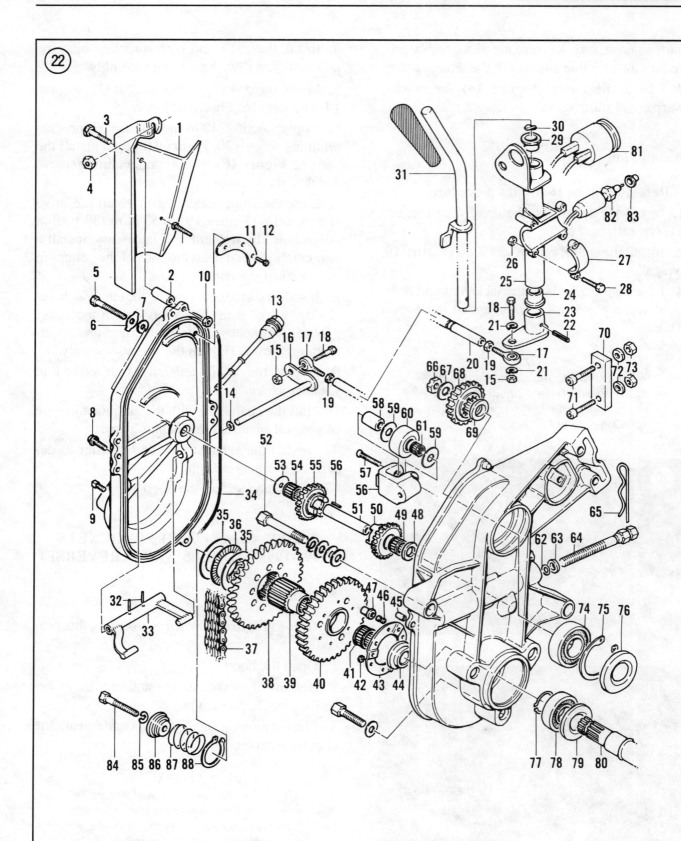

CHAINCASE, CHAIN AND SPROCKETS
(1993-1995 MODELS WITH REVERSE)

1. Deflector
2. Spacer
3. Bolt
4. Nut
5. Bolt
6. Lockplate
7. Washer
8. Bolt
9. Magnetic drain plug
10. Nut
11. Oil deflector
12. Screw
13. Dipstick
14. O-ring
15. Nut
16. Shift shaft
17. Rod end
18. Bolt
19. Locknut
20. Shift rod
21. Washers
22. Roll pin
23. Lever
24. Bushing
25. Upper bracket
26. Nut
27. Clamp
28. Bolt
29. Bushing
30. Spring washer
31. Shift handle
32. Roll pins
33. Shift fork
34. O-ring
35. Washers
36. Thrust bearing
37. Chain
38. Sprocket
39. Coupling shaft
40. Sprocket
41. Roller bearing
42. Nut
43. Retaining ring
44. Retaining ring
45. Dowel pin
46. Spring
47. Drive pin
48. Washer
49. Roller bearing
50. Sprocket
51. Reverse shaft
52. Alignment rod
53. Washer
54. Roller bearing
55. Sprocket
56. Tensioner block
57. Screw
58. Bushing
59. Washers
60. Roller
61. Roller bearing
62. O-ring
63. Washer
64. Adjuster
65. Hairpin clip
66. Castellated nut
67. Washer
68. Sprocket
69. Shim
70. Chain slider
71. Allen screws
72. Copper washers
73. Nuts
74. Ball bearing
75. Circlip
76. Oil seal
77. Circlip
78. Ball bearing
79. Oil seal
80. Drive shaft
81. Back-up alarm
82. Switch
83. Protector cap
84. Bolt
85. Lockwasher
86. Cap
87. Spring
88. Circlip

14

4. Remove the drain plug (A, **Figure 23**) and drain oil from the chaincase as described in Chapter Three.

5. Remove the screw from the shift coupling (B, **Figure 23**) and detach the coupling from the shift arm.

6. Bend the lock tab away from the screw (C, **Figure 23**), then remove the screw attaching the reverse shaft to the cover.

7. Remove the remaining screws attaching the cover to the chaincase.

8. Remove the cover while moving the cover toward the front to disengage the shift fork from the sliding gear. Discard the O-ring. Install a new O-ring when assembling.

9. Clean up as much oil as possible before proceeding with the removal.

10. Loosen chain tension as follows:
   a. Remove the pin (A, **Figure 24**).
   b. Turn the adjust bolt (B, **Figure 24**) counterclockwise and loosen chain tension.
   c. Check that chain tension is completely loose.

11. Remove cotter pin from the end of the jackshaft (**Figure 25**). Do not reuse this cotter pin.

12. Have an assistant apply the front brake, then loosen the drive sprocket nut (**Figure 25**).

13. Remove the screw (**Figure 26**) from the center of the sliding gear, then remove the sliding gear. Refer to **Figure 22**.

14. Remove the reverse idler gear, sprocket, spacers and axle (**Figure 27**).

15. Remove the drive sprocket retaining nut and washer (**Figure 25**).

16. Slide both sprockets from the shafts. Remove the chain and both sprockets as an assembly.

17. Remove the spacer from the jackshaft.

18. Remove the spacer from the drive axle.

Inspection

Refer to **Figure 22** for this procedure. Drive chain specifications are listed in **Table 1**.

1. Clean all components thoroughly in solvent. Remove any sealer residue or burrs from the cover and housing machined surfaces.

2. Inspect the drive and driven sprockets for cracks, deep scoring, excessive wear or tooth damage. Check gears and splines for the same abnormal conditions.

3. Check all radial bearings and thrust bearings. Refer to **Figure 22**. Check for roughness or discoloration.

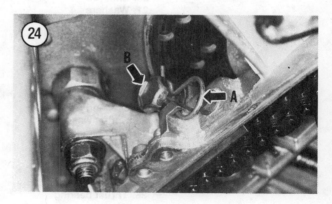

4. Replace any damaged parts. Install all parts of a bearing set as an assembly. The reverse idler sprocket and reverse idler gear are both equipped with needle bearings, but bearings are not interchangable.

5. If the sprockets and/or chain are severely worn or damaged, replace all 3 sprockets and the chain at the same time.

6. Check the chain tensioner for wear and damage. If you have to replace the chain and sprockets because of severe wear or damage, the chain tensioner gear should also be replaced.

7. Disassemble the chain tensioner (**Figure 16**). Check the bearing for damage and replace worn parts as necessary. Reverse the disassembly procedure to assemble and install the tensioner.

8. Check the cover (**Figure 14**) for cracks, warpage or other damage.

9. Check shift fork for damage or excessive wear. Drive the roll pins from the fork if removal is necessary.

10. Inspect the slider (70, **Figure 22**) for wear. If wear exceeds 1 mm (0.039 in.), install a new slider.

Installation

Refer to **Figure 22** for this procedure.

1. If removed, tighten the nuts (42, **Figure 22**) in a crossing pattern to 5 N•m (44 in.-lb.) torque.

2. Refer to **Figure 22** and **Figure 28** for assembling the sliding gear and related parts.

3. Install the spacer on the drive axle.

4. Install the spacer on the jackshaft.

5. Lubricate the ends of the jackshaft and drive axle with gear oil.

NOTE
When installing the sprockets in Step 6, fit the sprockets onto the drive chain so that the stamped markings on sprockets face out.

6. Install the drive sprocket, washer and nut on the jackshaft (**Figure 25**).

7. Install the chain and driven sprocket onto the drive axle and over the drive sprocket.

8. Install the alignment pin (**Figure 29**) in the reverse idler gear and align the pin with the hole in the sprocket (**Figure 30**).

9. Align the roll pin in the reverse axle (**Figure 27**) with the cutout of the housing (**Figure 31**) and install the axle.

14

10. Install the inner spacer (A, **Figure 32**) over the axle, then install the sprocket (B, **Figure 32**) and reverse gear (C, **Figure 32**) onto the shaft and into the housing.

11. After assembling the reverse idler gear and sprocket on the shaft, install the outer spacer (55, **Figure 22**).

12. Install the lower sliding gear assembly (**Figure 28**), then install the cap (86, **Figure 22**), washer and retaining screw. Tighten the screw to 48 N·m (35 ft.-lb.) torque.

13. Lock the front brake, then tighten the drive sprocket nut (**Figure 25**) to 48 N·m (35 ft.-lb.) torque. Align the holes in the nut with the holes in the shaft by tightening if necessary.

14. Install a *new* cotter pin and bend the ends of the cotter pin over against the nut.

15. Install the chain tensioner assembly (**Figure 33**) and adjusting bolt. Refer to **Figure 22**.

16. Install the sealing O-ring in the chaincase cover. Make sure the O-ring fits in the cover groove completely.

17. Install the cover, while aligning the ends of the shift fork between the sliding gear and the thrust washer. Make sure that the shift fork is in the correct location and that the cover fits against the chaincase before installing its attaching screws.

18. Install the screw (**Figure 34**) that passes through the reverse idler. Tighten this screw to 15 N·m (133 in.-lb.), then bend the locking tab against the flat of the screw.

19. Tighten the remaining cover retaining screws securely in a crossing pattern.

20. Attach the shift linkage and tighten the bolts to 10 N·m (89 in.-lb.).

21. Adjust the chain tension as described in Chapter Three.

22. Fill the chaincase with the amount and type of gear oil specified in Chapter Three.

23. Install the exhaust pipe and muffler as described in Chapter Eight.

24. Close and secure the hood.

CHAINCASE, BRAKE AND JACKSHAFT (ALL MODELS WITH MECHANICAL BRAKE)

All models except 1994-on MX Z and 1995 MACH 1 are equipped with a self adjusting mechanical disc brake installed in the top of the chaincase as shown in **Figure 35**.

The brake disc is located near the right end of the jackshaft. The jackshaft is installed horizontally at the rear of the engine compartment above the drive axle. The driven pulley is located on the left end of the jackshaft.

Refer to **Figure 36** and **Figure 37** for exploded views when performing procedures in this section.

Removal

1. Open and secure the hood.
2. Remove the air silencer as described in Chapter Six or Chapter Seven.
3. Remove the coolant reservoir.
4. Remove the oil injection tank.
5. Remove the heat guard from the right side.
6. Remove the chain and sprockets as described in this chapter.
7. Remove the driven pulley as described in Chapter Thirteen.
8. Pry the lock tab arms away from the caliper housing mounting nuts. Then loosen and remove the nuts and lock tab. See **Figure 36**.
9. Remove the 2 caliper housing attaching screws (**Figure 38**) and remove the outer caliper half (**Figure 39**).
10. Disconnect the brake cable (**Figure 40**) from the outer caliper half and remove the caliper half assembly.

NOTE
When removing the chaincase attaching screws in Step 11, note any shims placed between the chaincase and frame. These shims are used for chaincase alignment and must be installed during reassembly.

11. Remove the screws attaching the chaincase to the frame (**Figure 41** and **Figure 42**) and remove the chaincase. See **Figure 43**.
12. Loosen the lock collar Allen screw on the left side of the vehicle (**Figure 44**). Then use a punch and hammer and loosen the lock collar (**Figure 45**).

14

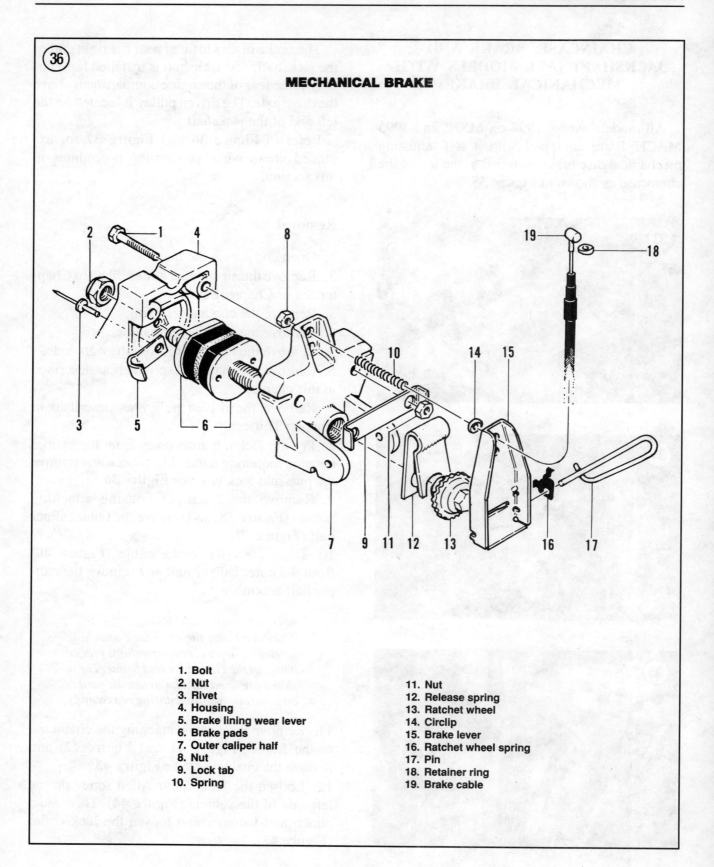

MECHANICAL BRAKE

1. Bolt
2. Nut
3. Rivet
4. Housing
5. Brake lining wear lever
6. Brake pads
7. Outer caliper half
8. Nut
9. Lock tab
10. Spring
11. Nut
12. Release spring
13. Ratchet wheel
14. Circlip
15. Brake lever
16. Ratchet wheel spring
17. Pin
18. Retainer ring
19. Brake cable

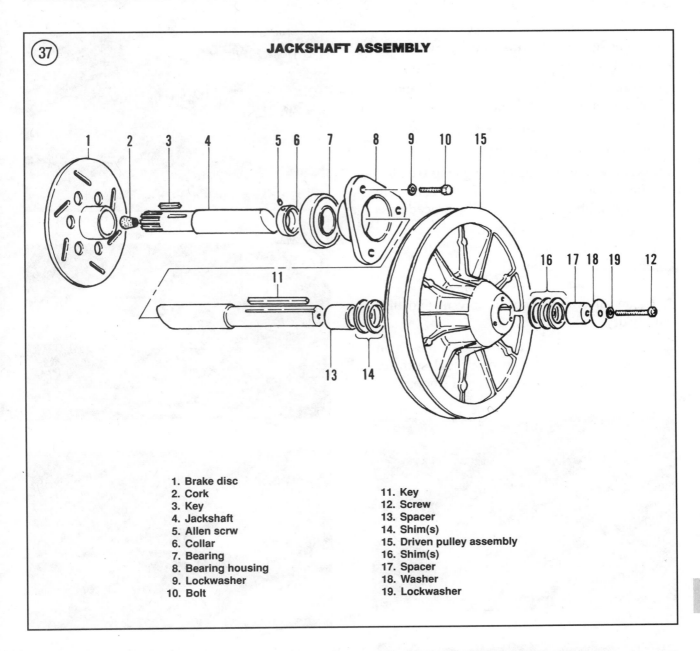

JACKSHAFT ASSEMBLY

1. Brake disc
2. Cork
3. Key
4. Jackshaft
5. Allen scrw
6. Collar
7. Bearing
8. Bearing housing
9. Lockwasher
10. Bolt
11. Key
12. Screw
13. Spacer
14. Shim(s)
15. Driven pulley assembly
16. Shim(s)
17. Spacer
18. Washer
19. Lockwasher

14

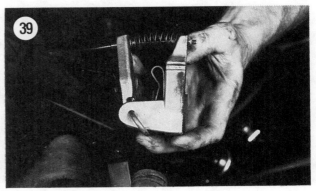

13. Remove the 3 bearing housing screws and washers (**Figure 46**).

14. Loosen the jackshaft (**Figure 47**) and remove the bearing (**Figure 48**).

15. Remove the jackshaft/brake disc assembly from the right side. See **Figure 49**.

16. Remove the bearing housing (**Figure 50**).

17. Inspect and service the different subassemblies as described in the following procedures.

Chain Case Inspection

1. Clean all components in solvent and thoroughly dry.

2. Check the machined surfaces of the chaincase and cover for sealer, burrs or rough surfaces. Sealing surfaces must be clean and smooth.

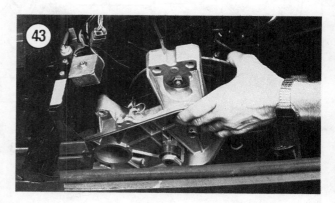

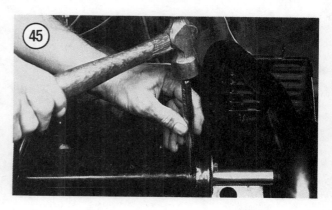

3. Check the chaincase oil seal (**Figure 51**) lip for cuts or damage. If necessary, replace the oil seal as follows:

a. Before removing the oil seal, notice and record the direction in which the lip of the seal faces for proper installation.

b. Carefully pry the oil seal from the chaincase with a large flat-tipped screwdriver (**Figure 52**). Place a rag underneath the screwdriver to prevent damage to the case.

c. Inspect the chaincase bearing as described in Step 4. If the bearing is worn or damaged, replace the bearing before installing the new oil seal.

d. The seal lips should face in the direction recorded during disassembly. After installation, pack the seal lip cavity with a low-temperature grease.

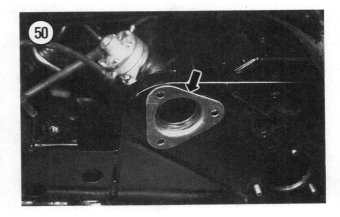

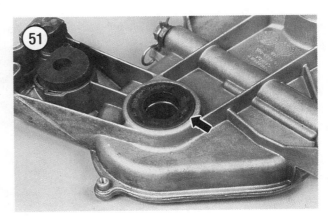

14

e. Install the new seal by driving it squarely into the chaincase with a suitable size socket placed on the outer portion of the seal (**Figure 53**).

4. Check the chaincase bearings (**Figure 54**). Turn the bearing inner race by hand and check for roughness or excessive noise. The bearing should turn smoothly. Visually check the bearing for cracks or other abnormal conditions. If the bearing is worn or damaged, replace it as follows:

a. Remove the adjoining oil seal.

b. Drive the bearing out of the chaincase with a suitable size socket placed on the outer bearing race (**Figure 55**).

c. Clean the chaincase bearing area with solvent and thoroughly dry.

d. Install the new bearing by driving it squarely into the chaincase with a socket placed on the outer bearing race (**Figure 53**).

e. Install the oil seal as described in Step 3.

Jackshaft Inspection

Refer to **Figure 37** for this procedure.

1. Clean the jackshaft in solvent and thoroughly dry.

2. Check the jackshaft (**Figure 56**) for bending.

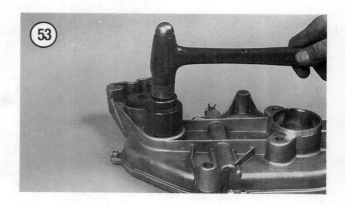

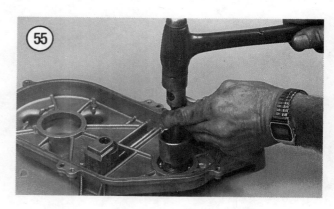

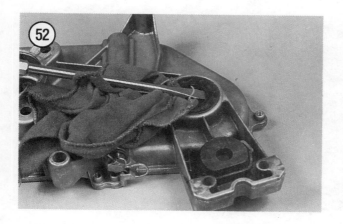

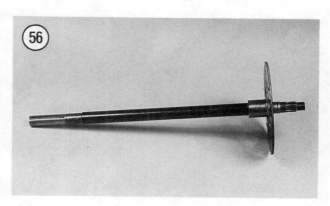

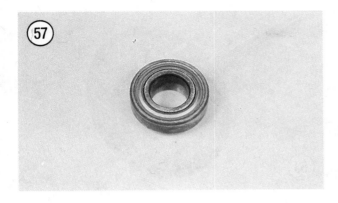

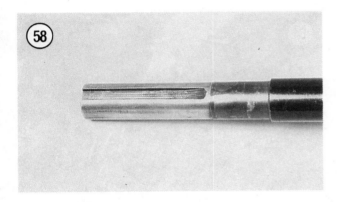

3. Turn the bearing (**Figure 57**) and check for excessive noise or roughness. Replace the bearing if worn or damaged.

4. Inspect both ends of the jackshaft for cracks, deep scoring or excessive wear. See **Figure 58** and **Figure 59**.

5. If the condition of the jackshaft is in question, repair or replace it.

Brake Component Inspection

> *WARNING*
> *The brake system is an important part of machine safety. If you are unsure about the condition of any brake component or assembly, have it checked by a qualified snowmobile mechanic.*

Refer to **Figure 36** for this procedure.

1. Clean all brake components (except brake pads) in solvent.

2. Check the brake pads for scoring, uneven wear, cracks or pad breakage. Replace the brake pads if necessary.

   a. Replace the fixed pad (**Figure 60**) by removing the nut (**Figure 61**).

   b. Replace the movable pad (**Figure 62**) by removing the rachet wheel (13, **Figure 36**).

   c. Reverse the procedure to install new pads. Tighten the fixed pad retaining nut to 8 N·m (71 in.-lb.) torque.

14

NOTE
A press is required to remove and install the brake disc from the jackshaft. Refer service to a Ski-Doo dealer or machine shop for removal of the old disc and installation of the new disc.

3. Inspect the brake disc (**Figure 63**) for cracks, deep scoring, heat discoloration or checking. Install a new brake disc if necessary.

CAUTION
Do not resurface the brake disc. If the brake disc surface is damaged or worn, replace the brake disc.

4. Check the ratchet wheel for wear or damage. Refer to **Figure 36** to replace the ratchet wheel. Observe the following:

   a. Apply a low-temperature grease to the ratchet threads and spring seat.

   b. Install the ratchet and turn until it is tight. Then back it off 1 turn.

5. If there is any doubt as to the condition of any part or assembly, replace it.

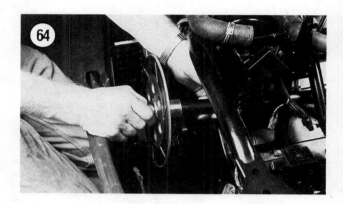

Installation

1. Pack the lip cavity of the seal (**Figure 51**) with low-temperature grease.

2. Install the bearing housing (**Figure 50**). Do not install the screws at this time.

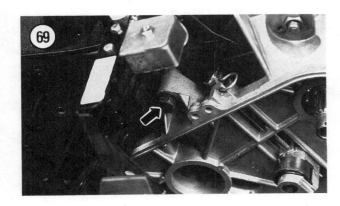

3. Insert the jackshaft (**Figure 64**) partway into the frame.

4. Install the lock collar over the jackshaft (**Figure 65**).

5. Install the bearing so that the shoulder (**Figure 66**) is toward the inside.

6. Push the jackshaft (**Figure 67**) all the way to the right side.

7. Position the chaincase over the jackshaft (**Figure 68**).

NOTE
When installing the chaincase in Step 8, be sure to install any shims that were placed between the chaincase and frame. These shims are used for chaincase alignment and must be installed in their exact original position.

8. Install the chaincase attaching screws and washers (**Figure 69** and **Figure 70**). Tighten the screws securely.

9. Insert the 2 caliper attaching screws (**Figure 71**) through the chain housing.

10. Reconnect the brake cable as shown in **Figure 72**. If necessary, turn the nut (8, **Figure 36**) to adjust the cable.

11. Position the holder (**Figure 73**) against the chain housing, install the lock tab and the 2 nuts. Tighten the nuts securely and bend the lock tabs over the nuts to lock them.

12. Adjust the jackshaft bearing as follows:

14

a. Check that the jackshaft is centered in the bearing housing. Then install the 3 bearing housing screws and washers (**Figure 74**). Tighten the screws securely.

> *NOTE*
> *If the jackshaft is not centered in the bearing housing, perform the **Chaincase Alignment Check and Adjustment** in this chapter.*

b. Install the chain and sprockets as described in this chapter.

> *NOTE*
> *The drive sprocket nut must be tightened before adjusting the jackshaft bearing.*

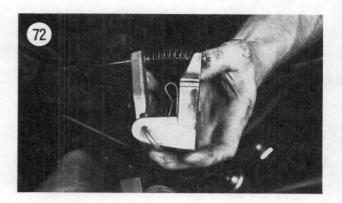

c. Slide the lock collar (**Figure 65**) toward the bearing. Then turn the lock collar to engage the collar and bearing. Engagement will probably require 1/4 turn. See **Figure 75**.

d. Turn the lock collar counterclockwise until the collar and inner race lock. Then insert a punch in the lock collar (**Figure 76**) and tighten it by tapping the punch with a hammer.

e. Apply Loctite 242 (blue) to the lock collar Allen screw. Then install and tighten the screw securely (**Figure 77**).

13. Install the chaincase cover as described in this chapter.

14. Reinstall the driven pulley as described in Chapter Thirteen

15. Reinstall the heat guard on the right side.

16. Install the oil injection tank.

17. Reinstall the coolant reservoir.

18. Reinstall the air silencer as described in Chapter Six or Chapter Seven.

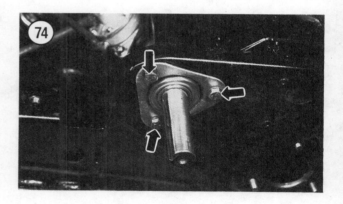

BRAKE PADS AND CALIPER (ALL MODELS WITH HYDRAULIC BRAKE)

The hydraulic brake caliper is attached to the top of the chaincase as shown in **Figure 78** or

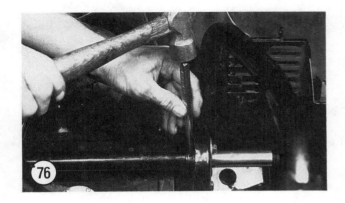

Figure 79. Brake pads can be removed and replaced without removing the caliper and the caliper can be removed from the chaincase without removing the chaincase.

Bleeding

Bleed air from the hydraulic brake system if the brake feels spongy, if there is a leak in the system, if any component of the system has been removed, or if the fluid has been replaced.

CAUTION
Immediately clean any spilled brake fluid. Wash spilled brake fluid from painted surfaces immediately, because it will damage the finish. Use soapy water and rinse with clean water.

1. Clean all dirt and foreign material from the top of the master cylinder. Remove the cover from the master cylinder and fill to the upper level mark with DOT 4 brake fluid.

WARNING
Use only brake fluid clearly marked DOT 4. Any other brake fluid may cause brake failure. Always use the same brand; do not intermix brake fluids. Some brands may not be compatible. Do not mix silicone based (DOT 5) brake fluid, because it can cause component damage when mixed with other fluids.

2. If the hose from the master cylinder to the brake caliper or the master cylinder was allowed to run dry, proceed as follows:

   a. Pump the brake lever several times, then hold the lever in.

   b. Loosen the hose attached to the master cylinder and allow some fluid and air to seep out, then tighten the hose connection.

   c. Repeat substeps a and b several times until all air is removed from the master cylinder.

   d. Refill the reservoir. Check the reservoir to make sure that it does not run dry during the bleeding process.

14

e. Continue to Step 3 when air has been removed from the master cylinder.

3. Pump the brake lever several times, then hold the lever in.

4. Connect a length of clear tubing to the bleeder valve (**Figure 78** or **Figure 79**) located toward the inside of the caliper. Place the other end of the tube into a clean container. Add enough DOT 4 brake fluid to the container to keep the end of the hose submerged, which prevents air from being drawn in during bleeding procedure.

5. Loosen the inner bleeder valve slowly and allow fluid and air to escape from the clear bleeder hose. Tighten the bleeder valve before releasing the brake lever.

6. Refill the reservoir. Check the reservoir frequently to make sure that it does not run dry during the bleeding process. Air will be pumped into the system if the reservoir is emptied while bleeding.

7. Repeat Step 5 several times until fluid without air bubbles is expelled from the bleeder tube.

8. Attach the bleeder tube to the outer bleeder valve as described in Step 4.

9. Continue bleeding from the outer bleeder valve as described in Steps 5-7.

10. Fill the reservoir and clean all spilled fluid.

Brake Pads

1A. On MX Z models, remove the retaining pin and brake pads as follows:

  a. Remove the pin as shown in **Figure 80**.

  b. Use a screwdriver or suitable tool to pry the caliper pistons and brake pads back.

  c. Pull the outer brake pad (**Figure 81**) from the caliper, then remove the inner pad (**Figure 82**).

1B. On MACH 1 models, remove the retaining pins and brake pads as follows:

  a. Remove the clips retaining the pins as shown in **Figure 83**.

  b. Pull the retaining pins from the the caliper and brake pads as shown in **Figure 84**.

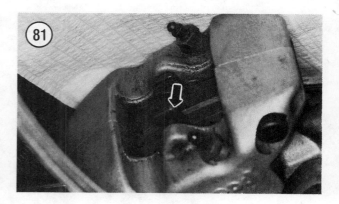

c. Remove the spring (**Figure 85**).

d. Use a screwdriver or suitable tool to pry the caliper pistons and brake pads back.

e. Pull the outer brake pad (**Figure 86**) from the caliper, then remove the inner pad.

2. Inspect the brake pads and rotor. New brake pads must be installed as a set.

3. Install the brake pads and retaining pins by reversing the removal procedure. If new pads are installed, it will probably be necessary to pry both brake pistons into the caliper completely.

4A. On MX Z models, make sure the retaining pin is correctly installed (**Figure 87**).

4B. On MACH 1 models, be sure to install clips (**Figure 83**).

Caliper Assembly

Repair parts for the caliper are not available. Service is limited to removal of the old part and installation of a new, similar part.

1. To remove the complete brake caliper assembly, first remove the brake pads as described in this chapter.

2. Disconnect the fitting (A, **Figure 88** or A, **Figure 89**) from the master cylinder and allow fluid to drain from the hose and master cylinder.

CAUTION
Immediately clean up any spilled brake fluid. Wash spilled brake fluid from

14

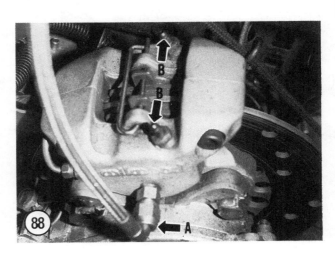

painted surfaces immediately, because it will damage the finish. Use soapy water and rinse with clean water.

3. Bend the locking tabs away from the two screws (B, **Figure 88** or B, **Figure 89**), then remove the two attaching screws.

4. Lift the caliper assembly from the chaincase and rotor.

5. Reinstall by reversing the removal procedure.

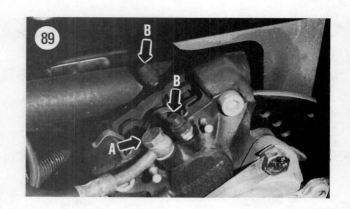

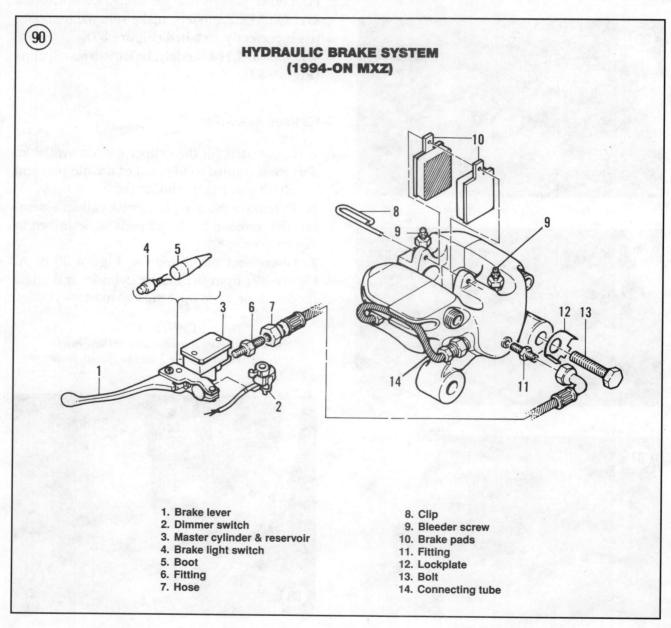

HYDRAULIC BRAKE SYSTEM (1994-ON MXZ)

1. Brake lever
2. Dimmer switch
3. Master cylinder & reservoir
4. Brake light switch
5. Boot
6. Fitting
7. Hose
8. Clip
9. Bleeder screw
10. Brake pads
11. Fitting
12. Lockplate
13. Bolt
14. Connecting tube

6. Bleed the hydraulic system as described in this chapter.

Master Cylinder

Repair parts for the master cylinder are not available. Service to the master cylinder is limited to removal of the old part and installation of a new, similar part. The brake light switch, hand lever and clamp parts are available. Refer to the exploded views in **Figure 90** or **Figure 91** when servicing.

1. Drain the master cylinder as follows:

   a. Attach a hose to the brake caliper bleeder valve.

   b. Place the open end of the hose in a clean container.

   c. Open the bleed valve and operate the brake lever to drain all fluid from the master cylinder reservoir.

   d. Close the bleeder valve and remove the drain hose.

   e. Discard the drained fluid. Do not attempt to reuse any brake fluid.

2. Disconnect the wires from the brake light switch.

3. Detach the hose from the master cylinder, then cover the openings to prevent the entrance of dirt.

4. Remove the clamping bolts and clamp attaching the master cylinder to the handlebar. Remove the master cylinder.

5. Install the master cylinder by reversing the removal procedure.

6. Fill the reservoir with DOT 4 brake fluid and bleed the system as described in this chapter.

> *WARNING*
> *Do not operate the snowmobile until the brake is operating properly.*

CHAINCASE, BRAKE DISC AND JACKSHAFT (ALL MODELS WITH HYDRAULIC BRAKE)

A hydraulic disk brake is used on 1994-on MX Z and 1995 MACH 1 models. The hydraulic brake caliper is attached to the top of the chaincase as shown in **Figure 78** or **Figure 79**.

The brake disc is near the right end of the jackshaft. The jackshaft is installed horizontally at the rear of the engine compartment above the drive axle. The driven pulley is located on the left end of the jackshaft.

Removal

1. Open and secure the hood.
2. Remove the air silencer as described in Chapter Six.
3. Remove the coolant reservoir.
4. Remove the oil injection tank.
5. Remove the heat guard from the right side.
6. Remove the chain and sprockets as described in this chapter.
7. Remove the driven pulley as described in Chapter Thirteen.
8. Remove the brake caliper as described in this chapter.

> *NOTE*
> *When removing the chaincase attaching screws in Step 9, note any shims placed between the chaincase and frame. These shims are used for chaincase alignment and must be installed during reassembly.*

9. Remove the screws attaching the chaincase to the frame (**Figure 92** and **Figure 93**), then remove the chaincase.
10. Remove the 3 Allen screws (A, **Figure 94**) attaching the bearing housing to the left side of the vehicle.
11. Remove the shims (B, **Figure 94**).
12. Loosen the jackshaft and remove the bearing.

14

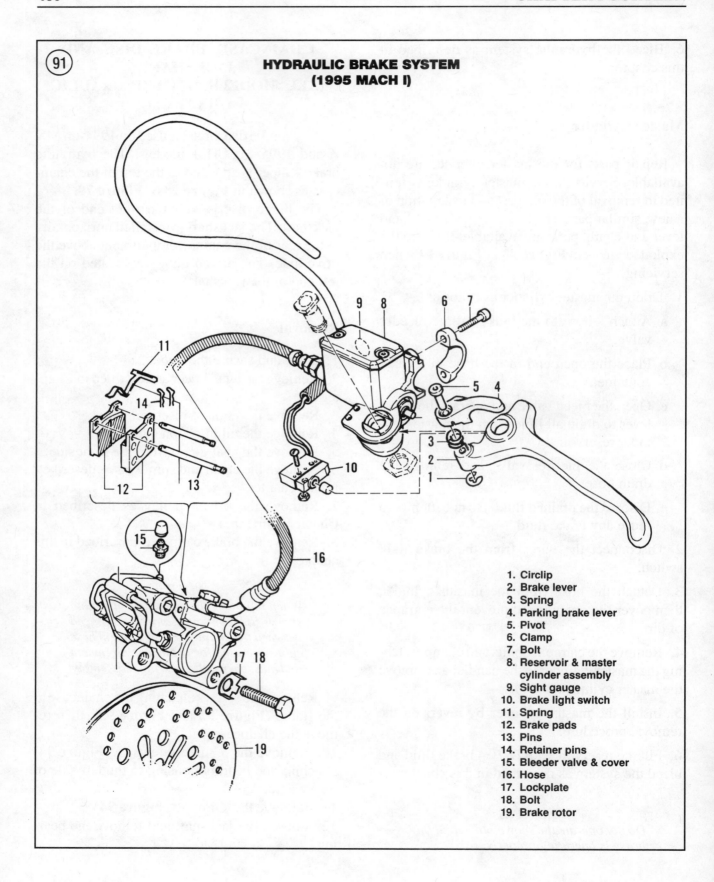

91

**HYDRAULIC BRAKE SYSTEM
(1995 MACH I)**

1. Circlip
2. Brake lever
3. Spring
4. Parking brake lever
5. Pivot
6. Clamp
7. Bolt
8. Reservoir & master
   cylinder assembly
9. Sight gauge
10. Brake light switch
11. Spring
12. Brake pads
13. Pins
14. Retainer pins
15. Bleeder valve & cover
16. Hose
17. Lockplate
18. Bolt
19. Brake rotor

13. Remove the jackshaft/brake disc assembly from the right side.

14. Inspect and service the different subassemblies as described in the following procedures.

Chain Case Inspection

Refer to **Figure 95** or **Figure 96** when servicing.

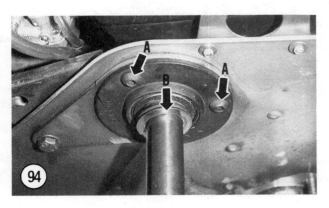

1. Clean all components in solvent and thoroughly dry.

2. Remove all sealer and any burrs from the machined surfaces of the chaincase and cover.

3. Check the chaincase oil seals for cuts or other damage. If necessary, replace the oil seals as follows:

   a. Before removing the oil seals, observe and record the direction in which the lip of each seal faces for proper reinstallation.

   b. Carefully pry the oil seal out of the chaincase with a large flat-tipped screwdriver. Protect the case from damage by placing a rag under the screwdriver.

   c. Check the chaincase bearing as described in Step 4. If the bearing is worn and damaged, replace the bearing before installing the new oil seal.

   d. The seal lips should face in the direction recorded during disassembly. After installation, pack the seal lip cavity with a low-temperature grease.

   e. Install the new seal by driving it squarely into the chaincase with a suitable size socket placed on the outer portion of the seal.

4. Inspect the chaincase bearings. Turn the bearing inner race by hand and check for roughness or excessive noise. The bearing should turn smoothly. Visually check the bearing for cracks or other abnormal conditions. If the bearing is worn or damaged, replace it as follows:

   a. Remove the adjacent oil seal.

   b. Drive the bearing out of the chaincase with a suitable size socket placed against the outer bearing race.

   c. Clean the bearing bore with solvent and thoroughly dry.

   d. Install the new bearing by driving it squarely into the chaincase with a socket placed against the outer bearing race.

   e. Install the oil seal as described in Step 3.

14

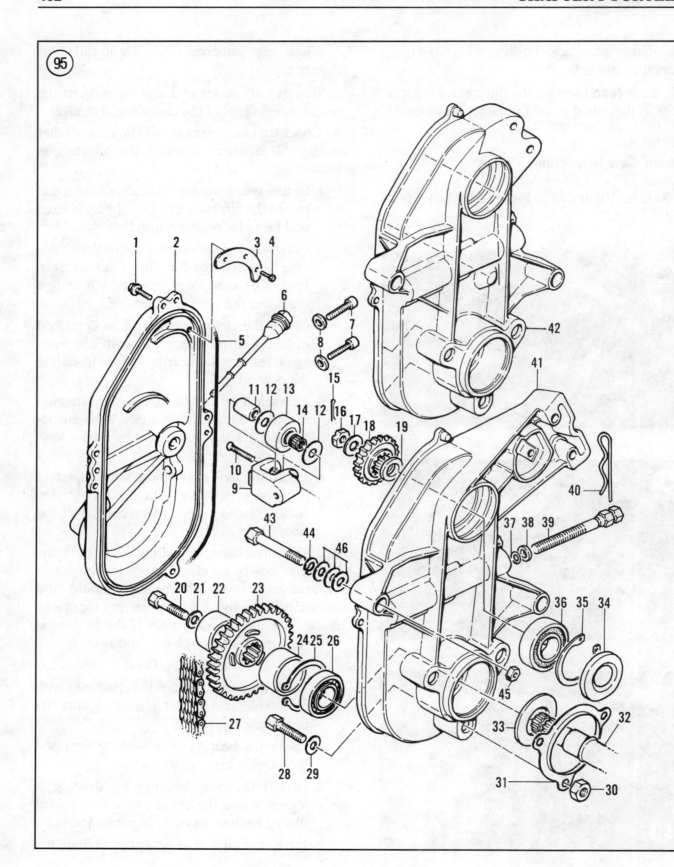

CHAINCASE, CHAIN AND SPROCKETS
(1993-1995 MODELS WITHOUT REVERSE)

1. Bolt
2. Cover
3. Oil deflector
4. Screw
5. O-ring
6. Dipstick
7. Allen screws
8. Washer
9. Tensioner block
10. Screw
11. Bushing
12. Washers
13. Roller
14. Roller bearing
15. Cotter pin
16. Castellated nut
17. Washer
18. Sprocket
19. Shim
20. Bolt
21. Lockwasher
22. Cap
23. Sprocket
24. Spacer
25. Circlip
26. Ball bearing
27. Chain
28. Bolt
29. Washer
30. Nut
31. Protector
32. Drive shaft
33. Oil seal
34. Oil seal
35. Circlip
36. Ball bearing
37. O-ring
38. Washer
39. Adjuster bolt
40. Hairpin clip
41. Chaincase
42. Chaincase
    (used on some models)
43. Lockwasher
44. Washers
45. Nut
46. Shims

14

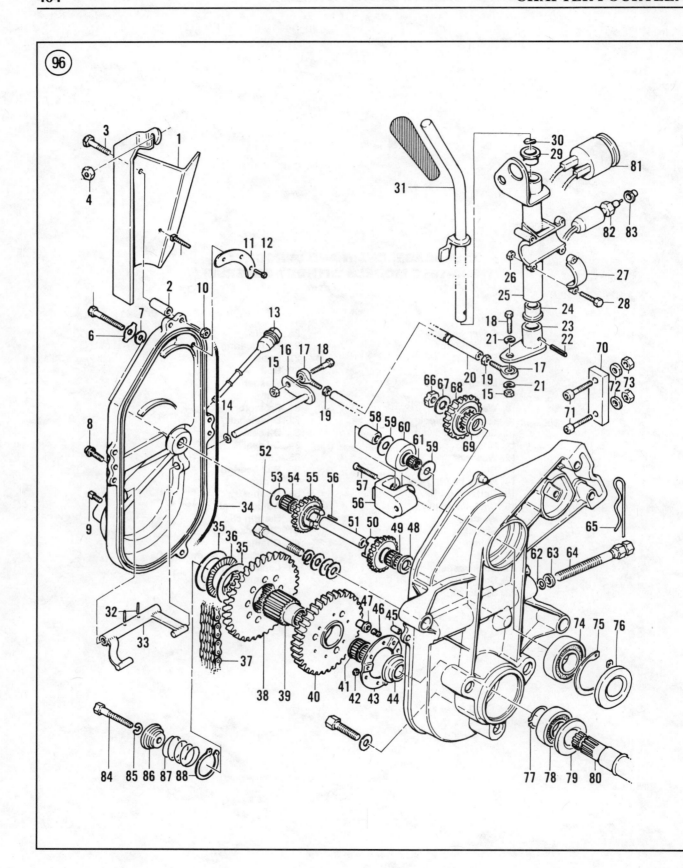

CHAINCASE, CHAIN AND SPROCKETS
(1993-1995 MODELS WITH REVERSE)

1. Deflector
2. Spacer
3. Bolt
4. Nut
5. Bolt
6. Lockplate
7. Washer
8. Bolt
9. Magnetic drain plug
10. Nut
11. Oil deflector
12. Screw
13. Dipstick
14. O-ring
15. Nuts
16. Shift shaft
17. Rod ends
18. Bolts
19. Locknuts
20. Shift rod
21. Washers
22. Roll pin
23. Lever
24. Bushing
25. Upper bracket
26. Nut
27. Clamp
28. Bolt
29. Bushing
30. Spring washer
31. Shift handle
32. Roll pins
33. Shift fork
34. O-ring
35. Washers
36. Thrust bearing
37. Chain
38. Sprocket
39. Coupling shaft
40. Sprocket
41. Roller bearing
42. Nut
43. Retaining ring
44. Retaining ring

45. Dowel pin
46. Spring
47. Drive pin
48. Washer
49. Roller bearing
50. Sprocket
51. Reverse shaft
52. Alignment rod
53. Sprocket
54. Roller bearing
55. Spacer
56. Tensioner block
57. Screw
58. Bushing
59. Washers
60. Roller
61. Roller bearing
62. O-ring
63. Washer
64. Adjuster
65. Hairpin clip
66. Castellated nut
67. Washer
68. Sprocket
69. Shim
70. Chain slider
71. Allen screws
72. Copper washers
73. Nuts
74. Ball bearing
75. Circlip
76. Oil seal
77. Snap ring
78. Ball bearing
79. Oil seal
80. Drive shaft
81. Backup alarm
82. Switch
83. Protector cap
84. Bolt
85. Lockwasher
86. Cap
87. Spring
88. Circlip

14

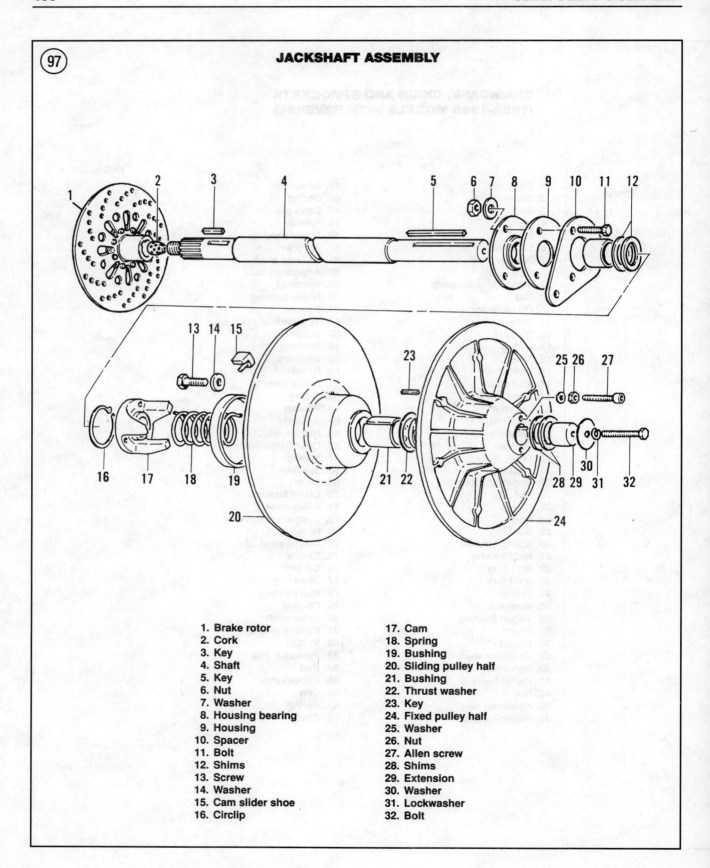

JACKSHAFT ASSEMBLY

1. Brake rotor
2. Cork
3. Key
4. Shaft
5. Key
6. Nut
7. Washer
8. Housing bearing
9. Housing
10. Spacer
11. Bolt
12. Shims
13. Screw
14. Washer
15. Cam slider shoe
16. Circlip
17. Cam
18. Spring
19. Bushing
20. Sliding pulley half
21. Bushing
22. Thrust washer
23. Key
24. Fixed pulley half
25. Washer
26. Nut
27. Allen screw
28. Shims
29. Extension
30. Washer
31. Lockwasher
32. Bolt

Jackshaft Inspection

Refer to **Figure 97** for this procedure.

1. Clean the jackshaft in solvent and thoroughly dry.

2. Check the jackshaft for bending.

3. Turn the bearing and check for excessive noise or roughness. Replace the bearing if worn or damaged.

4. Check both ends of the jackshaft for cracks, deep scoring or excessive wear.

5. If there is any doubt as to the condition of the jackshaft, repair or replace it.

Brake Rotor Inspection

WARNING
The brake system is an important part of machine safety. If you are unsure about the condition of any brake component or assembly, have it checked by a qualified snowmobile mechanic.

Inspect the brake disc for cracks, deep scoring, heat discoloration or checking. If necessary, replace the brake disc. A press is required to remove and install the brake disc. Refer service to a Ski-Doo dealer or machine shop.

CAUTION
Do not resurface the brake disc. If the brake disc surface is damaged or worn, replace the brake disc.

Installation

1. Pack the seal lip cavities with a low temperature grease.

2. Install the bearing housing (**Figure 94**). Do not tighten the screws at this time.

3. Insert the jackshaft through the frame and bearing.

4. Push the jackshaft all the way to the left side.

5. Position the chaincase over the right end of the jackshaft.

NOTE
When installing the chaincase in Step 6, be sure to install any shims, recorded during removal, that were placed between the chaincase and frame. These shims are used for chaincase alignment and must be installed in their exact original position.

6. Install the chaincase attaching screws and washers (**Figure 92** and **Figure 93**). Tighten the screws securely.

7. Tighten the 3 bearing housing screws (A, **Figure 94**) securely. Check that the jackshaft is centered in the bearing housing.

8. Install the brake caliper as described in this chapter.

9. Install the chain and sprockets as described in this chapter.

10. Install the chaincase cover as described in this chapter.

11. Install the driven pulley as described in Chapter Thirteen.

12. Install the heat guard on the right side.

13. Install the oil injection tank.

14. Install the coolant reservoir.

15. Install the air silencer as described in Chapter Six.

DRIVE AXLE

The drive axle receives power from the jackshaft through the drive chain assembly located on the right side. Refer to **Figure 98** when performing procedures in this section.

Removal

1. Remove the chain and sprockets as described in this chapter.

2. Remove the driven pulley assembly as described in this chapter.

3. Remove snap ring (25, **Figure 95** or 77, **Figure 96**).

14

4. Unbolt the cable protector from the bearing housing at the left end of the drive axle.

5. Disconnect the speedometer cable (**Figure 99**) from the bearing housing.

6. Remove the remaining screw, then remove the left end bearing housing.

7. Remove the rear suspension as described in Chapter Sixteen.

8. Alternately push the drive axle and sprockets toward the right side, then pull back toward the left until the bearing (26, **Figure 95** or 78, **Figure**

96) can be pulled from the chaincase bore and drive axle shaft.

9. Lift the drive axle from the track.

Inspection

This section describes drive axle inspection. A press is required to disassemble and reassemble the drive axle. Refer to **Figure 98**.

1. Inspect the bearings by spining the outer race by hand to check for roughness or excessive

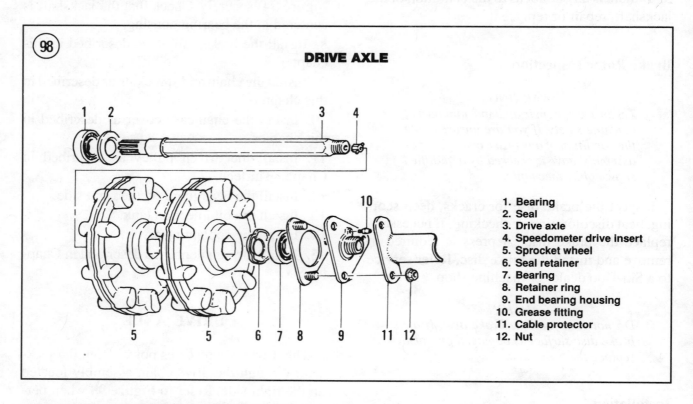

(98)

DRIVE AXLE

1. Bearing
2. Seal
3. Drive axle
4. Speedometer drive insert
5. Sprocket wheel
6. Seal retainer
7. Bearing
8. Retainer ring
9. End bearing housing
10. Grease fitting
11. Cable protector
12. Nut

(99)

(100)

noise. Also check the seals for damage. Replace the bearings and seals as necessary. Refer to **Figure 100**.

2. Check the drive axle for bending (**Figure 101**).

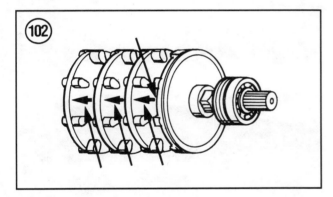

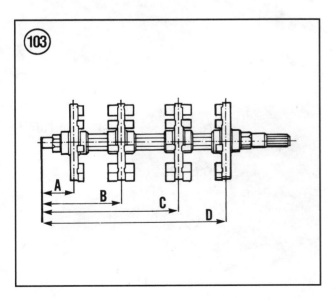

3. Check the drive axle splines for cracks or other damage.

4. Inspect the sprocket wheels (**Figure 101**) for excessive wear, cracks, distortion or other damage. If necessary, replace the sprocket as described in this chapter.

5. If there is any doubt as to the condition of any part, replace it.

Sprocket Replacement

A press is required to remove and install the sprockets. Refer to **Figure 98** for this procedure.

1. Purchase all new parts to have on hand before disassembly.

> *NOTE*
> *Before removing the right-side oil seal from the chaincase, note and record the direction in which the seal lip faces for proper reinstallation.*

2. Remove the bearing from left end using a suitable bearing puller.

3. Place the drive axle in a press and press each sprocket from the drive axle.

4. Clean the drive axle thoroughly. Remove all nicks with a file.

5. Observe the following when installing the sprockets:

   a. Each sprocket has an arrow mark that must align with the other sprockets when installed on the drive axle as shown in **Figure 102**. After installing the first sprocket wheel, press the remaining sprockets on so that all of the marks align.

   b. Press the sprockets onto the drive axle to the dimensions indicated in **Table 2**. Refer to **Figure 103** for measuring the spacing.

6. After installing the sprocket wheels, check synchronization as follows:

   a. Place the drive axle on a perfectly flat surface.

   b. Measure the gap between the sprocket wheels and the flat surface.

14

c. If the gap exceeds 1.5 mm (1/16 in.), the sprockets are not synchronized. Synchronization may be improved by changing one of the sprockets. The sprocket should not be removed, then reinstalled on the same drive axle.

d. When sprocket synchronization is within specification, proceed to Step 7.

7. When installing bearings and oil seals, refer to **Figure 98** and observe the following:

a. Install new oil seal in chaincase during assembly.

b. Install oil seals so that their open side faces inside the chaincase.

c. Install both bearings with their shielded side toward the sprocket wheels.

d. Install the bearing on left end of the drive axle so that it is flush with the drive axle as shown in **Figure 104**.

e. Install the bearing on the splined end after the track, axle and sprockets are in place.

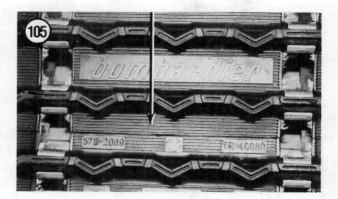

Installation

1. When installing the track, the V lugs should point in the direction of track movement as shown in **Figure 105**.

2. Position the track as shown in **Figure 106**.

3. Insert the splined end of the drive axle (**Figure 107**) through the seal and into the chaincase.

4. Position the bearing on the splined end of the drive axle, against the shoulder.

5. Pull the drive axle to the left while aligning the left bearing in its bore.

6. Continue pushing the bearing and shaft to the left until the bearing is seated in its bore in the chaincase.

7. Install the bearing retaining snap ring.

8. Install the spacer.

9. Install the chain, sprockets and cover as described in this chapter.

10. Install the left end bearing housing and reconnect the speedometer cable.

11. Perform the *Drive Axle Axial Play* in this chapter.

12. Adjust the chain and refill the chaincase with oil as described in Chapter Three.

13. Install the driven pulley as described in Chapter Thirteen.

14. Install the rear suspension as described in Chapter Sixteen.

DRIVE AXLE AXIAL PLAY

Chaincase Alignment
Check/Adjustment

Before checking axial play of the drive axle, make sure that the chaincase is properly aligned as follows.

1. Remove the driven pulley as described in Chapter Thirteen.

2A. On 1990 models, loosen the Allen screw (**Figure 108**) located in the lock collar on the left end of the jackshaft. Use a punch and hammer and loosen the lock collar (**Figure 109**). Turn the lock collar clockwise (**Figure 110**) to release the bearing. Remove the bearing from the retainer as shown in **Figure 111**, then slide the bearing back into its support (**Figure 112**). Interpret the ease of bearing installation as follows:

    a. If the bearing was easy to install, chaincase alignment is okay. Proceed to Step 4.

14

b. If the bearing was difficult to install, chaincase alignment is incorrect. Proceed to Step 3.

2B. On 1991 and later models, remove the screws attaching the bearing housing to the left side of the vehicle. Refer to A, **Figure 113**. Slide the bearing from the retainer, then slide the bearing back into its support. Interpret the ease of bearing installation as follows:

a. If the bearing was easy to install, chaincase alignment is okay. Proceed to Step 4.

b. If the bearing was difficult to install, chaincase alignment is incorrect. Proceed to Step 3.

NOTE
If it is necessary to install more than 1 shim to align the chaincase, install longer chaincase mounting screws.

3. Refer to **Figure 114** and observe at what position the difficulty was most noticeable. Refer to **Figure 114** and place shims between the chaincase and frame as indicated to correct

alignment. See **Figure 115** for shim positions. Recheck alignment after installing shims. Refer to *Chaincase, Brake Caliper and Jackshaft* to remove and install the chaincase.

4. Install the chain and sprockets as described in this chapter, if previously removed.

NOTE
*The drive sprocket nut (**Figure 116**) must be tightened before adjusting the jackshaft bearing.*

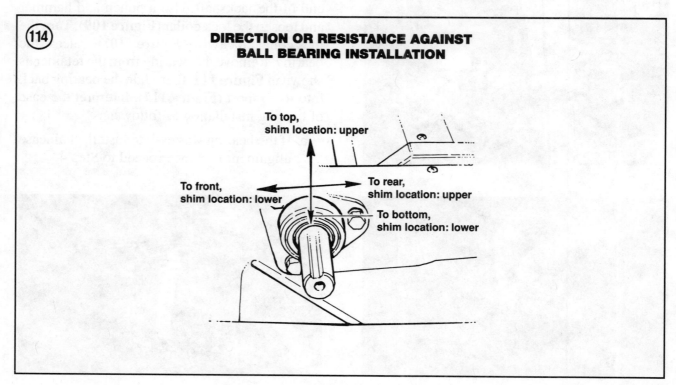

(114)
DIRECTION OR RESISTANCE AGAINST BALL BEARING INSTALLATION

To top,
shim location: upper

To front,
shim location: lower

To rear,
shim location: upper

To bottom,
shim location: lower

5A. On 1990 models, install the bearing so that the bearing shoulder faces toward the chaincase (**Figure 111**).

a. Slide the lock collar (**Figure 110**) toward the bearing.

b. Turn the lock collar to engage the collar and bearing. Engagement will probably require 1/4 turn. Turn the lock collar until the lock collar and inner race lock. Insert a punch in the lock collar (**Figure 109**) and tighten it by tapping the punch with a hammer.

c. Apply Loctite 242 (blue) to the lock collar Allen screw, then install and tighten the screw securely (**Figure 108**).

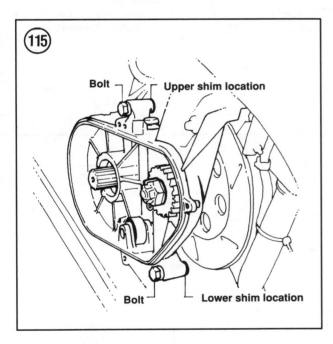

5B. On 1991 and later models, install the bearing and retainer (**Figure 113**). The bearing shoulder should face toward the chaincase.

> *NOTE*
> *Do not install the driven pulley until the axial play is adjusted.*

6. Proceed to *Axial Play Adjustment* to adjust the drive axle.

Axial Play Adjustment

Adjust the axial play of the dirve axle after first making sure that the chaincase is properly aligned. Refer to *Chaincase Alignment Check/Adjustment*.

1. Remove the *Drive Axle* as described in this chapter, then reinstall the drive axle without the track.

2. Push the drive axle toward the chaincase by hand, then measure the distance between the tunnel and sprocket as shown in **Figure 117**.

> *NOTE*
> *Make sure the drive axle bearing contacts the chaincase bearing bore completely when making the measurement in Step 2.*

3. Push the drive axle toward the left side end bearing housing by hand. Measure the distance between the tunnel and sprocket (**Figure 117**).

4. Subtract the measurement in Step 3 from the measurement in Step 2. The resulting difference in the measurements is the drive axle axial play. The axial play should be within 0-1.5 mm (0-0.060 in.). If the axial play is excessive, proceed to Step 5. If axial play is correct, proceed to Step 7.

> *NOTE*
> *Even though the end play should be near 0 when measured as described, be sure that the shaft does not have too many shims installed. Shaft bearings should not have preload.*

14

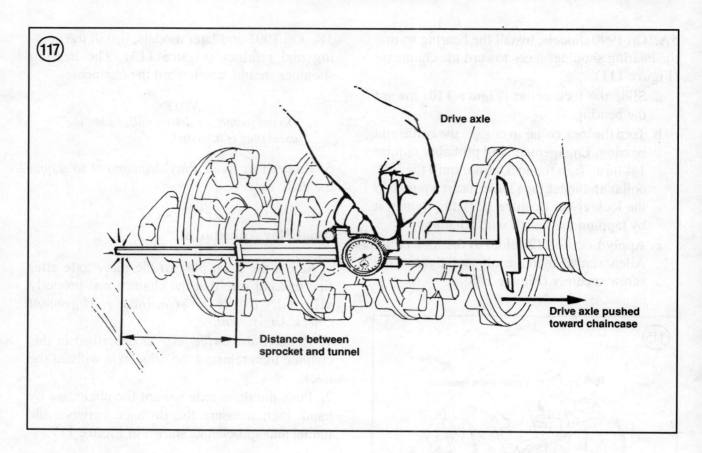

Drive axle

Distance between
sprocket and tunnel

Drive axle pushed
toward chaincase

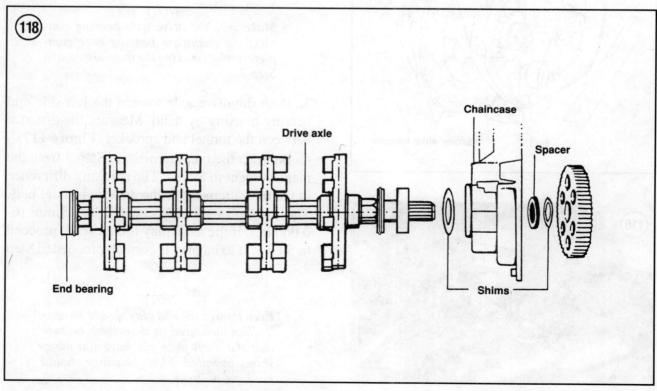

Chaincase

Spacer

Drive axle

End bearing

Shims

5. Select the correct shims to install as follows:

a. Remove the drive axle.

b. Select the specific shims required to obtain the correct drive axle axial play.

c. Refer to **Table 3** for correct positioning of the shims depending upon the quantity necessary to adjust the end play. For example, if only 1 shim is required, place the shim on the end bearing housing side. If 2 shims are required, place 1 shim on the end bearing housing side and 1 shim on the chaincase side. If 3 shims are required, place 2 shims on the end bearing side and 1 shim on the chaincase side.

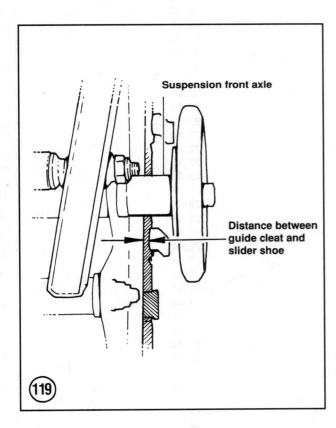

Distance between guide cleat and slider shoe

Suspension front axle

(119)

d. Install the selected shims on the drive axle. Install the same number of shims between the chaincase and drive axle bearing as installed between the drive chain sprocket and spacer. See **Figure 118**.

6. Reinstall the drive axle (without track) and recheck axial play. If end play is still incorrect, remove the drive axle and change the thickness of the shims again.

7. When drive axle axial free play is correct, install the track, drive axle and rear suspension. Adjust track tension and alignment as described in Chapter Sixteen.

8. Raise the vehicle enough to lift the track off of the ground, support the vehicle securely, then check the following:

a. Center the track as follows: Push the slide suspension to the right, then to the left. Observe the difference in both movements and center the track at this point by hand.

b. Check track alignment as follows: Measure the gap between the guide cleat and the slider shoe (behind front axle) on both sides of snowmobile. See **Figure 119**. Record the distance for each side. If the distance between the left and right sides exceeds 3 mm (1/8 in.), remove the drive axle and reposition shims as follows. If the difference recorded was 3-4.5 mm (1/8-3/16 in.), remove one shim from the larger gap side and add one shim to the smaller gap side. If the difference recorded was 4.5-6 mm (3/16-1/4 in.), remove 2 shims from the larger gap side and add 2 shims to the smaller gap side.

c. Reinstall drive axle and recheck alignment.

9. Reinstall all parts as required after adjustment is complete.

14

Table 1 DRIVE CHAIN SPECIFICATIONS

Model	Chain pitch* and length	Chain drive ratio
1990		
Formula MX	3/8-72	22:44
Formula MX LT	3/8-72	22:44
Formula Plus	3/8-68	20:38
Formula Plus LT	3/8-68	20:38
Formula MACH 1	3/8-70	22:40
Formula MACH 1 XTC	3/8-70	22:40
1991		
Formula MX	3/8-74	22:44
Formula MX E	3/8-74	26:44
Formula MX X	3/8-74	26:44
Formula MX XTC	3/8-74	26:44
Formula MX XTC E	3/8-74	26:44
Formula Plus	3/8-70	22:40
Formula Plus E	3/8-70	22:40
Formula Plus X	3/8-70	22:40
Formula Plus XTC	3/8-70	22:40
Formula Plus XTC E	3/8-70	22:40
Formula MACH 1	3/8-74	26:44
Formula MACH 1 X	3/8-74	26:44
Formula MACH 1 XTC	3/8-74	26:44
1992		
Formula MX	3/8-72	22:44
Formula MX XTC R	3/8-72	22:44
Formula Plus	3/8-70	23:40
Formula Plus E	3/8-70	23:40
Formula Plus XTC	3/8-70	22:40
Formula Plus XTC E	3/8-70	22:40
Formula Plus X	3/8-70	23:40
Formula MACH 1	3/8-74	26:44
Formula MACH 1 X	3/8-70	23:40
Formula MACH 1 XTC	3/8-74	24:44
1993		
Formula MX	3/8-72	26:44
Formula MX XTC R	3/8-70	22:44
Formula MX Z	3/8-74	24:44
Formula Plus	3/8-74	25:44
Formula Plus E	3/8-74	25:44
Formula Plus XTC	3/8-72	23:44
Formula Plus EFI	3/8-74	25:44
Formula Plus X	3/8W-74	25:44
Formula MACH 1	3/8W-74	25:44
Formula MACH 1 XTC	3/8W-74	25:44
Formula Grand Touring	3/8W-74	25:44
1994		
Formula MX	3/8-74	23:44
Formula MX Z	3/8W-74	23:44
Summit 470	3/8-72	22:44
Formula ST	3/8-72	23:44
Formula STX	3/8-74	25:44
Summit 583	3/8-72	23:44

(continued)

Table 1 DRIVE CHAIN SPECIFICATIONS (continued)

Model	Chain pitch* and length	Chain drive ratio
1994 (continued)		
Formula Z	3/8-74	25:44
MACH 1	3/8W-74	26:44
Grand Touring	3/8W-74	25:44
Grand Touring XTC	3/8W-72	23:44
Grand Touring SE	3/8W-74	26:44
1995		
MX	3/8-72	23:44
MX Z	3/8W-72	23:44
Formula SS	3/8W-74	26:44
Formula STX	3/8-74	25:44
Summit 583	3/8-72	23:44
Summit 670	3/8-74	25:44
Formula Z	3/8-74	25:44
MACH 1	3/8W-74	26:44
Grand Touring 470	3/8W-72	23:44
Grand Touring 580	3/8W-74	25:44
Grand Touring SE	3/8W-74	26:44

* All models use 3/8 in. pitch silent chain. Some 1993 and later models are equipped with chain that is wider than other models. The wide chain is 13 links wide, while the other chain is 11 links wide. The chain should not be shortened, lengthened or substituted. Only the original type of chain is recommended.

Table 2 SPROCKET WHEEL INSTALLATION SPECIFICATIONS

Model	Distance "A" mm (in.)	Distance "B" mm (in.)	Distance "C" mm (in.)	Distance "D" mm (in.)
1990-1992				
All models	64.5 (2 35/64)	166 (6 17/32)	289 (11 3/8)	390.5 (15 3/8)
1993				
Formula MX Z	53.9 (2 1/8)	155.4 (6 1/8)	278.4 (10 31/32)	379.9 14 31/32
Other models	4.5 (2 35/64)	166 (6 17/32)	289 (11 3/8)	390.5 (15 3/8)
1994				
MACH 1 & Grand Touring models	4.5 (2 35/64)	166 (6 17/32)	289 (11 3/8)	390.5 (15 3/8)
Other models	53.9 (2 1/8)	155.4 (6 1/8)	278.4 (10 31/32)	379.9 14 31/32
1995				
All models	53.9 (2 1/8)	155.4 (6 1/8)	278.4 (10 31/32)	379.9 14 31/32

14

Table 3 DRIVE AXLE SHIM POSITION AND QUANTITY

Shim(s)	Chaincase side			End bearing housing side
1				1
2	1			1
3	1			2

Chapter Fifteen

Front Suspension and Steering

All models are equipped with either Progressive Rate Suspension (PRS) as shown in **Figure 1** or with Direct Shock Action (DSA) front suspension system as shown in **Figure 2**. This chapter describes service to the skis, handlebar, steering assembly, steering column and tie rods of both systems. Ski alignment is described in Chapter Three.

Tables 1 and **Table 2** are at the end of the chapter.

SKIS

The skis are equipped with wear bars, or skags, that aid in turning the machine and protect the bottoms of the skis from wear and damage caused by road crossings and bare terrain. The bars are expendable and should be checked for wear and damage at periodic intervals and replaced when they are worn to the point they no longer protect the skis or aid in turning.

Removal/Installation

Refer to **Figure 3** or **Figure 4** for this procedure.

1. Support the front of the machine so both skis are off the ground.

> *NOTE*
> *Mark the skis with a L (left-hand) or R (right-hand). The skis should be installed on their original mounting side.*

2. Remove the cotter pin from the end of the ski pivot bolt. Loosen and remove the nut and bolt (A, **Figure 5**) and ski (B, **Figure 5**). Don't lose the collars from both sides of the ski pivot bolt hole.

3. If necessary, remove the ski boot (A, **Figure 6**) and the stop binding from the ski.

4. Inspect the skis as described in this chapter.

5. Installation is the reverse of these steps. Observe the following.

6. Clean all old grease from the pivot bolt, collar and washers.

7. Coat the pivot bolt and collar with a low-temperature grease before installation.

8. Reinstall the stop binding and ski boot, if removed.

9. When installing the skis, refer to the alignment marks made before removal.

10. Hold the ski in place, then install the collar, washers and pivot bolt.

11. Install the ski pivot bolt nut and tighten to the torque specification in **Table 1**.

12. Check that the ski pivots up and down with slight resistance. If the ski is tight, remove the ski and determine why.

13. Lock the pivot bolt by inserting a new cotter pin through the nut and bolt. Bend the ends of the cotter pin (**Figure 7**) over edges of nut.

Inspection

Refer to **Figure 3** or **Figure 4** for this procedure.

1. Check the rubber stoppers for wear, cracking or deterioration. Replace if necessary.

2. Check the skis for fatigue cracks or other damage. Repair or replace the ski(s) as required.

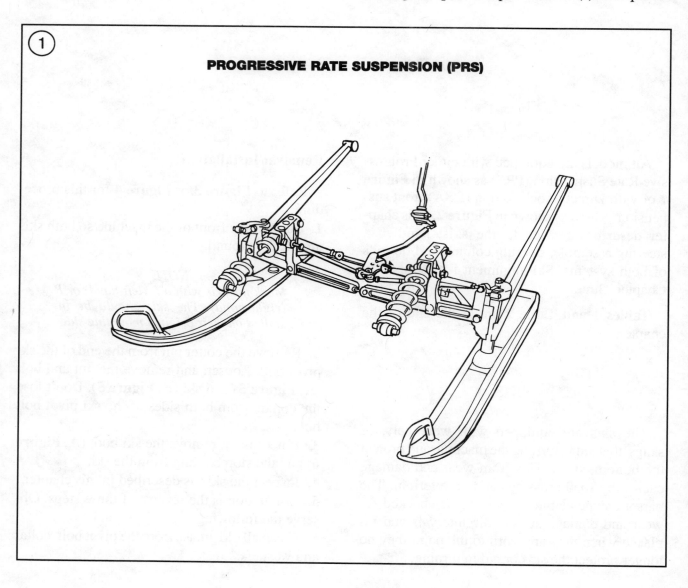

① **PROGRESSIVE RATE SUSPENSION (PRS)**

3. Check the wear bars (skags) on the bottom of the skis for severe wear or damage. If necessary, replace the wear bars as follows:

  a. Remove the rubber plugs from the top of the ski (B, **Figure 7**).

  b. Remove the nuts (**Figure 8**) holding the wear bars to the ski.

  c. Remove the cups from inside the ski.

  d. Remove the wear bar.

  e. Install the new wear bar by reversing these steps. Tighten the wear bar nuts to the specification in **Table 1**.

FRONT SUSPENSION (PROGRESSIVE RATE SUSPENSION)

The Ski-Doo Progressive Rate Suspension (PRS) is used on all 1990-1992 models, all 1993

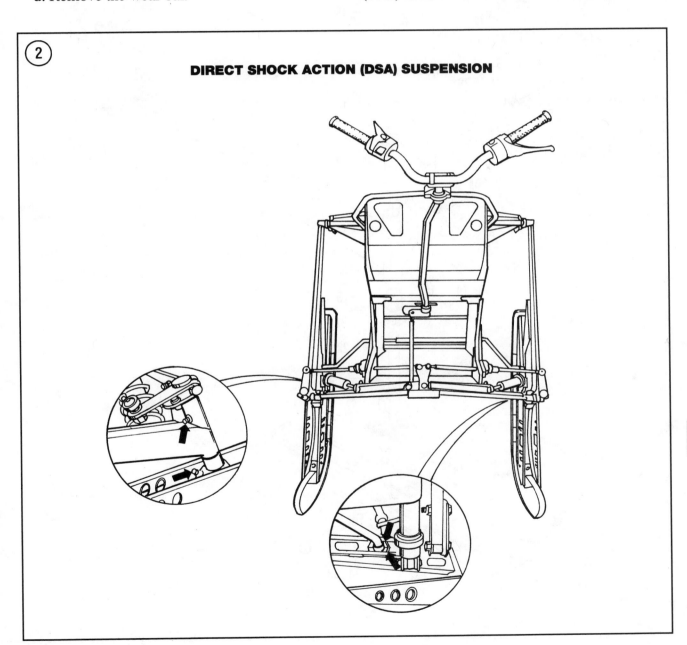

DIRECT SHOCK ACTION (DSA) SUSPENSION

15

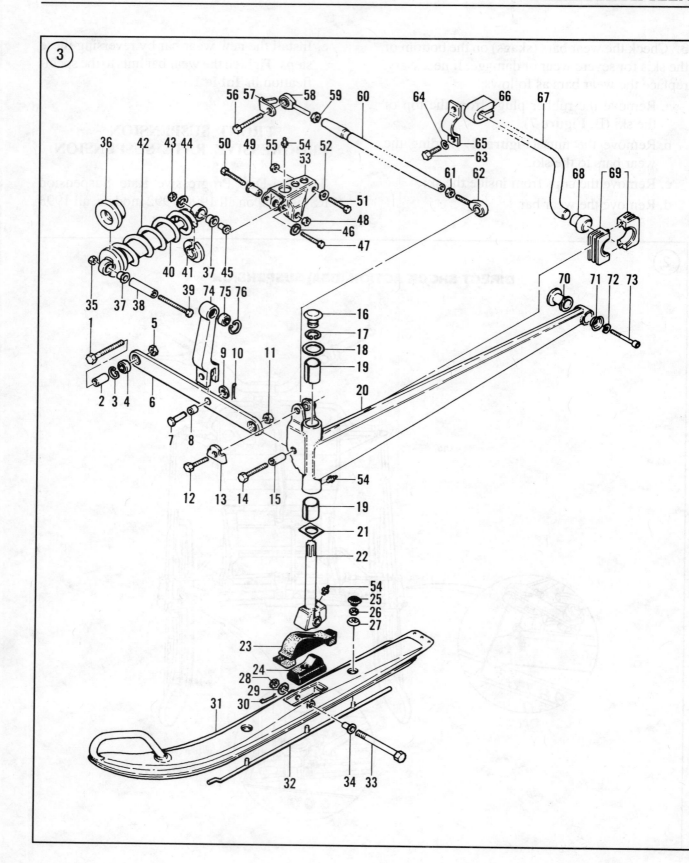

FRONT SUSPENSION AND SKI
(PROGRESSIVE RATE SUSPENSION)

1. Bolt	39. Bolt
2. Bushing	40. Shock absorber
3. Circlip	41. Spring stopper
4. Ball joint	42. Spring
5. Nut	43. Nut
6. Lower bracket	44. Washer
7. Clevis pin	45. Bushing
8. Bushing	46. Washer
9. Washer	47. Bolt
10. Cotter pin	48. Nut
11. Nut	49. Bushing
12. Bolt	50. Bolt
13. Lock tab	51. Bolt
14. Bolt	52. Washer
15. Bushing	53. Rocker arm
16. Cap	54. Grease nipple
17. Circlip	55. Nut
18. Thrust washer	56. Bolt
19. Housing	57. Screw stopper
20. Swing arm	58. Ball joint
21. Wear plate	59. Nut
22. Ski leg	60. Upper bracket
23. Ski boot	61. Nut
24. Stop binding	62. Ball joint
25. Cap	63. Bolt
26. Nut	64. Lockwasher
27. Cup	65. Clamp
28. Nut	66. Rubber clamp
29. Washer	67. Stabilizer bar
30. Cotter pin	68. Slider joint
31. Ski	69. Slider
32. Wear bar (skag)	70. Rubber damper
33. Bolt	71. Cup
34. Bushing	72. Lockwasher
35. Nut	73. Bolt
36. Stopper ring	74. Crank rod
37. Bushing	75. Ball joint
38. Spacer	76. Circlip

15

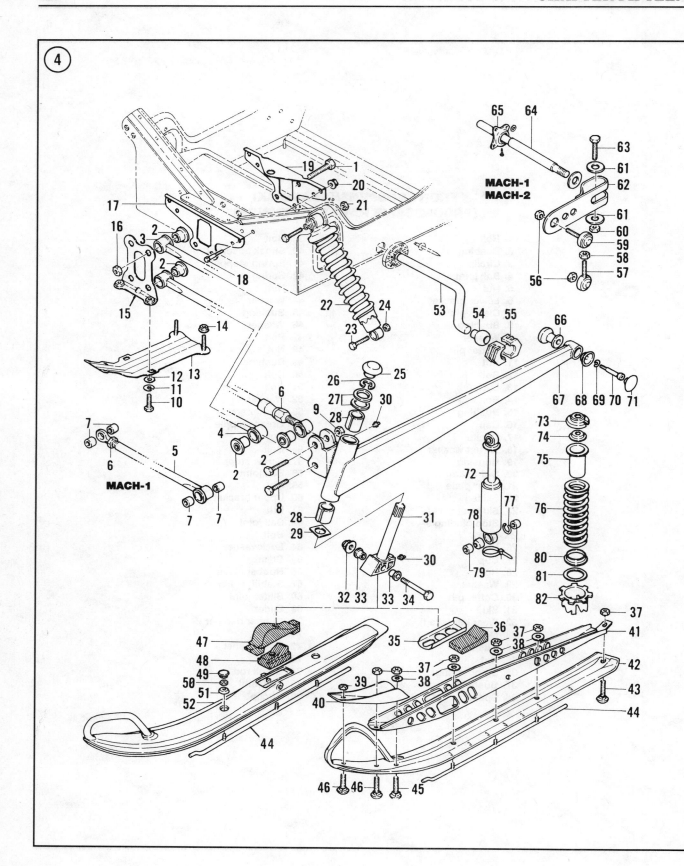

FRONT SUSPENSION (DIRECT SHOCK ACTION)

1. Bolt
2. Cushion
3. Upper arm
4. Lower arm
5. Lower arm
6. Lock nut
7. Spacers
8. Bolt
9. Nut
10. Bolt
11. Lockwasher
12. Washer
13. Plate
14. Nut
15. Link plate
16. Nut
17. Front link plate
18. Bolt
19. Rear link plate
20. Nut
21. Nut
22. Shock absorber
23. Bolt
24. Nut
25. Cap
26. Circlip
27. Washers
28. Bushings
29. Wear plate
30. Grease fitting
31. Ski leg
32. Nut
33. Cushion
34. Bolt
35. Stopper
36. Stopper
37. Nut
38. Washer
39. Nut
40. Reinforcement
41. Support

42. Plastic ski
43. Carriage bolt
44. Carbide wear bar (skag)
45. Carriage bolt
46. Carriage bolt
47. Ski protector
48. Stopper
49. Cap
50. Nut
51. Cupped washer
52. Ski
53. Stabilizer bar
54. Ball joint
55. Sliding block
56. Nuts
57. Connecting rod
58. Locknut
59. Rod end
60. Nut
61. Washers
62. Stabilizer lever
63. Bolt
64. Stabilizer bar
65. Bushing
66. Rubber damper
67. Swing arm
68. Bowl
69. Lockwasher
70. Bolt
71. Cap
72. Shock absorber
73. Spring retainer
74. Cap
75. Shield
76. Spring
77. Circlip
78. Cushion
79. Spacers
80. Spring seat
81. Washer
82. Adjuster

15

models except Formula MX Z, and 1994 MACH 1 and Grand Touring models. Refer to *Front Suspension (Direct Shock Action)* later in this chapter for other models.

Refer to **Figure 3** when performing procedures in this section. Because of the number of parts used in the suspension, identify parts during removal and store them in separate boxes.

Steering Arm, Ski Leg and Swing Arm Removal/Installation

1. Support the front of the machine so both skis are off the ground.
2. Remove the skis as described in this chapter.
3. Disconnect the tie rod from the steering arm (**Figure 9**).
4. Remove the steering arm and ski leg as follows:
    a. Remove the cap (**Figure 10**).
    b. Remove the snap ring (**Figure 11**) from the groove in the ski leg, of models so equipped.
    c. Remove the clamp bolt from the steering arm (**Figure 12**), then pull the steering arm from the ski leg.
    d. Remove the snap ring and washer (**Figure 13**).
    e. Remove the ski leg (**Figure 14**).
5. Disconnect the upper control arm from the swing arm (**Figure 15**).
6. Remove the swing arm as follows:

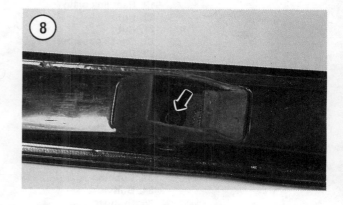

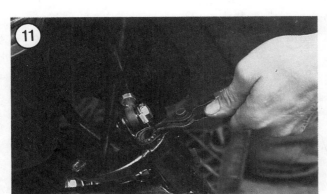

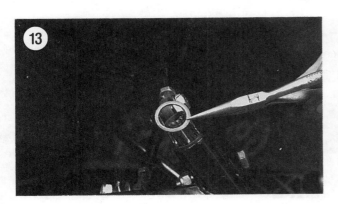

a. Remove the bolt (**Figure 16**) that attaches the lower control arm to the swing arm.

b. Remove the bolt that attaches the swing arm at the rear.

c. Remove the swing arm (**Figure 17**).

7. Inspect the swing arm and related parts as described in this section.

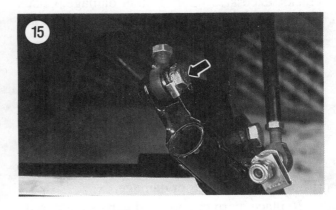

15

8. Install by reversing the removal procedure, observing the following:

    a. Tighten the swing arm rear bolt to the torque specification in **Table 1**.

    b. Tighten the steering arm pinch bolt to the torque specification in **Table 1**.

    c. Tighten the bolt attaching the upper control arm bolt to the swing arm to the torque specification in **Table 1**.

Inspection

1. Clean all components thoroughly in solvent. Remove all dirt and other residue from all surfaces.

> *NOTE*
> *If paint has been removed from parts during cleaning, touch up areas as required before assembly or installation.*

2. Inspect the steering arm (A, **Figure 18**) for cracks, excessive wear or other damage. Check splines (B, **Figure 18**) for damage. Check mating splines in the ski leg (A, **Figure 19**).

3. Check the ski leg (B, **Figure 19**) for cracks or other damage.

4. Check the lower end of the ski leg and wear plate (**Figure 20**) for damage.

5. Check the swing arm (**Figure 21**) for cracks, excessive wear or other damage. Check the housing, for cracks or damage. Check the bushing (**Figure 22**) for wear or damage.

6. Replace worn or damaged parts as required.

Lower Control Arm Removal/Installation

    Refer to **Figure 3** for this procedure.

1. Support the front of the machine so both skis are off the ground.

2. Open the hood.

3. Remove the bolt (**Figure 23**) that attaches the lower control arm to the swing arm.

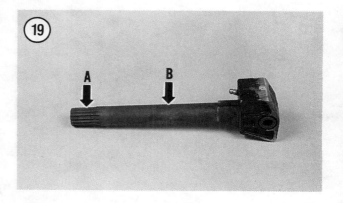

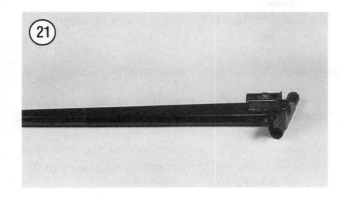

4. Remove the cotter pin from the clevis pin (**Figure 24**), then remove the clevis pin from the bellcrank rod.

5. Remove the bolt (**Figure 25**) that attaches the lower control arm to the frame.

6. Remove the lower control arm.

7. Check parts as described in the following *Lower Control Arm Inspection* procedure.

8. Installation is the reverse of removal. Observe the following:

    a. Tighten the lower control arm bolts to the torque specification in **Table 1**.

    b. Install the clevis pin assembly as shown in **Figure 3**, then secure the clevis pin with a new cotter pin.

Lower Control Arm Inspection

1. Clean the lower control arm in solvent and dry thoroughly.

2. If paint has been removed from the lower control arm during cleaning or through use, touch up areas before installation.

CAUTION
Do not paint over the radial ball joints in the lower control arm.

3. Check the lower control arm (**Figure 26**) for cracks or other damage. Control arm should be straight.

15

4. Check the radial ball joints (**Figure 27**) at both ends of the lower control arm for excessive wear or damage. Replace the radial ball joint by first removing the snap ring and driving the ball joint from the lower arm. Install new ball joint with a press or suitable tool.

5. Check the radial ball joint bushings for wear or damage.

6. Replace worn or damaged parts as required.

Stabilizer Bar
Removal/Installation

Refer to **Figure 3** for this procedure.

1. Remove the stabilizer bar mounting bolts and brackets, then remove the stabilizer bar.

2. Check parts as described in the following *Stabilizer Bar Inspection* procedure.

3. Reverse the removal steps to install. Tighten the stabilizer bolts to the torque specification in **Table 1**. Make sure the stabilizer has movement in its bushings.

Stabilizer Bar
Inspection

1. Clean the stabilizer bar in solvent and dry thoroughly.

2. If paint has been removed from the stabilizer bar during cleaning or through use, touch up areas before installation.

3. Check the stabilizer bar for wear, cracks or other damage.

4. Check the slider and slider joint for damage.

5. Replace worn or damaged parts as required.

Upper Control Arm
Removal/Installation

Refer to **Figure 3** for this procedure.

1. Open the hood.

2. Remove the bolt (**Figure 28**) attaching the upper control arm to the swing arm.

3. Remove the bolt (**Figure 29**) attaching the upper control arm to the frame.

4. Remove the upper control arm.

5. Check parts as described in the following *Upper Control Arm Inspection* procedure.

6. Installation is the reverse of the removal steps. Tighten the upper control arm bolts to the torque specification in **Table 1**.

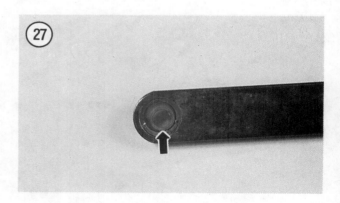

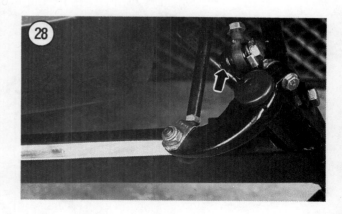

Upper Control Arm
Inspection

1. Clean the upper control arm in solvent and dry thoroughly.

2. If paint has been removed from the upper control arm during cleaning or through use, touch up areas before installation.

3. Check the upper control arm (**Figure 30**) for wear, cracks or other damage.

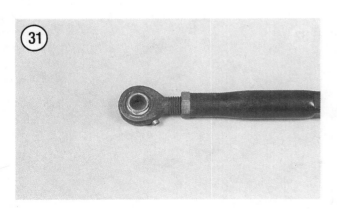

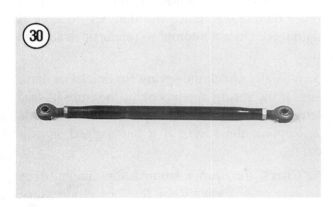

4. Check the ball joints (**Figure 31**) for excessive wear or damage. If damaged, loosen the nut and unscrew the ball joint. Reverse the procedure to install. When installing new ball joints, make sure the exposed thread length between the ball joint and the threaded rod does not exceed 15 mm (19/32 in.).

5. Replace worn or damaged parts as required.

6. If one or more ball joints were loosened or replaced, check *Steering Adjustment* as described in this chapter.

Rocker Arm
Removal/Installation

Disconnect all steering components from the rocker arm (53, **Figure 3**), then remove the rocker arm. Reverse the procedure to install. Apply Loctite 272 (red) to the rocker arm bolt during installation and tighten the bolt to the torque specified in **Table 1**.

Rocker Arm
Inspection

1. Clean the rocker arm in solvent and dry thoroughly.

2. If paint has been removed from the rocker arm during cleaning or through use, touch up areas before installation.

3. Check the rocker arm for wear, cracks or other damage.

4. Replace worn or damaged parts as required.

15

Shock Absorber
Removal/Installation

Refer to **Figure 3** for this procedure.

1. Support the front of the machine so both skis are off the ground.

2. Open the hood.

3. Remove the 2 bolts (**Figure 32**) attaching the shock absorber, then remove the shock absorber.

4. Check the shock absorber as described in *Shock Inspection* section in this chapter.

5. Installation is the reverse of these steps. Tighten the shock absorber attaching bolts to the torque specified in **Table 1**.

Spring Removal/Installation

Refer to **Figure 3** for this procedure.

1. Remove the shock absorber as described in this chapter.

2. Secure the bottom of the shock absorber in a vise with soft jaws.

3. Slide the rubber bumper down the shock shaft (**Figure 33**).

> *WARNING*
> *Do not attempt to remove or install the shock spring without the use of a spring compressor. Use the Ski-Doo spring remover (part No. 414 5796 00) or a suitable equivalent. Attempting to remove the spring without the use of a spring compressor may cause severe personal injury. If you do not have access to a spring compressor, refer spring removal to a Ski-Doo dealer.*

4. Attach a suitable spring compressor to the shock absorber following the compressor manufacturer's instructions. Compress the spring with the tool and remove the spring stopper from the top of the shock. Remove the spring.

> *CAUTION*
> *Do not attempt to disassemble the shock damper housing.*

5. Inspect the shock and spring as described in the following procedure.

6. Install the spring by reversing the removal steps. Make sure the spring stopper retains the spring securely.

Shock Inspection

1. Remove the spring from the shock absorber as described in this chapter.

2. Clean all components thoroughly in solvent and allow to dry.

3. Check the damper rod as follows:

   a. Check the damper housing for leakage. If the damper is leaking, replace it.

   b. Check the damper rod for bending or other damage. Check the damper housing for dents or other damage.

   c. Operate the damper rod by hand and check its operation. If the damper is operating correctly, a small amount of resistance should be felt on the compression stroke and a considerable amount of resistance felt on the return stroke.

   d. Replace the damper assembly if necessary.

4. Check the damper housing for crack, dents or other damage. Replace the damper housing if damaged. Do not attempt to repair or straighten it.

5. Visually check the spring for cracks or damage. If the spring appears okay, measure its free length and compare to the specification in **Table 2**. Replace the spring if it has sagged significantly.

6. Check the spring stopper for cracks, deep scoring or excessive wear. Replace if necessary.

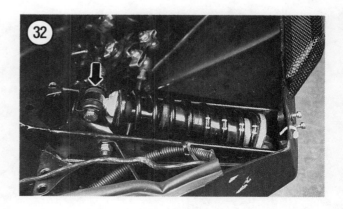

FRONT SUSPENSION (DIRECT SHOCK ACTION)

The Ski-Doo Direct Shock Action (DSA) is used on all 1995 models, the 1993 Formula MX Z model, and all 1994 models *except MACH 1 and Grand Touring models*. Refer to *Front Suspension (Progressive Rate Suspension)* in this chapter for other models.

Refer to **Figure 34** when performing procedures in this section. Because of the number of parts used in the suspension, identify parts during removal and store them in separate boxes.

Steering Arm, Ski Leg and Swing Arm Removal/Installation

1. Support the front of the machine so both skis are off the ground.

2. Remove the skis as described in this chapter.

3. Disconnect the tie rod from the steering arm (A, **Figure 35** or A, **Figure 36**).

4. Remove the steering arm and ski leg as follows:

   a. Remove the cap (**Figure 37**).

   b. Remove the clamp bolt (B, **Figure 35** or B, **Figure 36**) from the steering arm, then pull the steering arm from the ski leg.

   c. Remove the snap ring and washers, then pull the ski leg from the swing arm.

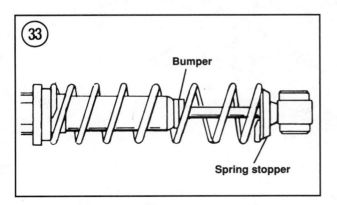

5. Remove the bolt (**Figure 38**) attaching the lower end of the shock absorber to the swing arm.

6. Remove the bolt (A, **Figure 39**) attaching the upper control arm to the swing arm.

7. Remove the bolt (B, **Figure 39**) that attaches the lower control arm to the swing arm.

8. Remove the bolt (**Figure 40**) that attaches the swing arm at the rear, then remove the swing arm.

9. Check the swing arm and related parts as described in this section.

10. Install by reversing the removal procedure, observing the following:

   a. Tighten the swing arm front and rear bolts to the torque values specified in **Table 1**.

   b. Tighten the steering arm pinch bolt and the shock absorber attaching bolt securely.

Inspection

1. Clean all components thoroughly in solvent. Remove all dirt and other residue from all surfaces.

NOTE
If paint has been removed from parts during cleaning, touch up areas as required before assembly or installation.

2. Inspect the steering arm for cracks, excessive wear or other damage. Check splines in steering arm and mating splines in ski leg carefully for wear or other damage.

3. Check the ski leg for cracks or other damage. Also check the shaft for being bent.

4. Check the lower end of the ski leg and wear plate for damage.

5. Check the swing arm for cracks, excessive wear or other damage. Check the housing, for cracks or damage. Check the bushings loacted in the swing arm for wear or damage.

6. Replace worn or damaged parts as required.

15

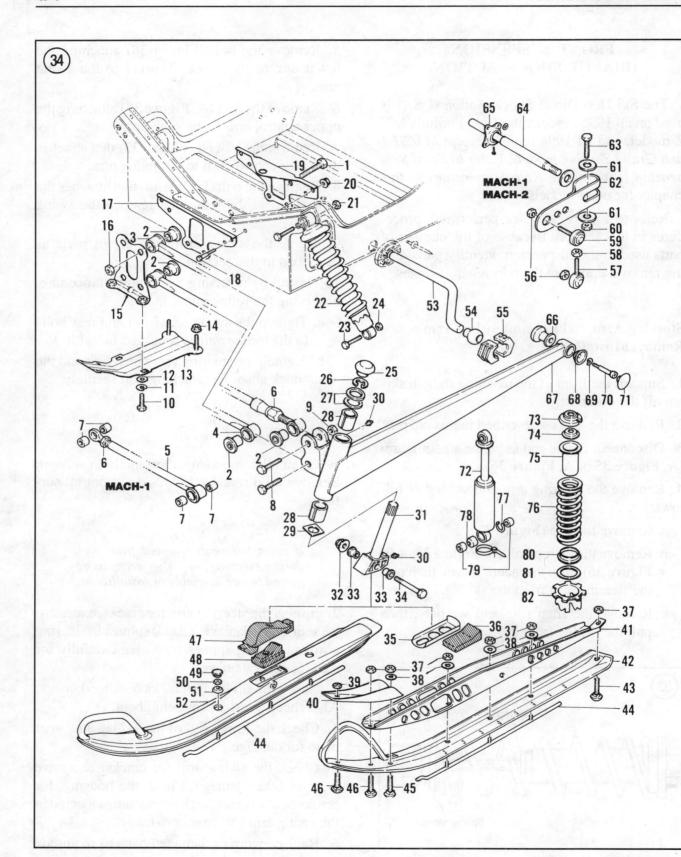

FRONT SUSPENSION
(DIRECT SHOCK ACTION)

1.	Bolt	42.	Plastic ski
2.	Cushion	43.	Carriage bolt
3.	Upper arm	44.	Carbide wear bar
4.	Lower arm	45.	Carriage bolt
5.	Lower arm	46.	Carriage bolt
6.	Lock nut	47.	Ski protector
7.	Spacers	48.	Stopper
8.	Bolt	49.	Cap
9.	Nut	50.	Nut
10.	Bolt	51.	Cupped washer
11.	Lockwasher	52.	Ski
12.	Washer	53.	Stabilizer bar
13.	Plate	54.	Ball joint
14.	Nut	55.	Sliding block
15.	Link plate	56.	Nuts
16.	Nut	57.	Connecting rod
17.	Front link plate	58.	Locknut
18.	Bolt	59.	Rod end
19.	Rear link plate	60.	Nut
20.	Nut	61.	Washers
21.	Nut	62.	Stabilizer lever
22.	Shock absorber	63.	Bolt
23.	Bolt	64.	Stabilizer bar
24.	Nut	65.	Bushing
25.	Cap	66.	Rubber damper
26.	Circlip	67.	Swing arm
27.	Washers	68.	Bowl
28.	Bushings	69.	Lockwasher
29.	Wear plate	70.	Bolt
30.	Grease fitting	71.	Cap
31.	Ski leg	72.	Shock absorber
32.	Nut	73.	Spring retainer
33.	Cushion	74.	Cap
34.	Bolt	75.	Shield
35.	Stopper	76.	Spring
36.	Stopper	77.	Circlip
37.	Nut	78.	Cushion
38.	Washer	79.	Spacers
39.	Nut	80.	Spring seat
40.	Reinforcement	81.	Washer
41.	Support	82.	Adjuster

15

Lower Control Arm
Removal/Installation

Refer to **Figure 34** for this procedure.

1. Support the front of the machine so both skis are off the ground.

2. Open the hood.

3. Remove the bolt (B, **Figure 39**) that attaches the lower control arm to the swing arm.

4. Remove the bolt (A, **Figure 41**) that attaches the lower control arm to the frame.

5. Remove the lower control arm.

6. Check parts as described in the following *Lower Control Arm Inspection* procedure.

7. Installation is the reverse of removal. Tighten the lower control arm bolts to the torque specification in **Table 1**.

Lower Control Arm
Inspection

1. Clean the lower control arm in solvent and dry thoroughly.

2. If paint has been removed from the lower control arm during cleaning or through use, touch up areas before installation.

3. Check the lower control arm for cracks or other damage. The control arm should be straight.

4. Check the cushions at both ends of the lower control arm for excessive wear or damage.

5. The lower control arm used on some models can be adjusted for length. Do not change this adjustment unless necessary. If changed, refer to *Camber Angle Adjustment* in this chapter. The standard length of the lower control arm for 1995 MX Z, Formula Z and MACH 1 models is 446 mm (17 9/16 in.).

6. Replace worn or damaged parts as required.

Stabilizer Bar

Refer to **Figure 34** for this procedure. Some models are equipped with arms clamped to the

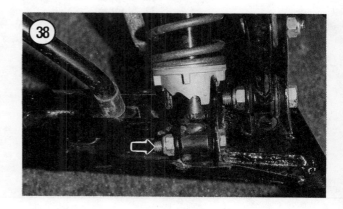

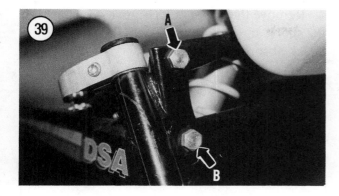

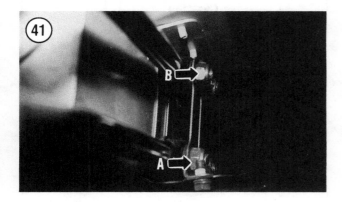

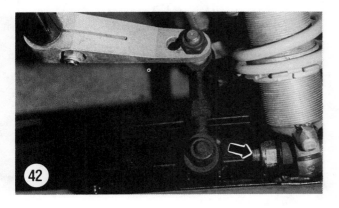

ends of the stabilizer bar as shown in **Figure 42** and adjustable linkage.

1. Remove the stabilizer bar mounting bolts and brackets, then remove the stabilizer bar.

2. Clean the stabilizer bar in solvent and dry thoroughly.

3. If paint has been removed from the stabilizer bar during cleaning or through use, touch up areas before installation.

4. Check the stabilizer bar for wear, cracks or other damage.

5. Check the slider and slider joint for damage.

6. Replace worn or damaged parts as required.

7. Reverse the removal steps to install and observe the following:

   a. If the removable arms have been removed, install with the arms nearly parallel with the ground.

   b. If equipped with link rod between the control arm and frame, the exposed threads of ball joint should not exceed 12 mm (15/32 in.). Tighten the lock nuts to 20 N•m (15 ft.-lb.) torque after aligning the ball joints.

   c. Tighten the stabilizer bolts securely.

   d. Make sure the stabilizer is free to move in its bushings.

Upper Control Arm Removal/Installation

Refer to **Figure 34** for this procedure.

1. Open the hood.

2. Remove the bolt (A, **Figure 39**) attaching the upper control arm to the swing arm.

3. Remove the bolt (B, **Figure 41**) attaching the upper control arm to the frame.

4. Remove the upper control arm.

5. Check parts as described in the following *Upper Control Arm Inspection* procedure.

6. Installation is the reverse of the removal steps. Tighten the control arm bolts to the torque specification in **Table 1**.

15

Upper Control Arm
Inspection

1. Clean the upper control arm in solvent and dry thoroughly.

2. If paint has been removed from the upper control arm during cleaning or through use, touch up areas before installation.

3. Check the upper control arm for wear, cracks or other damage. If a ball joint has been loose, threads in the upper control arm may be damaged.

4. Check the cushions for excessive wear or damage. If damaged, loosen the nut and unscrew the end. Reverse the procedure to install. When installing new ends, make sure the exposed thread length is the same as for the original installation.

5. Replace worn or damaged parts as required.

6. If one or more ball joints were loosened or replaced, check *Steering Adjustment* as described in this chapter.

Shock Absorber
Removal/Installation

Refer to **Figure 34** for this procedure.

1. Support the front of the machine so both skis are off the ground.

2. Open the hood.

3. Remove the lower bolt (**Figure 42**) attaching the shock absorber to the swing arm.

4. Remove the upper bolt (**Figure 43**) attaching the shock absorber to the frame, then remove the shock absorber.

5. Check the shock absorber as described in *Shock Inspection* section in this chapter.

6. Installation is the reverse of these steps. Tighten the shock absorber attaching bolts securely.

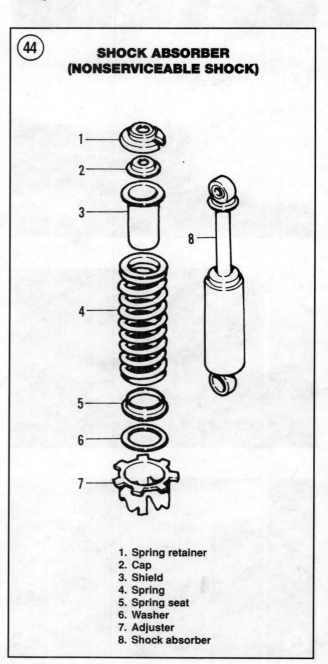

44

**SHOCK ABSORBER
(NONSERVICEABLE SHOCK)**

1. Spring retainer
2. Cap
3. Shield
4. Spring
5. Spring seat
6. Washer
7. Adjuster
8. Shock absorber

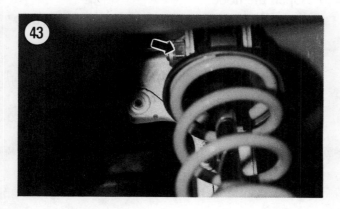

43

Spring
Removal/Installation

Refer to **Figure 44** or **Figure 45** for this procedure.

1. Remove the shock absorber as described in this chapter.

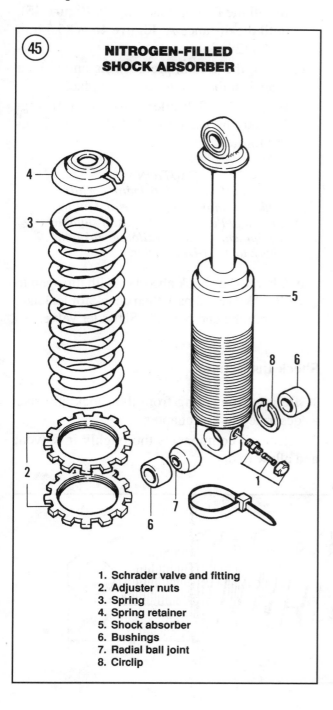

45 NITROGEN-FILLED SHOCK ABSORBER

1. Schrader valve and fitting
2. Adjuster nuts
3. Spring
4. Spring retainer
5. Shock absorber
6. Bushings
7. Radial ball joint
8. Circlip

2A. On models with the spring and shock absorber shown in **Figure 44**, proceed as follows:

  a. Secure the bottom of the shock absorber in a vise with soft jaws.

  b. Slide the rubber bumper down the shock shaft.

WARNING
Do not attempt to remove or install the shock spring without the use of a spring compressor. Use the Ski-Doo spring remover (part No. 414 5796 00) or a suitable equivalent. Attempting to remove the spring without the use of a spring compressor may cause severe personal injury. If you do not have access to a spring compressor, refer spring removal to a Ski-Doo dealer.

  c. Attach a suitable spring compressor to the shock absorber following the compressor manufacturer's instructions. Compress the spring with the tool and remove the spring stopper from the top of the shock. Remove the spring.

CAUTION
Do not attempt to disassemble the shock damper housing.

2B. On models with rebuildable and nitrogen charged shock absorber shown in **Figure 45**, proceed as follows:

CAUTION
The shock absorber is charged with nitrogen gas at 2070 kPa (300 psi). Wear eye protection and use extreme caution whenever you are working with high pressure gas. Do not attempt to remove the Schrader type valve before releasing all pressure.

  a. Clamp the upper end of the shock absorber in a soft-jawed vise.

  b. Remove cover protecting the Schrader valve and carefully release the pressurized nitrogen.

15

c. Remove the Schrader valve core after all pressure is released, then remove the fitting for the valve (1, **Figure 45**) from the dampener housing.

d. Use special tool (part No. 861 7439 00) to remove the spring preload rings (2, **Figure 45**).

e. Withdraw the spring (3, **Figure 45**) and the upper retainer (4, **Figure 45**) from the damper body.

3. Inspect the spring for cracks or damage. If the spring appears okay, measure its free length and compare to the specification in **Table 2**. Replace the spring if it has sagged significantly.

4. Check the spring retainer for cracks, deep scoring or excessive wear. Replace if necessary.

5A. On models with non-rebuildable shocks (**Figure 44**), install the spring by reversing the removal steps. Make sure the spring retainer holds the spring securely.

5B. On models with the nitrogen charged rebuildable shocks (**Figure 45**), install the spring as follows:

CAUTION
Be careful not to spill oil from the shock absorber while the Schrader valve is removed. If the amount of oil or if the condition of the shock absorber is questioned, the shock absorber should be taken to a dealer who is qualified to rebuild and tune the shock absorber.

a. Install the upper spring retainer (4, **Figure 45**) and the spring (3, **Figure 45**).

NOTE
Spring preload can be adjusted by changing the position of the preload ring, but initial setting is as follows.

b. Install the first preload ring (2, **Figure 45**), until the distance A, **Figure 46** is 85.5 mm (3 11/32 in.).

c. Install the second preload ring and tighten it against the first to lock it in place.

d. Install the Schrader valve and fitting. Tighten the valve to 1.5-2 N•m (13-17 in.-lb.) torque.

CAUTION
Use a suitable, regulated nitrogen filling tank, regulator, gauge, hose and fittings to charge the shock with gas. If suitable equipment is not available, take the shock to a Ski-Doo dealer.

e. Charge the shock absorber with nitrogen to 2070 kPa (300 psi), then check for leakage. Install the cap over the Schrader valve.

Shock Inspection

1. Remove the spring from the shock absorber as described in this chapter.
2. Clean all components thoroughly in solvent and allow to dry.

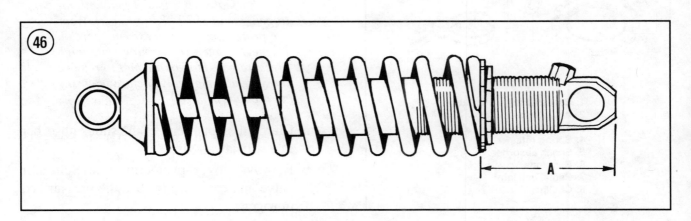

3. Check the damper rod as follows:

  a. Check the damper housing for leakage. If a non-rebuildable damper (**Figure 44**) is leaking, replace it. If a rebuildable damper (**Figure 45** is leaking, take it to a Ski-Doo dealer who can rebuild it.

  b. Check the damper rod for bending or other damage. Check the damper housing for dents or other damage.

  c. Operate the damper rod by hand and check its operation. If the damper is operating correctly, a small amount of resistance should be felt on the compression stroke and a considerable amount of resistance felt on the return stroke.

  d. Replace or repair the damper assembly if necessary.

4. Do not attempt any repair to the dampers shown in **Figure 44**. Do not attempt to straighten the damper rod of any type.

5. Check the spring stopper for cracks, deep scoring or excessive wear. Replace if necessary.

STEERING ASSEMBLY

This section describes service to the handlebar, steering column and tie rods.

Handlebar
Removal/Installation

Refer to **Figure 47** or **Figure 48** for this procedure.

1. Remove the steering pad assembly (**Figure 47** or **Figure 48**).

2. Remove the housings for the throttle and brake controls from the handlebar.

3. Remove the steering clamp bolts and steering clamp (**Figure 49**). Then remove the upper handlebar supports, handlebar and lower handlebar supports.

4. Install in reverse of the removal procedure, observing the following.

5. Install the lower handlebar supports, handlebar and upper handlebar supports. Then install the steering clamp and mounting bolts.

6. Position the handlebar and tighten the steering clamp bolts in a crisscross pattern to the torque specification in **Table 1**. Make sure the gap between the steering clamp steering column support is equal on all 4 sides.

WARNING
If the handlebar is positioned too high, the brake lever may contact the windshield while turning. Check clearance between the handlebar and the windshield before riding the snowmobile. If necessary, adjust the position to permit full handlebar movement.

7. Reinstall the steering pad assembly.

8. Reinstall the housings for throttle and brake control. Make sure that all controls have proper operation.

Handlebar Grips
Removal/Installation

1A. Observe the following when replacing handlebar *grips without heating element.*

  a. Grips can be removed and installed easily by blowing compressed air into the opposite handlebar end while covering the hole in opposite grip with a finger.

  b. To remove grips without compressed air, insert a thin-tipped screwdriver underneath the grip and squirt some electrical contact cleaner between the grip and handlebar or twist grip. Quickly remove the screwdriver and twist the grip to break its hold on the handlebar, then slide the grip off. To install new grips, squirt contact cleaner into the grip as before and quickly twist it onto the handlebar or twist grip. Allow plenty of time for the contact cleaner to evaporate before riding snowmobile.

1B. Observe the following when replacing *grips equipped with a heating element.*

15

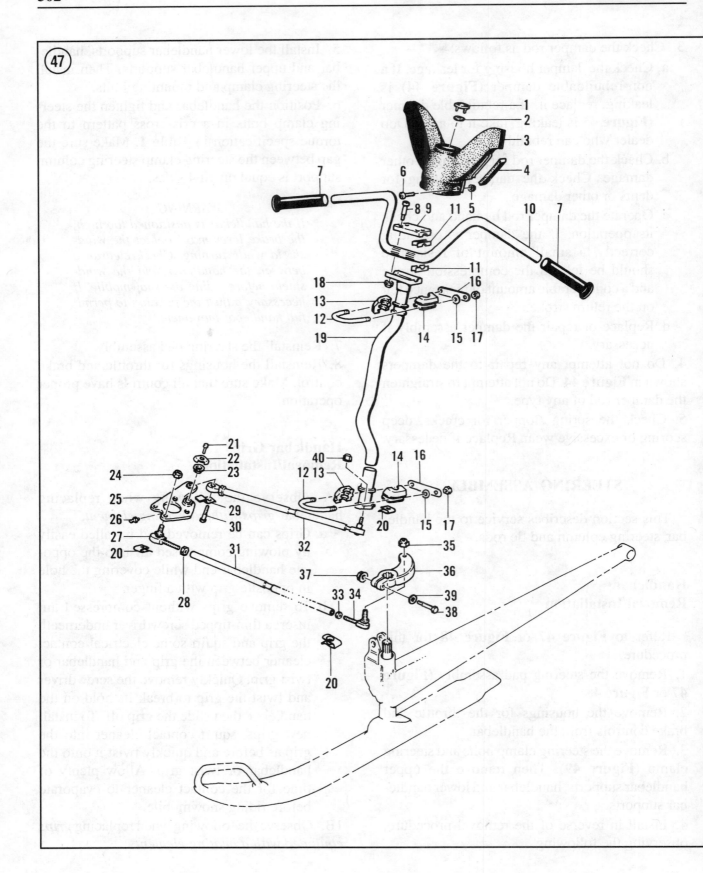

47

**STEERING ASSEMBLY
(EARLY MODELS, TYPICAL)**

1. Logo
2. Push nut
3. Cover
4. Clip
5. Nut
6. Screw
7. Hand grip
8. Bolt
9. Steering clamp
10. Handlebar
11. Steering support
12. U-clamp
13. Bushing
14. Bushing
15. Washer
16. Lock tab
17. Nut
18. Nut
19. Steering shaft
20. Lock tab
21. Screw
22. Screw stopper
23. Flange
24. Nut
25. Pivot arm
26. Grease fitting
27. Ball joint
28. Nut
29. Screw stopper
30. Bolt
31. Tie rod (long)
32. Tie rod (short)
33. Nut
34. Ball joint
35. Nut
36. Steering arm
37. Nut
38. Bolt
39. Washer

a. To remove a grip, locate the heating element wires on the grip. Then cut the grip on the opposite side away from the wires. Slowly peel the grip back and locate the gap between the heating element. Cut along this gap to completely remove grip.

b. When installing a new grip, route the heating element wires so that they do not interfere with brake or throttle operation. Bump the grips in position using a rubber mallet.

2. Make sure grips are *tight* before riding the snowmobile.

WARNING
Do not use any type of grease, soap or other lubricant to install grips. Loose grips can cause you to crash. Always replace damaged or loose grips before riding.

**Steering Column
Removal/Installation**

Refer to **Figure 47** or **Figure 48** for this procedure.

NOTE
The following procedure is shown with the engine removed for clarity.

1. Remove the handlebar as described in this chapter.
2. Disconnect the tie rod from the steering column (**Figure 50**).
3. Remove the upper and lower U-clamp and remove the steering column. Store the upper and lower steering bushings separately so they can be reinstalled in their original positions.
4. Inspect the steering column as described under *Inspection* in this chapter.
5. Install in the reverse of removal while observing the following.
6. Apply a low-temperature grease to the inner bearing halves before assembly.
7. If reinstalling the original steering bushings, install them in their original positions.

15

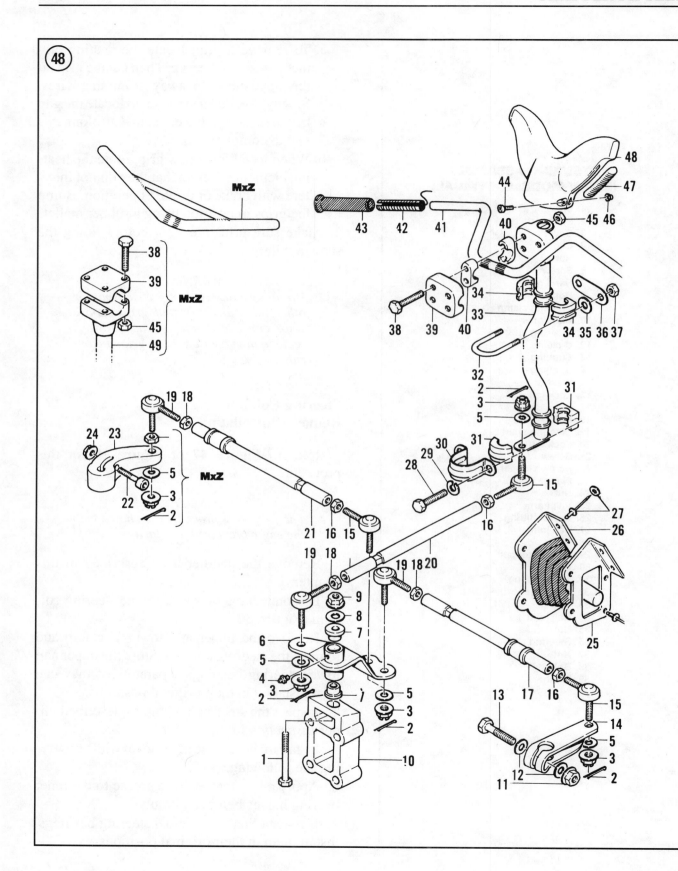

STEERING ASSEMBLY
(LATE MODELS, TYPICAL)

1. Pivot bolt
2. Cotter pins
3. Castellated nuts
4. Grease fitting
5. Washer
6. Pivot arm
7. Cushion
8. Washer
9. Nut
10. Center block
11. Nut
12. Washers
13. Clamp bolt
14. Steering arm (stamped)
15. Right hand rod ends
16. Right hand lock nut
17. Tie rod and bushing
18. Left-hand lock nut
19. Left-hand rod ends
20. Steering rod
21. Tie rod and bushing
22. Clamp bolt
23. Steering arm (aluminum)
24. Nut
25. Plate
26. Tie rod cap
27. Pop rivet
28. Bolt
29. Lockwasher
30. Lower support
31. Lower bushing
32. U clamp
33. Steering tube
34. Upper bushing
35. Washer
36. Lock plate
37. Nut
38. Bolt
39. Steering clamp
40. Steering support
41. Handle bar
42. Grip heater
43. Grip
44. Screw
45. Nut
46. Nut
47. Cover
48. Padding
49. Steering tube

15

8. Assemble the steering bushings and U-clamps as shown in **Figure 47** or **Figure 48**. Tighten the U-clamps to the torque specification in **Table 1**.

9. After tightening the bearing half mounting bolts, bend the lockwasher tabs over the bolts.

10. Check ski alignment as described in this chapter.

Steering Column Inspection

Refer to **Figure 47** or **Figure 48** for this procedure.

1. Clean all components thoroughly in solvent. Remove all grease residue from the bearing halves.

2. Inspect the steering column for cracks or deep scoring. Check the welds at the top and bottom of the shaft for cracks or breakage.

3. Inspect the steering bushings for cracks, deep scoring or excessive wear.

Tie Rod Removal/Installation

A short center tie rod connects the steering shaft to the center pivot arm. Two tie rods connect the center pivot arm to the steering arms located at the top of each ski leg. Refer to **Figure 47** or **Figure 48**.

> *NOTE*
> *It may be necessary to use a ratcheting box wrench as shown in **Figure 50** to remove and install the bolts attaching the tie rod ends. Views shown may have the engine removed for clarity. Clearance is tight, but it should be possible to remove the bolts from the rod ends with the engine in place.*

1. To remove the center tie rod, proceed as follows:

a. Disconnect the rear rod end from the steering column (**Figure 51**).

b. Disconnect the forward rod end from the pivot arm (A, **Figure 52**).

2. To remove the tie rods that operate from side to side between the center pivot arm and the ski leg steering arms, proceed as follows:

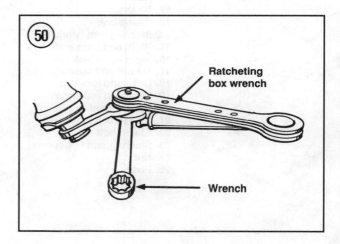

a. Disconnect the rod end located at the inner end from the center pivot arm (B, **Figure 52**).

b. Disconnect the outside rod end from the steering arm located at the top of the ski leg **Figure 53**.

3. Inspect the tie rod as described in the following procedure.

4. Installation is the reverse of these steps. Note the following.

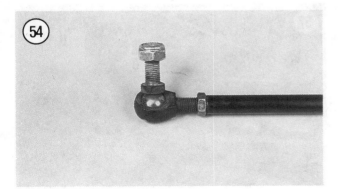

a. After installing the tie rods, check ski alignment as described in this chapter.

b. When ski alignment is correct, tighten tie rod bolts to the torque specification in **Table 1**. Secure bolts with lockwasher tab.

Tie Rod Inspection

1. Clean the tie rod in solvent and dry thoroughly.

2. If paint has been removed from the tie rod during cleaning or through use, touch up areas before installation.

3. Inspect the tie rod for dents, bends, cracks or other damage. Check the ball joints for deep scoring or excessive wear. If a ball joint has been loose, the threads in the tie rod may be damaged.

4. Check the ball joints (**Figure 54**) for excessive wear or damage.

a. If damaged, loosen the nut and unscrew the ball joint.

b. Reverse to install. When installing new ball joints, turn the new ball joint into the tie rod the same distance as the original.

WARNING
*The exposed threads between the ball joint and tie rod (**Figure 55**) should not exceed 15 mm (19/32 in.) for 1990-1992 models or 20 mm (25/32 in.) for 1993-on*

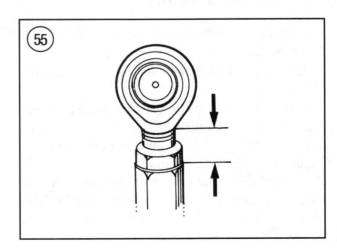

15

models. The number of exposed threads should be equal for ball joints at each end of the tie rod. If the tie rod is one of the two that operate from the center pivot to the steering arms on the ski legs, the number of exposed threads should be about the same for ball joints on both tie rods. The strength of the tie rod is weakened if the locknut is not tight or if the ball joint is not threaded in far enough.

  c. If a tie rod or ball joint was replaced, check *Steering Adjustment* as described in this chapter.

5. Replace worn or damaged parts as required.

6. If one or more ball joints were loosened or replaced, check steering adjustment as described in this chapter.

STEERING ADJUSTMENT

Incorrect ski alignment can cause difficult steering and result in lack of control. Accurate checks and adjustments are important. Steering adjustment is a 4 part procedure. The following adjustments must be performed in order:

  a. Pivot arm center adjustment.
  b. Camber angle adjustment.
  c. Handlebar alignment.
  d. Toe-out adjustment.

Pivot Arm Center Adjustment

1. Park the snowmobile on a level surface.

2. Open the hood.

3. Center the handlebars so they face straight ahead.

4A. For models with Progressive Rate Suspension (PSA), see **Figure 56**. Determine the centerline of the vehicle from the pivot bolt (A, **Figure 57**). Measure the distance from the vehicle centerline to the center of each tie rod ball joint (B, **Figure 57**) as shown in **Figure 56**. The distance should be the same for both tie rods. If not, perform the following:

  a. Turn the handlebar to the left to gain access to the front of the tie rod (C, **Figure 57**) that connects the steering shaft to the pivot arm.

  b. Loosen the ball joint jam nut on the tie rod (C, **Figure 57**), then remove the bolt attaching the ball joint to the pivot arm.

  c. Turn the ball joint into or out of the tie rod as required to correctly center the tie rod ends as shown in **Figure 56**.

NOTE
When adjusting the ball joint, make sure the exposed thread length between the ball joint and tie rod does not exceed 15

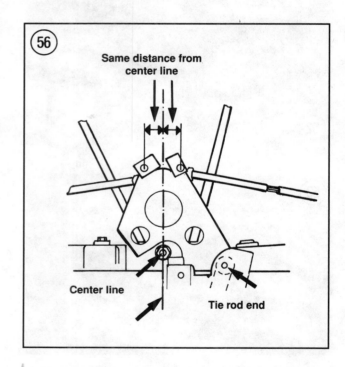

Same distance from center line

Center line

Tie rod end

mm (19/32 in.) on 1990-1992 models or 20 mm (25/32 in.) for 1993-on models.

d. When the handlebars and the pivot arm are both centered, tighten the tie rod attaching bolt to the torque specification in **Table 1**. Bend the lockwasher tab over bolt to lock it.

4B. For models with Direct Action Shocks (DSA) , see **Figure 58**. Determine the centerline of the vehicle from the pivot bolt (A, **Figure 59**). Measure the distance from the vehicle centerline to the center of each tie rod ball joint (B, **Figure 59**) as shown in **Figure 58**. The distance should be the same for both tie rods. If not, perform the following:

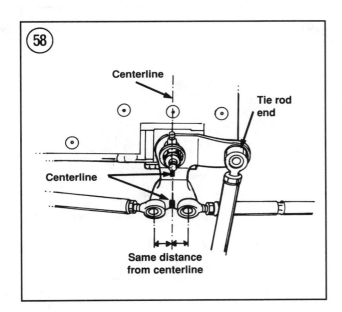

58

Centerline

Tie rod end

Centerline

Same distance from centerline

59

A

B

C

B

a. Loosen the ball joint jam nut on the tie rod (C, **Figure 59**), then remove the nut attaching the ball joint to the pivot arm.

b. Turn the ball joint into or out of the tie rod as required to correctly center the tie rod ends as shown in **Figure 58**.

NOTE
When adjusting ball joint, make sure the exposed thread length between the ball joint and tie rod does not exceed 20 mm (25/32 in.).

c. When the handlebars and the pivot arm are both centered, tighten the tie rod attaching nuts to the torque specification in **Table 1**.

Camber Angle Adjustment

1. Check the center position of the pivot arm center adjustment as described in the previous section in this chapter.

2A. On all except 1995 MX Z, Formula Z and MACH 1 models, raise and support the snowmobile so the skis are approximately 25 mm (1 in.) off the ground.

NOTE
Camber angle can only be measured when the front suspension is fully extended. Do not measure the angle with the skis on ground.

2B. On 1995 MX Z, Formula Z and MACH 1 models, the front shock absorber units must be removed and replaced with spacers of a specific length as follows:

a. Raise and support the snowmobile so the skis are off the ground.

b. Remove the front shock absorbers as described in this chapter.

c. Install the special 300 mm (11.8 in.) spacer bars (part No. 529 0278 00) in place of the shock absorbers.

15

NOTE
An angle finder or protractor is required to check and adjust the camber in Step 3 and Step 4. This tool is available from many tool suppliers and well-equipped building supply stores.

3. Place an angle finder on the main horizontal frame member as shown in **Figure 60** to check the vehicle level. If necessary, block the machine so the horizontal frame member is level.

NOTE
Do not place the angle finder on a decal or weld. This will give a false reading and will result in an incorrect camber adjustment.

4. Place the angle finder on one of the swing arms as shown in **Figure 61**. The camber reading should be 0° ±0.5°.

5A. On all except 1995 MX Z, Formula Z and MACH 1 models, if the adjustment is incorrect, loosen the locknut (**Figure 62**) on the upper control arm.

5B. On 1995 MX Z, Formula Z and MACH 1 models, if the adjustment is incorrect, loosen the locknut on the lower control arm.

6. Turn the upper (or lower) control arm to adjust the camber. Tighten the locknut securely and recheck the adjustment.

7. Repeat Step 5 and Step 6 for the opposite side.

8. On 1995 MX Z, Formula Z and MACH 1 models, remove the special 300 mm (11.8 in.) spacer bars and install the shock absorbers.

9. Lower skis to ground.

Handlebar Alignment

1. Raise and support the snowmobile so the skis are approximately 25 mm (1 in.) off the ground.

2. Turn handlebar until both skis face forward.

3. Check handlebar alignment as follows:
   a. Measure from the end of one handlebar grip to a point at the back of the snowmobile (**Figure 63**). Record the length.

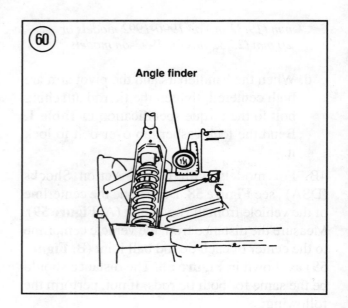

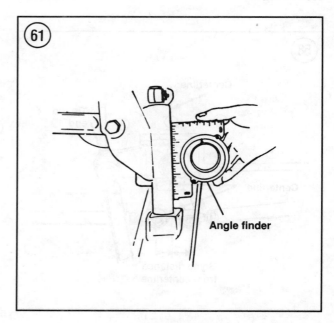

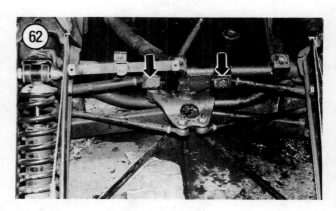

b. Repeat measurement for the opposite side (**Figure 63**). Make sure to use the same reference points. Record the length.

c. The distance recorded in substep b and c must be approximately the same. If adjustment is required, proceed to Step 4.

4. Loosen the 2 locknuts on each tie rod (**Figure 64**). Determine from Step 3 which direction the skis have to be turned to correctly align the handlebar. Then turn one tie rod to shorten its length and turn the opposite tie rod to lengthen it. Make sure to turn both tie rods the *same* amount so that you do not change the toe-out adjustment. Tighten locknuts and recheck adjustment.

> *NOTE*
> *When adjusting the ball joints, make sure the exposed thread length between the ball joint and tie rod does not exceed 15 mm (19/32 in.) on 1990-1992 models or 20 mm (25/32 in.) on 1993-on models.*

5. Check *Toe-Out Adjustment* as described in the following section of this chapter.

Toe-Out Adjustment

1. Check handlebar alignment as described in the previous section.

2. Raise and support the snowmobile so the skis are approximately 25 mm (1 in.) off the ground.

3. Turn the handlebar so the skis face forward.

4. Attach an elastic band (bungee) to the tips of the skis to pull the fronts of the skis together when checking toe-out.

5. Position a straightedge against the side of the track.

6. Measure the distance between the straightedge and the straight inner edge of the ski as shown in **Figure 65**. The skis should be straight or slightly toed-out. Try to measure as far forward and backward on the skis as possible. Pick a reference point or make chalk marks so the same measuring points are used for all measurements.

7. The difference between the front and rear measurements should be less than 1.5 mm (1/16 in.). The distance should never be more at the rear.

8. If the measurement is incorrect, loosen the tie rod locknuts (**Figure 64**) and turn the tie rods to

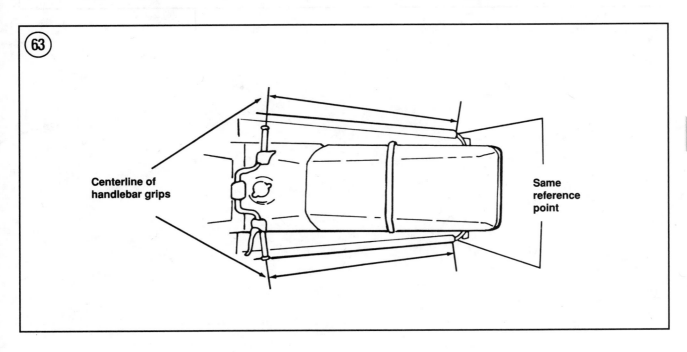

63

Centerline of
handlebar grips

Same
reference
point

15

increase or reduce toe-out as needed. Tighten
locknuts and recheck toe-out.

NOTE
When adjusting the ball joints, make
sure the exposed thread length between
the ball joint and tie rod does not exceed
15 mm (19/32 in.) on 1990-1992 models
or 20 mm (25/32 in.) on 1993-on models.

After adjusting one side, measure and adjust
toeout for the other ski following Steps 6-8.

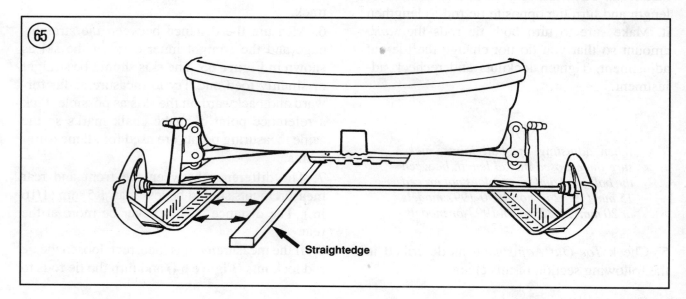

Straightedge

Table 1 FRONT SUSPENSION AND STEERING TIGHTENING TORQUES

	N·m	ft.-lb.
Models with Progressive Rate Suspension (PRS)		
Handle bar	26	19
Lower control arm		
At swing arm	85	63
At frame	52	38
Rocker arm bolt	48	35
Shock absorber bolts		
Front	29	21
Rear	35	26
Ski pivot bolt	40	30
Ski wear bar nuts	18	12 (159 in.-lb.)
Stabilizer bar bolts	15	11 (133 in.-lb.)
Steering arm pinch bolt	25	18
Steering column U-clamps		
Upper	26	19
Lower	9.5	7 (85 in.-lb.)
Swing arm bolts		
Front	29	21
Rear	25	18
Tie rod (sides)	29	21
Tie rod (center)		
At steering column	29	21
At pivot arm	48	35
Upper control arm bolts	29	21
Models with Direct Shock Action (DSA)		
Control arms (inner)	80	59
Handle bar	25	18
Plastic ski to support	10	8 (98 in.-lb.)
Ski wear bar nuts	14	10 (124 in.-lb.)
Steering column U-clamps		
Upper	26	19
Lower	25	18
Swing arm bolts		
Front	29	21
Rear	25	18
Steering tie rod		
Attachment at ends	40	30
Adjustment lock nuts	18	13 (159 in.-lb.)

15

Table 2 SPRING SPECIFICATIONS

	Color code	Free length
1990		
Formula MX	Green/Green	238.3-244.3 mm (9.38-9.62 in.)
Formula MX LT	White/Green	278.2-284.2 mm (10.95-11.19 in.)
Formula Plus	Green/Green	238.3-244.3 mm (9.38-9.62 in.)
	(continued)	

Table 2 SPRING SPECIFICATIONS (continued)

	Color code	Free length
1990 (continued)		
Formula Plus LT	White/Green	278.2-284.2 mm (10.95-11.19 in.)
Formula MACH 1	Green/Green	238.3-244.3 mm (9.38-9.62 in.)
Formula MACH 1 XTC	White/Green	278.2-284.2 mm (10.95-11.19 in.)
1991		
Formula MX	Green/Green	238.3-244.3 mm (9.38-9.62 in.)
Formula MX E	Green/Green	238.3-244.3 mm (9.38-9.62 in.)
Formula MX XTC	White/Green	278.2-284.2 mm (10.95-11.19 in.)
Formula MX XTC E	White/Green	278.2-284.2 mm (10.95-11.19 in.)
Formula Plus	Green/Green	238.3-244.3 mm (9.38-9.62 in.)
Formula Plus E	Green/Green	238.3-244.3 mm (9.38-9.62 in.)
Formula Plus XTC	White/Green	278.2-284.2 mm (10.95-11.19 in.)
Formula Plus XTC E	White/Green	278.2-284.2 mm (10.95-11.19 in.)
Formula MACH 1	Green/Green	238.3-244.3 mm (9.38-9.62 in.)
Formula MACH 1 XTC	White/Green	278.2-284.2 mm (10.95-11.19 in.)
All models optional	Yellow/Yellow	244.7-250.7 mm (9.63-9.87 in.)
1992		
Formula MX	Green/Red	223-229 mm (8.78-9.02 in.)
Formula MX XTC R	Red/Red	238-244 mm (9.37-9.61 mm)
Formula Plus	Green/Red	223-229 mm (8.78-9.02 in.)
Formula Plus E	Green/Red	223-229 mm (8.78-9.02 in.)
Formula Plus XTC	Red/Red	238-244 mm (9.37-9.61 mm)
Formula Plus XTC E	Red/Red	238-244 mm (9.37-9.61 mm)
Formula Plus X	Black	163-168 mm (6.42-6.61 in.)
Formula MACH 1	Green/Red	223-229 mm (8.78-9.02 in.)
Formula MACH 1 X	Black	163-168 mm (6.42-6.61 in.)
Formula MACH 1 XTC	Red/Red	238-244 mm (9.37-9.61 mm)
Formula MACH 1 XTC II	Red/Red	238-244 mm (9.37-9.61 mm)

(continued)

Table 2 SPRING SPECIFICATIONS (continued)

	Color code	Free length
1993		
Formula MX	Green/Yellow	224-230 mm (8.817-9.057 in.)
Formula MX (2)	Green/Yellow	224-230 mm (8.817-9.057 in.)
Formula MX XTC R	Green/White	224-230 mm (8.817-9.057 in.)
Formula MX Z	White	253.8-259.8 mm (9.99-10.23 in.)
Formula Plus	Green/Yellow	224-230 mm (8.817-9.057 in.)
Formula Plus (2)	Green/Yellow	224-230 mm (8.817-9.057 in.)
Formula Plus E	Green/Yellow	224-230 mm (8.817-9.057 in.)
Formula Plus XTC	Green/White	224-230 mm (8.817-9.057 in.)
Formula Plus EFI	Green/Yellow	224-230 mm (8.817-9.057 in.)
Formula Plus X	Black	162-168 mm (6.376-6.616 in.)
Formula MACH 1	Green/Yellow	224-230 mm (8.817-9.057 in.)
Formula MACH 1 (2)	Green/Yellow	224-230 mm (8.817-9.057 in.)
Formula MACH 1 XTC	Green/White	224-230 mm (8.817-9.057 in.)
Formula Grand Touring	Green/Yellow	224-230 mm (8.817-9.057 in.)
1994		
Formula MX	Yellow or Wh.	254-260 mm (10.00-10.24 in.)
Formula MX Z	Yellow or Wh.	254-260 mm (10.00-10.24 in.)
Summit 470 & 583	Black/White	236-242 mm (9.29-9.53 in.)
Formula ST	Red or White	254-260 mm (10.00-10.24 in.)
Formula STX	Red or White	254-260 mm (10.00-10.24 in.)
Formula STX II	Red or White	254-260 mm (10.00-10.24 in.)
Formula Z	Red or Wh./Bk.	257-263 mm (10.12-10.35 in.)
MACH 1	Green/Yellow	224-230 mm (8.817-9.057 in.)
Grand Touring	Green/Yellow	224-230 mm (8.817-9.057 in.)
Grand Touring XTC	Green/Yellow	224-230 mm (8.817-9.057 in.)
Grand Touring SE	Green/Yellow	224-230 mm (8.817-9.057 in.)

(continued)

15

Table 2 SPRING SPECIFICATIONS (continued)

	Color code	Free length
1995		
MX	Yellow	254-260 mm (10.00-10.24 in.)
MX Z	Yellow	254-260 mm (10.00-10.24 in.)
Formula SS	Red or White	254-260 mm (10.00-10.24 in.)
Formula STX	–	–
Formula STX (LT)	–	–
Summit 583	–	–
Summit 670	–	–
Formula Z	–	–
MACH 1	Raspberry	–
Grand Touring 470	–	–
Grand Touring 580	–	–
Grand Touring SE	–	–

Chapter Sixteen

Track and Rear Suspension

The rear suspension used on 1990 and 1991 models is shown in **Figure 1**. The rear suspension for 1992-1993 models with PRS (Progressive Rate Suspension) front suspension is shown in **Figure 2**. The rear suspension for 1993-1995 models with (DSA) Direct Shock Action) front suspension is shown in **Figure 3**. Adjustment procedures for all models are described in Chapter Four.

Track specifications are found in **Table 1**. **Tables 1-5** are at the end of the chapter.

REAR SUSPENSION

Removal

1. Loosen the locknuts on the track adjusting bolts (**Figure 4**) and back the bolts out to relieve track tension.

NOTE
The screws retaining the cross shaft are coated with Loctite upon assembly. To remove the screws, first loosen the screw on one side, then retighten that screw to hold the shaft while removing the screw from the opposite side. Return to the first screw and remove that screw.

2. On all long track models, unbolt and remove the rear-most cross shaft and wheels.

NOTE
If you do not have access to a suitable snowmobile jack, you will have to turn the snowmobile on its side when performing the following steps. If the snowmobile is going to be turned on its side during rear suspension removal, plug the oil injection reservoir cap and the chaincase filler cap vent holes to prevent leakage. In addition, place a large piece of cardboard next to the snowmobile before turning it on its side.

3. Raise the snowmobile so that the track is clear of the ground. Remove the bolts from both sides in the order shown in **Figure 5**.

4. Slide the track and suspension assembly away from the tunnel as shown in **Figure 6**, then lift the suspension assembly from the track to remove it.

Inspection

1. Clean all bolts, nuts and threaded holes thoroughly with solvent to remove all Loctite residue.

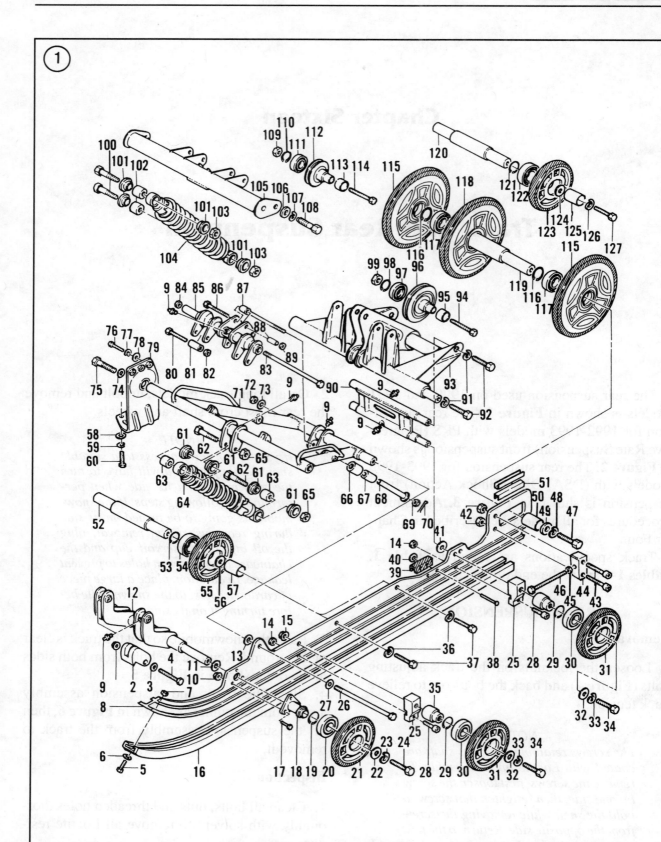

MULTILINK PROGRESSIVE REAR SUSPENSION
(1990-1991 MODELS)

1. Nut
2. Protector
3. Washer
4. Bolt
5. Bolt
6. Washer
7. Nut
8. Runner
9. Grease fitting
10. Nut
11. Washer
12. Front shackle
13. Washer
14. Nut
15. Nut
16. Slider shoe
17. Bolt
18. Housing
19. Circlip
20. Bearing
21. Idler wheel
22. Washer
23. Lockwasher
24. Bolt
25. Idler support
26. Bolt
27. Washer
28. Bolt
29. Circlip
30. Bearing
31. Idler wheel
32. Washer
33. Lockwasher
34. Bolt
35. Axle
36. Lockwasher
37. Bolts
38. Rivet
39. Rubber stopper
40. Push nut
41. Washer
42. Nuts
43. Bolts

44. Stopper
45. Locknut
46. Bolt
47. Bolt
48. Lockwasher
49. Washer
50. Outer spacer
51. Protector
52. Center axle
53. Circlip
54. Bearing
55. Idler wheel
56. Washer
57. Spacer
58. Washer
59. Lockwasher
60. Bolt
61. Cushions
62. Bolts
63. Spacers
64. Spring
65. Nuts
66. Cup
67. Stopper
68. Pin
69. Nut
70. Cotter pin
71. Front arm
72. Nut
73. Washer
74. Washer
75. Bolt
76. Bolt
77. Lockwasher
78. Washer
79. Shackle
80. Bolt
81. Spacer
82. Nut
83. Bolt
84. Nut
85. Front swing arm axle
86. Bolt

87. Stopper bolt
88. Spacer
89. Nut
90. Rear shackle
91. Lockwashers
92. Bolts
93. Rear arm
    and cross pivot
94. Bolt
95. Spacer
96. Idler wheel
    and axle
97. Bearing
98. Circlip
99. Nut
100. Bolts
101. Cushions
102. Spacers
103. Nuts
104. Spring
105. Shock pivot
106. Washer
107. Lockwasher
108. Bolt
109. Nut
110. Circlip
111. Bearing
112. Support wheel
113. Spacer
114. Bolt
115. Idler wheel
116. Circlip
117. Bearing
118. Idler wheel
119. Inner axle
120. Rear axle
121. Circlip
122. Bearing
123. Idler wheel
124. Washer
125. Spacer
126. Lockwasher
127. Bolt

16

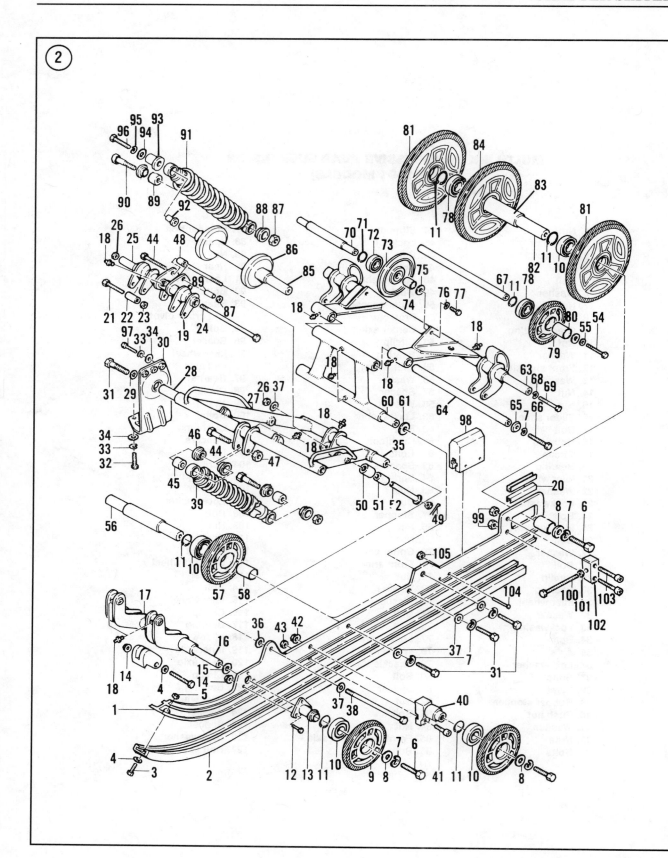

C7 MULTILINK PROGRESSIVE REAR SUSPENSION
(1992-1993 MODELS EQUIPPED WITH PRS FRONT SUSPENSION)

1. Runner
2. Slider shoe
3. Screw
4. Flat washer
5. Lock nut
6. Screw
7. Lock washer
8. Flat washer
9. Idler wheel
10. Ball bearing
11. Snap ring
12. Screw
13. Housing
14. Flanged lock nut
15. Flat washer
16. Front axle
17. Front shackle
18. Grease fitting
19. Front swing arm
20. Protector
21. Screw
22. Spacer
23. Lock nut
24. Long welded screw
25. Front swing arm axle
26. Lock nut
27. Front arm
28. Front arm upper axle
29. Flat washer & lock washer
30. Retainer plate
31. Screw
32. Screw
33. Lock washer
34. Flat washer
35. Lower axle

36. Flat washer
37. Flat washer
38. Short welded screw
39. Center shock
40. Idler support
41. Allen screw
42. Flanged lock nut
43. Lock nut
44. Screw
45. Spacer
46. Pad
47. Lock nut
48. Welded stoper
49. Cotter pin
50. Cup
51. Rubber stopper
52. Bushing
53. Lock nut
54. Screw
55. Lock washer
56. Center axle
57. Idler wheel
58. Spacer
59. Rear shackle
60. Rear shackle lower axle
61. Washer
62. Rear arm
63. Cross pivot
64. Rear shackle upper axle
65. Washer
66. Screw
67. Cross shaft
68. Lock washer
69. Screw
70. Axle

71. Snap ring
72. Ball bearing
73. Idler wheel
74. Spacer
75. Hardened washer
76. Lock washer
77. Screw
78. Ball bearing
79. Idler wheel
80. Spacer
81. Idler wheel
82. Rear axle
83. Inner spacer
84. Center idler wheel
85. Rear shock pivot
86. Protector
87. Lock nut
88. Pad
89. Spacer
90. Screw
91. Rear shock
92. Spacer
93. Pad
94. Washer
95. Lock washer
96. Screw
97. Screw
98. Rubber stopper
99. Lock nuts
100. Adjusting screw
101. Lock nut
102. Tenisoner stopper
103. Allen screw
104. Rivet
105. Push nut

16

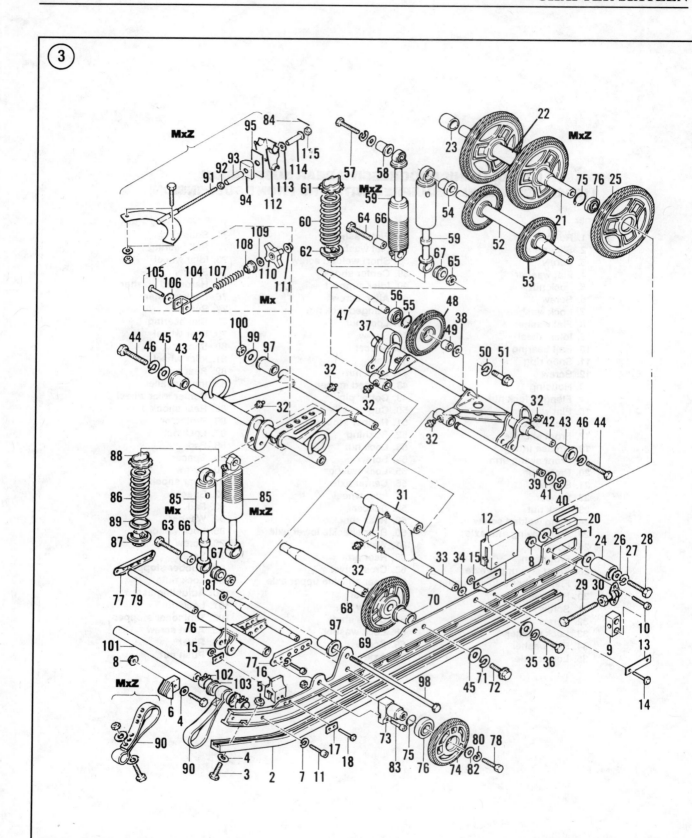

IMPROVED C7 REAR SUSPENSION
(1993-1995 MODELS EQUIPPED WITH DSA FRONT SUSPENSION)

1. Runner
2. Slider shoe
3. Screw
4. Flat washer
5. Lock nut
6. Runner protector
7. Lock washer
8. Flanged lock nut
9. Tensioner
10. Allen screw
11. Allen screw
12. Rear rubber stopper
13. Stopper portector
14. Rivet
15. Push nut
16. Front rubber stopper
17. Stopper protector
18. Rivet
19. Front arm
20. Protector
21. Rear axle
22. Long spacer
23. Short spacer
24. Outer spacer
25. Idler wheel
26. Flat washer
27. Lock washer
28. Screw
29. Adjusting screw
30. Lock nut
31. Rear arm pivot
32. Grease fitting
33. Lower axle
34. Hardened washer
35. Lock washer
36. Screw
37. Rear arm
38. Hardened washer
39. Upper axle

40. Snap ring
41. Flat washer
42. Upper axle
43. Cushion
44. Screw
45. Flat washer
46. Lock washer
47. Axle
48. Idler wheel
49. Spacer
50. Lock washer
51. Screw
52. Shock pivot
53. Protector
54. Pad
55. Snap ring
56. Ball bearing
57. Screw
58. Spacer
59. Rear shock
60. Spring
61. Spring seat
62. Spring stop
63. Screw
64. Screw
65. Lock nut
66. Spacer
67. Cushion
68. Center axle
69. Idler wheel
70. Spacer
71. Lock washer
72. Screw
73. Support
74. Idler wheel
75. Snap ring
76. Ball bearing
77. Retaining plate
78. Screw

79. Axle
80. Lock washer
81. Special washer
82. Flat washer
83. Allen screw
84. Cotter pin
85. Center shock
86. Spring
87. Spring stopper
88. Spring seat
89. Spring guide
90. Strap stopper
91. Belt tensioner
92. Lock nut
93. Bushing
94. Block
95. Rubber strip
96. Lower axle
97. Cushion
98. Long screw
99. Flat washer
100. Lock nut
101. Axle
102. Spring clamp
103. Washer
104. U-bracket
105. Washer
106. Pin
107. Spring
108. Adjuster bushing
109. Washer
110. Adjuster knob
111. Lock nut
112. Adjustment bracket
113. Rubber washer
114. Pusher piece
115. Lock nut
116. Idler wheel

16

2. Inspect the suspension attaching bolts for thread damage or breakage. Replace damaged bolts as required.

3. Inspect bolts for wear, cracks, bends or other abnormal conditions. If there is any doubt about the condition of a bolt, replace it.

4. Clean the complete suspension assembly and check for obvious damage.

5. Inspect the wheels and slides for damage. Replace parts as required.

6. Check the suspension components and frame for obvious damage. Refer to the appropriate sections in this chapter for inspection of specific components.

Installation

1. Pull the track away from the tunnel and open it (**Figure 7**) so suspension can be installed.

2. Install the rear suspension into the track, starting with the front of the suspension and working toward the rear.

NOTE
When installing the rear suspension mounting bolts in the following steps, do not tighten any bolt until all of the bolts are installed finger tight.

3. Install the rear suspension mounting bolts in the following order:

  a. Raise the front arm and align the retainer plate bolt holes with the frame. Install the bolts and washers finger tight. See **Figure 8**.

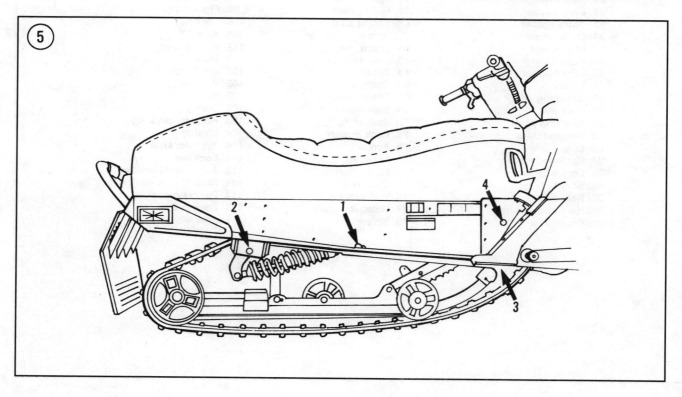

b. Install a spacer on the center axle outside of each shock (**Figure 9**), then install the shock pivot bolt (2, **Figure 5**) and washer.

c. Align the rear arm with the frame and install the rear arm bolts (**Figure 10**) and washers.

4. After the bolts have been installed, tighten all bolts securely in reverse of the sequence in **Figure 5**.

5. Remove the attaching bolts one at a time in reverse of the sequence shown in **Figure 5** and coat the threads with Loctite 271. Reinstall the bolts and tighten to the torque specified in **Table 1**.

6. Lower the track to the ground after all attaching screws are tightened.

7. If the snowmobile was placed on its side, it will probably be necessary to bleed the oil pump as described in Chapter Ten.

SLIDE SHOES

Inspection/Replacement

The slide shoes are mounted at the bottom of the runner and held in position with a single screw. Replace the slide shoes if worn or if they show signs of abnormal wear or damage.

Refer to **Figure 11** for 1990 and 1991 models, **Figure 12** for 1992-1993 models with PRS (Progressive Rate Suspension) front suspension, or **Figure 13** for 1993-1995 models with DSA (Direct Shock Action) front suspension.

16

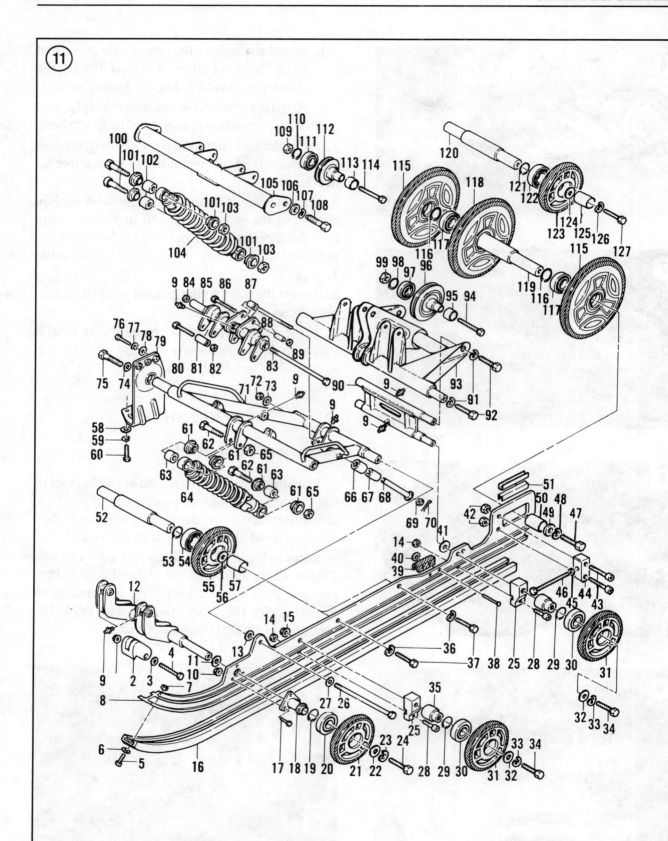

MULTILINK PROGRESSIVE REAR SUSPENSION
(1990-1991 MODELS)

1. Nut	44. Stopper	87. Stopper bolt
2. Protector	45. Locknut	88. Spacer
3. Washer	46. Bolt	89. Nut
4. Bolt	47. Bolt	90. Rear shackle
5. Bolt	48. Lockwasher	91. Lockwashers
6. Washer	49. Washer	92. Bolts
7. Nut	50. Outer spacer	93. Rear arm
8. Runner	51. Protector	and cross pivot
9. Grease fitting	52. Center axle	94. Bolt
10. Nut	53. Circlip	95. Spacer
11. Washer	54. Bearing	96. Idler wheel
12. Front shackle	55. Idler wheel	and axle
13. Washer	56. Washer	97. Bearing
14. Nut	57. Spacer	98. Circlip
15. Nut	58. Washer	99. Nut
16. Slider shoe	59. Lockwasher	100. Bolts
17. Bolt	60. Bolt	101. Cushions
18. Housing	61. Cushions	102. Spacers
19. Circlip	62. Bolts	103. Nuts
20. Bearing	63. Spacers	104. Spring
21. Idler wheel	64. Spring	105. Shock pivot
22. Washer	65. Nuts	106. Washer
23. Lockwasher	66. Cup	107. Lockwasher
24. Bolt	67. Stopper	108. Bolt
25. Idler support	68. Pin	109. Nut
26. Bolt	69. Nut	110. Circlip
27. Washer	70. Cotter pin	111. Bearing
28. Bolt	71. Front arm	112. Support wheel
29. Circlip	72. Nut	113. Spacer
30. Bearing	73. Washer	114. Bolt
31. Idler wheel	74. Washer	115. Idler wheel
32. Washer	75. Bolt	116. Circlip
33. Lockwasher	76. Bolt	117. Bearing
34. Bolt	77. Lockwasher	118. Idler wheel
35. Axle	78. Washer	119. Inner axle
36. Lockwasher	79. Shackle	120. Rear axle
37. Bolts	80. Bolt	121. Circlip
38. Rivet	81. Spacer	122. Bearing
39. Rubber stopper	82. Nut	123. Idler wheel
40. Push nut	83. Bolt	124. Washer
41. Washer	84. Nut	125. Spacer
42. Nuts	85. Front swing arm axle	126. Lockwasher
43. Bolts	86. Bolt	127. Bolt

16

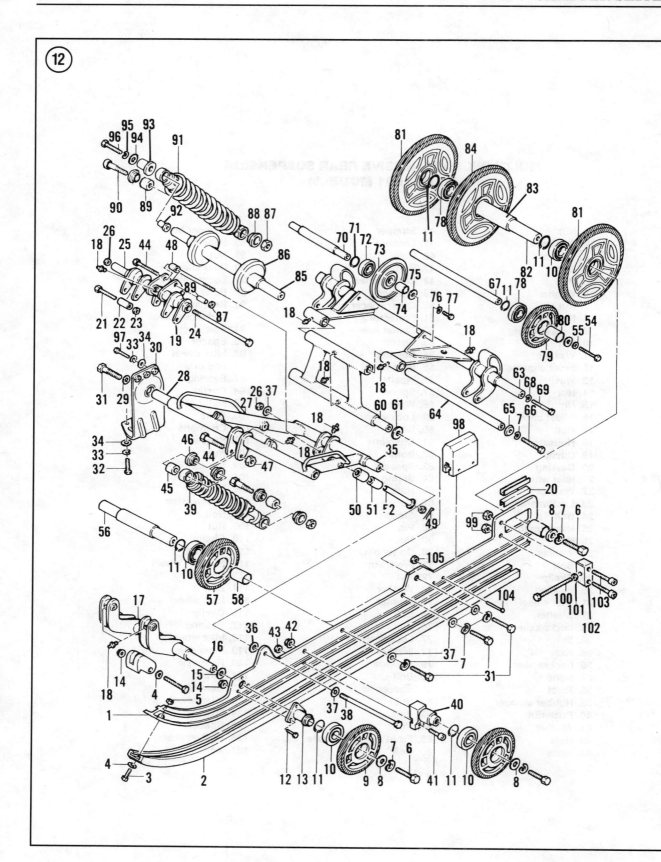

MULTILINK PROGRESSIVE REAR SUSPENSION
(1992-1993 MODELS)

1. Runner
2. Slider shoe
3. Screw
4. Flat washer
5. Lock nut
6. Screw
7. Lock washer
8. Flat washer
9. Idler wheel
10. Ball bearing
11. Snap ring
12. Screw
13. Housing
14. Flanged lock nut
15. Flat washer
16. Front axle
17. Front shackle
18. Grease fitting
19. Front swing arm
20. Protector
21. Screw
22. Spacer
23. Lock nut
24. Long welded screw
25. Front swing arm axle
26. Lock nut
27. Front arm
28. Front arm upper axle
29. Flat washer & lock washer
30. Retainer plate
31. Screw
32. Screw
33. Lock washer
34. Flat washer
35. Lower axle

36. Flat washer
37. Flat washer
38. Short welded screw
39. Center shock
40. Idler support
41. Allen screw
42. Flanged lock nut
43. Lock nut
44. Screw
45. Spacer
46. Pad
47. Lock nut
48. Welded stoper
49. Cotter pin
50. Cup
51. Rubber stopper
52. Bushing
53. Lock nut
54. Screw
55. Lock washer
56. Center axle
57. Idler wheel
58. Spacer
59. Rear shackle
60. Rear shackle lower axle
61. Washer
62. Rear arm
63. Cross pivot
64. Rear shackle upper axle
65. Washer
66. Screw
67. Cross shaft
68. Lock washer
69. Screw
70. Axle

71. Snap ring
72. Ball bearing
73. Idler wheel
74. Spacer
75. Hardened washer
76. Lock washer
77. Screw
78. Ball bearing
79. Idler wheel
80. Spacer
81. Idler wheel
82. Rear axle
83. Inner spacer
84. Center idler wheel
85. Rear shock pivot
86. Protector
87. Lock nut
88. Pad
89. Spacer
90. Screw
91. Rear shock
92. Spacer
93. Pad
94. Washer
95. Lock washer
96. Screw
97. Screw
98. Rubber stopper
99. Lock nuts
100. Adjusting screw
101. Lock nut
102. Tenisoner stopper
103. Allen screw
104. Rivet
105. Push nut

16

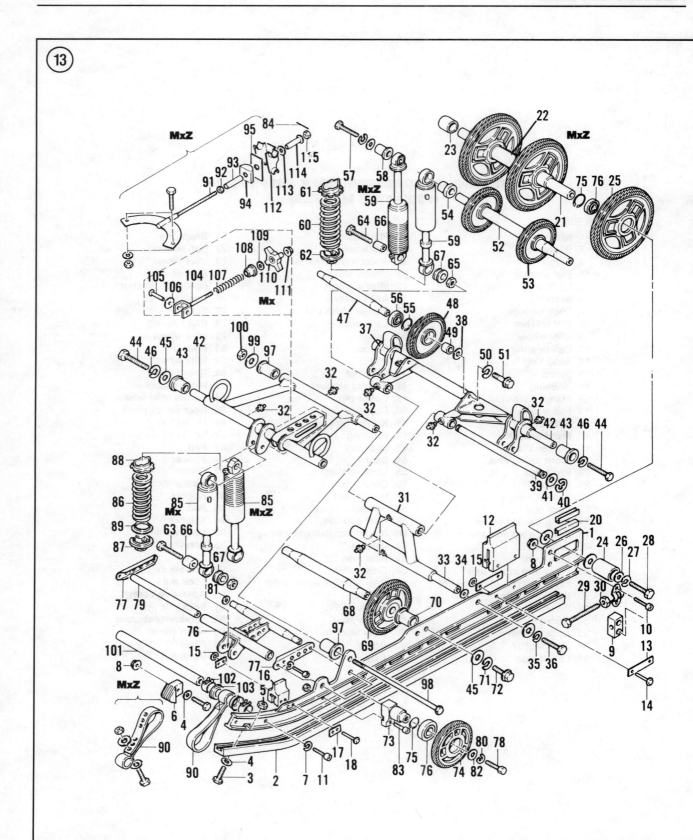

IMPROVED C7 REAR SUSPENSION
(1993-1995 MODELS)

1. Runner
2. Slider shoe
3. Screw
4. Flat washer
5. Lock nut
6. Runner protector
7. Lock washer
8. Flanged lock nut
9. Tensioner
10. Allen screw
11. Allen screw
12. Rear rubber stopper
13. Stopper portector
14. Rivet
15. Push nut
16. Front rubber stopper
17. Stopper protector
18. Rivet
19. Front arm
20. Protector
21. Rear axle
22. Long spacer
23. Short spacer
24. Outer spacer
25. Idler wheel
26. Flat washer
27. Lock washer
28. Screw
29. Adjusting screw
30. Lock nut
31. Rear arm pivot
32. Grease fitting
33. Lower axle
34. Hardened washer
35. Lock washer
36. Screw
37. Rear arm
38. Hardened washer
39. Upper axle
40. Snap ring
41. Flat washer
42. Upper axle
43. Cushion
44. Screw
45. Flat washer
46. Lock washer
47. Axle
48. Idler wheel
49. Spacer
50. Lock washer
51. Screw
52. Shock pivot
53. Protector
54. Pad
55. Snap ring
56. Ball bearing
57. Screw
58. Spacer
59. Rear shock
60. Spring
61. Spring seat
62. Spring stop
63. Screw
64. Screw
65. Lock nut
66. Spacer
67. Cushion
68. Center axle
69. Idler wheel
70. Spacer
71. Lock washer
72. Screw
73. Support
74. Idler wheel
75. Snap ring
76. Ball bearing
77. Retaining plate
78. Screw
79. Axle
80. Lock washer
81. Special washer
82. Flat washer
83. Allen screw
84. Cotter pin
85. Center shock
86. Spring
87. Spring stopper
88. Spring seat
89. Spring guide
90. Strap stopper
91. Belt tensioner
92. Lock nut
93. Bushing
94. Block
95. Rubber strip
96. Lower axle
97. Cushion
98. Long screw
99. Flat washer
100. Lock nut
101. Axle
102. Spring clamp
103. Washer
104. U-bracket
105. Washer
106. Pin
107. Spring
108. Adjuster bushing
109. Washer
110. Adjuster knob
111. Lock nut
112. Adjustment bracket
113. Rubber washer
114. Pusher piece
115. Lock nut
116. Idler wheel

16

1. Remove the rear suspension as described in this chapter.

2. Inspect the slide shoes for cracks or other damage **Figure 14**. If a crack is detected, replace the slide shoes as described in this procedure.

3. Install new slider shoes if the thickness is less than 10 mm (25/64 in.).

NOTE
The slide shoes must be replaced as a set.

4. Remove the slide shoes as follows:
   a. Turn the rear suspension over and rest it upside down on the workbench.
   b. Remove the screws (**Figure 15**) at the front of each shoe.
   c. Working at the front of the slide shoe, drive the shoe to the rear of the runner. If necessary, use a block of wood and hammer (**Figure 16**).

CAUTION
Do not use a steel punch to remove the slide shoes or the runner may become damaged.

5. Inspect the runner as follows:
   a. Clean the runner with solvent and dry thoroughly.
   b. Place a straightedge alongside the runner and check for bends. If a runner is bent, it must be straightened. If the bend is severe or if the runner is cracked or damaged, replace it.
   c. Check the runner for gouges or cracks along the runner path. Smooth any rough surfaces with a file or sandpaper.

6. Install the slide shoes as follows:
   a. Grease the runner mating surface lightly to ease installation.
   b. Working from the back of the runner, align the front of the slide shoe (end with hole) with the rear of the runner. Drive the slide shoe onto the runner with a wooden block and hammer as during removal.

c. Continue to drive the slide shoe onto the runner until the screw hole in the slide shoe aligns with the hole in the runner.

d. Install the screw, lockwasher and nut, then tighten securely.

RUNNER PROTECTOR

Inspect the runner protectors (**Figure 16**) for wear, cracks or other damage. Replace the pro-

tector by removing the nut, bolt and washer. Reverse to install.

SHOCK ABSORBERS

One shock absorber is located at the front of the rear suspension and 2 are located at the rear. Refer to **Figure 11** for 1990 and 1991 models, **Figure 12** for 1992-1993 models with PRS (Progressive Rate Suspension) front suspension, or **Figure 13** for 1993-1995 models with (Direct Shock Action) front suspension.

Front Shock
Removal/Installation

1. Remove the rear suspension as described in this chapter.
2. Loosen the limiter adjustment as follows:

a. Remove the cotter pin from the bottom of the limiter screw.

NOTE
The setting of the limiter screw controls weight transfer during acceleration. Count the number of threads visible from the base of the limiter screw to the end of the threads. Record this number so you can reinstall the limiter screw to the same setting. Adjustment of the limiter screw is covered in Chapter Four.

b. Loosen the limiter screw nut (**Figure 17**) until free play is obtained in the screw.
3. Remove the shock bolts and nuts and remove the front shock (**Figure 18**).
4. Remove the shock bushings and inspect them for wear or damage. Replace the bushings if necessary.
5. Inspect the shock absorbers as described in this chapter.
6. Installation is the reverse of the removal steps. Observe the following.
    a. Tighten the shock bolts to the torque in **Table 2**.
    b. Tighten the limiter screw nut (**Figure 17**) to the original setting recorded during disassembly. If necessary, refer to Chapter Four and adjust the limiter screw.
    c. Install a new cotter pin through the end of the limiter screw to prevent the nut from backing all the way off. Bend the ends of the cotter pin back to lock it.

Rear Shock Absorbers
Removal/Installation
(1990-1991)

Refer to **Figure 11** for this procedure.
1. Remove the rear suspension as described in this chapter.
2. Remove the bolts attaching the front of the shock absorber.
3. Remove the bolts attaching the rear of the shock absorber, then remove the shock absorber.

16

4. Repeat removal procedure for the other shock absorber.

5. Inspect the shock absorbers as described in this chapter.

6. Tighten the shock retainer bolts to the torque specification in **Table 2**.

Rear Shock Absorbers Removal/Installation (1992-1994 With PRS Front Suspension)

Refer to **Figure 12** for this procedure.

1. Remove the rear suspension as described in this chapter.

2. Remove the spacer (**Figure 9**) from cross shaft at the front of the shock.

3. Remove the bolt (**Figure 19**) attaching the rear of the shock absorber, then remove the shock absorber.

4. Repeat removal procedure for the other shock absorber.

5. Inspect the shock absorbers as described in this chapter.

6. Tighten the shock retainer bolts to the torque specification in **Table 2**.

Rear Shock Absorbers Removal/Installation (1993-1995 With DSA Front Suspension)

Refer to **Figure 13** for this procedure.

1. Remove the rear suspension as described in this chapter.

2. Remove the spacer (A, **Figure 20**) from cross shaft at the front of the shock.

3. Remove the bolts (B, **Figure 20**) attaching the rear of the shock absorber, then remove the shock absorber.

4. Repeat removal procedure for the other shock absorber.

5. Inspect the shock absorbers as described in this chapter.

6. Tighten the shock retainer bolts to the torque specification in **Table 2**.

Spring

The damper unit of the shock absorbers (**Figure 21**) used on most models cannot be disassembled or rebuilt. Service to this shock absorber is limited to replacement of the spring, bumper and the damper unit.

The shock absorber shown in **Figure 22** is gas charged, rebuildable and (to some degree internally) adjustable. It is necessary to release, then recharge the 2070 kPa (300 psi) nitrogen charge to remove the spring. If suitable equipment is not available, take the shock to a Ski-Doo dealer.

Removal/Installation

Refer to **Figure 21** or **Figure 22** for this procedure.

1. Remove the shock absorber as described in this chapter.

2A. On models with the spring and shock absorber shown in **Figure 21**, proceed as follows:

   a. Secure the bottom of the shock absorber in a vise with soft jaws.

   b. Slide the rubber bumper down the shock shaft.

WARNING
Do not attempt to remove or install the shock spring without the use of a spring compressor. Use the Ski-Doo spring remover (part No. 414 5796 00) or a suitable equivalent. Attempting to remove the spring without the use of a spring

compressor may cause severe personal injury. If you do not have access to a spring compressor, refer spring removal to a Ski-Doo dealer.

   c. Attach a suitable spring compressor to the shock absorber following the compressor manufacturer's instructions. Compress the spring with the tool and remove the spring stopper from the top of the shock. Remove the spring.

CAUTION
Do not attempt to disassemble the shock damper housing.

2B. On models with the rebuildable and nitrogen charged shock absorber shown in **Figure 22**, proceed as follows:

CAUTION
The shock absorber is charged with nitrogen gas at 2070 kPa (300 psi). Wear eye protection and use extreme caution whenever you are working with high-pressure gas. Do not attempt to remove the Schrader valve before releasing all pressure.

   a. Clamp the upper end of the shock absorber in a soft-jawed vise.

   b. Remove the cover protecting the Schrader valve and carefully release the pressurized nitrogen.

   c. Remove the Schrader valve core after all pressure is released, then remove the fitting for the valve (1, **Figure 22**) from the dampener housing.

   d. Use special tool (part No. 861 7439 00) to remove the spring preload rings (2, **Figure 22**).

   e. Withdraw the spring (3, **Figure 22**) and the upper retainer (4, **Figure 22**) from the damper body.

3. Inspect the spring for cracks or damage. If the spring appears okay, measure its free length and compare to the specification in **Table 3**. Replace the spring if it has sagged significantly.

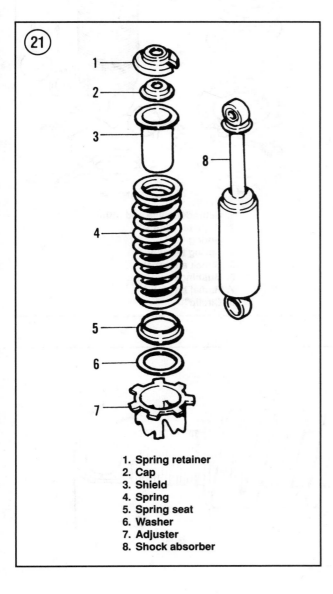

1. Spring retainer
2. Cap
3. Shield
4. Spring
5. Spring seat
6. Washer
7. Adjuster
8. Shock absorber

16

4. Check the spring retainer for cracks, deep scoring or excessive wear. Replace if necessary.

5A. On models with non-rebuildable shocks (**Figure 21**), install the spring by reversing the removal steps. Make sure the spring retainer holds the spring securely.

5B. On models with the nitrogen charged rebuildable shocks (**Figure 22**), install the spring as follows:

> *CAUTION*
> *Be careful not to spill oil from the shock absorber while the Schrader valve is removed. If the amount of oil or if the condition of the shock absorber is questioned, the shock absorber should be taken to a dealer who is qualified to rebuild and tune the shock absorber.*

a. Install the upper spring retainer (4, **Figure 22**) and the spring (3, **Figure 22**).

> *NOTE*
> *Spring preload can be adjusted by changing the position of the preload ring, but initial setting is as follows.*

b. Install the first preload ring (2, **Figure 22**), until the distance A, **Figure 23** is the length listed in **Table 3**.

c. Install the second preload ring and tighten it against the first to lock it in place.

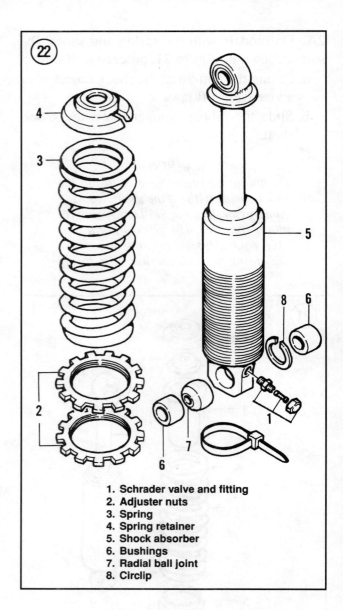

1. Schrader valve and fitting
2. Adjuster nuts
3. Spring
4. Spring retainer
5. Shock absorber
6. Bushings
7. Radial ball joint
8. Circlip

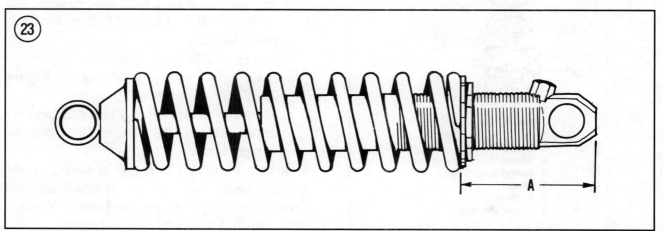

d. Install the Schrader valve and fitting. Tighten the valve to 1.5-2 N•m (13-17 in.-lb.) torque.

CAUTION
Use a suitable, regulated nitrogen filling tank, regulator, gauge, hose and fittings to charge the shock with gas. If suitable equipment is not available, take the shock to a Ski-Doo dealer.

e. Charge the shock absorber with nitrogen to 2070 kPa (300 psi), then check for leakage. Install the cap over the Schrader valve.

Shock Inspection

1. Remove the spring from the shock absorber as described in this chapter.
2. Clean all components thoroughly in solvent and allow to dry.
3. Check the damper rod as follows:

a. Check the damper housing for leakage. If a non-rebuildable damper (**Figure 21**) is leaking, replace it. If a rebuildable damper (**Figure 22** is leaking, take it to a Ski-Doo dealer who can rebuild it.
b. Check the damper rod for bending or other damage. Check the damper housing for dents or other damage.
c. Operate the damper rod by hand and check its operation. If the damper is operating correctly, a small amount of resistance should be felt on the compression stroke and a considerable amount of resistance felt on the return stroke.
d. Replace or repair the damper assembly if necessary.

4. Do not attempt any repair to the dampers shown in **Figure 21**. Do not attempt to straighten the damper rod of any type.
5. Check the spring stopper for cracks, deep scoring or excessive wear. Replace if necessary.

FRONT SHACKLE, FRONT SWING ARM AND FRONT ARM

Removal/Installation

Refer to **Figures 11-13** for this procedure.
1. Remove the rear swing arm as described in this chapter.
2. Loosen limiter screw (A, **Figure 24**) as follows:

a. Remove the cotter pin at the bottom of the limiter screw.

NOTE
Because the limiter screw controls vehicle weight transfer during acceleration, count the number of threads visible from the base of the nut to the end of the threads. Record this number so that you can reinstall the nut to the same setting. Adjustment of the limiter screw is covered in Chapter Four.

16

b. Loosen the limiter screw nut (**Figure 17**) until free play is obtained in screw.

3. Remove the nuts and bolts connecting the front shackle to the front swing arm (**Figure 25**).

4. Remove the shock absorber as described in this chapter.

5. Loosen the front swing arm pivot shaft nut (**Figure 26**). Then remove the nut and slide the pivot shaft from the front swing arm.

6. Loosen the front arm pivot shaft nut. Then remove the nut and slide the pivot shaft from the front arm.

7. If necessary, remove the retainer plates from the front arm (B, **Figure 24**).

8. Lift the subassemblies from the rear suspension unit.

9. Installation is the reverse of these steps. Observe the following.

10. When installing the retainer plates, turn the rear suspension assembly over. Then position the retainer plates so they face in approximately the same angle as shown in **Figure 24**.

11. Refer to **Table 2** or **Table 3** for tightening torques. If a fastener is not identified in **Table 2**, tighten it securely.

12. Tighten the limiter screw nut (**Figure 17**) to the original setting recorded during disassembly. Install a new cotter pin through the end of the limiter screw to prevent the nut from backing all the way of. Bend the ends of the cotter pin back to lock it.

Inspection

1. Clean all parts in solvent and dry thoroughly.

2. Inspect all welded joints for cracks or bends.

3. Check all pivot bolt surfaces for cracks, deep scoring or excessive wear.

4. If there is any doubt as to the condition of any part, repair or replace it as required.

5. Apply a low-temperature grease to all pivot shafts and bushings.

REAR SHACKLE AND REAR ARM

Removal/Installation
(1990-1991 Models)

Refer to **Figure 27** when performing this procedure.

1. Remove the rear suspension as described in this chapter.

2. Remove the rear shock absorbers as described in this chapter.

3. Disconnect the shock pivot (A, **Figure 28**) from the rear arm.

4. Remove the rear shackle bolts (B, **Figure 28**). Note the lower bolt hole position (**Figure 29**) so the rear shackle can be reinstalled in the same position.

5. Remove the rear arm bolts and washers.

6. Remove the rear shackle and rear arm subassemblies.

7. Installation is the reverse of these steps. Observe the following:

a. Install the rear shackle so the grease fittings (**Figure 30**) face forward.

b. Make sure to install the washers on the inside of the rear shackle.

c. Install the rear shackle in the same adjustment hole (**Figure 29**) as recorded during removal.

d. Install the rear arm so that the angle brackets face in the direction shown at (C, **Figure 28**.

e. Apply Loctite 242 (blue) to all mounting bolts. Then install the bolts and washers and tighten securely.

Inspection

1. Clean all parts in solvent and dry thoroughly.
2. Inspect all welded joints for cracks or bends.
3. Check all pivot bolt surfaces for cracks, deep scoring or excessive wear.
4. If there is any doubt as to the condition of any part, repair or replace it as required.
5. Apply a low-temperature grease to all pivot shafts and bushings.

Removal/Installation (1992-1995)

Refer to **Figure 12** or **Figure 13** when performing this procedure.

1. Remove the rear suspension as described in this chapter.
2. Remove the rear shock absorbers (A, **Figure 28**) as described in this chapter.
3. Remove the rear shackle upper axle bolts and washers (B, **Figure 28**). Then withdraw the upper axle.
4. Remove the rear shackle bolts at the runner. Observe the bolt hole position (**Figure 29**) so the rear shackle can be reinstalled in the same position.
5. Remove the rear arm bolts and washers.

6. Remove the rear shackle and rear arm subassemblies.
7. Installation is the reverse of these steps. Observe the following:
   a. Install the rear shackle so the grease fittings face forward. See **Figure 30**.
   b. Make sure to install the washers on the inside of the rear shackle as shown in **Figure 12** or **Figure 13**.
   c. Install the rear shackle in the same adjustment hole as recorded during removal (**Figure 29**).
   d. Install the rear arm so the angle brackets face in the direction shown in **Figure 28**. Refer also to **Figure 12** or **Figure 13**.
   e. Tighten the rear arm bolts to the torque specification in **Table 2**.
   f. Apply Loctite 242 (blue) to the rear shackle upper axle bolts and tighten the bolts securely.

REAR AXLE

Removal/Installation (1990-1991 Models)

1. Remove the rear suspension as described in this chapter.
2. Remove the idler wheel bolt and washers and remove the idler wheel. Repeat for the opposite wheel.
3. Remove the outer spacer (**Figure 31**).
4. Remove the runner from one side.
5. Remove the rear axle and its inner spacer.
6. Installation is the reverse of these steps. Observe the following:
   a. Install the rear axle so notch in the axle faces as shown in **Figure 31**.
   b. Install the outer spacer so the hole in the spacer faces toward the rear axle as shown in **Figure 31**.
   c. Tighten the idler wheel bolt to the torque specification in **Table 2**.

16

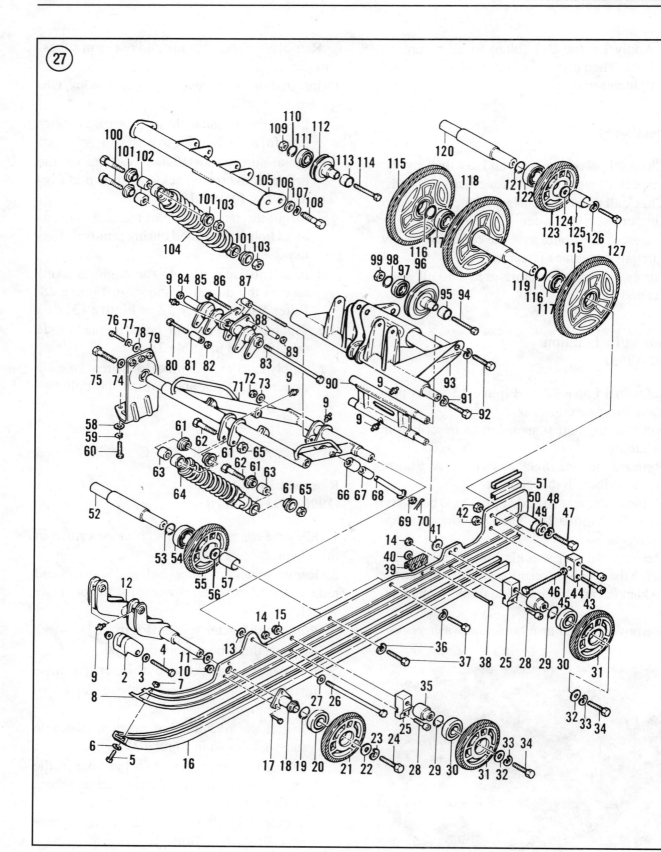

MULTILINK PROGRESSIVE REAR SUSPENSION
(1990-1991 MODELS)

1. Nut	44. Stopper	87. Stopper bolt
2. Protector	45. Locknut	88. Spacer
3. Washer	46. Bolt	89. Nut
4. Bolt	47. Bolt	90. Rear shackle
5. Bolt	48. Lockwasher	91. Lockwashers
6. Washer	49. Washer	92. Bolts
7. Nut	50. Outer spacer	93. Rear arm
8. Runner	51. Protector	and cross pivot
9. Grease fitting	52. Center axle	94. Bolt
10. Nut	53. Circlip	95. Spacer
11. Washer	54. Bearing	96. Idler wheel
12. Front shackle	55. Idler wheel	and axle
13. Washer	56. Washer	97. Bearing
14. Nut	57. Spacer	98. Circlip
15. Nut	58. Washer	99. Nut
16. Slider shoe	59. Lockwasher	100. Bolts
17. Bolt	60. Bolt	101. Cushions
18. Housing	61. Cushions	102. Spacers
19. Circlip	62. Bolts	103. Nuts
20. Bearing	63. Spacers	104. Spring
21. Idler wheel	64. Spring	105. Shock pivot
22. Washer	65. Nuts	106. Washer
23. Lockwasher	66. Cup	107. Lockwasher
24. Bolt	67. Stopper	108. Bolt
25. Idler support	68. Pin	109. Nut
26. Bolt	69. Nut	110. Circlip
27. Washer	70. Cotter pin	111. Bearing
28. Bolt	71. Front arm	112. Support wheel
29. Circlip	72. Nut	113. Spacer
30. Bearing	73. Washer	114. Bolt
31. Idler wheel	74. Washer	115. Idler wheel
32. Washer	75. Bolt	116. Circlip
33. Lockwasher	76. Bolt	117. Bearing
34. Bolt	77. Lockwasher	118. Idler wheel
35. Axle	78. Washer	119. Inner axle
36. Lockwasher	79. Shackle	120. Rear axle
37. Bolts	80. Bolt	121. Circlip
38. Rivet	81. Spacer	122. Bearing
39. Rubber stopper	82. Nut	123. Idler wheel
40. Push nut	83. Bolt	124. Washer
41. Washer	84. Nut	125. Spacer
42. Nuts	85. Front swing arm axle	126. Lockwasher
43. Bolts	86. Bolt	127. Bolt

16

Removal/Installation
(1992-1995 Models)

1. Remove the rear suspension as described in this chapter.

2. Remove the idler wheel bolt and washers and remove the idler wheel (**Figure 32**). Repeat for the opposite wheel.

3. Remove the outer spacer (**Figure 33**).

4. Remove the runner from one side.

5. Remove the rear axle and its inner spacer.

6. Installation is the reverse of these steps. Observe the following:

   a. Install the rear axle so the notch in the axle faces as shown in **Figure 33**.

   b. Install the outer spacer so the hole in the spacer faces toward the rear axle as shown in **Figure 33**.

   c. Tighten the idler wheel bolt to the torque specification in **Table 2**.

Inspection

1. Clean all components thoroughly in solvent.

2. Check the rear axle for cracks or other damage.

3. Check the inner spacer for cracks or damage.

4. Check the outer spacer for cracks or damage. Check the adjust bolt hole in the spacer for cracks.

5. If there is any doubt as to the condition of any part, repair or replace it as required.

6. Apply a low-temperature grease to all pivot shafts and bushings.

SUSPENSION AND GUIDE WHEELS

Refer to the following exploded views when servicing the suspension and guide wheels:

   a. **Figure 11**: 1990-1991 models.

   b. **Figure 12**: 1992-1994 models with PRS front suspension.

   c. **Figure 13**: 1993-1995 models with DSA front suspension.

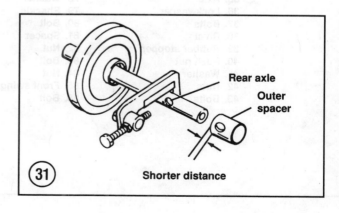

Rear axle

Outer spacer

Shorter distance

Inspection

1. Remove the rear suspension as described in this chapter.

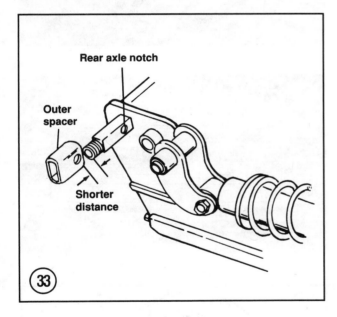

2. Spin the suspension and guide wheels. See **Figure 34** and **Figure 35**, typical. The wheels should spin smoothly without roughness, binding or noise. These abnormal conditions indicate worn or damaged bearings. Replace worn or damaged bearings as described in this chapter.

3. Check the wheel hubs for cracks.

4. Check the outer wheel surface for cracks, deep scoring or excessive wear.

5. If there is any doubt as to the condition of any part, replace it. Observe the following:

    a. Remove pressed on wheels with a universal-type bearing puller.

    b. When installing pressed on wheels, install the wheel by driving the bearing onto the shaft with a socket placed on the inner bearing race. Do not install by driving on the outer bearing race or bearing and/or wheel damage may occur.

6. When installing wheels, observe the following:

    a. Coat all sliding surfaces with a low-temperature grease.

    b. When installing circlips, make sure the circlip seats in the shaft groove or wheel groove completely.

    c. Spin each wheel and check its operation. If a wheel is tight or binding, remove the wheel and check the bearing.

16

Wheel Bearing Replacement

1. Remove the wheel from its shaft.

2. Remove the circlip from the groove in the wheel.

3. Using a socket or bearing driver, remove the wheel bearing.

4. Clean the wheel in solvent and thoroughly dry.

5. Check the circlip groove in the wheel hub (**Figure 36**) for cracks. Check the hub area for breakage or other damage. Replace the wheel if the hub is damaged.

6. Install the new bearing as follows:

   a. Align the new bearing with the hub.

b. Drive the bearing into the hub with a socket or bearing driver placed on the *outer* bearing race (**Figure 37**).

c. Drive the bearing squarely into the hub until it bottoms.

7. Secure the bearing with the circlip. Make sure the circlip seats in the hub groove completely.

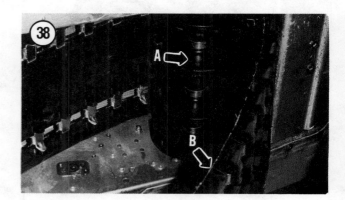

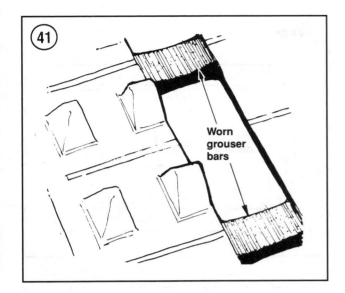

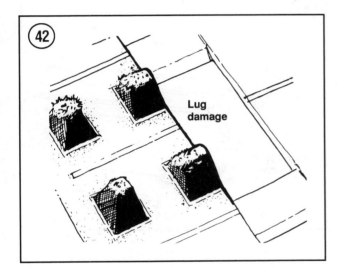

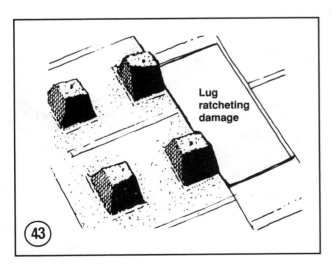

TRACK

Removal/Installation

1. Remove the rear suspension as described in this chapter.

2. Remove the driveshaft (A, **Figure 38**) as described in Chapter Fourteen.

3. Remove the track (B, **Figure 38**).

4. Installation is the reverse of these steps. Observe the following.

5. When installing the track, orient the track lugs to run in the direction shown in **Figure 39**.

Inspection

1. Check for missing or damaged track cleats. Replace cleats as described in this chapter.

2. Visually inspect the track for the following conditions:

    a. *Obstruction damage:* Cuts, slashes and gouges in the track surface are caused by hitting obstructions. These could include broken glass, sharp rocks or buried steel. See **Figure 40**.

    b. *Worn grouser bars:* Excessively worn grouser bars are caused by snowmobile operation over rough and non-snow covered terrain such as gravel roads and highway roadsides. See **Figure 41**.

    c. *Lug damage:* The lug damage shown in **Figure 42** is caused by lack of snow lubrication.

    d. *Ratcheting damage:* Insufficient track tension is a major cause of ratcheting damage to the top of the lugs (**Figure 43**). Ratcheting can also be caused by too great a load and constant "jack-rabbit" starts.

    e. *Over-tension damage:* Excessive track tension can cause too much friction on the wear bars. This friction causes the wear bars to melt and adhere to the track grouser bars. See **Figure 44**. An indication of this

16

condition is a sticky track that has a tendency to lock up.

f. *Loose track damage:* A track adjusted too loosely can cause the outer edge to flex excessively. This results in the type of damage shown in **Figure 45**. Excessive weight can also contribute to the damage.

g. *Impact damage:* Impact damage as shown in **Figure 46** causes the track rubber to open and expose the cord. This frequently happens in more than one place. Impact damage is usually caused by riding on rough or frozen ground or ice. Also, insufficient track tension can allow the track to pound

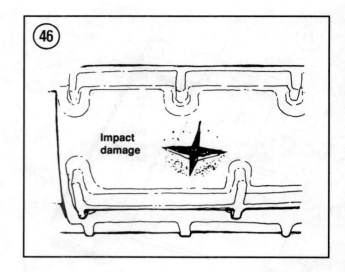

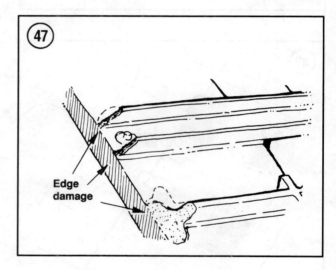

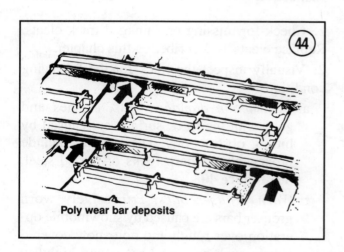

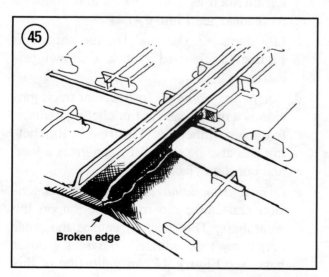

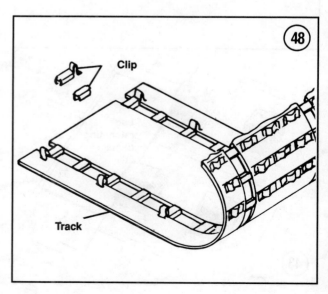

against the track stabilizers inside the tunnel.

h. *Edge damage:* Edge damage as shown in **Figure 47** is usually caused by tipping the snowmobile on its side to clear the track and allowing the track edge to contact an abrasive surface.

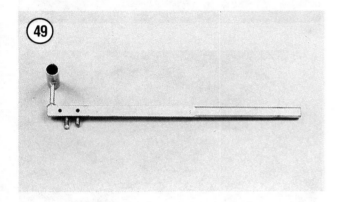

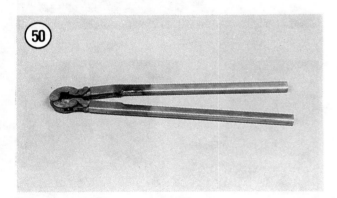

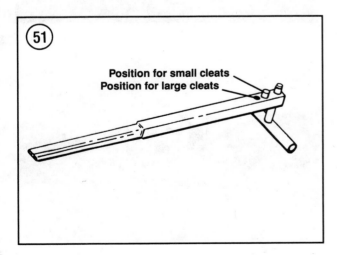

Cleat Replacement

Before removing the cleats, note that 2 types are used alternately along the track (**Figure 48**). Follow the same pattern when installing new cleats. Method 1 describes the use of Ski-Doo tools to remove and install cleats. Method 2 describes cleat removal using universal tools.

Method 1

The Ski-Doo track cleat remover (part No. 529 0082 00) (**Figure 49**), small track cleat installer (part No. 529 0085 00) and the large track cleat installer (part No. 529 0077 00) (**Figure 50**) are required to remove and install cleats.

1. Remove the track as described in this chapter.
2. Remove cleats as follows:
   a. Set the track cleat remover for small or large cleats. See **Figure 51**.
   b. Align tool with cleat and twist the tool to open and remove the cleat (**Figure 52**).
   c. Align the new cleat with the track. Then install a suitable size track cleat installer and bend the cleat (**Figure 53**) to secure it.

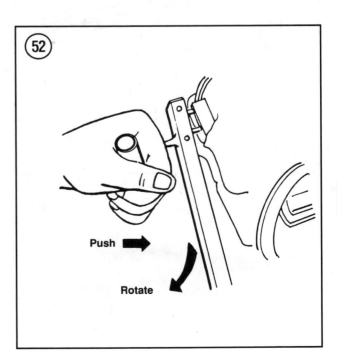

16

Method 2

A hand grinder, safety glasses and a universal track clip installer are required to remove and install new cleats. See **Figure 54**.

> *WARNING*
> *Safety glasses must be worn when using a hand grinder to remove cleats.*

1. Using a hand grinder (**Figure 55**), grind a slit in the corner of the cleat. See **Figure 56**.
2. Pry the cleat off of the track (**Figure 57**). Align the new cleat onto the track. Then install the cleat with the cleat installation tool (**Figure 58**). Check the cleat to make sure it is tight.

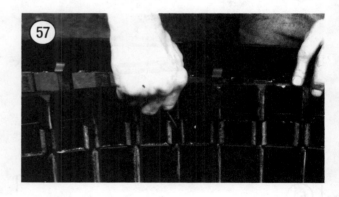

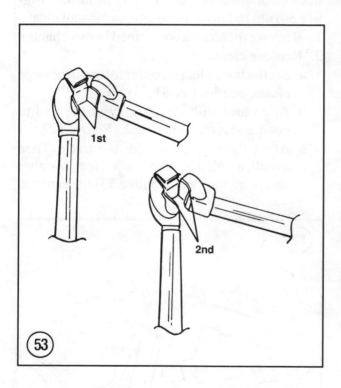

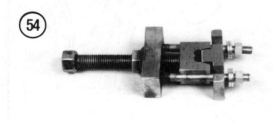

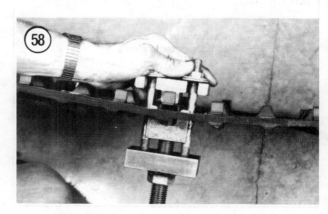

Table 1 TRACK SPECIFICATIONS

	Width	Length
1990-1992		
Standard track models	41 mm (16.1 in.)	307 mm (121 in.)
Long track models	41 mm (16.1 in.)	352 mm (138.6 in.)
1993		
Formula MX Z & Plus X	38.1 mm (15 in.)	307 mm (121 in.)
XTC models	41 mm (16.1 in.)	352 mm (138.6 in.)
Standard track models	41 mm (16.1 in.)	307 mm (121 in.)
1994		
Formula MX, MX Z & Z	38.1 mm (15 in.)	307 mm (121 in.)
Summit 470	38 mm (15 in.)	345.5 mm (136 in.)
Summit 583	38.1 mm (15 in.)	345 mm (135.8 in.)
Grand Touring & SE	41 mm (16.1 in.)	307 mm (121 in.)
Grand Touring XTC	41 mm (16.1 in.)	352 mm (138.6 in.)
MACH 1	41 mm (16.1 in.)	307 mm (121 in.)
1995		
MX, MX Z	38 mm (15 in.)	307 mm (121 in.)
Formula SS	38.1 mm (15 in.)	307 mm (121 in.)
Formula STX, STX LT	38.1 mm (15 in.)	307 mm (121 in.)
Formula Z	38.1 mm (15 in.)	307 mm (121 in.)
Summit 583	38.1 mm (15 in.)	345 mm (135.8 in.)
Summit 670	38.1 mm (15 in.)	345.5 mm (136 in.)
Grand Touring models	38.1 mm (15 in.)	345.5 mm (136 in.)
MACH 1	38.1 mm (15 in.)	307 mm (121 in.)
Suspension type		
1990-1991		
All models		
Front	PRS	
Rear	Multi-link progressive	
1992		
All models		
Front	PRS	
Rear	C-7 Multi-link progressive	
1993		
Formula MX Z		
Front	DSA	
Rear	Improved C-7	
Other models		
Front	PRS	
Rear	C-7 Multi-link progressive	
1994		
Grand Touring & MACH 1		
Front	PRS	
Rear	C-7	
Formula models & Summit models		
Front	DSA	
Rear	Improved C-7	
1995		
All models		
Front	DSA	
Rear	Improved C-7	

16

Table 2 REAR SUSPENSION TIGHTENING TORQUES

	N·m	in.-lb.	ft.-lb.
(1990-1991)			
Attaching bolts (refer to *Figure 5*)			
Center (1)	25		18
Rear (2)	48		35
Front (3 & 4)	15	133	11
Front swing arm spacer bolts	33		24
Idler support wheels	48		35
Idler wheel cross shaft	48		35
Rear shock pivot bolts	25		18
Retainer plate bolts	15	133	11
Shock retainer bolts	48		35
1992-1994 wth PRS front suspension			
Attaching bolts (refer to *Figure 5*)			
Bolts (1, 2 & 4)	48		35
Retainer plate bolts (3)	15	133	11
Front swing arm through bolt	33		24
Idler support wheels	48		35
Idler wheel cross shaft	48		35
Rear cross pivot	24		18
Rear shock pivot bolts	25		18
Retainer plate bolts	15	133	11
Shock retainer bolts	48		35
1993-1995 with DSA front suspension			
Attaching bolts (refer to *Figure 5*)			
Bolts (1, 2 & 4)	48		35
Retainer plate bolts (3)	15	133	11
Idler support wheels	48		35
Idler wheel cross shaft	48		35
Rear cross pivot	24		18
Shock retainer bolts	48		35

Table 3 GAS FILLED SHOCK ABSORBER SPECIFICATIONS

Front suspension	
Distance A, *Figure 23*	85.5 mm (3.11/32 in.)
Nitrogen charge pressure	2070 kPa (300 psi)
Rear suspension	
Front shock	
Distance A, *Figure 23*	104 mm (4.0 in.)
Nitrogen charge pressure	2070 kPa (300 psi)
Rear shocks	
Distance A, *Figure 23*	78 mm (3.0 in.)
Nitrogen charge pressure	2070 kPa (300 psi)

Table 4 SPRING SPECIFICATIONS

	Standard	Optional
Center shock		
Free length		
Color code		
Rear shock	Standard	Optional
Free length		
Color code		

Table 5 NITROGEN FILLED SHOCK SPECIFICATIONS

	Standard	Trail	Cross Country
Front shock			
Piston slits	4	4	4
Compression shims	8-30 mm × 0.152 mm	8-30 mm × 0.152 mm	6-30 mm × 0.152 mm
	2-15 mm × 0.114 mm	2-15 mm × 0.114 mm	1-24 mm × 0.114 mm
		1-21 mm × 0.114 mm	
Rebound shims	8-26 mm × 0.203 mm	8-26 mm × 0.203 mm	12-26 mm × 0.203 mm
	2-12 mm × 0.203 mm	1-12 mm × 0.203 mm	1-16 mm × 0.203 mm
Center shock			
Piston slits	6	6	0
Compression shims	9-30 mm × 0.152 mm	9-30 mm × 0.152 mm	12-30 mm × 0.203 mm
	2-15 mm × 0.114 mm	2-15 mm × 0.114 mm	1-24 mm × 0.114 mm
		1-21 mm × 0.114 mm	
Rebound shims	8-26 mm × 0.203 mm	8-26 mm × 0.203 mm	12-26mm × 0.203 mm
	2-15 mm × 0.114 mm	1-15 mm × 0.114 mm	1-16 mm × 0.203 mm
Rear shock			
Piston slits	6	6	2
Compression shims	8-30 mm × 0.203 mm	8-30 mm × 0.203 mm	7-30 mm × 0.203 mm
	6-15 mm × 0.114 mm	6-15 mm × 0.114 mm	1-24 mm × 0.114 mm
			1-20 mm × 0.152 mm
Rebound shims	10-26 mm × 0.203 mm	10-26 mm × 0.152 mm	10-26mm × 0.203 mm
	2-15 mm × 0.114 mm	2-15 mm × 0.114 mm	1-20 mm × 0.203 mm

16

Chapter Seventeen

Off-Season Storage

One of the most critical aspects of snowmobile maintenance is off-season storage. Proper storage will prevent engine and suspension damage and fuel system contamination. Improper storage will cause various degrees of deterioration and damage.

Preparation for Storage

Careful preparation will minimize deterioration and make it easier to restore the snowmobile to service later. When performing the following procedure, make a list of replacement or damaged parts so that they can be ordered and installed before next season.

1. Remove the seat and clean the area underneath the seat thoroughly. Wipe the seat off with a damp cloth and wipe a preservative over the seat to keep it from drying out. If you are concerned about the seat during storage, store it away from the snowmobile in a safe place.

2. Flush the cooling system as described in Chapter Three. Before refilling the cooling system, check all of the hoses for cracks or deterioration. Replace hoses as described in Chapter Eleven. Make sure all hose clamps are tight. Replace questionable hose clamps as required.

3. Change the chaincase oil as described in Chapter Three.

CAUTION
Do not allow water to enter the engine when performing Step 4.

4. Clean the snowmobile from front to back. Remove all dirt and other debris from the pan and tunnel. Clean out debris caught in the track.

5. Check the frame, skis and other metal parts for cracks or other damage. Apply paint to all bare metal surfaces.

6. Check all fasteners for looseness and tighten as required. Replace loose or damaged rivets.

NOTE
Refer to the appropriate chapter for the specified tightening torque as required.

7. Lubricate all pivot points with a low-temperature grease as described in Chapter Three.

8. Unplug all electrical connectors and clean both connector halves with electrical contact cleaner. Check the electrical contact pins for damage or looseness. Repair connectors as required. After the contact cleaner evaporates, apply a dielectric grease to one connector half and reconnect the connectors.

CAUTION
Dielectric grease is formulated for electrical use. Do not use a regular type grease on electrical connectors.

9. To protect the engine from rust buildup during storage, the engine must be fogged in. Perform the following:

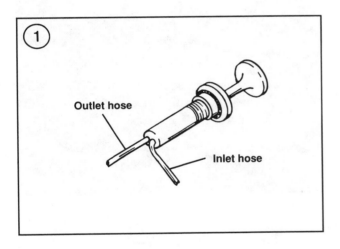

a. Raise the snowmobile so the track clears the ground.

b. Start the engine and allow it to warm to normal operating temperature. Then turn engine off.

WARNING
The exhaust gases are poisonous. Do not run the engine in a closed area. Make sure there is plenty of ventilation.

NOTE
A cloud of smoke will develop in substep c. This is normal.

c. Press the primer button (to prevent gasoline leakage) and disconnect the outlet primer hose from the primer valve. See **Figure 1**. Connect a can of Ski-Doo Storage Oil (part No. 496 0141 00) into the primer outlet hose previously disconnected. Then start the engine and allow it to idle. Spray storage oil through the primer outlet hose until 1/2 of the can has been injected into the engine or until the engine stalls.

d. Turn all switches OFF.

CAUTION
To prevent expensive engine damage, refer to CAUTION under Spark Plug Removal in Chapter Three.

e. Remove the spark plugs (**Figure 2**). Reconnect the spark plugs to their plug caps to ground them.

f. Spray approximately 150 cc of Ski-Doo Storage Oil (part No. 496 0141 00) into each cylinder. Pull the recoil starter handle to distribute the oil throughout the cylinder.

g. Wipe a film of oil on the spark plug threads and reinstall the spark plugs. Reconnect the high tension leads to the plugs.

h. Reconnect outlet primer hose.

CAUTION
During the storage period, do not run engine.

17

10. Plug the end of the muffler with a rag to prevent moisture from entering. Then tag the machine with a note to remind you to remove the rag before restarting the engine next season.

11. Remove the drive belt and store it on a flat surface.

12. Remove and service the primary and secondary sheaves as described in Chapter Thirteen. Replace worn or damaged parts as required.

13. Clean the jackshaft thoroughly. Then apply a light coat of low-temperature grease to the jackshaft (**Figure 3**). Wipe off excess grease before installing the secondary sheave.

14. Reinstall the primary and secondary sheaves. Tighten the bolts to the torque specification listed in Chapter Thirteen.

15. Close and secure the belt shield.

> *WARNING*
> *Some fuel may spill in the following procedure. Work in a well-ventilated area at least 50 ft. (15 m) from any sparks or flames, including gas appliance pilot lights. Do not smoke in the area. Keep a BC rated fire extinguisher handy.*

16. Using a suitable siphon tool, siphon fuel out of the fuel tank and into a gasoline storage tank.

17. When the fuel tank is empty, remove the drain plug (**Figure 4**) on each carburetor and drain the carburetors. Wipe up spilled gasoline immediately.

18. Protect all glossy surfaces on the chassis, hood and dash with an automotive type wax.

19. Then raise the track off the ground with wooden blocks. Make sure the snowmobile is secure.

20. Cover the snowmobile with a heavy cover that will provide adequate protection from dust and damage. Do not cover the snowmobile with plastic as moisture can collect and cause rusting. If the snowmobile must be stored outside, block the entire vehicle off the ground.

Removal From Storage

Preparing the snowmobile for use after storage should be relatively easy if proper storage procedures were followed.

1. Remove the plug from the end of the muffler.

2. Adjust track tension as described in Chapter Three.

3. Inspect the drive belt for cracks or other abnormal conditions. Then reinstall the drive belt as described in Chapter Thirteen.

4. Check the chaincase oil level. Refill as described in Chapter Three. If the oil was not

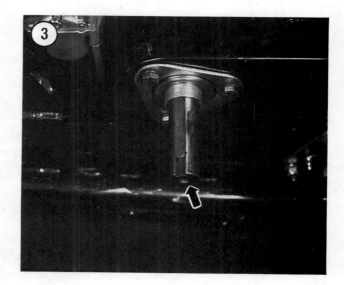

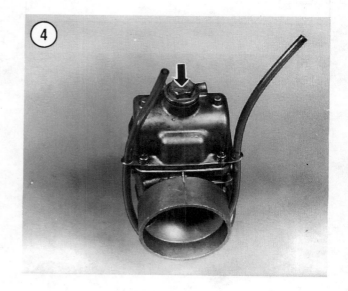

changed before storage, change the oil as described in Chapter Three.

5. Check and adjust drive belt tension.

6. Check the coolant level and refill if necessary.

7. Check all control cables for proper operation. Adjust as described in Chapter Three.

8. Fill the oil injection tank. If the tank was dry or if a hose was disconnected, bleed the oil pump as described in Chapter Ten.

9. Perform an engine tune-up as described in Chapter Three.

10. Check the fuel system. Refill the tank.

11. Make a thorough check of the snowmobile for loose or missing nuts, bolts or screws.

12. Start the engine and check for fuel or exhaust leaks. Make sure the lights and all switches work properly. Turn the engine off.

WARNING
The exhaust gases are poisonous. Do not run the engine in a closed area. Make sure there is plenty of ventilation.

13. After the engine has been initially run for a period of time, install new spark plugs as described in Chapter Three.

17

Index

WIRING
DIAGRAMS

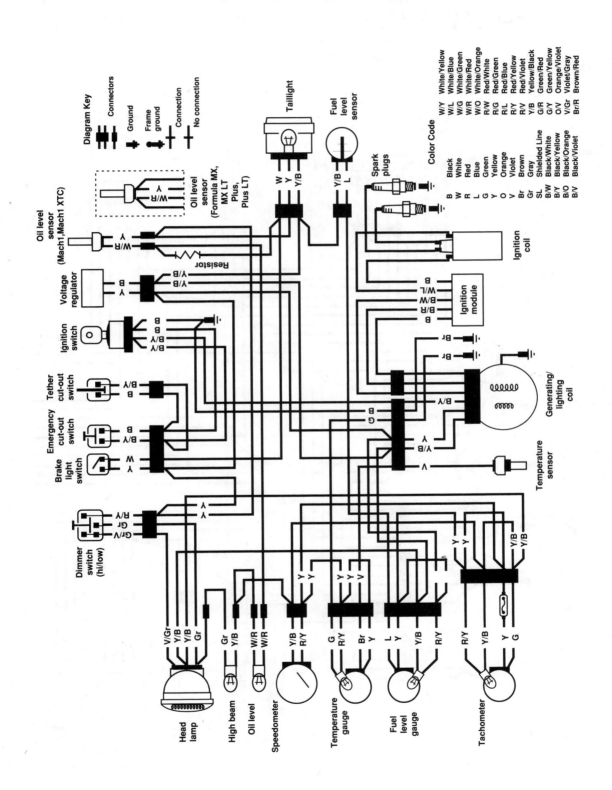

1990 FORMULA (MX, MX LT, PLUS, PLUS LT, MACH I)

Diagram Key

Connectors

Ground

Frame ground

Connection

No connection

Taillight

Fuel level sensor

Spark plugs

Color Code

B	Black	W/Y	White/Yellow
W	White	W/L	White/Blue
R	Red	W/G	White/Green
L	Blue	W/R	White/Red
G	Green	W/O	White/Orange
Y	Yellow	R/W	Red/White
O	Orange	R/G	Red/Green
V	Violet	R/L	Red/Blue
Br	Brown	R/Y	Red/Yellow
Gr	Gray	R/V	Red/Violet
SL	Shielded Line	Y/B	Yellow/Black
B/W	Black/White	G/R	Green/Red
B/Y	Black/Yellow	G/Y	Green/Yellow
B/O	Black/Orange	O/V	Orange/Violet
B/V	Black/Violet	V/Gr	Violet/Gray
		Br/R	Brown/Red

Oil level sensor (Mach1, Mach1 XTC)

Oil level sensor (Formula MX, MX LT Plus, Plus LT)

Ignition coil

Voltage regulator

Resistor

Ignition module

Ignition switch

Generating/ lighting coil

Tether cut-out switch

Emergency cut-out switch

Temperature sensor

Brake light switch

Dimmer switch (hi/low)

Head lamp

High beam

Oil level

Speedometer

Temperature gauge

Fuel level gauge

Tachometer

19

1991–1993 FORMULA (MX, MX II, MX XTC R, PLUS, PLUS II, PLUS E, PLUS ETC, MACH 1, MACH 1 II, MACH 1 XTC)

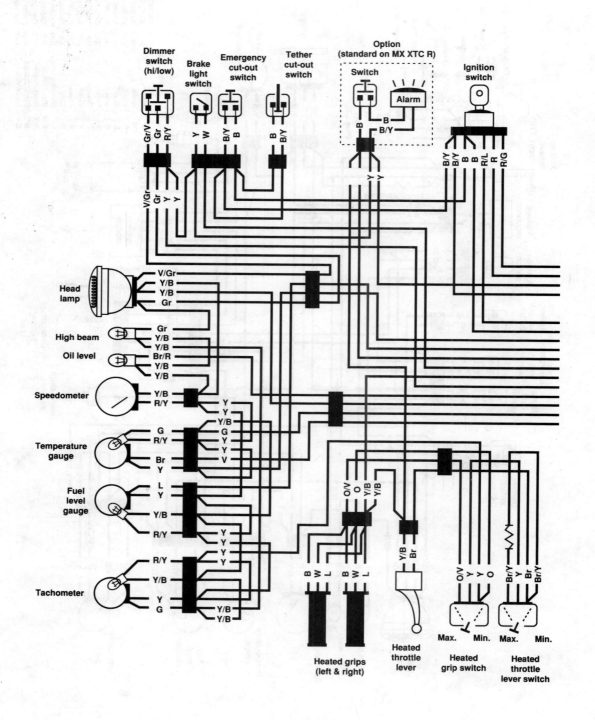

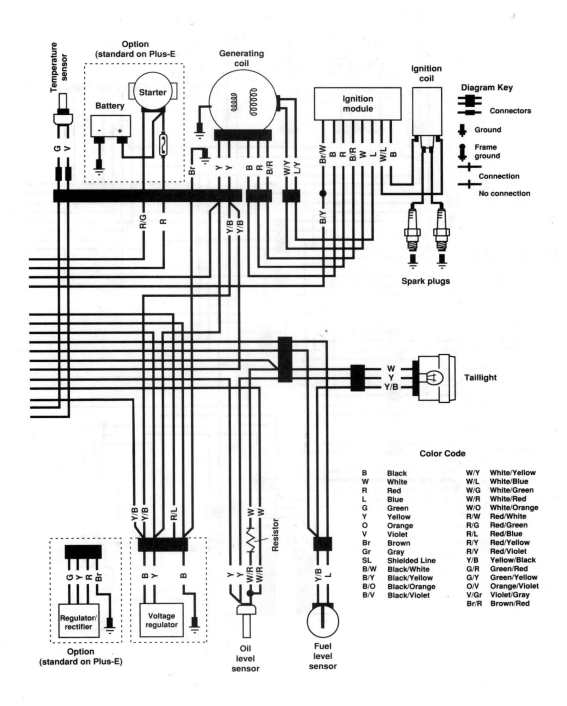

1993 EFI

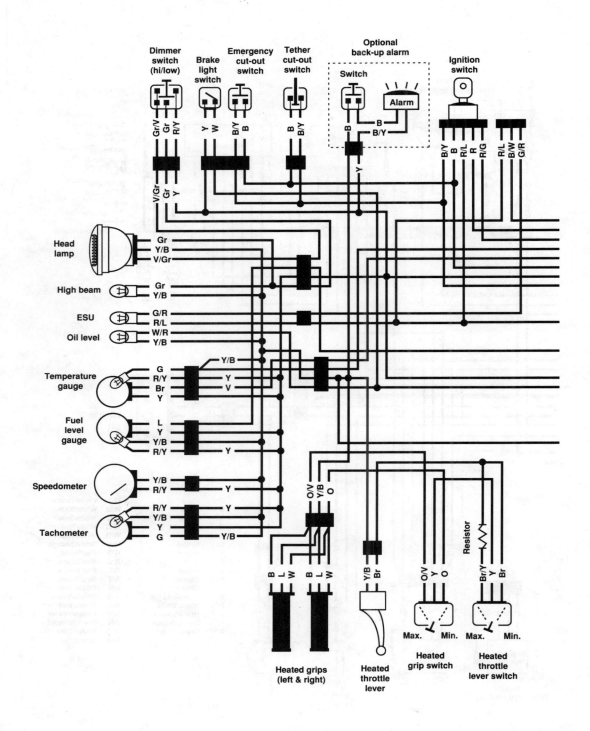

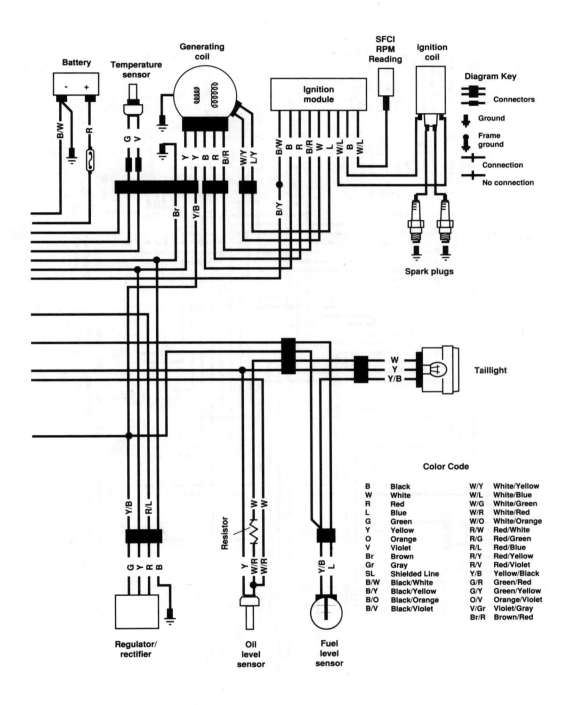

1993 FORMULA PLUS EFI

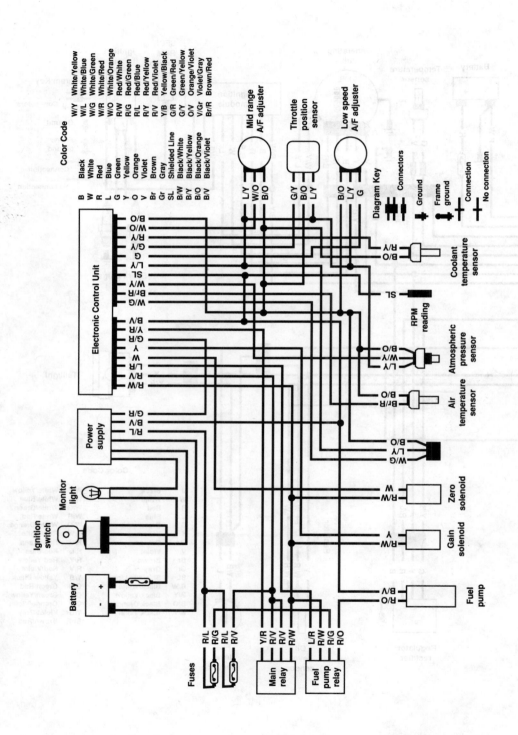

1993 EFI (SFCI)

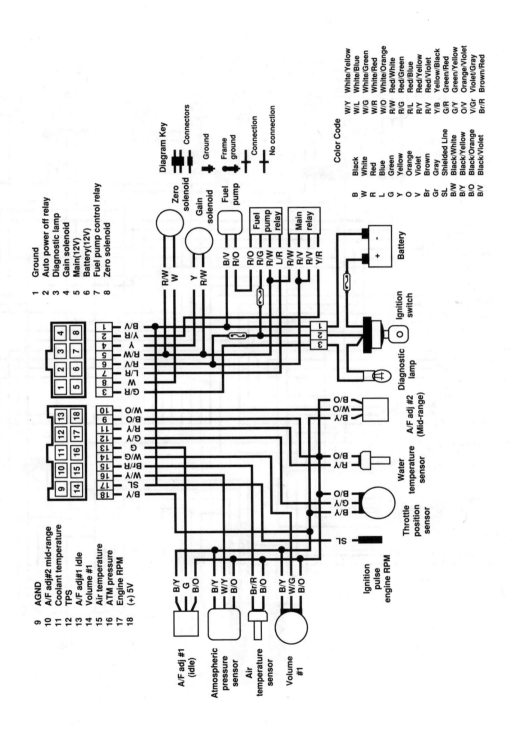

1994-ON

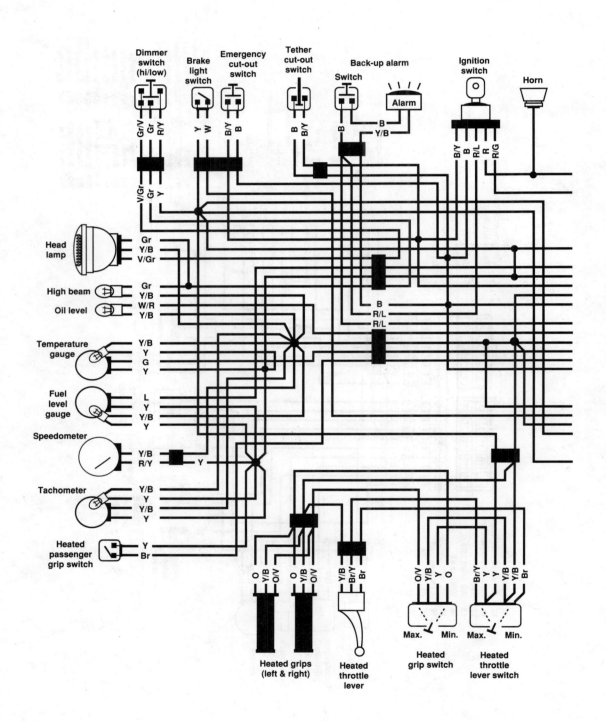

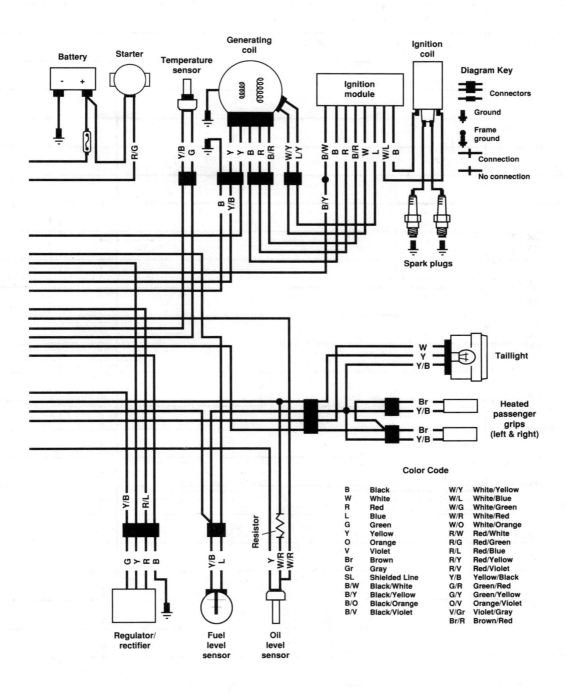

19

MAINTENANCE LOG

Date	Maintenance performed	Engine hours